Mike Meyers'

CompTIA Security+™

Certification Guide

ABOUT THE AUTHORS

Mike Meyers, CompTIA A+, CompTIA Network+, CompTIA Security+, is the industry's leading authority on CompTIA certifications and the best-selling author of ten editions of *CompTIA A+ Certification All-in-One Exam Guide* (McGraw Hill). He is the president and founder of Total Seminars, LLC, a major provider of PC and network repair seminars for thousands of organizations throughout the world, and a member of CompTIA.

Scott Jernigan, CompTIA ITF+, CompTIA A+, CompTIA Network+, CompTIA Security+, MCP, is the author or co-author (with Mike Meyers) of over two dozen IT certification books, including *CompTIA IT Fundamentals (ITF+) Certification All-in-One Exam Guide* (McGraw Hill). He has taught seminars on building, fixing, and securing computers and networks all over the United States, including stints at the FBI Academy in Quantico, Virginia, and the UN Headquarters in New York City, New York.

About the Technical Editor

Matt Walker is currently a member of the Cyber Security Infrastructure team at Kennedy Space Center with DB Consulting. An IT security and education professional for more than 20 years, he has served in multiple positions ranging from director of the Network Training Center and a curriculum lead/senior instructor for Cisco Networking Academy on Ramstein AB, Germany, to instructor supervisor and senior instructor at Dynetics, Inc., in Huntsville, Alabama, providing onsite certification-awarding classes for (ISC)^2, Cisco, and CompTIA. Matt has written and contributed to numerous technical training books for NASA, Air Education and Training Command, and the US Air Force, as well as commercially (*CEH Certified Ethical Hacker All-in-One Exam Guide*, now in its fourth edition), and continues to train and write certification and college-level IT and IA security courses.

Mike Meyers'

CompTIA Security+™

Certification Guide

Third Edition

(Exam SY0-601)

Mike Meyers
Scott Jernigan

New York   Chicago   San Francisco
Athens   London   Madrid   Mexico City
Milan   New Delhi   Singapore   Sydney   Toronto

Mike Meyers' CompTIA Security+™ Certification Guide, Third Edition (Exam SY0-601)

3 4 5 6 7 8 9   LCR   25 24 23 22 21

Library of Congress Control Number: 2021932335

ISBN   978-1-260-47369-8
MHID   1-260-47369-4

Sponsoring Editor
Tim Green

Technical Editor
Matt Walker

Production Supervisor
Thomas Somers

Editorial Supervisor
Janet Walden

Copy Editor
William McManus

Composition
KnowledgeWorks Global Ltd.

Project Manager
Neelu Sahu,
KnowledgeWorks Global Ltd.

Proofreader
Lisa McCoy

Illustration
KnowledgeWorks Global Ltd.

Indexer
Ted Laux

Art Director, Cover
Jeff Weeks

Acquisitions Coordinator
Emily Walters

CONTENTS AT A GLANCE

CONTENTS

ACKNOWLEDGMENTS

In general, we'd like to thank our amazing teams at McGraw Hill and KnowledgeWorks Global Ltd. for such excellent support and brilliant work editing, laying out, and publishing this edition. Special shout out to our co-workers at Total Seminars—Michael Smyer, Dave Rush, and Travis Everett—for listening to us rant and providing excellent feedback.

We'd like to acknowledge the many people who contributed their talents to make this book possible:

To **Tim Green, our acquisitions editor at McGraw Hill**: Thank you for the steady encouragement during this crazy year. You're the best!

To **Matt Walker, technical editor**: Excellent working with you! Thanks for laughing at our geeky jokes and sharing great stories.

To **Bill McManus, copy editor**: What an absolute delight to do this project with you! Your efforts made this a much better book.

To **Emily Walters, acquisitions coordinator at McGraw Hill**: Thanks for the Friday meetings and slightly menacing cat-on-lap petting. Way to keep us on track!

To **Neelu Sahu, project manager at KnowledgeWorks Global Ltd.**: Enjoyed working with you, Neelu. Hope the somewhat chaotic pacing wasn't too stressful!

To **Lisa McCoy, proofreader**: Fabulous job, thanks!

To **Ted Laux, indexer extraordinaire**: Well done!

To **KnowledgeWorks Global Ltd. compositors**: The layout was excellent, thanks!

To **Janet Walden, editorial supervisor at McGraw Hill**: Great to work with you on this project! Next time we'll make a few extra changes in page proofs just for you!

To **Tom Somers, production supervisor at McGraw Hill**: Thanks for waving that magic wand of yours and making so much happen as smoothly as possible.

INTRODUCTION

Most societies teem with a host of networked devices, from servers to smartphones, that provide the backbone for much of modern life. People and companies use these devices to produce and sell products and services, communicate around the globe, educate at every level, and manage the mechanisms of governments everywhere. Networked devices and the complex networks that interconnect them offer advances for humanity on par with, or perhaps beyond, the Agricultural and Industrial Revolutions. That's the good news.

The bad news is the fact that reliance on these devices creates a security risk to the resources placed on them. Networks can lose critical data and connections, both of which equate to loss of energy, confidence, time, and money. To paraphrase a few words from the American statesman, James Madison, if humans were angels, there'd be no need for security professionals. But humans are at best negligent and at worst petty, vindictive, and astoundingly creative in pursuit of your money and secrets.

Networked devices and the networks that interconnect them need security professionals to stand guard. The need for security professionals in information technology (IT) far outstrips demand, and we assume that's why you picked up this book. You see the trend and want to take the first step to becoming an IT security professional by attaining the acknowledged first security certification to get CompTIA Security+.

This introduction starts with an overview of the goals of security, to put a framework around everything you're going to learn. Second, we'll discuss the CompTIA Security+ certification and look at exam details. Finally, this introduction details the overall structure of the book, providing a roadmap for studying for the exam.

Goals of Security

Traditional computer security theory balances among three critical elements: functionality, security, and the resources available to ensure both. From a *functionality* standpoint, systems must function as people need them to function to process the data needed. Users and other systems need to interface with systems and data seamlessly to get work done. Don't confuse functionality with free rein. Allowing users to do whatever they wish with systems and data may result in loss, theft, or destruction of systems and data. Therefore, functionality must balance with security.

From the *security* standpoint, however, increasing the levels of protection for systems and data usually *reduces* functionality. Introducing security mechanisms and procedures into the mix doesn't always allow users to see or interact with data and systems the way they would like. This usually means a reduction in functionality to some degree.

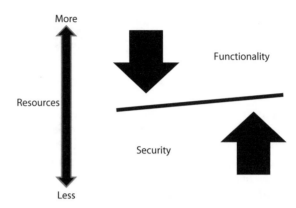

Figure 1
Balancing functionality, security, and resources

To add another wrinkle, the *resources* expended toward functionality and security, and the balance between them, are finite. No one has all the money or resources they need or as much functionality or security as they want. Keep in mind, therefore, that the relationship between functionality and security is inversely proportional; that is to say, the more security in place, the less functionality, and vice versa. Also, the fewer resources a person or organization has, the less of either functionality or security they can afford. Figure 1 illustrates this careful balancing act among the three elements of functionality, security, and resources.

Security theory follows three goals, widely considered the foundations of the IT security trade: confidentiality, integrity, and availability. Security professionals work to achieve these goals in every security program and technology. These three goals inform all the data and the systems that process it. The three goals of security are called the *CIA triad*. Figure 2 illustrates the three goals of confidentiality, integrity, and availability.

 NOTE The CIA triad is put into practice through various security mechanisms and controls. Every security technique, practice, and mechanism put into place to protect systems and data relates in some fashion to ensuring confidentiality, integrity, and availability.

Confidentiality

Confidentiality tries to keep unauthorized people from accessing, seeing, reading, or interacting with systems and data. Confidentiality is a characteristic met by keeping data secret from people who aren't allowed to have it or interact with it in any way, while making sure that only those people who do have the right to access it can do so. Systems achieve confidentiality through various means, including the use of permissions to data, encryption, and so on.

Figure 2
The CIA triad

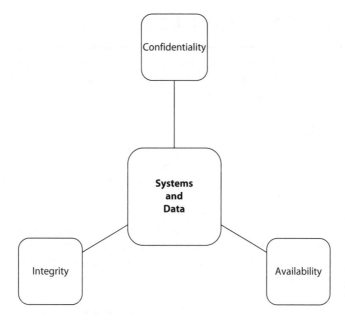

Integrity

Meeting the goal of *integrity* requires maintaining data and systems in a pristine, unaltered state when they are stored, transmitted, processed, and received, unless the alteration is intended due to normal processing. In other words, there should be no unauthorized modification, alteration, creation, or deletion of data. Any changes to data must be done only as part of authorized transformations in normal use and processing. Integrity can be maintained by the use of a variety of checks and other mechanisms, including data checksums and comparison with known or computed data values.

Availability

Maintaining *availability* means ensuring that systems and data are available for authorized users to perform authorized tasks, whenever they need them. Availability bridges security and functionality, because it ensures that users have a secure, functional system at their immediate disposal. An extremely secure system that's not functional is not available in practice. Availability is ensured in various ways, including system redundancy, data backups, business continuity, and other means.

During the course of your study, keep in mind the overall goals in IT security. First, balance three critical elements: functionality, security, and the resources available to ensure both. Second, focus on the goals of the CIA triad—confidentiality, integrity, and availability—when implementing, reviewing, managing, or troubleshooting network and system security. The book returns to these themes many times, tying new pieces of knowledge to this framework.

CompTIA Security+ Certification

The CompTIA Security+ certification has earned the reputation as the first step for anyone pursuing a career in the highly complex, highly convoluted, and still very much evolving world of IT security. Let's start with a description of CompTIA, then look at the specifics of the certification.

CompTIA

The *Computing Technology Industry Association (CompTIA)* is a nonprofit, industry-wide organization of just about everyone in the IT industry. The different aspects of CompTIA's mission include certification, education, and public policy.

As of this writing, CompTIA offers 13 vendor-neutral certifications covering a wide range of information technology areas. Examples of some of these areas and certifications include CompTIA Linux+ (focusing on the Linux operating system), CompTIA A+ (which focuses on computer technology support fundamentals), CompTIA Network+ (covering different network technologies), and, of course, CompTIA Security+.

CompTIA certifications are considered the *de facto* standard in the industry in some areas. Because they are vendor neutral, almost all CompTIA certifications cover basic knowledge of fundamental concepts of a particular aspect of IT. CompTIA works hard to develop exams that accurately validate knowledge that professionals must have in that area. This enables employers and others to be confident that the individual's knowledge meets a minimum level of skill, standardized across the industry.

The CompTIA Security+ Exam

Let's state up front that CompTIA does not have any requirements for individuals who want to take the CompTIA Security+ exam. There are no prerequisites for certification or definitive requirements for years of experience. CompTIA does have several recommendations, on the other hand, including knowledge that might be validated by other CompTIA certifications such as the CompTIA Network+ certification. In other words, the level of networking knowledge you are expected to have before you take the CompTIA Security+ exam is the level that you would have after successfully completing the CompTIA Network+ certification. Here are CompTIA's recommendations:

- Network+ certification
- Two years of experience in IT systems administration, with a focus on security

You should have experience in several areas, such as networking knowledge, basic information security concepts, hardware, software (both operating systems and applications), cryptography, physical security, and so on. The next few sections cover specific exam objectives that you need to know.

The following table shows the five domains in the CompTIA Security+ Certification Exam Objectives document for exam SY0-601. Each of these domains has very detailed exam objectives.

Domain	Name	Percent of Exam
1.0	Threats, Attacks, and Vulnerabilities	24
2.0	Architecture and Design	21
3.0	Implementation	25
4.0	Operations and Incident Response	16
5.0	Governance, Risk, and Compliance	14

Threats, Attacks, and Vulnerabilities

Domain 1.0 is all about the attacks, from malware to application attacks. It's critical you know your keyloggers from your RATs and your buffer overflows from your cross-site scripting. In addition, you should recognize the threat actors, from script kiddies to evil governments to incompetent users. Along with the threats and attacks, you should understand different types of vulnerabilities that enable these attacks to thrive and the two main tools you use to minimize those vulnerabilities, security assessments, and penetration testing.

Architecture and Design

Domain 2.0 explores a lot of topics under its benign-sounding title. You're expected to explain important security concepts, such as data protection, hashing, and site resiliency. The domain covers cloud models, such as infrastructure as a service (IaaS); you'll need to summarize containers, infrastructure as code, and virtualization. In addition, this domain covers the design of secure applications and security for embedded systems.

Domain 2.0 requires you to know how to use security devices, protocols, and tools. This domain covers the frameworks that enable secure IT, the design concepts such as defense-in-depth, and benchmarks used to measure security. This domain covers technologies to defend networks, such as VLANs, screened subnets, and wireless designs. In addition, this domain covers the design of secure applications and security for embedded systems. Domain 2.0 also covers physical security controls, such as fencing and fire prevention.

Finally, domain 2.0 expects knowledge of cryptographic concepts. You'll get questions on symmetric versus asymmetric cryptography, for example. The objectives explore public key encryption, keys, salting, hashing, and more.

Implementation

The key with domain 3.0 is in the name, "Implementation." Concepts discussed in other domains get scenario-level in this domain. Domain 3.0 goes into great detail about authentication, authorization, and accounting. It expects you to know and implement authentication and the many identity and access services such as LDAP and Kerberos.

The domain addresses authorization via user groups and accounts and the tools and methods used to control them. You'll need to know how to implement secure wireless and mobile solutions, plus apply cybersecurity solutions to cloud computing. Finally, the domain expects you to understand how to implement public key infrastructure.

Operations and Incident Response

Domain 4.0 explores organizational security, such as incident response policies and procedures. You'll need to know mitigation techniques and controls, plus practical forensic practices, such as how to acquire and handle evidence.

Governance, Risk, and Compliance

Domain 5.0 defines critical concepts in risk management, such as events, exposures, incidents, and vulnerability. You're expected to know risk-related tools, such as business impact analysis, assessments, incident response, and disaster recovery/business continuity. You'll need to understand the regulations, standards, and frameworks that impact operational security and explain policies that organizations use to implement security. Finally, the domain expects you to know how privacy and sensitive data use impacts security.

Getting Certified

This book covers everything you'll need to know for CompTIA's Security+ certification exam. The book is written in a modular fashion, with short, concise modules within each chapter devoted to specific topics and areas you'll need to master for the exam. Each module covers specific objectives and details for the exam, as defined by CompTIA. We've arranged these objectives in a manner that makes fairly logical sense from a learning perspective, and we think you'll find that arrangement will help you in learning the material.

 NOTE Throughout the book, you'll see helpful Notes and Exam Tips. These elements offer insight on how the concepts you'll study apply in the real world. Often, they may give you a bit more information on a topic than what is covered in the text or expected on the exam. And they may also be helpful in pointing out an area you need to focus on or important topics that you may see on the test.

End of Chapter Questions

At the end of each chapter you'll find questions that will test your knowledge and understanding of the concepts discussed in the modules. The questions also include an answer key, with explanations of the correct answers.

Using the Exam Objective Map

The Exam Objective map included in Appendix A has been constructed to help you cross-reference the official exam objectives from CompTIA with the relevant coverage in the book. References have been provided for the exam objectives exactly as CompTIA has presented them—the module that covers that objective, the chapter, and a page reference are included.

Online Resources

The online resources that accompany this book feature the TotalTester exam software that enables you to generate a complete practice exam or quizzes by chapter or by exam domain. See Appendix B for more information.

Study Well and Live Better

We enjoyed writing this book and hope you will enjoy reading it as well. Good luck in your studies and good luck on the CompTIA Security+ exam. If you have comments, questions, or suggestions, tag us:

Mike: desweds@protonmail.com
Scott: jernigan.scott@gmail.com

Risk Management

"It seems to me that if there were any logic to our language, trust would be a four-letter word."

—Joel Goodson, *Risky Business*

IT security professionals walk a tight line between keeping systems safe from inside and outside threats and making resources available to people who need them. Perfectly secure systems would allow no access, right? If attackers can't access the systems, they can't break or steal anything. But such "perfect" security clearly blocks legitimate users from using resources to produce anything of value. Conversely, a wide-open system provides great access for creativity and production, but also provides access to malicious people.

Security professionals provide a space in between, with enough security to stop attackers, yet enough access to enable good people to create and produce. With *risk management*, security folks identify and categorize risks and then systematically put controls in place to manage those risks and thus minimize their impact on the organization. As a science, risk management uses statistics, facts, scans, and numbers to align a vision, a design for the organization. As an art, security professionals craft a plan for risk management that people will buy into and actually follow.

This chapter tours IT risk management in eight modules:

- Defining Risk
- Risk Management Concepts
- Security Controls
- Risk Assessment
- Business Impact Analysis
- Data Security and Data Protection
- Personnel Risk and Policies
- Third-Party Risk and Policies

Module 1-1: Defining Risk

This module covers the following CompTIA Security+ objectives:

- **1.2 Given a scenario, analyze potential indicators to determine the type of attack**
- **1.5 Explain different threat actors, vectors, and intelligence sources**

In IT security, *risk* implies a lot more than the term means in standard English. Let's start with a jargon-filled definition, then examine each term in the definition. We'll review the definition with some examples at the end of the module.

> *Risk is the likelihood of a threat actor taking advantage of a vulnerability by using a threat against an IT system asset.*

This definition of risk includes five jargon terms that require further explanation:

- Asset
- Likelihood
- Threat actor
- Vulnerability
- Threat

Defining each jargon word or phrase relies at least a little on understanding one or more of the other jargon phrases. We'll cover these next, and then explore two related topics, vectors and threat intelligence, to round out the concept of risk. Let's do this.

Asset

An *asset* is a part of an IT infrastructure that has value. You can measure value either tangibly or intangibly. A gateway router to the Internet is an example of an asset with tangible value. If it fails, you can easily calculate the cost to replace the router.

What if that same router is the gateway to an in-house Web server? If that Web server is no longer accessible to your customers, they're not going to be happy and might go somewhere else due to lack of good faith or goodwill. Good faith doesn't have a measurable value; it's an intangible asset.

Here are a few more examples of assets:

- **Servers**   The computers that offer shared resources
- **Workstations**   The computers that users need to do their job
- **Applications**   Task-specific programs an organization needs to operate
- **Data**   The stored, proprietary information an organization uses
- **Personnel**   The people who work in an organization

- **Wireless access**   Access to the network that doesn't require plugging into an Ethernet port
- **Internet services**   The public- or private-facing resources an organization provides to customers, vendors, or personnel via the Web or other Internet applications

We will cover assets in much greater detail later in this chapter.

Likelihood

Likelihood means the probability—over a defined period of time—of someone or something damaging assets. Likelihood is generally discussed in a comparative nature. Here are a couple of examples:

- The company expects many attacks on its Web server daily, but few on its internal servers. The potential for a successful attack on the Web server is much more likely than on internal servers, and thus the *controls*—the things put in place to protect the systems—would vary a lot.
- Hard drives will likely fail after three years, with the probability of failure rising over time. The drive could fail right out of the box, but the likelihood of failure of a drive under three years old is much lower than a drive of three or more years old.

NOTE   You will also hear the term *probability* as a synonym for likelihood.

Threat Actor

A *threat actor* is anyone or anything that has the motive and resources to attack another enterprise's IT infrastructure. Threat actors manifest in many forms. Many folks think of a threat actor as a malicious person, such as a classic hacker bent on accessing corporate secrets. But a threat actor can take different guises as well, such as programs automated to attack at a specific date or time. A threat actor could be a respected member of an organization who has just enough access to the IT infrastructure but lacks the knowledge of what *not* to do. The word *actor* here simply means someone or something that can initiate a negative event.

The CompTIA Security+ exam covers nine specific types of threat actor:

- Hackers
- Hacktivists
- Script kiddies
- Insiders
- Competitors
- Shadow IT

- Criminal syndicates
- State actors
- Advanced persistent threat

Hackers—and more specifically *security hackers*—have the technical skills to gain access to computer systems. *White hat* hackers use their skills for good, checking for vulnerabilities and working with the full consent of the target. The malicious *black hat* hackers, in contrast, do not have the consent of the target. *Gray hat* hackers fall somewhere in the middle. They're rarely malicious, but usually do not have the target's consent.

 EXAM TIP The CompTIA Security+ objectives use bland and nonstandard descriptive terms for hacker types. Be prepared for either term to describe/ label a hacker.
—White hat = Authorized
—Black hat = Unauthorized
—Gray hat = Semi-authorized

A *hacktivist* is a hacker and an activist. These threat actors have some form of agenda, often political or fueled by a sense of injustice. Hacktivism is often associated with sophisticated yet loosely associated organizations, such as Anonymous.

Save the whales!

Script kiddies are poorly skilled threat actors who take advantage of relatively easy-to-use open-source attacking tools. They get the derogatory moniker because they don't have skills that accomplished hackers possess. Their lack of sophistication makes them notoriously easy to stop, most of the time.

Insiders (or *insider threats*) are people within an organization. As part of the targeted organization, these threat actors have substantial physical access and usually have user accounts that give them access to assets. In fact, the absolute best way to attack an organization is to be hired by them. You get hired; they hand you the keys to the kingdom; you're in. Insiders are often motivated by revenge or greed, but that's not universal. Some folks just do stupid things that cause all sorts of havoc.

Shadow IT describes information technology systems installed without the knowledge or consent of the main IT department. Almost never based on malicious intent, shadow IT springs up when users need to work around limitations imposed by IT departments for purposes of security, limitations that hamper their jobs.

Isn't it interesting that one attribute of the two previous threat actors is that they are inside the organization? The rest of the threat actors are external to the organization.

EXAM TIP   Take the time to recognize the attributes of threat actors: internal/external, intent/motivation, resources/funding, level of sophistication/capability.

Competitors are outside organizations that try to gain access to the same customers as the targeted company. Competitors, by definition in the same business, know precisely the type of secure information they want. Organizations practice *competitive intelligence gathering* to get information about competitors, their customers, their business practices, and so on. The information gathered can help shape business practices.

Criminal syndicates use extra-legal methods to gain access to resources. Also known as organized crime, criminal syndicates are a huge problem today. These groups are sophisticated, are well funded, and cause tremendous damage to vulnerable systems worldwide to make money.

State actors—or *nation states*—refers to government-directed attacks, such as the United States sending spies into Russia. Whereas criminal syndicates commonly use threats specifically to make money, state actors take advantage of vulnerabilities to acquire intelligence. Nation states have the resources—people and money—to collect *open-source intelligence (OSINT)* successfully—information from media (newspapers, television), public government reports, professional and academic publications, and so forth.

State actors are easily the best funded and most sophisticated of all threat actors. State actors often use *advanced persistent threats (APTs)*, where a threat actor gets long-term control of a compromised system, continually looking for new data to steal.

NOTE   Many state actors use criminal syndicates to conduct cyberattacks against other nation states.

Vulnerability and Threat

The terms vulnerability and threat go hand-in-hand, so it makes sense to talk about both at the same time. A *vulnerability* is a weakness inherent in an asset that leaves it open to a threat. A *threat* is an action a threat actor can use against a vulnerability to create a negative effect.

Vulnerabilities and their associated threats exist at every level of an organization. Not changing the default password on a router is a vulnerability; someone taking control of your router by using the default password is the threat. Giving a user full control to a shared folder (when that user does not need nor should have full control) is a vulnerability. That same user having the capability to delete every file in that folder is a threat.

Oh no!

Threats do not have to originate only from people or organizations. Forces of nature like earthquakes and hurricanes (a big deal here in Houston, Texas) can also be threats.

As you might imagine, dealing with threats by minimizing vulnerabilities is a core component of risk management. This chapter will develop this concept in detail.

NOTE   You will see two other terms associated with the jargon phrases covered in this section, attack and incident. An *attack* is when a threat actor actively attempts to take advantage of a vulnerability. When the target recognizes an attack, it is called an *incident*. Both attacks and incidents go beyond the concept of risk and are covered in Chapter 13.

Circling Back to the Risk Definition

Now that we have explored each jargon term in some detail, let's look at the definition of risk again and follow it with an example.

> *Risk is the likelihood of a threat actor taking advantage of a vulnerability by using a threat against an IT system asset.*

Here's an example of a risk:

> *There's a 15 percent chance in the next month that Sally the hacktivist will guess correctly John's password on the important company server to gain access to secret documents.*

The likelihood is 15 percent over the next month. The threat actor is Sally the hacktivist. John's lame password is a vulnerability; the threat is that Sally will get that password and use it to access the server. The assets are both the server and the secret documents. Got it? Let's move on.

Vectors

Threat actors use a variety of *attack vectors*—pathways to gain access to infrastructure— to carry out attacks. In the olden days, threat actors used floppy disks or optical media as vectors to install malware or tools. Today, the only commonly used removable media are USB thumb drives, the vector of choice for a threat actor who has physical access to a target system. Other attack vectors include the classic "hacker gets into your network through your router" (a.k.a. *direct access*), the ubiquitous vector of wireless networks (802.11, Bluetooth, cellular), and the relatively new cloud vector.

Don't limit yourself to thinking networking when you consider vectors. Almost any application that transfers information between systems might be a vector. Threat actors can use e-mail, social media, conferencing, and even shared document applications as vectors for an attack.

Smartphones and other mobile devices and the Internet of Things (IoT) offer serious and growing attack vectors for modern organizations. Just about everyone has a smartphone with sophisticated recording—video and sound—devices built in, plus always-on connectivity to the cellular network and the Internet. Any rogue or buggy app can create a pathway into a network. IoT devices controllable from outside the network also provide a point of entry to the network. It's a brave new world that attackers will try very hard to exploit.

The infamous Stuxnet worm that disrupted the Iranian nuclear program back in 2010 used a supply-chain vector. Threat actors (almost certainly the United States and Israel) infected printers with this worm that were then purchased by the Iranian government. This is a brutal example of a *supply-chain attack*.

Threat Intelligence

Cybersecurity professionals in organizations maintain and update information about past, current, and potential threats to the organization. This collection of information, called *threat intelligence*, helps those security professionals prepare for—and hopefully prevent—attacks on the organization.

Moreover, most security folks share information about vulnerabilities and associated threats with other professionals in the field. It's like one big, highly paranoid family out there!

Sources for threat intelligence come from many places. Dedicated *threat intelligence sources*—such as vulnerability databases available on the Internet—provide a wealth of information, of course. But so do what CompTIA calls *research sources*—things like academic journals and social media. Security professionals dive into all of these sources to build their threat intelligence.

This section explores the types of sources available for threat intelligence gathering and provides examples. This is not an exhaustive list of specific sources—impossible and instantly outdated—but a guide to the *types* of sources. We'll look at dedicated threat intelligence sources, then follow with research sources.

Threat Intelligence Sources

Dedicated threat intelligence sources enable security professionals to research potential threats to their organizations and share threats they discover with their peers. These sources reveal the past and current threats, explore potential threats by defining characteristics or signature types, and much more.

This section explores nine dedicated threat intelligence sources:

- OSINT
- Public/private information-sharing centers
- Dark Web
- Indicators of compromise
- Adversary tactics, techniques, and procedures
- Predictive analysis
- Threat maps
- File/code repositories
- Vulnerability databases

OSINT We discussed *open-source intelligence (OSINT)* sources earlier in this module. This category includes information gathered from media (newspapers, television), public government reports, professional and academic publications, and so forth. Security professionals rely heavily on OSINT for the big picture or the framework for the picture that can then get more specific in terms of nonpublic information layers.

Public/Private Information-Sharing Centers Motivated by the lack of coordinated information sharing between different federal organization after 9/11, the US government began a series of legislation establishing *information-sharing centers*, more commonly called Information Sharing and Analysis Centers (ISACs). Originally designed as government-based public entities just in the United States, most countries now have public ISACs as well as many private ISACs. ISACs communicate via *Automated Indicator Sharing (AIS)* tools to update each other's databases automatically.

The US Department of Homeland Security (DHS) sponsors several specifications for facilitating cybersecurity information sharing. *Trusted Automated eXchange of Intelligence Information (TAXII)* enables information sharing through services and message exchanges. TAXII provides transport for threat information exchange. *Structured Threat Information eXpression (STIX)* enables communication among organizations by providing a common language to represent information. *Cyber Observable eXpression (CybOX)* provides standardized specifications for communicating about cybersecurity phenomenon and elements, from malware types to event logging. DHS has made these specifications available globally for free.

 EXAM TIP You might see a question on the CompTIA Security+ exam about DHS-sponsored specifications for cybersecurity information sharing. Only TAXII and STIX are in the objectives, though. CybOX is not mentioned.

Dark Web The *Dark Web* refers to Internet sites that are inaccessible without using specific applications such as the Tor network. Dark Web sites run the gamut from illegal drug sales to terrorist groups to interesting puzzles, with just about everything

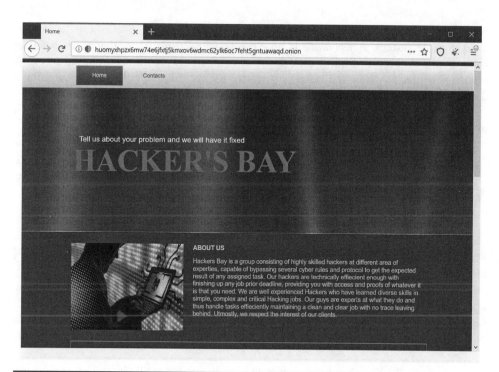

Figure 1-1   A sketchy site on the Dark Web

in between (Figure 1-1). Dark Web sites are "dark" because search engines, like Google, don't index them. You can't find these sites with a typical Internet search, in other words, but they function just like any other Web site.

The Dark Web can provide a lot of important information, especially about criminal activity through sting operations conducted by law enforcement agents posing as Dark Web site visitors interested in engaging in illegal transactions. Plus, a lot of Dark Web sites offer highly entertaining, completely legal content. It's the Wild West, so take care if (*when*) you venture in.

Indicators of Compromise   It's almost impossible for a threat actor to attack a system and not leave behind clues of the actor's presence. An IT security person must recognize the artifact of an intrusion, known as an *indicator of compromise (IoC)*. IoCs take on many forms. A sudden increase in outgoing network traffic, malware signatures, strange changes in file permissions—all of these are examples of IoCs. IoCs feature as key evidence collected in forensic investigations.

Recognizing IoCs enables cybersecurity professionals to monitor networks and provide threat monitoring tools as *threat feeds*—real-time data streams to recognize threats. Threat feeds work with internal networks as well as outside networks.

Adversary Tactics, Techniques, and Procedures   The term *adversary tactics, techniques, and procedures (TTP)* describes the actions of threat actors to gain access to your infrastructure. A *tactic* is the goal of the attacker, such as to gain initial access to a network or system. A *technique* is how the attacker implements that tactic, such as using a valid account or finding a weakness in your supply chain to gain initial access. A *procedure* is precisely how the attacker performs the technique; for example, watching a user's keyboard as the user enters an account password.

The MITRE ATT&CK framework incorporates TTP, breaking tactics into a dozen or so categories and providing common techniques associated with those tactics. Check it out here: https://attack.mitre.org.

EXAM TIP CompTIA places threat feeds and TTP as types of research sources, but many researchers consider them part of dedicated threat intelligence sources. Either way, the key for the exam is that both sources enable you to enhance threat intelligence.

Predictive Analysis Every IT security professional could use a crystal ball enabling him or her to know an incident is about to take place. That's the world of *predictive analysis*: using software, often artificial intelligence, to look for trends to anticipate any upcoming problems. Predictive analysis isn't perfect for every aspect of IT security, but for issues like hardware failure prediction and network loads, predictive analysis is a powerful tool.

NOTE Check out the Predictive Analytics portal at CIO for the latest news on the subject: https://www.cio.com/category/predictive-analytics/.

Threat Maps *Threat maps* are graphical representations of the geographical source and target of attacks (Figure 1-2). Threat maps are certainly pretty, but they aren't real time and they lack any form of deep detail about the attacks. They work well for presentations, especially to show broader trends.

File/Code Repositories A *repository* is a storage area for data files or code. Unlike archive data, repository data/code is stored in such a way that the data/code is sorted or indexed based on certain information pertinent to that data or code. Log files for an entire network over a certain number of years is one example of a file repository. Code repositories are a different matter. These are used by developers to produce and control code development. It's rare to find anything written these days that doesn't use a code repository like GitLab (Figure 1-3).

EXAM TIP CompTIA lumps file and code repositories into a single term, *file/code repositories*.

Vulnerability Databases The IT industry aggressively looks for vulnerabilities and their associated threats. Many governments and organizations host *vulnerability databases*,

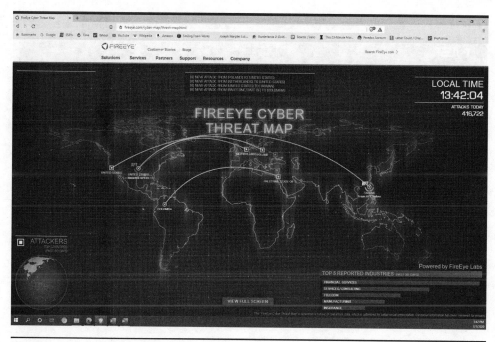

Figure 1-2   Cyber Threat Map from FireEye

Figure 1-3   GitLab

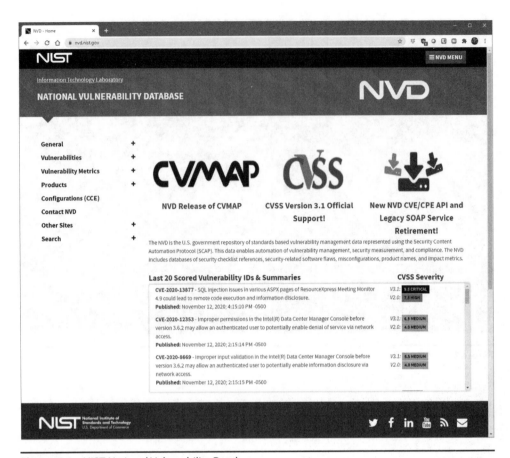

Figure 1-4 NIST National Vulnerability Database

collections of all the known problem areas or weaknesses in deployed software. One of the most important vulnerability databases in the United States is the National Institute of Standards and Technology's National Vulnerability Database (Figure 1-4).

Another great source for vulnerabilities is the Common Vulnerabilities and Exposures (CVE) list provided by MITRE Corporation: https://cve.mitre.org.

Also, check out the open-source, community-driven vulnerability database, VULDB: https://vuldb.com.

There are a lot more vulnerability databases out there, but these three should get you started.

NOTE CompTIA's division between research sources and threat intelligence sources is somewhat arbitrary. In practice, these two areas overlap.

Research Sources

Research sources aren't devoted exclusively to the idea of threat intelligence, but they're always good places to look for problems in a more generic way. Whether you're just checking a vendor forum or chatting at a conference, if security issues are out there, they're always a hot topic. This section looks at seven common research sources:

- Vendor Web sites
- Vulnerability feeds
- Conferences
- Academic journals
- Requests for comments
- Local industry groups
- Social media

If you want to know anything about a product, go directly to the *vendor Web site* to do some good research (Figure 1-5). Who else knows more about a product (hopefully) than the vendor who makes or sells it? Find a support forum and dig in!

If you want to stay on the bleeding edge of vulnerabilities and you want them basically delivered to you, *vulnerability feeds* make your research easy (easier) by delivering RSS feeds, tweets, social media posts, or other methods to let you see what's out there. There are hundreds of these types of feeds. The NVD, mentioned earlier, has a great feed.

Get out there and hit some *conferences*! There are plenty of great conferences at the regional, national, and international level. Every IT security person should make a trip to the famous Black Hat conference, held annually in Las Vegas and in other locations internationally (such as Black Hat Europe and Black Hat Asia).

Reading *academic journals* is the ultimate egghead research path, but many vulnerabilities are first brought to public attention using journals. The only challenge to reading about vulnerabilities in academic journals is that the articles often only discuss a theoretical vulnerability without showing how to do it (in many cases, someone usually does create a practical attack after an article is published).

Requests for comments (RFCs) started as the original ARPANET documents that literally defined the Internet. While this is still true, RFCs evolved to cover every aspect of TCP/IP communication and are issued by Internet Engineering Task Force (IETF), the Internet Research Task Force (IRTF), and the Internet Architecture Board (IAB). If you want the gritty details on any technology that is part of TCP/IP communications, RFCs are the place to go (Figure 1-6). All RFCs are public and can be accessed via www .rfc-editor.org.

Many security issues are industry specific, so joining *local industry groups* is almost always the best way to connect with the folks who deal with similar issues in your industry. These are often the only reliable source for industry-specific or closed/proprietary information. Search in your area for a local Information Systems Security Association International (ISSA) chapter. They're super good: https://issa.org.

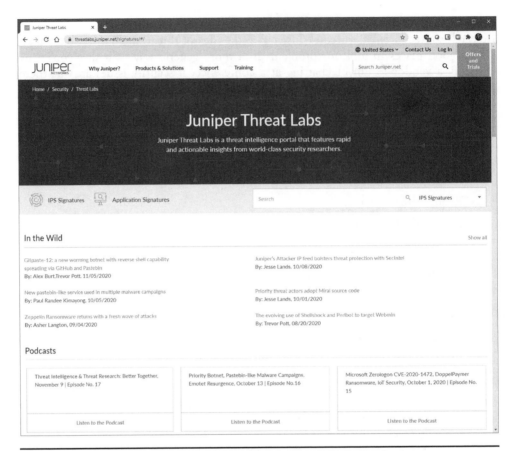

Figure 1-5   Advanced networking device manufacturer Juniper's support forums

Virtually every company or organization that provides hardware, software, services, or applications has some form of *bug bounty* program. These programs reward people who report vulnerabilities with money, swag, and acclaim (Figure 1-7). Before you get too excited and start hacking your favorite (fill in the blank), know that all of these programs have very specific scopes and parameters. Going beyond the scope could get you in serious legal trouble. Look before you leap! And get permission before you start.

Social media, such as Twitter and Reddit, provide a wealth of threat intelligence sources. Numerous Twitter feeds are dedicated to cybersecurity. Check out @Dejan_Kosutic— for hourly updates. The r/threatintel subreddit, while not quite as hyperactive as the Twitter feeds, has some great information as well. IT security professionals use a lot of tools to combat risk. These tools get lumped together under the term "risk management." Primarily, the tools reduce the impact of—*mitigate*—threats posed to an organization. Module 1-2 explores risk management concepts; later modules expand on the toolsets available. Let's leave Module 1-1 with a definition of the job of an IT security professional:

> *IT security professionals implement risk management techniques and practices to mitigate threats to their organizations.*

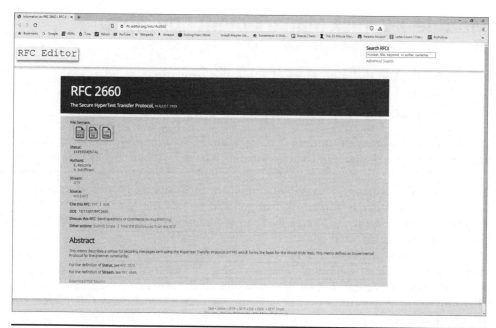

Figure 1-6   RFC for HTTPS

Figure 1-7   Facebook vulnerability reporting

Module 1-2: Risk Management Concepts

This module covers the following CompTIA Security+ objectives:

- **5.2 Explain the importance of applicable regulations, standards, or frameworks that impact organizational security posture**
- **5.3 Explain the importance of policies to organizational security**

Module 1-1 ended with a pithy job description: IT security professionals implement risk management techniques and practices to mitigate threats to their organizations. To get to the "implement" stage requires knowledge, naturally, and the term "risk management" is loaded with meaning. This module explores four aspects of risk management: infrastructure, security controls, risk management frameworks, and industry-standard frameworks and reference architectures. Later modules build on this information to get you to the "implement" step.

The term *security posture* (or *cybersecurity posture*) refers to the security status of every aspect of an organization. That includes the security of networks, systems, physical property, and intellectual property, plus all the systems, policies, and controls that implement that security. Security posture includes external entities that affect the organization, such as partners, vendors, and the supply chain. This module takes some of the theory and concepts from Module 1-1 and begins the journey to understanding the security posture.

Infrastructure

In IT risk management, the term *infrastructure* applies to just about every aspect of an organization, from the organization itself to its computers, networks, employees, physical security, and sometimes third-party access.

Organization

At its most basic, an organization is who you work for: your company, your corporation, your nonprofit, your governmental department. These are good potential examples of an organization, but in some cases, you might need more details. A single organization, for example, might look like a collection of smaller organizations in terms of risk management (Figure 1-8).

The big difference here is how autonomous your IT management is in relation to the overall organization. The more decisions the main organization lets a smaller group handle, the more the smaller group should look at itself as an organization. A smaller organization might be a single physical location in a different city or perhaps a different country. It might be a division of a corporation, or a regional governmental agency.

 NOTE A quick way to determine the scope of any IT infrastructure is to identify the bigwigs. A single IT infrastructure should never have more than one chief security officer, for example.

Figure 1-8
What's your
organization?

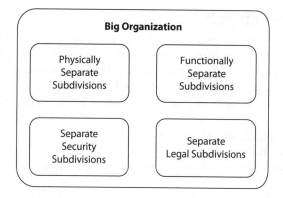

Systems

Computers and network equipment are part of an IT infrastructure, but there are many more components. People matter, such as IT managers, IT techs, human resources, chief security officer, chief information officer, and legal staff; even individual users are part of the IT infrastructure. See Figure 1-9.

Physical Security

Physical security is also an important part of an IT infrastructure. Fences, cameras, and guards protect your infrastructure just as well as they protect the rest of your organization. We'll cover physical security in Chapter 7, Module 7-8.

Third-Party Access

Third parties that your organization contracts with are part of your IT infrastructure. Does your organization have an intranet that enables suppliers to access your equipment? Then those suppliers are part of your IT infrastructure. Have a maintenance contract on all your laser printers? There's another part of your infrastructure. The company that hosts all your Web servers? Yes, they are part of your IT infrastructure as well. We'll cover third-party access in Module 1-8.

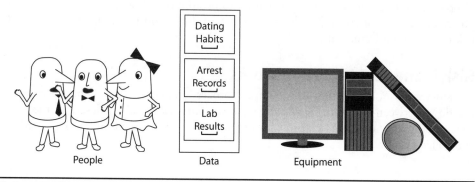

Figure 1-9   We are your infrastructure.

Security Controls

The action of strengthening a vulnerability to reduce or eliminate the threat is called a *security control*. A security control is a directed action you place on some part of your infrastructure. Security controls don't say how to perform the steps needed to mitigate a threat, only that they must be performed.

Here is an example of a security control in the *NIST Special Publication 800-53 (Rev. 4)*.

IA-5 Authenticator Management
Control Description
The organization manages information system authenticators by:

    a. Verifying, as part of the initial authenticator distribution, the identity of the individual, group, role, or device receiving the authenticator;

    b. Establishing initial authenticator content for authenticators defined by the organization;

    c. Ensuring that authenticators have sufficient strength of mechanism for their intended use;

Plus about seven other points that collectively make up the security control.

You don't have to know what all of that means yet, but do note that the controls are guidelines, not specific implementation steps. Steps required to implement the controls will vary among operating systems and network systems. The bottom line for your job as a security professional is to locate vulnerabilities and apply security controls. It's what we do.

 NOTE The security control listed here comes from the NIST NVD in case you want to look it up: https://nvd.nist.gov/800-53/Rev4/control/IA-5.

As you might imagine, the typical infrastructure probably has thousands, if not tens of thousands, of security controls that need to be applied. How does a lone IT security pro create this list of controls? The answer is, you don't. You use a bit of magic called a risk management framework.

Risk Management Frameworks

A framework is a description of a complex process, concentrating on major steps and the flows between the steps. A *risk management framework (RMF)* describes the major steps and flows of the complex process of applying security controls in an organized and controlled fashion.

EXAM TIP The CompTIA Security+ 601 objectives use the term *key frameworks* as an umbrella term for the various risk management frameworks discussed in this module. That's an objectives organizational term rather than an industry term.

One popular RMF is the *National Institute of Standards and Technology (NIST) Risk Management Framework (RMF)*. See Figure 1-10. This RMF is described in NIST Special Publication (SP) 800-37, Revision 2, *Risk Management Framework for Information Systems and Organizations: A System Life Cycle Approach for Security and Privacy*. Originally designed as an RMF expressly for US federal organizations, the NIST RMF has been adopted as the *de facto* RMF by many in the IT security industry.

The NIST RMF isn't the only well-known framework. NIST RMF was originally designed only for government agencies (although the latest version of RMF changed its name from "Federal Information Systems" to "Information Systems and Organizations"). Not too many years after developing the NIST RMF, NIST introduced the *NIST Cybersecurity Framework (CSF)*, geared more towards private industry. The NIST CSF is a similar, less comprehensive framework than the NIST RMF.

International Organization for Standardization/International Electrotechnical Commission (ISO/IEC) 27001 is the international standard for best-practice information security management systems (ISMS), roughly like the NIST RMF. ISO/IEC 27002 is the international standard to help organizations *enumerate*—list, define—their security controls. ISO/IEC 27002 lists categories of security controls, not actual individual controls. ISO/IEC 27701 extends the ISO/IEC 27001 standard to address personal information and privacy issues.

Figure 1-10
NIST RMF from
NIST.SP.800-37r2
.pdf

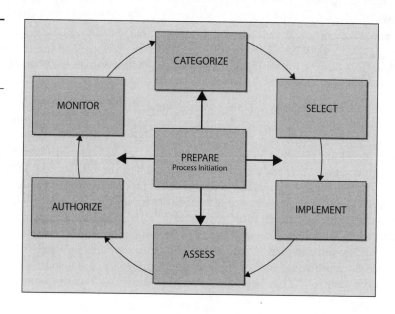

NOTE ISO 27001 and 27002 are certainly frameworks, but think of them more as frameworks with teeth! The EU can selectively choose to require organizations to use these frameworks as a compliance check, making them more of a standard than a simple recommendation like the NIST's publications.

ISO 31000 provides a broad, higher-level, and less technical overview of risk management concepts and tools to implement risk management frameworks from the executive standpoint.

The Center for Internet Security (CIS) publishes *CIS Benchmarks*, an interesting and respected framework. The fact that CIS is a nonprofit, nongovernmental organization makes its framework attractive to many security professionals. Additionally, the CIS Benchmarks framework explicitly works with small, medium, and large organizations—the only framework that addresses the "little guy."

ISACA—a professional association devoted to risk management, auditing, and security controls management—produces the *COBIT* framework designed for enterprise-wide management and governance of information processing and technology. Currently at COBIT 2019, the framework has wide adoption in the industry.

Although it might at first seem odd to throw accounting frameworks into the security mix, the auditing aspect of accounting certainly applies. The American Institute of Certified Public Accountants (AICPA) publishes the Statement on Standards for Attestation Engagements (SSAE) as a guide to financial reporting. In 2017, AICPA updated the standard from SSAE 16 to SSAE 18 to include a cybersecurity risk management reporting framework. It includes System and Organization Controls (SOC) to guide organizations in their reporting. This framework has been updated since. SOC 2 reports come in two forms, called Type I and Type II. These refer to evaluations of controls in place (Type I) and the efficiency of those controls over time (Type II).

 EXAM TIP The CompTIA Security+ exam objectives use the term "SSAE SOC 2 Type I/II" for the SSAE 18 framework as it applies to cybersecurity.

The Cloud Security Alliance (CSA) created the *Cloud Controls Matrix (CCM)*, a framework for security controls designed exclusively for cloud computing. Additionally, CSA produces *reference architectures*—templates, really—for both broad and very-specific cloud security. Plus, the CSA CCM works well with—and was designed to complement—other industry frameworks, such as the NIST and CIS frameworks.

The two biggest players in cloud computing today, Microsoft Azure and Amazon Web Services (AWS), have frameworks for security in networks that use their services. Amazon has extensive documentation for its *AWS Well-Architected Framework*, for example, providing guidelines for every aspect of security. Curious? Check out AWS's Five Pillars of the Framework: https://wa.aws.amazon.com/wat.pillars.wa-pillars.en.html.

Organizations use one or more of the frameworks discussed above to apply various security controls. That begs the question: Where do security controls originate? Let's dive into the sources of some controls, such as legislation and regulations, standards, best practices, and security policies.

Legislation/Regulations

Many *laws* affect how and what types of security controls your organization may use. Governments from states/territories and nations affect those whose businesses work or operate in the respective locations.

The United States has many laws that IT security professionals should know, such as the *Patriot Act* (2001), the *Electronic Communications Privacy Act of 1986* (ECPA), the *Computer Security Act of 1987*, the *Health Insurance Portability and Accountability Act of 1996* (HIPAA), and the *Sarbanes-Oxley Act of 2002* (SOX). There are many more, but a couple of descriptions should do for this introduction.

HIPAA provides data privacy and security provisions for safeguarding medical information. These include provisions for who may have access to patient records and how to properly store records. SOX has many provisions, but the one that is most important to many companies is the requirement for private businesses to retain critical records for specific time periods. Both HIPAA and SOX are discussed in more detail in Module 1-6.

 NOTE The CompTIA Security+ exam barely scratches the surface of what security professionals need to know about laws that affect our field. You cannot skip over legal guidelines, though, because they will bite you . . . and make your security career short and unpleasant.

In response to demands by the public to protect the privacy of users visiting Web sites, the European Union (EU) created the General Data Protection Regulation (GDPR). Since GDPR became effective in 2018, odds are good you've seen a GDPR notification on Web sites such as shown in Figure 1-11.

GDPR is an interesting law, as in theory it applies globally to any organization or country that processes or stores personal information of any EU citizen. As of this writing, the EU hasn't attempted to sanction or fine any non-EU organization, but it's just a matter of time. GDPR is unique to the EU, but many national, state, and territorial governments have adopted similar legislation. The state of California, for example, adopted the California Consumer Privacy Act (CCPA).

Standards

A *standard* is a ruleset voluntarily adopted by an industry to provide more uniform products and services. It might be more accurate to replace the word *voluntarily* with the word *voluntold*, because many standards are often required for participation in certain industries. Easily the most far-reaching standard from the standpoint of IT security is the *Payment Card Industry Data Security Standard (PCI DSS)*. This industry-specific framework, adopted by everyone who processes credit card, debit card, prepaid card, or gift card transactions, provides for several highly detailed security controls to mitigate credit card fraud. Vendors who accept credit cards but fail to abide by PCI DSS rules quickly find themselves cut off from their ability to accept cards.

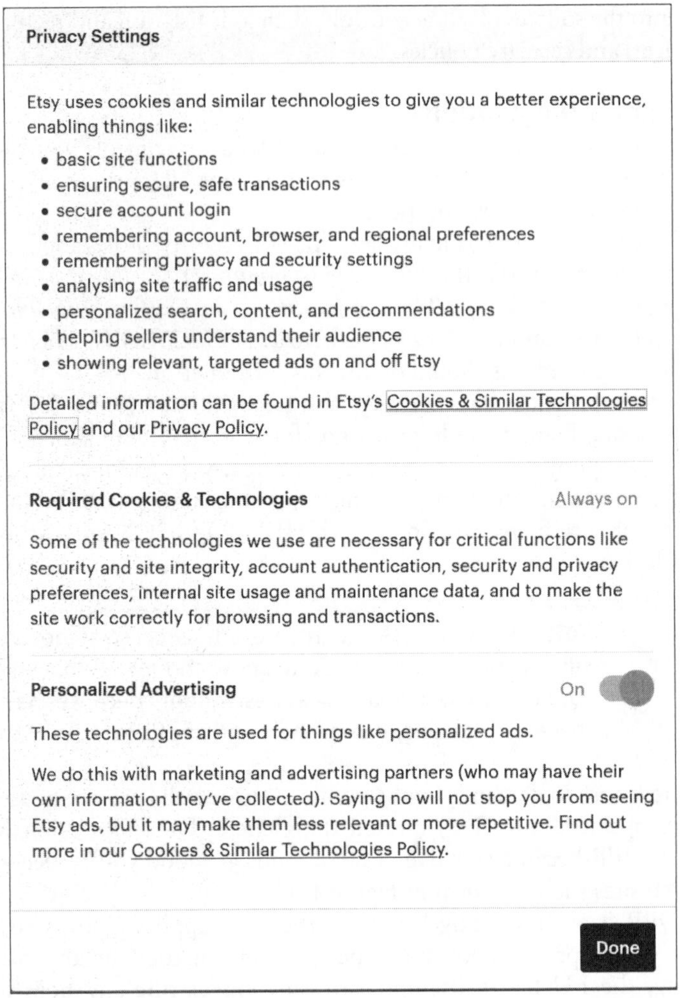

Figure 1-11
GDPR
notification

Privacy Settings

Etsy uses cookies and similar technologies to give you a better experience, enabling things like:

- basic site functions
- ensuring secure, safe transactions
- secure account login
- remembering account, browser, and regional preferences
- remembering privacy and security settings
- analysing site traffic and usage
- personalized search, content, and recommendations
- helping sellers understand their audience
- showing relevant, targeted ads on and off Etsy

Detailed information can be found in Etsy's <u>Cookies & Similar Technologies Policy</u> and our <u>Privacy Policy</u>.

Required Cookies & Technologies   Always on

Some of the technologies we use are necessary for critical functions like security and site integrity, account authentication, security and privacy preferences, internal site usage and maintenance data, and to make the site work correctly for browsing and transactions.

Personalized Advertising   On

These technologies are used for things like personalized ads.

We do this with marketing and advertising partners (who may have their own information they've collected). Saying no will not stop you from seeing Etsy ads, but it may make them less relevant or more repetitive. Find out more in our <u>Cookies & Similar Technologies Policy</u>.

Done

Benchmarks/Secure Configuration Guides

Benchmarks and secure configuration guides are knowledgeable recommendations that lack the enforceability of legislation and standards, but are an important consideration of any IT security framework. Benchmarks and guides come from governments (if you want to be accurate, even the NIST RMF is just a guide), industry groups, and vendors. In most cases benchmarks and guides tend to be very specific, directed toward a platform such as Microsoft Windows, Apache Web servers, application servers, network infrastructure devices, and so on.

NOTE Add the term "best practices" to benchmarks and guides, as they are basically the same thing.

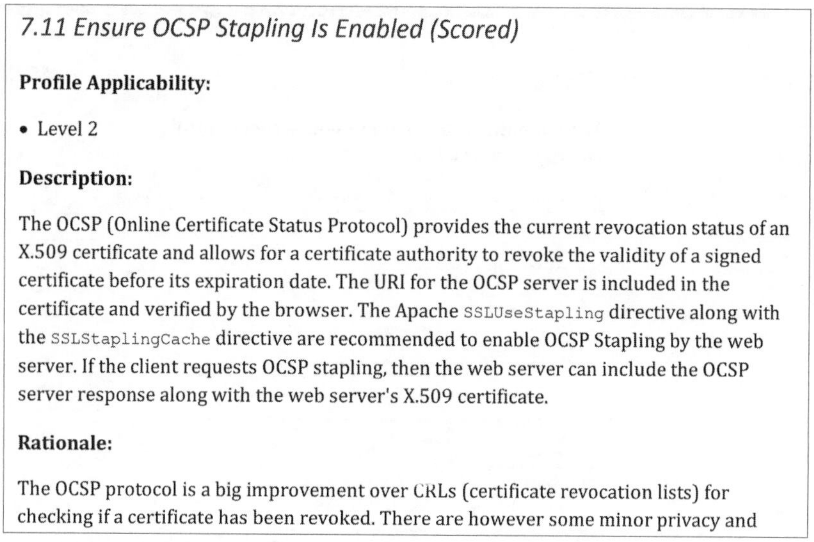

7.11 Ensure OCSP Stapling Is Enabled (Scored)

Profile Applicability:

- Level 2

Description:

The OCSP (Online Certificate Status Protocol) provides the current revocation status of an X.509 certificate and allows for a certificate authority to revoke the validity of a signed certificate before its expiration date. The URI for the OCSP server is included in the certificate and verified by the browser. The Apache `SSLUseStapling` directive along with the `SSLStaplingCache` directive are recommended to enable OCSP Stapling by the web server. If the client requests OCSP stapling, then the web server can include the OCSP server response along with the web server's X.509 certificate.

Rationale:

The OCSP protocol is a big improvement over CRLs (certificate revocation lists) for checking if a certificate has been revoked. There are however some minor privacy and

Figure 1-12 Excerpt from CIS Benchmark for Apache HTTP Server

One excellent example of benchmarks is the collection of CIS Controls from the Center for Internet Security, the same folks who made the CIS Benchmarks mentioned earlier. These *platform-specific* benchmarks are wonderfully detailed and are an excellent tool for those of us who need a more step-by-step guide for securing a broad cross-section of platforms. Figure 1-12 shows a few lines from CIS's excellent guide to securing the popular Apache Web server.

Sometimes it's down to the users of equipment to tell others about their security experiences. Any organization can create or use a *Security Technical Implementation Guide (STIG)* to standardize security protocols throughout their networks. A typical STIG provides details on how to optimize desktop computer security, for example, and best practices for patching and security updates. STIGs also cover configuration and security details for every common networking device, from routers to firewalls.

 EXAM TIP The CompTIA Security+ exam will test your knowledge of the European legislation GDPS, US laws (HIPAA and SOX), and standards such as PCI DSS.

The entire IT industry is filled with *vendor-specific guides*, providing best practices that vendors recommend you follow. From configuring access control lists for a Cisco router to hardening Remote Desktop on Windows Server 2019, there's a benchmark (or best practice) for you. Microsoft provides incredibly detailed best practices for all its products (Figure 1-13).

Figure 1-13   Best practices for a Microsoft product

Security Policies

A security policy is a document that organizations generate to declare what actions and attitudes they will take for certain critical aspects of their infrastructure. An organization may have hundreds of policies, but, generally, policies most commonly define security controls for the trickiest assets in every organization—the people. Later modules will delve deeply into policies; for now, let's look at one of the most common, an acceptable use policy.

An *acceptable use policy (AUP)* defines exactly what users may or may not do on systems in the organization. Here are a few lines from an example AUP pulled from one of many free boilerplates available on the Web:

- Users must not attempt to access any data, documents, e-mail correspondence, and programs contained on systems for which they do not have authorization.

- Users must not share their account(s), passwords, personal identification numbers (PIN), security tokens (i.e., smart card), or similar information or devices used for identification and authorization purposes.

- Users must not use non-standard shareware or freeware software without the appropriate management approval.

- Users must not engage in activity that may degrade the performance of Information Resources; deprive an authorized user access to resources; obtain extra resources beyond those allocated; or circumvent computer security measures.

- Users must not download, install, or run security programs or utilities such as password cracking programs, packet sniffers, or port scanners that reveal or exploit weaknesses in the security of a computer resource unless approved by the CISO (chief information security officer).

Module 1-3: Security Controls

This module covers the following CompTIA Security+ objective:

- **5.1 Compare and contrast various types of controls**

The previous module covered the concept of security controls and even showed you a few examples. This module delves deeply into the organization of security controls. This organization makes it easier to consider the types of controls available and to classify them into specific groups based on what they do to mitigate threats. The CompTIA Security+ objectives group controls into two broad areas: categories and types. Let's look at both to see how they work.

Control Categories

Control categories define who or what aspect of the enterprise deals with them or who or what aspect of the infrastructure they affect. In this case, we break security controls into managerial, operational, and technical.

Managerial Controls

You can categorize controls by defining the people responsible for those controls. A *managerial control* (or management control), for example, is a broad control that covers the entire organization. All employees, no matter their location, must use a 12-character password updated every 30 days—that's a managerial control. These require some form of management overview. Management controls are reviewed periodically, such as yearly or monthly.

Operational Controls

Operational controls apply to a single unit in an organization and deal with how things get done. An example of an operational control would be a requirement that a certain PC controller must be reset daily. Operational controls rarely need management overview and are reviewed far more frequently than management controls.

Technical Controls

Technical controls are security controls applied to technology. If you specify a security control that states, "All edge routers must be able to communicate on SNMPv3," then you've made a technical control.

Control Types

Thus far, the book has defined a security control as an action performed on a vulnerability to mitigate the impact of a risk. But what form of action can a control take? At first glance you might be tempted to look at a security control as an action to block an attack. It's tempting, for example, to think of placing 20-character, complex WPA2 passwords on all the wireless access points (WAPs) in an organization as a security control that will stop anyone from hacking the 802.11 network. This is a strong security control

Figure 1-14
Mitigation isn't
perfection.

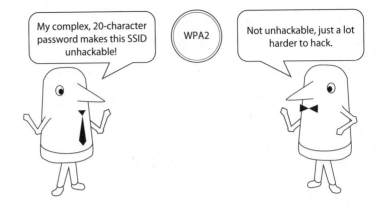

no doubt, but it can't absolutely stop a determined attacker. Even long passwords can be hacked, although the probability of a successful attack is greatly reduced (Figure 1-14).

Mitigation doesn't mean stopping an attack. Attacks happen. Therefore, it's helpful to define security controls based on when they work relative to the phase of an attack. A security control might work before, during, or after an attack. These are generally known as *control types*. You need to know five control types for both essential skills and the CompTIA Security+ exam: deterrent, preventive, detective, corrective, and compensating.

 EXAM TIP The CompTIA Security+ objectives include *physical* as a control type. The physical control *category* includes options for securing physical areas from unauthorized access, such as fences, bollards, and so on. See Chapter 10, Module 10-1 for physical controls in depth.

Deterrent Control

A *deterrent control* is designed to deter a potential attacker from even attempting an attack. Good lighting or signage around your building might deter an intruder from entering. Not building a server building near a fault line is another example. Figure 1-15 shows the welcome banner from a Secure Shell (SSH) server. Surely that will deter any potential hacker!

Figure 1-15
Mike's SSH
warning

```
login as:root

Welcome to Mike's SSH server!

*****************************************
* WARNING! AUTHORIZED USERS ONLY!       *
*                                       *
* YOUR IP ADDRESS IS BEING TRACKED!     *
*                                       *
*****************************************
root@10.11.12.101's password:_
```

Preventive Control

A *preventive control* attempts to keep an active attack from succeeding. The earlier example of using a 20-character password on WPA2 is a great example of a preventive control. Putting a lock on the server room door is another example of a preventive control. Doing thorough background checks on potential new employees would be a third example.

NOTE Most security controls are preventive controls.

Detective Control

A *detective control* works during an attack. As the name implies, these controls actively look for an attack and alert security professionals to the presence of an active, ongoing attack. An intrusion detection system, for example, watches a network for activity that indicates an intrusion attack. A security camera detects someone trying to go into a place he or she does not belong.

EXAM TIP Some security controls cross phases. A security guard can be classified as a deterrent control, preventive control, or detective control, for example, depending on the role that the security guard is playing at any given moment.

Corrective

A *corrective control* applies after an attack has taken place and fixes/mitigates the result of the incident. Restoring data from backups is probably the most common example of a corrective control.

Compensating

Sometimes you need to provide a temporary solution to a vulnerability that's less than optimal. Perhaps someone tried to drive through a fence and you need to hire an extra guard for a short time. Maybe all users have to log into a system as root until a completely new system comes online, so you add extra logs to track usage more closely. These are *compensating controls.* You use compensating controls to keep going until a better control is available or possible.

Module 1-4: Risk Assessment

This module covers the following CompTIA Security+ objective:

- **5.4 Summarize risk management processes and concepts**

Previous modules discussed risk and the security controls used to mitigate risk. So, you might think that risk management is nothing more than an ongoing process

Figure 1-16
Probably not
worth it

of identifying each vulnerability and then applying some form of security control to mitigate the risks that vulnerability exposes. Applying security controls is important, but the actual step of applying a security control is the end of a complex process. Risk management is much more nuanced.

This nuance comes from the fact that every risk has a different vulnerability and impact. A risk with very low impact might not be worth the cost of mitigation. Equally, a risk with very low impact might motivate you to ignore the risk. Also, consider the fact that IT security teams have a limited amount of money, time, and resources to apply to addressing all the risks.

Consider the risk of a meteor hitting your facility (Figure 1-16). If you could get a *Star Wars* ion cannon for the low, low price of $47 trillion, how would you feel about sending that bill to your accounting department?

These variables require a good IT security professional to develop a *risk assessment*, which is a carefully organized plan, more nuanced than simply trying to mitigate everything. A good risk assessment uses several tools and methods to enable the IT security professional to react to all threats in a realistic and practical way. This module starts by defining some of the main concepts and tools of risk assessment. The module describes existing frameworks you can use to help you perform a comprehensive risk assessment.

Risk Assessment Processes and Concepts

Risk assessment brings a lot of jargon into play to describe specific aspects or nuances in security. This section explores risk assessment terms that define common processes and concepts: risk awareness, risk and controls, risk assessment methods, threat sources and events, vulnerabilities, likelihood and impact, and risk register.

Risk Awareness

Risk awareness is the process by which people recognize risk. It's one of those terms that sounds obvious but really isn't. Sure, we want to be aware of risk, but how does that awareness manifest? Knowing how we are aware of a risk often helps us mitigate that risk. First of all, maybe it doesn't manifest at all. Perhaps the awareness comes from careful analysis, or perhaps the person identifying the risk has some form of bias about that risk.

Risk and Controls

There's more to risk than simply mitigating through controls. You can't just recognize a risk and slap on a control to mitigate that risk. You need to consider the ramifications of the control before applying it to a risk. Does the control mitigate the risk? What happens without the control? How much mitigation does the control provide? Is it worth it? Does the application of the control create other risks that also have to be mitigated? That creates three states: the risk with no control applied; the risk after a control; new risks developed because of the control.

Inherent risk represents the amount of risk that exists in the absence of controls. *Residual risk* is the amount of risk that remains after accounting for controls. *Control risk* is the probability of loss resulting from the malfunction of internal control measures implemented to mitigate risks.

Once a control is applied, it's important to make a control assessment. These assessments manifest in many ways, but you should know the two ways to perform that assessment: a *risk control assessment* is when you use an outside source to inspect and judge the quality of your controls. This might be important especially to comply with laws or regulations that affect control risk or *risk posture*—the overall scope of risk for an organization. Otherwise, an organization can simply perform a *risk control self-assessment*—as in you use in-house resources to do the assessment.

Risk Assessment Methods

In addition to hiring knowledgeable and experienced risk management personnel, organizations can implement and follow a formalized process or methodology in assessing risk. Developing this process can be quite an undertaking, but, fortunately, organizations can use existing methods created by experts in the risk management profession. One such common method of conducting risk assessments is NIST SP 800-30, Rev. 1, *Guide for Conducting Risk Assessments*. Another assessment methodology comes from ISACA, a professional association devoted to risk management, auditing, and security controls management. This methodology is *The Risk IT Framework*. Both methodologies describe detailed processes for conducting risk assessments, and both can be adapted for any organization to use.

NIST SP 800-30, Rev. 1, prescribes a four-step risk assessment process:

1. Prepare for assessment.

2. Conduct assessment:

   A. Identify threat sources and events.

   B. Identify vulnerabilities and predisposing conditions.

   C. Determine likelihood of occurrence.

   D. Determine magnitude of impact.

   E. Determine risk.

3. Communicate results.

4. Maintain assessment.

After initial preparation, the IT security professional begins the assessment. First, identify threat actors (sources) and threat events, and then identify vulnerabilities associated with assets and other risk factors. You then calculate likelihood and impact values, which define the risk. Communicating the risk assessment results means reporting the assessment to management, so that risk response options can be carefully considered. Maintaining the assessment means implementing the response options and closely monitoring the risk, periodically reassessing it to ensure the effectiveness of the response options and to determine whether the risk has changed.

NOTE Although you likely will not be tested on either the NIST or ISACA methodologies, they're good to know for use on the job, especially if you are assigned any type of risk assessment duties for your organization.

Identifying Threat Sources and Events

The first step in *threat assessment* is to identify the threat sources and to categorize them into groups. The process of categorizing threats may seem daunting, but NIST and ISACA provide some good basic categories to begin the process. Referencing NIST SP 800-30, Rev. 1, Table D-2, one possible categorization might look something like Figure 1-17.

You're not required to use this categorization. Some organizations simply break all threat sources into no more than the following four categories. Compare these to similar categories listed in Figure 1-17 to get an idea as to how different organizations can use totally different categories to cover the same types of threats.

- **Environmental**   Natural disasters outside the control of humans
- **Person-made**   Any threat that is not environmental; includes disasters caused by people
- **Internal**   Threat generated by internal sources, usually an insider to the organization
- **External**   Threat generated from outside your infrastructure

Vulnerabilities

As a refresher from Module 1-1, a *vulnerability* is a weakness inherent in an asset that leaves it open to a threat. Vulnerabilities in an organization vary according to the unique components of that organization, so it's hard to provide anything concrete here that applies universally. Broadly speaking, though, just as with threat sources, organizations can have internal and external vulnerabilities.

Internal vulnerabilities include *legacy systems* and *software compliance/licensing* issues. As a business grows over time, that "old Windows 7 computer in the corner that has one job" might not have any security support anymore. Assessing all the systems in use throughout an organization is essential to finding vulnerabilities. Likewise, software that is out of compliance or license creates a financial vulnerability—get caught in an audit and pay stiff penalties.

TABLE D-2: TAXONOMY OF THREAT SOURCES

Type of Threat Source	Description	Characteristics

ADVERSARIAL
- Individual
  - Outsider
  - Insider
  - Trusted Insider
  - Privileged Insider
- Group
  - Ad hoc
  - Established
- Organization
  - Competitor
  - Supplier
  - Partner
  - Customer
- Nation-State
	Individuals, groups, organizations, or states that seek to exploit the organization's dependence on cyber resources (i.e., information in electronic form, information and communications technologies, and the communications and information-handling capabilities provided by those technologies).	Capability, Intent, Targeting

ACCIDENTAL - User - Privileged User/Administrator	Erroneous actions taken by individuals in the course of executing their everyday responsibilities.	Range of effects

STRUCTURAL
- Information Technology (IT) Equipment
  - Storage
  - Processing
  - Communications
  - Display
  - Sensor
  - Controller
- Environmental Controls
  - Temperature/Humidity Controls
  - Power Supply
- Software
  - Operating System
  - Networking
  - General-Purpose Application
  - Mission-Specific Application
	Failures of equipment, environmental controls, or software due to aging, resource depletion, or other circumstances which exceed expected operating parameters.	Range of effects

ENVIRONMENTAL
- Natural or man-made disaster
  - Fire
  - Flood/Tsunami
  - Windstorm/Tornado
  - Hurricane
  - Earthquake
  - Bombing
  - Overrun
- Unusual Natural Event (e.g., sunspots)
- Infrastructure Failure/Outage
  - Telecommunications
  - Electrical Power
	Natural disasters and failures of critical infrastructures on which the organization depends, but which are outside the control of the organization.
	
	Note: Natural and man-made disasters can also be characterized in terms of their severity and/or duration. However, because the threat source and the threat event are strongly identified, severity and duration can be included in the description of the threat event (e.g., Category 5 hurricane causes extensive damage to the facilities housing mission-critical systems, making those systems unavailable for three weeks).
		Range of effects

Figure 1-17   Example taxonomy of threat sources (from NIST SP 800-30, Rev. 1)

Multiparty affiliations can expose external vulnerabilities, such as the communications among the entities, or a shared database in the cloud with users from each entity. Having valuable intellectual property presents a prototypical vulnerability, *IP theft* by external hackers.

Combine these vulnerabilities with willing and able threat actors, then define the likelihood of occurrence (described next). These are classic risks for which you need to implement security measures to protect the organization.

 NOTE CompTIA uses the term "risk types" to describe vulnerabilities like those outlined in this section. The vulnerabilities become risks when you add threats and likelihood.

Likelihood and Impact

Once you have collected all the different data on threats, vulnerabilities, and assets, you can assess likelihood of occurrence and impact. *Likelihood of occurrence* is the probability that a threat actor will initiate a threat or the probability that a threat could successfully exploit a given vulnerability. *Impact* is the degree of harm or damage caused to an asset or the organization. Both can be viewed in either objective or subjective terms.

Objectively, likelihood or impact could be expressed in terms of numerical values. In a subjective expression, both elements may be termed qualitatively, or using a range of descriptions on a scale. These two ways of expressing likelihood and impact are the two risk assessment types discussed in the upcoming sections: *quantitative* (objective or numerical) and *qualitative* (subjective) assessment types.

Risk Register

A *risk register* is a scatter-plot graph that compares probability to impact. Risk registers are handy tools for detecting otherwise easily missed risks.

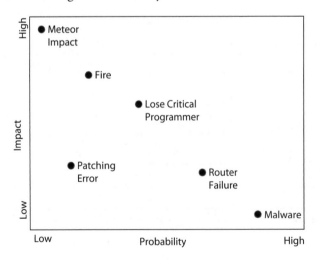

Taxonomy of Threat Sources

Quantitative Risk Assessment

An organization uses a *quantitative risk assessment* when it requires exact figures on risk equated to likelihood and impact. Exact dollar values, for instance, can be used to describe impact or loss of an asset. A quantitative risk assessment requires that the organization measure and obtain certain pieces of data, because the assessment depends upon the accuracy and completeness of the data fed into it.

A quantitative risk assessment is based on *objective* data—typically, numerical data. A quantitative assessment is objective in that the data fed into it is measurable and independently verifiable. For example, cost expressed as a dollar value is a measurable and concrete piece of data often used to perform quantitative analysis. Other types of numerical data may include statistical analysis of different aspects of likelihood, for instance.

In the next few sections, we'll look at five data elements required to perform a quantitative assessment: asset value, exposure factor, single-loss expectancy, annualized rate of occurrence, and annualized loss expectancy. Note that these are very simplistic data elements; in more complex assessments, other data elements might be required as well.

Asset Value and Exposure Factor

A quantitative risk assessment starts with determining *asset value*, a monetary figure that reflects various factors, such as replacement or repair cost, cost over time, and more. First, determine an asset's replacement cost. Some organizations may need to consider depreciation values over time, however, which would reduce the amount of money they may have available to replace an asset. Another consideration is repair cost versus replacement cost. If an asset simply needs repair to return to an operational condition, then the organization should consider different costs for different components required to repair the asset. (See Module 1-5 for more on component failure measurements.)

Beyond cost to replace or repair the asset, you must also look at the revenue the asset generates. To replace a failed server, for example, costs $5000; the amount of revenue that the server brings in every day, due to the data that's processed on it, is $3000. So even if you pay the $5000 to order a new server, if the vendor can't get it to you and installed within four days, you've lost $12,000 in revenue in addition to the cost of the server. Those considerations may require you to reevaluate the value of the asset. It's not only about the cost of replacement for the asset, but also how much value it gives to the organization.

 NOTE   When valuing an asset, consider not only the replacement cost but also the revenue the asset generates, as this will be lost as well if the asset is not available.

Along with asset valuation, organizations should consider the *exposure factor*, the percentage of an asset's value that could be lost during a negative event. Realistically, you will not always lose 100 percent of the value; you may lose only 30 percent or 50 percent, for example. Exposure factor considers the percentage of the asset's value (or the revenue derived from the asset) lost in the event of an incident.

You can use exposure factors when performing risk assessments to determine realistically how much of a loss your organization may suffer during an incident. This in turn affects how much money or other resources you should devote to budgeting for risk response. Exposure factors are normally expressed mathematically as a decimal number. An exposure factor of 0.4, for example, is a 40 percent loss, and an exposure factor of 1 is a 100 percent loss.

Single-Loss Expectancy

The *single-loss expectancy (SLE)* is a value that's computed simply by multiplying the asset's value (in dollars) by the exposure factor (percentage of loss). Use this simple formula as the initial step in describing risk from a quantitative point of view. The SLE indicates what the loss would be in a single circumstance of a negative incident affecting the asset. The formula can also be described as follows:

SLE (single-loss expectancy) = AV (asset value) × EF (exposure factor)

Given this formula, suppose you had an asset worth $5000, and during a single-loss event such as a fire, you'd expect to lose 50 percent of that asset's value. This would be expressed as:

SLE = $5000 (AV) × 0.50 (EF) = $2500

Obviously, this is a very simple scenario. When calculating SLE, you must look at other aspects of the loss, such as the event that might cause the loss, its likelihood, revenue generated from the asset, and so on. Additionally, exposure factor can be a difficult value to nail down. You might use statistical analysis, or even the "best guess" by a committee of experts, to determine exposure factor for different assets.

 EXAM TIP Know the formula for single-loss expectancy:
SLE = AV (asset value) × EF (exposure factor)

Annualized Rate of Occurrence

The *annualized rate of occurrence (ARO)* is how many times per year you would expect a negative event to occur, resulting in a loss of the asset. This value relates more to likelihood than impact and serves to establish a baseline of how likely a specific threat is to occur, affecting the asset.

This value can result from several different sources. First, you could look at historical trends. For example, let's say that your business is in an area prone to tornadoes. You can gather information from the National Weather Service on how many tornadoes normally occur in your region every year. This would be the ARO for that threat. Obviously, other events would have other rates of occurrence. Some of these would be difficult to quantify without more in-depth information. For instance, obtaining the ARO for attacks from hackers would be problematic, since that would not necessarily be limited to a geographical area. You might have to gather data and perform statistical analysis to determine how often serious attacks occur, given specific circumstances, attack methods, level of attack, and so on, with regard to your type of industry or business. Some of this data might come from published industry trends, and some information may come from law enforcement or threat intelligence sources (introduced in Module 1-1) that provide aggregate analysis of this particular type of data. In the end, this might simply be an educated guess, based upon the best data you have available to you. In any case, what you're after is an end number that you can use as a factor in determining how often a particular threat might occur on an annual basis. You'll use this number during the next calculation, the ALE.

Annualized Loss Expectancy

The *annualized loss expectancy (ALE)* essentially looks at the amount of loss from the SLE and determines how much loss the organization could realistically expect in a one-year period. Viewing potential loss on an annual basis makes it easier to craft budgets and allocate resources toward risk management, since most organizations function on a fiscal-year basis. Additionally, this allows the organization to project how many times in a given year a particular event may occur. The formula for ALE is also quite simple:

ALE (annualized loss expectancy) = SLE × ARO

Let's use an example to make this formula clear.

The Bayland Widgets Corporation has a data center in Totoville, Kansas. Totoville averages about seven major tornados a year. The ARO of a tornado is therefore 7. A serious tornado hit to the $2,000,000 facility would likely cause about 20 percent damage. Put those numbers together to create the SLE:

SLE = AV ($2,000,000) × EF (20% or 0.2)
SLE = $400,000

If all seven major tornadoes that occurred during the year actually hit and caused this level of damage to the facility, then the ALE would be $400,000 (SLE) × 7 (ARO) = a *potential* loss of $2,800,000 (ALE). This would be the worst-case scenario. Realistically, since all seven are not likely to hit the facility, you can lower the ARO to a lesser number.

Obviously, this is a very simplistic (and most likely remote) scenario; the object here is to show you the different data elements and demonstrate how the formulas work. These simple formulas don't take into account realistic values or other risk factors that may affect likelihood and impact. However, they do demonstrate the basics of how you might calculate these two risk elements. You'll find that these particular formulas are prevalent throughout the Security+ exam as well as other higher-level information security exams, such as the CISSP.

 EXAM TIP   Understand the formula for computing the annualized loss expectancy:
ALE = SLE (single-loss expectancy) × ARO (annualized rate of occurrence)

Qualitative Risk Assessment

Quantitative risk assessments seem to be, on the surface, the way to go if an organization wants a very accurate, data-driven view of risk. Quantitative analysis, however, has a couple of weak points. First, a lack of data can force organizations to use incomplete or subjective numerical values. Second, even exact numbers can be misleading, simply because of the different methods people and organizations use to arrive at numerical values. Yet another issue is the fact that even when you're talking about exact numbers, they can still be subjective. People, because of their own opinions or limitations of their data collection and analysis processes, sometimes have to make educated guesses about numerical values. These issues can cause data to be incomplete, inexact, or simply incorrect. Another big shortfall with quantitative analysis is that many other types of data cannot be easily quantified or measured. Some of these pieces of data are also subjective. In other words, they are dependent upon the point of view of the person collecting and analyzing the data. This is why a qualitative analysis is often preferred.

A *qualitative risk assessment* doesn't necessarily use numerical values; it relies on a *risk appetite*. Risk appetite is a relative term of how much risk is perceived by the organization. Organizations usually assign a descriptive value, such as low, medium, or high when defining a risk appetite for a particular risk. They take into consideration less tangible ideas such as experience, opinion, trend analysis, or best estimates. For example, what would the impact be to an organization if it suffered a loss of reputation in the marketplace?

Reputation cannot be easily quantified numerically. Those are typically the values (or some similar range of descriptive values) that qualitative analysis uses. In the case of loss of reputation, the impact might be designated as *high*, for instance.

Even risk elements that could normally be assigned a numerical value can be expressed qualitatively. The likelihood of a threat exploiting a vulnerability could be expressed in a range of descriptive values, such as very low, low, moderate, high, and extreme. The same could be said for impact. Of course, these values are subjective; what one person believes to be a *high* likelihood, another may believe to be an *extreme* likelihood. In qualitative analysis, the organization must come to a consensus over what qualitative values mean and the relationships among values.

We can use tools such as a *risk matrix* to help organize risk assessment. A risk matrix is a table that plots the likelihood of occurrence of a risk against the severity of the impact. Imagine a scenario where a server room becomes inoperable. Plotting severity of impact against likelihood, we could see something like the risk matrix shown in Table 1-1.

		Impact			
		Marginal	**Minor**	**Important**	**Critical**
	Certain	Moderate	High	Extreme	Extreme
Likelihood	**Likely**	Moderate	High	High	Extreme
	Possible	Low	Moderate	High	High
	Unlikely	Low	Low	Moderate	Moderate
	Rare	Very Low	Very Low	Low	Moderate

Table 1-1   Risk Matrix

TABLE D-3: ASSESSMENT SCALE – CHARACTERISTICS OF ADVERSARY CAPABILITY

Qualitative Values	Semi-Quantitative Values		Description
Very High	96–100	10	The adversary has a very sophisticated level of expertise, is well resourced, and can generate opportunities to support multiple successful, continuous, and coordinated attacks.
High	80–95	8	The adversary has a sophisticated level of expertise, with significant resources and opportunities to support multiple successful coordinated attacks.
Moderate	21–79	5	The adversary has moderate resources, expertise, and opportunities to support multiple successful attacks.
Low	5–20	2	The adversary has limited resources, expertise, and opportunities to support a successful attack.
Very Low	0–4	0	The adversary has very limited resources, expertise, and opportunities to support a successful attack.

Figure 1-18   Qualitative and semi-qualitative values (from NIST SP 800-30, Rev. 1)

This sample risk matrix is fairly easy to read, but as a matrix gets larger it's often handy to add color to the matrix to represent the risk by color: red the highest and green the lowest. This is called a *heat map*.

Despite the subjective nature of qualitative analysis, this type of assessment can be very meaningful and accurate. The organization can develop a method of calculating risk based upon the relative values of impact and likelihood, even given descriptive values. In Figure 1-18, taken from NIST SP 800-30, Rev. 1, risk can be calculated from a qualitative perspective using descriptive likelihood and impact values.

It's also worth mentioning here that another type of scale could be used, one that does use numeric values. You could have a scale that uses values from 1 to 10, for example. In this case, the scale will be referred to as *semi-quantitative*, because these numbers could be averaged together to get aggregate values. Since it is still a subjective measurement, however, it is really a qualitative type of analysis.

Putting It All Together: Risk Analysis

Although qualitative risk analysis is probably most often used because it can accept a wide variety of data, including elements that are not easily quantifiable, most organizations use a combination of qualitative and quantitative analyses. To calculate the impact, for example, the organization might use quantitative assessments. To calculate likelihood, the organization may go with a qualitative approach. For some risk scenarios, either one or both may be more appropriate. Which method an organization uses depends upon what type of data it has and what type of data it wants to obtain from the analysis.

Also, although risk scenarios typically revolve around a single threat, vulnerability, and asset at a time taken together in context, these risks are usually calculated and then rolled up into a larger level of risk that applies to the entire organization. Figure 1-19, also taken from NIST SP 800-30, Rev. 1, illustrates how the use of qualitative values can be used to describe overall risk. At first glance, Figure 1-19 seems almost identical to Figure 1-18, but read the descriptions. Figure 1-18's description is concerned with

TABLE D-4: ASSESSMENT SCALE – CHARACTERISTICS OF ADVERSARY INTENT

Qualitative Values	Semi-Quantitative Values		Description
Very High	96–100	10	The adversary seeks to undermine, severely impede, or destroy a core mission or business function, program, or enterprise by exploiting a presence in the organization's information systems or infrastructure. The adversary is concerned about disclosure of tradecraft only to the extent that it would impede its ability to complete stated goals.
High	80–95	8	The adversary seeks to undermine/impede critical aspects of a core mission or business function, program, or enterprise, or place itself in a position to do so in the future, by maintaining a presence in the organization's information systems or infrastructure. The adversary is very concerned about minimizing attack detection/disclosure of tradecraft, particularly while preparing for future attacks.
Moderate	21–79	5	The adversary seeks to obtain or modify specific critical or sensitive information or usurp/disrupt the organization's cyber resources by establishing a foothold in the organization's information systems or infrastructure. The adversary is concerned about minimizing attack detection/disclosure of tradecraft, particularly when carrying out attacks over long time periods. The adversary is willing to impede aspects of the organization's missions/business functions to achieve these ends.
Low	5–20	2	The adversary actively seeks to obtain critical or sensitive information or to usurp/disrupt the organization's cyber resources, and does so without concern about attack detection/disclosure of tradecraft.
Very Low	0–4	0	The adversary seeks to usurp, disrupt, or deface the organization's cyber resources, and does so without concern about attack detection/disclosure of tradecraft.

Figure 1-19   Qualitative assessment of risk (from NIST SP 800-30, Rev. 1)

the attacker, whereas the description in Figure 1-19 describes the risk in terms of how it might affect infrastructure.

NOTE   Remember the difference between qualitative and quantitative assessment methods. Qualitative methods use descriptive terms, while quantitative methods primarily use numerical values.

Risk Response

After you've identified and analyzed risk for assets and the organization, you must then decide how to respond to the risks produced as a result of the analysis. Responding to risk means to attempt to minimize its effects on the organization. *Risk management strategies* fall into four categories:

- Mitigation
- Transference
- Acceptance
- Avoidance

An organization chooses risk mitigation, risk transference, risk acceptance, or risk avoidance depending on several factors, including cost, effectiveness, and what value it places on the asset in question. Often, risk responses could include implementing technologies or controls that cost more than the asset is worth, and the organization has to decide whether it is worth it to deal with the risk.

Risk mitigation is an attempt to reduce risk, or at least minimize its effects on an asset. This may mean reducing the likelihood of occurrence, reducing or eliminating the exposure of the vulnerability, or reducing the impact if a negative event does occur. Mitigation usually involves adding security controls to protect an asset against a threat, reducing likelihood, exposure, or impact in some way.

Be aware that most risk management theory states that risk can never be completely eliminated; it can only be reduced or mitigated to an acceptable level. The acceptable level may be an extremely low likelihood of occurrence or an extremely low impact if the risk were to be realized.

Risk transference (also sometimes called *risk sharing*) deals with risk by sharing the burden of the risk, especially the impact element. In risk transference, an organization contracts with another party to share some of the risk, such as the cost to the organization if the threat were realized.

The standard example of risk transference you will often hear about in the security community is the use of *cybersecurity insurance*. Buying insurance to protect a business in the event of a natural disaster, for example, alleviates the burden to the business by reducing the impact of cost if a natural disaster occurs. The insurance pays the business if equipment or facilities are damaged, reducing the impact. Note that this doesn't lessen the likelihood of the threat occurring; it only lessens the financial impact to the business.

Another example of risk sharing is through the use of third-party service providers, such as those that provide infrastructure or data storage services. In this example, the business contracts with a third party to store and protect the business's data in a different location. Such an arrangement could be beneficial to the business because it might reduce the likelihood of a threat occurring that would destroy data (by providing additional security controls and data redundancy, for example) as well as the impact.

 NOTE Transferring risk does not also mean transferring legal responsibility or liability from the organization. Ultimately, the responsibility for protecting data and following legal governance still belongs to the organization.

Risk acceptance means the organization has implemented controls and some risk remains. It does not mean simply accepting an identified risk without taking any action to reduce its effects on the organization. Risk acceptance isn't the act of ignoring risk.

Risk acceptance occurs when an organization has done everything it can do to mitigate or reduce risk inherent to an asset, yet finds that some small level of risk remains even after these efforts (called *residual risk*). Remember that risk can never be *completely* eliminated; it may simply be reduced to a very unlikely level or to a very insignificant impact.

As an example, suppose that an organization believes there is significant risk to one of its most valuable information technology assets, a critical server that processes real-time financial transactions. If this server costs $20,000 to replace, the organization may spend $3000 in security controls to protect the server. After it has spent this money, the organization may find that the risk is reduced to a very small level. The residual risk is very unlikely, and even if it were to occur, it would have only a very slight impact. The organization could reduce the risk even more by spending an additional $2000 on more controls, but if the risk is very small, would spending the additional money be worth it? At this point, the organization has to decide whether to spend the additional money or simply accept the residual risk.

Risk avoidance means that the organization could choose not to participate in activities that cause unnecessary or excessive risk. Note that this doesn't mean that the risk is ignored and that the organization does not take steps to reduce it. In some cases, a business pursuit or activity may be too risky to undertake, for example. The organization may perform a risk analysis on a proposed activity and simply decide that the risk is not worth the potential negative effects to the asset or organization.

Often, an organization will use a combination of these responses to address the many and varied risks it encounters; there is no one perfect response solution that fits all organizations, assets, and activities. The decision of how to respond to a particular risk scenario involves many complex factors, which include cost, effectiveness of the response, value of the asset, and the ability of the organization to implement a particular response successfully. Additionally, as risk factors and conditions change over time, the organization must continually monitor and revisit risk responses from time to time to ensure that they are still effective.

 EXAM TIP Remember the four possible risk responses: risk mitigation, risk transference, risk acceptance, and risk avoidance, as well as their definitions.

Module 1-5: Business Impact Analysis

This module covers the following CompTIA Security+ objectives:

- **1.6   Explain the security concerns associated with various types of vulnerabilities**
- **5.4   Summarize risk management processes and concepts**
- **5.5   Explain privacy and sensitive data concepts in relation to security**

A good risk assessment requires analysis of the impact of incidents against the IT infrastructure. You should consider the impact of an incident in terms of how it affects the work of an organization. To do this, security professionals perform a *business impact analysis (BIA)* that predicts both the consequences of incidents and the time and resources needed to recover from incidents.

This module starts with an overview of the steps involved with performing a BIA, using my company, Total Seminars, as an example. The rest of the module focuses on three important BIA functions: types of impact, location of critical resources, and calculating impact.

NOTE A business impact analysis is designed to mitigate the effects of an incident, not to prevent an incident.

BIA Basics

NIST SP 800-34, Rev. 1, *Contingency Planning Guide for Federal Information Systems,* offers a detailed, three-stage BIA (Figure 1-20):

1. ***Determine mission/business processes and recovery criticality.*** *Mission/Business processes supported by the system are identified and the impact of a system disruption to those processes is determined along with outage impacts and estimated downtime.*

   My interpretation: Make sure you know which workflows and processes your organization depends on to operate, in other words, the *mission-essential functions.* Determine the types of impact and consider the impact of the failure of each of these workflows and processes. Estimate how long it takes to bring those workflows and processes up to speed.

2. ***Identify resource requirements.*** *Realistic recovery efforts require a thorough evaluation of the resources required to resume mission/business processes and related interdependencies as quickly as possible.*

   My interpretation: What are the critical tools your organization uses to do these workflows and processes? Where are they? How do they work? In other words, a BIA provides *identification of critical systems.*

Figure 1-20
NIST SP 800-34,
Rev. 1

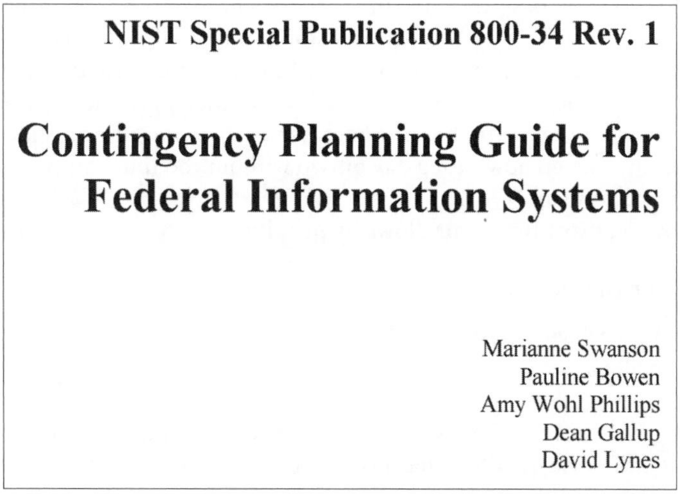

NIST Special Publication 800-34 Rev. 1

Contingency Planning Guide for Federal Information Systems

Marianne Swanson
Pauline Bowen
Amy Wohl Phillips
Dean Gallup
David Lynes

3. *Identify recovery priorities for system resources.* *Based upon the results from the previous activities, system resources can be linked more clearly to critical mission/ business processes and functions. Priority levels can be established for sequencing recovery activities and resources.*

My interpretation: Once you understand all the resources that make a workflow/ process work, determine the priority of bringing them back up to speed if they fail. Make sure you know the *mission-essential functions* of the organization; this helps you prioritize recovery.

 NOTE A BIA is part of a broader field of study in IT security called *contingency planning (CP)*. CP covers almost everything an IT security person needs to consider to keep an infrastructure humming in the face of an incident. CP goes way beyond the scope of the CompTIA Security+ exam, but note for future studies that the two go together.

A typical small business provides an excellent example for a BIA in action. Total Seminars (or TotalSem, for short) writes books, generates online content, builds test banks, and makes lots of videos (shameless plug: check out hub.totalsem.com).

Determine Mission/Business Processes and Recovery Criticality

TotalSem has three critical workflows:

- The online store (www.totalsem.com) for selling products
- Internet access for R&D and customer communication
- Video production facility consisting of workstations and a few critical local servers

The three workflows differ in what the company can do to protect them. Amazon Web Services hosts the Web site and store, so there is little to do to mitigate the impact of AWS going down, other than wait. Internet access has two components. The cable company provides the pipe—not much to do there, just like with AWS—and TotalSem techs control access to the Internet for each workstation. Video production, while important, can go down for a day or two without too much impact (unless you're waiting for my next video!).

Now, let's sort these workflows by priority.

1. Internet access
2. Video production
3. Web store

The Web store generates company profits and, from a business sense, should have top priority. Because TotalSem has no direct control over the store, however, it drops to the bottom of this list.

Once you've determined priorities, move to the next BIA stage.

Identify Resource Requirements

At the second stage, you should analyze all the resources required for each mission/process outlined in the first stage. Total Seminars' Internet access provides a good example.

Total Seminars' Internet access isn't very complex. A single Internet service provider (ISP) provides a cable modem that's owned by the ISP. Locally, TotalSem has a midrange edge router (Cisco ASA) that supports a public-facing DNS server. The TotalSem internal network moves through a second NAT router (with a built-in switch) to individual systems.

The resources for Internet access therefore consist of a cable modem, a server, and a couple of routers/switches.

After outlining all resource needs for each mission/process, move to the next stage.

Identify Recovery Priorities for System Resources

At the final stage, prioritize recovery steps. If TotalSem completely lost Internet access, for example, the priority would be (other people may have a different opinion as to this order):

1. Repair/restore/replace cable modem (must have for Internet).

2. Repair/restore/replace edge router (need the protection for DNS server).

3. Repair/restore/replace DNS server (critical to access certain systems).

4. Repair/restore/replace NAT router (for workstations).

At this stage, you should identify recovery priorities for system resources that support every mission/process outlined in stage one.

Types of Impact

To analyze the impact of an incident, focus first on the consequences in terms of business processes supported by the affected resources. A typical BIA looks at (at least) five types of impact:

- Financial
- Reputation
- Availability loss
- Privacy
- Data

Financial

Financial impact manifests in several ways. It might mean lost or delayed sales. It might also lead to increased expenses, such as overtime, outsourcing, and fines. The one good aspect of financial impact is that it has a quantitative dollar value.

Reputation

How does a potential customer feel if he or she heads to www.totalsem.com only to find the Web site down (Figure 1-21)? *Reputation* is an important impact to consider, but it's

Figure 1-21
Reputation is
critical.

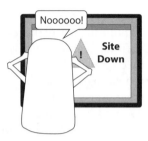

also difficult to quantify. There are studies that can give a financial estimate of loss of reputation, but even these are very specific (such as sales loss due to lost customers due to a data breach).

Availability Loss

Every organization relies on critical data. If that data becomes unavailable, it can have a massive negative impact on the organization. Here are some examples: customer lists deleted; file storage disconnected and unavailable; an expired certificate that makes access to a company Web site fail; all these describe *availability loss*.

Privacy

Any organization that keeps individuals' personal information takes on several risks with serious legal and financial impacts, both to itself and to the individuals whose data is being stored. The next module, Module 1-6, goes into great detail on the concept of privacy. I'll save the details until then but address the concept of privacy impact here.

An organization performs a *privacy impact assessment (PIA)* to determine the impact on the privacy of the individuals whose data is being stored and to ensure that the organization has sufficient security controls applied to be within compliance with applicable laws or standards.

To create a PIA, an organization performs a *privacy threshold assessment (PTA)* on its infrastructure to locate personal information, determine what personal information is stored, and from whom the personal information is collected. Once the PTA is complete, the PIA can then be applied.

Data

Bad things can happen to good data, from outright loss to unauthorized access by untrusted sources. Problems with data can have impacts in many categories. *Data loss* reduces productivity, because the data needs to be re-created. Worse, it has a financial impact—the time to re-create the data costs money. Finally, data loss can hurt reputationally; for example, a deliverable not getting to a client on time because of data loss besmirches the organization.

Data breaches occur when confidential information has been exposed, whether by accident or by malicious intent. *Data exfiltration* is a type of data breach, specifically involving bad actors/malware performing an unauthorized transfer of data. The impact of such data breaches and exfiltration will undermine customer confidence, impacting the organization's reputation. The financial impact can come from getting sued over the breach and paying legal fees as well.

Locating Critical Resources

Analyzing critical resources as part of a BIA can reveal unexpected vulnerabilities. Resources needed for TotalSem's Internet access provides a good example.

Total Seminars' Internet access relies on four basic resources:

- Cable modem
- Edge router
- DNS server
- NAT router

The BIA clearly shows several *single points of failure*: if any one of these resources fails, TotalSem loses its business process of Internet access. The impact of losing this process could cause negative financial consequences for the company: pretty much every employee stops working.

You should mitigate single points of failure if possible. In the case of resources needed for Internet access, for example, several actions could mitigate the problems:

- **Cable modem**   Add a second ISP into the mix. This could act as a failover if the primary ISP fails.
- **Edge router**   Cisco produces very reliable routers, but a quick check of the Cisco Web site shows the router model used by TotalSem accepts dual power supplies. This will help increase the MTBF (see the next section) significantly.
- **DNS server**   A single DNS server is never a good idea. TotalSem could add a second DNS server or create a secondary lookup zone on a cloud server.
- **NAT router**   TotalSem uses a low-quality router, but has spares ready to go. There will be a time impact to install the replacement, but having the spare onsite is far better than running to the store.

Calculating Impact

The process of calculating impact has the same problem that calculating risk in earlier modules had: is it qualitative or quantitative? The CompTIA Security+ exam touches only on qualitative business impact analysis, and only on a few well-known factors: MTBF, MTTF, and MTTR.

The *mean time between failures (MTBF)* factor, which typically applies to hardware components, represents the manufacturer's best guess (based on historical data) regarding

	Capacity	
	Routing table size	512 entries (IPv4), 256 entries (IPv6)
	MAC address table size	16384 entries
Reliability	MTBF (years)	52.79
Environment	Operating temperature	23°F to 113°F (-5°C to 45°C)
	Operating relative humidity	10% to 90%, noncondensing
	Nonoperating/Storage temperature	-40°F to 158°F (-40°C to 70°C)

Figure 1-22 Router datasheet showing MTBF

how much time will pass between major failures of that component (Figure 1-22). This is, of course, assuming that more than one failure will occur, which means that the component will be repaired rather than replaced. Organizations should take this risk factor into account because it may affect likelihood and impact of the risks associated with critical systems.

The *mean time to failure (MTTF)* factor indicates the length of time a device is expected to last in operation. In MTTF, only a single, definitive failure will occur and will require that the device be replaced rather than repaired.

Lastly, the *mean time to repair (MTTR)* is the average time it takes to repair (or replace) a hardware component. *Mean time to recovery (MTTR)* is the time it takes for a hardware component to recover from failure. (The two MTTR definitions are frequently used interchangeably.)

 EXAM TIP You should understand the difference between mean time between failures (MTBF), mean time to failure (MTTF), and mean time to repair (MTTR) measurements for hardware failure.

Calculating Downtime

When systems go down, they affect other systems as well. The *recovery time objective (RTO)* is the maximum amount of time that a resource should remain unavailable before an unacceptable impact on other system resources occurs. The *recovery point objective (RPO)* defines the amount of time that will pass between an incident and recovery from backup. If a company backed up yesterday, for example, the RPO is 24 hours. If data changes so rapidly (an accounts receivable database, for example) that any backup more than an hour old requires calling customers or other extraordinary actions, then the RPO is one hour. The RTO and RPO help IT professionals calculate how much an organization can or will lose if a system goes down before backup systems can be brought online.

Module 1-6: Data Security and Data Protection

This module covers the following CompTIA Security+ objectives:

- **1.6** **Explain the security concerns associated with various types of vulnerabilities**
- **2.1** **Explain the importance of security concepts in an enterprise environment**
- **2.7** **Explain the importance of physical security controls**
- **5.3** **Explain the importance of policies to organizational security**
- **5.5** **Explain privacy and sensitive data concepts in relation to security**

IT security professionals protect data. Proprietary data is the lifeblood of many companies. Those companies put a premium on securing that data (Figure 1-23).

The complexity of data security presents a challenge to IT security professionals. Data manifests throughout an infrastructure in many ways: from a single user's personal folders containing a few Word documents to massive multiterabyte databases, accessed by hundreds or even thousands of users.

The complexity of access and control of data adds another challenge to IT security professionals. Every database program, every operating system, and many Internet services offer settings that give administrators impressively fine control when configuring which users and groups may access specific classes of data and what they are permitted to do with that data. But how do we control that access? How do we look at the data and determine the amount of access any given entity receives? We'll answer these questions in Chapter 3.

Handling certain types of data involves serious legal and privacy issues. Organizations need to protect data aggressively. If your databases contain individuals' private medical information, customers' personal credit card numbers, or even a young offender's rap sheet, you are under tremendous pressure to maintain that privacy (Figure 1-24).

This module covers the basics of data security and privacy. The module starts by covering common methods of data organization, then delves into legal compliance and privacy. We'll look at tried and true methods for data destruction. The module closes by covering privacy breaches.

Figure 1-23
Data is precious.

Figure 1-24
Storing
personal data
brings heavy
responsibilities.

Organizing Data

Attaining data security starts with organization. Analyze individual chunks of data, such as databases, spreadsheets, access control lists, and so on. Then determine the importance—the *sensitivity*—of that data. After accomplishing both tasks, sort the data into different classifications based on sensitivity. These classifications help security professionals to determine the amount of security control to apply to each data set.

The dynamic nature of data requires more than just classification of the data. Every data set needs to be administered by one or more people. The roles of the people who manage the data and the users who access that data need classification as well.

NOTE The NIST Federal Information Processing Standards (FIPS) Publication 199, *Standards for Security Categorization of Federal Information and Information Systems*, is considered by many sources as the *de facto* framework for IT data classification.

Data Sensitivity

IT security professionals need to apply appropriate security controls to data, making decisions based on the sensitivity of that data. Organizations can apply a dizzyingly large number of security controls to data. Some data sets need stringent security controls. Other data sets need less complex security controls. Not all data in an organization has the same sensitivity. The more sensitive the data, the more controls we apply to ensure its security.

Organizations spend a lot of time thinking about their data and coming up with classifications to enable them to identify the sensitivity to in turn address their handling. One way to consider sensitivity is by the impact of an incident that exposes the data. NIST FIPS 199 provides one way to consider the impact by looking at the *confidentiality, integrity, and availability (CIA)* of the data and breaking the impact into three levels: low, moderate, and high (Figure 1-25). It's also very common to differentiate between commercial and government/military to classify data.

Security Objective	POTENTIAL IMPACT		
	LOW	MODERATE	HIGH
Confidentiality Preserving authorized restrictions on information access and disclosure, including means for protecting personal privacy and proprietary information. [44 U.S.C., SEC. 3542]	The unauthorized disclosure of information could be expected to have a **limited** adverse effect on organizational operations, organizational assets, or individuals.	The unauthorized disclosure of information could be expected to have a **serious** adverse effect on organizational operations, organizational assets, or individuals.	The unauthorized disclosure of information could be expected to have a **severe or catastrophic** adverse effect on organizational operations, organizational assets, or individuals.
Integrity Guarding against improper information modification or destruction, and includes ensuring information non-repudiation and authenticity. [44 U.S.C., SEC. 3542]	The unauthorized modification or destruction of information could be expected to have a **limited** adverse effect on organizational operations, organizational assets, or individuals.	The unauthorized modification or destruction of information could be expected to have a **serious** adverse effect on organizational operations, organizational assets, or individuals.	The unauthorized modification or destruction of information could be expected to have a **severe or catastrophic** adverse effect on organizational operations, organizational assets, or individuals.
Availability Ensuring timely and reliable access to and use of information. [44 U.S.C., SEC. 3542]	The disruption of access to or use of information or an information system could be expected to have a **limited** adverse effect on organizational operations, organizational assets, or individuals.	The disruption of access to or use of information or an information system could be expected to have a **serious** adverse effect on organizational operations, organizational assets, or individuals.	The disruption of access to or use of information or an information system could be expected to have a **severe or catastrophic** adverse effect on organizational operations, organizational assets, or individuals.

Figure 1-25   Impact table for data (FIPS 199)

Commercial Classifications   Classifying data using commercial labels works well for most private-sector organizations. Most security pros in the nongovernmental sector start with some variation of the following list:

- **Public**   Information that is not sensitive. The prices of all the products on eBay is one example.

  Private   Information that specifically applies to an individual, such as a Social Security number.

- **Sensitive**   A generic label that is often tied to both commercial and government/military label types.

- **Confidential**   Information that one party offers to a second party. Usually secured via a non-disclosure agreement (NDA). A common example is internal company information used by its employees.

- **Critical**   Data without which an organization could not function or fulfil its essential mission.

- **Proprietary**   Information owned by a company that gives the company certain competitive advantages. The secret formula to Coca-Cola is an example.

- **Customer data**   Information about the customer, such as personally identifiable information and personal health information (covered later in this module).

 NOTE   Public information may not have confidentiality, but it still needs integrity and availability.

Government/Military Labels   If you enjoy spy novels, most government/military labels should sound familiar. In fact, these types of labels predate computers to a time when paper documents literally had physical labels (or stamps) signifying their sensitivity. Experts disagree on exactly what these labels mean, although not as much as with commercial labels. Here in the United States, security professionals refer to Executive Order 13526 of December 29, 2009, "Classified National Security Information," which defines the labels for *government data*—property of the government—as follows:

- "Top Secret" shall be applied to information, the unauthorized disclosure of which reasonably could be expected to cause exceptionally grave damage to the national security that the original classification authority is able to identify or describe.

- "Secret" shall be applied to information, the unauthorized disclosure of which reasonably could be expected to cause serious damage to national security that the original classification authority is able to identify or describe.

- "Confidential" shall be applied to information, the unauthorized disclosure of which reasonably could be expected to cause damage to the national security that the original classification authority is able to identify or describe.

Data Roles

Every data set needs some number of people with clearly defined roles who manage that data at various levels. Data roles help define both the various responsibilities and the responsible parties for the different jobs. Let's go through the data roles listed by the CompTIA Security+ exam objectives.

Data Owner   The *data owner* is the entity who holds the legal ownership of a data set. This includes any copyrights, trademarks, or other legal possession items that tie the data set to the entity. The data owner can rent, sell, or give away the data set as the owner sees fit. Data owners are almost always the organization itself and not an actual person. This entity has complete control over the data and will delegate responsibility for the management of that data set to persons or groups to handle the real work on that data.

Data Controller   The *General Data Protection Regulation (GDPR)* in the European Union outlines in great detail how organizations should deal with private information. GDPR went into force in 2018 and includes a few roles added to the traditional ones, notably the data controller and data processor. Many countries have subsequently adopted similar regulations, so, naturally, many multinational corporations comply with those regulations throughout their organizations.

A *data controller* controls the data, which sounds silly, but means the person must ensure that data complies with the protections of personally identifiable information (PII) thoroughly, according to the regulations in the GDPR. The data controller must create systems about data processing and report on them as well.

Data Processor   A *data processor* in GDPR parlance doesn't have as much control over the data as a data controller. The data processor essentially works under the guidance of the data controller, handling data according to the controller's guidelines.

Data Custodian   A *data custodian* ensures that the technical aspects of the data set are in good order. Data custodians are the folks who make sure the data is secure, available, and accurate. They audit the data and ensure they have both the appropriate storage capacity and proper backups.

Data Steward   A *data steward* makes sure that the data set does what the data is supposed to do for the organization. Data stewards interface with the users of the organization to ensure *data governance*: to cover data requirements, to ensure legal compliance, and to make sure the data ties to company or industry standards. Data stewards update the data as needed to conform to needs. Data stewards also define how users access the data.

NOTE   Data stewards and data custodians always closely interact.

Data Protection Officer   The GDPR requires organizations to staff the role of *data protection officer (DPO)*, a leadership role responsible for making sure the enterprise complies with GDPR rules. Specifically, the DPO oversees an organization's policies and procedures for protection of data.

Legal and Compliance

Most countries have laws, regulations, and standards designed to protect different forms of data. As introduced in Module 1-2, in the United States, the Health Insurance Portability and Accountability Act (HIPAA) and Sarbanes-Oxley Act (SOX) provide strict federal guidelines for the handling, storage, and transmission of data. In addition, the Payment Card Industry Data Security Standard (PCI DSS), while not a law, has equally stringent guidelines for the handling, storage, and transmission of credit card data. In all these cases, the job of IT security changes from securing the IT infrastructure to making sure the organization doesn't get fined (and no one gets arrested!) for lack of compliance.

Many companies use *digital rights management (DRM)* technologies to protect their intellectual property, methods to stop easy copying (and redistributing) of music, movies, and so on. Many governments, in turn, supplement these efforts with laws criminalizing tampering with or circumventing the DRM technologies, such as the *Digital Millennium Copyright Act (DMCA)* in the United States.

> **NOTE** The US government has levied millions in fines and has imprisoned individuals for violations of both HIPAA and SOX. Credit card companies have revoked credit card processing from a huge number of businesses for failure to comply with PCI DSS standards.

Rather than break down these individual laws/standards, it's often better to concentrate on some of the more important aspects. Focus on personally identifiable information, protected health information, data retention, and data sovereignty.

Personally Identifiable Information

Personally identifiable information (PII) is any information referencing an individual that either by itself or with other information could identify that individual, allowing persons to contact or locate that individual without their permission. The idea of PII has been around since the early 1970s, but came into stronger prominence with HIPAA in the mid-1990s. PII is also very important for PCI DSS.

While there is no single definition of PII, NIST SP 800-122, *Guide to Protecting the Confidentiality of Personally Identifiable Information (PII)*, (Figure 1-26) provides many examples:

- Name, such as full name, maiden name, mother's maiden name, or alias
- Personal identification numbers, such as Social Security number (SSN), passport number, driver's license number, taxpayer identification number, or financial account or credit card number
- Address information, such as street address or e-mail address
- Personal characteristics, including photographic image (especially of face or other identifying characteristic), fingerprints, handwriting, or other biometric data (e.g., retina scan, voice signature, facial geometry)
- Information about an individual that is linked or linkable to one of the above (e.g., date of birth, place of birth, race, religion, weight, activities, geographical indicators, employment information, medical information, education information, financial information)

Different laws and standards vary the definition of what entails PII. For example, here are a few examples of PII by PCI DSS standards:

- Account number
- Cardholder name

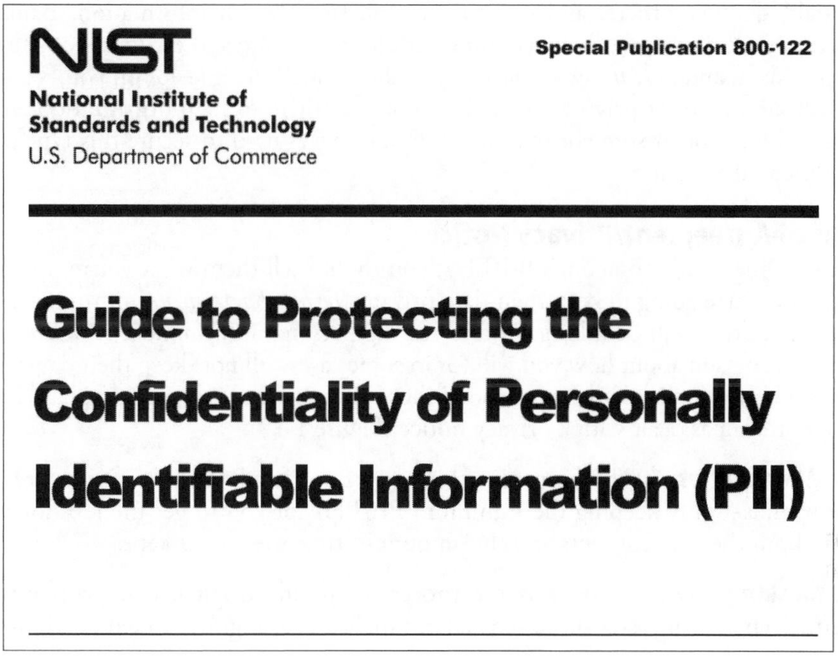

NIST
National Institute of
Standards and Technology
U.S. Department of Commerce

Special Publication 800-122

Guide to Protecting the Confidentiality of Personally Identifiable Information (PII)

Figure 1-26 NIST SP 800-122

- Expiration date
- Magnetic strip or chip data
- PIN
- CVC2/CVV2/CID

Protected Health Information

Protected health information (PHI) is any form of personal health information (treatment, diagnosis, prescriptions, etc.) electronically stored or transmitted by any health provider, insurer, or employer. This health information must be tied to the individual's PII to be considered PHI. In other words, a blood pressure reading combined with age and race is alone not PHI. A blood pressure reading combined with a name, address, or SSN is PHI.

Financial Information

Personal financial information is any information that provides insight into an individual's finances. This includes bank account numbers, credit scores, or user name and login information for electronic payment applications.

Privacy Enhancing Technologies

Consider the types of PII and PHI just described and ask yourself, "What types of organization might store this type of data?" The answer is that PII/PHI exists everywhere!

Hospitals, doctors' offices, and governments all store health information. Banks and financial institutions store financial information. Every store and e-commerce site stores customer data, and *only the government knows* how much PII it keeps on you.

There are plenty of privacy enhancing tools out there to help organizations protect PII/PHI. Let's look at some of the more common ways used to secure this type of data from potential exposure.

Terms of Agreement/Privacy Notice

If you're going to use someone's PII/PHI, you should tell them what you're doing with it and how you're going to keep their data private. *Terms of agreement* inform parties that your organization will be asking for and storing personal information. A *privacy notice* informs the person about how you will (or in some cases will not) keep their data private. Anyone who's ever clicked through one of those screens on a Web page that has "I agree" on the bottom has dealt with a privacy notice (Figure 1-27).

Data Minimization   Why keep something you don't need? *Data minimization* is just like it sounds—only keeping the minimum PII/PHI for you to get the job done. This reduces both the data contents and the amount of time the data is kept.

Data Masking   *Data masking* is the process of hiding original data with modified content, such as using asterisks to hide all but the last four digits of a credit card number.

Tokenization   Why send around sensitive data like a credit card number when you can replace it with a random value, or *token*, that's only known by a single source to tie

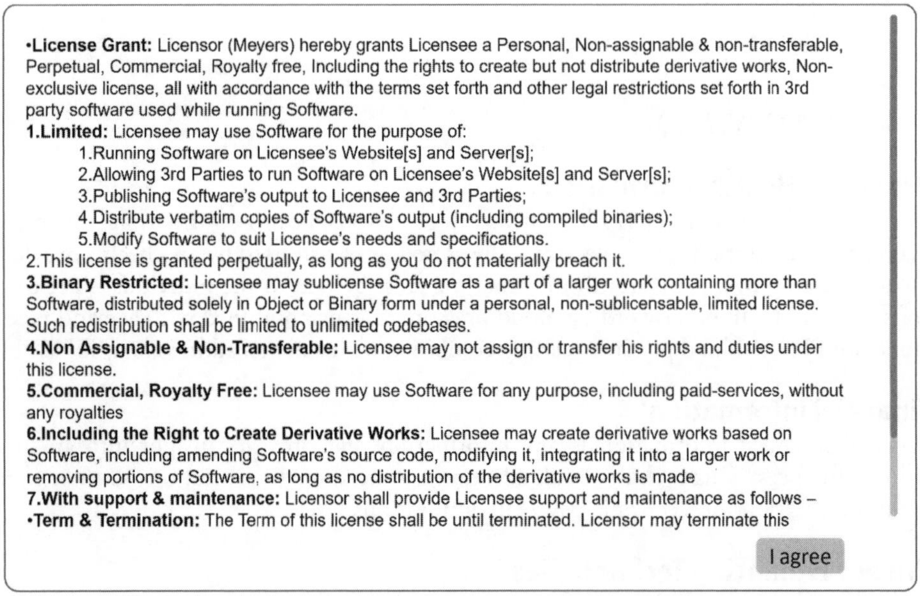

•**License Grant:** Licensor (Meyers) hereby grants Licensee a Personal, Non-assignable & non-transferable, Perpetual, Commercial, Royalty free, Including the rights to create but not distribute derivative works, Non-exclusive license, all with accordance with the terms set forth and other legal restrictions set forth in 3rd party software used while running Software.
1.Limited: Licensee may use Software for the purpose of:
      1.Running Software on Licensee's Website[s] and Server[s];
      2.Allowing 3rd Parties to run Software on Licensee's Website[s] and Server[s];
      3.Publishing Software's output to Licensee and 3rd Parties;
      4.Distribute verbatim copies of Software's output (including compiled binaries);
      5.Modify Software to suit Licensee's needs and specifications.
2.This license is granted perpetually, as long as you do not materially breach it.
3.Binary Restricted: Licensee may sublicense Software as a part of a larger work containing more than Software, distributed solely in Object or Binary form under a personal, non-sublicensable, limited license. Such redistribution shall be limited to unlimited codebases.
4.Non Assignable & Non-Transferable: Licensee may not assign or transfer his rights and duties under this license.
5.Commercial, Royalty Free: Licensee may use Software for any purpose, including paid-services, without any royalties
6.Including the Right to Create Derivative Works: Licensee may create derivative works based on Software, including amending Software's source code, modifying it, integrating it into a larger work or removing portions of Software, as long as no distribution of the derivative works is made
7.With support & maintenance: Licensor shall provide Licensee support and maintenance as follows –
•**Term & Termination:** The Term of this license shall be until terminated. Licensor may terminate this

I agree

Figure 1-27   Terms of Agreement

back to the actual number? Data *tokenization* is extremely common. For example, once a patient's record is stored in a database, just assign a patient number to that record so things like name and address don't have to be associated with that patient number.

Anonymization There's a lot of useful information that comes from PII/PHI that doesn't require actually identifying the people whose information is part of the data set. How many people in Houston, Texas, are morbidly obese? What's the average age for women in the United States to have their first child? How many complaints came in last month about our new smartphone app? These types of statistics are very helpful, but it's up to the data set provider to ensure that no PII/PHI is retrieved by implementing *anonymization* of the data.

TIP Anonymization removes all PII/PHI. Pseudoanonymization tokenizes the PII/PHI.

Sometimes the process of extracting anonymous data from a PII data set creates problems—or worse yet might accidently allow exposure of PII. One way to avoid this issue is to create a second data set and replace all PII with token data that looks random. This is called *pseudoanonymization*.

Data Retention

A number of laws and regulations have strict requirements regarding how long types of organizations must retain different types of data. Data retention is part of the *information life cycle*. The Sarbanes-Oxley Act is easily the most far-reaching law affecting the types of data public companies must retain and the length of time they must retain that data. In particular, IT departments must react to two parts of the law covered in Section 802(a):

> Whoever knowingly alters, destroys, mutilates, conceals, covers up, falsifies, or makes a false entry in any record, document, or tangible object with the intent to impede, obstruct, or influence the investigation … shall be fined under this title, imprisoned not more than 20 years, or both.

Yipe! But at least it also gives some idea as to the length of time companies need to retain records:

> Any accountant who conducts an audit of an issuer of securities … shall maintain all audit or review workpapers for a period of 5 years from the end of the fiscal period in which the audit or review was concluded.

It's not that hard to keep contracts, accounts, audits, and such for five years, but this also includes e-mail. Managing and storing e-mail for an entire company can be a challenge, especially because e-mail is usually under the control of individual users (ever deleted an e-mail?). SOX alone changed everything, requiring publicly traded companies to adopt standard practices outlined in the law and making lots of storage providers very happy indeed!

EXAM TIP The *information life cycle* is generally understood to have five phases, from creation to storage, usage, archival, and then destruction. Data retention falls into cycles two and four. We'll see cycle five a little later in this module.

Data Sovereignty

Governments have laws in place to give them access to data. That data could help solve crimes, protect people, and so on; and the desire for access is clear. The question that begs in a world of multinational corporations and cloud computing as the normal way to store data is, which laws apply to data stored in which countries? Let's explore this through a scenario.

Microsoft has servers based in Ireland. Some e-mail accounts hosted on those servers belong to people who might have committed crimes in the United States. Microsoft Corporation is a US-based company. If the US government decides that it needs access to those e-mail account records, which US law or laws permit such access, and what can or should Microsoft do in response?

The concept of *data sovereignty* determines that the laws of the country of origin of data apply to that data. The e-mail accounts hosted by a server in Ireland (an EU member nation), therefore, must abide by—and are protected by—EU laws, not US laws. This isn't just a hypothetical scenario, by the way. Microsoft argued and won against the US government that US laws did not apply to its Ireland-based holdings.

Data Destruction

When it's time to get rid of storage media, you should also destroy the data stored on that media. But how do you destroy media in such a way to ensure the data is gone? Let's take a moment to talk about *secure data destruction/media sanitization*. NIST SP 800-88, Rev. 1, *Guidelines for Media Sanitization*, provides some great guidelines (Figure 1-28).

NIST Special Publication 800-88
Revision 1

Guidelines for Media Sanitization

Richard Kissel
Andrew Regenscheid
Matthew Scholl
Kevin Stine

Figure 1-28 NIST SP 800-88, Rev. 1

The CompTIA Security+ exam covers a number of different data destruction methods that apply to specific types of data. Stored data fits into one of two categories: legacy media (paper, film, tape, etc.) or electronic media (hard drives, SD cards, optical media, etc.). Each category has different methods for data destruction.

 NOTE The terms data destruction, data sanitization, and data purging are interchangeable.

Legacy Media

Given that most legacy media isn't completely erasable, the best way to eliminate the data is to destroy the media. Paper, film, and tape are all extremely flammable, so *burning* is an excellent method to destroy the data. For "greener" organizations, *pulping* water-soluble media (paper) enables them to recycle the media and not pollute the environment.

Electronic Media

Almost all electronic media is erasable, so in many cases you can nondestructively remove the data. Simple erasing, however, even reformatting, isn't enough. A good forensic examiner can recover the original data from a hard disk that's been erased as many as nine times. You need to go through a specific wiping process that removes any residual data. NIST SP 800-88, Rev. 1, describes the ATA Secure Erase command built into PATA and SATA drives. *Third-party solutions* can help here. Several programs can perform a secure erase. Figure 1-29 shows DBAN 2.3.0 (Darik's Boot and Nuke), a popular secure erase utility (and it's free!).

```
Darik's Boot and Nuke

Warning: This software irrecoverably destroys data.

This software is provided without any warranty; without even the implied
warranty of merchantability or fitness for a particular purpose. In no event
shall the software authors or contributors be liable for any damages arising
from the use of this software.  This software is provided "as is".

http://www.dban.org/

* Press the F2 key to learn about DBAN.
* Press the F3 key for a list of quick commands.
* Press the F4 key for troubleshooting hints.
* Press the ENTER key to start DBAN in interactive mode.
* Enter autonuke at this prompt to start DBAN in automatic mode.

boot: _
```

Figure 1-29 DBAN 2.3.0 (Darik's Boot and Nuke)

To ensure complete data destruction, destroy the media. A common method is degaussing the media through a *degaussing* machine. A degausser uses a powerful electromagnet both to wipe the data and make the media useless.

Pulverizing or *shredding* are great methods for destroying media as well. Pulverizing means to smash completely. Shredding works for both legacy media and electronic media. A classic shredder can shred paper, optical media, and many types of flash media. There are several types of shredding cuts (Figure 1-30).

Shredding doesn't stop with paper! There are machines available that shred (or pulverize, or crush) just about any media, reducing them to bits of metal for you to recycle. You'll see those machines, and much more about data sanitizing, in Chapter 5, Module 5-7.

Privacy Breaches

We talked about data breaches back in Module 1-5 and the reputational and financial impact to an organization. Organizational consequences of privacy and data breaches involving PII or PHI have a whole order of magnitude more impact. You've likely heard of data breaches of health insurance companies, dating Web sites, and other hosts of PII and PHI. These breaches have led to horrific *reputational damage*, *identity theft* of customers, intellectual property stolen (*IP theft*), civil court cases with massive *fines* . . . and in a few cases, people going to jail. The serious consequences of privacy breaches like these require organizations to address any incidents quickly and aggressively.

First, organizations that are subject to industry or governmental regulations, such as PCI, HIPAA, and so on, are required to *escalate* these incidents by reporting to the proper government agencies. These regulations are important. Before they came into force, organizations would try to hide privacy breaches or even deny they happened at all. Last, organizations, through moral or legal reasons, should provide *public notification and disclosure* of the type of data exposed to lessen reputational damage and avoid legal actions based on failure to disclose. An organization should not only make a public notification of the breach, they also should make a best attempt to inform those affected. Web sites such as https://haveibeenpwned.com, for example, provide the public with easy access to determine if an e-mail address has been breached.

 EXAM TIP Expect a question on the CompTIA Security+ exam that asks about proper company response to breaches and private or sensitive data loss. The organization must provide notification of breaches to customers, escalation of response to government agencies, and public notifications.

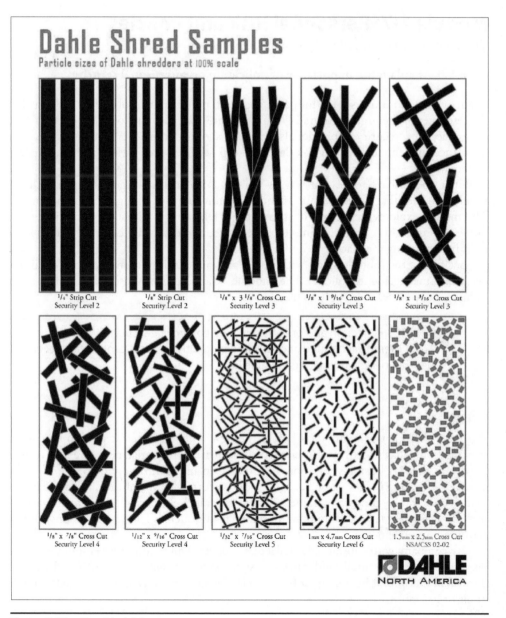

Figure 1-30 Shredded drive

Module 1-7: Personnel Risk and Policies

This module covers the following CompTIA Security+ objective:

- **5.3 Explain the importance of policies to organizational security**

An organization's users—the human beings who perform their jobs every day by using the resources of the organization's IT infrastructure—are also one of the biggest IT risk issues faced by security professionals. Human actions, from accidental to innocent, from incompetent to downright criminal, keep security pros awake at night in fear and loathing.

But it doesn't have to be that way. A well-organized risk management plan includes detailed policies that define security controls to mitigate risk brought on by personnel. This module explores the lifespan of an employee's relationship with an organization, from hiring day to exit day, and examines the risk concepts and security controls used to keep users from trashing the place.

Specifically, the module starts with hiring and onboarding, then goes into detail on personnel management policies. The module wraps up with discussions about user training and policies that apply to user habits.

 NOTE Policies in and of themselves *do not provide security*. Well-designed policies implemented and followed diligently by users can provide security. What people do matters a whole lot.

Hiring

Personnel risk management starts before the new employee ever steps into the infrastructure. In today's security-conscious environment, a potential new hire is screened heavily. At the very least, it's common for someone in an organization to do a *social media analysis*—checking Facebook or Instagram (or the current flavor of the day) for behavior that doesn't fit the company's values—and a general Web search. Many organizations perform *background checks* to look for potential issues, such as felony convictions, and to verify résumé statements.

Any company with substantial intellectual property will require new employees—and occasionally even potential candidates—to sign a *non-disclosure agreement (NDA)*, a legal document that prohibits the signer from disclosing any company secrets learned as a part of his or her job.

Onboarding

Onboarding is the process of giving a new hire the knowledge and skills he or she needs to do the job, while at the same time defining the behaviors expected of the new hire within the corporate culture. A lot of onboarding has nothing to do with IT security, but some part of the process usually is dedicated to helping new hires understand the expectations and attitudes toward IT security that are important to the organization. One of the biggest issues is their understanding of the organization's personnel management policies.

That Onboarding Moment

Personnel Management Policies

A *personnel management policy* defines the way a user works within the organization. An organization will invest in one or more personnel management policies to help mitigate a number of different types of personnel risks. Let's go through all of these personnel management policies to see how they work to make an infrastructure less vulnerable to risks.

Standard Operating Procedures

An important part of the onboarding process is making sure new hires understand the *standard operating procedures (SOPs)*—that is, how they do things according to the organization's best practices—for their job functions. Some SOPs that are particularly important for IT security include login procedures, usable data storage locations, use of security credentials, and procedures for lost or damaged equipment.

Necessary Knowledge

Mandatory Vacations

Many industries (for example, the US banking industry) require all employees to take off work for a minimum of two weeks every year, a *mandatory vacation*. Mandatory vacations are an important security control mainly to make it harder to perpetuate embezzlement.

Any embezzlement scheme usually requires the embezzler to monitor orders constantly, manipulate records, or deal with issues that might arise to keep themselves from being detected.

 NOTE Mandatory vacations have benefits beyond IT security, but for the exam think "embezzlement."

Job Rotation

Job rotation involves periodically switching people around to work in different positions. This practice enables different people to become proficient in a variety of job roles so that the organization doesn't have to depend solely on one person to perform certain critical functions or tasks. If something were to happen to an individual occupying a critical position, for example, another person could step in to do the job.

When people become too comfortable with a job, they might believe that they can get away with performing actions they are not authorized to perform. Rotating people into different positions increases the potential to detect fraud or misuse in that position and can discourage or prevent nefarious activities.

Job rotation is difficult for many organizations, for the same reasons that organizations don't always implement mandatory vacations. A shortage of trained personnel as well as positions that require substantial training and commitment are two reasons why job rotation isn't always performed.

Separation of Duties

In the *separation of duties* concept, a single individual should not perform all critical or privileged-level duties. These types of important duties must be separated or divided among several individuals.

Separation of duties ensures that no single individual can perform sufficiently critical or privileged actions that could seriously damage a system, operation, or the organization. These critical or privileged actions can be split among two or more people, requiring some level of checks and balances. Security auditors responsible for reviewing security logs, for example, should not necessarily have administrative rights over systems. Likewise, a security administrator should not have the capability to review or alter logs, because he or she could perform unauthorized actions and then delete any trace of them from the logs. Two separate individuals are required to perform such activities to ensure verifiability and traceability.

Separation of duties is considered an administrative control, because it's related to policy. Closely related to the concept of separation of duties is the technique of using multiperson control to perform some tasks or functions.

 NOTE A related concept to separation of duties is the *principle of least privilege*—don't give people access to anything beyond what they need to accomplish their jobs. CompTIA adds least privilege as a personnel policy, but it's more of a principle. You'll find more discussion in Chapter 3.

Multiperson Control

Multiperson control means that more than one person is required to accomplish a specific task or function. An organization might implement multiperson controls, for example, to ensure that one person, by herself, could not initiate an action that would cause detrimental consequences for the organization, resulting in loss of data, destruction of systems, or theft.

Organizations implement multiperson control by dividing up critical tasks to require more than one person to accomplish those tasks. In a banking environment, for example, one person may be authorized to sign negotiable instruments, such as checks, for up to $10,000. Beyond the limit of $10,000, however, requires two signatures to process the transaction. This would help prevent one malicious person from stealing more than $10,000. Although it's conceivable that two people could conspire to use their assigned abilities to commit an unauthorized act, fraud in this case, separation of duties and multiperson control make this more difficult. In this case, counter-signing a check is a multiperson control. In an information security environment, multiperson control could be used to access sensitive documents, recover passwords or encryption keys, and so on.

Training

User training should take place at two very distinct points in the user's relationship with an organization: during the onboarding process to get the new hire to understand and subscribe to critical policies and good user habits and, possibly even more importantly, as an ongoing continuing-education process. Let's look at role-based training and various training techniques.

 NOTE   Just as policies do not achieve security if they are not implemented, training does not achieve security if its lessons aren't implemented. Users need ongoing, memorable training, because people forget details over time or, worse, choose not to follow best practices because they're too hard. Training requires enforcement to make it stick.

Role-Based Training

User training differs according to the role an individual plays in an organization. *Role-based training* targets five broad categories: user, privileged user, executive user, system administrator, and data owner/system owner. Let's look at all five.

User   A *user* must understand how his or her system functions and have proper security training to recognize common issues (malware, unauthorized user at his or her system, etc.).

Privileged User   A *privileged user* has increased access and control over a system, including access to tools unavailable to regular users. Like a regular user, the privileged user needs a basic understanding of his or her system's functions; the privileged user must also have security awareness that ties to access level. A regular user may run anti-malware software, for example, but a privileged user may update the anti-malware program as well as run it.

Executive User   An *executive user* concentrates on strategic decisions including policy review, incident response, and disaster recovery.

System Administrator   The *system administrator* has complete, direct control over a system. His or her training would include best practices for adding and removing users, applying permissions, and doing system maintenance and debugging.

Data Owner/System Owner   From a role-based training aspect, these two otherwise slightly different functions are very similar in that in almost all cases the data owner is the organization. In these cases, the main security role here is to know how to delegate security awareness to the proper authority. For data, this is usually the data custodian; for systems, it is usually the system administrator.

Training Techniques

Ongoing user training is critical to keep users aware of potential attacks on the organization's infrastructure. The downside of ongoing training is that it can get very, very boring, and users will tune out or ignore the training. Thus, keeping users' attention requires incorporating a *diversity of training techniques*. Change those PowerPoint presentations into videos. Change those videos into games. Change those instructional memos into classroom training. With *computer-based training (CBT)* these days, it's easy to provide diversity in training.

Gamification   *Gamification* turns learning about security into games. The term encompasses a wide variety of activities, from tablet-based mini games to full-on competitions among users that feature points, badges, a leaderboard, and more.

Capture the Flag   *Capture the flag* means to direct someone to accomplish something on a remote system. For training purposes, we can challenge entry-level security personnel to apply what they've learned in a controlled environment. It's fun to talk about SQL injections or cross-site scripting, but it really lights people up the first time you let them do these attacks. (And it's best if the attacks don't actually destroy your network or someone else's network.) See Modules 7-1, 11-3, and 12-2 in later chapters for discussion of specific cyberattacks.

Phishing Campaigns   Phishing attacks represent the greatest threat to company security that involves users specifically. *Phishing* is an attempt to get personal information from people through e-mail, social media, instant messaging, and other forms of electronic communications. The most classic form of phishing is sending e-mail messages with links to fraudulent Web sites that purport to be legitimate Web sites. It might look like a message from your bank, but that "link" goes to the fraudulent Web site to grab your information.

The best way to create user awareness about phishing is through an in-house *phishing campaign*. Send out e-mail messages to your users and see just how many of them go to the fraudulent Web site you've created. Phishing campaigns are a way to see who needs training. Not comfortable making a phishing campaign from scratch? Plenty of vendors sell software packages or Web sites for *phishing simulations*.

Policies

If people are going to use your organization's equipment, they need to read, understand, and, in most cases, sign policies that directly affect the user's experience. Two policy types handle this job: acceptable use policies and security policies.

Acceptable Use Policy/Rules of Behavior Policy

An *acceptable use policy (AUP)*, also called a *rules of behavior policy*, defines what a user may or may not do on the organization's equipment. These policies tend to be very detailed documents, carefully listing what users may and may not do. Some examples of issues covered in an AUP include

- Company data can only be used for company business uses.
- Users will not access illegal or unacceptable Internet sites.
- Users will not introduce malware into a system.
- Users will work aggressively to protect company systems and data.

General Security Policies

People use *social media networks* and *personal e-mail* to exchange information and photographs and keep in touch with family members and friends. Unfortunately, some people post way too much information on social media networks and through *social media applications*—hello, Snapchat—decreasing their (and others') level of privacy.

Although organizations may have very little control over what individual employees post to social media sites and send in their e-mail, it's a good idea to create a relevant policy and train users on what they should and should not post on social media or e-mail to others. For example, users should be briefed that they should not post any sensitive or proprietary information on their social media sites that would compromise the organization or result in any type of unauthorized access or breach of information.

User Habits

In addition to policy-related topics, topics that concern the actions and habits of users must be addressed in training programs. Many such items will also be set forth in policy, but that doesn't mean that users don't need training and reinforcement to break bad habits where they exist. We'll look at some of these bad habits in the next few sections and, where appropriate, discuss how they also may be established in policy and why they should be included in any organizational information security training program.

Password Behaviors

By now, you should be aware that password issues can pose serious problems in an organization. Users forget passwords, write them down where they can be easily discovered by others, share passwords, use simple passwords, and so on. These are the causes of most password security issues, and the reasons why users need training regarding how to create and use passwords properly in the organization. Following are some key points that should be emphasized:

- Users should create long passwords.
- Users should create complex passwords.
- Users must try to create passwords that don't use dictionary words.
- Users should never share their passwords or write them down.
- Users should change their passwords *often* to thwart password attacks.

Of course, you should also use technical measures to reinforce some of these rules, including configuring systems to allow only complex passwords of a certain length, as well as password expiration rules. Periodically check around the users' work areas to make sure they haven't written down passwords, and ensure that multiple people aren't using the same accounts and passwords to log into systems. In addition, check to see if your password policies are being complied with by occasionally engaging in password cracking yourself—with the appropriate approval from management, of course. The problems associated with password behaviors, as well as the speed and ease with which passwords can be cracked by sophisticated attackers and systems, are the main reasons why organizations should consider multifactor authentication methods. (Check out Chapter 3, Module 3-2 for more details on multifactor authentication.)

Clean Desk Policies

A *clean desk space policy* isn't about asking employees not to leave old soda cans and candy wrappers on their desks! Instead, it creates a process for employees to clear sensitive data out of work areas so that it is stored securely at the end of the workday. Sensitive data must not be exposed to unauthorized people such as janitors, maintenance personnel, guards, and even other employees when an authorized employee is away from his or her desk.

A clean desk policy can apply to any time employees are using sensitive data at their desks and they need to leave the area. The goal is to make sure that sensitive data is not unattended and available. This policy should be developed and implemented as a formal written policy, and all employees should be trained on it.

Preventing Social Engineering Attacks

Users should be briefed on the general concepts of social engineering and how it works, and they should also be briefed on the specific types of attacks they may encounter, such as shoulder surfing, tailgating, dumpster diving, and so on. By being aware of these attacks, they can do their part in helping to prevent them. Tailgating, in particular, exposes the organization and others to serious harm or danger if an unauthorized person is allowed to enter the facility. Users should be trained on how to spot potential social engineering attacks, including tailgaters, and how to respond to them by following organizational policies and procedures.

Personally Owned Devices

Users should get training on risks posed by bringing *personally owned devices* to work and how they might help prevent these risks. Using such devices in the organization can lead to a loss of privacy by the individual, as well as loss of both personal and organizational data if the device is lost or stolen. If the organization allows individuals to manage their own devices, while allowing their use in the organization to process the organization's data, then the organization incurs a huge risk. Users must be trained on those risks and how serious their responsibilities are.

If the organization centrally manages mobile devices with *mobile device management (MDM)* software, the risk is significantly lowered because the organization can use remote capabilities to lock, encrypt, or wipe data on the device. Users should be briefed on these capabilities if they are used within the organization to manage devices, because users must accept organizational control of their devices and the policies that may be enforced on them.

Many companies around the globe have clear policies on *bring your own device (BYOD)*, the catchy phrase for incorporating employee-owned technology (such as laptops, tablets, and smartphones) in the corporate network. As the trend intensifies, just about every organization should have such policies.

Offboarding

When employees leave an organization, the organization must perform a number of important steps to ensure a tidy and professional separation. This process, called *offboarding*, varies among organizations, but includes several common steps:

- Termination letter
- Equipment return
- Knowledge transfer

Termination Letter/Exit Interview

An employee should provide a written *termination letter*, defining the final day of employment. In many organizations, this is also the time to perform an exit interview. *Exit interviews* give the soon-to-be-separated employee an opportunity to provide insight to the employer about ways to improve the organization. Some example questions include

- What are your main reasons for leaving?
- What procedures can we improve upon?

Return of Equipment

All organizations should use a checklist to ensure that all equipment owned by the organization is returned by the departing employee. This includes computers, phones, and tablets, as well as any other issued equipment. Also, this is the time to return keys, ID cards, and other access tools.

Knowledge Transfer

Knowledge transfer is the process that makes sure a separating employee provides any and all knowledge needed by the organization. In some cases knowledge transfer may last weeks. In other cases it's no more than part of the exit interview.

Module 1-8: Third-Party Risk and Policies

This module covers the following CompTIA Security+ objectives:

- **1.6 Explain the security concerns associated with various types of vulnerabilities**
- **5.3 Explain the importance of policies to organizational security**

Every organization interacts with third parties. Every infrastructure has vendors, contractors, business-to-business (B2B) intranets, partnerships, service providers—the list of third parties touching an infrastructure in one way or another is endless. The challenge with all these third parties is risk. For example, in 2019, two Facebook apps—developed by third parties that interact with Facebook—gashed out over 500 million personal records in hacks. Those records included usernames, groups, passwords, likes, movies, photos, music, and much more. Home Depot in 2014 had over 50 million customer credit card numbers stolen by a hack of its third-party payment systems. This list can go on for a very long time.

What can IT security professionals do to mitigate risks potentially created by those outside the infrastructure? General security practices hold third parties to certain levels of security through several types of agreements (Figure 1-31). This module considers the concept of third-party risk and risk management and then looks at some of the more common types of agreements used between parties.

Third-Party Risk Management

If your organization works with vendors, then it must use *vendor management*, the process of handling everything from selecting vendors and negotiating contracts or agreements with them to eventually terminating those vendor relationships. Vendor management is critically important when it comes to IT security.

Figure 1-31
It's all in the
agreement.

It's said that the devil is in the details; this is definitely true when it comes to security considerations that involve multiple parties. When you negotiate a contract with a third-party provider or business partner, you must ensure that several considerations are specified in your business agreements. You should have representatives from your security, privacy, and legal departments review any business agreements with third parties to ensure that certain security-related stipulations are included in the agreements and the day-to-day business transactions with outside entities. Let's look at a few of these security considerations next.

Data Storage

Whether it's a supplier accessing your inventory databases or a group of programmers creating your next great Web app, vendors will need to access data stored on your organization's systems directly or store your organization's data on their own systems. Controls over *data storage* must match the same level regardless of whether your organization or the third party maintains that data.

Just as your organization has its own security policies, procedures, and processes, third-party organizations have their own as well. Before your organization conducts business with another organization, the two parties need to negotiate how to handle any conflicts between their respective policies, procedures, and processes regarding data storage that might affect the business relationship.

In some cases, contract agreements may specify security policies and procedures that both parties must follow regarding shared data or contracted services. This applies to all third parties: software developers, service providers, business associates, subcontractors, and so on. Security policies and procedures agreed upon in advance ensure that external entities protect your organization's data to the level your organization would protect the data internally.

Data Privacy Considerations

Your organization must ensure privacy when exchanging data with any third party. If you contract services with a third party, make sure to agree on data privacy safeguards prior to entering into any business agreements. Privacy considerations include employee data privacy; privacy related to the type of data itself, such as financial data, personally identifiable information (PII), and protected health information (PHI); and how the third party will treat this data.

Legal or regulatory governance may provide you some protection, in that the third party has to obey laws with regard to data privacy, but you may find that your organization has additional requirements that need to be met by the third party. It's also possible that the agreement could be too restrictive in favor of the service provider, and your organization requires more flexible terms to ensure data privacy to your standards.

In any case, ensure to specify in any agreements made between your organization and a third-party provider or business associate how to handle private data, including how it is stored, processed, accessed, and especially transmitted to other third parties. For example, the HIPAA security regulations require that any third-party providers (referred to as "business associates" in HIPAA parlance) that could possibly have access to PHI be subjected to strict access control and handling requirements for that type of data.

Unauthorized Data Sharing

Security policies set forth in third-party agreements should cover unauthorized data sharing and access control. In addition to setting forth minimum requirements for access control, which include administrative, technical, and operational controls, the agreement should set forth mechanisms that an organization must use in order to share data with other authorized parties, as well as conditions under which the third party must comply with the law in sharing data with government and law enforcement agencies. The agreement should also cover how the organizations will respond in the event of a data breach or unauthorized access. Last, the agreement specifies who is liable for any fines or damages stemming from unauthorized data sharing.

Data Ownership

Organizations must define the types of data to which they claim ownership initially and how they would classify that data in terms of its sensitivity and protection requirements. The organizations must also determine how they will decide on ownership of data that is created during the contract term and who will control it. Some third parties that process data for an organization specifically agree that any data created during the contract term still belongs to the originating organization, but other third-party providers may maintain that they have legal ownership over any data that is created on their systems, based upon their unique processes or proprietary methods. This issue must be resolved prior to engaging in business with a third party. Issues with data ownership can lead to disputes over copyrights and patents, as well as unauthorized disclosure issues between two parties that both claim to own the data produced.

Supply Chain Concerns

Ensuring the security of *supply chains*—equipment, software, online services that collectively make products happen—requires proactive measures. IT security folks conduct *supply chain assessments* to ensure the availability of those critical components, to secure alternative processes, and to verify the security of data.

Two important aspects of supply chain assessment are *end of life (EOL)* and *end of service life (EOSL)*. These two terms are similar but have important, if subtle, differences. All products have a life cycle. Software versions are abandoned after a new version comes out. When a software or hardware vendor releases a new version of its product, it abandons any effort to update, market, or sell the prior version.

Vendors must let us know when a product reaches the end of its life. A *lack of vendor support* clearly marks a risk in dealing with third parties. A vendor releases an EOL to inform its customers that it will no longer sell a particular product, although the vendor may provide upgrades, patches, or maintenance.

End of service life marks the moment that an organization stops supporting a product. Microsoft might continue to provide updates and security patches for Windows 8.1, for example, but Highland Gadgets Corporation no longer provides support for operating systems older than Windows 10. The latter enterprise therefore announces the EOSL for Windows 8.1.

System Integration

There are many situations where two organizations might find it beneficial to perform many types of *system integration*, linking or matching networks, software, security, services, and so forth. To share data securely, for example, a third-party vendor might integrate its domain to your Active Directory forest and then create trust relationships.

System integration comes with all the risks of any single system. Users from the third party must be created with proper passwords. Both parties must use careful trust relationships to make sure no one has access to the other's data and resources unless needed. Third-party systems need acceptable anti-malware … this list goes on and on!

Measurement Systems Analysis

Having systems in place to test or check production and services provides necessary data about third-party contributions to the organization. *Measurement systems analysis (MSA)* tests the accuracy of those systems and data collection using math.

As an example of how MSA is helpful in managing third-party risk, a supply-chain supervisor gets complaints that some part coming from Source Alpha seems to be causing all sorts of problems with the end product. The supervisor checks production and finds that Source Alpha follows every guideline for production to the letter. What could cause the problem? If the calibration or measurements used for production were off by just a little, the end product could be off by a lot. MSA checks the accuracy of the measurements to discover errors.

Agreement Types

When your organization enters into any type of business partnership or agreement with a third-party business partner or service provider, the agreements and contract documents created serve to protect both organizations from a legal perspective as well as establish the terms of the business relationship. You'll need to be familiar with several types of documents for the exam, covering various aspects of data protection, interoperability, interconnection, and so on. They basically define the interoperability relationship between the two (and sometimes more) parties. Obviously, these types of agreements will be negotiated by the business contracting and legal personnel in each organization, but advice and input should also come from other affected functions within the businesses, such as security, privacy, IT support, and so on. Let's take a look at a few of these types of business agreements.

Sales and Purchase Agreement

A *sales and purchase agreement (SPA)* is a legal document obligating a buyer to buy and a seller to sell a product or service. SPAs are critical and common for large, complex purchases. An SPA not only defines prices but payment amounts and time frames for deposits. On the seller's side, an SPA defines how and when the property is to be transferred to the seller, acceptable condition of the goods or services, and any details that might impede the transfer.

You'll often see SPAs used in the cabling industry. Pulling cable, especially in an existing building, is complex. A good SPA for cabling covers all of the issues, such as when the installation will take place, when it will be complete, what types of cabling will be used, where the cable runs will go, how the runs will be labeled, how technicians will enter your facility, and whether the vendor is paid at once or at certain completion points.

Service Level Agreement

A *service level agreement (SLA)* is a legal document that defines the level of service that a third-party provider guarantees it will provide to the organization. The provider guarantees the service that it provides to be up and running and usable by the organization either for a certain percentage of time or to a certain level of standards. If the provider is storing or processing data for the organization, the SLA may state that the data will be available in a particular format, through a particular application or system, in a specified format, and to authorized users within the organization. If the provider is offering a service such as outsourced network or Web-based transactional services, for example, the SLA states that the services will be available for authorized users whenever they need them. The SLA may describe technologies and redundant systems used to ensure availability for the customer's data and services, as well as specify what actions the provider will take in the event of incidents that may affect availability of services, and how long the provider has to restore full access for the organization. Finally, most SLAs specify penalties for failure to provide the specified service.

NOTE Time is an important element for an SLA—length of time of the agreement, uptime guarantees, and response time for problems.

Business Partnership Agreement

The *business partnership agreement (BPA)* specifies what type of relationships the different parties will have, usually from a legal perspective. An entirely separate company may be established for the business venture, combining elements of both individual businesses; this is usually for long-term or large-scale ventures. Usually, however, legal agreements dictate the type of partnerships or customer–provider relationships. These partnerships are usually distinguished by scope, term length, and level of product, service, data access, and so forth provided to each party in the agreement.

NOTE A BPA rarely has a time frame but it will have clear methods for ending the partnership.

Memorandum of Understanding

A *memorandum of understanding (MOU)*, sometimes called a *memorandum of agreement (MOA)*, is a document often used within a large business or government agency that establishes an agreement between two independently managed parties that may be working together on a project or business venture. In this type of agreement, a contract isn't necessarily in place (nor required), simply because both parties work for the same overall organization. An MOU is established so that each party will agree to provide certain services or functions to the other party. Since both parties may work for the same higher-level organization, money doesn't necessarily change hands, but it could in a fee-for-service model where funds are transferred from one party's account to another's within the same company, for example. An example of this type of MOU would be if a division of the company provides data center services to other divisions of the same company; this MOU would outline the division's responsibilities and guaranteed levels of services to another division that uses it for data storage and protection.

You'll also see an MOU type of agreement between different government agencies; a military base, for example, may agree to provide network infrastructure services for another nonmilitary government agency that resides on the base (think of NASA, for example, which may have divisions housed on various US Army and US Air Force bases throughout the world).

You could also see an MOU between two businesses, of course, as part of a larger contract agreement; this may simply serve to define functions and interactions between two lower-level functions or departments located in each organization that weren't specified in the overall contract. The MOU may be agreed to and signed off by the middle-level managers of each department.

Non-Disclosure Agreement

There are plenty of situations where your organization needs to provide a vendor private/proprietary information. A *non-disclosure agreement (NDA)* is a legally binding agreement by your vendor that it will not release or expose the information your organization provides to it to any person not specifically listed in the NDA.

Interconnection Security Agreement

Telecommunication companies will use an *interconnection security agreement (ISA)* when connecting to each other's network to handle essential details about technology and personnel. An ISA is not a legal document used to cover technical issues between two parties. An ISA may detail how two independently owned and managed network infrastructures are connected to each other. The businesses that own each network may require interconnections to share and access each other's data, and may use this type of agreement to specify the technical details needed for the connections. The ISA may specify security requirements, such as firewall and VPN use, encryption levels and methods, authentication types, allowed protocols, and so forth. The ISA may be an attachment or amendment to the overall contract between parties.

Verifying Compliance and Performance

Any agreement between business parties and providers should specify how each party can verify compliance and performance standards. The parties may specify certain common standards and performance levels that each party has to meet, as well as legal or governance compliance. Audits or periodic inspections may be used by either party to verify the other party's compliance and performance. Access control checks, data integrity checks, and review of availability mechanisms (such as backup and restore devices and processes) may be addressed in this part of the agreement. Performance and security metrics such as throughput, availability times, backup frequency, limits on data permissions, and so forth may be specified and used to measure whether or not each organization is adhering to compliance and performance standards. Details regarding noncompliance and failure to perform up to standards should also be addressed in such agreements to give each party an avenue of redress against the other.

Questions

1. A script kiddie is a classic example of a(n) _____.

   A. attacker

   B. criminal

   C. threat

   D. threat actor

2. Risk is often considered formulaically as

   A. Risk = Probability × Threat

   B. Risk = Threat × Impact

   C. Risk = Vulnerability × Threat

   D. Risk = Probability × Impact

3. A company makes a document called "Acceptable Use" that defines what the company allows users to do and not do on their work systems. The company requires new employees to read and sign this. What is this type of document called?

   A. Standard

   B. Policy

   C. Procedure

   D. Control

4. A _____ is a description of a complex process, concentrating on major steps and the flows between the steps.

   A. law

   B. procedure

   C. framework

   D. control

5. A *No Trespassing* sign is an example of a _____ control.

    A. deterrent

    B. preventive

    C. detective

    D. corrective

6. A lock on the door of a building is an example of a _____ control.

    A. deterrent

    B. preventive

    C. detective

    D. corrective

7. An asset's exposure factor is measured in _____.

    A. dollars

    B. percentages

    C. units

    D. reputation

8. Which of the following equations is correct?

    A. Single-Loss Expectancy = Asset Value × Exposure Factor

    B. Annualized Rate of Occurrence = Asset Value × Exposure Factor

    C. Annualized Loss Expectancy = Asset Value × Exposure Factor

    D. Single Rate of Occurrence = Asset Value × Exposure Factor

9. Financial is one type of business impact. Which of the following names another?

    A. Pride

    B. Technical

    C. Device

    D. Reputation

10. Which of the following represents the component manufacturer's best guess (based on historical data) regarding how much time will pass between major failures of that component?

    A. MTTR

    B. MTBF

    C. MTMB

    D. MOAB

Answers

1. **D.** A script kiddie is a classic example of a threat actor.

2. **D.** Risk is often considered formulaically as Risk = Probability × Impact.

3. **B.** Policies are normally written documents that define an organization's goals and actions. Acceptable use policies are very common.

4. **C.** A framework is a description of a complex process, concentrating on major steps and the flows between the steps.

5. **A.** A deterrent control deters a threat actor from performing a threat. A *No Trespassing* sign is a good example.

6. **B.** A preventive control stops threat actors from performing a threat. Locks are a notable example.

7. **B.** Exposure factor is measured in terms of a percentage of loss to the value of that asset.

8. **A.** The only correct equation is Single-Loss Expectancy = Asset Value × Exposure Factor.

9. **D.** Of the choices listed, only reputation is a common business impact.

10. **B.** Mean time between failures (MTBF) represents the component manufacturer's best guess (based on historical data) regarding how much time will pass between major failures of that component.

Cryptography

Now he had learned that a machine, simple in its design, could produce results of infinite complexity.

—Neal Stephenson, *Cryptonomicon*

Every organization has private data, data accessible by authorized users and not accessible to outsiders. This data includes customer databases; e-mails with critical business strategies; file servers with proprietary recipes and manufacturing processes; cameras sending images of security gates; and Web sites where people type in their names, addresses, and credit card information. Organizations need to keep this data secure. Encryption gives organizations the tools to accomplish this goal.

Encryption is a reversible process of converting data such that to a third party the data is nothing more than a random binary string. Note the phrase *reversible process*. This means a good encryption method must make it easy for someone who knows something secret to encrypt the data and to reverse the process to return the data from an encrypted state to an unencrypted state. *Decrypting* makes encrypted data readable.

This chapter explores *cryptography*, the science of encrypting and decrypting data, in nine modules:

- Cryptography Basics
- Cryptographic Methods
- Symmetric Cryptosystems
- Asymmetric Cryptosystems
- Hashing Algorithms
- Digital Signatures and Certificates
- Public Key Infrastructure
- Cryptographic Attacks
- Other Cryptosystems

Module 2-1: Cryptography Basics

This module covers the following CompTIA Security+ objectives:

- **2.1 Explain the importance of security concepts in an enterprise environment**
- **2.8 Summarize the basics of cryptographic concepts**

Cryptography provides methods and technologies to enable people and systems to exchange information securely, from local connections to enterprise environments that span the globe. Cryptography ensures *confidentiality*—the encrypted data can be unencrypted and read only by the intended recipient. Cryptography also affords *integrity*, so the recipient can know that the data received matches the data sent—that the data hasn't been altered in some way. To accomplish these tasks, developers and programmers have created immensely complicated and awesome systems...and those systems come with a ton of epic jargon and details.

This module begins the exploration into the systems that make up modern cryptographic methods. It starts with basic building block concepts, such as plaintext and ciphertext. You'll look at early cryptography to understand the methods with simple examples. The module finishes with an overview of the essential components of every cryptographic system.

Essential Building Blocks

Cryptography has terms that describe the state of data, tools used to affect that data, and the movement of data from one state to another. This section discusses these terms:

- Plaintext and ciphertext
- Code and cipher
- Data at rest, data in use, data in transit

Plaintext and Ciphertext

IT professionals use the terms *plaintext* and *ciphertext* to describe the current readability of data. Humans and machines can easily read plaintext. Ciphertext, on the other hand, is unreadable. The process of converting plaintext information into ciphertext information is called *encryption*. The goal of encryption is to *obfuscate* the plaintext—to make it unreadable, to look as though it were simply a random jumble of data. Essentially, encryption is about *data protection*. The reverse of encryption, converting ciphertext back into plaintext, is called *decryption*. Figure 2-1 shows the icons used here when discussing plaintext and ciphertext.

 NOTE Don't mistake the "text" portion of the words *plaintext* and *ciphertext* to mean only letters of the alphabet. Any form of easily readable binary data is plaintext. Any form of encrypted binary data is ciphertext.

Figure 2-1
Plaintext and
ciphertext

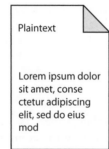

Plaintext

Lorem ipsum dolor
sit amet, conse
ctetur adipiscing
elit, sed do eius
mod

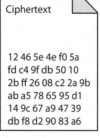

Ciphertext

12 46 5e 4e f0 5a
fd c4 9f db 50 10
2b ff 26 08 c2 2a 9b
ab a5 78 65 95 d1
14 9c 67 a9 47 39
db f8 d2 90 83 a6

Code and Cipher

IT professionals use the terms code and cipher to describe generically the ways tools encrypt and decrypt. A *code* is a representation of an entire phrase or sentence, whereas a *cipher* tends to represent text on a character-by-character basis. For example, a coded version of the phrase "We attack at dawn" might be "Mother bought some brown eggs at the store." Codes are not typically transformative; that is, there is usually no formal process to convert the true meanings of messages into their coded equivalents or back. Codes usually require a *codebook*, a predefined dictionary that translates codes to their plaintext messages and back. The need for a codebook limits the range of messages that can be sent and received via codes. Codes were common before computers, but are not at all common today in modern cryptography.

Ciphers, on the other hand, use some form of formal, usually mathematical process to work instead of a fixed codebook. This makes the range of potential messages that can be sent using ciphers essentially unlimited, because these processes are usually done on the fly. Modern cryptographic methods with computers tend to use ciphers.

You may sometimes hear the terms *encode* and *decode* (as well as *encipher* and *decipher*) thrown around. In encoding, data *transforms*, changes from one form to another. For example, you can encode a sound file from uncompressed WAV format into an MP3 file format. This saves space, but has nothing to do with security. In cryptography, *encipher* and *encrypt* mean the same thing, although the former is not in common use. Since IT security focuses on ciphers, this book sticks to the terms that apply to ciphers: encrypt and decrypt.

NOTE Codes are entire words and phrases; ciphers are individual characters. The cryptography methods discussed in this book focus on ciphers.

Data at Rest, Data in Use, and Data in Transit

Dealing with cryptography for computer data depends on the location of the data and the actions of that data at any given moment. The process of encrypting and decrypting data sitting on a hard drive, for example, differs from the process of encrypting and decrypting data moving wirelessly between a wireless access point and a wireless client. Three terms define the current state of data:

- Data at rest
- Data in use
- Data in transit

Data at Rest   *Data at rest* describes data that resides in storage. This data is not currently accessed, transmitted, or received, nor used by the computer. Data at rest is normally represented by data stored in static files on a hard drive or other storage media, when the device that holds that media is powered down. In other words, data on a laptop computer, powered down and sitting in Steve's bag, is data at rest.

 NOTE   Once Steve has logged into his computer at the airport lounge, the data on the laptop's SSD *could* change at any time. So is it truly data at rest? Cybersecurity professionals argue this point a lot, and some call the data subject to change *data at rest (inconstant)*. You won't see that phrase on the CompTIA Security+ exam.

Data in Use   *Data in use* describes data currently in use by a computing device and not at rest or in transit. Data in a computer's RAM and accessed by the computer's CPU, operating system, and applications is data in use. Operating systems and applications take data at rest and put it into use on a constant basis, transforming it, using it as input to processes, and so on. A Microsoft Word document Susan is currently editing is an obvious example.

Lots of techniques target data in use. *Shoulder surfing*—a social engineering technique where someone literally or figuratively looks over a user's shoulder to view/record the contents on the screen—can grab data in use. A fairly simple USB keycatcher—easy to install when a user isn't looking—can record or transmit via wireless everything the user types. Data in use is very much *data in danger*!

 EXAM TIP   The CompTIA Security+ objectives use the term *data in processing* as an alternative label for data in use. Don't be thrown off by the odd term.

Data in Transit   *Data in transit* describes data currently in transport. This data is being transmitted or received from one person or host to another. Examples of data in transit include information moving over a network, over an Internet connection, from computer to computer over an Ethernet connection, or even over wireless networks. The data is not in storage; it has been transformed and formatted to be transmitted and received.

Data in transit has high requirements for confidentiality. It's relatively easy for malicious actors to intercept transmitting data, so we need good encryption. Data in transit also has very high requirements for integrity. The recipient must have assurance that the data received is the same as the data sent.

 EXAM TIP The CompTIA Security+ objectives describe a key facet of data protection as dealing with data *in transit/motion*. The industry term used here, data *in transit*, means the same thing. Don't get tripped up by the wording.

Outstanding! The module has covered enough terms to enable a brief survey of the history of cryptography. Pay attention here, as almost everything done hundreds of years ago is still used today on modern computers.

Early Cryptography

People throughout the past few thousand years have used cryptography to protect personal secrets, military troop movements, diplomatic messages, and so on. Historians have discovered several examples of the uses of crude, but effective, cryptographic methods, such as the Spartan *scytale*, which was a baton or stick with a strip of parchment wound around it several times, from one end of the stick to the other (Figure 2-2). After the parchment was wrapped on the baton, a person wrote a message in plaintext. Once the parchment was removed from the stick, the words on the strip of parchment made no sense, since they were effectively encrypted. To "decrypt" the message, the receiver had to know the exact dimensions of the baton and have an identical one so that he could rewrap the parchment the same way around the baton and read the message.

Figure 2-2
Author's home-made scytale
(Attack at dawn)

Other historical uses of cryptography involved using different techniques to scramble letters of the alphabet so that only the sender and recipient would know how to unscramble and read them. The next sections of the chapter discuss those methods. Still other, more modern ways of using cryptography involved the use of specially built machines to encrypt and decrypt messages. The classic example is the Enigma machine used by the Germans during World War II. This machine used encryption techniques that were considered unbreakable, until Dr. Alan Turing, a British mathematician, figured out how the machine worked and the methods it used to encrypt its information. Turing, now considered the father of modern cryptography and, to a large degree, computers, decrypted intercepted German messages. The capability of the British government to decrypt German military communications gave the Allies incredible insight into enemy troop movements, invasion plans, and so forth, effectively turning the tide of the war.

Alan Turing didn't invent cryptography, but many of the concepts used today were quantified by him in the huge number of academic papers Turing wrote. Turing clarified the ideas of substitution and transposition, the two pillars of cryptography.

Substitution

A *substitution* cipher swaps letters of the alphabet for other letters. To make a substitution cipher work, rotate the letters of the alphabet by some number of characters, then swap the letters that will substitute for them. A typical rotation shifts the alphabet 13 characters, called ROT13. Here's the standard alphabet:

ABCDEFGHIJKLMNOPQRSTUVWXYZ

And here's the same alphabet with ROT13 applied:

NOPQRSTUVWXYZABCDEFGHIJKLM

Note that the letter N replaces letter A. Letter G replaces letter T. Line the two up so you can see the full replacement scheme:

ABCDEFGHIJKLMNOPQRSTUVWXYZ
NOPQRSTUVWXYZABCDEFGHIJKLM

Now apply an example. The plaintext phrase, WE ATTACK AT DAWN, would change to JRNGGNPXNGQNJA in ROT13 encryption.

 NOTE ROT13 is not the only ROT cipher. You can do ROT2, ROT10, ROT25, and so on.

This type of cipher is also called a *shift cipher* because it essentially shifts the entire alphabet down 13 spaces and then starts over with the first letter. Still other methods of using substitution ciphers might use different words to begin the substitution alphabet and then follow those words with the rest of the alphabet in normal order.

NOTE Julius Caesar used a substitution cipher in his military campaigns for sensitive communications. Thus, a substitution cipher is commonly referred to as a *Caesar cipher*.

A *Vigenère cipher* takes the Caesar cipher to its extreme. Figure 2-3 shows a *tabula recta*, a table of all 26 possible ROT ciphers that creates a grid. The Vigenère cipher uses a repeating *key word* to determine which row to use for encryption.

Here's how to use the *tabula recta* and key word to encrypt the plaintext. Find the plaintext letter at the top (column), then use the key word letter along the side (row). The matching column and row intersection provides the encrypted letter. An example will make this clear.

Again our plaintext is WE ATTACK AT DAWN. And we'll use a key word of MIKE (repeated here to match the text):

```
WEATTACKATDAWN
MIKEMIKEMIKEMI
```

```
    A B C D E F G H I J K L M N O P Q R S T U V W X Y Z
  A A B C D E F G H I J K L M N O P Q R S T U V W X Y Z
  B B C D E F G H I J K L M N O P Q R S T U V W X Y Z A
  C C D E F G H I J K L M N O P Q R S T U V W X Y Z A B
  D D E F G H I J K L M N O P Q R S T U V W X Y Z A B C
  E E F G H I J K L M N O P Q R S T U V W X Y Z A B C D
  F F G H I J K L M N O P Q R S T U V W X Y Z A B C D E
  G G H I J K L M N O P Q R S T U V W X Y Z A B C D E F
  H H I J K L M N O P Q R S T U V W X Y Z A B C D E F G
  I I J K L M N O P Q R S T U V W X Y Z A B C D E F G H
  J J K L M N O P Q R S T U V W X Y Z A B C D E F G H I
  K K L M N O P Q R S T U V W X Y Z A B C D E F G H I J
  L L M N O P Q R S T U V W X Y Z A B C D E F G H I J K
  M M N O P Q R S T U V W X Y Z A B C D E F G H I J K L
  N N O P Q R S T U V W X Y Z A B C D E F G H I J K L M
  O O P Q R S T U V W X Y Z A B C D E F G H I J K L M N
  P P Q R S T U V W X Y Z A B C D E F G H I J K L M N O
  Q Q R S T U V W X Y Z A B C D E F G H I J K L M N O P
  R R S T U V W X Y Z A B C D E F G H I J K L M N O P Q
  S S T U V W X Y Z A B C D E F G H I J K L M N O P Q R
  T T U V W X Y Z A B C D E F G H I J K L M N O P Q R S
  U U V W X Y Z A B C D E F G H I J K L M N O P Q R S T
  V V W X Y Z A B C D E F G H I J K L M N O P Q R S T U
  W W X Y Z A B C D E F G H I J K L M N O P Q R S T U V
  X X Y Z A B C D E F G H I J K L M N O P Q R S T U V W
  Y Y Z A B C D E F G H I J K L M N O P Q R S T U V W X
  Z Z A B C D E F G H I J K L M N O P Q R S T U V W X Y
```

Figure 2-3 Vigenère cipher table, or *tabula recta*

Use the *tabula recta* to create the encrypted phrase. Here are the first five letters:

```
W → M = I
E → I = M
A → K = K
T → E = X
T → M = F
```

And so on . . .

Note that the second "T" encrypts to a different letter than the first "T" because of the difference in the key word letter. Sweet! Here's the fully encrypted phrase:

```
IMKXFIMOMBNEIV
```

If the recipient knows the key word, he or she can quickly decipher the code. Without the key word, deciphering becomes more difficult (and relies on repetition analysis and so forth).

Vigenère ciphers were popular for centuries. Examples of substitution ciphers can be found in the standard word puzzle books you see on magazine racks in supermarkets and bookstores.

In cryptography, *confusion* means that every character in a key is used to make the ciphertext more random looking. Adding a key to change the ROT value of every character adds confusion, making a Vigenère cipher much harder to crack than a ROT.

Vigenère ciphers have a weakness. Encrypt the plaintext WE ATTACK AT NOON with the MIKE key, but each letter in the key only affects the plaintext character directly underneath it. A better encryption should act in such a way that even the smallest change in the key makes for very different ciphertext. This is called *diffusion*. The Vigenère cipher lacks diffusion. Modern codes do not!

Transposition

A *transposition* cipher transposes or changes the order of characters in a message using some predetermined method that both the sender and recipient know. The sender transposes the message and sends it. The recipient applies the same transposition method in reverse, decrypting the message. There are a variety of different transposition methods, including columnar, rail fence, and route ciphers. Current computer-based cryptography uses both substitution and transposition together in wildly complex ways.

Cryptanalysis

For as long as people have encrypted and decrypted data (or messages or whatever), others have tried to crack those messages. *Cryptanalysis* is the study of breaking encryption, the opposite of cryptography. You perform cryptanalysis on ciphertext data to reverse it to a plaintext state when you do not have access to the methods used to encrypt the data in the first place. Both security professionals and malicious actors perform cryptanalysis when attempting to decrypt ciphertext. There are hundreds, if not thousands, of methods for performing cryptanalysis, but many of them depend upon having a piece of plaintext that can be compared to its corresponding ciphertext, and vice versa, when you have some knowledge of the methods used to encrypt and decrypt the text. The next few modules discuss various methods of cryptanalysis.

Cryptography Components

Cryptography has several basic components that make the process work. These include algorithms, keys, XOR functions, shifts, rounds, and cryptosystems. While this module covers only the basics of these components, the remaining modules on cryptography discuss in depth how these different components work together.

Algorithms and Keys

Algorithms and keys work together to create cryptographic methods used to encrypt and decrypt messages. (They also can create cryptographic hash functions, used for digital signatures and more, a subject covered in depth in Module 2-5.)

Algorithms are mathematical constructs that define how to transform plaintext into ciphertext, as well as how to reverse that process during decryption. An individual algorithm might be very simple or very complex. A very simple algorithm used in a substitution cipher, for example, only requires shifting a letter several spaces to the right. Almost all the real-world algorithms used in IT encryption/decryption are extraordinarily complex. A single algorithm will contain a dizzying number of mathematical manipulations.

A *key* applies a variable used by the algorithm for the final cryptosystem (see the upcoming section "Cryptosystems"). In a ROT13 cryptosystem, ROT is the algorithm—to implement the encryption/decryption, shift letters of the alphabet. The 13 is the key or *cryptovariable* that defines how many letters to shift.

Algorithms often don't change. Keys change to keep bad actors guessing.

Keys are kept secret. Keys are typically not simplistic numbers. They are often complex, lengthy strings of numbers or characters. A key might also be a password, passphrase, personal identification number (PIN), code word, and so on. Algorithms and keys are used to encrypt or decrypt text, as illustrated in Figure 2-4.

Figure 2-4
Algorithms and keys

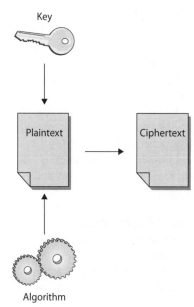

Key

Plaintext → Ciphertext

Algorithm

Algorithms are generally well known and tested, giving cryptographers and security professionals a level of confidence in their strength and ability to protect data. *Kerckhoffs' principle* states that the algorithm should not be the secret part of the cryptographic process or method used; the key should be kept secret, not the algorithm. Most security professionals follow this principle.

NOTE Dutch cryptographer Auguste Kerckhoffs developed Kerckhoffs' principle in the late 19th century. This stuff has been around for a while!

Key escrow grants knowledge or copies of keys to a third party. Businesses and other organizations use key escrow to store keys securely in the event that they are lost, they become corrupt, or an individual in the company with the only knowledge of the keys is terminated or quits. Key escrow provides an exception to Kerckhoffs' principle.

EXAM TIP An algorithm is a mathematical construct or rule that dictates how data will be encrypted and decrypted. Algorithms are generally well known and not kept secret. Secret algorithms are not needed. Keys are the variables that algorithms use to ensure secrecy and randomness in the cryptographic process. Keys should be kept secret.

Key length or *key size* refers to the number of bits in a key; this number implies security—a hacker can readily break a short key, for example. With the unbelievable growth in computing power today, on the other hand, a long key doesn't necessarily equate to better security. You'll see various key lengths used in practical cryptography in Modules 2-3 and 2-4.

The most secure keys would come from truly randomly generated numbers, numbers that no one could predict. Such a number would have an *entropy* value of 1, meaning full entropy or complete unpredictability. The reverse of this, with a completely *deterministic* system, would have an entropy value of 0. The ROT13 system discussed earlier, for example, with its predictable, fixed system, is such a deterministic system.

Computers are not random, though, but very much predictable. Many will use software to generate *pseudorandom numbers* based on some mathematical system. Not surprisingly, the type of software used in cryptography is called a *cryptographically secure pseudorandom number generator (CSPRNG)*, or simply *cryptographic random number generator (CRNG)*. The factor to keep in mind here is that the keys come from some system and thus provide a place for threat actors to attack. We'll see more of this in Module 2-8, "Cryptographic Attacks."

Block and Streaming Algorithms

Algorithms have a wide variety of characteristics that include mathematical foundation, strength, and how they operate on plaintext. Modules 2-3 and 2-4 go into detail about specific algorithms used in *cipher suites* (groups of algorithms used to secure network connections), but for now, let's discuss an important distinction within algorithms: block and streaming.

Remember the distinction between codes and ciphers and how they work with entire phrases (codes) or on individual characters (ciphers)? The algorithms discussed in this book work on binary digits (bits) of plaintext, either individually or in specified groups. A *block algorithm* operates on a predefined size of a group of bits, known as a *block*. Different block algorithms use different block sizes, but typical sizes are 16-, 64-, and 128-bit blocks. Most of the algorithms discussed in this book are block algorithms.

Streaming algorithms operate on individual bits, one bit at a time. Streaming algorithms don't work on blocks of text; instead, they look at each individual bit and perform a mathematical operation on that bit and then move on to the next bit. Streaming algorithms tend to work much faster than block algorithms and are used in cryptographic methods that support fast communications requirements, such as wireless technologies.

 EXAM TIP Block algorithms work on predefined sizes of plaintext blocks, while streaming algorithms work on single bits of plaintext. CompTIA refers to streaming algorithms as *stream algorithms*.

Streaming algorithms have a problem. Since they only encrypt one bit at a time, they need a piece of arbitrary value or string to get the encryption process started. This code, called an *initialization vector (IV)*, provides the necessary randomness for the algorithms. There are also some interesting situations where IVs work in a block protocol as well. See "DES" in Module 2-3 for more.

XOR Functions

Computing devices use binary data. Hard drives store Word documents in binary format. YouTube videos stream to a browser in binary format. Caesar ciphers use alphabets, not bits, so they don't readily apply to binary data. Computers need mathematical tools to encrypt, to transpose and substitute ones and zeros. The most commonly used binary math function used in cryptography is called *eXclusive OR (XOR)*. XOR compares two bits to determine difference.

With XOR, any bits that compare and are the same (two binary 0's, for example) yield a resultant bit of *false* (and produce a 0-bit as the output). Any bits that compare and are different (a binary 1 and a binary 0) produce a *true* value, and an output bit of 1 is generated. Figure 2-5 illustrates this process. (If you've taken the CompTIA Network+ exam, then you know about XOR comparison from subnetting. The 1's in the subnet mask compare to the IP address to differentiate the network ID from the host ID.)

 NOTE XOR results might seem a little weird at first. Keep in mind that XOR determines *differences* in compared data. A *true* result means that the compared data is *not* the same. A *false* result means the data is the same.

Here's an example of XOR in action, encrypting the *randomly selected* name, Mike, as the data:

MIKE

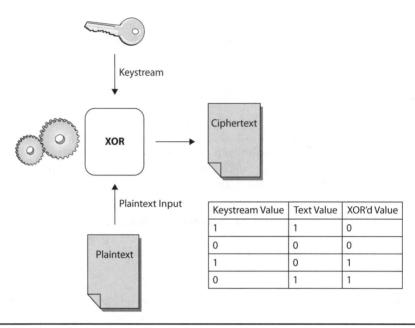

Figure 2-5 The XOR function in action

As a first step, convert these four letters into binary. For this example, we'll use ASCII code. ASCII converts every letter of the English alphabet in 8-bit binary values:

```
M = 01001101
I = 01001001
K = 01001011
E = 01000101
```

So, MIKE in binary is 01001101010010010100101101000101. This string of bits is the *plaintext*.

The XOR function compares two binary values, right? To encrypt with XOR requires another value to compare with the plaintext. To XOR encrypt this binary data, therefore, we need a binary key. Let's *arbitrarily* choose the ridiculously easy key of 0110. To encrypt, repeatedly place the key under the plaintext, as follows:

```
01001101010010010100101101000101 (plaintext)
01100110011001100110011001100110 (key repeated)
```

Now go one bit at a time, using XOR to encrypt:

```
01001101010010010100101101000101
01100110011001100110011001100110
00101011001011110010110100100011 (ciphertext)
```

Congrats! You've just done binary encryption, in this example using XOR. Want to decrypt the ciphertext? Just XOR it against the repeated key, as follows:

```
00101011001011110010110100100011  (ciphertext)
01100110011001100110011001100110  (key repeated)
01001101010010010100101101000101  (plaintext)
```

Using XOR solely, especially with such a short key, creates an easily cracked ciphertext. Let's make it harder by adding a shift.

Shifts

As the name implies, a *shift* in binary means moving the ciphertext left or right. Let's shift the ciphertext four digits to the left. Here's the initial ciphertext:

```
00101011001011110010110100100011
```

Now, take the first four binary values on the far left and move them to the end on the far right, as follows:

```
10110010111100101101001000110010
```

Adding a shift increases the complexity involved in decrypting. You need the key, plus knowledge of the shift.

A simple shift makes better encryption, but a powerful computer can figure out this shifty trick in milliseconds! Let's enhance the encryption by doing the whole XOR/left-shift multiple times.

Rounds

Repeating the XOR/left-shift iteration more than once—such as five times—makes the encryption harder to crack. It also means it will take longer to encrypt and decrypt, because every encryption and decryption must repeat the iteration five times. (That's the price required for security.) Each of these XOR/left-shift iterations is called a *round*. Most modern algorithms use multiple rounds, repeating the process several times to ensure that the process is effective.

Cryptosystems

A *cryptosystem* includes everything in a cryptographic process, such as the algorithms, keys, functions, methods, and techniques. The example used here—the Mike Meyers Excellent Cryptosystem—includes four components:

- A four-bit key
- An XOR
- A four-digit left shift of the ciphertext
- The XOR/left-shift iteration repeated in five rounds

Cryptosystems use algorithms and keys as basic components to stir up the binary data and also implement them in ways that enable the encryption/decryption to be faster, more efficient, or stronger.

Module 2-2: Cryptographic Methods

This module covers the following CompTIA Security+ objectives:

- **2.1 Explain the importance of security concepts in an enterprise environment**
- **2.8 Summarize the basics of cryptographic concepts**

You can differentiate cryptographic methods by the encryption method used, either symmetric or asymmetric. These two types of cryptography focus more on the aspect of the keys used than the algorithms, although each type has its own algorithms, as discussed in later modules.

This module explores symmetric cryptography first, followed by asymmetric cryptography. The third section in the module describes a unique type of cryptography called hashing. The fourth section explores the relative limitations between symmetric and asymmetric cryptographic systems. The fifth section puts symmetric cryptographic systems, asymmetric cryptographic systems, and hashing together in hybrid cryptography. The final section discusses what makes a perfect cryptosystem.

Symmetric Cryptography

Symmetric cryptography uses a single key that both encrypts and decrypts data. All parties that require access to a piece of encrypted data know that key. If someone encrypts a file or sends a secure message to another person, both persons must have the key used to encrypt the data to decrypt it.

NOTE The industry uses the terms "symmetric cryptography" and "symmetric-key cryptography" interchangeably. You'll see that here and in a similar form with "asymmetric cryptography" used interchangeably with "asymmetric-key cryptography."

Symmetric keys are sometimes called *secret* keys or *session* keys. Session keys, more specifically, are created and used for a single communications session. They are not reused after the communications session ends. If the parties want to communicate again using symmetric cryptography, new session keys are generated by either party or by the cryptosystem in use. Figure 2-6 shows how two parties use symmetric keys to exchange sensitive data.

EXAM TIP Symmetric key cryptography uses a single key that both encrypts and decrypts data.

Figure 2-6
Symmetric keys
in use

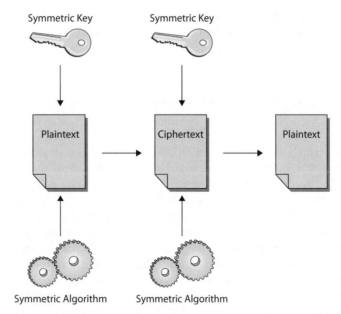

Symmetric key cryptography is both *low latency* (quick to respond) and good at handling large amounts of data, such as storage or transmission of large files. Symmetric keys require minimal computational overhead. Since only one key is involved, in communications limited to only two parties, symmetric key cryptography works great.

Symmetric key cryptography has a couple of weaknesses in scaling and key exchange. First, when multiple parties require access to the same encrypted data (such as a group of friends or business associates), the exchange uses the same key. The more people who have the key, the greater the chances that it will get inadvertently disclosed to an unauthorized person. Second, getting the key into the hands of only the desired users presents challenges.

Let's look at an example of the scaling problem. User Meghan wants to communicate with user Amy. Both need only one secret key. Adding more users, such as Tim, Bobby, and Dawn, means each must have the same key to access the encrypted data.

What if, however, Meghan wants only Amy to view a piece of data, and she doesn't want Tim, Bobby, or Dawn to see it? Meghan must maintain separate symmetric keys for each party with whom she wants to communicate. Among a few people this scenario might be manageable. But imagine what happens if Meghan needs to maintain separate keys for 100 people? Meghan has a lot of keys!

Worse yet, what if each of the 100 people required secure, unique communication with every other user? How many total keys must be generated?

Math comes to the rescue here. The total number of keys required is equal to the number of people in the group, multiplied by that same number less 1, and then divided by 2. Here's the formula:

$K = N \times (N - 1)/2$

- K is the total number of keys required.
- N is the number of people in the group.

So: $K = 100 \times (100 - 1)/2 = 4950$. As you can see, with 100 users, a lot of keys must be generated, issued, and exchanged among each pair of users in the group who must securely communicate. Symmetric key cryptography does not scale very well in larger groups or entities that must securely communicate with one another.

Key exchange refers to the process used to exchange keys between users who send a message and those who receive it. Without the key, an authorized user or message recipient can't decrypt the message; the message will simply remain as ciphertext.

Since only one key is used in a symmetric communication, there must be a way to deliver the key securely to the right users, with an assurance that it won't be intercepted and compromised. E-mail is usually not the most secure way, although sometimes people send their secret keys via an e-mail message. Manual methods offer a little more security, such as giving someone a key stored on a USB memory stick.

Most of the time, especially in large organizations or when communicating with someone over greater distances, manual exchange isn't practical. The problem with key exchange, therefore, is getting the key to someone using a means that is considered secure—so that the key will not be intercepted and used by an unauthorized person, rendering the entire process useless. Symmetric key cryptography has problems with secure key exchange.

Key exchange has two terms to describe the exchange methods:

- In-band
- Out-of-band

In-band key exchange involves using the same communications channel you are using to send the message to send the key. This may not be the most secure way, since that channel may be monitored by a malicious person.

Out-of-band key exchange involves the use of a separate, independent channel, such as snail mail, USB stick, or even a different network connection, to send the key to the authorized users. In smaller groups of users that reside near each other, key exchange may not be much of a problem. In large organizations, however, in which users may be geographically separated, key exchange can be an issue, especially when using only symmetric key cryptography.

 EXAM TIP Symmetric key cryptography excels in speed, efficiency, and the ability to handle large amounts of data easily. The disadvantages primarily involve scalability and key exchange.

Asymmetric Cryptography

Asymmetric cryptography uses two separate keys—a *key pair*—for secure communication. Data encrypted with one key requires the other key in the key pair for decryption.

In *public key cryptography*—the primary asymmetric implementation—these keys are called a *public key* and a *private key*. Each user is issued or generates a key pair for his or her own use. The user gives the public key to anyone, even posting it on the Internet. The user keeps the private key, on the other hand, secret. With public key cryptography, what one key encrypts, only the other key can decrypt, and vice versa. If the key in the pair is used to encrypt a message, it cannot decrypt the same message. This makes the cryptography process, particularly sending and receiving confidential messages, different from the process used in symmetric key cryptography.

 EXAM TIP Public key cryptography uses two mathematically related keys in a pair, a public key and a private key. What one key encrypts, only the other key in the pair may decrypt, and vice versa. In current systems, the public key encrypts and the private key decrypts. (See Module 2-6 for the only use for reversing this process, validating a certificate by viewing the digital signature.)

Jack and Jill want to communicate using public key cryptography. They need to follow specific steps. First, each must generate a unique key pair. Second, each user makes his or her public key readily available, such as posting it to the Internet.

Jack acquires Jill's public key, encrypts a message using that key, and sends it to Jill. Jill receives the message and decrypts it with her private key. Her private key is the only way to decrypt a message encrypted with her public key.

For Jill to send a message to Jack securely, she reverses the process. She gets his public key and uses it to encrypt the message. Upon receipt, Jack decrypts the message using his private key. It's an elegant system. Figures 2-7 and 2-8 demonstrate this process.

Asymmetric key cryptography has several advantages over symmetric key cryptography, the major one being key exchange. The process eliminates key exchange issues, since no

Figure 2-7
Distribution
of public and
private keys

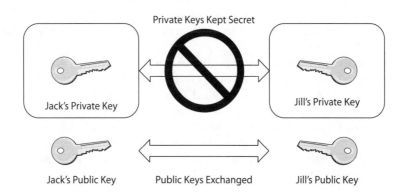

Figure 2-8
Using asymmetric key cryptography

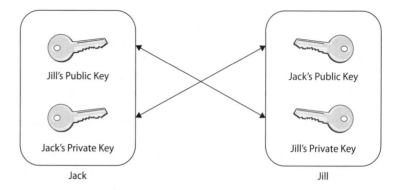

one really has to exchange a key. Anyone can acquire the public key. The sending party encrypts the message with the receiving person's public key, and only the recipient who possesses the private key can decrypt it.

Asymmetric key cryptography has a couple of disadvantages as well. First, it's slower than symmetric key cryptography and more computationally intensive to generate keys. Second, it works well only with small amounts of data; it's not suited for bulk data encryption or transmission. Module 2-7 will discuss the primary uses of asymmetric key cryptography, which involve public key infrastructure, or PKI, and uses of digital certificates and signatures.

EXAM TIP Asymmetric key cryptography does great key exchange, but features slower speed compared to symmetric key cryptography and doesn't handle large amounts of data very efficiently. Expect a question or two on the CompTIA Security+ exam that asks you to contrast *symmetric vs. asymmetric* encryption concepts and methods.

Hashing

Hashing provides integrity in the confidentiality, integrity, availability (CIA) triad of security by creating unique numbers for data and originators of information. Hashing helps verify that data came from a specific source and that the data did not change from what was sent.

In the hashing process, variable-length text, such as a document or spreadsheet, or even a password, is exposed to a cryptographic algorithm that produces a cryptographic sum, or *hash* (also sometimes called a *message digest*), of the document. This hash is only a representation of the text; it is not the same thing as the text itself. Think of a hash as a unique fingerprint that identifies a very specific piece of plaintext. The piece of plaintext can be any length, and it generally does not matter how large the input plaintext is. The resulting hash will always be a fixed-length piece of ciphertext, usually expressed in a hexadecimal format. An example of a typical hash is shown in Figure 2-9.

Figure 2-9   A hash value computed for a file

Unlike the encryption and decryption process, hashing was not designed to be reversible. In other words, you don't simply encrypt text with a hashing function with the expectation of decrypting it later. Hashing is a one-way mathematical function whose sole purpose is to produce the cryptographic sum of the input plaintext. Think of the hashing process as sort of a measuring process for the data, with the resultant hash being the actual measurement itself.

Although its purpose is not to decrypt text, the cryptographic sum produced by hashing has some uses. First, hashing is used to provide for integrity of data. A hash is unique to a particular piece of text. If one letter or word of the text is altered in any way, if even one binary digit changes, the resulting hash will differ from the original hash. *Hashing assures the integrity* of a piece of plaintext, since any changes would produce an easily detected different sum. Figure 2-10 shows the hashing process.

Data transmitted over a network can be hashed before transmission and after reception, and the two resulting hashes can be compared. If the hashes match, you have unaltered data. If they differ, you can assume that the data has changed in some way during transmission. We'll discuss hashing in more depth in Module 2-5, with specific examples of hashing methods.

NOTE   The term "message" generically refers to any piece of variable-length text, be it a password, text document, spreadsheet, picture file, or any other type of data.

Figure 2-10
The hashing
process

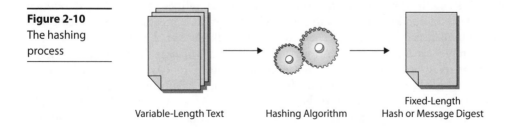

Variable-Length Text   Hashing Algorithm   Fixed-Length
                                                          Hash or Message Digest

Limitations in Symmetric vs. Asymmetric Cryptography

You need to have clarity on the relative strengths and weaknesses of symmetric and asymmetric cryptography in concept before you delve into the next two modules, which layer on all the specific implementations of those systems. Limitations of systems include

- Speed
- Size
- Weak keys
- Time
- Longevity
- Predictability
- Reuse
- Entropy
- Computational overheads
- Resource vs. security constraints

The module has discussed several of these limitations already, notably *speed, size, weak keys*, and *computational overheads*, noting that symmetric encryption is faster and has lower computational overhead than asymmetric encryption and that small-sized keys are weak keys. Size also relates to symmetric encryption handling larger files more efficiently than asymmetric encryption. The other limitations require a little more discussion.

No encryption scheme is unbreakable. Developers instead strive to create an encryption scheme that provides strong enough security to make it too difficult—in terms of *time* and *computational power* needed—to crack. Because technology advances rapidly increase the computing power available to hackers, on the other hand, the relative security of any cryptosystem is a moving target. Folks at the National Institute of Standards and Technology (NIST) keep track of these things, rating the *longevity* of each active cryptosystem, as in how many years a cryptosystem remains secure in the current computing environment. We'll save the details for the next couple of modules, but current cryptosystems are pretty awesome, and increasing the size of keys by just a single bit makes a cryptosystem twice as hard to crack.

Modern cryptographic systems generate some kind of key to encrypt and decrypt messages, but those keys usher in limitations and vulnerabilities. We discussed the *entropy* level of pseudorandom numbers in the previous module, a measure of how predictable those numbers can be. The four characters in the Mike Meyers Excellent Cryptosystem, for example, have a very low entropy level, meaning a hacker could predict or guess them pretty quickly. Other cryptosystems might seem to have much tougher keys, such as 64-bit keys, but if 32 bits of the key have high *predictability*, the overall key is vulnerable to attack. There's also the *reuse* factor for keys. An 8-bit key, for example, would generate numbers between 0 and 255, which means the numbers would quickly be reused, making the 8-bit key weak. In contrast, a one-time password that's never reused? Almost uncrackable.

Finally, *resource vs. security constraints* boils down to the relationship between how much computing power goes into the system and the security of the system. Higher key lengths offer more security but require more computing power to deal with. A million-character one-use key would be utterly secure, but to generate that every time a message gets encrypted/decrypted would kill modern systems. Every cryptosystem works on this balancing principle, defining an inherent limitation.

Hybrid Cryptography

Many modern implementations of cryptography combine symmetric key and asymmetric key functions with hashing to create a highly secure mashup generically called *hybrid cryptography*. Symmetric key cryptography handles large data well, but is weak at key exchange. Asymmetric does key exchange well, but encrypts/decrypts more slowly than symmetric. Both pretty much *define* confidentiality, but lack integrity. Hashing provides the missing integrity aspect.

Here's an example of hybrid key cryptography in action. A common method of key exchange involves the creation of a "secret" between the two parties. This secret is then run through a hash to create the one-and-only unique, cannot-be-reversed (supposedly) key to be used on the symmetric side. Encrypt and send this hash via your asymmetric system and voilà! You've securely exchanged a viable key for your symmetric side.

Nothing is perfect, of course, and there are many variables—using certificates to identify each party, encryption streams within the exchange, and so on. But for the purposes of this discussion, just remember hybrid encryption means to use combinations of symmetric, asymmetric, and hashing to ensure better confidentiality and integrity.

 EXAM TIP   Hybrid cryptography leverages the advantages of both symmetric and asymmetric key cryptography and eliminates their disadvantages.

The Perfect Cryptosystem

Cryptosystems should render unclear or unintelligible—*obfuscate*—any plaintext into what anyone who can't decrypt would see as nothing more than random data. This obfuscation makes data secure. *Security through obfuscation* is what cryptography is all about!

 EXAM TIP   Look for questions on the CompTIA Security+ exam that ask you to recognize *common use cases* of cryptography *supporting obfuscation*. You'll see more use cases when we tackle specific cryptosystems in Modules 2-3 and 2-4.

Proponents of *security through obscurity* argue that hiding how cryptosystems work hardens those systems. If you invent a great cryptosystem, full of interesting math using all kinds of substitutions, transpositions, and shifts over lots of rounds, and, in the implementation, count on the fact that no one else knows the algorithm, you have the perfect, uncrackable cryptosystem.

NOTE Many IT security professionals argue that making a target appear uninteresting adds a level of protection. This differently nuanced definition of security through obscurity applies to situations such as a bank versus a would-be robber. The robber might spend all of his time on the vault door, so storing vital stuff in a simple locked janitor closet would work.

Security through obscurity misses one essential fact: every cryptosystem is crackable over time. What seems impossible today becomes child's play with tomorrow's technologies.

Rather than hiding how cryptosystems work, modern cryptography makes algorithms public. Making the systems available for everyone to attack exposes vulnerabilities and weaknesses that can be addressed. Make the underlying algorithm unassailable, as Kerckhoffs suggested, but keep the specific key used secret. Because of this attitude, new, more resilient cryptosystems come out every few years. The creators of these cryptosystems happily send them out for academic rigor, making sure the code has *high resiliency*, that it holds up against cracking.

Finally, that elusive perfect cryptosystem should hold up over time. In some cases, keys might be used for weeks, months, or even years perhaps. *Forward secrecy* means to protect a cryptosystem from one key giving away some secret that makes it easier to crack. If an algorithm achieves this, we call it *perfect forward secrecy*. There is no such thing as perfect forward secrecy other than using a key only once and throwing it away—a *one-time pad*.

Module 2-3: Symmetric Cryptosystems

This module covers the following CompTIA Security+ objective:

- **2.8 Summarize the basics of cryptographic concepts**

Developers have created and deployed numerous symmetric key cryptosystems over the years to provide fast and secure data communications. This module explores the six most common symmetric cryptosystems. Some of the data here is historical, but all of it informs modern cryptosystems. Let's look at these cryptosystems:

- DES
- 3DES
- AES
- Blowfish
- Twofish
- RC4

DES

The *Data Encryption Standard (DES)* is an older, now obsolete standard for commercial-grade encryption within the United States. DES uses an algorithm called Lucifer, developed by IBM. In the DES implementation, Lucifer has a 64-bit key size. Eight of those bits are used for computational overhead, so the true key size is only 56 bits. DES is a symmetric block algorithm and uses 64-bit block sizes. Blocks that are less than 64 bits in size are padded.

 EXAM TIP The CompTIA Security+ exam will quiz you on block sizes, so make notes throughout this module!

DES works in *modes of operation*, defined methods that determine how a plaintext block is input and changed to produce ciphertext. Each of these modes processes input blocks of text in different ways to encrypt the data. Modes also use certain mathematical functions to transform the data for stronger encryption. DES uses 16 rounds for each mode. So, for whichever mode is used, that process is repeated 16 times on a block of plaintext to produce the output ciphertext.

DES uses five different *block cipher modes of operation*:

- ECB
- CBC
- CFB
- OFB
- CTR

In the *electronic code book (ECB)* mode, plaintext blocks of 64 bits are manipulated to produce ciphertext. With ECB mode, a given piece of plaintext will always produce the same corresponding piece of ciphertext. Unfortunately, this makes ECB mode very predictable, and it can easily be broken if an attacker has specific pieces of plaintext and ciphertext to compare.

The *cipher block chaining (CBC)* mode produces much stronger encryption by XORing the previous block to the block being encrypted. The very first block introduces an initialization vector (IV) into the process. This ensures that every block of plaintext input into the process produces a uniquely different piece of ciphertext. So even when the same block of plaintext is input repeatedly, the resultant ciphertext will not be identical to any previous outputs.

Cipher feedback (CFB) mode is like CBC except the plaintext is XORed into the IV after each round.

Output feedback (OFB) mode is very similar to CFB mode, but instead of the previous block's ciphertext being the next block's IV, it takes the result of the previous encryption of the IV and key *before* the plaintext is XORed.

In DES, *counter (CTR)* mode uses a random 64-bit block as the first IV, then increments a specified number or counter for every subsequent block of plaintext. CTR mode offers the best performance.

Figure 2-11 illustrates how complex even the simple ECB mode is in DES; this screenshot was taken from the freely available open-source CrypTool cryptography learning program (www.cryptool.org).

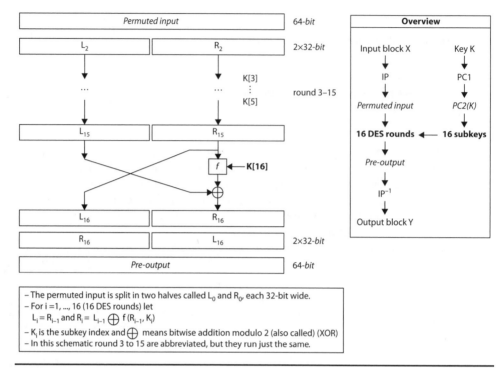

The permuted input is split in two halves called L_0 and R_0, each 32-bit wide.
- For i =1, ..., 16 (16 DES rounds) let
  $L_i = R_{i-1}$ and $R_i = L_{i-1} \oplus f(R_{i-1}, K_i)$
- K_i is the subkey index and $\oplus$ means bitwise addition modulo 2 (also called) (XOR)
- In this schematic round 3 to 15 are abbreviated, but they run just the same.

Figure 2-11   Illustration of how DES ECB mode works (screenshot from the CrypTool cryptography learning program)

 EXAM TIP   You need to know the different characteristics of DES for the exam—16 rounds of encryption, 64-bit blocks, 56-bit keys, and five cipher modes of operation.

Authenticated Encryption

The modes of operation used in symmetric cryptosystems can run in a couple of different ways, as *unauthenticated* or *authenticated*. The strength of the encryption doesn't change either way, but unauthenticated modes offer a flaw when used in online applications. An attacker can use an attack called a chosen ciphertext attack to intercept, modify, and, eventually, decrypt messages.

You can implement cryptosystems that fix this flaw in a couple of ways, but such implementations have traditionally been optional, presumably because the encryption standards were good enough and faster without the added layers of protections. The most common way today to secure modes of operation is to use *authenticated encryption (AE)* modes that both encrypt and authenticate messages. (See the description of GCM in the upcoming discussion of AES for a very commonly used AE mode.) Alternatively, you could use the more complicated *message authentication code* to add more protection. (See "HMAC" in Module 2-5 for more details.)

EXAM TIP Look for questions on the Security+ exam that ask about unauthenticated vs. authenticated encryption modes of operation. Bottom line? Unauthenticated = bad. Authenticated = good.

3DES

Triple DES (3DES or *TDES)* is a later iteration of DES designed to fix some of the problems found in DES. It basically puts plaintext blocks through the same type of DES encryption process, but it does so in three distinct iterations. Where DES uses single 56-bit keys, 3DES uses three 56-bit keys. Many IT folks—and the CompTIA Security+ exam—combine the three keys, so describe 3DES as having a *168-bit key.*

3DES uses the same modes that DES uses; it just repeats them three times using three different keys. Other than the number of iterations, there are no differences between the two algorithms. This similarity causes 3DES to suffer from some of the same weaknesses as DES. These weaknesses motivated the industry to replace 3DES with more modern algorithms, particularly AES, discussed next.

EXAM TIP 3DES made up for some of DES's weaknesses, but it did not significantly change the algorithm. It puts plaintext through more iterations than DES, but it still suffers from some of the same weaknesses.

AES

The *Advanced Encryption Standard (AES)* is a symmetric block cipher that can use block sizes of 128 bits, with key sizes of 128, 192, and 256 bits. It uses 10 rounds for 128-bit keys, 12 rounds for 192-bit keys, and 14 rounds for 256-bit keys. Like DES, AES can use different modes to encrypt and decrypt data. Most attacks on AES are theoretical in nature—referred to as *side-channel* attacks, which take advantage of ineffective implementations of the AES algorithm in the cryptosystem, versus the algorithm itself.

EXAM TIP AES is the *de jure* encryption standard for the US government and the *de facto* standard for private and commercial organizations. It is a block cipher that uses 128-bit block sizes, with 128-bit, 192-bit, and 256-bit keys. It uses 10, 12, and 14 rounds, respectively, for these keys.

AES supports all the modes listed under DES, but tends to use the much lower-latency mode called *Galois/Counter Mode (GCM)*. GCM starts with CTR mode, but adds a special data type known as a Galois field to add integrity. GCM is an authenticated encryption mode of operation.

NOTE You'll sometimes hear AES called by its original name, Rijndael, derived from the last names of its two Belgian developers, Vincent Rijmen and Joan Daemen.

Blowfish

Blowfish is a block cipher that accepts 64-bit blocks and has a wide range of variable key links, from 32 bits all the way up to 448 bits. It uses 16 rounds of encryption, just as DES does. It is widely implemented in different software encryption solutions and is considered a good choice for a strong encryption algorithm, since there have been no more effective complete cryptanalysis solutions published to date. The designer, Bruce Schneier, placed Blowfish in the public domain, free for all to use.

Twofish

Twofish is a symmetric block algorithm that uses a 128-bit block size. It can use 128-bit, 192-bit, or 256-bit keys. Like DES, it uses 16 rounds of encryption. It is viewed as a successor to Blowfish. Although there have been some published partial theoretical attacks against Twofish, there are currently no publicly known attacks against it. Like Blowfish, Twofish has been placed in the public domain, making it freely available for anyone to use.

 EXAM TIP Although AES is the official US standard, both Blowfish and Twofish are exceptionally good encryption algorithms. Both use 64-bit blocks, and both perform 16 rounds of encryption. Blowfish can use key sizes from 32 to 448 bits, and Twofish uses key sizes of 128 bits, 192 bits, and 256 bits. Longer keys provide better key strength.

RC4

Rivest Cipher 4 (RC4) is a streaming symmetric algorithm (unlike the block algorithms discussed previously in the module). Because it is a streaming cipher, it uses only one round of encryption. RC4 can use key sizes from 40 to 2048 bits in length. It's a very fast protocol, as all streaming ciphers are. RC4 uses a *key stream* (stream of pseudorandom bits injected into the encryption process), which is then combined with plaintext using the XOR function to encrypt them into ciphertext.

RC4 is most popularly used in wireless encryption with the older, now obsolete and cryptographically broken Wired Equivalent Privacy (WEP) protocol. It can also be found in versions of the Secure Sockets Layer (SSL) and Transport Layer Security (TLS) protocols. RC4 has some documented weaknesses, which makes it unsuitable for future implementations. Current software vendors advise against its use, and the Internet Engineering Task Force's (IETF) RFC 7465 eliminated its use in TLS.

 EXAM TIP RC4 is likely the only example of a streaming cipher you will see on the exam. All the other symmetric algorithms discussed throughout this book are block ciphers.

Summary of Symmetric Algorithm Characteristics

Table 2-1 summarizes the characteristics of the different symmetric algorithms.

Symmetric Algorithm	Block or Streaming	Block Size	Rounds	Key Size	Notes
DES	Block	64-bit	16	56 bits (64 bits total, with 8 bits for parity overhead)	Uses five modes of operation: ECB, CBC, CFB, OFB, and CTR.
3DES	Block	64-bit	16	168 bits (three 56-bit keys)	Repeats DES process three times.
AES	Block	128-bit	10, 12, and 14 (based on key size)	128, 192, and 256 bits	Encryption standard for the US government; GCM mode is popular.
Blowfish	Block	64-bit	16	32–448 bits	Public domain algorithm.
Twofish	Block	128-bit	16	128, 192, and 256 bits	Public domain algorithm.
RC4	Streaming	N/A	1	40–2048 bits	Used in WEP, SSL, and TLS; largely deprecated in current technologies.

Table 2-1 Summary of Symmetric Algorithms

Module 2-4: Asymmetric Cryptosystems

This module covers the following CompTIA Security+ objective:

- **2.8 Summarize the basics of cryptographic concepts**

Developers have created and deployed numerous asymmetric key cryptosystems over the years to provide robust key exchange and secure data communications. This module explores the five most common asymmetric cryptosystems. Some of the data here is historical, but all of it informs modern cryptosystems. Let's look, in order, at these cryptosystems:

- RSA
- Diffie-Hellman
- PGP/GPG
- ECC
- ElGamal

RSA

The *RSA* cryptosystem enables you to create and use a public-private key pair. It generates keys based on the mathematical problem of the difficulty of factoring two very large prime numbers (each generally up to several hundred digits in length). RSA uses one round of encryption, and its typical key sizes range from 1024 to 4096 bits.

Although RSA is considered very secure, keys of smaller sizes have been broken in various published attacks. Still, these attacks are largely based upon faulty implementations of the protocol, rather than the protocol itself.

RSA is pretty much the *de facto* asymmetric algorithm used in most public key cryptography implementations today. Figure 2-12 demonstrates how RSA works, using simple prime numbers and the CrypTool learning program.

 NOTE RSA is the *de facto* asymmetric protocol used for generating public-private key pairs. The name RSA reflects the first letters of its creators, Ron Rivest, Adi Shamir, and Leonard Adleman.

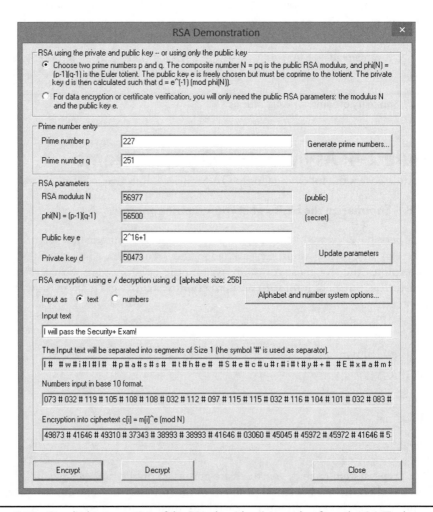

Figure 2-12 Simple demonstration of the RSA algorithm (screenshot from the CrypTool cryptography learning program)

Diffie-Hellman

The *Diffie-Hellman (DH)* protocols enable you to use asymmetric key exchange to give both sides of a conversation a single symmetric key. This means that two parties can use a nonsecure channel to establish a secure communications session. This secure key exchange works even when the parties have no previous relationship.

DH offers a much faster connection compared to RSA. RSA provides great security, but requires a lot of computation and complex key exchange procedures. If you prefer speed over security, DH is the asymmetric algorithm for you!

DH uses discrete logarithms, modulo arithmetic, and prime numbers to generate key pairs randomly that derive a symmetric key without ever sending any private information. Part of the DH key exchange process requires each side to create a temporary key, called an *ephemeral key*, which is used in only one exchange and then discarded. This ephemeral key usage is called *Diffie-Hellman Ephemeral (DHE)*.

DH relies on pseudorandom number generation to create the ephemeral keys. In most cases, this relies on pseudorandom number code that uses aspects of the underlying system like dates, MAC address of the network interface card (NIC), and other seemingly random information to make these values. Unfortunately, dates and MAC addresses really aren't random; in theory, a malicious actor can use this against you. To fight against this, several alternatives exist.

One alternative is to use a larger *modulus*: an important value that helps DH derive keys. A preset modulus of a specific size is called a *DH group*. As long as both sides agree to a group size, we can improve DH while still providing backward support for systems that only can derive smaller keys. Here are a few examples of DH groups:

- **Group 1**   768-bit modulus
- **Group 2**   1024-bit modulus
- **Group 5**   1536-bit modulus
- **Group 14**   2048-bit modulus

Another alternative is to skip ephemeral keys with DH and use something more resilient, such as *Elliptic-Curve Diffie-Hellman Ephemeral (ECDHE)*. ECDHE skips pseudorandom number generation and instead uses ephemeral keys calculated using elliptic-curve cryptography, discussed later in this module. ECDHE is negotiated by groups as well:

- **Group 19**   25-bit elliptic curve
- **Group 20**   384-bit elliptic curve
- **Group 21**   521-bit elliptic curve

 NOTE   Many applications (such as secure Web sites) use RSA for authentication and DH for key exchange.

PGP/GPG

Pretty Good Privacy (PGP) is a cryptography application and protocol suite used in asymmetric cryptography. PGP can use both asymmetric and symmetric keys for a wide variety of operations, including bulk encryption, data at rest encryption (including both file and full disk encryption), key-pair generation, and key exchange. Unlike other public key cryptography schemes, PGP uses a *web-of-trust* rather than a public key infrastructure. (See Module 2-7 for details.) Although PGP is considered a commercialized, proprietary version, it has an open-source equivalent, Gnu Privacy Guard (GPG). The various versions of PGP and GPG comply with the OpenPGP standard, an IETF standard published as RFC 4880.

 EXAM TIP   With PGP/GPG, think e-mail here. That's where you'll see these standards in play.

ECC

Elliptic-curve cryptography (ECC) is an asymmetric method of cryptography based on problems involving the algebraic structure of elliptic curves over finite fields. (Say that three times fast!) ECC has many uses, including variations that apply both to encryption and digital signatures.

ECC has special uses involving mobile devices. It requires low computational power and memory usage, so ECC has been widely implemented in smartphones and other low-power mobile devices.

 EXAM TIP   Expect a question on common use cases involving *low-power devices*, such as smartphones, on the exam. ECC provides the answer.

ECC typically uses much smaller key sizes than other asymmetric algorithms, but these smaller-sized ECC keys are also harder to break. The largest known ECC key broken to date is only a 112-bit key, for example, compared to a 768-bit key size that has been broken with RSA.

ElGamal

ElGamal is an asymmetric algorithm that can be used for both digital signatures and general encryption. (See Module 2-6 for the details on digital signatures.) Taher Elgamal based his eponymous algorithm partially on Diffie-Hellman key exchange algorithms. ElGamal uses mathematical problems related to computing discrete logarithms.

You'll see ElGamal used in hybrid cryptosystems, where ElGamal encrypts the comparatively tiny symmetric key and some other (faster) scheme encrypts the message. It's also widely used in open standards and cryptosystems, including PGP and GPG.

The US government's Digital Signature Algorithm (DSA) is based upon the ElGamal signature scheme.

Module 2-5: Hashing Algorithms

This module covers the following CompTIA Security+ objectives:

- **2.1** **Explain the importance of security concepts in an enterprise environment**
- **2.8** **Summarize the basics of cryptographic concepts**

IT professionals use several hashing algorithms to ensure the integrity of data and source. This module starts with a brief discussion of how hashing works—a rehash of the introduction in Module 2-2, so to speak. [Insert groan here at bad pun.] Then we'll explore the four most common hashing algorithms:

- MD5
- SHA
- RIPEMD
- HMAC

Hashing Process

Encryption necessarily implies decryption. Plaintext transformed through encryption into an unreadable state can be decrypted and returned to a plaintext state.

Hashing does not encrypt text; it generates a representation of that text, which is the hash or message digest. A hash is not the plaintext itself, but rather a unique identifier for the text, like a fingerprint. Note that hashing does not use keys at all, only algorithms, also making it less like encryption and decryption.

Theoretically, an identical piece of plaintext will always produce the same hash value, assuming that you use the same hashing algorithm. Likewise, no two different pieces of plaintext *should* ever produce the same hash, given the same algorithm, although it happens.

These accidentally matching hashes, called *collisions*, can enable a miscreant in theory to generate a piece of data with the right hash to fool others as to its integrity. Figure 2-13 illustrates the collision process a bit more clearly, where two differing texts run through the hashing algorithm, but result in identical hashes.

Several older hashing algorithms can produce collisions. As this module addresses the different hashing algorithms, we'll point out the older, collision-prone algorithms.

 NOTE Hashing is not the same thing as encryption and decryption. Hashes cannot be reversed or decrypted; they can only be compared to see if they match.

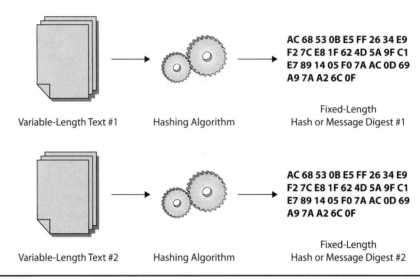

Figure 2-13   The hashing process and collisions

Hashing supports confidentiality (in the case of hashing passwords, for instance) and integrity. For confidentiality, you can hash a password (run it through the hashing algorithm) and send the resulting hash over an untrusted network for authentication. You would not need to transmit the actual password (Figure 2-14).

When the authenticating server receives the hash, it takes the password hash it has stored in the credentials database and compares it to the hash it received. If they match, the server knows that the user also knew the correct password, and it allows authentication. If the hashes don't match, the server refuses authentication, because the user obviously did not know the correct password, which in turn did not generate the correct hash. Hashing thus supports authentication as well as confidentiality and integrity.

   EXAM TIP   Expect questions on common use cases for supporting authentication, confidentiality, or integrity. Hashing provides all three.

Some systems encrypt password hashes during transmission using symmetric key cryptography and then decrypt them on the receiving end to protect the hash during transmission. This action blocks an obvious attack option.

Figure 2-14
Sending a password's hash instead of the password itself

An attacker can intercept a password hash as it travels over a network. The attacker won't have the actual password at that point, of course, and can't reverse the hash to get it, but she can use various methods to perform the same type of hash comparisons against a list of potential passwords and generate an identical hash, letting her discover the original password. An encrypted hash blunts that capability.

Because identical pieces of plaintext always produce the same hash value, using the same hashing algorithm on both enables you to tell if a piece of text has changed, even by one binary digit (bit). If even a single 1 or 0 bit changes in the text, the hash produced will differ from the hash of the original piece of text. In this way, comparing hashes of two supposedly identical pieces of plaintext can verify the integrity of the original. If the hashes match when compared, the samples of text are identical and have not been altered. If the hashes differ when compared, however, then a change has occurred between the original text and what was received, violating integrity.

 EXAM TIP   Hashing can be used to assure both confidentiality and integrity.

MD5

The *Message Digest 5 (MD5)* algorithm generates a 128-bit hash, 32 hexadecimal characters long, and it replaced an earlier version of the MD series, MD4. MD5 has weaknesses, however, and researchers have demonstrated collisions (and thus vulnerability to collision attacks) many times, even using off-the-shelf consumer laptops. Despite deprecation by security experts—as in, "don't use this broken thing!"—many low-security situations still use it, even in 2020. MD5 is also used as part of other cryptographic methods, including the Extensible Authentication Protocol (EAP), as part of its EAP-MD5 implementation.

 EXAM TIP   MD5 produces a 128-bit message digest, consisting of 32 hexadecimal characters, regardless of the length of the input text.

SHA

The US National Security Agency (NSA) developed the *Secure Hash Algorithm (SHA)* standards to provide cryptographic hash functions, starting in 1993. Since the initial release—SHA-0, SHA has seen several iterations, including SHA-1, SHA-2, and SHA-3.

The 160-bit SHA-1 algorithm, originally designed as the standardized Digital Signature Algorithm for the United States, produces 40-character hashes. SHA-1 was a contemporary of MD5 and had similar cryptographic flaws. SHA-2 is made up of two separate algorithms, SHA-256 and SHA-512, but each has minor versions that include SHA-224 and SHA-384. SHA-3 uses a hash function called Keccak that makes it different internally than SHA-1 and SHA-2. It has the same hash lengths as the SHA-2 versions.

EXAM TIP SHA-1 and SHA-2 have been replaced by the latest iteration of SHA, known as SHA-3, which is an implementation of the Keccak hashing function. Also, you might see SHA on the exam as Secure *Hashing* Algorithm, so don't get confused. The exam means SHA.

RIPEMD

RACE Integrity Primitives Evaluation Message Digest (RIPEMD) is a hashing algorithm not often seen in practical implementation. It was developed in an open-standard type of environment, as opposed to SHA. RIPEMD comes in 128-, 160-, 256-, and 320-bit versions. Again, it is not in widespread use, despite the relatively stable and secure implementation of the RIPEMD-160 iteration, which is the most common.

HMAC

Hash-based Message Authentication Code (HMAC) is used in conjunction with a symmetric key both to authenticate and verify the integrity of the message. HMAC can use either MD5 or SHA series of hashing algorithms (and noted as HMAC-MD5 or HMAC-SHA1/2/3, respectively). The HMAC process produces a hash value, the *message authentication code (MAC)*, whose length and strength correspond to whichever hashing algorithm was used to create it. Here's how it works.

You already know that a given piece of plaintext or message produces the same hash every time, as long as you use the same hashing algorithm. This can be used to verify integrity; however, anyone can send a message that can be verified in terms of integrity, if the hashes match. But you cannot verify the authenticity of the message—that is, who sent it—and you cannot verify who will be able to receive it.

HMAC uses a secret (symmetric) key with the hashing process, so that a given message produces a unique hash using that symmetric key. If someone does not have the key, she cannot reproduce the hash of the message, so that neither integrity nor authenticity can be verified. Only someone who has the secret key can successfully produce the same hash. This verifies not only integrity but also authenticity, since only the person having the secret key could have produced that unique hash and sent the message.

EXAM TIP HMAC can use hashing functions and symmetric keys to produce a message authentication code (MAC), used to ensure both integrity and authenticity of a message.

Module 2-6: Digital Signatures and Certificates

This module covers the following CompTIA Security+ objectives:

- **2.8 Summarize the basics of cryptographic concepts**
- **3.9 Given a scenario, implement public key infrastructure**

Figure 2-15
Secure Web site,
Hello!

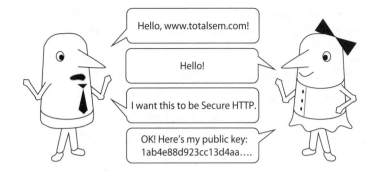

Asymmetric encryption relies heavily on trust. When you access a secure Web site to make a purchase, for example, you need to trust in the security of the connection between the Web server and your client before putting in a credit card number. Two related cryptographic functions create this security, digital signatures and digital certificates.

Digital Signatures

Secure Web sites use RSA keys for asymmetric encryption. Every connection to a secure Web site requires a key exchange. At the very least, the Web server provides its public key to the client so the client can encrypt messages securely. In some cases, the client will share its public key (Figure 2-15).

The challenge to key exchange isn't handing out the keys. The Web server and client can automatically share their public keys the moment they connect. The problem comes with the key itself. Imagine a scenario where a third party intercepts the data and tries to send a bogus public key to the client (Figure 2-16). Digital signatures address this scenario.

To send a message in a typical asymmetric encryption cryptosystem, the sender encrypts using the recipient's public key; the recipient decrypts using her private key. The reverse, however, can also work. The sender can encrypt with his *private* key; the only key that would enable decryption is his *public* key. This concept makes digital signatures possible. Here's the full process of creating a digital signature.

Figure 2-16
Third parties can
be evil!

To prove that the public key your client receives came from the proper server, the Web server adds a digital signature. The Web server takes the current Web page and does the following:

1. Encrypts the page with the client's public key.

2. Hashes the page.

3. Encrypts the hash with the server's private key.

4. Sends the page, the public key, and the hash to the client.

Now it's the client's turn:

1. The client decrypts the hash using the server's public key to verify it really came from the server. (Only the server's public key can decrypt something encrypted with the server's private key.)

2. The client decrypts the message with the client's private key.

Figure 2-17 helps describe this process.

The hash value encrypted with the private key and that accompanies the public key is a *digital signature*.

 NOTE Digital signatures are one of the very few places where private keys are used to encrypt. Normally, public keys encrypt and private keys decrypt.

Digital signatures alone work great to verify the identity of a source. Successfully decrypting the message using the source's public key means the message could only have come from that source.

Figure 2-17
Proof that the
message came
from the owner
of the private key

Figure 2-18 Who can you trust?

Digital Certificates

A digital signature is only good for verifying that the entity who sent you a public key is legitimately the one who possesses the corresponding private key. But how do you know that public key really came from the Web site, or the owner of that e-mail address, or the VPN service, or whatever other thing you want to connect to that you need to know you can trust? You need something more than a digital signature (Figure 2-18).

You might at this point say, "I know I'm on the right Web site because it says so in the address bar" or, "I know this e-mail came from mike@totalsem.com, because that's who the e-mail said it came from." This is not acceptable. First, it's easy to make another Web site look just like one you know (Figure 2-19). Equally, it's easy to make another service—e-mail is a great example—look like it came from a known source. This process

Figure 2-19 It's easy to deceive.

Figure 2-20
A certificate
should have
a third-party
signature.

is called *spoofing*. Simply relying on the fact that something looks like it's a legitimate source isn't good enough. (And how closely do most people look at URLs anyway?)

Worse, a fiend can use Unicode to whack out URLs to the point where you could swear you know where you are, but you are at a completely different URL.

To create trust in this scenario requires a *digital certificate*, an electronic file specifically formatted using industry standards that contains identifying information. That's a mouthful!

Think of a digital certificate like a Word document with a bunch of spaces to fill in with specific information. There are different digital certificate "forms" for different jobs (e-mail, Web servers, code signing, and many more). Any digital certificate will store a public key with a digital signature, personal information about the resource (URL, e-mail address, phone numbers, whatever), and a second digital signature from a third party you both trust (Figure 2-20).

The rest of this module concentrates on the types of digital certificates and their formats and tours a typical certificate on a PC.

NOTE Module 2-7 goes into depth on maintaining digital certificates.

Touring a Certificate

Let's look at a digital certificate. In Windows, you can see your certificates by opening any Web browser's Settings and locating a certificates option. In Microsoft Edge, for example, click the icon with three horizontal dots in the upper-right corner and choose Settings. Select Privacy and Services, then click the Manage Certificates button to open the Certificates dialog box (Figure 2-21).

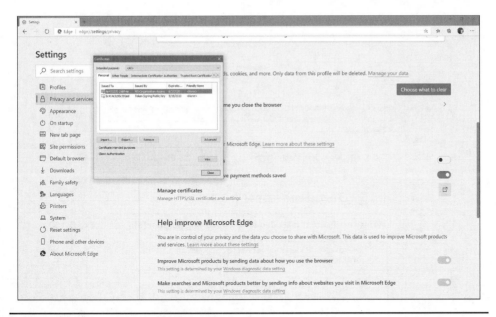

Figure 2-21 Getting to the Certificates dialog box in Microsoft Edge

NOTE All Web browsers have a certificate location. Take your time, you'll find it.

The Certificates dialog box features several tabs. For this module, pick any tab, select any certificate on that tab, and then click View (or whatever your system says) to see the certificate in detail. You should see something like Figure 2-22.

Now click the Details tab at the top. On the Show pull-down menu, select Version 1 Fields Only to see something like Figure 2-23. Click each field as you read through the following descriptions to see what each value stores.

- **Version**   The common certificate format is *X.509*. It started with version 1. Modern certificates are version 3. This field shows the X.509 version of this certificate.
- **Serial number**   A unique number given to this certificate by the issuing body.
- **Signature algorithm**   The type of encryption and hash used by this certificate.
- **Signature hash algorithm**   Same as signature algorithm. (It's a Microsoft thing.)
- **Issuer**   X.509 formatted name of issuer of this certificate. (See "Certificate Attributes" next.)
- **Valid from**   Time the certificate was granted.
- **Valid to**   Time the certificate expires.
- **Subject**   To what this certificate is issued in X.509 format.
- **Public key**   The public key for the certificate.

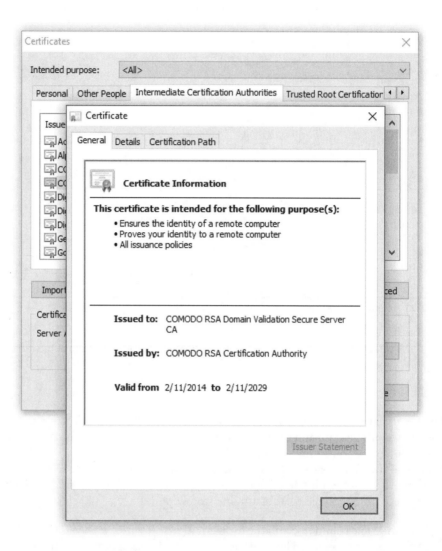

Figure 2-22 Certificate view in Windows

There's a lot more to see if you change Show: to <ALL>, but there are two fields that warrant note here:

- **Thumbprint**   The certificate's digital signature.
- **Authority Key Identifier**   The third party's digital signature.

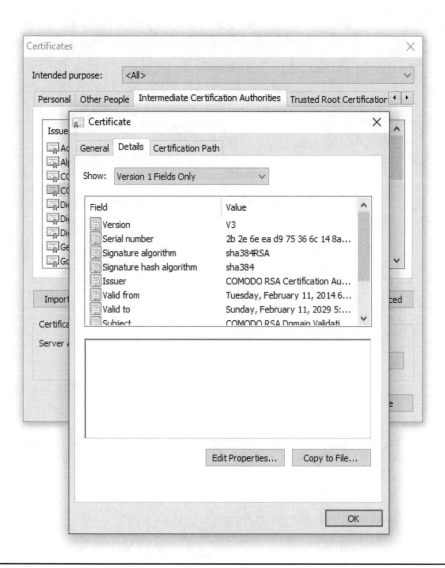

Figure 2-23 Typical certificate details in Windows

Certificate Attributes

Digging deeper into certificates reveals a lot more information, specifically certificate attributes that vary according to the purpose of the certificate. Figure 2-24 shows a local Trusted Root Certification Authority certificate from COMODO ECC Certification Authority.

Figure 2-24
Local Trusted
Root CA
certificate

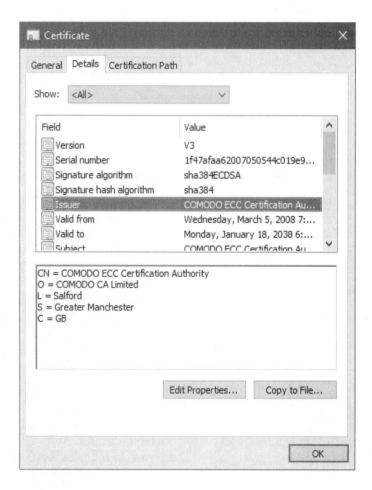

Note the Issuer details in the bottom pane:

- **CN**   The canonical name, the full name of the issuing body
- **O**   The organization, COMODO CA Limited
- **L**   The locality, Salford
- **S**   The state or province, Greater Manchester
- **C**   The country or origin, Great Britain

Contrast the certificate shown in Figure 2-24 with the certificate shown in Figure 2-25, which comes from the Chrome Web browser connected to https://www.amazon.com. The Details tab is selected again, but the Subject is chosen in the top pane rather than Issuer. As you might expect, it reveals the details about Amazon, including the CN, O, L, S, and C; Amazon's headquarters are in Seattle, Washington, United States of America.

Figure 2-25
Web certificate attribute details

Getting a Certificate

Virtually all cryptosystems that use asymmetric cryptography require a certificate. Probably the best example is a secure Web site. Let's say you want to set up a secure (HTTPS) Web server. You can spin up your own server and load some Web server software on your own, but if you want to use HTTPS, you'll need a certificate.

To get a certificate, submit information to a certificate issuing organization, called a *certificate authority (CA)*. There are a handful of these organizations, though three dominate the market: IdenTrust, DigiCert, and Sectigo (formerly Comodo). Before you give a certificate issuing organization your credit card details, you need to generate a *certificate signing request (CSR)* on your Web server, as described in the "Certificate Life Cycle" section of Module 2-7. Figure 2-26 shows part of this process in Microsoft Internet Information Services (IIS).

Once you create the CSR, cut and paste the information into an online form. Depending on the certificate, you'll get your certificate sent via e-mail or through a Web interface. In most cases, the certificate installs itself. You can import if necessary.

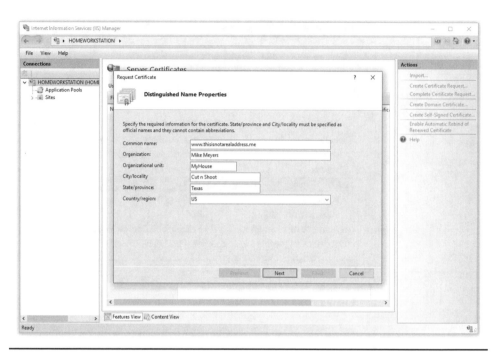

Figure 2-26 Creating a CSR in IIS

NOTE You don't have to pay for third parties to sign certificates (e.g., Let's Encrypt, https://letsencrypt.org, is a popular free certificate issuer, backed by IdenTrust). Self-signed certificates work just fine *within* your network for services that require certificates—applications and such on the corporate intranet, for example. There's no reason to pay for certificates for internal use. Make certain those self-signed or untrusted-signed certificates never see the rest of the world.

Module 2-7: Public Key Infrastructure

This module covers the following CompTIA Security+ objectives:

- **2.8 Summarize the basics of cryptographic concepts**
- **3.9 Given a scenario, implement public key infrastructure**

Public key infrastructure (PKI) implementations combine symmetric and asymmetric key cryptographic methods with hashing to create robust and secure systems. This module puts together all the information in Modules 2-1 through 2-6 of this chapter to describe these systems.

The module starts with keys, algorithms, and standards. The second section explores PKI services. The third section discusses digital certificates and PKI structure. We'll look at key safety next and then finish with trust models.

PKI puts cryptography into practical application. IT professionals use PKI to implement strong authentication and encryption schemes to protect data confidentiality and integrity and to ensure non-repudiation. Let's get started.

Keys, Algorithms, and Standards

Hybrid cryptographic systems incorporate the advantages of asymmetric and symmetric algorithms, while at the same time making up for the disadvantages each has. Symmetric algorithms are fast, and they can encrypt large amounts of data efficiently. Symmetric cryptography suffers from key exchange and scalability problems. Asymmetric cryptography, on the other hand, has no issues with key exchange. It's also very scalable, since it only requires that each individual have a public and private key pair. Unfortunately, asymmetric cryptography doesn't do very well with speed or encrypting large amounts of data.

PKI takes advantage of these different positive aspects of both asymmetric and symmetric key cryptography and uses each, along with hashing algorithms, for different aspects of identification, authentication, encryption, and non-repudiation. Let's look now at keys and algorithms that relate to PKI.

 EXAM TIP   PKI is composed of several components and technologies, as well as the infrastructure and processes used to manage certificates.

Keys

Asymmetric cryptographic systems use a public and private key pair. Both keys are mathematically related, but you cannot use one to derive the other. The keys are generated using various mathematical algorithms. What one key in a pair encrypts, only the other key in the same pair can decrypt. Public keys are given to anyone who wants them, and private keys are kept confidential, protected by the individuals who own them. To exchange messages between two parties, each must have a public and private key pair. Each party must also possess the public key of the other party.

When one person wants to send an encrypted message to the other, the sender encrypts the message using the receiver's public key. Then, the receiver decrypts it using the receiver's private key, since that's the only key in the pair that can decrypt what the public key encrypts. This is demonstrated in Figure 2-27.

Figure 2-27
Communicating using public and private keys

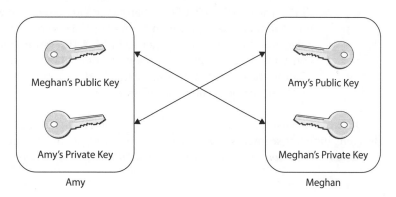

Symmetric cryptography, on the other hand, uses only one key. Both parties must possess that same key to encrypt and decrypt data. Getting the same key to each party securely poses the major obstacle in symmetric cryptography.

In a hybrid cryptographic system, party A generates a symmetric key—often called a *session key*—and encrypts that key using party B's public key, and then sends the encrypted key to party B. Party B, the receiving party, decrypts the encrypted session key with party B's private key. After that, faster communications can take place using the symmetric session key.

Using this hybrid approach with asymmetric and symmetric keys ensures confidentiality, since both data and the session keys are encrypted. It doesn't, however, ensure authenticity or integrity of the message, nor does it provide for non-repudiation. Adding hashing algorithms into the process provides those services; we'll discuss those momentarily.

EXAM TIP The CompTIA Security+ SY0-601 objectives use specific wording on this topic. So a common use case for cryptography is *supporting confidentiality*. The hybrid cryptographic system clearly accomplishes this goal.

Algorithms

Previous modules discussed the algorithms, both symmetric and asymmetric, employed in PKI. These include symmetric algorithms such as AES and asymmetric algorithms such as RSA for key generation and Diffie-Hellman for key exchange. PKI also uses hashing algorithms, such as MD5, RIPEMD, and the SHA family of algorithms. Let's look at specific PKI standards to see how they put the algorithms together.

PKI Standards

PKI implementations use one of several standards. The primary standard is X.509; other standards apply to specific industries.

The ITU Telecommunication Standardization Sector (ITU-T) *X.509* standard describes how digital certificates are constructed, including what information they will contain, their uses, and their formatting. The X.509 standard also describes processes involved with issuing certificates, as well as other processes in the certificate life cycle.

NOTE The initialism "ITU" has changed meaning over the years, from International Telegraph Union, formed in 1865, to the International Telecommunication Union, created in 1932. ITU-T morphed from the Comité consultatif international téléphonique et télégraphique (CCITT), formed in 1956, to the current initialism, created in 1993. (And none of this brief history lesson shows up on any CompTIA exam.)

Other somewhat proprietary standards that you'll encounter in PKI come from different industry segments, but usually comply with open standards. One set of these standards is the *Public Key Cryptography Standards (PKCS)*, developed by RSA Security.

The PKCS describe certificate construction and use. Cryptosystems use a PKCS #7 file digital certificate, for example, to sign or encrypt messages, such as e-mail. A PKCS #12 file contains public and private keys and is encrypted for secure key storage.

Other vendors, such as Microsoft and Apple, for example, also have proprietary ways of issuing and managing certificates throughout the certificates' life cycle, although these standards usually comply with the X.509 standards.

EXAM TIP   The primary standard used in PKI is the X.509 standard, which describes the certificate format and how it is used.

PKI Services

In addition to confidentiality, PKI provides for secure key exchange, message authentication and integrity, and non-repudiation. The next few sections discuss how PKI provides these different services. We'll also revisit digital signatures.

Key Generation and Exchange

PKI has technologies and methods built in for several different processes. Among those are key generation and key exchange. *Key generation* is the process of creating a public and private key pair, which is then issued to an individual, based upon his or her confirmed identity. RSA is the most popular key generation algorithm, although there are others. *Key exchange* is a process, typically using Diffie-Hellman algorithms, that assists in the creation and secure exchange of symmetric keys, typically session keys used for one communications session only. After keys are generated, public and private keys are used to encrypt and decrypt session keys once they are transmitted and received, respectively, by both parties.

Non-repudiation

Non-repudiation means that a person cannot deny that he or she took a specific action. The person's identity has been positively verified, and any actions that person takes are traced back to that identity.

PKI assures non-repudiation by using public and private keys. The certificate authority must positively identify and authenticate an individual before the CA issues a key pair. After issuing that key pair, the CA digitally signs the individual's certificate using the CA's private key. This signing confirms the CA has validated the user's identity. Finally, because only the issuing organization can sign with its private key, this verifies that the certificate came from a valid issuing organization.

Once Jack gets his key pair from the certificate authority, any message he signs using his private key verifies he sent the message. This assumes that Jack did the right thing and protected his private key, of course. If a message is signed using a key pair owned by Jack, in other words, he cannot deny that he sent the message. This assures non-repudiation.

EXAM TIP   The CompTIA Security+ SY0-601 objectives use specific wording on this topic. So a common use case for cryptography is *supporting non-repudiation*. PKI clearly accomplishes this goal.

Message Integrity

PKI can provide message integrity through hashing algorithms. Using hashing algorithms such as SHA-512, for instance, you can hash messages to generate unique fingerprints, or *hashes*, that can be checked both before transmission and after the message is received. If the hashes compare and match, you can be assured of data integrity. If they compare and do not match, you know that something (or someone) has changed the integrity of the message. Message integrity can be altered accidentally through simple "bit-flipping" during bad transmission conditions or intentionally by some malicious actor.

Message integrity is assured by also incorporating hashing algorithms into the PKI process. Although there are several possible ways to do this, the simplest way is to hash the message and encrypt both the message and the hash and send them on to the recipient, so that when the recipient gets the message, he can simply decrypt the message with his private key and then rehash the message to generate a hash that he can compare to the hash he received. The recipient doesn't do this manually; the automatic PKI processes take care of these steps at the application level.

 EXAM TIP The CompTIA Security+ SY0-601 objectives use specific wording on this topic. So a common use case for cryptography is *supporting integrity*. PKI clearly accomplishes this goal.

Digital Signatures

PKI systems incorporate digital signatures to authenticate the source of a message. Encrypting a message with a private key assures the recipient of the source when the corresponding public key decrypts that message. Add in the hashing component of digital signatures and you've got a winning combination, as discussed back in Module 2-6.

Digital Certificates and PKI Structure

This section explores how a basic public key infrastructure organization works, describing some of the elements in a PKI, such as the certificate and registration authorities, as well as the certificate revocation list. First, however, we'll take another look at digital certificates and describe them in more detail.

Digital Certificates

As mentioned earlier, digital certificates are simple electronic files. The X.509 and PKCS standards determine the specific formats for digital certificates, as well as the file types and formats. Digital certificates come in a variety of file formats, including those with .cer and .pem file extensions. (We'll cover all of these in detail in Module 11-5.) Additionally, there is a variety of types of certificate files, and each of these may fulfill a unique function in a PKI, such as a certificate request file. Digital certificates can be stored on several types of media, such as USB sticks, mobile devices, internal computer storage, and even centralized repositories on a network or the Internet.

Certificates come in a variety of types, each type serving one or more purposes such as the following:

- Signing and encrypting e-mails
- Identifying and authenticating networks
- Identifying servers
- Digitally signing software, verifying its authenticity from a publisher

Certificates typically contain a variety of information, known as *certificate attributes*, including the public key of the individual and information that identifies that person, the issuing organization, and valid dates and functions for the certificate to be used (Figure 2-28). Cryptographic systems can use *certificate attribute filters* to allow or deny specific access. A filter might examine the organization (O) attribute and allow only traffic that comes from Total Seminars, for example.

 EXAM TIP   The CompTIA Security+ SY0-601 objectives use specific wording on this topic. So a common use case for cryptography is *supporting authentication*. Certificates clearly accomplish this goal.

Figure 2-28
A digital
certificate

Certificate Life Cycle

Managing a digital certificate from issuance, through use, and finally disposal refers to the process of *managing the certificate over its life cycle*. That life cycle follows four main stages:

1. Registration by an entity
2. Issuance of certificate from certificate authority
3. Maintenance by the certificate authority
4. End of life through expiration, suspension, or revocation

The sections below explore both the life cycle stages and the entities involved. We'll look at certificate registration, certificate authorities, certificate servers, and certificate end of life features.

Certificate Registration   A certificate's life cycle begins when a user registers to receive a certificate. The person requesting the certificate must provide valid identification to the *certificate authority (CA)*, the entity that issues and controls the digital certificates. *Registration* usually means the user must present identification that the issuing organization authenticates, thus verifying the person's identity. Valid forms of identification that a requester may submit include her driver's license, birth certificate, passport, photographs, and any other identification that the issuing organization requires. Once a user has submitted the required identification, the CA decides whether to issue the certificate and under what circumstances.

 NOTE   Before issuing a certificate to an individual, the certificate authority must verify the individual's identity.

Certificate Authority   As just mentioned, the *certificate authority* issues and controls digital certificates. The CA might be a commercial organization, such as GoDaddy, or it could be the user's organization. Often, private organizations have internal CAs that issue digital certificates used specifically within the logical bounds of the organization. The CA also manages the *certificate server* (sometimes called the *CA server*), the host computer that generates keys and produces digital certificate files.

The CA normally handles all user registration, identification, and validation processes, and it issues digital certificates to the user. In larger organizations, to help balance the workload for the CA, registration functions may be delegated to a separate *registration authority (RA)*, which verifies user identities and then passes the information on to the CA for certificate generation.

The CA makes decisions on whether to issue the certificate, under what circumstances, and with what caveats. When an entity requests a certificate, it submits a *certificate signing request (CSR)*. The CA reviews the CSR, which contains the information that will be embedded in the digital certificate, including the public key, organization name, common

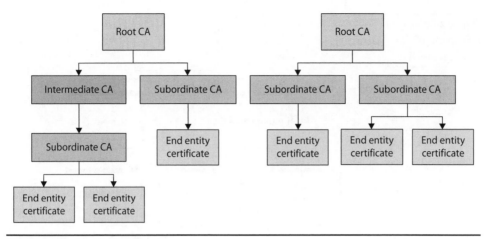

Figure 2-29   Simple CA hierarchy

name, and so on. The CA then generates a certificate for the requesting entity. That certificate is called an *end entity certificate*. After generating certificates, the CA must also perform actions on them, such as renewing, suspending, or revoking them, as needed.

   EXAM TIP   A certificate authority (CA) is the primary element in PKI.

Depending on a host of factors, such as geographical considerations, supply chains, and so forth, a "single" CA—the root CA—creates a hierarchy of trust to subordinate CAs. The subordinate CAs have a chain of trust with the root CA; they in turn grant the end entity certificates. Additionally, a subordinate CA might also need its own subordinate CAs. The CA in the middle of the chain is called an *intermediate CA* (Figure 2-29).

Certificate Servers   Smaller organizations may use only one or two servers that manage all their certificate needs. Larger organizations, however, may have an entire hierarchy of servers. At the top of this hierarchy is the single master server, called the *root CA server*. The root issues its own *self-signed certificate*, unless the organization purchases and receives one from an external certificate authority. Whether self-signed or received from an external CA, the root CA server has the *root certificate* for the organization. All other certificates in the hierarchy derive from this trust point.

   NOTE   Module 11-5 goes into much more detail on the various types of certificates. This module is an overview to help make PKI concepts make sense.

The root CA server can also issue certificates for any other use, but it typically issues trusted certificates only to intermediate or subordinate servers. These intermediate

Figure 2-30
A hierarchy of
certificate servers

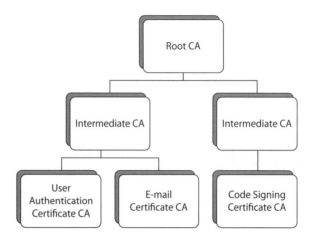

servers may perform all the different certificate authority functions, or they may perform only very specific functions, depending upon the needs of the organization. Normally, once an organization has set up intermediate or subordinate servers, they take the root CA server offline to protect it against possible compromise. The root CA server may be brought back up online only occasionally for maintenance or to update certificate information. Figure 2-30 shows a typical arrangement of a hierarchy of certificate servers in an organization.

 NOTE   An organization normally takes the root CA server offline after setting up intermediate and subordinate CA servers, to prevent compromise of the server and the root certificate. If the root certificate is compromised, all subordinate certificates that have been issued or signed by the root are also considered compromised and should be treated as no longer valid or trustworthy.

Certificate Expiration, Suspension, and Revocation   Certificates do not last forever. Certificates remain valid only for a specific period of time, and after that time they expire. This is because, like passwords, certificates could be compromised. Certificate *expiration* enables a user and the CA to monitor certificate compromise and periodically reissue certificates to ensure that a compromised certificate isn't used over long periods of time.

CA rules determine certificate lifetimes. An average time might be three years, but it may be a longer or lesser period, depending upon the circumstances under which the certificate was issued. For example, a temporary employee might receive a digital certificate that's good for only a year. Before a certificate expires, the user and the issuing organization must take steps to revalidate the user, as well as their need for the certificate, and reissue it. A user cannot use an expired and thus invalid certificate. Most browsers and applications will display errors when trying to use or accept an expired certificate. Figure 2-31 gives an example of an expired certificate.

Figure 2-31
An expired
certificate

Certificates can lose their validity even before their expiration dates. This usually requires some intervention from the CA and is usually because of adverse circumstances. A certificate may be suspended, which renders it invalid for a temporary, indefinite time period. Normally a certificate would be suspended if the user is on extended leave, or during an investigation, for instance. *Suspending* a certificate means that it could be reinstated, allowing a user to continue using the certificate, but only if and when the CA makes a conscious decision to do so.

Revoking a certificate, on the other hand, means that the certificate is permanently rendered invalid. Once a digital certificate has been revoked, it can't be reissued or reused. The CA might revoke a certificate if a user no longer needs it, if the user has been terminated or retires, or if the certificate has been misused or compromised in any way. If a certificate has been revoked, the CA must reissue a totally different certificate to the user if the CA determines that the user requires it.

The CA publishes a *certificate revocation list (CRL)* that contains the certificates the entity has issued and subsequently revoked. Users can access this list to determine the validity of a certificate. If a certificate has been revoked, it is considered no longer valid

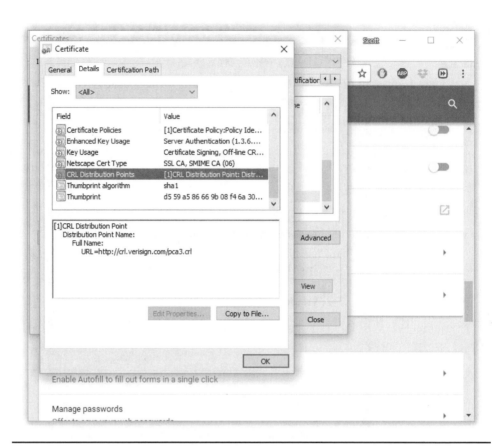

Figure 2-32 A small sample of a CRL entry from Verisign

and cannot be used. Certificate revocation lists can be published online, or they can be part of an automated process that application software checks from a centralized repository.

Similarly, the *Online Certificate Status Protocol (OCSP)* is used to automate certificate validation, making checking the status of certificates seamless and transparent to the user. Most modern browsers and other applications that use digital certificates can use OCSP to check CRLs automatically for certificate validity. A sample from a CRL, downloaded to a user's browser, is shown in Figure 2-32.

OCSP permits users (through Internet browsers and other certificate-aware applications) to check for certificate expiration, suspension, and revocation before the certificate is accepted. In Figure 2-33, you can see an example of a revoked certificate, which in this case is a famous example of a certificate erroneously issued to a fraudulent party claiming to be Microsoft. The certificate was quickly revoked after the error was discovered.

Figure 2-33
A *revoked certificate*

 EXAM TIP   Suspended certificates can be reused after the organization determines it is safe to reactivate them. Revoked certificates are never reused and are considered invalid forever.

Key Safety

Keys in PKI encrypt and decrypt data; losing a key means losing access to any data encrypted by the other key in the pair. That would be a bad thing! Two *key management* options protect organizations from such a loss, recovery agents and key escrow.

Recovery Agent

A *recovery agent* is a designated person or entity who has the authority to recover lost keys or data in the event the person holding the keys is not available. Recovery agents can work in a few different ways. One way requires the individual to store his private key in a secure area that a recovery agent can access in the event the individual is terminated or unavailable to decrypt data, for example, that had been encrypted with his private key. This would be the least desirable way, however, since non-repudiation would suffer because private keys are supposed to be kept private and confidential and accessible only by the user. Another, more common way would be to have the recovery agent maintain a different key that can decrypt any data encrypted by an individual.

Key Escrow

As you'll recall from Module 2-1, *key escrow* is the practice of maintaining private keys, sometimes by an independent third party, so that they can be accessed in the event individuals are not able or unavailable to use them to recover data that has been encrypted. Organizations should approach this practice with caution, however, because, as mentioned previously, this can create issues with non-repudiation. Before an organization puts key escrow into practice, it should identify a secure, carefully executed, and transparent method of key escrow. An organization may want to implement key escrow to guard against the possibility that an individual will encrypt sensitive data and then leave the company suddenly, without a way for the organization to recover the data.

Trust Models

Most commercial certificate authorities are generally trusted by most browsers and applications, since their root certificate is usually contained in the root certificate store of most devices. Private CAs, however, such as an internal CA that issues certificates only to its own employees, may not generally be trusted by outside organizations. This would render the certificates they have issued as untrusted by anyone outside their own organization. Because of this, some *trust models* have evolved over the years to enable organizations to take advantage of each other's digital certificates, permitting some level of trust between them. Let's look at three trust modules:

- Hierarchical trust
- Cross-trust
- Web-of-trust

Hierarchical Trust

A *hierarchical trust* is normally found within an organization, particularly a larger organization, and involves trust in digital certificates within organizational boundaries. Often, there are intermediate or subordinate CAs within a large organization that must trust each other. One subordinate CA may issue e-mail certificates, for example, and another may issue code-signing certificates. All the certificates, however, can be traced back and trusted through the originating root CA. This is possible with a hierarchical trust model, such that all subordinate and intermediate CAs trust each other because they trust the original root CA. Look again at Figure 2-29, shown earlier, as an example of a hierarchical trust model.

Cross-Trust

A *cross-trust* model is often used between two different organizations. In this trust model, organizations typically have their own certificate authorities and issuing servers. However, because of business partner arrangements, they must trust each other's certificates so that their personnel can authenticate to access resources in each other's security domains. A cross-trust model enables organizations to have their root CAs trust each other (and the certificates they generate) or even have specific subordinate CAs trust each other. This type of trust can be open to any certificate or limited only to very specific certificates issued under particular circumstances.

Web-of-Trust

A *web-of-trust* model is not typically used in a PKI. You'll most often see this type of model used in smaller groups or organizations, typically in those that allow individual users to generate their own public and private key pairs. The use of Pretty Good Privacy (PGP) and Gnu Privacy Guard (GPG) between small groups of users is a prime example of a web-of-trust. In this model, there is no central issuing authority that validates user identities. It is left up to each individual user to trust another user's certificates. While this works well in small groups, where each user has some level of assurance of the identity of another user, it's typically not scalable to large groups of people or organizations.

Module 2-8: Cryptographic Attacks

This module covers the following CompTIA Security+ objectives:

- **1.2 Given a scenario, analyze potential indicators to determine the type of attack**
- **1.3 Given a scenario, analyze potential indicators associated with application attacks**
- **2.8 Summarize the basics of cryptographic concepts**
- **4.1 Given a scenario, use the appropriate tool to assess organizational security**

Cryptanalysis, the science of breaking encryption, is as old as encryption itself. From Louis XVI at his palace in Versailles to the latest state-sponsored attacks, encryption has been successfully attacked many times. This module looks at some of the more common cryptographic attacks and the tools used to perform them. Understanding these attacks and their tools provides a better understanding on how to keep data secure. (Plus, it's really fun to crack stuff!)

The module starts with a general discussion of attack strategies and then examines attackable data. The third section explores password-oriented attacks and the tools commonly used in the attacks. The fourth section describes how to defend password storage. The module finishes with a look at a few attacks unrelated to passwords.

Attack Strategies

Every cryptosystem has an underlying algorithm, a key (or in the case of hashes, a digest), or some implementation of the cryptosystem itself, all of which the attacker understands.

All cryptographic algorithms are known and rarely change, in accordance with Kerckhoffs' principle (introduced in Module 2-1). Every cryptographic attack starts by careful inspection of the cryptosystem and aggressively probing and experimenting to find some form of weakness in one of those three aspects.

NOTE Every cryptosystem currently in use has countries, universities, private organizations, and individuals who constantly experiment with them, looking for weaknesses. We need this research so that a weakness may be discovered and shared with others in IT security and adjustments may be made.

Attack the Algorithm

Every cryptographic algorithm is crackable given enough time to research. This is why organizations and agencies such as the National Security Agency (NSA) update encryption standards every few years. As of this writing, the only symmetric encryption algorithm that has not shown any substantial weakness is AES. (Although that happy state of affairs could have already changed between my typing and your reading of the printed work!) The danger here is that many modern cryptosystems can use pre-AES encryptions such as RC4 or DES. In this case, skilled cryptographers can crack a "secure" cryptosystem by attacking the underlying algorithm.

NOTE No secure Web server package will easily allow you to use non-AES encryptions.

Attack the Key

Given that virtually every cryptosystem uses some form of key, it's obvious that cryptanalysis will look at the key for weaknesses or, more importantly, attempt to determine the key simply by attacking at the ciphertext. One of the great weaknesses is key length. Modern increases in computing power make it easier to crack keys that were once considered too long to crack.

Consider a bike lock with only four wheels versus a bike lock with many more than four (Figure 2-34). Which of these is faster to crack? The same concept applies to keys. Taking a piece of ciphertext and trying every possible key until something that looks like plaintext appears is a brute-force attack. (More on that type of attack shortly.)

DES has an effective key length of only 56 bits. That means it has a *key space* (the total number of possible keys) of 2^{56} or 72,057,594,037,927,936 different combinations. This number seems like an impossibly large number of combinations, but specialized computing systems like the Electronic Freedom Federation's Deep Crack cracked a DES key in 22 hours ... back in 1998. Today, a high-end desktop computer's processing power isn't too far from that same power.

Figure 2-34
Two bike locks—
which is easier to
crack?

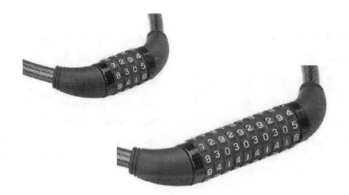

Attack the Implementation

Some implementations of new cryptosystems have some inherent flaw that causes an unanticipated weakness that is no fault of the underlying algorithm. *Wired Equivalent Privacy (WEP)* was marketed as a complete 802.11 encryption cryptosystem, introduced with the first generation of 802.11 wireless access points (WAPs) in 1999. Widely adopted, within a year cryptographers discovered that WEP poorly implemented the way it used the underlying RC4 encryption. That flaw enabled a simple cryptanalysis to derive the key simply by collecting enough encrypted data.

NOTE WEP was not a true encryption mechanism, but instead provided the expectation of privacy the users would get from a wired network connection. In practice, as noted, it quickly failed to protect much of anything.

Attackable Data

No cipher attack is going to work if you don't have access to something crackable. This crackable data can be divided into two different types: ciphertext or hashes. Before we go about attacking anything, let's first create two example scenarios: one with ciphertext and another with hashes. Then we'll attack.

Ciphertext Scenario

Let's use a simple example of an 802.11 network encrypted with Wi-Fi Protected Access Pre-Shared Key (WPA-PSK). When a client connects to a WAP, the client goes through a simple handshake procedure that determines that each side stores the same PSK. This process does not transmit the key, but contains enough information to provide the key to a skilled hacker. Programmers have developed applications that can capture WPA handshakes. Figure 2-35 shows the popular Aircrack-ng program grabbing a handshake.

```
[CH 9 ][ Elapsed: 13 mins ][ 2019-03-01 12:21 ][ WPA handshake: 12:23:45:AB:CD:EF

BSSID              PWR    Beacons      #Data #/s  CH  MB   ENC   CIPHER AUTH ESSID

C5:EE:BE:90:2B:AE  -52      2344        592   4   9  54e  WPA2  CCMP   PSK  NSA Van 45
D0:DA:DF:51:A2:D5  -56       329         34   0   9  54e  WPA2  CCMP   PSK  Private
0A:75:9F:30:34:D1  -89        72         29   0   9  54e  WPA2  CCMP   PSK  Frood

BSSID              STATION              PWR    Rate    Lost   Frames  Probe

D0:DA:DF:51:A2:D5  12:34:11:2A:1E:6C    -96    0 - 1      0        2  NSA Van 45
0A:75:9F:30:34:D1  CC:2A:91:F3:AE:15    -31    0e- 1e    81      399  Frood
```

Figure 2-35 Aircrack-ng grabbing a WPA handshake

NOTE An online attack is executed against data in transit. An offline attack is done against data at rest.

Once this handshake is captured, the attacker has a value upon which to apply a 128-bit key. If the attacker places the correct 128-bit key, she can determine the PSK.

Hash Scenario

Many cryptographic attacks target cracking passwords. Let's start this scenario with a review of the where, how, and why of passwords.

A computer system or application that requires password authentication must contain a database or *table* of passwords. Because these password tables are potentially vulnerable to anyone with the technical knowledge to locate them and try to crack them, storing a plaintext password is dangerous. It is extremely common, therefore, not to store the password itself, but instead store a cryptographic hash of the password in the database.

The following is a sample of a hypothetical password list, consisting of four user names with their associated passwords stored as MD5 hashes. How can you tell they are MD5? Simply by counting the number of characters! This sample could be used for many applications. This example uses a text file; a password list could be a text file, a binary file, a cookie, or registry settings, depending on the application or the operating system that uses the passwords.

Mike, bd4c4ea1b44a8ff2afa18dfd261ec2c8
Steve, 4015e9ce43edfb0668ddaa973ebc7e87
Janet, 8cbad96aced40b3838dd9f07f6ef5772
Penny, 48cccca3bab2ad18832233ee8dff1b0b

Once you have the hashes, you can hash every possible conceptual password to see if you can match the hash.

Attack Scenarios

The ciphertext and hash scenarios previously presented have common features. Both rely on a single data point: either ciphertext or a hash. Both have a clearly understood algorithm: WPA and MD5. Finally, you can use an attack to apply a key to obtain plaintext. But how do bad actors *perform* this attack? What tools do they use to read that ciphertext or hash and try to extract the plaintext key or password? They use programs called *password crackers* or *password recovery tools* to perform these *password attacks*.

Password crackers have legitimate use in assessing organizational security and recovering forgotten passwords. Such tools belong in every network security professional's toolbox. In the wrong hands, though, tools to help can readily turn into tools to harm.

Password crackers come in a broad assortment of functions and interfaces. A Linux-based attacker, for example, uses Jack the Ripper or Hashcat (Figure 2-36). A Windows-based attacker might employ the venerable Cain & Abel (Figure 2-37).

```
root@et:~/hashcat# ./hashcat -m 15100 -a 3 -w 3 hash.txt ?l?l?l?l?l?lt
hashcat (v3.5.0) starting...

OpenCL Platform #1: NVIDIA Corporation
========================================
* Device #1: GeForce GTX 1080, 2026/8107 MB allocatable, 20MCU
* Device #2: GeForce GTX 1080, 2028/8114 MB allocatable, 20MCU
* Device #3: GeForce GTX 1080, 2028/8114 MB allocatable, 20MCU
* Device #4: GeForce GTX 1080, 2028/8114 MB allocatable, 20MCU

Hashes: 1 digests; 1 unique digests, 1 unique salts
Bitmaps: 16 bits, 65536 entries, 0x0000ffff mask, 262144 bytes, 5/13 rotates

Applicable optimizers:
* Zero-Byte
* Single-Hash
* Single-Salt
* Brute-Force

Watchdog: Temperature abort trigger set to 90c
Watchdog: Temperature retain trigger set to 75c

$sha1$20000$46487265$5EZzAHiEWP.Hwufke.kRNWOA.sg1:hashcat

Session..........: hashcat
Status...........: Cracked
Hash.Type........: Juniper/NetBSD sha1crypt
Hash.Target......: $sha1$20000$46487265$5EZzAHiEWP.Hwufke.kRNWOA.sg1
Time.Started.....: Wed Apr  5 11:37:22 2017 (2 mins, 8 secs)
Time.Estimated...: Wed Apr  5 11:39:30 2017 (0 secs)
Guess.Mask.......: ?l?l?l?l?l?lt [7]
Guess.Queue......: 1/1 (100.00%)
Speed.Dev.#1.....:   184.8 kH/s (91.44ms)
Speed.Dev.#2.....:   184.9 kH/s (91.24ms)
Speed.Dev.#3.....:   184.8 kH/s (91.30ms)
Speed.Dev.#4.....:   184.8 kH/s (91.53ms)
Speed.Dev.#*.....:   739.3 kH/s
Recovered........: 1/1 (100.00%) Digests, 1/1 (100.00%) Salts
Progress.........: 93716480/308915776 (30.34%)
Rejected.........: 0/93716480 (0.00%)
Restore.Point....: 0/11881376 (0.00%)
Candidates.#1....: harinat -> hmldcot
Candidates.#2....: waktltt -> wltxslt
Candidates.#3....: wkjytrt -> wqcduct
Candidates.#4....: wswsbut -> wwpfsit
HwMon.Dev.#1.....: Temp: 53c Fan:100% Util:100% Core:1936MHz Mem:4513MHz Bus:1
HwMon.Dev.#2.....: Temp: 59c Fan:100% Util:100% Core:1949MHz Mem:4513MHz Bus:1
HwMon.Dev.#3.....: Temp: 54c Fan:100% Util:100% Core:1949MHz Mem:4513MHz Bus:1
HwMon.Dev.#4.....: Temp: 55c Fan:100% Util:100% Core:1936MHz Mem:4513MHz Bus:1

Started: Wed Apr  5 11:37:17 2017
Stopped: Wed Apr  5 11:39:30 2017
```

Figure 2-36   Hashcat

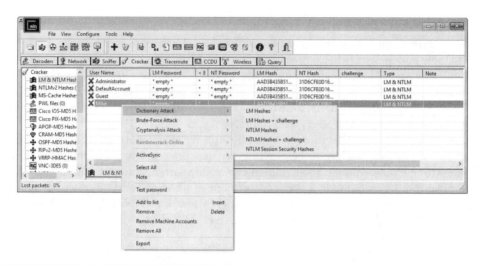

Figure 2-37 Cain & Abel

In general, all these tools follow similar patterns. First, they grab the ciphertext or hashes you want to attack. Second, they analyze the data to determine the type of encryption (or they know the encryption by the source). Finally, they give you the option to attack in most, if not all, of the ways listed in this module.

Let's look at five common attack types that apply to these password-based scenarios:

- Brute-force attack
- Dictionary attack
- Rainbow-table attack
- Password spraying attack
- Plaintext/unencrypted attack

NOTE There is no such thing as a do-it-all single password cracker. There are hundreds of different password crackers, each with a different niche depending on your needs.

Brute-Force Attack

A *brute-force attack* is the simplest and least-efficient type of attack against known ciphertext/hashes. A brute-force attack attempts to derive a password or key by inspecting either ciphertext or a hash and then trying every possible combination of key or hash until it can decrypt the plaintext or generate a match. The challenge to brute force is the total number of iterations necessary to try every possible key combination. Consider a captured WPA handshake. The key is 128-bit, so it can go from 128 zeros to 128 ones, plus all the combinations in between.

So, how long does it take to try 2^{128} combinations? Longer means more combinations and therefore harder, so 2^{128} is equal to

$$3.4028236692093846346337460743176821 1456 \times 10^{38}$$

That's a huge number, but computers are powerful. A single, very high-end Intel Core i7 can process at half a *trillion* floating point operations per second (FLOPS), and you can readily source a computer with a lot of these CPUs. Additionally, password crackers are carefully optimized to take advantage of all those FLOPS. In fact, the better crackers can even take advantage of powerful graphics processing units (GPUs) on video cards as well as special-purpose application-specific integrated circuit (ASIC) devices that work hundreds or even thousands of times faster than a CPU (Figure 2-38).

So, without spending outrageous text on the intricacies of CPUs, FLOPS, GPUs, and such, we can arguably say that a very high-end cracking system could process 1 trillion cracking attempts per second. It would take something like 10,790,283,070,806,014,188 years to try every possible key. If that seems like an impossibly long time to you, it is. Keep in mind that the key might be all zeros, which means you will get the WPA key on the very first try. Alternatively, the key might be all ones, which means you would have to try all 2^{128} combinations.

This might make you think that brute force is useless, and it is for relatively large keys. Shorter keys, however, can easily be cracked. For example, a 56-bit DES key can be cracked (using the preceding assumptions) in about 20 hours. As computing power increases, what was once a long key or hash becomes short. That's why keys and hashes get longer and longer over the years.

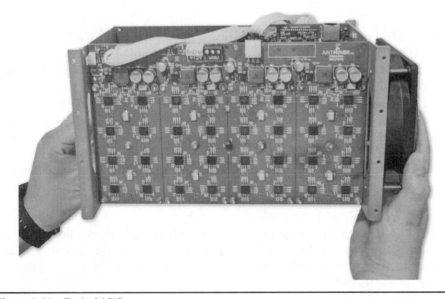

Figure 2-38 Typical ASIC

But even if we can run a brute-force attack in hours, why not come up with attacks that speed up the process? How can we narrow down the possible number of keys to try?

Dictionary Attack

Easily the weakest aspect to passwords is the fact that human beings create them. People produce passwords like this one:

Password123

This is a great password, right? It mixes upper- and lowercase letters and numbers. Hmm … not so much when it comes to modern cryptographic attacks.

People rarely create a password that looks like this:

1x3^^7vEssde6)

That's a far more awesome password, but it's just not what typical people create.

With this thought in mind, we can tell our cracking program to read a text file filled with all the common words in the (in this case) English language—a *dictionary file*. The cracking software will then use this dictionary file instead of brute force in a *dictionary attack*. Here is a tiny, tiny piece of a dictionary file downloaded from the Internet:

A
AA
AAA
AAAA
a
aa
aaa
aaaa

As you can see, most dictionary files include lots of non-words as well. That's because non-words like "AAAA" or "QWERTY" or "NASA" are commonly used for passwords. A small dictionary file might only store a few million passwords. The largest dictionary files contain many millions of passwords.

NOTE   If you recall the discussion of password policies from Chapter 1, you might see a nice attack opportunity here. A perpetrator who obtains a copy of an organization's security policies could readily see specific password policies. If the policy sets password length to 16+ characters, for example, the perp won't waste time or computational power on shorter passwords, but rather cut straight to the chase.

Good dictionary attack tools don't try only passwords in the dictionary list. Check out the dictionary attack settings for Cain & Abel in Figure 2-39. Note the options that allow you to modify the dictionary. If your dictionary file has the word *cheese*, for example, Cain & Abel will let you

- Reverse the word: eseehc
- Double pass: cheesecheese

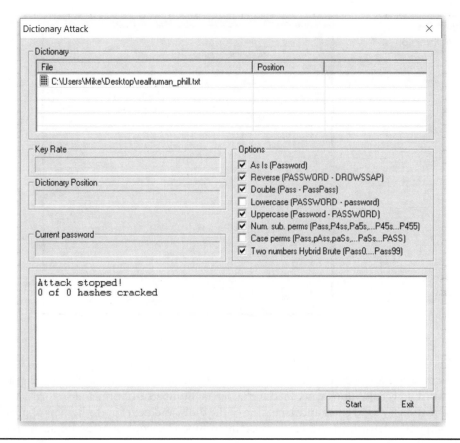

Figure 2-39   Cain & Abel dictionary options

- Uppercase to lowercase: not applicable, as cheese is all lowercase
- Lowercase to uppercase: CHEESE
- Number substitution: ch33s3
- Case permutations: Cheese, cHeese, etc.
- Add one or two numbers to the end: cheese1, cheese44

You can argue that these options add a brute-force aspect to a dictionary attack. A dictionary attack combined with brute-force options such as these is called a *hybrid attack*.

NOTE   As a quick mental exercise, ask yourself this question: Would the Cain & Abel tool be able to derive any of the passwords you use?

Figure 2-40
Hydra in action

Keep in mind there's a huge difference in the quality of dictionary files. I keep a set of dictionary files, accumulated over the years from many sources, sorted by length of password, lowercase/uppercase, special characters, numbers in front, and so forth. With good dictionary files, good understanding of the tools, and belief in the laziness of people to use poor passwords, I can crack most any offline password in a few hours, a classic *offline attack* scenario.

What if you don't have any ciphertext to attack? What if you just want to try a few million passwords to try to log into a Web site? That's a classic *online attack* situation and it's no problem! There are plenty of online dictionary attack password crackers such as the popular Hydra (Figure 2-40). Online attacks are slow, but it's easy to start an attack and let it run for days or weeks.

Rainbow-Table Attack

The challenge to dictionary attacks, particularly when you are trying to crack hashed passwords, is the fact that you have to take a word in the dictionary, hash it, then compare the hash to the hash in the password file. You could include hash values for all the entries in a dictionary file using common hashing algorithms to increase the effectiveness of a dictionary attack. The SHA-256 hash for "password" will always be

5e884898da28047151d0e56f8dc6292773603d0d6aabbdd62a11ef721d1542d8

So, what if we edited our dictionary files to include the hash? Sure, it might take weeks to generate the billions of hashes and save them in our dictionary file, but once it's done,

Figure 2-41
Simple dictionary files with hashes are too massive for practical use.

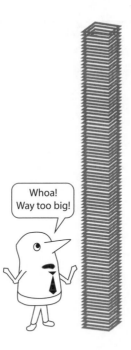

we have a file that includes the dictionary word as well as the hash. Such a dictionary file would start like this:

a, ca978112ca1bbdcafac231b39a23dc4da786eff8147c4e72b9807785afee48bb
aa, 961b6dd3ede3cb8ecbaacbd68de040cd78eb2ed5889130cceb4c49268ea4d506
aaa, 9834876dcfb05cb167a5c24953eba58c4ac89b1adf57f28f2f9d09af107ee8f0
aaaa, 61be55a8e2f6b4e172338bddf184d6dbee29c98853e0a0485ecee7f27b9af0b4

Using such an inclusive dictionary file could make a dictionary attack brutally effective. Except there's a huge problem. Files like these are massive, potentially in the hundreds of petabytes range for dictionary files that include really long passwords. They are simply too big for practical use (Figure 2-41).

Math comes to the rescue! Using complicated math well outside the scope of the CompTIA Security+ exam, a password cracker can create a *rainbow table*, a dramatically reduced-sized dictionary file that includes hashed entries.

 NOTE Online vs. offline, which is better? You can run brute-force, dictionary, and rainbow table attacks either way, but offline is faster if you have a key.

Rainbow tables are binary files, not text files. Figure 2-42 shows the contents of one set of rainbow tables, designed to help crack the old Windows XP–style List Manager passwords files. Rainbow tables for more advanced operating systems can be much larger, although always much smaller than a traditional dictionary file with hashes.

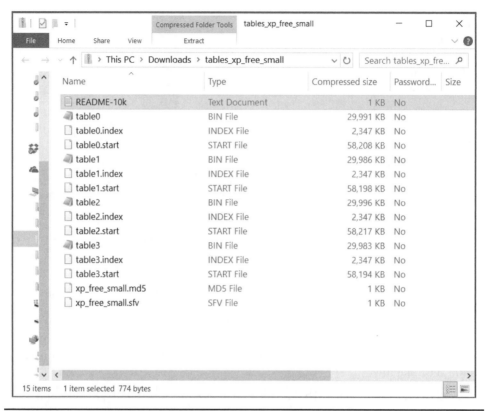

Figure 2-42   Rainbow tables for Windows XP passwords

Rainbow tables were long the first choice for cracking passwords; such attacks are fast and generally very successful. Rainbow tables were so popular that you can find online services that let you load hashes to crack, and powerful systems will crack a password for just a few dollars (Figure 2-43). (Or, you can use GPU brute force, which is how modern hackers do it.)

Password Spraying Attack

In a *password spraying attack*, an actor applies a few common passwords to many accounts in an organization. By applying "123456" or "password1" to 100 different accounts, for example, the attacker tries to find an entry into the network while avoiding lockouts and remaining undetected. Single sign-on (like in a Windows domain) and cloud accounts provide the most tempting targets of password spraying.

Plaintext/Unencrypted Attack

Attackers can use packet sniffing software to monitor and capture traffic on a network. If passwords are sent in plaintext or unencrypted, it's game over instantly. Depending on the encryption strength, attackers can decrypt a lot of encrypted traffic given

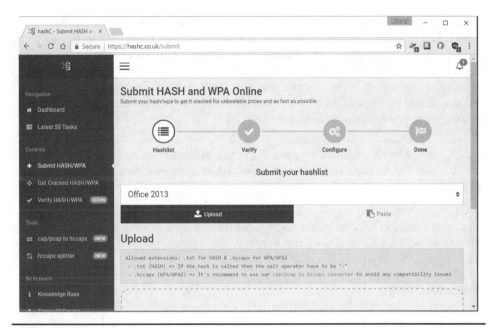

Figure 2-43   One of many online cracking services

enough time. CompTIA uses the term *plaintext/unencrypted* as a type of password attack, but it's more commonly referred to as a generic packet sniffing attack.

EXAM TIP   The simplest and most effective password attack is to ask the user for his password. It works (allegedly, not that I've done anything like this!).

Defending Password Storage

Between brute-force, dictionary, and rainbow attacks, traditional hash password storage has been under prolonged attack, making it important for cryptographers to come up with methods to make password storage more robust against these attacks. Salts and key stretching offer protections.

Salts

A *salt* is an arbitrary value, usually created by the application or operating system storing passwords, added to the end of a password before it is hashed. If a user's password is 1234567, for example, a system might add an eight-character preset value, a salt, to the end of the password as such:

1234567akxcf3sf

When hashed (in this example SHA256), it looks like this:

a75f22d3cd5aea740f2a17b0275bfacd0c822aca

Salts defeat rainbow tables simply because (hopefully) there are no rainbow tables that include dictionary terms plus the string akxcf3sf. Salts are common in just about everything that stores passwords. The downside is that a salt must be stored. If someone had access to your hashes, they also have access to the salt. They can run dictionary attacks, but now they must add the salt every time and recalculate the hash, slowing cracking down immensely. Also, it is possible to grab a salt and re-create a rainbow table, although this is also a slow process.

 EXAM TIP All modern operating systems use salts in password storage. You'll see the term "salting" on the CompTIA Security+ exam to mean "using a salt."

Cryptosystems often use a nonce instead of, or along with, a salt to enhance security. A *nonce* is a *n*umber used *once* that helps in the transmission of shared keys, among many other uses. Because it's used once and not repeated, a nonce prevents common attacks—called *replay attacks*—from cracking encryption.

Key Stretching

Another trick used to make cracking harder is key stretching. Keys are almost always generated from some plain English password. If we just hash the password, it doesn't take a lot of time for an attacker to pick a potential password, hash it, then compare the results to a password hash file. But what if we were to make the process by which a key is derived from a password more complex? We can do so with a *key derivation function*. What if, for example, we hashed an initial password five times to then derive the key? This would require the attacker to run not just one hash, but five hashes for every iteration. Using key derivation functions that intentionally slow this derivation of keys is *key stretching*.

There are several key stretching key derivation functions; two stand out: PBKDF2 and bcrypt.

Password-Based Key Derivation Function 2 (PBKDF2) combines adding a very long salt and a huge number of hashing iterations to make a key. PBKDF2 doesn't set the number of hash iterations. Some operating systems that employ PBKDF2 use 10,000 iterations!

bcrypt generates hashes based on the Blowfish cipher. In many ways similar to PBKDF2, it also has flexible hash iterations. bcrypt has a very long key derivation process and is considered stronger than PBKDF2.

Other Attack Options

Several types of cryptographic attacks deviate from the crack-the-password variety. This section explores three such attack types:

- Collision attacks
- Known-plaintext attacks
- Implementation attacks

Collision Attack

A *collision attack* exploits the fact that hashes have a finite size, and there will be times when two different values create the same hash, a *hash collision* (as described in Module 2-5). Given that hashes provide integrity, an attacker may take advantage of collisions to do harmful things. For example, if an attacker can create a collision with a digital signature; she doesn't need to know the actual private key, just a value to make an identical signature.

There's no magic to creating a collision. You use brute force on millions of hashes until you get one that collides. This is a big job, but there are some interesting aspects of hashes that make it a bit easier. The most well-known is the *birthday attack*.

It seems that every undergraduate statistics class begins with the teacher looking out at his or her class and saying, "There are 30 students in this classroom. What are the odds that two people share the same birthday?" They are surprisingly high; for 30 students, about 70 percent.

The same situation happens with hash collisions. A 64-bit hash has approximately 1.8×10^{19} different outputs. While this number is huge, the goal here is to find another identical hash. That's where the birthday statistic applies. It only takes roughly half (5.38×10^{9}) to generate a collision using brute force.

Known-Plaintext Attack

A *known-plaintext attack* isn't a true attack as much as it is an attack strategy. If you have both a known plaintext and the ciphertext, you can sometimes derive the key itself. Known-plaintext attacks have worked many times in the past. It's how the British cracked the Nazi Enigma code in World War II. Military messages followed rigid forms, for example, so some words would always be in the same relative place. Messages would end with *Heil Hitler*, in other words, and *wetter* (weather) was consistently placed.

Implementation Attack

Any cryptosystem has weaknesses or aspects that attackers may use to help them. Attacking the WEP weakness described earlier is a classic example of a weak implementation attack. Download and replay attacks exploit weaknesses in implementation.

Downgrade Attack   Almost all of today's cryptosystems give a client multiple ways to access a system. One of the best examples is TLS. A Web server using TLS supports several authentication and encryption methods to give flexibility for different Web browsers. In TLS, a client and a server traditionally request the most robust encryption. In a *downgrade attack*, the attack makes a legitimate request to the Web server to use a weak, deprecated algorithm that's easier to crack (Figure 2-44) in hopes of then successfully getting keys, passwords, and so forth.

 NOTE   A *deprecated algorithm* is an algorithm deemed obsolete or too flawed for use by the IT community. *Deprecated* means no one should use it in the future.

Figure 2-44
Downgrade
attack against TLS

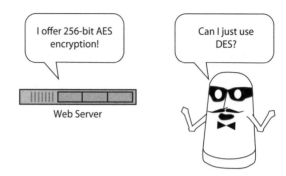

Replay Attack In many situations, an attacker can *sniff* or capture traffic on a network, monitoring the different communications taking place. A *replay attack* is an attack where the attacker captures some type of legitimate traffic and resends it as needed to do something malicious. Here's an example:

Bob: "Hey Joe, I need you to send the encryption keys for this session to me."
Joe: "Okay, Bob, here you go."
Bad Guy Mike: "Hey Joe, I need you to send the encryption keys for this session to me."
Joe: "Okay, Bob. I thought I just did, but whatever. Here you go."
Bad Guy Mike: "Mwuhuhahahahaha…."

NOTE True replay attacks tend to be more complicated than the Bad Guy Mike scenario. A hacker might steal all the back and forth in a certificate exchange, for example, and then boot the originator off just before completion. Then the hacker would resend the same stream. But you get the idea.

Module 2-9: Other Cryptosystems

This module covers the following CompTIA Security+ objective:

- **2.8 Summarize the basics of cryptographic concepts**

Several cryptosystems—current and speculative—fall outside the classic paradigms of symmetric and asymmetric cryptosystems. Depending on the field you wind up in as an IT security professional, you might encounter and need to work with one or more of these non-classical cryptosystems. This module explores four cryptosystem fields:

- Homomorphic encryption
- Blockchain
- Quantum cryptography
- Post-quantum cryptography

Homomorphic Encryption

A clear challenge to storing data in the cloud is ensuring that personal data remains private. An organization cannot risk the possibility that an individual's medical data, for example, could be shared or mined or even known without the explicit permission of the individual. Cryptographers have kicked around the problem and sought solutions since the late 1970s, but the beginnings of practical answers finally came in 2009 with the publication of Craig Gentry's Stanford University PhD thesis, "Fully Homomorphic Encryption Using Ideal Lattices." We'll spare you the details on how Gentry's initial scheme worked and how subsequent developments (with input from other awesome cryptographers) made current cryptosystems work.

Homomorphic encryption enables manipulation of encrypted data—without decrypting—that then applies to that data when it's decrypted. Wrap your head around that for a moment. Private, encrypted data can be outsourced to the cloud without compromising the privacy of that data. It means researchers can run analytical scans on encrypted data, get amazing amounts of information, and never compromise the private records of individuals.

Cryptographers see the current state of homomorphic encryption as the third generation. Gentry and his collaborators continue to innovate in the field. The world awaits the future.

Blockchain

E-commerce on the Internet relies on hierarchical cryptosystems. Certificate authorities (CAs) provide certificates to organizations; that creates *trust*. We can buy from https://amazon.com or https://linengarb.com with trust that our financial information (credit card numbers and such) won't be compromised. Encryption, hashing, and other aspects of cryptography provide the secure connection between our computers and the e-commerce servers. Moreover, traditional institutions such as banks and credit card companies facilitate the flow of our money to vendors. Users of e-commerce, therefore, rely heavily on institutions that are *not* the seller.

Blockchain radically disrupts this model, creating a decentralized, peer-to-peer system for secure interaction between buyer and seller. Here are the details.

The shadowy figure Satoshi Nakamoto—real identity unknown—invented blockchain in 2008 to support the bitcoin cryptocurrency. *Bitcoin* is a topic for a whole other book, but in a nutshell, it's money, called *cryptocurrency*, that's not tied to any bank or nation state. Blockchain provides the peer-to-peer record—*public ledger*, in bitcoin speak—of all the transactions among people using bitcoin. You buy a pizza and pay for it using bitcoins, for example; that transaction goes into all the computers connected into the blockchain. The pizza joint now has bitcoins to spend on something else available in the market.

Bitcoin and blockchain rely on public key infrastructure (PKI) cryptosystems to ensure safe storage of the currency and the transactions as well. You know about PKI from previous modules. Everything you learned applies here. Private keys must stay private (or else your bitcoins will get stolen); public keys are just that, public. Encryption/decryption works the same.

The fundamental difference between traditional e-commerce and commerce conducted with bitcoin and blockchain is the decentralized structure of the latter.

Quantum Cryptography

The nascent field of *quantum cryptography* uses the vast power of quantum computers to fundamentally transform cryptosystems used today. Huh? The math works, but the machines barely exist today. Here's the scoop in layman terms.

Researchers postulate that we can build computers that can transmit data based on qubits, rather than simple binary digits. A *qubit* is a particle that's a binary digit but captured in time, so it's almost a 1, for example, or transitioning to a 0. The math is a lot more precise than the terms used here, of course. The key for security is that the state of a qubit is fragile; a hacker intercepting a stream would get only 1's and 0's because the qubits would collapse to the full binary state closest to its relative position. Think of this as rounding up or rounding down, like in basic math.

This sounds like science fiction, but for relatively short distances, quantum computers work. The field of *quantum communication*, for example, has established connections between quantum computers over fiber-optic lines that regularly transact business using quantum key distribution (QKD). The connection between Shanghai and Beijing banks using quantum communication is over 2000 kilometers!

Quantum cryptography relies on quantum computers to accomplish a couple of things. First, future complex quantum computers (theoretically) can easily crack modern secure cryptosystems, especially RSA and Diffie-Hellman. Second, key distribution using something called *quantum entanglement* holds the promise that it should become completely secure, a positive development.

Quantum cryptography remains in the realm of theory, not practical application today. The math works, but building machines that can handle the complexities involved seems a decade or more in the future.

If quantum computing breaks much of classic cryptography, does this mean the end? Not at all. Quantum computing may be wonderful at breaking classic "easy one way but hard the other way" forms of encryption, but cryptographers are already preparing for the future. The flip side to quantum cryptography, called *post-quantum cryptography*, speculates cryptographic algorithms that can withstand any attack using quantum computers. Wildly complex forms of encryption are already being developed, although it will be years before any form of encryption algorithm will be forwarded for public use.

Questions

1. Which of the following types of algorithms encrypts specified sizes of groups of text at a time?

   A. Asymmetric

   B. Symmetric

   C. Streaming

   D. Block

2. You must implement a cryptography system in your organization. You need to be able to send large amounts of data quickly over the network. The system will be used by a very small group of users only, and key exchange is not a problem. Which of the following should you consider?

   A. Asymmetric cryptography

   B. Symmetric cryptography

   C. Hybrid cryptography

   D. Key escrow

3. Which of the following asymmetric algorithms uses a maximum key size of 4096 bits?

   A. AES

   B. Diffie-Hellman

   C. RSA

   D. ECC

4. Which of the following asymmetric algorithms is widely used on mobile devices because of its low computational power requirements?

   A. ECC

   B. ElGamal

   C. Diffie-Hellman

   D. GPG

5. Which type of algorithm is typically used to encrypt data at rest?

   A. Symmetric

   B. Asymmetric

   C. Streaming

   D. Block

6. Which of the following places secrecy of the key versus secrecy of the algorithm as the most important factor in developing secure and reliable cryptosystems?

   A. Data Encryption Standard (DES)

   B. Advanced Encryption Standard (AES)

   C. Kerckhoffs' principle

   D. Digital Signature Algorithm (DSA)

7. Which of the following algorithms produces a 40-character message digest?

   A. MD5

   B. SHA-1

   C. RIPEMD-128

   D. Blowfish

8. If an individual encrypts a message with his own private key, what does this assure?

   A. Confidentiality

   B. Message authenticity

   C. Integrity

   D. Availability

9. Which of the following entities can help distribute the workload of the CA by performing identification and authentication of individual certificate requestors?

   A. Subordinate CA

   B. Root CA server

   C. Authentication authority

   D. Registration authority

10. Which of the following serves as the master certificate server in an organization?

   A. Intermediate CA server

   B. Root CA server

   C. Subordinate CA server

   D. Kerberos KDC

Answers

1. **D.** Block algorithms encrypt entire groups of bits of text, usually of specific sizes.

2. **B.** In this scenario, symmetric key cryptography would probably be the best choice, since the user group is very small and key exchange is not a problem. You also have the requirements of speed and efficiency, as well as the ability to send large amounts of data. All are advantages of using symmetric key cryptography.

3. **C.** RSA uses key sizes between 1024 and 4096 bits.

4. **A.** Elliptic-curve cryptography (ECC) is an asymmetric algorithm widely found in use on mobile devices because it requires low amounts of computational power.

5. **A.** Symmetric algorithms are typically used to encrypt data that resides in storage.

6. **C.** Kerckhoffs' principle states that reliable cryptosystems should depend upon the secrecy of the key, rather than the secrecy of the algorithm.

7. **B.** SHA-1 is a 160-bit hashing algorithm that produces a 40-character hexadecimal message digest, or hash.

8. **B.** If an individual encrypts a message with his private key, this ensures message authenticity, since he is the only person who could have encrypted it.

9. **D.** The registration authority (RA) can help distribute the workload of the CA by performing identification and authentication of individual certificate requestors.

10. **B.** A root CA server is the master certificate server in an organization.

Identity and Account Management

Be who you are and say what you feel because those who mind don't matter and those who matter don't mind.

—Dr. Seuss

Everything that is networking, everything that is the Internet, the whole reason to run cables, set up routers, configure firewalls and applications, and sit on the phone for hours with balky ISPs is really only to do one job: share resources. These resources are Web pages, e-mail messages, VoIP conversations, games…. The interconnected world has millions of resources for people to use to make work and leisure more convenient, more efficient, more inexpensive … and more fun (Figure 3-1).

Resources are useless unless there's someone or something accessing and using them. A Web page has no value unless someone accesses it. A shared folder does nothing unless users read, modify, and delete files stored in those folders. E-mail messages sit on a server unread until you read them. Users must run client software to use those resources.

Offering a resource for anyone to use has major pitfalls. Users are at best ignorant, often nosy, and at worst, downright evil (Figure 3-2). IT professionals manage how users access the many resources.

This chapter dives deeply into *identity and account management*: using methods and technology to control who accesses resources and what they can do with those resources once they have access (Figure 3-3).

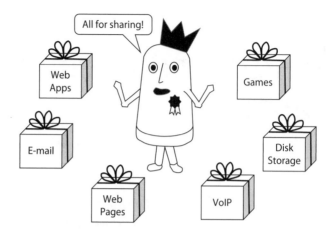

Figure 3-1
Lots of resources!

This chapter covers various distinct aspects of access control in six modules:

- Understanding Authentication
- Authentication Methods and Access Controls
- Account Management
- Point-to-Point Authentication
- Network Authentication
- Identity Management Systems

Figure 3-2   Unmanaged access to resources is foolhardy.

Figure 3-3
Controlling
resources

Module 3-1: Understanding Authentication

This module covers the following CompTIA Security+ objectives:

- **2.4 Summarize authentication and authorization design concepts**
- **3.8 Given a scenario, implement authentication and authorization solutions**

Identity and access management, like most CompTIA Security+ topics, brings a ton of concepts and specific jargon that serious students need to digest before implementing systems in the real world. This module explores identification and AAA (authentication, authorization, and accounting), then looks at concepts of trust, such as authentication structures and federated authentication.

Identification and AAA

Identification, authentication, authorization, and accounting work together to manage assets securely. This section briefly reprises what you read about in the Introduction on core security concepts.

Imagine an asset, a shared resource, as a box. *Authentication* functions like a lock on that box. For a user to access the box, he must have some kind of key or *credentials* to get through the lock (Figure 3-4). The information in those credentials identifies the user with respect to that system. (That's the *identification* part.) In analogy terms, it's a pretty complicated lock that opens different portions of the box depending on the key used.

Authorization determines what the user can do with the contents of the box with the specific credentials he used. Authorization is nuanced, because of variables in what people can do. Consider a shared folder on a Windows system in a local area network (LAN) that contains a single file. You can do a lot to that file. You can view the file, edit the file, or delete the file. (You can do much more than this, but this is enough for now.) Authorization defines what a user may do to that file. Think of authorization as a checklist (Figure 3-5).

Figure 3-4
Authentication as
a lock

Figure 3-5
Authorization as
a checklist

Accounting means to keep a historical record of what users do to shared resources. Look at accounting as a sign-in sheet associated with the shared resource (Figure 3-6).

Identification and Authentication

The typical locked box and key analogy struggles when taken from physical access to electronic access. Granting access in the physical world, like a door lock on a real door, works fine because people don't generally hand out a key to someone they can't identify. In the electronic world, how do we identify individual users?

Back in the early days of PC networking—for example, early versions of Windows that predated NTFS—this problem was simply ignored. Resources such as shared folders had no associated user accounts. If you wanted to share a folder, you just gave that folder a single password, which in turn was passed out to everyone to whom you wanted to give access (Figure 3-7).

More commonly today, user accounts identify individual users. A user account is generally nothing more than a line in a table (remember the user names in password

Figure 3-6
Accounting as a
sign-in sheet

storage in the previous chapter?) that identifies an individual user by some value, such as a User Name, UserID, Social Security Number, and so on. Figure 3-8 shows one example of a user account in Windows Server.

A user account must include some authentication factor(s) or attribute(s) to provide any kind of security. Identification is by itself insufficient for authentication.

Figure 3-7
Old Windows
shared folder

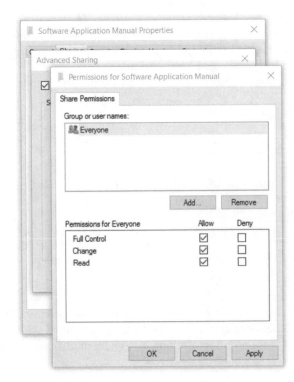

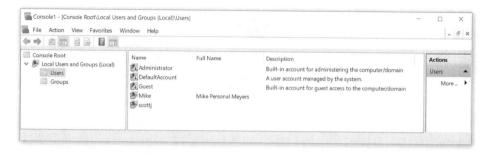

Figure 3-8 Windows Server user account

An authentication factor or attribute reveals some unique aspect of the identified user. Passwords are very common but just scratch the surface. Let's look at authentication factors and attributes in a lot more detail.

Authentication Factors and Attributes

Authentication systems use different characteristics of identification to identify a user and validate her credentials. These different methods—*factors* and *attributes*—depend upon the method of identification used. Several different factors and attributes can be used either separately or, preferably, together. *Single-factor authentication* uses only one factor or attribute. *Multifactor authentication (MFA)* uses more than one factor or attribute. (You'll also see the term *two-factor* authentication to describe systems that use two factors or attributes.) Using more than one factor or attribute at a time provides more security and represents better authentication.

There are three authentication factors used in computing:

- Something you know
- Something you have
- Something you are

There are four common attributes:

- Something you do
- Somewhere you are
- Something you exhibit
- Someone you know

EXAM TIP The CompTIA Security+ exam will test you on the difference between single-factor and multifactor authentication. Single-factor authentication uses only one factor or attribute; multifactor uses at least two factors or attributes.

Figure 3-9
Knowledge
factor

Something You Know   The *knowledge factor* relates to something you know, typically used when you identify yourself to a system with a user name and password combination. You know your user name and password, and use your memory to present them to the system (Figure 3-9).

Although you use two details for this credential, it is still considered a single-factor form of authentication because it involves only something you know. This single-factor form of authentication can be compromised easily if someone gains access to it—in this case, if they learn your user name and password. If you've written them down somewhere or told someone your user name or password, you have effectively transferred that factor to the other person, and it could be considered compromised.

Something You Have   The *possession factor* relates to something you have. You physically possess an object to use as an authenticator. Scanning a gym membership card to gain access, for example, uses something you have. When used in this manner, the card alone is a single-factor form of authentication.

More often than not, however, these types of authenticators require some additional method of authentication. Typically, this could be something you know, such as a personal identification number (PIN) or password. When used in this manner, the card and PIN are a multifactor form of authentication. You use two different *types* of factors: the possession factor and the knowledge factor.

Smart cards and tokens are probably the most commonly used multifactor form of authentication that uses the possession factor. *Smart cards* are plastic cards with electronic chips in them that contain a limited amount of information related to the user, such as public and private keys. Smart cards enable users to access facilities, secure areas, and computer systems.

Physical tokens usually display a complex series of changing numbers. When a token is used to access a system, the user must also enter a PIN or password known only to her in conjunction with the token and its own number. The system uses these two factors to validate the user. Figure 3-10 shows an example of a token.

Something You Are   The *inherence factor* relates to something you are, relying on a person's unique physical characteristics that can be used as a form of identification, such as fingerprints, retinal eye patterns, iris patterns, handprints, and voiceprints (Figure 3-11). These unique biometric characteristics of a person are difficult to replicate or fake. (See "Biometrics" in Module 3-2 for more specific details on how organizations incorporate biometric scanning in security.)

Figure 3-10
Possession factor

Inherence factors can also be used in conjunction with an additional factor in an MFA system. Newer laptops and smartphones often arrive with a fingerprint scanner built into them, for example, and the user must scan his fingerprint and enter a PIN or password to access the system. Secure facilities may also require fingerprint or handprint factors in their authentication systems. It's also not unusual to see multiple inherence factors used for an even stronger authentication system.

Something You Do   Something you do, meaning that when you present your credentials to the system, you must perform an action (Figure 3-12), is a common attribute that accompanies authentication factors. The best example of this type of authentication attribute is when you use a finger or hand gesture on a smartphone or tablet to log in. The pattern you create using your finger or hand is the something you do. The user credentials database of the system you access stores that pattern. When the authentication system confirms that these patterns match, you gain access to the device or system.

Some forms of authentication that use this type of gesture are single-factor if that's the only thing you're required to do to access the system. Other authentication systems may also require an additional factor, such as entry of a PIN, making it a multifactor form of authentication.

 EXAM TIP   CompTIA Security+ objective 2.4 adds another word to describe the action attribute: *something you can do*. Describing a *potential* action as an authentication attribute seems a little odd, to say the least. Just don't miss this on the exam.

Figure 3-11
Inherence factor

Figure 3-12
Action attribute

Somewhere You Are The *location attribute* relates to your location when you authenticate. This attribute could use either physical or logical locations and requires you to be in a certain location when you authenticate to the system (Figure 3-13). From a physical perspective, for example, in a highly secure facility, you may need to use a specific workstation, located in a certain room, to authenticate to the system before you can work on it from any other location. Because you would likely have to authenticate with other physical protections and controls to get into this room, this very secure form of authentication would allow only a limited number of people to access the system.

From a logical perspective, a location attribute could be used as an authentication attribute if you are required to authenticate from a certain device that has a specific digital certificate assigned to it, or from behind a certain network device, physical port, or even a subnet. This doesn't necessarily limit you by requiring authentication from a single physical location; rather, the logical location with respect to the network and the authentication system being used would be important. This might ensure that you do not attempt to authenticate from an untrusted network or device.

Something You Exhibit *Something you exhibit* can refer to something neurological that can be measured or scanned; it could be a personality trait or a mannerism. Speech analysis systems could very easily identify Barak Obama from the cadence of the way he talks, for example, with distinctive pauses. This is not a commonly used attribute today in cybersecurity.

Someone You Know The *someone you know* attribute reflects a trust relationship. John Bob—known and trusted by the system—vouches for Rebecca Sue.

Figure 3-13
Location
attribute

NOTE An additional authentication attribute that you won't see on the CompTIA Security+ exam is *temporal*, relating to some*when* you are. Systems can set specific login times and restrict others, for example. You'll definitely hear arguments that the temporal attribute is a control, not an authentication attribute, and thus belongs in authorization.

Knowledge-Based Authentication

In *knowledge-based authentication (KBA)*, users provide answers to questions or shared secrets to prove their identities. You'll see KBA implemented in scenarios involving online banking systems, for example, where users authenticate (or recover a forgotten password) by stating common authentication factors (such as name) and also answer questions presumably only they would know, such as "What was your first pet's name?" or "What was your first car?" The use of pre-agreed or pre-shared secrets is also known as *static KBA*.

Dynamic KBA, in contrast, uses information about the user gleaned from public data—what the authenticating system can gather from a Web search—and private data, such as a credit history. A lack of shared secrets makes dynamic KBA more secure than static KBA, though it's more difficult to implement.

NOTE As you progress through this chapter, keep in mind the balance among cost, implementation time, and expertise required to put systems in place. The Woodland Heights Community Bank might have the need for multifactor, layered authentication plus serious physical controls. Jane's coffee shop Wi-Fi network, on the other hand, might need a far lighter touch. Security folks weigh cost versus need when recommending and implementing systems.

Authorization

Authentication gets you in the door of a shared resource; the key unlocks the box. Authorization defines what you can do once you authenticate. Users have rights or permissions to do certain things to shared resources. This presents some unique challenges because different resources often have wildly different permissions based on the type of resource.

To get an idea of how resources can vary, let's consider two different types of resources: a printer and a Web page. Figure 3-14 shows permissions you can assign to a shared printer in Windows. Note three permissions: Print, Manage this printer, and Manage documents. These permissions make sense, as these are the actions we need to do to a printer.

Compare printer permissions to the permissions of a Web server program, shown in Figure 3-15. A simple HTTP server only has two permissions: allow access or deny access.

The downside to applying permissions to user accounts is that users and their permissions change over time. People quit, employees get promoted, customers leave, students graduate, and so on. Keeping up with the process of creating/deleting users and adding/changing permissions when people's situations change can be an administrative nightmare.

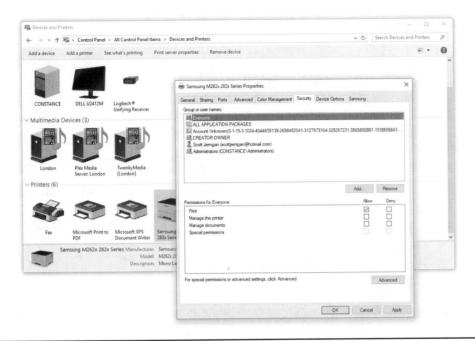

Figure 3-14 Printer permissions in Windows 10

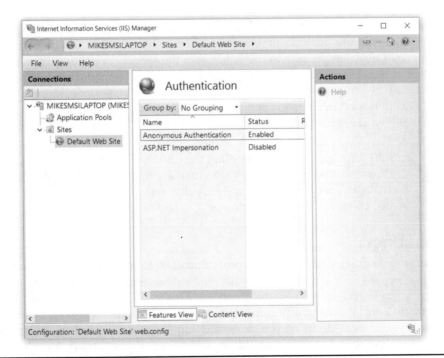

Figure 3-15 Web permissions in Internet Information Services

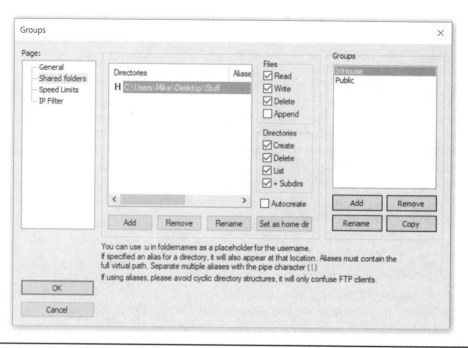

Figure 3-16   Groups in FileZilla

Groups streamline this process by organizing similar users into collections. Applying permissions to groups lowers administrative work. When a user needs permission changes, you can assign the user to the group with the appropriate permissions. Almost every type of authorization uses the idea of groups. Figure 3-16 shows group settings for FileZilla, an FTP server program.

Authorization goes deeper than simply users, groups, and permissions, but this level of detail should suffice for now. We'll dive deeper into authorization throughout this chapter.

NOTE   We touched on onboarding and offboarding policies way back in Chapter 1. Such policies can have a dramatic impact on organizations. That's why security staffs spend a lot of time analyzing and reviewing decommission and termination policies and procedures.

Accounting

Accounting or *auditing* enables security professionals to keep track of the accesses that take place on any given resource over time. Windows enables administrators to set audit policies on many aspects of the computer. Figure 3-17 shows the Local Security Policy snap-in on a standalone Windows 10 computer. Note the categories of audits in the background; the window on top shows auditing set to track failed logon attempts. Windows domain administrators would use the Group Policy Management Console (GPMC) to audit domain-level access to resources.

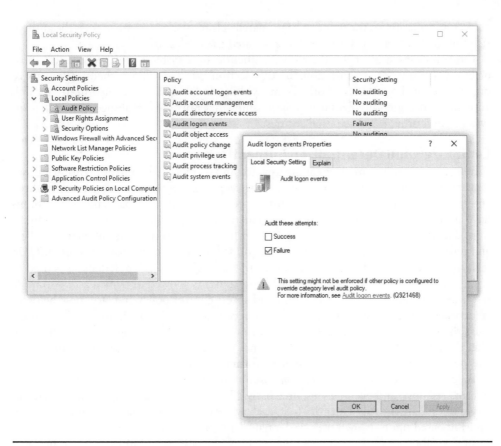

Figure 3-17 Local Security Policy snap-in

The technologies that support authentication, authorization, and accounting are known as AAA. We'll delve into these technologies in more detail in later chapters, but for now make sure you understand that accounting/auditing is very much a part of access management.

 EXAM TIP You can use Event Viewer in Windows to view logs of what you've set the computer or domain to audit. Pay attention to the wording of the question to know whether you're setting audit policy or viewing logs of audit events, then pick the right tool.

Trust

Access management builds on the concept of *trust* in several ways. First, the system must trust that the user presenting credentials is in fact the user represented by those credentials. Second, the system must trust the integrity of the user credentials database, in that the data is current and correct and the system is functioning normally and returns the correct information so the user can be validated. Third, the system must trust the authenticity of the hardware or software that generated the credentials.

Organizations must trust their own authentication systems and, sometimes, those of another entity or organization. In this section, we'll discuss authentication across organizational boundaries, both from within and outside an organization. This authentication often involves trust relationships that must be established between hosts, systems, and other organizational entities.

Centralized and Decentralized Authentication

When an organization manages all its user accounts, credentials, and authentication systems as one unified system, this is said to be *centralized authentication*. In a centralized enterprise authentication system, credentials are stored in one database and user accounts have uniform security policies and requirements that apply across the entire organization. The authentication system performs authentication services for all systems, data, and resources across the enterprise. Often, you will hear the term *single sign-on (SSO)* in relation to a centralized system; this means that a single set of user credentials is used to access resources across the enterprise. Whether a user is allowed or denied access to those resources depends on the authorization and access control policy in place, not the user's credentials in the authentication process. In a centralized model, all hosts and resources trust the central credentials database to take care of authenticating the user for them; after that, it's merely an issue of whether or not that user has the correct rights, privileges, and permissions to access a resource or perform an action.

By contrast, in a *decentralized authentication* model, authentication occurs on a per-system, per-host, and even per-resource basis. No centralized authentication mechanism serves to validate the user's identity first; each system or resource makes an authentication decision based upon its own user credentials database or access control list.

In a small office setting, for example, each user may be an administrator for her own workstation and have the ability to create accounts on that workstation. If another user wants to access a shared folder on another user's workstation, he would need a separate user name and password—on that workstation—just for that resource. It usually won't be the same user name and password he uses for his own workstation; even if an effort is made to duplicate these across workstations, both accounts still reside in separate databases on each workstation and are therefore not technically the same. If a password in one set of credentials changes, for example, this doesn't guarantee that the other set of credentials on the other workstation will be updated as well.

Decentralized systems do not trust each other's credentials database or authentication mechanisms; they require a user to authenticate using his own systems and credentials. Decentralized authentication also means that user account and password policies will be different as well.

Trusts and Federated Authentication

Outside of organizational boundaries, users must often be authenticated to systems within another organization's infrastructure. Examples of this include business partner relationships, where employees need to access documents in the partner company's network, or university students who must access an affiliate university's shared library resources.

In these examples, each organization may have its own centralized authentication system that trusts its own users and systems but not users outside the organization's boundaries. Two ways of allowing outside users to access resources internal to an organization, and authenticating those users, are though trust relationships and federated systems.

Authentication systems can establish a *trust relationship*, enabling users from each system to authenticate to the other's resources. The authentication system in one company, for instance, may trust the authentication decisions (and vice versa) of a partner company, allowing its users to access sensitive resources such as shared folders and files. Trusts can be one-way or two-way (bidirectional); two entities may trust each other's authentication systems, but the relationship can also be such that entity A trusts entity B's authentication systems and decisions, but the reverse is not true.

One variation on this trust relationship is called a *transitive trust*. In this type of trust relationship, there are more than two entities; if Company A trusts Company B's authentication systems, and Company B trusts Company C, then Company A may also trust Company C's systems by default. More often than not, though, trust relationships between entities must be explicitly established instead of defaulting to transitive trusts.

A *federated* system involves the use of a common authentication system and credentials database that multiple entities use and share. This ensures that a user's credentials in Company A would be acceptable in Company B and Company C, and only access permissions would be the determining factor in accessing systems and data. Windows Active Directory is a good example of a federated system in practice; user credentials from different domains could be used in other domains if they are all part of the same Active Directory forest.

 EXAM TIP   The CompTIA Security+ objectives refer to use of federated systems as *federation*.

Attestation

Strong MFA schemes can incorporate attestation into their authentication. *Attestation* assures that the hardware or software that created the authentication factors matches the standards and protocols it's supposed to use. Your key might look great, but was it made on a Cyclon RXP Key machine running genuine BluePart software? As you might expect, enabling attestation requires a lot more work and upkeep.

Module 3-2: Authentication Methods and Access Controls

This module covers the following CompTIA Security+ objectives:

- **2.4   Summarize authentication and authorization design concepts**
- **3.7   Given a scenario, implement identity and account management controls**
- **3.8   Given a scenario, implement authentication and authorization solutions**
- **5.3   Explain the importance of policies to organizational security**

Identity, authentication, and authorization enable secure access of resources, as you know from the previous module. This module explores the nuts and bolts involved in implementing these schemes. We'll start with authentication methods, explore biometrics, and finish with access control schemes employed in authorization.

Authentication Methods

Organizations need real-world methods, real-world mechanisms to identify, authenticate, and authorize. They need tools that verify the authentication factors (something you know, something you have, and something you are) you learned in Module 3-1. Let's explore the technologies used to implement authentication.

NOTE There are a lot of authentication methods, but the CompTIA Security+ objectives only cover a few of the most important and common ones. In addition, the exam goes into great detail on some of these methods, while barely touching others. To make sure we cover the exam objectives, some of the methods listed in this module (user name/password is a great example) get quite a bit more coverage later in the book.

User Name/Password

The user name/password combination has been around from the earliest days of authentication. You'd be hard-pressed to find an application or operating system that doesn't use user name/password as the primary authentication mechanism, from logging into a Linux system to connecting to a game server (Figure 3-18).

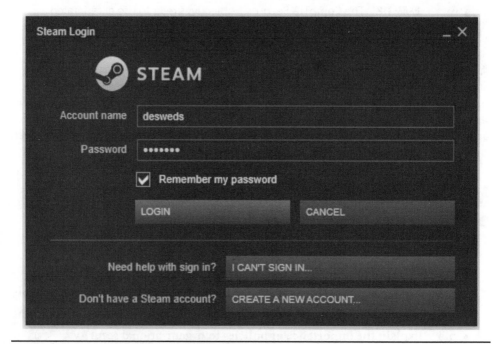

Figure 3-18   Author's Steam account login

Operating systems rely on user accounts, secured by user name and password, for basic file system security. The permissions associated with a user account say what that user can do with data stored on the system, such as adding, deleting, or taking ownership. User accounts are a fundamental authentication mechanism for every operating system.

Many applications likewise rely on user names and passwords for authentication. You can set up database programs, for example, to require an additional login before a user can access or manipulate data. Such fundamental database security begins with a user name and password.

User accounts, user names, and passwords are so important, both to the real world and to the CompTIA Security+ exam, that Module 3-3, "Account Management," is dedicated to user accounts, groups, permissions, and the many aspects of user name/password used for authentication and access control.

There's a good reason that just about everything turns to user name/password for authentication. User name/password is fast, it takes little storage on systems, it leans completely on the something you know authentication factor (so nothing to lose or accidently drop in a toilet), and possibly most importantly, people are used to entering user names/passwords for just about anything.

 EXAM TIP Expect a question on the CompTIA Security+ exam on *static codes* for authentication. These refer to personal identification numbers (PINs) that you use to log into a Microsoft account, for example, or to finish authenticating with an automated teller machine (ATM) at the bank. Most smartphones require a static code for login (i.e., authentication).

Password Vaults

Relying on user name and password for logging into a single system or application works well enough for many situations, but consider an all-too-familiar scenario where a user needs to log into multiple applications and keep track of multiple passwords. Although a lot of Web applications allow you to establish an identity and verify that identity using a Google or Facebook account that functions similar to single sign-on (discussed in Module 3-1), that's not always practical or desired.

Many organizations and individuals turn to applications called *password vaults* to retain all the passwords—or *password keys*—for you. A typical commercial password vault such as Bitwarden can store hundreds of discreet passwords securely. All you have to remember is your master key (and to make very certain it's robust). The downside to password vaults is that they need to be installed on individual systems and don't give you the ultimate in flexibility.

One-Time Passwords/Tokens

In any form of authentication, the best type of password is one that's used one time then never again. A *one-time password (OTP)* is generated and used only once, and it is never repeated. But how can two separate parties somehow magically know the same password if it's only to be used once and then thrown away?

The trick to using an OTP is there must be some type of independent, third-party, separate-from-the-two-sides-of-a-secure-communication tool that generates these passwords/keys in such a way that both sides of a communication trust the third party. This third-party password generator is known generically as a *token* or *token key*. Hardware tokens are physical devices such as a USB *security key* linked to a specific account and plugged into the client computer. Software tokens are applications that generate OTPs. Figure 3-19 shows a software token used for a *World of Warcraft* account.

People use the WoW authenticator for a specific game, but you can also use general *authentication applications* as a part of two-factor authentication at various Web sites. The https://login.gov Web site, for example, enables users to add one of various apps to their smart devices, such as Google Authenticator, Authy, LastPass, or 1Password, to create that second authentication factor.

Hardware and software tokens are great examples of one-time passwords in action. The OTP provided by a token is used in conjunction with another mechanism, such as a regular password, to provide better security in a multifactor environment.

Another example of one-time password use is during a secure communications session, where the secure protocols automatically generate a session key that is used only during that session. The session key could be considered a one-time password. *Diffie-Hellman Ephemeral (DHE)* keys are a great example of OTPs.

Figure 3-19
WoW software
token

Many security systems use standard communication methods to convey an OTP. Common systems send an OTP via *short message service (SMS)* to a smartphone, for example, or *push notifications* to a computer. Other systems make an automated voice *phone call* to verify and authenticate.

TOTP   A one-time password, like any password, is going to work whether you use it instantly or later, so it's important to give a time limit to any OTP you generate. Also, given that no date and time is ever the same, time is a great factor to help generate totally unique OTPs. A *time-based one-time password (TOTP)* uses time as a factor to assist in generating the OTP. In the previous example regarding a token, the TOTP changes very often, sometimes after only a few seconds. Therefore, it must keep its time synchronized exactly with the authentication database. If the user is even one or two seconds off from using the correct TOTP displayed on the token, authentication fails.

Normally, the user has a set number of seconds to input the correct password before it changes and another one must be used. This has many advantages, including the prevention of replay attacks. Another advantage is that it can be very difficult to predict TOTPs, based upon the time factor that is input into the algorithm used to create them. This can make it very difficult for an attacker to guess what TOTPs might be used.

Tokens are not the only devices that can use TOTPs. Google, using strong authentication practices, for example, may send a TOTP to a personal device, such as a smartphone, that you would be required to have in your possession during authentication. Your Google account may require you to input this TOTP within a certain amount of time, and after you receive a text message with the TOTP, you would input this password, usually a set of digits, into the corresponding field on the screen. You would then be authenticated and allowed to access your Google account. Figure 3-20 shows TOTP codes for different applications on a smartphone.

 EXAM TIP   The CompTIA Security+ exam may ask about using one-time passwords. OTPs typically are generated by tokens or mobile devices to facilitate multifactor authentication.

HOTP   One algorithm used to generate OTPs is the *HMAC-based one-time password (HOTP)* algorithm. If you recall from Chapter 2, the Hash-based Message Authentication Code (HMAC) provides for message authentication and data integrity. HMAC can use either MD5 or the SHA series of hashing algorithms and various key sizes. In the case of HOTP use, the user is authenticated against the centralized authentication database, and the authentication server calculates the HMAC value and sends it to the user via an authentication device such as a token. Several popular authentication mechanisms that use mobile devices, such as smartphones, make use of HOTP.

Certificate-Based Authentication

Asymmetric encryption, using the exchange of public keys, is a powerful authentication tool. The exchange of public keys, especially in the form of robust PKI certificates, makes a level of identification that's hard to beat (Figure 3-21).

Figure 3-20
TOTP codes from
a smartphone

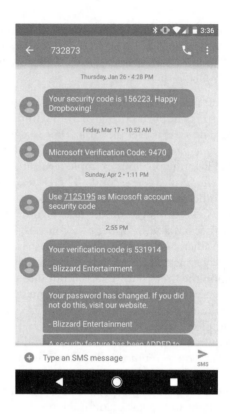

Figure 3-20
TOTP codes from
a smartphone

The challenge to using tools like certificates is that they are tricky to carry around for individuals. Since a certificate is nothing more than binary data, there needs to be a method for individuals to carry their certificates. In such a scenario, smart cards, PIV cards, and common access cards ride to the rescue for *certificate-based authentication*.

Smart Cards   Adding a storage chip to a standard credit card–sized plastic card creates a way for an individual to store personal information, a *smart card*. The term "smart card"

Figure 3-21
Certificate as an
identity tool

Figure 3-22
Smart card contacts

isn't a standard by itself, although a number of standards for data organization, physical dimensions, contact versus contactless, voltage, and so on fit under the term. Figure 3-22 shows a few examples of smart card–enabled credit cards. Note the slightly different contact types.

Smart cards can store any binary data, not just certificates. Some applications use smart cards that store symmetric keys, digital signatures, PINs, or personally identifiable information (PII). There is no law of physics or law of humans that says how you use a smart card or what is stored on that card. Two NIST documents—Special Publication 800-78-4 and FIPS 201-2—provide frameworks for the adoption, organization, and administration for smart cards.

NOTE The most common symmetric key type used on smart cards is 3DES; the most common asymmetric key type is RSA.

Personal Identity Verification Card Smart cards for authentication certainly predate the NIST's involvement, but there were no well-received standards. Almost anyone using smart cards up until the early 2000s used vendor-specific systems and, as you might imagine, there was little to no interoperability. The framework provided by Special Publication 800-78-4 and FIPS 201-2 and the subsequent adoption of that framework by civilian departments in the US federal government spurred the industry to create a single method to use smart cards for identity and authentication.

The result of these publications is the *Personal Identity Verification (PIV)* card. If you're a civilian and you work for or directly with the US federal government, you almost certainly have been issued a PIV card (Figure 3-23).

PIV card standards provide a wide range of interoperability, ease of administration, tremendous flexibility, and rock-solid access control. The PIV standard gives individual agencies quite a bit of leeway as to exactly what is stored on a PIV, but it gives very strict rules on how that data is stored if you choose to use it. This includes physical as well as electronic data. PIV cards must be constructed and printed to strict rules. Specific areas of the card are reserved for a head shot photo, expiration date, smart chip, and so forth (Figure 3-24).

Figure 3-23
PIV card

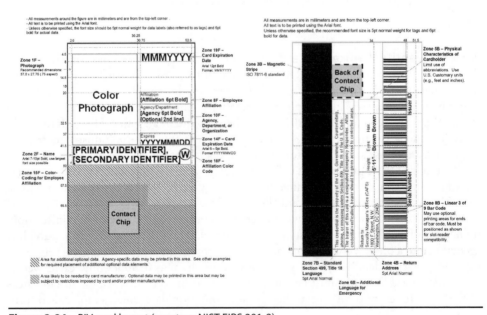

Figure 3-24   PIV card layout (courtesy NIST FIPS 201-2)

Common Access Card   The US Department of Defense has its own version of PIV card called the *common access card (CAC)*. CAC builds on the PIV standard, adding different versions for active military, civilian employees, contractors, and so on.

Biometrics

Biometrics use a person's physical characteristics (something you are—the *inherence factor*) to provide strong user identification and verification. The CompTIA Security+ exam objectives list numerous biometric factors, such as fingerprints, retina and iris patterns, voice patterns, and facial features. These physical characteristics are unique to every individual and are very difficult to mimic or fake. This makes biometric authentication an extremely secure form of authentication in theory, although sometimes the methods used to implement it are not as secure and can be circumvented. You should understand some terms and concepts in biometric authentication for the exam and as a security professional.

Fingerprints

Every person has unique fingerprints, making those swirls and lines perfect for biometric authentication. *Fingerprint scanners*, like the one shown in Figure 3-25, are common in many keyboards, laptops, and mobile devices.

Figure 3-25
Android finger-
print scanner

Figure 3-26
Retinal scanner
in *Half-Life* game

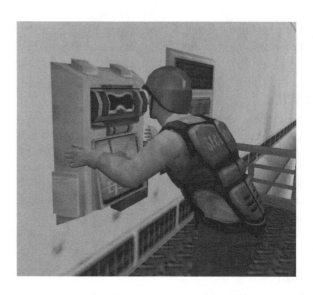

Retina/Iris Patterns

The human retina and iris have unique patterns that lend themselves to identification. *Retinal scanners* for access controls date back to the early 1990s, but their cost relegated them to extremely secure environments. They've made a huge impression in popular culture (Figure 3-26).

Improvements in camera resolution, computing power, and hardware pricing brought iris scanners into the forefront. *Iris scanners* are far more common than retinal scanners, while providing almost the same degree of accuracy (Figure 3-27).

Voice Recognition

Voice recognition for speech to text holds a strong niche for dictation. Most mobile devices—like smartphones—and personal assistant hardware use voice recognition tools such as Google Assistant, Amazon Alexa, and Apple Siri. But voice recognition as authentication hasn't gained any real acceptance due to its low accuracy compared to other biometric technologies.

Figure 3-27
Iris scanner

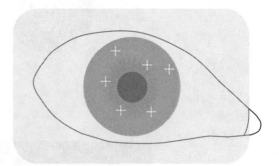

Figure 3-28   Windows Hello

NOTE   It's a lot easier to fake a person's voice than a person's iris pattern.

Facial Recognition

Facial recognition has become a popular and powerful authentication method for several applications. The Windows Hello API, built into every version of Windows 10, is a *facial recognition* tool (Figure 3-28). Most facial recognition tools require extra functionality, especially cameras that include infrared so the camera can differentiate between a real face and a photograph.

Vein Matching and Gait Analysis

Two biometric areas show promise in authentication, though they're not as widely implemented as the five physical characteristics previously discussed: vein matching and gait analysis. *Vein matching* uses the patterns of a person's blood vessels to identify that person. The patterns in the palm of the hand, for example, provide data 100 times more unique than fingerprints, can be scanned without touching the skin, and ignore damage to the skin. Vein-matching systems are in use in some hospital systems around the globe.

Gait analysis measures the unique way a person walks or runs by using machine vision–based tools—external cameras, in other words—or via the sensors built into existing smartphones. This latter technology shows a lot of promise, because it can tap into the accelerometer every current smartphone has to authenticate the user continuously.

The current systems only offer approximately 75 percent accuracy, so more work needs to be done, but gait analysis shows promise.

Biometric Efficacy Rates

Biometric systems are not foolproof. The efficacy rates of various systems depend on a lot of factors, such as error rates, security, privacy, user acceptance, and usability. The previous discussions of specific physical characteristics mentioned some of these factors, such as the difficulty of getting affordable and acceptable retinal scanners. Two other specific terms describe efficacy rates: false rejection rate and false acceptance rate.

The *false rejection rate*, or *FRR* (also known as a type I error), is the rate at which a biometric system erroneously rejects authorized users who should in fact be identified and authenticated as valid users. The *false acceptance rate*, or *FAR* (also known as a type II error), is the rate at which a biometric system erroneously identifies and authenticates unauthorized individuals as valid users. Both error rates can be dealt with by tuning the relative sensitivity of the biometric system in question; however, tuning it too much to reduce one type of error usually results in increasing the other type, so a trade-off is involved. This trade-off is usually tuned to the level of the *crossover error rate (CER)*, which is the point at which one error rate is reduced to the smallest point that does not result in an increase in the other error rate. Figure 3-29 illustrates this concept.

EXAM TIP   The CompTIA Security+ exam may ask questions about the difference between the false rejection rate and the false acceptance rate in biometrics. The FRR is the rate of errors from incorrectly rejecting authorized users. The FAR is the rate of errors from incorrectly authenticating unauthorized users. The crossover error rate (CER) is the point at which the system must be tuned to reduce both types of errors effectively without increasing either one of them.

Figure 3-29
The crossover error rate

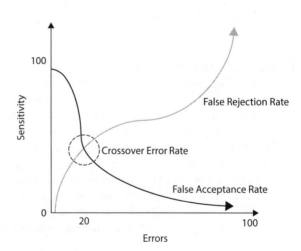

Authorization and Access Control Schemes/Models

Authentication verifies identity and lets a user in the door to access systems in an enterprise. Authorization determines what that user can do once she's inside. Access controls further refine what that user can do based on specific security policies. We talked about security policies in general way back in Chapter 1, but let's take it a step further now.

A familiar (and perhaps overused) example sets the scenario for this section: a bank. The Woodland Heights Community Bank serves the good people of Woodland Heights. Security policies determine which employees have access to information and assets of the bank. *Credential policies* define things like how personnel log into the network (password policies, for example), what kind of access third-party companies get, and how service accounts and administrator/root accounts are set up and given to people. Credential policies also apply to devices accessing the network, such as what remote Computer A can share with, store on, and back up to internal Server B.

Policies govern which people get access according to a set of rules. The bank tellers, for example, should be able to log into the main system and have access to client records. That way they can accept money and put it into the proper account, for example, and give money to verified users from the proper account. Bank tellers wouldn't have access to the security camera records; the security team and management would have that additional access. Management would have access to the vault with all the gold bullion, but additional controls would restrict and record their access too.

This process of determining who gets what is the basis for the *principle of least privilege*: only give access to people who need access; restrict access for those who do not. All of this leads to specific access controls that enforce the polices. And all of that is encompassed in the process of authorization. Got it? Enough preamble. Let's get to the meat (or tofu, depending on your preference).

The introduction of electronically stored data in the early days of computing compelled IT entities to start thinking about ways to organize access to ensure good security. Several entities developed access control schemes, but it wasn't until the US Department of Defense *Trusted Computer System Evaluation Criteria (TCSEC)* "Orange" book (Figure 3-30) that robust models emerged.

The TCSEC quantified several well-known access control schemes; over time, more have been added. Many access control schemes are used in the industry; the CompTIA Security+ exam objectives list several: mandatory access control, discretionary access control, role-based access control, rule-based access control, attribute-based access control, and conditional access. We'll tack physical access control on the end for completeness.

 NOTE The international *Common Criteria* standard replaced TCSEC way back in 2005. That was your history lesson for the day. All the access control schemes/models listed here apply.

Mandatory Access Control

Mandatory access control (MAC) applies to highly secure environments, such as defense or financial systems. With mandatory access control, a user is granted access to a system

Figure 3-30
TCSEC cover

or data based upon his security clearance level. Data is assigned different labels that designate its sensitivity and the security clearance required to access it. Administrators grant users, who also have security clearances assigned to their accounts, access to specific systems or data, based upon their need-to-know requirements. Even on the same system, users who have the requisite security clearances don't always get access to all of the data at the same clearance level. Each user's job requirements must also indicate a valid need to access the data. MAC models are typically either confidentiality or integrity models. A *confidentiality model* emphasizes protection against unauthorized access, and an *integrity model* emphasizes the need to protect all data from unauthorized modification.

Discretionary Access Control

Discretionary access control (DAC) is what most users encounter on a normal basis. Microsoft Windows, as well as macOS and Linux systems, typically use DAC in both standalone and network environments. With DAC, the user who has created or owns an object, such as a file or folder, has the discretion to assign permissions to that object as she sees fit. The file system, such as NTFS in Windows, provides the security to do such *filesystem permissions*. (Note that CompTIA removes the space, so *filesystem permissions*, rather than file-system permissions.) Administrator-level access isn't required to assign permissions; any user who creates or owns the resource can do so. Discretionary access control is a very flexible model, and users can assign rights, permissions, and privileges both to individuals and to groups of users, which can be logically created in the system based upon different functional or security needs.

 EXAM TIP The discretionary access control model is the only model that allows normal users to dictate who has permissions to objects such as files, folders, or other resources.

Role-Based Access Control

Role-based access control, on the surface, sounds like access control using groups, but this isn't necessarily the case. Although DAC models can be used to assign permissions, rights, and privileges to traditional groups, role-based access controls almost exclusively use predefined roles rather than groups or users. These predefined roles must already exist in the system, and users must be assigned to these roles to have the access levels granted to the roles.

A role-based access control model is *not* discretionary. The creator or owner of a resource cannot necessarily assign a user to a particular role simply to give him access. Normally an administrative-level user must assign a user to a role. Roles might include supervisory roles, administrative roles, management roles, or data change roles that have an increased level of access to systems, data, or other objects.

Rule-Based Access Control

Rule-based access control is a model that is rarely seen as a standalone type of access control model. It's typically integrated with other access control models, such as discretionary or mandatory access control. In rule-based access control, all accesses granted in the system are based upon predefined rules, which might include restrictions on when, how, where, and under what circumstances a user may access a system or resource. A rule, for example, may state that between the business hours of 8 A.M. and 11 A.M., only the accounting department may have write access to a particular database, but between 1 P.M. and 4 P.M., users in accounting, marketing, and production may have read and write access to the database.

Rules may apply to users or groups of users, and they may even specify the workstations that must be used, the type of permissions that apply to the resource, and so on. An example of rule-based access control is that used in more advanced firewalls, which lists a series of rules that users, network devices, hosts, and network traffic must meet in order to access other hosts and resources on the network.

Attribute-Based Access Control

All of the previous access control models share a user-centric attitude toward access. Users are important, but limiting. In the last few years a number of more granular, more powerful access control models have been adopted. The *attribute-based access control (ABAC)* model replaces users with attributes. While an attribute may be any form of identifying information, it's commonly divided into functional groups, such as subject attributes (name, clearance, department) or object attributes (data type, classification, color). We then connect policies to the access control. When someone wants to access data, ABAC uses preset rules that consider attributes and policies to make a decision about access.

Conditional Access

Conditional access policy means to grant specific users or groups access when certain (usually dire) conditions occur. A conditional access policy might apply in case cellular networks go down in an area and two-factor authentication becomes impossible. You'll see this sort of policy implemented in a lot of modern systems, especially cloud-based systems like Microsoft Azure. Azure offers various "as a service" offerings, such as platform as a service (PaaS), software as a service (SaaS), and infrastructure as a service (IaaS). Having aggressive policies in place to deal with catastrophic circumstances like floods and fires makes perfect sense when your product should be available to customers always.

Microsoft 365—as in Office 365, a powerful productivity suite of applications—offers a good example of a current security architecture that includes a layered approach and multiple controls. At the heart of the system is the data storage and configuration, controlled by administrators, *privileged accounts*. That heart is protected by what's called *privileged access management (PAM)*, a control to isolate or limit the affect a compromised privileged account can have on the overall system. Layered on that is conditional access. Layered on that is RBAC. In practice, this layered security protects the system from abuse and the users from loss.

Physical Access Control

Physical access control describes the mechanisms for admitting and denying user access to your space. This applies to doors, door locks, and facilities in general. More specifically, the term refers to the objects used to enable users to gain secure access. Smart cards, discussed previously, can function as physical access control mechanisms. *Proximity cards* rely on a different frequency, but function similarly. Another typical tool is a *key fob* (Figure 3-31). These are used at places like gyms that allow 24/7 access.

Module 3-3: Account Management

This module covers the following CompTIA Security+ objectives:

- **3.7   Given a scenario, implement identity and account management controls**
- **5.3   Explain the importance of policies to organizational security**

User accounts and passwords provide the bedrock of identity and account management control. This module explores user account types, issues with mingling accounts on a single machine, and managing permissions. We'll also analyze account policies and account administration best practices.

Figure 3-31   Key fob

User Accounts

User accounts provide a method to identify, authenticate, and authorize individual users to a resource. In a common scenario, you have some type of server software offering a resource and some type of client software trying to access that resource (see Figure 3-32).

 NOTE   Server software is not necessarily running on the same physical computer as the resource it shares, although it often does.

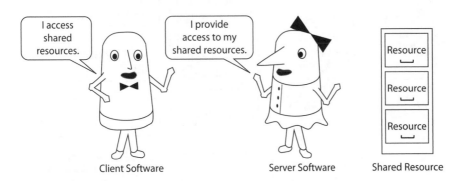

Figure 3-32   Client, server, and resource

Figure 3-33   Authenticating to a server

User accounts are data structures, usually stored on the serving system, that store two discrete features: a unique identifier (a user name) that identifies the user and a shared secret (a password) used to handle the authentication (Figure 3-33).

Assuming a successful login, the client authenticates and can access any resource the server allows. The server issues to the client software some form of access token. The server software uses the access token to handle the authorization, defining the permissions the user has to the shared resources via some form of access control list. Figure 3-34 shows an access control list as attributes assigned to each resource.

NOTE   In Windows, the access token is known as a *security identifier (SID)*.

Note that when you run a server offering shared resources, sometimes there are housekeeping or security issues—issues that have nothing to do with the resources

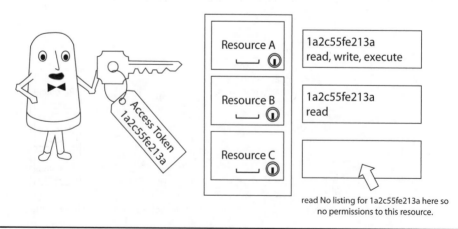

Figure 3-34   An access token handles authorization.

themselves, but rather the server as a whole—that you must deal with to support good authentication and authorization. For example, what if the server cares about the user's password length? We call these *rights* or *privileges*, and we'll see more of these shortly.

Account Types

Serving systems that employ user accounts organize their accounts into different types to help categorize their use and apply the principle of least privilege discussed back in Module 3-2. You should know these user account types: user, administrator/root, privileged, service, and guest.

User   The *user account* is created for and allocated to the people needing access to shared resources. In a perfect world, every individual needing access to resources has his or her own user account, although sometimes there are exceptions.

Administrator/Root   Every serving system, in particular every operating system, has an account that has complete power over the resource as well as the complete serving system. This super account is often automatically created when the OS is installed. In Windows this account is called *administrator* (often shortened to *admin*); in macOS and Linux/UNIX, this account is called *root*.

The admin/root account is powerful. It has complete and total access to all resources on the serving system. It has access to all permissions to the system. In general, avoid using these powerful accounts unless you are performing a job that requires them.

Privileged   A *privileged account* sits between a user account and an admin/root account. We generally create privileged accounts to delegate some aspect of system or account management. For example, an admin might assign the right to update software to a user account, making it privileged.

Service   In some cases individual processes, not actual people, need rights and/or permissions to a serving system. A backup program, for example, might need read access to any file on a computer to make a proper backup. In these cases we create (or the operating system automatically creates) *service accounts*.

 NOTE   Service accounts usually aren't held to password complexity or password changing controls, making them a vulnerability to protect. They're often overlooked or ignored and thus make a great entry point for bad guys.

Guest   *Guest accounts* have minimal rights and privileges, often used for temporary access to resources. In most cases guest accounts are premade by operating systems, and in almost every case they are disabled by default. Note the down arrow on the guest account in Figure 3-35 showing that it is disabled.

Mingling Accounts

Sometimes it's impossible or impractical to assign a single user account to every individual in your organization. Two important considerations in managing accounts are the use of multiple accounts, usually by one individual, and the use of shared accounts,

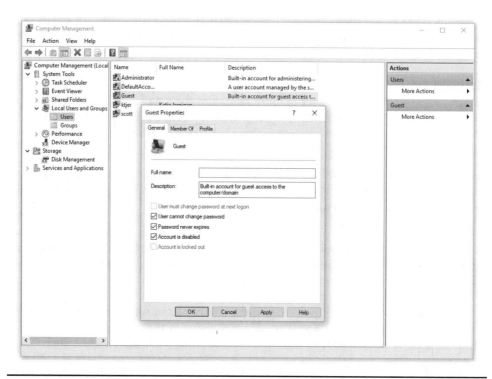

Figure 3-35   Disabled guest account on Windows 10 Professional

which may be used by multiple individuals. In some circumstances, the use of multiple user accounts, or even shared accounts, may be required. In these cases, we have to balance this functionality with security.

Multiple Accounts   Normal user accounts are allowed to perform typical user actions, such as editing documents, checking e-mail, and performing daily work. Higher-level account privileges on the host or network may be required by administrative-level or privileged users because of their duty or job position requirements. But if we assign the normal user account higher-level privileges, it increases the potential for bad things to happen. First, the user could routinely abuse his privileges. Second, if a malicious entity obtains the user's account and password, she could perform harmful actions using those elevated privileges. Finally, if the user is logged into the system with that privileged account, any malware or software that requires elevated user privileges can take advantage of that account, potentially taking harmful and sometimes unknown actions on the system.

The answer to this problem is through the controlled use of *multiple accounts*—in other words, a user would have a normal user account with lower-level privileges, plus a second user account with very specific higher-level privileges. The user would use her lower-level account to perform routine duties—actions such as accessing e-mail and files, editing documents, and other actions that require no special privileges. When the user needs to use higher-level privileges, such as creating accounts, installing devices, and updating software, she could authenticate to the privileged account and log out of the account when the action is complete. This way, the user restricts her use of the privileged account only to the times when it is needed, and she is not constantly authenticated as a privileged user. This reduces the attack surface on the system or network and the possibility of those privileges being abused. It also makes it easier to hold the user accountable for any actions performed using those higher-level privileges by auditing those accounts.

Some general rules for maintaining multiple accounts include the following:

- Use different login names, different passwords, and different permissions and privileges for both accounts.
- Different group assignments should be made for those accounts, plus a higher degree of auditing of their use.
- Users should not stay logged into the system using privileged accounts; they should be allowed to log into the accounts only when they need them.
- Users should have to follow a process of logging in and authenticating to the system with those accounts before they are allowed to use them.
- Users should be allowed to perform only certain actions while they are logged into those accounts and should be required to log out when they're done.
- Audit multiple accounts, particularly privileged ones, periodically to determine current needs and proper use. Too often, users can get a little lazy and stop using their "lesser" account. Regular audits should keep such misbehavior minimized.

Shared Accounts   In a *shared account*, several users can log in using the same user name and password for the account—in other words, several people can access the same account. You can quickly see how sharing accounts could cause issues with accountability and non-repudiation. If someone used that account to change file permissions, delete data, or even create another user account with elevated permissions, who would you trace the action to? The abuser could be anyone who has access to the account and knows its user name and password. Even strictly auditing the account would not tell you who used it (Figure 3-36).

Figure 3-36
Not me! Must have been the other User22!

Don't use shared accounts/credentials (referred to as *shared and generic accounts/ credentials* in CompTIA Security+ objective 3.7), period. They represent a gigantic security hole. Administrators can always take over in a pinch, so having multiple people able to access the same systems with the same account credentials is a poor security practice.

Although they should be avoided whenever possible, shared accounts should be carefully controlled if they are used. Anyone who has access to the shared account should be documented and briefed on its care and use. Some systems may allow a user to be logged in as a normal user and then authenticate to the shared account. In this case, the system may audit the use of the shared account, the time it is used, the actions performed with it, and the authenticating user, thus ensuring accountability. If the system does not have this capability, users should have to log their use of a shared account manually, as well as what actions they took while using it. These manual and system logs should be scrutinized carefully and often to make sure that people are using the account for its intended purpose, and securely.

 EXAM TIP   Shared and generic accounts/credentials should be used as minimally as possible. When their use is absolutely required, shared accounts must be documented, audited, and carefully controlled.

Managing Permissions and Rights with User Accounts

Permissions and rights are generally assigned on an individual basis to user accounts or to logical groups that have been created for common functional and security needs. We'll look at both methods and discuss the need to review and monitor privileges periodically to ensure that they're being used appropriately.

The principle of *least privilege*, as you'll recall from Module 3-2, guides policies about account permissions and rights, meaning that administrators never give a user account more rights and permissions—the least amount of privilege—than is needed for the user to do his or her job. A great example of a least privilege policy is *time-based logins* to make sure that users have access to their systems only during the times they should be at their machines. There's no reason for Penny in Accounting to have access to her system at 2 A.M. on a Sunday morning (unless Penny works strange hours)!

User-Assigned Access Control
One of the reasons to create individual user accounts is that it enables administrators to assign the accounts specific rights and permissions. User accounts allow users to identify and authenticate themselves to the system, access and interact with resources, and perform their daily jobs. Set up properly, these accounts also enable administrators to trace the actions performed by the user account to the physical user. When a user requires access to a system or resource, an administrator assigns specific privileges to her user account. When that user requires access to yet another resource, the administrator assigns her even more privileges. At some point, the user may no longer require access to certain resources or privileges to perform actions on the system. When that happens, the administrator can also reduce the user's privileges or revoke certain permissions.

These types of actions occur daily with most user accounts in large organizations. You'll find, however, that many user accounts have common functional needs and security requirements. Managing permissions on an individual user account basis can be inefficient and difficult. Although certain user account permissions need to be administered on an individual basis, the preferred way of managing permissions is by assigning them to groups, discussed next.

Group-Based Access Control   On a system, a *group* is a logical collection of user accounts that have common functions, access, and/or security needs. The most efficient way to assign user rights and permissions is to assign them to groups. This allows the appropriate privileges to be assigned to the entire group of users only once, rather than assigning privileges to individual user accounts each time new users require the same privileges (Figure 3-37).

User accounts can be placed in and removed from groups easily. You can assign user accounts to multiple groups to reflect different functional and security needs.

One disadvantage to group-based privileges is that a user account may be placed in a group and eventually forgotten about. Later, if the organization does not want a user to have certain privileges, an admin examining the individual user account wouldn't see the group privileges there. Another disadvantage is that group privileges are often cumulative. For example, if a user is assigned to the administrators group, he usually has elevated privileges. If he is assigned to a functional group as well, such as accounting or marketing, he may use his administrative-level privileges to affect certain transactions that are not authorized.

Group membership should be examined closely, as well as cumulative permissions and the continuing need to have them. Reviewing privilege requirements and continuously monitoring them is important.

NOTE   Use groups to assign user rights and permissions to resources whenever possible. This makes the process much more efficient and secure.

Figure 3-37
Groups assign permissions to users with common functions.

Account Policies

Organizations develop and implement *account policies* to ensure uniformly created and maintained accounts. Network administrators apply technical policy settings within the system to implement the written account policy for the organization. For example, Windows has several account policy settings that you can use to enforce certain restrictions on user accounts. The following sections explore different aspects of *account policy enforcement*, including password policies, and circumstances that may require user accounts to be locked out or disabled. Figure 3-38 shows some of the technical policy settings in Windows used to manage accounts.

 EXAM TIP Policies that determine what a user account can do in a system are also referred to as *access policies*.

Password Length and Complexity

Every security professional harps on the need to have strong passwords. But what makes up a strong password? In the early days of computers and the Internet, people used their dog's and children's names, birthdays, and other common, easy-to-remember things as

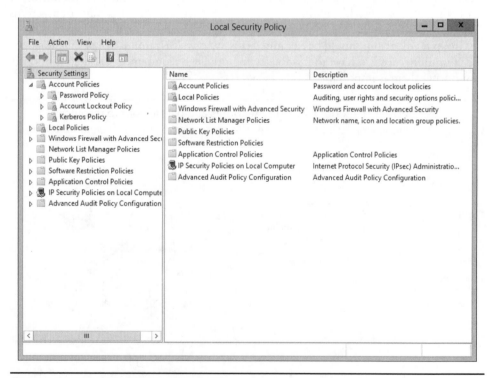

Figure 3-38 Windows Server security policies

Figure 3-39
Fido, good boy!

passwords. Passwords were usually very short, five or six letters at best, and normally made up of letters of the alphabet (Figure 3-39).

As malicious hackers came on the scene, however, they quickly learned to guess and defeat passwords using simple mathematics (since short passwords did not yield a lot of different combinations to try) or by guessing the users' passwords by learning different characteristics about them and their personal lives (Figure 3-40).

Best practice avoids the use of simple user names and passwords for identification and authentication, but most folks don't practice . . . *best*. Although businesses and government agencies use multifactor methods such as smart cards, PINs, and biometrics, the average user (business users included) still relies on user name and password combinations in many of their applications (Figure 3-41). So security professionals still have to account for the possibility that passwords will be stolen and cracked by malicious entities. To make it harder for hackers to steal and crack passwords, create password construction rules that make password guessing and brute-forcing more difficult.

A password consists of several linear characters. Fewer characters means easy crackability. If, for example, the password was constructed of only numbers, then a four-character password would have only 10,000 possible combinations. This might seem difficult for a human to guess, but a computer could crack this password in seconds. Even if you added one more character, the password would have 100,000 possibilities—still very easy for a computer to figure out.

Figure 3-40
Simple pass-
words crack
easily.

Figure 3-41
Too easy

Today, the general rule is that the longer the password the better, because the different combinations of password possibilities makes it harder to crack. These days, most organizations recommend, and sometimes require, a password length of at least 14 to 20 characters. A computer can break even a password this long in a matter of minutes, however, if the password uses only numbers or letters. That's where complexity comes in.

Password complexity takes into account the number of character sets that can be used to construct a password. In a four-character password that uses only numbers, for each possible character, there are only 10 possibilities (digits 0–9). Add another character set, such as all lowercase letters of the alphabet, and the number of potential characters increases to 36 possibilities per character (digits 0–9 and lowercase alphabetic letters a–z). This increases the character space and the complexity of the password. A four-character password increases from 10,000 possible combinations to 1,679,616. Again, this sounds like an awful lot of combinations, and it would be very difficult for a human to crack this password in a reasonable amount of time (Figure 3-42). Computers can attempt thousands of combinations per second, however, so it wouldn't take long to crack a four-character password, even with this many combinations.

Adding additional character sets increases the number of password combinations. Rather than using only numbers and lowercase letters, most organizations require the use of uppercase letters and special characters. Ideally, users should construct *long* passwords that use at least one of *each* of those four character sets, preferably at least two of each. *Password length* fundamentally impacts security—the longer the better.

Figure 3-42
Better boy, Fido!

The more complex a password is, the less likely the user will be able to remember it, and that means he'll probably write it down; this is something to consider when requiring complex passwords. Users must be trained on how to develop secure passwords that they can remember without compromising them by writing them down. Many users find that constructing a password from an easily remembered phrase is a viable solution to this problem. I'm a military aviation fan, so one of my old passwords was Mikelikesthef14tomcatsapg-71radar. (Yes, I'm a serious nerd.)

Watch out for *keyboard walks*, the process of making a password by just moving up or down the keys on the keyboard. The password Mju7Nhy6Bgt% looks like a really complex password, for example, but watch the keyboard while you type it. It's a keyboard walk and every password cracker knows it.

EXAM TIP Password complexity consists of increased length and character sets. Both contribute to the character space (number of possible combinations) and a password's security.

Password Reuse and History

Essential account policies restrict password reuse and maintain a password history. It does no good to require users to change their password periodically if they revert to the same password they've used for years. A *password reuse* account policy restricts users from reusing the same password frequently. For example, setting a password reuse policy to 10 would prevent users from using their last ten passwords, thus ensuring a fresh password.

TIP Good account policy restricts password reuse. Also, not on the exam, but worth noting is that good policies can restrict password *resemblance* as well as reuse. Edgar changes his password from An3wPWD4here1! to An3wPWD4here2! when required by the network policy. Is the new password a complex, long password? Yes, but it differs only one digit from his previous password. That's not good security!

The password history, which stores the user account's passwords for a certain number of password change cycles, helps enforce the password reuse policy. If the password history policy is set to 10, for example, the system would store the user's last ten passwords. Beyond this setting, the user can, of course, reuse a password, but setting stringent password aging requirements would prevent the user from reusing passwords for a period of time. If, for example, passwords are required to be changed every 90 days and the password history is set to 10, then the soonest a user could reuse a password would be 900 days. By that time, the user probably won't even remember the old passwords, so odds are an old password won't be reused. Figure 3-43 shows a Windows Server password policy management console that includes password history settings and complexity requirements.

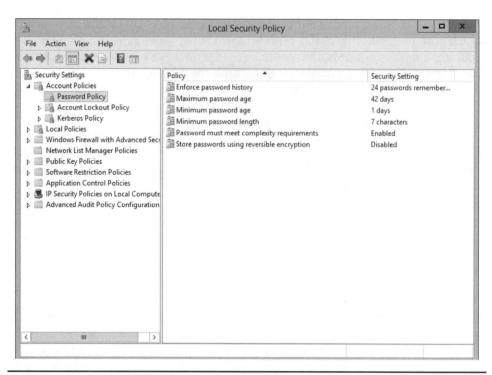

Figure 3-43 Managing password policies in Windows Server

Account and Password Expiration

Accounts and passwords shouldn't last forever; in fact, some accounts and passwords *should* be set to expire. Accounts for temporary workers, for example, could be set to expire after a predetermined period of time, such as 90 days. These accounts could be reviewed shortly before the time period expires to see if they are still needed.

Passwords, on the other hand, should be set to expire for everyone in the organization, to include administrators and even senior executives, because, over time, passwords could become cracked by malicious hackers, lost, or otherwise compromised. Password expiration shortens the amount of time that an attacker has to crack and use a password (Figure 3-44). Depending on password length and complexity, it can take an inordinate amount of time to crack. The idea is to make sure the passwords expire before they are cracked.

When the password is set to expire, the system should notify users a certain number of days (set by the system's account or password policy) ahead of time so that they have ample opportunity to change to a new password. If a user does not change her password within the allowed amount of time, her account should lock, so that she cannot use the account again until the password is changed. This forces the user to change her password, and when she again creates a new password, the expiration time for that password resets.

Figure 3-44
Drats, foiled
again!

Disabling Accounts

Administrators disable accounts temporarily for various reasons. The organization may not want to revoke, retire, or delete the account permanently, since the user may need it at a later date. Perhaps a user has repeatedly input an incorrect password—the system would automatically disable the account to prevent its compromise in case an attacker is attempting to brute-force the account. Or an administrator may temporarily disable an account when a user takes a vacation—or if he is under investigation for a crime involving the computer. The user may not be allowed to use the account during either of these two circumstances, so an administrator would manually disable the account until management determines that it can be re-enabled.

 EXAM TIP The CompTIA Security+ objectives use the term *disablement* to describe the process of disabling user accounts. It's all part of account policy enforcement, an essential aspect of IT security.

For whatever reason an account is disabled, it prevents its use for a set duration. An administrator must re-enable the account and should include a documented reason as to why she both disabled and re-enabled the account. It may be organizational policy to disable an account for a predetermined amount of time after a user has left the organization; in those cases, policies should also set a time after which the account will be permanently deleted.

 EXAM TIP *Disable* accounts temporarily whenever a user does not need access to the system. Don't permanently *delete* accounts until you determine that a user will never need access to the system again.

Account Lockout

Account *lockout* policies protect user accounts from being compromised. A typical policy disables an account after a number of incorrect password attempts, for example. The account can be locked for a predetermined period, such as an hour or two, or until an administrator manually re-enables the account. This prevents brute-force password attacks. Account lockouts also normally show up in audit logs and could alert the administrator to a potential attack—or, at a minimum, a user who has issues with his account or password. Most account lockout thresholds are set to a small number, usually between three and ten, sufficient to prevent a brute-force attack but forgiving of a user who may have simply forgotten or mistyped his password. Figure 3-45 illustrates the default lockout policy settings in Windows.

 EXAM TIP You should always set account lockout as part of your organization's account policies. Without account lockout, a malicious user could use brute-force techniques to guess a password and access an account.

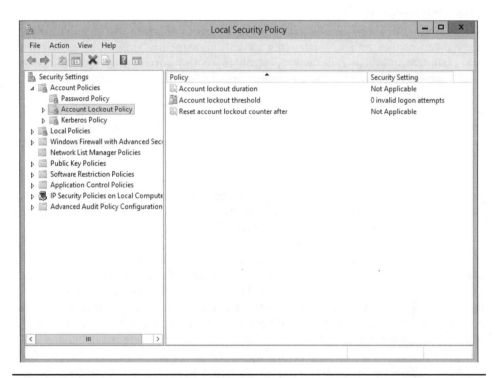

Figure 3-45 Default lockout policy settings in Windows

Figure 3-46
Maybe we should
just fire the guy?

Account and Password Recovery

Proper account policies incorporate account and password recovery. Account recovery policies should cover both disabled and deleted accounts. Password recovery generally applies only to forgotten passwords. Those people and their shoddy memories (Figure 3-46)!

Account recovery options vary a lot between disabled and deleted accounts. An administrator can easily re-enable a disabled account whenever management or policy dictates. A deleted account, whether by accident or by intent, offers challenging recovery options. Simply re-creating an account isn't the same thing as re-enabling it. Even if you were to re-create the account with the same user name, the *identifier* that the system uses for it will differ. The system uses identifiers to assign privileges and allow access to different areas of the system. Re-creating an account means that you've created a new account, so the user rights and privileges used on the original account would not apply to the new account—you must reassign them from scratch.

NOTE In Windows, the account identifier is known as the *security identifier*, or *SID*. In UNIX- and Linux-based systems, account identifiers are known as *user identifiers*, or *UIDs*.

You can also recover an account by restoring part of the accounts database from a backup. This isn't always the preferred method, however, because it is difficult to restore only discrete pieces of the database pertaining to the user account. Typically, the entire database might have to be restored, which would also undo any other changes that were made since the account was lost or deleted.

Password recovery typically occurs only if the password has been stored somewhere offline, such as in a secure file or container. Often, organizations will record highly sensitive passwords for system services or critical personnel and store them in secured and encrypted files or in a secure container, such as a safe, for example. If passwords have not been stored offline, recovery could be difficult if a system goes down. Some older systems might store passwords in plaintext, which is highly undesirable, but it might make passwords easier to recover. The best way to "restore" a password is to create a new one, especially with a lost or potentially compromised password.

Location-Based and Time-Based Policies

The prevalence of accessing e-mail on smartphones has led to security policies based on the *network location* of devices. If an employee loses a company smartphone that's set up to receive and send e-mail messages, this presents a clear danger. Smartphones know where they are, for the most part, because of interaction with cell towers. Companies can implement policies that restrict features of smartphones, like e-mail, when the user goes outside a given geographic area. Or the policies can be set up to provide an automated notification about an unsafe location, such as when travelling abroad.

In addition to location-based policies, administrators often add *time-based login* policies as well, providing authentication that includes when a user should or could log in. John logs in successfully each morning at the office at 8:00 A.M., Monday through Friday. Policy determines that he should not log in at 6:00 A.M. during the week, for example, nor at 8:00 A.M. on the weekend.

Anomaly Detection Policy

Implementing a system based on Microsoft Azure Active Directory, a cloud-based network solution, provides a typical scenario for account policies. Many of the network assets are remote rather than local and thus add a dimension to the account policies beyond a locally based network. Microsoft Cloud App Security offers specific policy options that apply to their Azure AD system, such as anomaly detection policies.

Fully automated, these policy options include such gems as *impossible travel time*, *risky login*, and *activity rate monitoring*. After a user logs off from Azure AD at a specific physical location and time, the system can detect if that user attempts to log in at another physical location that is sufficiently distant to represent an impossible travel time from the location of the previous logout. Erin can't log off her work computer in Houston, Texas, at 5:00 P.M., for example, and then log into her work computer remotely at 5:30 P.M. from Dallas, Texas. The system is smart enough to recognize VPN logins, which reduces the number of false positives. A positive detection triggers a security alert so that administrators can take appropriate action.

A risky login reflects a risky IP address, generally from an unknown or suspect location. Erin logs off from her remote connection in Houston on Friday night. She logs in on Monday from an IP address that's in Brazil, and the system has no clue if she's on a business trip or somebody hacked her account. Security alerts are triggered and administrators can take appropriate action.

Microsoft Cloud App Security policies dictate the degree to which unusual activity gets flagged. This activity can include all sorts of things, from unusually high downloads to excessive file sharing or file deletion. The system will trigger an alert, and administrators can take appropriate action.

The cool part about policy systems like Microsoft Cloud App Security is that administrators can fine-tune them to work accurately for their network needs. All of the policies can and should be tweaked over time.

Account Administration

The typical network administrator has common repetitive tasks that affect company security. Policies determine how to handle most of these tasks. Let's look at onboarding/ offboarding, user audits and reviews, and continuous monitoring.

Onboarding/Offboarding

Policies on onboarding and offboarding of personnel apply explicitly to the status of the user account. We touched on these back in Module 1-7, but they're worth putting into context here. During the onboarding process, a new employee should have a new account created, using some form of standard naming convention to enable ease of use by everyone.

 NOTE Failure to use a standard naming convention is the bane of small businesses that start to grow. Even tiny companies should always pick a standard naming convention for all user names and stick to it.

Offboarding is even trickier. When an employee separates, administrators do not typically delete the user account. Instead, they reset the user account with a new password used only by the administrator and the account is disabled for a set amount of time. This makes data recovery easy.

Account Audits and Review

Network administrators should periodically audit access to systems and resources for several reasons. First, compliance with any organizational access control policy may require periodic review. Second, users often are transferred within an organization, they may be hired or terminated, or they may be promoted or demoted. In all of those cases, users likely don't require the same access to systems and data. Unfortunately, if access is not reviewed on a periodic basis, users may move around within the organization and retain privileges even when they no longer need them. This is a problem commonly called *privilege creep*, and it violates the principle of least privilege.

The best way to perform these *account audits* is by looking at two very specific areas: *account permissions* auditing and review and usage auditing and review. What permissions does the user account have across all shared resources? What resources is he actually using (usage audit)? Is he using all he has? Does he have too many permissions due to privilege creep? Here is where the administrator makes changes to rights and permissions to stick with least privilege. This audit process is an essential part of *account maintenance*, the collective procedures to make sure users have access to what they need over time, with changing projects and responsibilities, and nothing else.

Some highly sensitive systems or data require periodic access reviews called *recertification* to ensure that unauthorized users have not been inadvertently given inappropriate permissions to sensitive data. Access reviews involve reviewing audit logs, object permissions, access control lists, and policies that specifically direct who should have access to systems and data and under what circumstances. That's another reason it's a good idea to document exactly who has access to sensitive systems and data and when that access will expire; it makes access reviews a great deal easier.

Continuous Monitoring

Continuous monitoring is a form of auditing that involves examining audit trails, such as logs and other documentation, to ensure accountability for actions any user performs. With continuous monitoring, administrators can continuously check to ensure that systems and data are being accessed properly and by authorized personnel. Monitoring may involve automated means or manual review of logs or documentation. In any event, administrators look for signs of improper access by unauthorized persons or unauthorized actions authorized people may take, such as unauthorized use of account privileges; use of accounts by unauthorized users; unauthorized creation, deletion, or modification of data; and so on.

Continuous monitoring enables administrators to be sure that users are performing only the authorized actions they are allowed to perform on the network. This supports the security concepts of authorization and non-repudiation, as well as accountability. Figure 3-47 shows the different options available for auditing in Windows, a necessary part of reviewing user access and continuous privilege monitoring.

 EXAM TIP The organization should review the need for higher-level privileges on a frequent basis and continually monitor the use of those privileges. This ensures accountability and prevents security incidents from occurring.

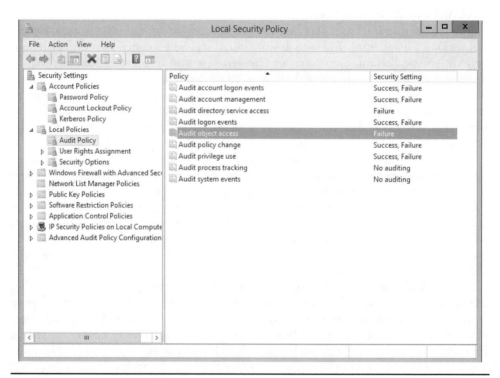

Figure 3-47 Audit Policy settings in Windows

Module 3-4: Point-to-Point Authentication

This module covers the following CompTIA Security+ objective:

- **3.8   Given a scenario, implement authentication and authorization solutions**

Now that this chapter has covered most of the critical concepts of access management, it's time to move from the theoretical into the practical. This module looks at the protocols and methods that enable a client to access a server securely.

The best place to start this is at the beginning of the Internet; a time when cable modems, cellular WANs, and fiber to the premises weren't considered; a time when computers sat in your house, unconnected to any network. If you wanted to connect to the Internet, you had to make a remote connection from your computer to a remote server of an ISP that in turn connected to the Internet.

Back in the early 1990s, just about everyone had a physical telephone line. Using an analog modem and a telephone number, we could dial in to a system that was connected to the Internet, and then we were connected as well (Figure 3-48).

The protocol that made all this work was the *Point-to-Point Protocol (PPP)*. In essence, PPP turned a modem into a network interface card (NIC). The PPP client dialed up the remote PPP server and made a virtual Ethernet connection, just as if your computer at home was connected to the switch at the remote server's location. From here the PPP server would send out Dynamic Host Configuration Protocol (DHCP) requests just like a modern system does.

 NOTE   Point-to-point in this context means taking a single computer and making a single, one-to-one connection to a remote network. Don't confuse these remote connections with modern technologies such as virtual private networking. A VPN requires a system *already* on the Internet to make a private connection. A point-to-point connection means your client is not on any network.

The problem with PPP was that it was remote. A PPP server had a phone number that anyone could call and PPP servers weren't cheap, so PPP came with several authentication protocols. Three of these protocols—PAP, CHAP, and MS-CHAP—dominated and continue to dominate point-to-point authentication.

Figure 3-48
Ancient connec-
tion options

PAP

The *Password Authentication Protocol (PAP)* is the oldest authentication protocol used to pass user names and passwords to a central authentication server. PAP was usually seen with older dial-up remote connection methods and actually predates PPP. Unfortunately, PAP does not pass user names and passwords securely during authentication by default; this information is generally sent over the network in clear text, making it easily intercepted by someone using a network sniffer.

EXAM TIP The ancient and non-secure PAP has been deprecated. You should always use an authentication protocol that hashes or encrypts user credentials that travel across a network connection.

CHAP/MS-CHAP

The *Challenge-Handshake Authentication Protocol (CHAP)* is an Internet standard method (described in RFC 1994) of authenticating users or a host to a centralized authentication server. CHAP is an older protocol that replaced sending user name and password information over clear text, as non-secure implementations of PAP did. CHAP was primarily used over PPP connections, and it was the first of several different versions of challenge-response authentication protocols. In CHAP, the authentication server sends a challenge message to the user or host. The user inputs his password, and the system hashes the combination of the password and challenge together, using a one-way hash function. The host then sends this hashed response back to the authentication server. The authentication server, which knows the user's password, repeats the hashing process with the password and challenge and produces its own hash value. If the hash values match, then the authentication server knows that the user input the correct password and the user can be authenticated. If the hash values do not match, authentication fails. Figure 3-49 illustrates how this process works.

CHAP periodically reauthenticates clients during a session; this process uses a three-way handshake. CHAP can prevent replay attacks and also enables the user to authenticate without directly sending his password over non-secure network connections. Microsoft developed its own version of the CHAP protocol, MS-CHAP, and later MS-CHAP v2,

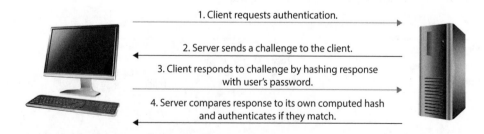

1. Client requests authentication.

2. Server sends a challenge to the client.

3. Client responds to challenge by hashing response with user's password.

4. Server compares response to its own computed hash and authenticates if they match.

Figure 3-49 The CHAP authentication process

which was used in earlier versions of Microsoft Windows. It is been all but deprecated on all recent versions of Windows in favor of more secure authentication mechanisms such as Kerberos.

 EXAM TIP CHAP relies on challenge and response messages and hashed passwords, as do other modern protocols. This ensures that passwords or other user credentials are never sent over the network in clear text.

Remote Access Connection and Authentication Services

This section explores various remote authentication services and protocols that enable external authorized users and hosts to authenticate into an internal network. These methods are normally used for older dial-up and Integrated Services Digital Network (ISDN) connections, but we'll also look at the two primary tunneling protocols that can provide remote access services for VPN connections—the subject of later modules, so we won't go much in depth here.

Authentication, authorization, and accounting (AAA) apply to functions performed by authentication services, such as remote authentication services. In this context, *authentication* and *authorization* mean the same thing, although there might be intermediary devices that provide certain related services rather than having a host authenticate directly with a centralized authentication server or database.

The accounting function, when used in the context of remote access, describes the process of accounting for connection time and billing functions, another throwback to the older days of dial-up, when users paid for their connection to an ISP by the minute or hour. These days, users typically connect via a broadband method that is "always on," such as DSL or cable modem. Although users are still charged for their service, it's typically on a flat-rate basis and not by the minute or hour. Still, the accounting function of remote access takes care of this aspect of the connection, including time of connection, the traffic that was used over the connection, and which hosts connected at which times to make use of the connection.

RADIUS

The *Remote Authentication Dial-In User Service (RADIUS)* protocol was originally developed to provide for remote connections through older dial-in services. RADIUS provides AAA services to clients and providers. It is a standardized Internet specification and falls under several different RFCs, including RFC 2865, RFC 2866, and others. A basic client/server protocol, RADIUS uses User Datagram Protocol (UDP) as its transport protocol on ports 1812 (for authentication and authorization) and 1813 (for accounting functions).

RADIUS has a few interesting terms you need to know. A *RADIUS client* is not the host attempting to connect; it is the network access server itself, to which remote hosts connect. This server is an intermediary that processes the connection request and passes it on to other servers, called *RADIUS servers*, which provide authentication services and can be either Windows or UNIX-based servers. Active Directory, in fact, can provide for authentication services to RADIUS clients, acting as a RADIUS server, through the Microsoft remote access and VPN services. In terms of security, though, RADIUS is a bit lacking. Although the communications between the RADIUS client and the RADIUS server are encrypted, communications between the RADIUS client and the remote host are not. Unfortunately, user name and password information could be intercepted between the remote host and the RADIUS client. RADIUS can support a variety of authentication methods, including some of the older ones, including PPP, PAP, and CHAP.

 EXAM TIP A RADIUS client is the network server that receives the connection request from the remote host and communicates with the RADIUS server. It is not the remote host itself.

Diameter

Diameter is an AAA protocol proposed to replace RADIUS. Its name is actually a pun and doesn't really stand for anything. It makes sport of the fact that the diameter of a circle is twice the radius. Diameter supports a wider variety of authentication protocols, including the Extensible Authentication Protocol (EAP). It uses TCP port 3868 instead of the UDP that RADIUS uses. It also can handle more advanced security using IPsec and Transport Layer Security (TLS).

 NOTE Module 7-1, "Networking with 802.11," covers wireless authentication protocols such as EAP and 802.1X in detail.

TACACS, XTACACS, and TACACS+

The *Terminal Access Controller Access Control System (TACACS)* supplanted RADIUS and allows a remote user to connect and authenticate to a network via an intermediary TACACS server. It works pretty much the same way as RADIUS, with a few exceptions. XTACACS, which stands for Extended TACACS, provides additional functionality for the TACACS protocol. It also separates the authentication, authorization, and accounting functions out into separate processes, even allowing them to be handled by separate servers and technologies. TACACS+ is a Cisco-designed version of the older TACACS protocol that enables newer, more secure authentication protocols to be used over it, such as Kerberos and EAP. It also permits two-factor authentication. It has become an open standard. Unlike the issues that plague RADIUS with encryption between the remote host and the RADIUS client, TACACS+ encrypts all traffic between all connection points, to include user names and passwords. Unfortunately, TACACS+ is not backward-compatible with the earlier versions of the protocol. TACACS uses TCP or UDP port 49 by default.

Module 3-5: Network Authentication

This module covers the following CompTIA Security+ objectives:

- **2.4   Summarize authentication and authorization design concepts**
- **3.1   Given a scenario, implement secure protocols**
- **3.8   Given a scenario, implement authentication and authorization solutions**

The point-to-point authentication methods described in the previous module are powerful tools for solutions to situations where a single client needs to authenticate to a single server acting as a gatekeeper to a larger network. Yet what do we do when we have many systems already connected on a single LAN? Unlike point-to-point, a client computer wanting to authenticate connects to many computers at all times (Figure 3-50).

Authentication on a LAN has serious issues that methods such as MS-CHAP or RADIUS simply do not or cannot address. Let's look at issues a LAN brings to access management and then look at the authentication methods and protocols used in most LANs to provide network authentication.

The Challenge of LAN Access Management

LANs change the concept of access management in a number of ways. First, LANs are much more permanent compared to most point-to-point connections. The desktop computer in your office, connected by a Gigabit Ethernet connection to your main switch, is probably going to spend a few years connected to your LAN. This means that the system needs some form of initial authentication to identify that computer to the network. Plus, you also need some method to authenticate *any* user who sits down in front of that computer to access network resources. Second, LANs are very fast compared to most

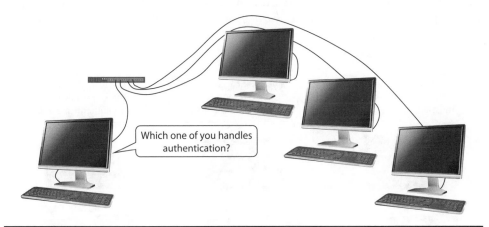

Figure 3-50   Network authentication is a different animal.

Figure 3-51
Network access
control must be
flexible.

point-to-point connections. If you are going to authenticate, you need fast protocols that allow systems to authenticate quickly. Third, most anything done on LANs is broadcast to every other computer on the broadcast domain, requiring authentication methods that allow for many systems to authenticate and authorize each other (Figure 3-51).

The permanency of LANs is motivation for a feature you don't see in point-to-point connections. With a LAN, the systems tend to be relatively fixed and permanent, but users tend to move around. This means that a good LAN access solution has the flexibility to enable any user to sit at any computer and authenticate themselves to the network as a whole.

The last and possibly biggest issue is the concept that any single system may offer shared resources to properly authenticated and authorized users on any system. This creates an issue in that every system on the network has its own authentication database, almost always user accounts/passwords. Unless something else is done, a user must authenticate to every system on the LAN individually (Figure 3-52).

Every computer on a LAN has an operating system that comes with networking tools for naming systems, sharing resources, and authenticating users. And every modern operating system can easily share files among each other. For sharing, for example, Windows, macOS, and Linux/UNIX use the *server message block (SMB)* protocol (also known generically as *Windows file sharing*), so all three operating system families can easily share (Figure 3-53).

Figure 3-52   In a LAN each system is an island.

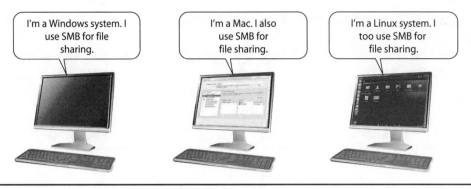

Figure 3-53 Everybody speaks Windows file sharing!

Each operating system also has tools for authentication, particularly for logging into Windows machines. Because Windows dominates the marketplace, Windows authentication methods loom large. The next section explores Windows authentication methods in detail.

Microsoft Networking

Microsoft networking has been around for a very long time and has gone through an incredible number of changes and iterations, but we can make a few straightforward breakdowns. First, all Windows systems are organized in one of two ways: workgroups or domains. In a workgroup, every Windows system stores local user names and passwords and controls access to its own resources. In a domain, all computers authenticate to a single authentication server known as a domain controller (Figure 3-54). A modern Windows domain stores far more than just user names and passwords. This more advanced, very powerful domain type is known commonly as Active Directory (AD).

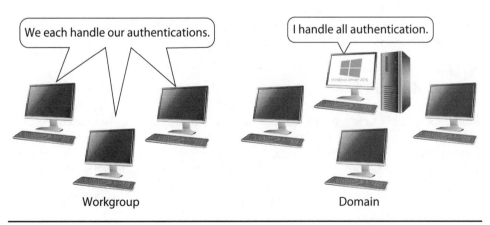

Figure 3-54 Workgroup vs. domain

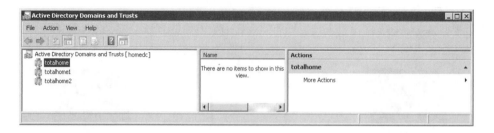

Figure 3-55 Windows Server domains

Every Windows computer on earth is a member of either a workgroup or a domain. Using workgroups is the default network organization and is very common in homes and small offices. In a workgroup, a user must have an account on every system from which they wish to access shared resources. A common way to get around this issue is to make the same account with the same password on every system. Domains require a system running special, powerful, and expensive Windows Server operating systems (Figure 3-55). Every computer on the network then goes through a special process of joining the domain. Once a computer joins the domain, it authenticates to the domain controller. A user can log onto any system in the domain and log onto the domain—the perfect example of single sign-on in action.

 NOTE Windows' domain single sign-on function is so popular that other operating systems will use Samba to enable individual systems to log onto a Windows domain controller even if they have no interest in sharing folders.

Workgroups and domains are very important in that Windows uses very different authentication methods depending on whether there is a workgroup or a domain. In a workgroup, Windows uses the very old, slightly vulnerable but easy to implement and backward-compatible NT LAN Manager (NTLM). Windows domain controllers use the powerful and robust Kerberos authentication protocol.

NTLM

Microsoft developed a series of proprietary authentication protocols early on during Windows development, and for the most part, they have been deprecated and are no longer included in new versions of the Windows operating system. You should be aware of them for the exam, however, and you may actually run into some of these from time to time in your professional career. The *LAN Manager (LANMAN)* protocol was developed and included in Microsoft Windows NT. Like any first attempt, it had weaknesses. For example, its hash-stored passwords are easily broken if they are obtained by an attacker. LANMAN was disabled by default starting in Windows Vista and shouldn't be used unless you're running legacy clients that require it.

New Technology LAN Manager (NTLM) was created by Microsoft to replace LANMAN and is backward-compatible with the older protocol. It's also a very non-secure protocol, and it was quickly replaced by NTLM version 2. Both versions are challenge-response authentication protocols and work similarly to CHAP. Version 2 is used in modern iterations of Windows, but only for workgroup authentication. Kerberos is the default authentication protocol for Windows domains (see the next section), but there are still times when NTLM v2 is used, even in domains. These instances include authenticating to a server using only an IP address, authenticating to a different AD network that has a legacy trust enabled, or authenticating a host to a non-AD domain. In these instances, Windows will default to using NTLM v2.

 EXAM TIP   Understand the situations in which Windows will default to using NTLM v2 instead of Kerberos for its authentication protocol. Usually this occurs where there is no AD environment and the host is communicating in a workgroup setup.

Kerberos

The *Kerberos* network authentication protocol is used in modern Active Directory implementations. It began as a project of the Massachusetts Institute of Technology (MIT) and has been implemented as a centralized, single sign-on authentication mechanism. It is an open standard, supported officially as an Internet standard by RFC 4120. As of this writing, the most current version of Kerberos widely in use is version 5.

Kerberos uses a system based on authentication tickets and time stamps that are issued to the authenticated user. Time stamps help prevent replay attacks because the tickets expire after a short time and must be refreshed, requiring that the user be reauthenticated and the ticket reissued. Kerberos's time stamps rely heavily on authoritative time sources throughout the network architecture, so many implementations also provide for a network time server.

Time synchronization is critical in Kerberos. A classic usage case is the "I can't log into my domain" problem. If clients are outside a certain tolerance for time difference with the Kerberos server, the users logging into those clients will not be authenticated. The default tolerance for time differences is 5 minutes in an Active Directory network, although this can be changed. Windows systems lean heavily on time synchronization and constantly keep their time synchronized with their domain controller.

Kerberos uses several components, which you should be familiar with for the exam. First is the *Kerberos Key Distribution Center (KDC)*, which is responsible for authenticating users and issuing session keys and tickets. In Active Directory implementations, the domain controller serves as the KDC. There is also an *Authentication Service (AS)* and a *Ticket-Granting Service (TGS)*. Although they are not required to be on the same host, these services frequently are, for simplicity and efficiency's sake, on AD domain controllers in a Windows environment and are part of the KDC implementation.

When a user logs into the system, the AS verifies her identity using the credentials stored in AD. The user is then issued a *Ticket-Granting Ticket (TGT)* by the AS, which can be used to access resources throughout the domain. The TGT expires after a certain

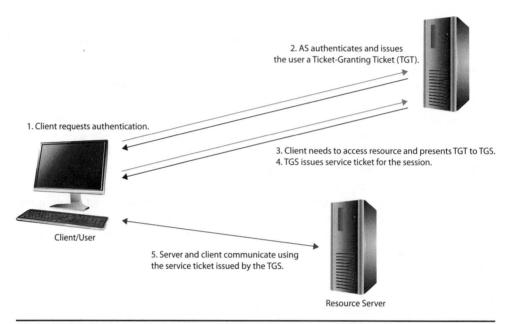

Figure 3-56   Kerberos process in Windows environments

amount of time, so it must be periodically reissued. When a user wants to access a resource in the domain, the TGT is presented to the TGS for authentication and the TGS generates a session key for the communications session between the user and the resource server. This is known as a *service ticket* and is used for the duration of the access to the resource. When a user later needs access to the same or a different resource, the older ticket is not reused and a new service ticket is generated.

Note that the process we've described is specific to Windows AD implementations of Kerberos, but the principles are the same regardless of what operating system and LDAP-based implementation are in use. A network that uses Kerberos as its authentication protocol is called a *Kerberos realm*. Kerberos uses both TCP and UDP ports 88, and it uses symmetric key cryptography. Figure 3-56 illustrates the Kerberos process in Windows AD.

LDAP and Secure LDAP

The power of modern Active Directory networks requires a language that allows different domain controllers to query each other's ADs. This is where LDAP comes into play. The *Lightweight Directory Access Protocol (LDAP)* isn't an authentication protocol; it's used to assist in allowing already authenticated users to browse and locate objects in a distributed network database (like a Windows AD spread out among two or more domain controllers). It's also used to facilitate authentication and authorization for these objects. LDAP is a modern replacement for older X.500 *directory services* protocols (used for authentication). Although the most popular iteration of LDAP (its current version is version 3) can be found in AD, other platforms use LDAP as well, including the popular OpenLDAP. LDAP uses both TCP and UDP ports 389. There is a secure version of LDAP that uses TCP port 636. It's primarily *Lightweight Directory Access Protocol over SSL (LDAPS)*, and it has been deprecated with LDAP version 2.

NOTE   Keep in mind that LDAP is not an authentication protocol, but it does facilitate authentication and resource access.

Module 3-6: Identity Management Systems

This module covers the following CompTIA Security+ objectives:

- **3.7   Given a scenario, implement identity and account management controls**
- **3.8   Given a scenario, implement authentication and authorization solutions**

Single sign-on (SSO) for network authentication has been around for a long time. We've already covered single sign-on in a LAN with Microsoft Windows domains as probably the best single example. As powerful as single sign-on is for LANs, it traditionally has never been used on the Internet. Anyone who has spent any amount of time bouncing from one secure Web site to another appreciates the hassle of remembering user names and passwords for every site.

With the proliferation of Internet services comes *password fatigue*, the user-based syndrome of "I have to set up yet another user account and password to remember for [insert name of new, must-have Web site] service too? Not again!" (Figure 3-57).

NOTE   In fairness, Windows' domain single sign-on can span multiple LANs, but it's not commonly used to secure public Web sites.

Figure 3-57
Many passwords
to memorize

The idea of one user name and password to rule them all has merits, certainly, but also opens a huge discussion about how to keep that identity secure. Plus, it requires understanding how to establish trusts such that a user can sign on to one site and in some way then transfer that authentication to other sites in a secure fashion. This module explores *identity management systems (IMSs)*, tools used to simplify secure access to multiple Internet-based services via single sign-on. We'll start with the physical, with security tokens, then look at shared authentication schemes. The module finishes with single sign-on options.

Trust

One of the great powers of a Windows domain SSO is the fact that there is always a domain controller (and maybe a few secondary domain controllers) that stores a single repository of users and their associated passwords. When you log onto a Windows domain, you log onto a domain controller. Once your user account authenticates, the different servers provide authorization to their resources via your Windows security identifier. Every computer on the domain trusts the domain controller.

Web sites have no domain controller to handle authentication. To make some form of IMS work for the most distributed of all networks, the Internet, requires trust. Every IMS begins by giving any Web site that wants to use it some way to trust someone big like Google, Facebook, or Twitter. The Web site treats the sign-in you use with a trusted big platform as an option or a replacement for your signing in at the Web site itself. The individual sites, however, still handle their own authorization (Figure 3-58).

In general, an IMS provides a connection to log into one of these big platforms and, in turn, provides a token that the little sites use. Module 3-2 touched on the concepts of tokens, physical objects that enable access to restricted areas or content. A *security token* in an online IMS can be a physical thing, like a smartphone, that contains authentication or password information. It might also be a bit of data that stores some form of descriptor for the authentication used. You see this sort of token manifest in game systems, for example, where you change something online and a message is sent to your smartphone. The change will go through only by entering the security code sent to the phone. The stored security information in security tokens is often hashed to prevent access in the event of theft or loss of the device.

Figure 3-58
This site has a lot of trust.

EXAM TIP The CompTIA Security+ exam objectives refer to security tokens as simply *tokens*.

Shared Authentication Schemes

Shared authentication schemes use various protocols, languages, and mechanisms to provide easier access to online resources for people. The two most prominent schemes are SAML and OpenID.

The *Security Assertion Markup Language (SAML)* provides a format for a client and server to exchange authentication and authorization data securely. SAML defines three roles for making this happen: principal, identity provider, and service provider. The client or user is often the *principal*. The principal wants something from the *service provider (SP)*, the latter often a Web service of some kind. The *identity provider (IdP)* contains information that can assure the SP that the principal is legitimately who he says he is. Systems using SAML can use any number of methods for authentication, including passwords and user names.

Many companies—big ones, like Amazon, Google, and Microsoft—use *OpenID* as an alternative to SAML, enabling users to log into other services using their respective credentials. Figure 3-59 shows a typical use of OpenID. The user accesses a new (to him) Web-based service and can log in using his Google account.

Figure 3-59
Sign in with
Google!

OpenID handles the authentication part of the identification process, but relies on *OAuth* for authorization. OAuth enables things like users granting information to Web sites without revealing their passwords.

Many SSO standards rely on SAML for secure communication between principals and SPs. The SSO standards differ from the previous standards in that the latter require additional use of the same user credentials. SSO standards do not.

The *Shibboleth* SSO system, for example, uses SAML (versions 1.3 and 2.0) to authenticate to various federations of organizations. As discussed in Module 3-1, federations enable content providers to provide content without retaining any personal information about clients or principals. This applies to Web-based systems as well as LAN- and domain-based systems.

Questions

1. Which of the following terms describes the process of allowing access to different resources?

   A. Authorization

   B. Authentication

   C. Accountability

   D. Identification

2. Which of the following states that users should be given only the level of access needed to perform their duties?

   A. Separation of duties

   B. Accountability

   C. Principle of least privilege

   D. Authorization

3. Which of the following access control models allows object creators and owners to assign permissions to users?

   A. Rule-based access control

   B. Discretionary access control

   C. Mandatory access control

   D. Role-based access control

4. An administrator wants to restrict access to a particular database based upon a stringent set of requirements. The organization is using a discretionary access control model. The database cannot be written to during a specified period when

transactions are being reconciled. What type of restriction might the administrator impose on access to the database?

A. Access restricted by the database owner

B. Access based upon membership in a logical group

C. Access from a particular workstation

D. Time-of-day and object permission restrictions

5. Which of the following allows a user to use one set of credentials throughout an enterprise?

A. TACACS

B. RADIUS

C. Single sign-on

D. TACACS+

6. Which of the following is used to prevent the reuse of passwords?

A. Account disablement

B. Account lockout

C. Password complexity

D. Password history

7. Which of the following are the best ways to ensure that user accounts are being used appropriately and securely? (Choose two.)

A. Periodically review assigned privileges.

B. Allow users to maintain their privileges indefinitely, even during promotion or transfer.

C. Continuously monitor accounts, through auditing, to ensure accountability and security.

D. Ensure that users' permissions stay cumulative, regardless of which group or job role they occupy.

8. Which of the following authentication factors would require that you input a piece of information from memory in addition to using a smart card?

A. Possession

B. Knowledge

C. Inherence

D. Temporal

9. You are implementing an authentication system for a new company. This is a small company, and the owner has requested that all users be able to create

accounts on their own individual workstations. You would like to explain to the owner that centralized authentication might be better to use. Which of the following are advantages of centralized authentication? (Choose two.)

A. Centralized security policies and account requirements.

B. Ability of individuals to set their own security requirements.

C. Ability to use single sign-on capabilities within the entire organization.

D. Requirements have different user names and passwords for each workstation and resource.

10. Under which of the following circumstances would a Windows host use Kerberos instead of NTLM v2 to authenticate users?

A. Authenticating to a server using only an IP address

B. Authenticating to a modern Windows Active Directory domain

C. Authenticating to a different Active Directory forest with legacy trusts enabled

D. Authenticating to a server in a Windows workgroup

Answers

1. **A.** Authorization describes the process of allowing access to different resources.

2. **C.** The principle of least privilege states that users should be given only the level of access needed to perform their duties.

3. **B.** The discretionary access control model allows object creators and owners to assign permissions to users.

4. **D.** The administrator would want to impose both a time-of-day and object permission restriction on users to prevent them from writing to the database during a specified time period.

5. **C.** Single sign-on allows a user to use one set of credentials throughout an enterprise to access various resources without having to reauthenticate with a different set of credentials.

6. **D.** The password history setting in the account policy is used to prevent the reuse of older passwords.

7. **A, C.** Periodic reviews and continuous monitoring are two ways to ensure that accounts and privileges are used in accordance with organizational policy and in a secure manner.

8. **B.** The knowledge factor would require that you input a piece of information, such as a password or PIN, from memory in addition to using a smart card.

9. **A, C.** Centralized system security policies as well as the ability to use single sign-on throughout the organization are two advantages of centralized authentication.

10. **B.** When authenticating to a modern Windows Active Directory domain, Windows uses Kerberos as its authentication protocol by default.

CHAPTER 4

Tools of the Trade

I have a thing for tools.

—Tim Allen

IT security professionals use a lot of tools to keep networks secure. These tools range from go-to utilities that run from the command-line interface of just about every operating system to more complex tools for scanning network activity. Security professionals spend a phenomenal amount of time setting up and monitoring logs of system activities so that when that bad actor steps in or some odd action occurs, they're ready to save the day.

This chapter explores essential IT security tools in four modules:

- Operating System Utilities
- Network Scanners
- Protocol Analyzers
- Monitoring Networks

Module 4-1: Operating System Utilities

This module covers the following CompTIA Security+ objectives:

- **3.7   Given a scenario, implement identity and account management controls**
- **4.1   Given a scenario, use the appropriate tool to assess organizational security**

Windows, macOS, and every Linux distro come with a host of tools for security professionals. The tools enable you to query network settings, explore routing options, diagnose connection problems, and much more. Built-in tools give you flexibility and availability—you need to know them.

This module covers many of the utilities included in Windows and UNIX/Linux systems. These utilities are listed in the CompTIA Security+ objectives and, more importantly, every good tech should recognize all of these as well as know where and when to use them (Figure 4-1).

Figure 4-1
We love utilities!

The CompTIA Security+ objectives break these tools into three groups (no doubt to keep the organization a bit easier): network reconnaissance and discovery, file manipulation, and shell and script environments.

Network Reconnaissance and Discovery

Sometimes you need to find out details about your system's network settings and how that system communicates with both your local network and extended network. Both Windows and Linux come with plenty of tools, many of them the same or nearly the same, to do exactly that job. Let's explore a dozen or so tools:

- ping
- ipconfig
- ifconfig
- ip
- arp
- netstat
- route
- netcat
- tracert/traceroute
- pathping
- TCPView
- PingPlotter
- nslookup
- dig

ping

The *ping* utility enables you to query another system on a TCP/IP network to determine connectivity. ping uses Internet Control Message Protocol (ICMP) packets at OSI Layer 3, Network, for queries. It's not a perfect tool, because many systems disable ICMP traffic to avoid attacks, but ping is quick and effective enough that you'll find it very useful.

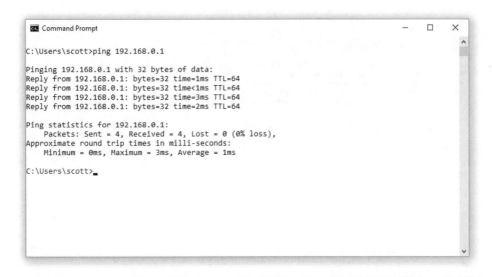

Figure 4-2   ping in Windows

When one system successfully pings another host, you automatically know that the other system is connected and is properly IP addressed. Figure 4-2 shows a successful ping running in a Windows terminal. We know it's successful because it shows replies from the pinged system (192.168.0.1).

By default, ping runs four times in Windows and stops automatically. In Linux, ping runs continuously until you press CTRL-C. To get ping to run continuously in Windows, use the –t switch.

The ping utility has uses beyond simply verifying connectivity. Running ping using a DNS name, for example, is a great way to verify you have a good DNS server. Look at Figure 4-3. Note that the ping is unsuccessful (shows *Destination port unreachable*), but the ping successfully resolves the DNS name (www.cheese.com) to an IP address (195.149.84.153).

The ping utility offers many more features that IT security professionals use all the time. Here's a list of some of the more useful switches:

- **–a** Resolve addresses to hostnames
- **–t** Run continuously
- **–f** Set Don't Fragment flag in packet (IPv4 only)
- **–4** Force using IPv4
- **–6** Force using IPv6

```
Command Prompt                                          —    □    ×

C:\Users\scott>ping www.cheese.com

Pinging www.cheese.com [195.149.84.153] with 32 bytes of data:
Reply from 195.149.84.244: Destination port unreachable.
Reply from 195.149.84.244: Destination port unreachable.
Reply from 195.149.84.244: Destination port unreachable.
Reply from 195.149.84.244: Destination port unreachable.

Ping statistics for 195.149.84.153:
    Packets: Sent = 4, Received = 4, Lost = 0 (0% loss),

C:\Users\scott>
```

Figure 4-3   ping resolving an IP address

 NOTE   Administrators disable ICMP—and thus, ping requests—for a variety of reasons, but most notably because people can use ping maliciously. The *ping of death* sends malformed packets to a computer, possibly causing a crash. Continuous ping requests—as a *denial-of-service* attack—can also crash systems. You'll see more about attacks such as these in Chapter 5.

ipconfig

Use the *ipconfig* command in Windows to show the current status of the network settings for a host system. Figure 4-4 shows sample output from ipconfig in Windows 10. You can see the various IPv6 addresses plus the IPv4 address and subnet mask. Typing **ipconfig** by itself also shows the default gateways.

Using switches enhances the ipconfig output; the following six switches are particularly useful. Typing **ipconfig /all**, for example, lists virtually every IP and Ethernet setting on the system.

- **/all**   Get exhaustive listing of virtually every IP and Ethernet setting
- **/release**   Release the DHCP IP address lease
- **/renew**   Renew the DHCP IP address lease
- **/flushdns**   Clear the host's DNS cache
- **/displaydns**   Display the host's DNS cache

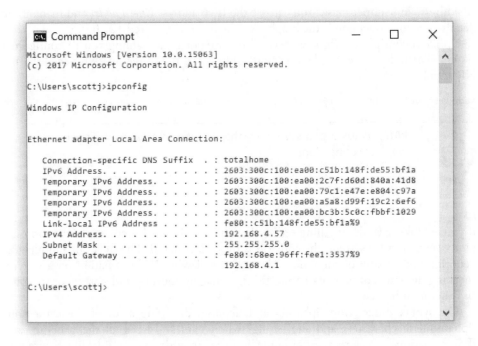

Figure 4-4 Results from running ipconfig

ifconfig

Use the *ifconfig* command in UNIX/Linux and macOS operating systems to show the current status of the network settings for a host system. Figure 4-5 shows ifconfig running in Ubuntu Linux. This shows a lot of configuration settings for the Ethernet connection (*enp0s3*), including the MAC address (*HWaddr*), IPv4 address (*inet addr*), broadcast

```
student@Student01: ~
student@Student01:~$ ifconfig
enp0s3    Link encap:Ethernet   HWaddr 08:00:27:85:17:1e
          inet addr:10.0.2.15  Bcast:10.0.2.255  Mask:255.255.255.0
          inet6 addr: fe80::4f34:ca79:e046:eb2a/64 Scope:Link
          UP BROADCAST RUNNING MULTICAST  MTU:1500  Metric:1
          RX packets:311085 errors:0 dropped:0 overruns:0 frame:0
          TX packets:66871 errors:0 dropped:0 overruns:0 carrier:0
          collisions:0 txqueuelen:1000
          RX bytes:381380061 (381.3 MB)  TX bytes:4634396 (4.6 MB)

lo        Link encap:Local Loopback
          inet addr:127.0.0.1  Mask:255.0.0.0
          inet6 addr: ::1/128 Scope:Host
          UP LOOPBACK RUNNING  MTU:65536  Metric:1
          RX packets:907 errors:0 dropped:0 overruns:0 frame:0
          TX packets:907 errors:0 dropped:0 overruns:0 carrier:0
          collisions:0 txqueuelen:1
          RX bytes:90729 (90.7 KB)  TX bytes:90729 (90.7 KB)
```

Figure 4-5 ifconfig in Ubuntu

IP address, and subnet mask. You can see the IPv6 address (*inet6 addr*) and many more details. The lo connection is the loopback, which is the expected 127.0.0.1.

Unlike ipconfig, ifconfig goes beyond basic reporting, enabling you to configure a system. The following example sets the IP address and the subnet mask for the Ethernet NIC eth0:

```
sudo ifconfig eth0 192.168.0.1 netmask 255.255.255.0
```

 NOTE   Linux systems also have the *iwconfig* command exclusively for wireless connections.

ip

If you're looking to do anything serious in terms of IP and Ethernet information on a Linux (not macOS) system, the cool kid is the *ip* command. The ip command replaces ifconfig, doing many of the same tasks, such as viewing IP information on a system, checking the status of network connections, managing routing, and starting or stopping an Ethernet interface.

The syntax differs from ipconfig and ifconfig, dropping a lot of the extra non-alphanumeric characters and shortening switch names. To see all the Ethernet and IP information for a system, for example, just type **ip addr** to get results like Figure 4-6.

You can see the loopback address (lo) for both IPv4 (127.0.0.1/8) and IPv6 (::1/128) and the IPv4 and IPv6 addresses assigned to the Ethernet port (eth0). Typing ip addr does not show the MAC address. For that you'd type **ip link**.

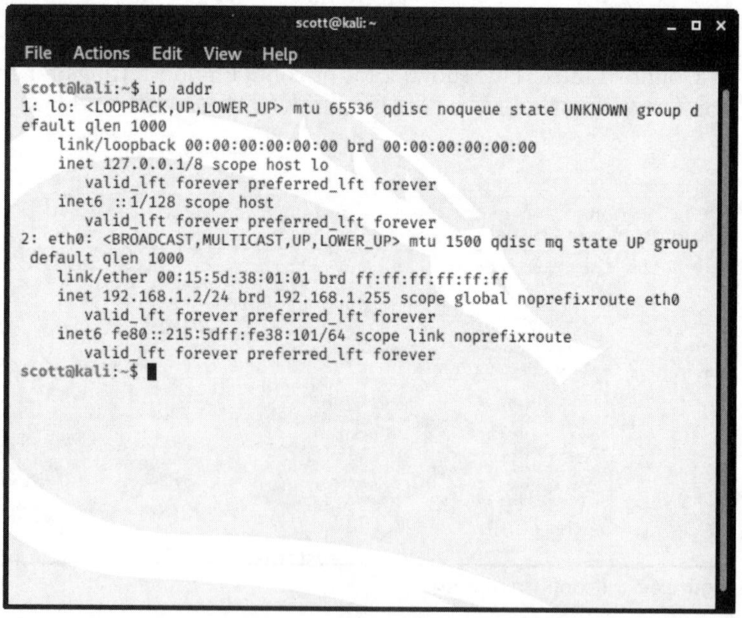

Figure 4-6
Running the command ip addr in Kali Linux

```
                              scott@kali: ~                    _ □ ✕
   File  Actions  Edit  View  Help
scott@kali:~$ ip addr
1: lo: <LOOPBACK,UP,LOWER_UP> mtu 65536 qdisc noqueue state UNKNOWN group d
efault qlen 1000
    link/loopback 00:00:00:00:00:00 brd 00:00:00:00:00:00
    inet 127.0.0.1/8 scope host lo
       valid_lft forever preferred_lft forever
    inet6 ::1/128 scope host
       valid_lft forever preferred_lft forever
2: eth0: <BROADCAST,MULTICAST,UP,LOWER_UP> mtu 1500 qdisc mq state UP group
 default qlen 1000
    link/ether 00:15:5d:38:01:01 brd ff:ff:ff:ff:ff:ff
    inet 192.168.1.2/24 brd 192.168.1.255 scope global noprefixroute eth0
       valid_lft forever preferred_lft forever
    inet6 fe80::215:5dff:fe38:101/64 scope link noprefixroute
       valid_lft forever preferred_lft forever
scott@kali:~$ ▮
```

arp

Every host on a network keeps a cache of mapped IPv4-to-Ethernet addresses for the local network. The *arp* command enables you to observe and administer this cache. Interestingly, both the Windows version and the Linux version use almost the same switches. If you want to see the current cache, type the command as follows (Windows version):

```
C:\>arp -a
Interface: 192.168.1.75 --- 0x2
  Internet Address      Physical Address     Type
  192.168.1.1           14-dd-a9-9b-03-90    dynamic
  192.168.1.58          88-de-a9-57-8c-f7    dynamic
  192.168.1.128         30-cd-a7-b6-ff-d0    dynamic
  192.168.1.255         ff-ff-ff-ff-ff-ff    static
  224.0.0.2             01-00-5e-00-00-02    static
  224.0.0.22            01-00-5e-00-00-16    static
  224.0.0.251           01-00-5e-00-00-fb    static
```

(Several output lines have been removed for brevity.)

The dynamic entries in the Type column show listings under control of DHCP. Static types are fixed (the multicast addresses that start with 224 never change) or are for statically assigned IP addresses.

NOTE The arp command is only for IPv4 addresses. IPv6 uses the Neighbor Discovery protocol.

The arp command enables detection of *ARP spoofing*, when a separate system uses the arp command to broadcast another host's IP address. Look carefully at this arp command's output and note that two systems have the same IP address:

```
C:\>arp -a
Interface: 192.168.1.75 --- 0x2
  Internet Address      Physical Address     Type
  192.168.1.1           14-dd-a9-9b-03-90    dynamic
  192.168.1.58          88-de-a9-57-8c-f7    dynamic
  192.168.1.58          23-1d-77-43-2c-9b    dynamic
```

Given that most operating systems return an error when this happens, you might think using arp isn't helpful. But arp at least provides the MAC address for the spoofing system, which might help you determine the offending system. (A lot of modern switches employ Dynamic ARP Inspection [DAI] to deal with ARP spoofing automatically, though that's beyond the discussion here.)

NOTE The arp command (lowercase) displays information on aspects of the system that use the Address Resolution Protocol (ARP). The mapped cache of IP-to-Ethernet addresses, for example, is the ARP cache. arp and other command-line utilities listed here are lowercase to reflect the case-sensitivity of UNIX/Linux systems.

netstat

The *netstat* command is the go-to tool in Windows and Linux to get any information you might need on the host system's TCP and UDP connections, status of all open and listening ports, and a few other items such as the host's routing table.

Typing **netstat** by itself shows all active connections between a host and other hosts:

```
C:\Users\Mike>netstat
Active Connections
   Proto  Local Address          Foreign Address                State
   TCP    127.0.0.1:5432         MiKESLAPTOP:50165              ESTABLISHED
   TCP    127.0.0.1:5432         MiKESLAPTOP:50168              ESTABLISHED
   TCP    127.0.0.1:5432         MiKESLAPTOP:50175              ESTABLISHED
```

You can see that the first few lines of any netstat show a number of active connections with the loopback address (the 127.*x.x.x*). These are used by Microsoft for several different information exchanges such as the Cortana voice recognition utility. Other connections show up as more varied IP addresses:

```
   TCP    192.168.1.75:57552     167.125.3.3:https              CLOSE_WAIT
   TCP    192.168.1.75:58620     msnbot-25-52-108-191:https     ESTABLISHED
   TCP    192.168.1.75:60435     61.55.223.14:33033             ESTABLISHED
   TCP    192.168.1.75:60444     92.190.216.63:12350            ESTABLISHED
   TCP    192.168.1.75:60457     42.122.162.208:https           ESTABLISHED
   TCP    192.168.1.75:60461     62.52.108.74:https             ESTABLISHED
   TCP    192.168.1.75:60466     a14-112-155-235:https          CLOSE_WAIT
   TCP    192.168.1.75:60537     65.55.223.12:40027             CLOSE_WAIT
```

The preceding netstat output shows the open connections on this system, mainly HTTPS connections for Web pages. In the State column on the right, ESTABLISHED identifies active connections and CLOSE_WAIT indicates connections that are closing.

Typing **netstat** in Linux gives the same information, but in a slightly different format. At the very bottom are the associated UNIX sockets. A socket is an endpoint for connections. This data is very long and not very useful. Figure 4-7 shows just the first few lines.

Typing **netstat –a** in Windows or Linux shows the same information as netstat alone, but adds listening ports. This is a very powerful tool for finding hidden servers or malware on a host. Look carefully at the following command. Notice that HTTP port 80 and HTTPS port 443 are listening. This instantly tells you that the host is an HTTP/HTTPS server. You must then answer the question: "Should this system be running a Web server?"

```
C:\Users\Mike>netstat -a
Active Connections
   Proto  Local Address          Foreign Address         State
   TCP    0.0.0.0:135            MiKESLAPTOP:0           LISTENING
   TCP    0.0.0.0:445            MiKESLAPTOP:0           LISTENING
   TCP    0.0.0.0:3780           MiKESLAPTOP:0           LISTENING
   TCP    127.0.0.1:9990         MiKESLAPTOP:0           LISTENING
   TCP    127.0.0.1:17600        MiKESLAPTOP:0           LISTENING
   TCP    192.168.1.75:80        MiKESLAPTOP:0           LISTENING
   TCP    192.168.1.75:443       MiKESLAPTOP:0           LISTENING
   TCP    192.168.1.75:6698      MiKESLAPTOP:0           LISTENING
   TCP    192.168.1.75:13958     MiKESLAPTOP:0           LISTENING
```

(Lines removed for brevity.)

```
mike@VirtualUbuntu:~$ sudo netstat
Active Internet connections (w/o servers)
Proto Recv-Q Send-Q Local Address          Foreign Address          State
tcp        0      0 10.0.2.15:39822         atl14s77-in-f4.1e:https  ESTABLISHED
tcp        0      0 10.0.2.15:35096         avocado.canonical.:http  ESTABLISHED
tcp        0      0 10.0.2.15:46080         dfw25s27-in-f14.1:https  TIME_WAIT
tcp        0      0 10.0.2.15:34910         dfw28s02-in-f3.1e:https  ESTABLISHED
tcp        0      0 10.0.2.15:47550    .    13.32.188.5:https        ESTABLISHED
tcp        0      0 10.0.2.15:38942         ec2-52-33-209-128:https  ESTABLISHED
tcp        0      0 10.0.2.15:45932         dfw25s27-in-f14.1e:http  ESTABLISHED
tcp        0      0 10.0.2.15:60528         dfw25s27-in-f3.1e:https  ESTABLISHED
tcp        0      0 10.0.2.15:39332         ec2-52-31-101-251:https  ESTABLISHED
tcp        0      0 10.0.2.15:47408         ec2-52-36-207-192:https  ESTABLISHED
tcp        0      0 10.0.2.15:41358         atl14s77-in-f4.1e1:http  ESTABLISHED
tcp        0      0 10.0.2.15:46082         dfw25s27-in-f14.1:https  ESTABLISHED
tcp        0      0 10.0.2.15:50714         dfw25s12-in-f46.1:https  ESTABLISHED
tcp        0      0 10.0.2.15:45204         ec2-52-34-28-127.:https  ESTABLISHED
tcp        0      0 10.0.2.15:53268         13.32.188.161:https      ESTABLISHED
tcp        0      0 10.0.2.15:35900         72.21.91.29:http         ESTABLISHED
tcp        0      0 10.0.2.15:45664         server-54-230-204:https  ESTABLISHED
Active UNIX domain sockets (w/o servers)
Proto RefCnt Flags       Type       State       I-Node   Path
unix  2      [ ]         DGRAM                  18094    /run/user/1000/systemd/notify
unix  17     [ ]         DGRAM                  10886    /run/systemd/journal/dev-log
unix  2      [ ]         DGRAM                  10887    /run/systemd/journal/syslog
unix  7      [ ]         DGRAM                  10800    /run/systemd/journal/socket
```

Figure 4-7   netstat in Linux

Running netstat with the –b option displays the executable file making the connection. Here's netstat running in Windows PowerShell (introduced later in this module) using both the –b and –a options (with many lines removed for brevity):

```
PS C:\WINDOWS\system32> netstat -a -b
Active Connections
  Proto  Local Address          Foreign Address          State
  TCP    0.0.0.0:135            MiKESLAPTOP:0            LISTENING
 [svchost.exe]
  TCP    0.0.0.0:80             MiKESLAPTOP:0            LISTENING
 [svchost.exe]
  TCP    0.0.0.0:17500          MiKESLAPTOP:0            LISTENING
 [Dropbox.exe]
  TCP    0.0.0.0:47984          MiKESLAPTOP:0            LISTENING
 [NvStreamNetworkService.exe]
  TCP    192.168.1.75:6698      MiKESLAPTOP:0            LISTENING
 [SkypeHost.exe]
  TCP    192.168.1.75:58620     msnbot-65-52-108-191:https  ESTABLISHED
 [Explorer.EXE]
  TCP    192.168.1.75:62789     msnbot-65-52-108-205:https  ESTABLISHED
 [OneDrive.exe]
```

Researching open ports and processes in netstat is nerve wracking. What are these programs? Why are they listening? A quick Web search of the filename often gives you excellent guidance as to which programs are good, which are evil, and which you simply don't need.

NOTE   The netstat command works perfectly well with IPv6.

netstat is an incredibly powerful tool, and this short description barely touched its capabilities. For the CompTIA Security+ exam, you should experiment with netstat both in Linux and in Windows.

route

The *route* command enables you to display and edit a host's routing table. Inspecting a routing table enables you to find problems if packets leave your system but never get a response. In Linux you type **route** to see the routing table; in Windows you type **route print**. Here's an example of this in Linux:

```
mike@mike-VirtualBox:~$ route
Kernel IP routing table
Destination     Gateway         Genmask         Flags Metric Ref    Use Iface
default         _gateway        0.0.0.0         UG    100    0        0 enp0s3
10.0.2.0        0.0.0.0         255.255.255.0   U     100    0        0 enp0s3
link-local      0.0.0.0         255.255.0.0     U     1000   0        0 enp0s3
```

The operating system automatically generates routing tables on individual hosts based on the network settings. So using route to display the routing table seems logical.

On the other hand, you can use route to make changes to the routing table for a variety of reasons. You could set up a static route for security purposes, for example, or remove a route to a specific host to force a secondary gateway.

 NOTE The route command rarely comes with Linux distros. Use the apt or rpm command to install the net-tools package, which includes plenty more than route as well.

netcat

netcat (or *nc*) is a terminal program for Linux that enables you to make any type of connection and see the results from a command line. With nc, you can connect to anything on any port number or you can make your system listen on a port number. Figure 4-8 shows nc connecting to a Web page.

The nc command is a primitive tool. To get any good information from the connection, the user must know the protocol well enough to type in properly formed input data. Since this is a Web page, type **get index.html HTTP/1.1**, as this is what the Web server is expecting. Figure 4-9 shows the result.

The challenge and the power of nc come from the fact that it's a tool for people who know how to type in the right commands, making it great for penetration testing or, if you're evil, hacking. Imagine making a connection to a server and typing in anything you want to try to fool the server into doing something it's not supposed to do!

```
mike@VirtualUbuntu:~$ nc -v www.google.com 80
Connection to www.google.com 80 port [tcp/http] succeeded!
```

Figure 4-8 Connecting to www.google.com with nc

```
mike@VirtualUbuntu:~$ nc -v www.google.com 80
Connection to www.google.com 80 port [tcp/http] succeeded!
GET / HTTP/1.1

HTTP/1.1 200 OK
Date: Tue, 06 Jun 2017 01:50:18 GMT
Expires: -1
Cache-Control: private, max-age=0
Content-Type: text/html; charset=ISO-8859-1
```

Figure 4-9 Successful connection to www.google.com with nc

The nc command even works as a handy scanning command. Find a server, guess on a port number, and try connecting! The nc command works perfectly with scripts. It's relatively easy to write a script that tries 1024 port numbers one after the other, automating the scanning process.

 NOTE   Windows lacks an equivalent to netcat, but Ncat from https://nmap .org/ncat/ has very similar functionality.

tracert/traceroute

If you want to know how packets are routed from a host to an endpoint, try the Windows *tracert* command. Linux can use the almost identical command called *traceroute* (although it's not installed by default on many distros, including Ubuntu).

Either command sends packets to each connection between the host and the endpoint, checking the time to live (TTL) between those connections. Running tracert returns something like this:

```
C:\>tracert www.robotmonkeybutler.com
Tracing route to www.robotmonkeybutler.com [64.98.145.30]
over a maximum of 30 hops:

  1     5 ms      9 ms      5 ms   192.168.4.1
  2     5 ms     18 ms     10 ms   10.120.17.101
  3    15 ms     14 ms     19 ms   ae201-sur04.airport.tx.houston.comcast.net
[68.85.253.229]
  4    14 ms     10 ms     17 ms   ae-0-sur03.airport.tx.houston.comcast.net
[68.85.247.29]
```

(Hops 5 through 12 removed for brevity.)

```
 13    71 ms     66 ms    179 ms   xe-0-10-0-3-5.r05.asbnva02.us.ce.gin.ntt.net
[130.94.195.234]
 14    63 ms     60 ms     69 ms   iar02-p3.ash.tucows.net [64.98.2.10]
 15    65 ms     68 ms     70 ms   csr-p6.ash.tucows.net [64.98.128.14]
 16    59 ms     58 ms     67 ms   url.hover.com [64.98.145.30]

Trace complete.
```

The power of tracert comes by running it before there are any problems. If you look at the previous example, you see the first two hops use a private IP address. This is correct, because this network has two routers between the host and the ISP—in this case, Comcast. Let's say we run this command again and get this result:

```
C:\>tracert www.robotmonkeybutler.com
Tracing route to www.robotmonkeybutler.com [64.98.145.30]
over a maximum of 30 hops:
  1      5 ms      9 ms      5 ms   192.168.4.1
  2      5 ms     18 ms     10 ms   10.120.17.101
  3    [10.120.17.101] reports: Destination host unreachable
```

The tracert successfully made it through both internal routers, but couldn't make it to the ISP. In this case we know there's something wrong between the gateway and the ISP. It could be that the ISP simply blocks ICMP packets (the protocol used with tracert in Windows). You can test this by running traceroute in Linux or macOS, which use UDP rather than ICMP by default.

pathping

pathping, a Windows-only utility, is an interesting combination of tracert and ping. pathping first runs a traceroute, but then pings each hop 100 times. All this pinging determines latency much more accurately than tracert does. Pathping is slower than tracert. The following example of pathping forces no DNS resolution and requires only IPv4 addresses.

```
C:\System32\pathping -n -4 www.ibm.com
Tracing route to user-att-108-66-144-0.e2874.dscx.akamaiedge.net [104.94.70.94]
over a maximum of 30 hops:
  0   172.18.13.117
  1   172.18.13.1
  2   104.186.12.1
  3      *         *         *
Computing statistics for 50 seconds...
                Source to Here   This Node/Link
Hop   RTT     Lost/Sent = Pct   Lost/Sent = Pct   Address
  0                                                172.18.13.117
                                  0/ 100 =   0%    |
  1     0ms     0/ 100 =   0%     0/ 100 =   0%    172.18.13.1
                                  0/ 100 =   0%    |
  2     1ms     0/ 100 =   0%     0/ 100 =   0%    104.186.12.1
Trace complete.
```

NOTE In Linux, try either the mtr command or tracepath command rather than the old and often not-even-installed traceroute. Neither tool is mentioned in the CompTIA Security+ SY0-601 objectives, but we think you'll find them useful.

TCPView and PingPlotter

Need something a little more graphical in your life? There are many interesting graphical tools that enable you to access these commands graphically. Graphical tools often

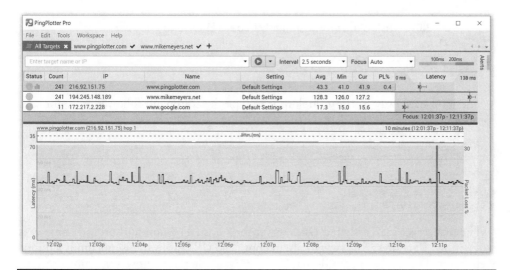

Figure 4-10   PingPlotter in action

provide easier-to-grasp information that the command-line tools lack. Finding netstat a little frustrating? Try *TCPView* from Windows Sysinternals instead of netstat. Or maybe replace boring old ping/traceroute with *PingPlotter* from Pingman Tools (Figure 4-10). There are a ton of great tools out there. Take your time, do some research, and find the ones you enjoy.

 NOTE   tracert is often a great way to determine the ISP just by looking at the router names.

DNS Tools

DNS security issues can create huge problems for IT security professionals. Techniques such as spoofing or replacing a host's DNS server settings give an attacker tremendous insight as to whom the host is communicating with. While there are multiple tools and techniques used to diagnose DNS issues, two built-in OS utilities can be very useful: nslookup and dig.

nslookup   The *nslookup* tool, built into both Windows and Linux, has one function: if you give nslookup a DNS server name or a DNS server's IP address, nslookup will query that DNS server and (assuming the DNS server is configured to respond) return incredibly detailed information about any DNS domain. For example, you can run nslookup to ask a DNS server for all the NS (name server) records for any domain.

This power of nslookup has been used for evil purposes. For that reason, almost no public DNS server supports nslookup anymore for anything but the simplest queries. But there are still good reasons to use nslookup.

NOTE nslookup works similarly in both Linux and Windows.

The most basic way to run nslookup is to type the command followed by a domain. For example:

```
C:\WINDOWS\system32>nslookup www.totalsem.com
Server:  cdns01.comcast.net
Address:  2001:558:feed::1
Non-authoritative answer:
Name:    www.totalsem.com
Address:  75.126.29.106
```

The first server is an assigned DNS server for a host. The non-authoritative answer is the returned IP address for www.totalsem.com. The URL www.totalsem.com is a public Web server. The totalsem.com domain has a private file server, however, named server1 .totalsem.com. If that URL is queried by nslookup the following happens:

```
C:\WINDOWS\system32>nslookup server1.totalsem.com
Server:  cdns01.comcast.net
Address:  2001:558:feed::1
*** cdns01.comcast.net can't find server1.totalsem.com: Non-existent domain
```

This is good. The authoritative DNS server is configured to protect this private server and therefore not respond to an nslookup query.

nslookup can tell you if an IP address is a functioning DNS server. Run nslookup interactively by typing **nslookup** to get a prompt:

```
C:\WINDOWS\system32>nslookup
Default Server:  cdns01.comcast.net
Address:  2001:558:feed::1
>
```

Then type in the IP address of the DNS server you want to check:

```
> server 8.8.8.8
Default Server:  google-public-dns-a.google.com
Address:  8.8.8.8
>
```

Note that it returns a DNS name. This means there is a reverse DNS zone; a very good sign, but still not proof. Let's make it resolve a known-good DNS name:

```
> www.totalsem.com
Server:  google-public-dns-a.google.com
Address:  8.8.8.8

Non-authoritative answer:
Name:    www.totalsem.com
Address:  75.126.29.106
>
```

But look at this alternate response:

```
DNS request timed out.
    timeout was 2 seconds.
*** Request to [4.7.3.4] timed-out
>
```

This could mean that the server IP address is not a functional DNS server. Or, at the very least, that the DNS service on this particular server isn't working.

dig   The *dig* command is a Linux-based DNS querying tool that offers many advantages over nslookup. dig works with the host's DNS settings, as opposed to nslookup, which ignores the host's DNS settings and makes queries based on the variables entered at the command line. dig also works well with scripting tools. The dig tool is unique to Linux, although you can find third-party Windows dig-like tools. dig is simple to use and provides excellent information with an easy-to-use interface. Figure 4-11 shows a basic dig query.

Try other dig options. For example, if you want to know all the mail server (MX) servers for a domain, just add the MX switch, as shown in Figure 4-12.

NOTE   The Linux *host* command isn't listed on the CompTIA Security+ objectives, but is a great tool and one of our favorites. Know nslookup and dig for the exam, but check out the host command too!

File Manipulation

Commands generate readable output. If you want to preserve output from a command for future reference, you can save the command output as a text file. In Linux, pretty

```
mike@VirtualUbuntu:~$ dig totalsem.com

; <<>> DiG 9.10.3-P4-Ubuntu <<>> totalsem.com
;; global options: +cmd
;; Got answer:
;; ->>HEADER<<- opcode: QUERY, status: NOERROR, id: 11252
;; flags: qr rd ra; QUERY: 1, ANSWER: 1, AUTHORITY: 0, ADDITIONAL: 1

;; OPT PSEUDOSECTION:
; EDNS: version: 0, flags:; udp: 1280
;; QUESTION SECTION:
;totalsem.com.                  IN      A

;; ANSWER SECTION:
totalsem.com.           1799    IN      A       75.126.29.106

;; Query time: 27 msec
;; SERVER: 127.0.1.1#53(127.0.1.1)
;; WHEN: Wed Jun 07 12:17:22 CDT 2017
;; MSG SIZE  rcvd: 57
```

Figure 4-11   Simple dig query

```
mike@VirtualUbuntu:~$ dig robotmonkeybutler.com MX

; <<>> DiG 9.10.3-P4-Ubuntu <<>> robotmonkeybutler.com MX
;; global options: +cmd
;; Got answer:
;; ->>HEADER<<- opcode: QUERY, status: NOERROR, id: 46722
;; flags: qr rd ra; QUERY: 1, ANSWER: 5, AUTHORITY: 0, ADDITIONAL: 9

;; OPT PSEUDOSECTION:
; EDNS: version: 0, flags:; udp: 1280
;; QUESTION SECTION:
;robotmonkeybutler.com.          IN      MX

;; ANSWER SECTION:
robotmonkeybutler.com.   900    IN      MX      10 ALT4.ASPMX.L.GOOGLE.com.
robotmonkeybutler.com.   900    IN      MX      1 ASPMX.L.GOOGLE.com.
robotmonkeybutler.com.   900    IN      MX      5 ALT1.ASPMX.L.GOOGLE.com.
robotmonkeybutler.com.   900    IN      MX      5 ALT2.ASPMX.L.GOOGLE.com.
robotmonkeybutler.com.   900    IN      MX      10 ALT3.ASPMX.L.GOOGLE.com.
```

Figure 4-12   Querying for MX records (output reduced for brevity)

much all log files (we're diving into log files later in Module 4-4) are text files that you can review, search, and edit. Several Linux utilities provide this capability: cat, chmod, grep, head, tail, and logger.

 NOTE   The CompTIA Security+ objectives don't mention several important commands that you should know as an IT security professional, such as sudo, ls, cd, cp, mv, and delete. Because of their practical importance as IT security tools, you should review them.

cat

The *cat* command enables you to combine—*concatenate*—files. Concatenate two files to the screen with the following command:

```
cat file1.txt file2.txt
```

To concatenate these same two files and create a new file, use the following command:

```
cat file1.txt file2.txt > file3.txt
```

The cat utility also enables you to view the contents of any text file. Just type **cat** followed by the text file you wish to see and it appears on the screen:

```
mike@mike-VirtualBox:~/Desktop$ cat onelinefile.txt
This is the one line in this file
```

The cat utility provides a quick, powerful, and versatile tool for working with text files from the command line. You can view log files, for example, and combine multiple logs. To search the log files, you can combine cat with grep (which is discussed shortly). cat is a go-to tool for Linux users.

NOTE   cat is a fine tool, but explore another tool for current systems (that's not on the exam) called *less*.

chmod

All files on a Linux system, including all log files and text files, have file permissions, or *modes*. File permissions are read (r), write (w), and execute (x). Type **ls -l** to see these permissions:

```
mike@mike-VirtualBox:~/Desktop$ ls -l
-rw-rw-r-- 1 mike mike 18626 Jul 11 16:09 file2.txt
-rw-rw-r-- 1 mike mike 18635 Jul 11 16:14 file3.txt
-rw-rw-r-- 1 mike mike     9 Jul 11 15:50 file.txt
-rwxrwxrwx 1 mike mike    31 Jul 11 16:42 program.bin
drwxrwxr-x 2 mike mike  4096 Jul 11 16:43 timmy
```

Examining this output from left to right, the first character determines the type of entry: a hyphen denotes a regular file and a d denotes a directory. You can see the file or directory name on the far right of each line. The first four lines show the permissions for regular files, and the last line shows the permissions for the directory named timmy.

Permissions are listed in three sets of three permissions each, all in a row. The first set shows the permissions for the owner/creator; the second set defines the group permissions; the third set describes permissions for everyone else, or *other* (Figure 4-13). If a set includes r, w, and x, it means all three of those permissions are assigned. A hyphen in place of a letter means that specific permission is *not* assigned. For example, the file2 .txt file in the previous ls -l output has read and write permissions assigned for the owner and group, but only read permission for other. No one has execute permission (probably because it really is just a text file!). The directory timmy, in contrast, shows read, write, and execute permissions for both the owner and the group, plus read and execute (but not write) for other.

The *chmod* command enables you to change permissions—or *change modes*—for a file or directory. A common way to edit these permissions is to give each set of three permissions a single numeric value between 0 and 7, representing the combined values of read (4), write (2), and execute (1). For example, if owner is assigned 0, owner has no

Figure 4-13
Linux permis-
sions

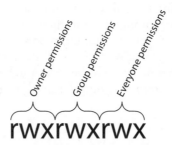

permissions for the file or directory; if assigned 7, owner has all three permissions. Using three numbers with chmod can set permissions for any file. Here are some examples:

- **chmod 777 <filename>** sets permissions to rwxrwxrwx
- **chmod 664 <filename>** sets permissions to rw-rw-r--
- **chmod 440 <filename>** sets permissions to r--r-----

Suppose you have a file called mikeconfig.pcap with the following permissions:

```
-rw-r----- 1 mike mike 18626 Sep 22 8:09 mikeconfig.pcap
```

If you wanted to give read and write permissions to everyone, you'd type this command:

```
chmod 666 mikeconfig.pcap
```

grep

Text files sometimes get large, making it challenging to find a specific bit of data in them you need. The *grep* command looks for search terms (strings) inside text files and returns any line of that text file containing the string you requested. To illustrate, here is a text file called database.txt that contains four lines of personal data:

```
mike@mike-VirtualBox:~$ cat database.txt
mike meyers 1313 mockingbird lane Houston TX
scott jernigan 555 garden oaks Houston TX
dave rush 1234 anytown Spring TX
nasa wissa 5343 space center blvd Clear Lake TX
```

Watch the following grep commands and see the result.

- Find the word "mike" in database.txt:

```
mike@mike-VirtualBox:~$ grep mike database.txt
mike meyers 1313 mockingbird lane Houston TX
```

- Find the phrase "dave rush" in database.txt and identify the line on which it is found:

```
mike@mike-VirtualBox:~$  grep -n "dave rush" database.txt
3:dave rush 1234 anytown Spring TX
```

The grep utility isn't limited to files. You can take any output to the terminal and then "pipe" the output through grep to filter out anything you don't want. The handy ps aux command shows all the running processes on a Linux system, but the output can be massive. Let's say you want to see all the Firefox processes on your system. The command ps aux | grep firefox tells the system to send (to pipe) the output to the grep command, not to the screen. The output runs through the grep command and then goes to the screen.

```
mike@mike-VirtualBox:~$ ps aux | grep firefox
mike        2970 16.5 13.4 3234952 273148 ?        Sl   15:13   0:06 /usr/lib/
```

```
firefox/firefox -new-window
mike        3019 23.9 14.7 2719736 299288 ?       Sl   15:13   0:08 /usr/
lib/firefox/firefox -contentproc -childID 1 -isForBrowser -prefsLen 1
-prefMapSize 219196 -parentBuildID 20200630195452 -appdir /usr/lib/firefox/
browser 2970 true tab
```

The grep utility is a wonderful tool to filter output to and from files or the screen. This quick introduction is just that—an introduction and enough to get you through the exam—but anyone who works with Linux should on their own dig deeper into grep.

head/tail

Sometimes you want to see only the beginning of a text file to get a clue about what data is stored in that file. Alternatively, there are times where you just want to see the end of a text file, maybe to see if records were added. That's where head and tail are used. *head* displays the first ten lines of a text file. *tail* shows the last ten lines.

logger

The *logger* command enables you to add text to log files manually. You would do this when you want to add comments. We'll get to log files in Module 4-4.

Shell and Script Environments

Security experts understand operating system *shells*, the command-line interfaces (such as Command, Bash, Terminal, etc.) that enable you to do a ton of things quickly and with authority. And the CompTIA Security+ objectives aggressively assume that knowledge.

 EXAM TIP   CompTIA inadvertently listed Open*SSL* rather than Open*SSH* in objective 4.1. Expect to see OpenSSH (discussed later in this section) on the exam.

A huge part of working at the command prompt is using scripting languages. Scripting languages enable automation of complex tasks and, with the right shells, take advantage of powerful operating system features (like updating registry settings in Windows) that would otherwise require writing actual compiled code. The funny part is that the CompTIA Security+ objectives only mention one shell—Windows' PowerShell—and only one scripting language, Python. OK, PowerShell also includes its own scripting language, but CompTIA Security+ seems to skip popular shells such as GNU Bash (a Linux shell) and scripting languages like JavaScript.

PowerShell

For decades, Microsoft leaned heavily and exclusively on the Command shell. Compared to UNIX/Linux, Command was (and still is) extremely primitive and Microsoft knew this. After a few (better forgotten) attempts, Microsoft introduced PowerShell back in 2006. Since then PowerShell has gone through multiple improvements, making it arguably the best combination of shell and scripting language, certainly for the Windows platform. Figure 4-14 shows the default PowerShell interface.

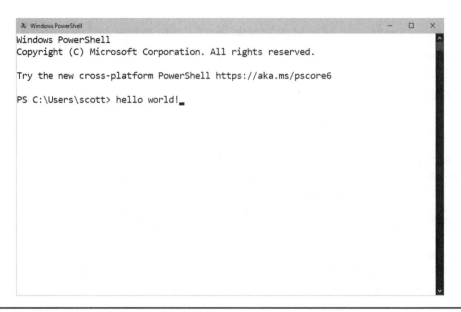

Figure 4-14 Windows PowerShell interface

PowerShell's built-in scripting language has a unique feature that makes it vastly more powerful than any other language when it comes to working with the Windows operating system, a direct connection to the internals of Windows. Want to see a list of local users on a system? Try this PowerShell *cmdlet* (pronounced "command let"):

```
Get-LocalUser | Select *
```

Need to see a setting for a key in the Windows registry? That's easy for PowerShell:

```
Get-ItemProperty -Path HKCU:\Software\ScriptingGuys\Scripts -Name version).
version
```

Feel free to integrate PowerShell cmdlets into the powerful scripting language to do, well, anything you can imagine. Create GUIs, access databases . . . PowerShell can do it all.

 NOTE PowerShell scripts normally end with a .ps1 file extension.

Don't feel like using PowerShell scripting in your PowerShell terminal? No worries. The PowerShell terminal supports other languages such as JavaScript and Python. PowerShell is a fabulous shell as well as scripting language, and if you're working on or developing on a Windows platform, you need to know how to use it.

Python

Most security folks consider Python to be the "go to" scripting language for anything that's cross platform, because Python works perfectly and equally on Windows, macOS, and UNIX/Linux systems. Python has been around for a very long time, is totally free, is well known and well supported, and has easy-to-find tutorials and support.

NOTE PowerShell is also cross platform (but good luck finding anyone who runs PowerShell for a living outside of Windows systems).

SSH

Sometimes you just can't physically be in front of a machine to open a terminal and do whatever you need to do. That's where the *Secure Shell (SSH)* protocol comes into play. Applications using the SSH protocol can manifest a terminal to a remote machine, assuming you have a user name and password on that remote machine (and that remote machine is running an SSH-compatible server). SSH runs on TCP port 22, and almost every operating system comes with a built-in SSH client, if not an SSH server as well.

SSH servers and clients must first create an encrypted connection. The SSH protocol has several ways to do this, but one of the more common methods is for the SSH server to generate *SSH keys*: a traditional RSA asymmetric key pair. The server then treats one key as public and the other as private. When an SSH client attempts to access an SSH server for the first time, the server sends the public key (Figure 4-15).

Most SSH implementations today rely on the *OpenSSH* suite of secure networking utilities. First released in 1999 and in continuous development since then, OpenSSH offers best-in-class secure connectivity between systems.

NOTE OpenSSH is hosted at https://www.openssh.com/. Check it out— maybe you can use OpenSSH to develop the next great SSH server!

Module 4-2: Network Scanners

This module covers the following CompTIA Security+ objective:

- **4.1 Given a scenario, use the appropriate tool to assess organizational security**

What is on your network? This is one of the most important questions a good IT security professional must answer. When you want to see what's on a network, you need to go through the process of network reconnaissance and discovery. Several software and hardware tools, known collectively as *network scanners*, help you to complete this process.

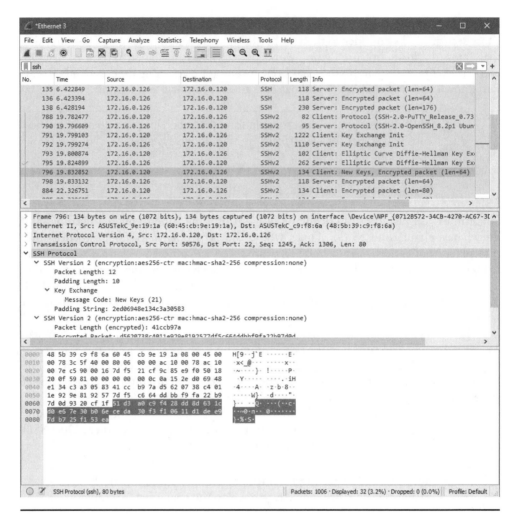

Figure 4-15 SSH client receiving a server key

Network scanners use protocols on a network, almost always a LAN, to determine as much information about the LAN as possible. In essence, a scanner is an inventory tool. There's no single standard or type of network scanner. Different network scanners use a variety of protocols, standards, and methods to query the hosts on the LAN. Given that virtually every network in existence uses the TCP/IP protocol stack, it might be more accurate to use the term *IP scanner* when describing these tools.

 EXAM TIP IP scanners are any class of network scanner that concentrates on IP addresses for network discovery.

Scanning Methods

Every scanner scans differently, but they try to find certain common data. Here's a short list of some of the more important items every network scanner will inventory:

- Topology
- MAC addresses
- IP addresses
- Open ports
- Protocol information on open ports
- Operating systems

A good network scanner compiles this information and presents it in a way that enables security people to understand what's going on in the network. A network scanner enables *network mapping* on many levels.

The one area that IP scanners do not usually cover are protocols underneath TCP/IP. For example, a TCP/IP scanner isn't commonly going to verify the Ethernet speed/type. Some network scanners do inventory lower protocol information, but they tend to be more specialized. With that in mind, let's dive into network IP scanners. In general, we turn to this information for two reasons: baselining and monitoring.

Scanning Targets

Think of a *baseline* as a verification of the network assets. Security professionals run baselines to make sure of exactly what is on the network. This a great time to build an "official" inventory that defines and details every computer, server, printer, router, switch, and WAP in the network infrastructure.

Once you know what's on a network, you can then occasionally reapply a network scan to verify that there are no surprises on the network. Compare recent scans to the baseline and look for differences. Any sort of *baseline deviation*—things that have changed—can help secure the network. In such a scenario, monitoring enables *rogue system detection*, such as finding rogue WAPs, unauthorized servers, and other such security breaches.

Network scanners are everywhere. If you go into Network and Sharing Center in Windows (assuming your firewall settings aren't too restrictive), you'll see a perfectly functional, although very simple, network scanner (Figure 4-16).

Scanner Types

Network scanners tend to fit into one of two categories: simple or powerful. Simple scanners make quick, basic scans. They require little or no actual skill and only provide essential information. Powerful network scanners use many protocols to drill deeply into a network and return an outrageous amount of information.

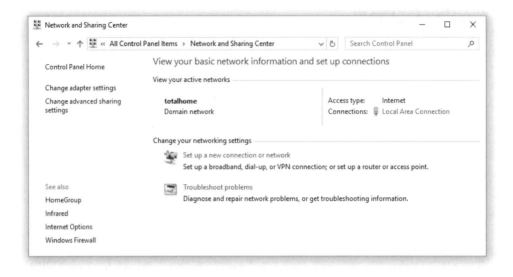

Figure 4-16 Windows network information

 NOTE You won't see anything on the CompTIA Security+ exam that divides network scanner types into simple versus powerful. We make that distinction purely for ease of teaching the subject.

Simple Network Scanners

Simple scanners are easy to use and invariably have pretty graphical user interfaces (GUIs) to improve usability. The free and surprisingly powerful *Angry IP Scanner* from Anton Keks (https://angryip.org) does a good job using simple protocols, mainly ping, to query a single IPv4 address or an address range. If you just want to count the systems in a simple LAN and you have confidence that your internal network isn't blocking ICMP messages, Angry IP Scanner is a great tool (Figure 4-17). Angry IP Scanner is good for a single network ID and it does some basic port scanning, but that's about it.

 NOTE Angry IP Scanner and, in fact, most scanning tools will set off your anti-malware tools. In most cases you'll need to shut off the anti-malware; or better yet, go through whatever process is needed to make these scanners exempt from the anti-malware software.

Simple scanners aren't limited to Windows. macOS users have similar tools. One of the more common and popular is *IP Scanner* by 10base-t Interactive (https://10base-t .com). Like Angry IP Scanner, this tool uses only the simplest protocols to query a local network. Compare Figure 4-18 to Figure 4-17 and see how they share a somewhat similar interface.

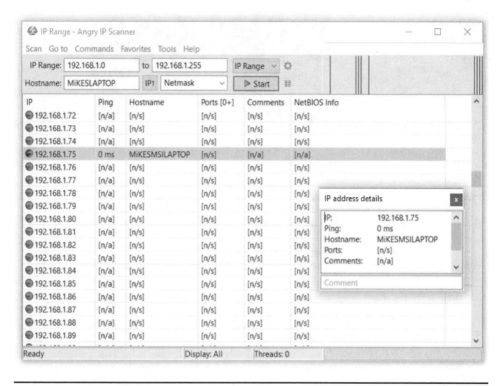

Figure 4-17   Angry IP Scanner

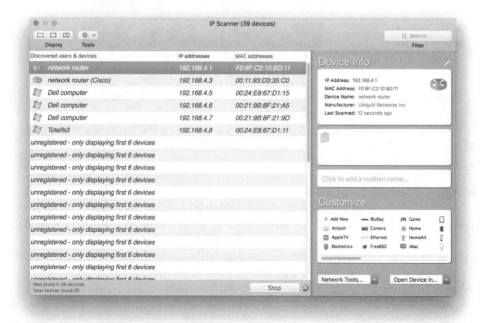

Figure 4-18   IP Scanner

Figure 4-19

Fing scanner on
Android

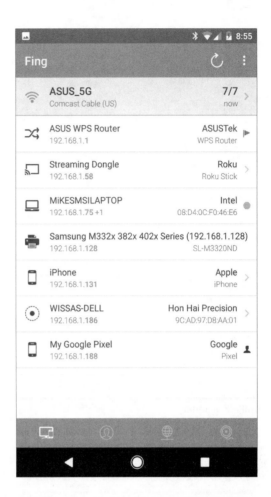

There are also several excellent simple network scanners for smart devices running Android and iOS operating systems. Given that these devices all have dedicated 802.11 connections, almost all of these simple IP network scanners tend to give excellent wireless information. One of our favorite scanners is Fing (https://www.fing.com). Note the screenshot of Fing in Figure 4-19.

Nmap: A Powerful Network Scanner

Simple scanners are wonderful tools if you're looking for quick scans that grab IP addresses, open ports, and maybe a Windows network name, but little else. But what if you're looking for more? What if you have multiple address ranges? What if you have a routed network and you want to install multiple sensors that all report back to a single system? In that case you'll need to turn to a powerful network scanner.

Among the many contenders in the network scanner market, the one that every security professional should know, and the one explicitly listed in the CompTIA

```
Port         State        Service
22/tcp       open         ssh

No exact OS matches for host

Nmap run completed -- 1 IP address (1 host up) scanneds
# sshnuke 10.2.2.2 -rootpw="Z10N0101"
Connecting to 10.2.2.2:ssh ... successful.
Attempting to exploit SSHv1 CRC32 ... successful.
Reseting root password to "Z10N0101".
System open: Access Level <9>
# ssh 10.2.2.2 -l ro
```

Figure 4-20 Nmap used in *The Matrix*

Security+ exam objectives, is Nmap (from https://nmap.org). Originally written back in the mid-1990s by Gordon Lyon, Nmap established itself as the gold standard for TCP/IP network scanners early on and has retained its prominence through ongoing updates from the Nmap community. Nmap is so popular that it shows up in popular media, such as the movies *The Matrix* (Figure 4-20) and *Judge Dredd*.

 NOTE Nmap runs on most operating systems, but it runs best on Linux/ UNIX systems.

Having said all these nice things about Nmap, be warned: Nmap is a command-line tool with a powerful and incredibly complex number of switches and options. Nmap is complicated to master; there are many thick books and long online Web page Nmap tutorials that do a great job showing you the power of Nmap. (Also, GUI overlays that run on top of Nmap are available, such as Zenmap, discussed shortly.) It is impossible to give you any more than the lightest of touches on Nmap in this module. Fortunately, the CompTIA Security+ exam will not test you intensely on this tool, but it will expect you to have a good understanding of its capabilities and some of the basic syntax, and that we can do here. Do yourself a favor, download Nmap and try it.

Nmap Basics   In its simplest form, Nmap is run from a command line. I can run a very simple Nmap command, as shown in Figure 4-21, against my home router. Nmap scans the 1000 most common port numbers by default. In this case it located four open ports: 53 (my router is a DNS forwarder), 80 (the router's Web interface), and 515 and 9100 (I have a printer plugged into the network).

Nmap can just as easily scan an entire network ID. For example, this Nmap command will run the same command except generate a very long output to the terminal:

```
nmap 192.168.1.*
```

```
mike@VirtualUbuntu:~$ nmap 192.168.1.1

Starting Nmap 7.01 ( https://nmap.org ) at 2017-06-08 23:05 CDT
Nmap scan report for router.asus.com (192.168.1.1)
Host is up (0.0061s latency).
Not shown: 996 closed ports
PORT     STATE SERVICE
53/tcp   open  domain
80/tcp   open  http
515/tcp  open  printer
9100/tcp open  jetdirect

Nmap done: 1 IP address (1 host up) scanned in 0.16 seconds
mike@VirtualUbuntu:~$
```

Figure 4-21   Basic Nmap command

By adding a few extra switches, –A to tell Nmap to query for OS version and –v to increase the "verbosity" (in essence telling Nmap to grab more information), you can get a lot more information. Nmap also works perfectly fine for any public-facing server. Figure 4-22 shows part of the Nmap scan against Nmap.org's purpose-built public server scanme.nmap.org.

```
Scanning scanme.nmap.org (45.33.32.156) [1000 ports]
Discovered open port 22/tcp on 45.33.32.156
Discovered open port 80/tcp on 45.33.32.156
Increasing send delay for 45.33.32.156 from 0 to 5 due to 11 out of 36 dropped probes since last inc
rease.
Discovered open port 9929/tcp on 45.33.32.156
Discovered open port 31337/tcp on 45.33.32.156
Completed Connect Scan at 23:53, 7.65s elapsed (1000 total ports)
Initiating Service scan at 23:53
Scanning 4 services on scanme.nmap.org (45.33.32.156)
Completed Service scan at 23:53, 6.14s elapsed (4 services on 1 host)
NSE: Script scanning 45.33.32.156.
Initiating NSE at 23:53
Completed NSE at 23:53, 5.45s elapsed
Initiating NSE at 23:53
Completed NSE at 23:53, 0.00s elapsed
Nmap scan report for scanme.nmap.org (45.33.32.156)
Host is up (0.061s latency).
Other addresses for scanme.nmap.org (not scanned): 2600:3c01::f03c:91ff:fe18:bb2f
Not shown: 992 closed ports
PORT      STATE    SERVICE       VERSION
22/tcp    open     ssh           OpenSSH 6.6.1p1 Ubuntu 2ubuntu2.8 (Ubuntu Linux; protocol 2.0)
| ssh-hostkey:
|   1024 ac:00:a0:1a:82:ff:cc:55:99:dc:67:2b:34:97:6b:75 (DSA)
|   2048 20:3d:2d:44:62:2a:b0:5a:9d:b5:b3:05:14:c2:a6:b2 (RSA)
|_  256 96:02:bb:5e:57:54:1c:4e:45:2f:56:4c:4a:24:b2:57 (ECDSA)
25/tcp    filtered smtp
80/tcp    open     http          Apache httpd 2.4.7 ((Ubuntu))
|_http-favicon: Unknown favicon MD5: 156515DA3C0F7DC6B2493BD5CE43F795
| http-methods:
|_  Supported Methods: GET HEAD POST OPTIONS
|_http-server-header: Apache/2.4.7 (Ubuntu)
|_http-title: Go ahead and ScanMe!
135/tcp   filtered msrpc
139/tcp   filtered netbios-ssn
445/tcp   filtered microsoft-ds
9929/tcp  open     nping-echo    Nping echo
31337/tcp open     tcpwrapped
Service Info: OS: Linux; CPE: cpe:/o:linux:linux_kernel
```

Figure 4-22   Part of a more aggressive Nmap scan

Note that not only does Nmap detect open ports, it pulls detailed information about each port, including the RSA key for the SSH server, the HTTP server version, and the title to the index page as well as NetBIOS ports.

CAUTION Before you grab a copy of Nmap and start blasting away at random public-facing servers, a word of caution. Don't! Multiple laws protect businesses and individuals from unauthorized scanning. You could end up in a world of legal hurt if you don't have permissions to scan. Getting those permissions as an authorized (white hat) hacker or penetration tester— someone who tests networks to help identify potential security holes—is a great idea. Be careful out there!

Zenmap Nmap outputs can be massive, so in many cases security professionals don't use this interactive mode of terminal screen output; instead, they direct output to XML files other tools can analyze, including graphical tools. Nmap provides a wonderful GUI called Zenmap that enables you to enter Nmap commands and then provides some handy analysis tools. Figure 4-23 shows the topology screen from Zenmap, showing a complete network.

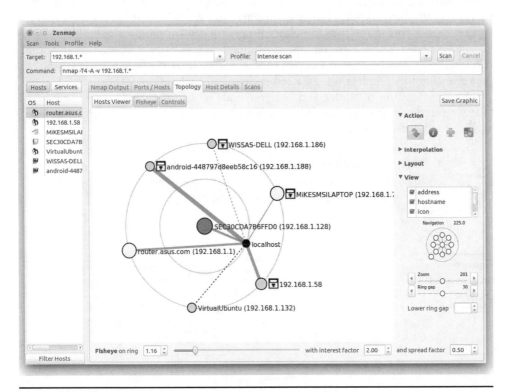

Figure 4-23 Zenmap

As previously mentioned, this is just the lightest of tastes of the powerful Nmap scanner. Nmap is a critical part of many Linux security packages, including the powerful Metasploit framework.

Module 4-3: Protocol Analyzers

This module covers the following CompTIA Security+ objectives:

- **4.1 Given a scenario, use the appropriate tool to assess organizational security**
- **4.3 Given an incident, utilize appropriate data sources to support an investigation**

Protocol analyzers collect and inventory the network traffic on a network. The CompTIA Security+ exam uses the term *protocol analyzer*, but that's a fairly broad term. The IT industry defines protocol analyzers as any type of hardware or software that analyzes any form of communication. In IP networks, all data transmits via Ethernet frames or IP packets contained in those frames, so the better term is *packet analyzer* (Figure 4-24). Yet another term you'll hear many folks in the IT industry use is *packet sniffer* (or just *sniffer*).

If something is going to analyze packets, it is first going to need, well, packets! It needs some program that can put a NIC into promiscuous mode so that the NIC grabs every packet it sees. This frame/packet grabber program needs to monitor or sniff the wired or wireless network and start grabbing the frames/packets. So, a packet analyzer is really two totally separate functions: a packet sniffer that captures the frames/packets, and the packet analyzer that replays the collected packets and analyzes them (Figure 4-25).

This combination of sniffer and analyzer leads to a funny name issue. Any of the following terms are perfectly interchangeable: packet analyzer, network sniffer, network analyzer, and packet sniffer.

NOTE Different network technologies need different sniffers. If you want to analyze a wired network, you need a wired sniffer. If you want to sniff a wireless network, you need a wireless sniffer.

Figure 4-24
I'm a protocol analyzer.

Figure 4-25
Sniffers and
analyzers

Networks generate a huge number of packets. Even in a small home network, moving a few files and watching a few videos generates hundreds of thousands of packets. A good analyzer needs two features. First, it must provide some type of interface that allows the security professional a way to inspect packets. Second, it must provide powerful sorting and filtering tools to let you look at the packets that interest you while eliminating the ones you do not want to see.

Why Protocol Analyze?

Collecting and analyzing data via a protocol analyzer enables you to perform wildly detailed analyses. A protocol analyzer enables security professionals to access and use data sources to support an investigation in case of an incident. The *protocol analyzer output*—the data source—can provide critical information.

A protocol analyzer can reveal all sorts of information, providing huge benefits to the security of your network. Here are six examples:

- Count all the packets coming through over a certain time period to get a strong idea as to your network utilization.

- Inspect the packets for single protocols to verify they are working properly (of course, this means you must know how these protocols work in detail).

- Monitor communication between a client and a server to look for problems in the communication.

- Look for servers that aren't authorized on the network.

- Find systems broadcasting bad data.

- Find problems in authentication by watching each step of the process in detail.

 NOTE Protocol analyzers require skilled operators with a firm grasp of TCP/IP protocols. The more a tech understands protocols, the more useful a protocol analyzer will be.

You can find quite a few protocol analyzers today, but the CompTIA Security+ exam focuses on two very good protocol analyzers: Wireshark and tcpdump. Both tools enable packet capture and replay. You can get some great work done without detailed knowledge of either tool, but in the hands of a skilled professional who understands both the tool and TCP/IP, a protocol analyzer can answer almost any question that arises in any network.

The CompTIA Security+ exam isn't going to ask detailed questions about protocol analyzers, so we'll only cover a few of the more basic aspects of these tools. But like Nmap from the previous module, it would behoove you to make an investment in learning and using one or the other of these amazing tools.

Wireshark

Wireshark is the Grand Old Man of packet analyzers, originally developed in 1998 by Gerald Combs as Ethereal. In 2006, Ethereal was forked from the original development team and renamed Wireshark. Wireshark may be old, but it has an amazing development team that keeps this venerable tool sharp with a huge number of updates.

Wireshark is not only powerful but completely free and works on all major operating systems (and quite a few not so common ones as well). Its default GUI is so common that even a few competing protocol analyzers copy it for theirs.

 NOTE   Some anti-malware programs will flag Wireshark. It's stupid, but they do. You might need to disable anti-malware to get results.

Let's start with that interface, as shown in Figure 4-26. The interface has three main panes. At the top is a list of all the frames currently captured. (Wireshark shows each

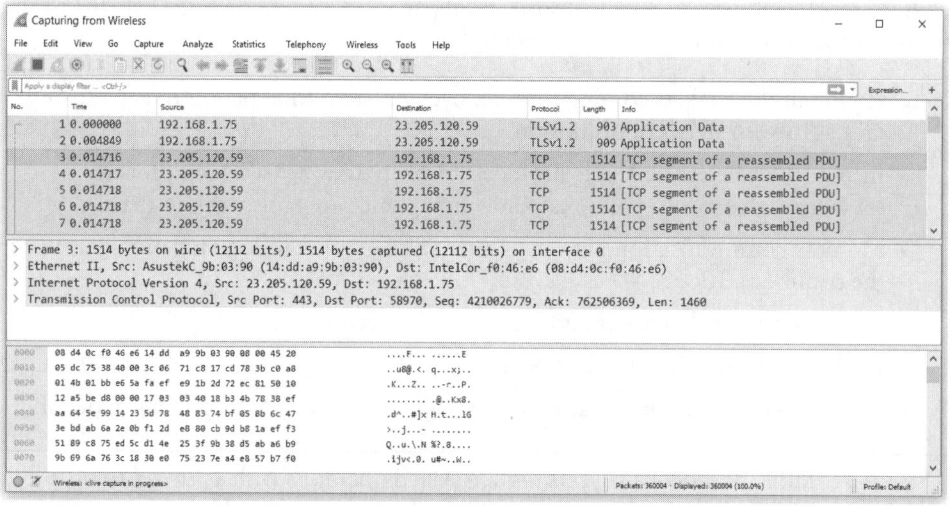

Figure 4-26   Wireshark main screen

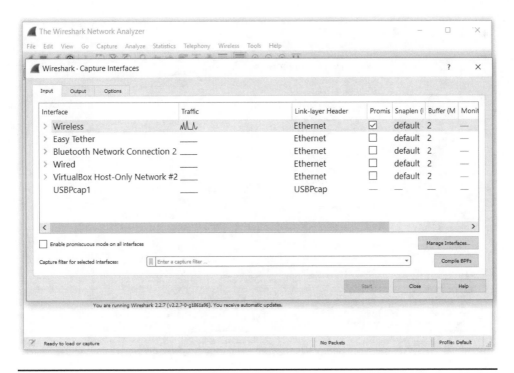

Figure 4-27   Selecting a network interface

Ethernet frame, a feature that few other protocol analyzers provide.) In the middle are the gritty details of the frame currently selected in the top frame. At the bottom is the raw frame data in hexadecimal.

Wireshark employs an application programming interface (API) to enable a NIC to ingest all traffic passing by, rather than the default of only traffic intended for the box. Wireshark uses the *libpcap* API in Linux or the *WinPcap* API on Windows systems.

You begin the process of using Wireshark by starting a capture. As shown in Figure 4-27, Wireshark locates your network interfaces and gives you the opportunity to select which interface you want to start capturing.

Once you start a capture, at some point you then stop the capture. From there you can filter and sort the capture by source or destination IP address, source or destination port number, protocol, or hundreds of other criteria. Wireshark has an expression builder to help you with complex filters. In Figure 4-28 the expression builder is creating a filter for a DHCP server response that is passing out the IP address 192.168.1.23.

NOTE   You can use a filter on the incoming packets or you can just sniff everything and filter afterward.

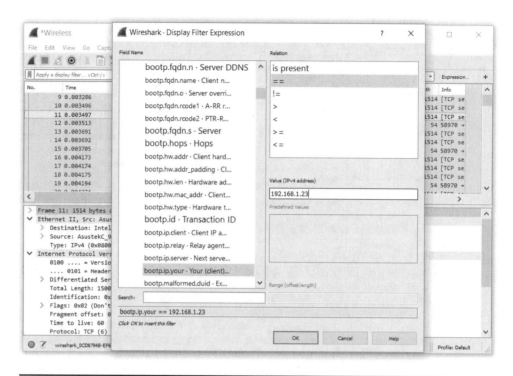

Figure 4-28   Expression builder

Wireshark by default captures and analyzes packets in real time, so you can analyze as things happen. Sometimes, on the other hand, you need to record data over a period of time and then run tools for analysis for baselining or historical reference. Imagine a situation in which a tech wants to capture all HTTP traffic between 12 A.M. and 4 A.M. on a specific server. In this case, instead of running Wireshark all night, he or she will turn to a capture-only tool such as TShark. TShark is a command-line tool that works well with scripting and scheduling tools (Figure 4-29). TShark saves the capture in a format called pcap that a tech can load into Wireshark the next day for analysis.

```
PS C:\Program Files\Wireshark> .\tshark -D
1.  \Device\NPF_{7AAB8953-B1FF-4C05-B7B4-8FE73B9F1C5D} (Local Area Connection* 10)
2.  \Device\NPF_{0FF11516-B476-439D-A881-7D602CF86E0E} (Local Area Connection* 9)
3.  \Device\NPF_{D6CC7E27-6AB2-44D2-80D4-1B26B031652A} (Npcap Loopback Adapter)
4.  \Device\NPF_{1DA7160C-F255-46FD-BB35-C017BD637DA1} (Bluetooth Network Connection)
5.  \Device\NPF_{174CD92A-32DA-4E7D-8F55-14A27F0BFAF7} (Local Area Connection* 11)
6.  \Device\NPF_{597E72A6-E268-484A-8348-90535E77B6B9} (VirtualBox Host-Only Network)
7.  \Device\NPF_{07B2D520-E047-4A6E-9E02-9F924A6E7927} (Local Area Connection)
8.  \Device\NPF_{E3AB0328-FA73-4C9D-A173-6EF6AA130632} (Ethernet)
PS C:\Program Files\Wireshark> .\tshark -i8
Capturing on 'Ethernet'
    1   0.000000 192.168.44.2 → 192.168.4.8  NBSS 55 NBSS Continuation Message
    2   0.187179 192.168.4.8 → 192.168.44.2 TCP 94 445→51072 [ACK] Seq=1 Ack=2 Win=260 Len=0
    3   1.886295 192.168.44.2 → 192.168.4.12 DNS 78 Standard query 0x8207 A beacon.dropbox.com
    4   1.911807 192.168.44.2 → 192.168.4.12 DNS 78 Standard query 0x8207 A beacon.dropbox.com
    5   2.146493 192.168.4.12 → 192.168.44.2 DNS 220 Standard query response 0x8207 A beacon.dropbox.com CNAME beacon.v.dro
pbox.com A 162.125.34.129
    6   2.147157 192.168.44.2 → 192.168.4.12 DNS 78 Standard query 0xad09 A beacon.dropbox.com
    7   2.171178 192.168.44.2 → 192.168.4.12 DNS 78 Standard query 0xad09 A beacon.dropbox.com
    8   2.171253 192.168.4.12 → 192.168.44.2 DNS 220 Standard query response 0xad09 A beacon.dropbox.com CNAME beacon.v.dro
pbox.com A 162.125.34.129
    9   2.198842 192.168.4.12 → 192.168.44.2 DNS 220 Standard query response 0xad09 A beacon.dropbox.com CNAME beacon.v.dro
pbox.com A 162.125.34.129
```

Figure 4-29   TShark in action

```
student@Student01:~$ sudo tcpdump
tcpdump: verbose output suppressed, use -v or -vv for full protocol decode
listening on enp0s3, link-type EN10MB (Ethernet), capture size 262144 bytes
21:47:03.901138 IP 10.13.212.153.netbios-ns > 10.13.212.255.netbios-ns: NBT UDP
PACKET(137): QUERY; REQUEST; BROADCAST
21:47:03.963882 IP 10.13.212.205.16290 > 10.13.212.1.domain: 6713+ PTR? 255.212.
13.10.in-addr.arpa. (44)
21:47:03.987695 IP 10.13.212.1.domain > 10.13.212.205.16290: 6713 NXDomain 0/0/0
 (44)
21:47:03.987890 IP 10.13.212.205.46128 > 10.13.212.1.domain: 29782+ PTR? 153.212
.13.10.in-addr.arpa. (44)
21:47:04.011270 IP 10.13.212.1.domain > 10.13.212.205.46128: 29782 NXDomain 0/0/
0 (44)
21:47:04.011517 IP 10.13.212.205.19145 > 10.13.212.1.domain: 18048+ PTR? 1.212.1
3.10.in-addr.arpa. (42)
21:47:04.035326 IP 10.13.212.1.domain > 10.13.212.205.19145: 18048 NXDomain 0/0/
0 (42)
21:47:04.035526 IP 10.13.212.205.26167 > 10.13.212.1.domain: 54489+ PTR? 205.212
.13.10.in-addr.arpa. (44)
21:47:04.646279 IP 10.13.212.153.netbios-ns > 10.13.212.255.netbios-ns: NBT UDP
PACKET(137): QUERY; REQUEST; BROADCAST
21:47:05.398838 IP 10.13.212.153.netbios-ns > 10.13.212.255.netbios-ns: NBT UDP
PACKET(137): QUERY; REQUEST; BROADCAST
```

Figure 4-30   tcpdump

tcpdump

As popular as Wireshark is, especially in Windows, many Linux/UNIX techs swear by *tcpdump*. tcpdump predates Wireshark by almost a decade and was the only real protocol analyzer option for Linux/UNIX until Wireshark was ported over in the very late 1990s (Figure 4-30).

tcpdump is amazing at sniffing packets, but it can be time consuming to use as a protocol analyzer, relying on complex command-line switches for sorting and filtering. No worries! Plenty of graphical protocol analyzers, even Wireshark, run on Linux (Figure 4-31).

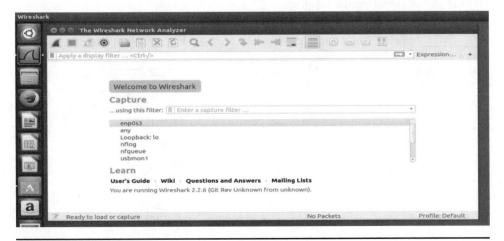

Figure 4-31   Wireshark in Linux

Module 4-4: Monitoring Networks

This module covers the following CompTIA Security+ objectives:

- **1.7 Summarize the techniques used in security assessments**
- **4.3 Given an incident, utilize appropriate data sources to support an investigation**

Every organization with proper security includes continuous network monitoring to recognize and address performance and security events. This monitoring manifests as the collection of data from a wide variety of sources, one being the standard device and system logs inherent to every operating system. The *metadata* from applications, such as Microsoft Office 365, provides a great source, because it includes e-mail logs, mobile device records, Web traffic, and file manipulation details. Another source is logs from devices running protocols designed specifically for network monitoring, such as the Simple Network Management Protocol (SNMP).

SNMP data collected for network monitoring includes intrusion detection/prevention system alerts, firewall alerts and logs, and real-time network monitoring. Real-time network monitoring involves protocol and traffic monitoring (also known as *sniffing*) using a protocol analyzer, so that the data may be collected and stored for later analysis. SNMP provides bandwidth monitoring in real time, enabling security professionals to assess data in the face of an incident.

Similarly, the Cisco-based NetFlow and the more generic sFlow offer analytical tools for security people by assessing the flow of IP traffic. Such tools are invaluable when an incident occurs.

More complex systems rely on advanced monitoring tools such as a *security information and event management (SIEM)* application that monitors log files—brought into the monitoring tools using protocols like SNMP—to provide managers powerful, easy to read and understand toolsets. These toolsets enable them to react to situations on their network in real time (Figure 4-32).

Figure 4-32

A security event

To understand the critical process of network monitoring, let's begin by exploring the many types of log files found on devices in a network. From there, we'll see how these files can be centralized for easier monitoring and then finish with a discussion on log file management and analysis.

Exploring Log Files

Logs are databases, usually distinct files that record events on systems. You'll most commonly hear them referenced as *event logs*, as in the case of Microsoft Windows operating systems. Linux systems refer to them as *syslogs*, or system logs. Whatever the name, log files are everywhere! You'd be hard-pressed to find a networking device or almost any form of software that doesn't make log files, or at least has the capability to create log files as needed.

Operating systems also store log files in various locations and in various formats. Security personnel often refer to these logs as *security* or *audit trail*, or sometimes as *audit log*, because they provide information on events that are of a security interest. Security logs audit access to a particular resource or system. Audit logs can record very specific information about an event, to include user names, workstation or host names, IP addresses, MAC addresses, the resource that was accessed, and the type of action that occurred on the resource. This action could be something such as a file deletion or creation; it also could be use of elevated or administrative privileges.

Very often, security personnel may audit when users with administrative privileges create additional user accounts, for example, or change host configurations. Figure 4-33 shows an example of a Linux audit trail.

Visitor logs are resource-oriented and list all the different types of access that occur on a resource (such as a shared folder, file, or other object). Most systems can produce visitor logs for a specific resource, but often this must be configured on the resource itself to generate those logs. You can use visitor logs that are not system-generated. For example, you can have manually generated visitor logs for entrance into a facility or restricted area. Security experts work hard to keep up with all the different log files available and use them in the most efficient and reasonable way possible.

Log File Examples

Students of CompTIA Security+ reasonably ask what they need to know about log files to pass the exam. It's a fair question, but rarely do people like my answer: "You need to know very little about log files other than what's inside the log files themselves." What I'm trying to say is that if you think about what a log records, then you should have a good feel about the types of data stored in that log file. Luckily for students of the SY0-601 exam, CompTIA has specific types of log files for consideration, all listed prettily under objective 4.3! Let's run down that list.

Network   It you have a device or a piece of software that deals with networking, then you almost certainly have some kind of network log. A *network log* varies by the type of device using the network. A router might have a network log that tracks the number of connections per hour on every route. A switch might record packets per seconds for VLANs. On an individual host, you might log the usage of a particular NIC.

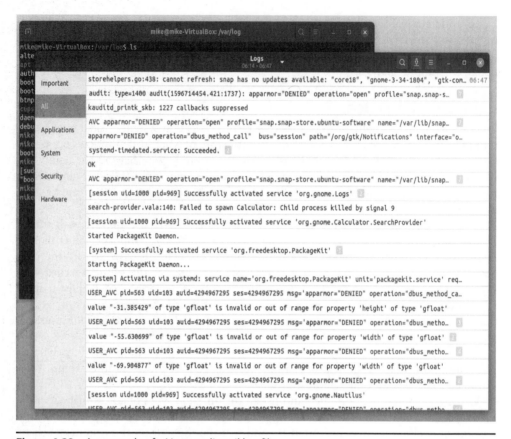

Figure 4-33   An example of a Linux audit trail log file

System   A *system log* file records issues that directly affect a single system but aren't network functions. System log files will show reboots, executable files starting, and edited files on the system, for example.

Application   An application may have its own log file. What appears in this *application log* file requires some knowledge of the application that is using the log. Probably one of the most common application logs is for a Web server. Web server software is an application to share Web pages. In this case, since we know what Web servers do, we can assume the *Web log* keeps track of the number of pages served per hour/minute, perhaps even a listing of the different IP addresses asking for the Web page, or maybe the number of malformed HTTPS packets.

Security   Both systems and applications typically include *security logs* that record activities that potentially impact security. Security logs might track all successful and/or unsuccessful logon attempts. They track the creation or deletion of new users and also keep track of any permission changes to resources within the system or application.

DNS Any good DNS server is going to keep a log. *DNS logs* are application logs that keep track of things appropriate to a DNS server application. DNS logs typically include entries for activities such as the creation of new forward lookup zones, cache updates/clearing, and changes to critical settings like root server.

Authentication An *authentication log* is a special type of security log that tracks nothing other than users attempting to log onto a system. This includes tracking failed logons as well as successful logons.

Dump Files On some operating systems, a dump file is generated when an executable program crashes. These *dump files* record memory locations, running processes, and threads. Dump files are almost always used exclusively by the developers of the executable file that needs . . . dumping.

VoIP and Call Managers *Voice over IP (VoIP)* and *call manager* software solutions create logs that store information about the calls themselves. Phone numbers and duration of calls are the two most common items logged, but items from other VoIP tools such as billing might also be included.

Session Initiation Protocol Traffic *Session Initial Protocol (SIP) traffic* is usually a subset of VoIP traffic but exclusive to the SIP protocol. In this case, a *SIP traffic log* tracks where the IP address to/from is logged as well as any details about the call itself.

Windows Log Tools

Every Windows systems contains the venerable *Event Viewer* as the go-to log observation tool. Event Viewer contains a number of preset logs (notice the System logs folder in Figure 4-34). You can create new logs here or in the local security policy application.

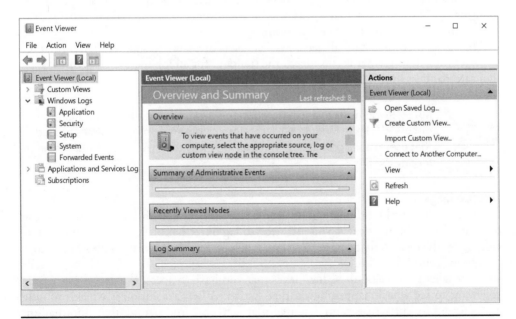

Figure 4-34 Event Viewer

```
mike@mike-VirtualBox:~$ journalctl | grep warn
Jul 07 08:35:47 mike-VirtualBox NetworkManager[529]: <warn>  [1594128947.7311] config: unknown key 'w
ifi.cloned-mac-address' in section [device-mac-addr-change-wifi] of file '/usr/lib/NetworkManager/con
f.d/no-mac-addr-change.conf'
Jul 07 08:35:47 mike-VirtualBox NetworkManager[529]: <warn>  [1594128947.7311] config: unknown key 'e
thernet.cloned-mac-address' in section [device-mac-addr-change-wifi] of file '/usr/lib/NetworkManager
/conf.d/no-mac-addr-change.conf'
Jul 07 08:35:47 mike-VirtualBox thermald[566]: I/O warning : failed to load external entity "/etc/the
rmald/thermal-conf.xml"
Jul 07 08:35:49 mike-VirtualBox NetworkManager[529]: <warn>  [1594128949.3655] ifupdown: interfaces f
ile /etc/network/interfaces doesn't exist
Jul 07 08:35:49 mike-VirtualBox NetworkManager[529]: <warn>  [1594128949.4339] Error: failed to open
/run/network/ifstate
Jul 07 08:35:49 mike-VirtualBox /usr/lib/gdm3/gdm-x-session[758]:                  (WW) warning, (EE) error, (
NI) not implemented, (??) unknown.
```

Figure 4-35   Linux journalctl log viewer

Linux Logs

Linux loves to make log files, dedicating an entire folder to nothing but all the logs you'll ever need. In most distros, this folder is called /var/log. Log files end with a .log extension and, unlike in Windows, there is no single log viewing app. You can add various GUI log readers, such as LOGalyze or glogg.

The go-to log viewer on most Linux systems, *journalctl*, displays all logs in a system in a single format. journalctl also takes all the common Linux terminal arguments. Figure 4-35 shows journalctl using grep commands to filter on the term "warn."

Linux logs are almost as simple as Windows logs in that there's basically a single source for all your log needs: *syslog*. OK, that's not exactly true, as syslog is over 30 years old and has been supplanted by two improved syslog versions: *rsyslog*, which came out in the late 1990s and is basically just an improved syslog, and *syslog-ng*, which is an object-oriented version of syslog. Right now syslog is probably the most popular version of these three syslog-like tools, but deciding which tool is best is really up to the individual user, as syslog, rsyslog, and syslog-ng all have their fans and detractors. In most cases, you'll end up using the form of syslog that works best for whatever system you want to use. (See the upcoming "Centralizing Log Files" section.)

The one good thing about all versions of syslog is their superb standardized format for all log entries. This format is considered the standard for all log files. Even Windows log files can manifest in this format.

NOTE   If you need to add a notation to syslog, use the *logger* command, discussed back in Module 4-1. It creates a single entry, properly timestamped, that users can access later. It's an excellent way to make inline documentation for any log file.

Device Logs

Every enterprise-level (and many SOHO-level) devices come with some form of logging built into them. In most cases, you just need to log onto that device (often a Web interface) to see the logs on that device in action. Figure 4-36 shows one example of these logs on a home router.

The challenge to using these log files is that you have to access the device every time you want to see what's happening on that system. A better solution is where multiple devices send log files to a central source that can, in turn, analyze that information.

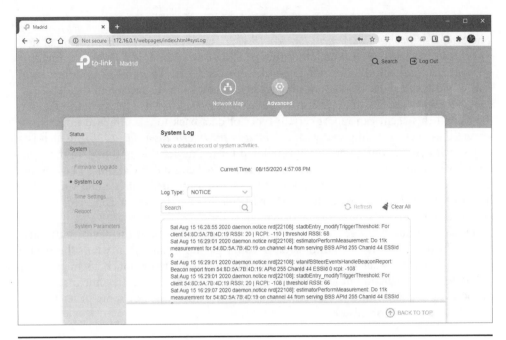

Figure 4-36 Home router log file

Then that centralized analysis can display what's happening on the network in a way that administrators can react to the needs of the network. To do that requires centralization of far-flung log files into a single source.

Centralizing Log Files

The idea of gathering log files from disparate hosts within a network and placing them in a central location for storage and analysis isn't a new idea. Many tools and protocols help you accomplish exactly this task. Let's start by organizing some of the major players out there for centralization and eventually lead to the Holy Grail of network monitoring, SIEM.

syslog

syslog and its alternative forms are more than just log tools. syslog is a complete protocol for the transmission and storage of Linux logs into a single syslog server, configured by the network administrators. Once all the files are stored in a single location, we can use tools such as journalctl to monitor the entire network.

NOTE Can you imagine using syslog to combine log files from all over a network? Imagine the complexity of just trying to read, analyze, and store these files. This is a big shortcoming of syslog and the reason we use other tools on top of syslog to do the big-picture jobs of network monitoring. Keep reading!

SNMP

The *Simple Network Management Protocol (SNMP)* enables proactive monitoring of network hosts in real time. Among other things, SNMP is a *bandwidth monitor*, providing up-to-the-second information for network administrators. This real-time information can provide critical data sources to support investigations in the face of an incident.

Devices that use SNMP have a small piece of software known as an *agent* installed on them, and this agent can report certain types of data back to a centralized monitoring server. This agent is configured with a *Management Information Base (MIB)*, which is a very specific set of configuration items tailored for the device. Using the MIB, the agent can relay very specific event information to a centralized console in real time. These events are known as *traps* and are essentially specific events configured with certain thresholds. If a configured threshold is reached for a particular event, the trap is triggered and the notification or alert is sent to the management console.

These traps and messages can let an administrator know about the device status and health. In other words, the administrator could get information on when the device is up or down, whether its hardware is functioning properly or not, if its memory or CPU use is too high, and other interesting details about the device. In some cases, these trap messages could indicate an active attack against the device or some other type of unauthorized access or misuse.

NOTE   Chapter 8 covers SNMP security in more detail.

NetFlow/sFlow

The Cisco-based NetFlow utility provides real-time information about all the IP traffic in a system. sFlow provides similar information, but, unlike NetFlow, runs in hardware. NetFlow is a software implementation. Numerous switch and router manufacturers deploy sFlow chips/technology, so it is not limited to Cisco hardware.

In concept, a flow represents the movement of an IP packet through a network. By monitoring such information, NetFlow/sFlow can pick up very quickly when patterns diverge from what would be considered normal traffic. Flow information is stored in logs or flow caches that the tools can analyze.

Spawned from NetFlow version 9, *Internet Protocol Flow Information Export (IPFIX)* provides more flexibility in the types of information that can be combined and saved for analysis, such as mail records, HTTP URL information, SIP data, and more. IPFIX is an Internet Engineering Task Force (IETF) specification (RFC 7011), is backwardly compatible to NetFlow v9, and is widely adopted in the industry.

EXAM TIP   CompTIA uses title case for NetFlow, so *Netflow*. Cisco uses camel case, so that's what we use too.

NXLog

NXLog is one example of many solutions out there that provide centralized log monitoring. NXLog is cross platform and takes advantage of darn near every and any protocol out there (including syslog and SNMP) to bring log data together. On Linux systems, NXLog reads from both a local system's syslog and NXLog's installed daemon. On Windows, NXLog runs its own agent and also uses SNMP.

NXLog is a powerful logging tool, but it is not designed to provide pretty desktops or to analyze the log data. NXLog is ready and able to give this log data to those types of systems, but that means we need to start talking about SIEM.

Security Information and Event Management

The traditional way to manage logging and monitoring in a network was to sit down at a system and look at the log files generated by the system, reviewing them for the events of interest. This is not the most efficient way to manage network monitoring and analysis activities.

Almost every organization now uses *security information and event management (SIEM)*, an enterprise-level technology and infrastructure that collects data points from every host on the network, including log files, traffic captures, SNMP messages, and so on. SIEM can collect all this data into one centralized location and correlate it for analysis to look for security and performance issues, as well as negative trends, all in real time.

NOTE   SIEM is pronounced "sim" most frequently, not "seem" or "see-em." For clarity, network professionals can simply enunciate the initials.

Note that although SIEM requires real-time monitoring technologies, just because you're using some of these real-time technologies doesn't necessarily mean you are using SIEM. SIEM unifies and correlates all the real-time events from a multitude of disparate sources, including network alerts, log files, physical security logs, and so on. You could still have real-time monitoring going on, but without combining and correlating all those different event sources. A true unified SIEM system is required to do that.

SIEM Infrastructure

SIEM isn't a law or a standard. It's an integrated approach to monitoring networks that enables security professionals to react on a timely basis to incidents. SIEM systems employ certain components, discrete or combined with others, but you can count on the following:

- Sensors/collectors
- Server
- Analyzers
- Dashboard

Sensors/Collectors   All SIEM solutions rely on *sensors/collectors* to acquire data about the network. These collectors manifest as special software running on a Windows system, an SNMP connection to a switch, or perhaps a third-party tool like NXLog providing information from a gateway router. Whatever the case, these devices must work together to bring the data into a single source, a SIEM server.

Server   A *SIEM server* stores all the data coming in from multiple collectors. A single SIEM server might be a subserver that in turn reports to a main SIEM server.

Analyzers   *Analyzers* take data from SIEM servers and, using a myriad of tools, look at the data to try to locate signatures of something that an organization would consider an incident.

Dashboard   A SIEM *dashboard* presents the analyzed data in a way that makes sense to those monitoring the data and informs them of incidents taking place. Most SIEM dashboards provide graphs and counters. Figure 4-37 shows one style of dashboard from Elastic Cloud, a popular SIEM solution available today.

A good SIEM dashboard provides *security monitoring*—tools for watching and recording what's happening on your network. Beyond that, though, you can count on a SIEM dashboard to supply the following information:

- **Sensor list/sensor warning**   If an incident is taking place at a certain point, which sensor is giving that information? The sensor list or sensor warning provides that information.

- **Alerts**   Alerts enable the SIEM dashboard to inform the person(s) monitoring of a potential incident. This can be a warning ribbon at the bottom of the screen, an audible alarm, or a log entry shown in red.

- **Sensitivity**   How sensitive is a certain setting that might detect an incident? Too high and you'll get false positives. Too low and you'll get false negatives.

- **Trends**   Certain incidents make more sense when seen as a trend as opposed to an alert. Network usage is one good example. Techs can watch usage grow on a chat and consider those implications, as opposed to just getting some alert. Anyone who owns an automobile with an oil pressure gauge instead of an idiot light knows this feeling.

- **Correlation**   A good dashboard will recognize relationships between alerts and trends and in some way inform the person(s) monitoring of that correlation. This is often presented as line graphs with multiple data fields.

SIEM Process

The SIEM process closely maps to the infrastructure. Let's discuss some of the more important parts of this process as data goes through a typical SIEM infrastructure.

Data Inputs   SIEM solutions grab data from many different sources. Most SIEM solutions use *log collectors*—tools for recording network events—and SNMP inputs, of course, but many go far beyond those sources. For example, it's not uncommon for a

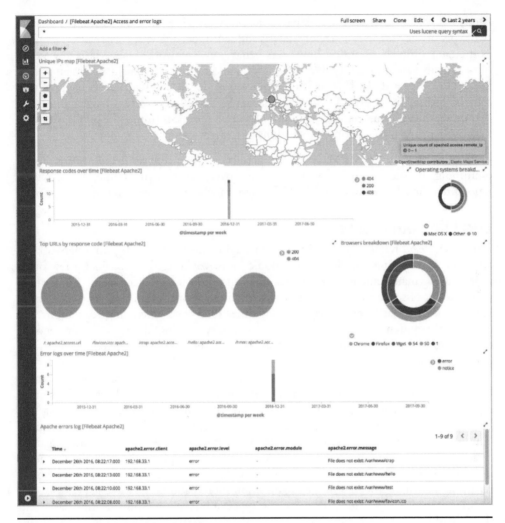

Figure 4-37 Elastic Cloud dashboard

SIEM solution to employ agents that perform *packet capture* for situations where that might be needed.

Log Aggregation   SIEM servers can't just have data dumped on them. First, data needs to be *normalized*, to regularize the same type of data among multiple logs. One great example of this is *log aggregation*. What if one log stores all source IP address information as "SRC_IP" while another log stores the same data as "Source"? Proper log aggregation will make the data output under a single label. Another example is too much data. Does the server need to store every IP packet going through a switch if all it really needs to know is the number of packets per second?

Analysis   SIEM analysis is a massive topic, but CompTIA only wants you to consider two types of analyses, user behavior analysis and sentiment analysis. *User behavior analysis*, as the name implies, considers how users behave on a network. Does Maria always log onto the same machine every day? Does Mario add new users to his department within a day after they are hired? When users move outside their anticipated behaviors, that may be indicative of trouble. *Sentiment analysis* tries to parse actual language used to determine the meaning behind that use. The system monitors things like publications for negative sentiment to determine intentions of a threat group, for example.

Review Reports   No SIEM system is perfect. Review reports detail the results of examining the success rate of a SIEM system over a certain timeframe. These review reports tell the administrators of the SIEM system where they need to improve.

Log File Management

Log management refers to the logistics of managing all the device logs in a network. In addition to reviewing log files on a periodic basis, you'll need to consider a few other aspects of log management. First, you should decide how long to keep log files, since they take up a lot of space and may not exactly contain a lot of relevant information—unless you need to look at a specific event. Sometimes *governance*, including regulations and other legal requirements, may require you to keep system log files for a certain amount of time, so log management is also concerned with retention of archived log files for a defined period.

Secure storage, retention, and retrieval of archived logs are required simply because log files can contain sensitive information about systems and networks, as well as other types of sensitive data. You must ensure that only personnel authorized to view log files have access to them and protect those log files from unauthorized access or modification. You must also be able to retrieve the log files from storage in the event of an investigation or legal action against your organization, as well as comply with audit requirements imposed by law. Log management applies to all of these things, and effective policy regarding managing the logs in the organization should address all these issues.

Security professionals look for particular types of information on a routine basis, and thus should configure logging to provide only that pertinent information. This helps to find the relevant information and eliminate the massive amounts of unnecessary information. For event-specific information, such as a major performance issue, an outage, or even a significant security event, a lot more information may be needed during those specific circumstances only. In such a case, security professionals may temporarily configure logging to provide far more detailed information. Getting that level of detail on a routine basis, however, would likely make logs unmanageable and limit their usefulness.

For example, let's say that you are monitoring a potential hacking attempt. You may change the audit level of your network devices or internal hosts to include more detailed information on processes, threads, and interactions with lower-level hardware. This level of detail can produce a vast amount of logs very quickly, which can fill up device storage and be very unwieldy to examine. Because of this, you'd want to enable this level of logging only for a short while, just long enough to get the information you need. After that, you'd want to reduce the logging level back to normal.

Questions

1. What does nslookup do?

   A. Retrieves the name space for the network

   B. Queries DNS for the IP address of the supplied host name

   C. Performs an ARP lookup

   D. Lists the current running network services on localhost

2. What is Wireshark?

   A. Protocol analyzer

   B. Packet sniffer

   C. Packet analyzer

   D. All of the above

3. One of your users calls you with a complaint that he can't reach the site www
   .google.com. You try and access the site and discover you can't connect either but
   you can ping the site with its IP address. What is the most probable culprit?

   A. The workgroup switch is down.

   B. Google is down.

   C. The gateway is down.

   D. The DNS server is down.

4. What command do you use to see the DNS cache on a Windows system?

   A. ping /showdns

   B. ipconfig /showdns

   C. ipconfig /displaydns

   D. ping /displaydns

5. Which of the following tools enables you to log into and control a remote
   system securely?

   A. ipconfig

   B. remoteconfig

   C. rlogin

   D. SSH

6. Which protocol do tools use to enable proactive monitoring of network hosts in
   real time?

   A. ipconfig

   B. nslookup

   C. SNMP

   D. SSH

7. The Windows tracert tool fails sometimes because many routers block _____ packets.

   A. ping

   B. TCP

   C. UDP

   D. ICMP

8. Which tools can you (and hackers) use to query LISTENING ports on your network? (Choose three.)

   A. Port scanner

   B. Nmap

   C. Angry IP Scanner

   D. Hostname command

9. Which tool enables you to view the contents of a text file in Linux?

   A. cat

   B. dig

   C. notepad

   D. nslookup

10. Which of the following commands would change the permissions of the file timmy.exe to read-only for all users but execute for the owner?

    A. chmod 440 timmy.exe

    B. chmod 664 timmy.exe

    C. chmod 744 timmy.exe

    D. chmod 777 timmy.exe

Answers

1. **B.** The nslookup command queries DNS and returns the IP address of the supplied host name.

2. **D.** Wireshark can sniff and analyze all the network traffic that enters the computer's NIC.

3. **D.** In this case, the DNS system is probably at fault. By pinging the site with its IP address, you have established that the site is up and your LAN and gateway are functioning properly.

4. **C.** To see the DNS cache on a Windows system, run the ipconfig /displaydns command at a command prompt.

5. D. Use Secure Shell (SSH) to log in and control a remote system securely. rlogin is an alternative to SSH, by the way, but lacks encryption.

6. C. The protocol for tools to do real-time network monitoring is SNMP.

7. D. The Windows tracert tool fails because it relies on ICMP packets that routers commonly block.

8. A, B, C. The hostname command simply returns the host name of the local system. All other tools mentioned can scan ports to locate network vulnerabilities.

9. A. The cat command enables you to view and combine text files in Linux.

10. C. Using the command chmod 744 timmy.exe sets the permission as rwxr--r-- for the file. The owner has read, write, and execute permissions. The group and others have only read permissions.

Securing Individual Systems

Adapt what is useful, reject what is useless, and add what is specifically your own.

—Bruce Lee

A typical security professional bandies about the term *attack surface*, meaning a cumulation of all the vulnerabilities for a specific infrastructure item. For a gateway router, for example, the attack surface refers to every option that an attacker might use to compromise that router, from misconfiguration to physical damage or theft (Figure 5-1).

This chapter explores the attack surface of one of the most vulnerable parts of networks, the individual systems. An *individual system* for the purposes of this chapter is a single computer running Windows, macOS, Linux/UNIX, or Chrome OS, in use every day. This includes desktops, laptops, servers, and workstations. It also includes mobile devices, but only to a lesser degree. We'll see more of those systems in later chapters.

The typical individual system on a network has hardware, software, connections, and applications, all of which are vulnerable to attack. The chapter first examines some of the more common attack methods, building on concepts that you learned in earlier chapters. This follows with an extensive discussion of the effects malware can have. Module 5-3 examines system resiliency options and methods. Subsequent modules explore different angles of individual system attack surfaces, from hardware to operating systems and applications, including host-based firewalls and intrusion detection (Figure 5-2). The chapter finishes with a brief discussion of ending the life of individual systems securely.

Figure 5-1
An attack surface

NOTE One attack surface variety this chapter does *not* cover is Internet applications—that is, Web apps. While these applications certainly run on individual server systems, local users on a LAN generally do not use those systems. These applications have their own class of problems that warrant their own chapter. We'll go into Internet application attacks—and how to stop them—in Chapter 11.

This chapter explores methods for securing individual systems in six modules:

- Types of System Attacks
- Malware
- Cybersecurity Resilience
- Securing Hardware
- Securing Endpoints
- System Recycling

Figure 5-2
We need to
protect systems.

Module 5-1: Types of System Attacks

This module covers the following CompTIA Security+ objectives:

- **1.3 Given a scenario, analyze potential indicators associated with application attacks**
- **1.4 Given a scenario, analyze potential indicators associated with network attacks**
- **1.6 Explain the security concerns associated with various types of vulnerabilities**

Any network is nothing more than a series of systems connected via fiber, copper, or wireless connections. But a physical connection isn't enough. To function on a network, the system must possess the necessary hardware and software to connect to a LAN and communicate via IP, sending and receiving properly formatted TCP/UDP/ICMP segments/datagrams (lumped together here as TCP/IP packets).

To perform this, a system consists of four independent features: network-aware applications, a network-aware operating system, a network stack to handle incoming and outgoing packets, and proper drivers for the network interface. Collectively, these features are the attack surface for an individual system.

 NOTE Physical access to a system provides a rather robust attack surface, although most of these topics fall outside the scope of CompTIA Security+. Module 5-4 explores this further.

To understand the types of attacks unleashed on systems, let's put all these features in order, as shown in Figure 5-3. We can then explore how bad actors can take advantage of vulnerabilities in each of these features to compromise individual systems.

Figure 5-3
Individual systems' attack surfaces

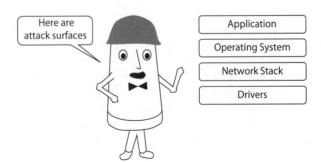

Attacking Applications

Applications contain their own unique set of vulnerabilities, but the impact of the vulnerabilities often remains, such as taking control of the application, shutting down the application, and accessing data from the application. This section looks at several attack surfaces for applications:

- Race conditions
- Improper input handling
- Error handling
- Memory/buffer vulnerabilities
- Pointer/object dereference
- Resource exhaustion
- Weak encryption
- DLL injection
- API attacks
- Privilege escalation
- Services

NOTE Just about every application attack type listed starts with or interacts with the operating system on which the application runs. This section could have easily been titled "Exploiting Operating System Vulnerabilities to Attack Applications," but we went with the shorter title. You'll see this interaction between OS and apps throughout.

Race Conditions

Most applications take advantage of multitasking to run multiple processes/functions at the same time. Sometimes the effect of two or more simultaneous transactions can result in undesired results called a race condition. *Race conditions* manifest as counters, totals, and other usually integer (whole number) values that simply don't add up correctly, such as when a program runs subroutine A and subroutine NOT A at the same time. Another bug that can happen with a race condition is *time-of-check to time-of-use (TOCTOU)*, where exploits can happen between the program checking the state of something and doing something about the results. Attackers can create or exploit race conditions. The impact of race conditions varies from incorrect values in Web carts to system stops to privilege escalation (see "Privilege Escalation" for more details on the last).

EXAM TIP The CompTIA Security+ objectives drop the hyphens and the "to" for TOCTOU, so you'll see the term on the exam as *time of check/time of use.*

Improper Input Handling

Programmers write software to take in and output data and results. That seems fairly obvious from a user standpoint, whether it's typing in Microsoft Word or changing data in an Access database and seeing changes made appear on the screen. Programs also get input from less visible sources and need to validate that input. A poorly written program—or a great program attacked by a clever attacker—can take in or handle improper information. This *improper input handling* can lead to unauthorized access to data, unexpected or undesired commands executed on a Web server, and more.

 NOTE Programmers write apps with certain expectations. Users provide input, processors process, and the app provides output. *Input validation* routines accept proper input and, in theory, reject improper input. Unexpected input can wreak havoc, though, so app developers will hire folks to throw all sorts of stuff at their app, just to see if it will break. That's part of the programming process. (You won't be tested on this, but thought you might like to know.)

Error Handling

What happens following an *exception*, an unexpected input or result, depends on how the programmers anticipated *error handling* by the application. Attackers could exploit a weak configuration or a bug in the code to do some serious damage. As a result of such vulnerabilities, some programs might crash, while others might reboot or restart. A more graceful response would send the application or server into a safe state that stops a bad actor from continuing an attack or malformed packets from causing problems. A Web server could restart in a maintenance mode, for example, so bad guys couldn't keep manipulating it. The Web server could inform administrators that it has switched to the error/maintenance mode. These would be good examples of error handling.

 NOTE Programmers dance delicate steps with error handling and reporting. Saving logs or error reports helps developers find and fix unexpected issues. Too precise an error report, on the other hand, can tell an attacker exactly what happened. That can lead the attacker to a new, more effective path, and that's not a good thing.

Memory/Buffer Vulnerabilities

All code uses memory to handle the active operation of that code. RAM may be cheap these days, but applications must be programmed properly to be aware of the amount of memory they're using. The CompTIA Security+ objectives include three vulnerabilities that are so closely related that it makes sense to treat them as a single issue:

- Memory leak
- Integer overflow
- Buffer overflow

All three of these vulnerabilities describe some part of memory being filled beyond the programmed capacity. A *memory leak* is a general issue where a single process begins to ask for more and more memory from the system without ever releasing memory. Eventually, the system reaches a memory full state and stops working.

Integer overflows are when a value greater than an integer variable causes the application to stop working. The program might have a field that accepts whole numbers from 0–64,535, for example, and receive a number of 128,000. Ouch!

A buffer is a temporary storage area in memory to hold data, such as the results of a form input. Buffers are fixed in size. If too much data gets into the buffer, causing unpredictable results, that's a *buffer overflow*.

The impact of all these situations is similar in that the system will at best kick out an error (that hopefully is well handled) and at worst cause a system lockup.

Pointer/Object Dereference

A pointer is an object used in most programming languages that "points to" another value in memory. Unlike a variable, a pointer references a memory location. When a pointer accesses the stored value, this is known as *pointer/object dereference*. If a bad actor can get a pointer to point incorrectly, a dereference can cause havoc to the code. If the bad actor can get a pointer to point to *no* memory location—a null pointer dereference—this can cause some very negative results. The impact of this vulnerability mirrors the impacts of previously discussed vulnerabilities, such as crashes, freezes, reboots, and worse.

Resource Exhaustion

Resource exhaustion isn't a vulnerability itself but rather the result of an attack that takes advantage of one or more of the memory-specific vulnerabilities previously described to bring down the system. Another example is sending malformed packets to a system, such as bad pings, that cause the server to churn so hard that it becomes inoperable. Resource exhaustion is the basis for denial-of-service (DoS) attacks that seek to make resources (servers, services, and so on) unavailable for legitimate users. (We'll see more on DoS and related attacks in Chapter 8.)

Weak Encryption

Securing any app is an ongoing battle between the good guys keeping encryption strong versus bad guys working to crack that encryption. One of the most obvious examples of this ongoing battle is in wireless networking. When Wi-Fi first arrived, WEP for security was fine-ish, but it was quickly cracked. Weak configurations and, in this case, weak encryption exposed wireless users to vulnerabilities. The industry came out with WPA, then WPA2, and then WPA3, trying to stay ahead of the bad guys. You'll remember all this from your CompTIA A+ and Network+ studies. The same vulnerabilities apply to every type of encryption used in modern networks.

 NOTE Many people will argue that WEP wasn't/isn't an encryption standard. As its name implies, Wired Equivalent Privacy was intended to provide security and confidentiality as good as a wired network. We get it.

Part of the struggle faced by developers is maintaining backward compatibility with older encryption standards while supporting newer, more secure encryption standards. A typical Web server can support 10–20 different types of encryption to enable different clients to connect and do business securely. A clever bad actor can take advantage of this by requesting the weakest type of encryption from a Web server in the hopes of getting something easily crackable. Organizations need to update and patch operating systems, firmware, and applications regularly just to keep up with the bad guys. You'll see this evolution and battle as we discuss encryption implementations in subsequent chapters.

NOTE The *Padding Oracle On Downgraded Legacy Encryption (POODLE)* attack from a few years back offers a stark example of clever attacks like the one listed above. Attackers used exploits to make apps drop from TLS to SSL security and then took advantage of known vulnerabilities of SSL to get information. We'll look at more attacks like this in Chapter 6.

DLL Injection

A dynamic-link library (DLL) is a file used in Windows systems that provides support code to executable files. Every Windows system has hundreds of DLLs, most commonly stored in the \Windows\System32 folder (Figure 5-4). Most applications provide their own DLLs as well. DLLs help reduce code size and speed up processing.

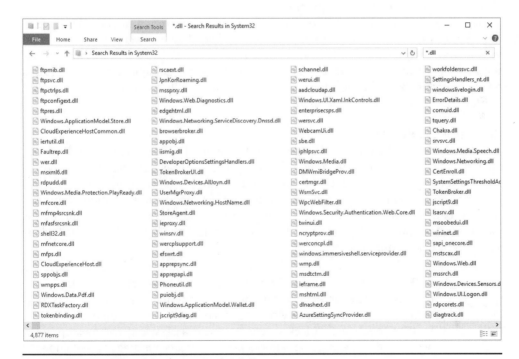

Figure 5-4 Just a few of the DLLs on Mike's laptop

DLL injection is a technique used by bad actors to get users to run malicious code. The code runs in the address space of another process and loads a malicious DLL. Once the DLL runs, all the usual impacts come into play: system control is one of the most common, used to zombify systems for distributed denial-of-service (DDoS) attacks—where attackers use many systems to hammer a server to try to shut it down. (See Chapter 8 for more details about DDoS and related attacks.)

NOTE Injection-style attacks don't stop with DLLs. You'll see them again with SQL, XML, and more in Module 11-3. (I see you trembling with anticipation!)

API Attacks

No program is an island. When you fire up Microsoft Word, for example, you're actually starting a program called winword.exe. The winword.exe executable acts as an orchestra conductor, automatically opening dozens or hundreds of other executables and DLLs as needed to enable Word to open and close files, to spell check, to access files across a network, and more. Interconnecting applications requires functions and procedures— programming—that can bridge the gap to, in effect, translate from one application to the other. These helper/translator applications are called *application programming interfaces (APIs)*. Like most things in computing, APIs started with little to no security. This has changed over time and version updates.

Bad actors look for unpatched or earlier versions of APIs in use to take advantage of discovered weaknesses and perform an *API attack*. If you have software of any form, that software uses one or more APIs, and at some time or other, bad guys have figured out ways to take advantage of that software. Web browsers, for example, interact with APIs on Web servers. Bad actors exploit weaknesses in these APIs to intercept data, disrupt systems, take down systems, and so forth.

Privilege Escalation

Privilege escalation, the process of accessing a system at a lower authentication level and upgrading (escalating) authentication to a more privileged level, presents attack opportunities against applications. All of the common operating systems require every user and every process accessing the system to go through some form of authentication/authorization procedure. If an attacker can access a system using a low-level access account such as public, everyone, or guest, he or she may find a bug that gets him or her to the highest access levels (root, administrator, etc.).

NOTE A *service account*, unlike an account used by people (guest, user, root), is used by some process running on the system that needs access to resources. The nature of service accounts prevents typical authentication methods because they lack anyone to type in a password. This makes service accounts a prime target for attacks. Over the years hundreds of well-known exploits have used service account privilege escalation as an attack surface.

Operating systems are designed to prevent privilege escalation. Attackers need to find some type of bug, sometimes even through an application running on the operating system, that gives them higher privilege. Alternatively, attackers can find an alternative login that may not have a higher privilege but might give access to something that lets them do what they need to do. If an attacker wants to access a printer, he doesn't need root access, just some account that has access to that printer.

NOTE Well-patched operating systems are extremely resilient to privilege escalation.

Services

Operating system services provide an attack surface for bad actors to attack applications. For a Windows-centric person, a *service* is any process that works without any interface to the Windows Desktop. You can access all running Windows services using the aptly named Services app (Figure 5-5).

Attacking a Windows service is pretty much the same as attacking an application. Attackers can use man-in-the middle attacks if possible, or they can use privilege escalation if they can find an exploit.

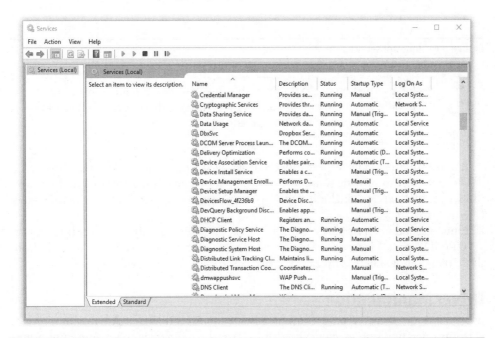

Figure 5-5   Services in Windows

```
Administrator: Command Prompt - netstat -a -b                          —    □    ×
  TCP    127.0.0.1:57537         Constance:57539       ESTABLISHED        ^
 [Dropbox.exe]
  TCP    127.0.0.1:57539         Constance:57537       ESTABLISHED
 [Dropbox.exe]
  TCP    127.0.0.1:58741         Constance:50041       ESTABLISHED
 [EXCEL.EXE]
  TCP    127.0.0.1:65001         Constance:0           LISTENING
 [nvcontainer.exe]
  TCP    127.0.0.1:65001         Constance:49642       ESTABLISHED
 [nvcontainer.exe]
  TCP    172.16.0.120:139        Constance:0           LISTENING
 Can not obtain ownership information
  TCP    172.16.0.120:8096       LONDON:58617          TIME_WAIT
  TCP    172.16.0.120:8096       LONDON:58633          TIME_WAIT
  TCP    172.16.0.120:8096       LONDON:58634          TIME_WAIT
  TCP    172.16.0.120:8096       LONDON:58635          TIME_WAIT
  TCP    172.16.0.120:8096       LONDON:58667          TIME_WAIT
  TCP    172.16.0.120:8096       LONDON:58672          TIME_WAIT
  TCP    172.16.0.120:50720      US-DEN-ANX-R008:http  ESTABLISHED
 [TeamViewer_Service.exe]
  TCP    172.16.0.120:50721      US-DEN-ANX-R008:http  ESTABLISHED
 [TeamViewer_Service.exe]
  TCP    172.16.0.120:50725      52.242.211.89:https   ESTABLISHED
 WpnService
 [svchost.exe]
  TCP    172.16.0.120:50809      17.248.241.143:https  CLOSE_WAIT
 [iCloudPhotos.exe]
  TCP    172.16.0.120:50810      17.248.241.143:https  CLOSE_WAIT
 [iCloudDrive.exe]                                                       v
```

Figure 5-6   Internet services

NOTE   The CompTIA Security+ objectives version 3 changed man-in-the-middle attacks to on-path attacks. We'll discuss these sorts of attacks in much more detail in Chapters 6 and 11.

A more Internet-centric person would define *services* as processes that listen on a TCP/UDP port to provide some sort of (again aptly named) service. In Windows, you can see TCP/IP services, including the process providing that service, using netstat –a –b (Figure 5-6).

Linux users don't have this confusion. A Linux service is only a process listening on a TCP/UDP port. Linux does not separate processes that interface to the desktop from those that do not. There is no Linux equivalent to Windows' Services app.

Driver Manipulation

Every piece of hardware on a computer (with the exception of RAM) communicates with the operating system via device drivers. Attackers either can send communications to device drivers to make them do things they were never supposed to do, or can replace the device drivers with corrupted device drivers to gain privilege escalation or launch spoofing attacks.

There are two attack surfaces to manipulate device drivers to do malicious things, driver refactoring and driver shimming. Neither attack surface is unique to device drivers—both are present in any type of code—but they are the two best ways to attack an individual system via its device drivers.

Refactoring

Programming is all about inputs and outputs. A piece of code takes input and, based on that input, does some type of output. For software developers, *refactoring* means to rewrite the internals of a piece of code without changing the way it reacts to input or how it performs output.

The many device drivers that talk to system hardware are certainly code. Hardware manufacturers always want to make their drivers faster and smaller, so refactoring is a common feature with device drivers.

Refactoring can have a slightly different, malevolent definition. *Refactoring* can mean to reprogram a device driver's internals so that the device driver responds to all of the normal inputs and generates all the regular outputs, but also generates malicious output. A refactored printer driver that works perfectly but also sends all print jobs to an evil remote server is an example of this other type of refactoring.

 EXAM TIP Every operating system provides a method of driver signing that is designed to prevent refactoring attacks on device drivers.

Shimming

Refactoring was a very common attack for many years, but today all operating systems use *driver signing* that confirms the exact driver files used. The operating system detects any changes and deals with them in one way or another, so replacing a device driver's files isn't as easy as it used to be. To get around this issue as an attacker, instead of replacing a signed file (or files), why not just throw another file or two (with the extra evil code) into the system?

A *shim* is a library that responds to inputs that the original device driver isn't designed to handle. Inserting an unauthorized shim, called *shimming* or a *shim attack*, is more common than refactoring because it does not require replacing an actual file—it merely relies on listening for inputs that the original device driver isn't written to hear.

Malicious Code or Script Execution

Modern computing systems are filled with tools to enable properly written code or scripts to do all kinds of powerful actions to the operating system or applications. CompTIA's Security+ objective 1.4 lists the following: two shells, PowerShell and Bash; one compiled general-purpose language, Visual Basic for Applications (VBA); one interpreted general-purpose scripting language, Python; and the word "macros" (a lovely generic term that the author assumes CompTIA uses to refer to the combination and automation of commands built into an application like Microsoft Excel).

Figure 5-7 We're totally different, but we can do the same jobs!

These five *things* are very different in what they do, where they work, and how they're used. Yet collectively these five shells/languages/macros provide virtually identical tools to write amazing code to get work done (Figure 5-7).

 NOTE I don't want to enumerate these five shells/languages/macros every time they come up, so let's have a little fun and invent a term, just for this one small section: *PPBMV* (PowerShell, Python, Bash, Macros, Visual Basic for Applications). Once we're done here, feel free to forget it.

Let's consider one example, changing file permissions. Every single member of PPBMV can change file permissions. PowerShell has the set-acl command to change NTFS permissions. Bash and Python can just run a chmod. VBA and most macros in Windows applications can change file permissions as well.

Changing file permissions is just one example of what PPBMV can do. These tools can edit the registry (in Windows), change IP addresses or computer network names, manipulate files; this list goes on and on. These capabilities enable PPBMV to do good work, and we want PPBMV to have these features. But there's a downside. Actions such as changing file permissions is also a dangerous thing done maliciously. We provide security to systems by first limiting what PPBMV can do and second, by watching for indicators of compromise such as unauthorized changes in permissions. Don't blame the tool; blame the way it is used (Figure 5-8)!

Limiting what PPBMV can do is done on a platform-by-platform basis. You can enable features such as execution policies and Constrained Language mode to limit what PowerShell can do, for example. You can isolate PPMBV on hosts with host-based firewalls. You can even completely delete these tools from your host unless they are needed. The trick here is understanding the power of PPBMV and doing your best to limit that power unless you need it.

Figure 5-8
Don't blame
PPBMV, blame
the attacker

Module 5-2: Malware

This module covers the following CompTIA Security+ objective:

- **1.2   Given a scenario, analyze potential indicators to determine the type of attack**

Programmers with evil intent write software that attacks systems to gain control, do damage, or extract financial gain. This malicious software—*malware*—comes in many forms, for evil programmers can be just as clever as good programmers. The CompTIA Security+ exam will challenge you with scenario questions that expect you to recognize the symptoms of certain types of malware. Let's go through the following types and make sure you're aware of the differences:

- Virus
- Cryptomalware/ransomware
- Worm
- Trojan horse
- Potentially unwanted programs (adware, spyware, crapware)
- Bots/botnet
- Logic bomb
- Keylogger
- RAT
- Rootkit
- Backdoor

Each section explores the malware, then finishes with a description of the symptoms and action(s) you should or could take to deal with an attack of that type. Some of the fixes involve actions to ameliorate the problems; others just acknowledge the obvious and recommend rebuilding and cutting your losses. Let's take a look.

Virus

A *virus* is a piece of malicious software that must be propagated through a definite user action. In other words, it normally cannot spread by itself. It requires a user to initiate, in some way, the execution of the virus. Sometimes this action is very subtle, and the unsuspecting user may not even know that his actions are executing a virus. For example, he may open an infected file or executable, spawning the virus. Normally, viruses are propagated via download from malicious Internet sites, through removable storage media (USB sticks, for example) passed along from person to person, or through the transmission of infected files from computer to computer via e-mail or file sharing.

Viruses have a variety of effects on computers and applications. These effects range from affecting performance by slowing down the system, filling up storage space, and slowing down the host's network connections, to more serious impacts, such as recording passwords and other sensitive information, and rendering the host completely unusable or even unbootable. Some viruses infect files, while others, usually more serious ones, infect the boot sector of media. These boot-sector viruses automatically execute in the computer's memory when the host boots up; at that moment, there is no OS-based anti-virus software loaded to detect or eradicate it, so it has already done its damage by the time the OS loads. Usually, the only way to get rid of a boot-sector virus is to boot the host off of a known good (meaning clean and free of malware) media, such as a new hard drive, bootable optical disc, or a USB stick. The boot media should also have specialized antivirus software loaded on it to detect and clean the infection.

A particularly vicious form of malware—called *fileless malware* (CompTIA calls it *fileless virus*)—behaves in some ways like a virus, attacking and propagating, but differs in one fundamental aspect. Fileless malware lives only in memory, not writing any part of itself to mass storage. Fileless malware often uses tools built into the operating system, such as PowerShell in Windows, to attack that very system. Anti-malware software struggles to identify, let alone mitigate, fileless malware.

You might have wondered why it seems so easy for hackers to create viruses that can do so much damage; in fact, there are many programs on the Internet that help hackers create viruses easily. Some require extensive programming skills, and others are simple graphical programs that require almost no knowledge at all. Figure 5-9 gives an example of one such program, TeraBIT Virus Maker, but there are hundreds more out there.

- **Symptoms:** System slowdown; some action against your system.

- **Action:** Use an anti-malware program from a live boot to clear the virus from the system.

Figure 5-9   TeraBIT Virus Maker, a virus creation program

Cryptomalware/Ransomware

Cryptomalware uses some form of encryption to lock a user out of a system. Once the cryptomalware encrypts the computer, usually encrypting the boot drive, in most cases the malware then forces the user to pay money to get the system decrypted, as shown in Figure 5-10. When any form of malware makes you pay to get the malware to go away, we call that malware *ransomware*. If a cryptomalware uses a ransom, we commonly call it *crypto-ransomware*.

Crypto-ransomware is one of the most troublesome malwares today, first appearing around 2012 and still going strong. Zero-day variations of cryptomalware, with names such as CryptoWall or WannaCry, are often impossible to clean.

- **Symptoms:** System lockout; ransom screen with payment instructions.
- **Action:** Use anti-malware software from a live boot to clear the cryptomalware from the system.

NOTE   Most cryptomalware propagates via a Trojan horse. See the upcoming "Trojan Horse" section for more information.

Figure 5-10 CryptoWall, an infamous crypto-ransomware

Worm

A *worm* is much like a virus, in that it can cause disruptions to the host, slow down systems, and cause other problems. However, a worm is spread very differently from a virus. A worm is usually able to self-replicate and spread all over a network, often through methods such as instant messaging, e-mail, and other types of network-based connections. The big difference between a virus and a worm is that a virus can't spread itself; in other words, a virus requires a user action to replicate and spread. A worm doesn't have this problem and can automatically replicate over an entire network with very little user intervention. This unfortunate characteristic of a worm is what causes it to be a significant problem in large networks. Examples of famous worm infections include MyDoom, Blaster, and the Win32Conficker worm.

- **Symptoms:** System slowdown; unauthorized network activity; some action against your system.
- **Action:** Use an anti-malware program from a live boot to clear the worm from the system.

Trojan Horse

A *Trojan horse* isn't really a type of malware; it's more a method by which malware propagates. Named after the Greek Trojan Horse of mythological fame, a Trojan horse is a piece of software that seems to be of value to the user. It could be in the form of a game, utility, or other piece of useful software. It is malware, however, and serves a specific function. Usually a Trojan horse has the goal of collecting personal information from a user, including user credentials, financial information, and so on. It can also be used as a generic container used to spread viruses and worms. (Note that symptoms and actions will follow the payload type, so will vary a lot.)

EXAM TIP The CompTIA Security+ exam refers to Trojan horse malware as simply "Trojans."

Potentially Unwanted Programs

Although technically not malware, some programs installed on your computer have negative or undesirable effects. Makers of the programs resented labels such as adware, spyware, bloatware, crapware, and so on, and sued the anti-malware companies to stop the use of such terms. For legal reasons, therefore, the industry adopted the term *potentially unwanted programs (PUPs)* as a blanket term for these programs that have negative effects on your computer.

PUPs differ from malware because users consent to download them. That "consent" typically is obtained through sneaky, deceitful, or underhanded means. Often the user might seek to download a perfectly legitimate, useful application, but then clicks what seems to be the download option, only to install some PUP instead.

Figure 5-11 shows a common bait-and-switch operation. Using a reputable third-party download site—CNET—I clicked the option to download CPU-Z (an excellent system hardware reporting tool, by the way). Rather than the download starting immediately, I was kicked to the page in Figure 5-11. At the top of the page in fine print it says "Your download will begin in a moment. If it doesn't, restart the download." Fine; companies like CNET make money off ads. That's just capitalism. But at the bottom of the page, you see the giant "Start" button? Click that and you'll install a nasty PUP, not the desired utility program.

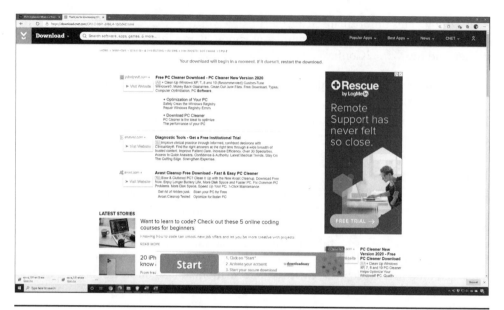

Figure 5-11   Underhanded and sneaky ad trying to trick user into installing a PUP

Adware

Adware is the name given to annoying advertisements that come in the form of pop-up messages in a user's browser or on a user's screen outside of a browser session. These messages usually want the user to visit a site, buy a product, or click the ad itself. At best, these messages can be irritating, interrupting a user's activities with the pop-up message, but sometimes they are a real hindrance to productivity, often redirecting the user's home pages in the browser or spawning several (sometimes dozens to hundreds) of pop-ups or Web sites at once.

Computers get adware infections pretty much the same way they get other types of malware. The user may click a Web link or download something that changes browser or other configuration settings on the host, resulting in the continuous stream of pop-ups. Adware can even be included with purposefully downloaded, seemingly unrelated applications. Sometimes the user is asked to allow the installation of an add-in or browser helper object (BHO) to view a certain file type or run a piece of browser-based software. Most of the time, unsuspecting users will allow the installation by default, opening the door to pop-ups, automatically spawned programs, and browser redirection.

- **Symptoms:** Unauthorized Web browser redirection; pop-up ads.
- **Action:** Use an anti-malware program from a live boot to clear the adware off the system.

Spyware

Spyware isn't a type of malware; it's more of a goal for some types of malware. Spyware is a virus or Trojan horse in form, but we tend to classify spyware by its function rather than type. Spyware is used for the specific purpose of surreptitiously observing a user's actions and recording them, as well as stealing sensitive data, such as passwords, credit card information, and so forth. Spyware can send data back to the attacker, quietly of course, so that the user can't easily detect it. Spyware can also dump data into a file so an attacker can later retrieve it directly from the system if she has physical access. Spyware can affect hosts through various means, in usually the same way that other malware does.

 NOTE The spyware aspect of a malware can take many forms. Look to the specific payload type for all the malware symptoms and the actions you should take to combat it.

Crapware

The rather derogatory term *crapware* describes software that purports to help users accomplish tasks, but instead directs the users to sites that primarily benefit the software developers. The most common of these programs are the free, additional toolbars that install in Web browsers. These have built-in search and help features, but they don't take you to the excellent Google or Bing search tools. Instead, they send the unsuspecting user to ad-filled mediocre search pages, track user searches, and more. Educate users not to install these foul things!

Bots/Botnets

A *botnet* is a distributed type of malware attack that uses remotely controlled malware that has infected several different computers. The idea is to create a large robot-like network used to wage large-scale attacks on systems and networks. Once the malware is installed on the host, the attacker can control hosts remotely and send malicious commands to them to be carried out. The hosts are called *bots*, or *zombies*, because they obey only the orders of the attacker once the attack begins.

One of the common implementations of bots and botnets involves servers that control the actions of the bots. These *command and control (C2)* protocols try to automate the control, not requiring human interaction after the initial programming. See Chapter 8 for more details about C2 protocols, botnets, and the brutal attacks they can deliver, such as DDoS attacks.

Among the different attack methods that botnets can use is sending massive amounts of malware to different computers, sending large volumes of network traffic, and performing other methods designed to slow down or completely disable hosts and networks. Botnet attacks can spread rapidly once activated and can be very difficult to counter.

In fact, one of the attack methods used during an attack is to infect other hosts and have them join the botnet:

- **Symptoms:** Usually undetectable until activated. System slowdown in some cases.
- **Action:** Use an anti-malware program from a live boot to clear the bot from the system.

Logic Bomb

A *logic bomb* is often a script set to execute either at a specific time or if a certain event or circumstance takes place on the system. It is designed to take malicious actions when it executes. An example of a logic bomb is a script that has been written to begin erasing file shares or disk storage at a certain time or date. Most logic bombs are timed to execute by including them as a scheduled event using the operating system's event scheduling facility, such as the AT command in Windows or the cron utility in Linux-based systems. A logic bomb is *not* necessarily a form of malware—at least it's not the kind that can easily be detected by anti-malware software.

Logic bombs are usually planted by a malicious insider or a disgruntled administrator; most of the logic bomb attacks recently sensationalized in the news media involved a rogue administrator dissatisfied with an employer for whatever reason. Detecting a logic bomb can be troublesome; it usually requires examining any files, utilities, and scheduled jobs the malicious user had access to, as well as auditing the user's actions and reviewing the access logs that recorded any use of his privileges.

- **Symptoms:** Usually undetectable until activated. System damage, data loss.
- **Action:** Restore system from backups.

Keylogger

A *keylogger* is a piece of malware that records keystrokes. Most keyloggers store a certain number of keystrokes and then send the stored keystrokes as a file to the bad actor. Recorded keystrokes are one of the best ways to collect passwords, filenames, and other highly personalized types of information. Keyloggers are not all evil. They are a very common feature for parental control software. Figure 5-12 shows one example, Spyrix Free Keylogger.

 NOTE   Keyloggers also manifest as malicious hardware dongles that sit between your keyboard and your system.

Hardware keyloggers manifest as tiny USB adapters that fit between a keyboard USB connector and the USB port on the system. They're nondescript and do not show up as system devices, so you won't know they're present without physical inspection. They

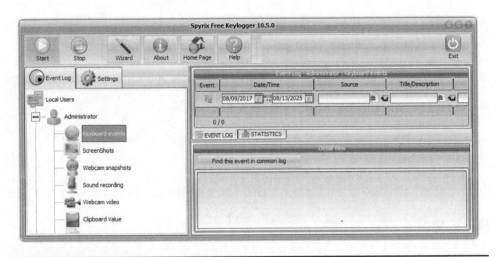

Figure 5-12   Keylogger interface

come in a couple of varieties. Some have flash memory built in and require periodic physical removal for scanning. Others transmit wirelessly to a receiving system.

- **Symptoms:** Often no symptoms at all. System slowdown; unauthorized network activity.
- **Action:** Use anti-malware software from a live boot to remove the keylogger software. Removing keylogger hardware requires suspecting such a device might exist, finding it, and physically removing it from the system. Then smashing it with a hammer.

RAT

RAT stands for one of two things. First, RAT stands for *remote administration tool*, which is some form of software that gives remote access for administrators and IT support. We use this kind of RAT all the time in IT to log into servers, remote cameras, Internet of Things (IoT) devices (lightbulbs, thermostats, etc., connected to the network), and to provide support for users all over local networks and the Internet.

Second, RAT also stands for *remote access Trojan*, which is a remote administration tool maliciously installed as a Trojan horse to give a remote user some level of control of the infected system. This can be as simple as just opening a Telnet server on the infected system to full-blown, graphical remote desktops. RATs are often an important part of a botnet.

- **Symptoms:** Usually undetectable until activated. System damage, data loss.
- **Action:** Restore system from backups.

Rootkit

A *rootkit* is a piece of malware that attempts to infect critical operating system files on the host. Often, anti-malware software cannot easily detect rootkits, so they can reside on the system for quite a while before detection. Additionally, rootkits can thwart anti-malware software because they can send false system information to it, preventing it from detecting and eradicating not only itself but other malware as well.

- **Symptoms:** Often no symptoms at all. System slowdown; unauthorized network activity.

- **Action:** Although you can find anti-malware software that claims it can remove a rootkit, always opt for the better solution: wipe the drive and reload.

Backdoor

A *backdoor* is an entry method into a piece of software (application or operating system) that wasn't intended to be used by normal users. Most backdoors are created as a maintenance entry point during software development, usually by the programmers creating the software. These maintenance backdoors should be closed prior to software release, but often they are either forgotten about or left open intentionally to bypass security mechanisms later after the software is released, either by the programmer or a malicious entity.

 NOTE   A few smartphones and other mobile devices manufactured in China have been found to have backdoors.

Backdoors can also be created by hackers during an intrusion into a system; often their goal is to have a way back into the system if their primary entry point is taken away or secured. Again, backdoors usually bypass security mechanisms that normally require identification and authorization, so this is a serious security issue. Vulnerability testing can often detect these unauthorized entry points into a system, but sometimes more in-depth testing methods, such as penetration testing or application fuzzing, may be required to find them.

 NOTE   Like Trojan horses, a backdoor is a method of entry into a system, not a malware type. Look for the specific payload type to determine symptoms and actions you should take to protect or remediate.

Module 5-3: Cybersecurity Resilience

This module covers the following CompTIA Security+ objective:

- **2.5   Given a scenario, implement cybersecurity resilience**

Figure 5-13
I rebuff your pathetic attempts!

What if you could design a system such that even if successfully attacked, the system could in some way quickly (as in a matter of seconds) rebuild itself or, even better, weather an attack without the attack being able to do any real damage? That's the idea behind *cybersecurity resilience*: adding technologies and processes that don't stop attacks, but enable the system to recover easily (Figure 5-13).

 EXAM TIP   Resilient systems don't eliminate risk. That's impossible! Resilient systems fight off attacks more readily than systems with less resilience. They handle risks better, in other words. The principles here apply to individual systems and to larger "systems," such as an enterprise network.

There are many ways to make systems more resilient, but it helps to organize these methods into three main categories: non-persistence, redundancy, and diversity. *Non-persistence* simply means to possess a method to bring a system back quickly to its pre-attack state. *Redundancy* means to have more than one of some functioning feature of a system or even another complete system. *Diversity* refers to the practices of using a variety of technologies, vendors, cryptographic systems, and controls to avoid the possibility that all systems have the same vulnerability and can be taken out en masse.

Non-persistence

A typical individual system is *persistent* in that it has a fixed set of hardware, a fixed operating system, and a fixed configuration. If you turn off a system and turn it back on, you have the same hardware, the same operating system, and the same configuration. It is persistent.

The downside to a persistent system is that if an attack takes place, that attack will in some way change some aspect of that persistent state. The attack might wipe a hard drive. It might inject evil device drivers. It might create privileged users you don't want on the OS. If any attack takes place, there's a good chance you'll have to go through some painful recovery process. This might include reinstalling an operating system or rebuilding from backups. These are time-consuming processes and ones to avoid by using less persistent systems.

Achieving non-persistence means pursuing one of these options:

- Virtualization/snapshots
- Revert to known state
- VMs and automation
- Live boot media

Virtualization/Snapshots

There are many reasons virtualization has taken over the world of serving systems these days. One reason is the ease of recovery by simply shutting down a virtual machine (VM) and then restarting it without affecting any of the underlying hardware. But another feature, and the one that very much fits under the idea of non-persistence, is the snapshot. A *snapshot* is the stored difference between the files in one version of a VM and the files in another version. While the snapshot procedure varies from one virtualization platform to another, imagine a perfectly functional VM where you change a single device driver, only to discover over time that the device driver is buggy and keeps causing your VM to crash. If this were a classic persistent system, you'd have to reinstall the device driver. If you made a snapshot of the system before you installed the device driver, however, you could simply revert to the earlier snapshot and bring the system back to its original function (Figure 5-14).

Snapshots are a critical non-persistence tool for VMs. Every time you change a driver, update an application or service, patch a client OS, or take any other action that makes any significant change to your VM, run a snapshot.

Revert to Known State

Every technician has made some change to an operating system, only to find that the change he or she made is flawed in some way. A bad driver, a poorly distributed patch, or an OS update that fails to perform the way the tech thought and causes problems can

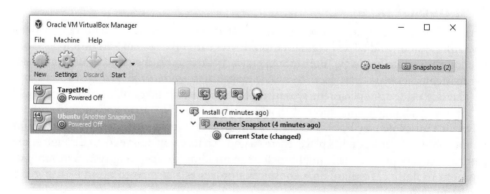

Figure 5-14   Snapshots in VirtualBox

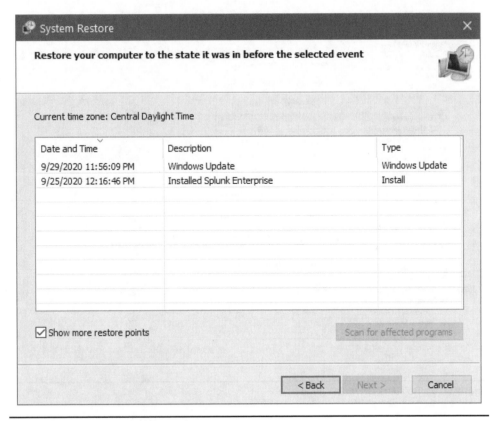

Figure 5-15   Restore points in Windows

make the tech want to go back to the way things were before the change was made. If you have a virtual system, you can easily erase such changes via a snapshot. On a fixed traditional system, it's not that easy.

Every major OS has some form of *revert/rollback* method to bring a system back to a previous state, what the CompTIA Security+ objectives call *revert to known state*. All revert/rollback methods work by making the OS aware of changes and then storing files or settings in such a way that techs can look up previous states and tell the OS to go back to one of those states.

Microsoft Windows enables you to create a *restore point*—a capture of the overall operating system and drivers at that moment in time—that enable you to revert the operating system to an earlier configuration (Figure 5-15). Windows restore points aren't perfect. They don't save user information or installed applications; but other than those two issues, restore points are very powerful.

Device drivers, especially video card drivers, often have unforeseen problems that motivate a return to a previous driver version. Equally, a refactored device driver might wreak havoc on an otherwise perfectly good system. Again, Windows has an elegant solution in the Roll Back Driver feature, as shown in Figure 5-16.

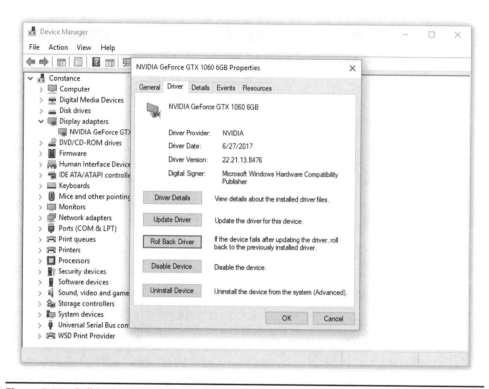

Figure 5-16　Roll Back Driver in Windows

Apple macOS machines rely on *Time Machine*, a program that records snapshots of the state of the computer over time to an external drive (Figure 5-17). If you support Macs, establish Time Machine for every system.

Apple macOS doesn't have a roll back driver feature similar to that in Windows for two reasons. First, Apple checks all drivers much more aggressively than Microsoft; so bad, refactored, or shimmed drivers almost never happen. Second, Time Machine supports drivers as well, making a separate rollback feature unnecessary.

EXAM TIP　Older Windows versions (such as Windows 7) offered a boot feature called *last known good configuration* that enabled quick recovery from installation of a buggy driver. The feature was especially useful with buggy video card drivers. The inability to get into the Windows graphical user interface made troubleshooting or uninstalling problematic. Windows 10 has much more powerful tools through Advanced Recovery options. Not sure why CompTIA left *last known-good configuration* in the Security+ objectives, but now you know what it is.

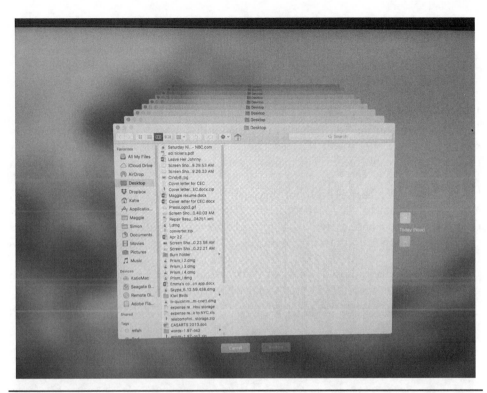

Figure 5-17   Time Machine in macOS

VMs and Automation

Many modern networks use virtualization technologies to provide both rollouts and rollbacks of many systems all at once. With a *master image*—the desktop environment for users of very specific hardware and configurations—a central server can push that image to every local computer. Automation/scripting can make rollouts regular, such as after patch Tuesday—and configuration validation (i.e., it works!)—so users always have up-to-date builds. This kind of automated course of action helps keep systems current.

EXAM TIP   You'll see this aspect of VMs—the capability to push out multiple identical copies—categorized as *replication* on the CompTIA Security+ exam.

Plus, master images enable network administrators to respond very quickly to problems. With continuous monitoring, as you'll recall from Chapter 3, network administrators keep up with the reporting from network monitoring and managing tools. If a recent rollout hits snags, the network techs can fix the master image and, with a manual rollout, essentially "roll back" the problematic build. Similarly, if a new bug or attack causes problems, a fixed and validated master image can be quickly deployed.

NOTE Virtual machine developers, like VMware, enable you to create a *template* of a completed VM that you can use to create identical versions of the VM. Templates provide excellent flexibility and rapid deployment of additional servers as needed.

Live Boot Media

If you want the ultimate in non-persistence on a non-VM system, you can always use some kind of live boot media. *Live boot media* are complete, installed operating systems that exist on bootable media. The names change to match the media. On optical media, for example, they're called *live CDs*; for consistency, bootable flash-media drives should be called *live sticks* (they're not), but they're usually just called *bootable USB flash drives*. You boot a system to the live boot media and use the OS as configured. Your system doesn't even need a hard drive. Live boot media are very popular in Linux environments, giving you an opportunity to try a Linux distro without installing it on your hard drive (Figure 5-18).

Live boot media go way beyond test-driving Linux. You can easily install a carefully configured system, say a DNS server, to a live boot and run the entire server in that fashion. As long as the serving system doesn't need to store any persistent data (like a database

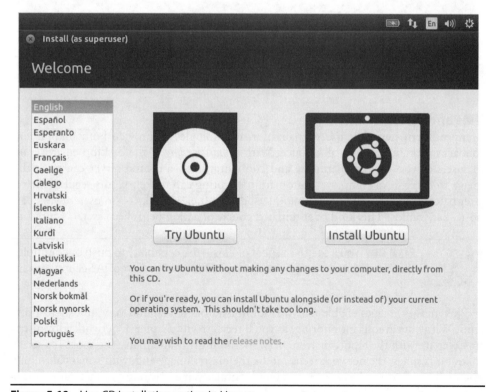

Figure 5-18 Live CD installation option in Linux

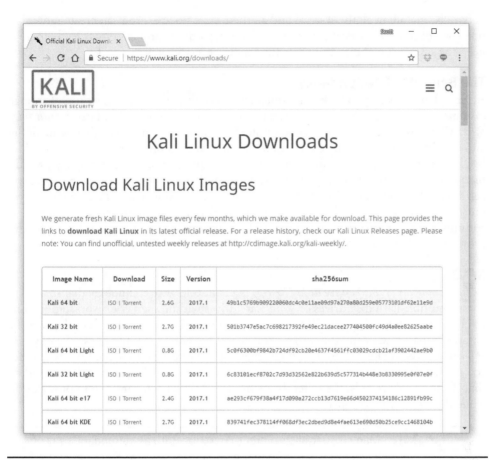

Figure 5-19 Kali Linux downloads

that changes), you can run almost any OS/application combination from a live boot media. One of the most popular live boots is Kali Linux, the go-to Linux distro, stuffed full of many IT security tools (Figure 5-19).

Redundancy

Non-persistence provides excellent resiliency in most cases, but falls short in data storage when there are big changes in the state of the stored data. Snapshots/reverts are wonderful for subtle changes in operating systems, such as a security patch or a driver update, as they don't require much mass storage space. They simply aren't designed to deal with big changes to data, such as customer databases, inventories, users' file storage, and other such data that requires a lot of hard drive space. Traditionally, this type of data is backed up daily; in this situation, turn to redundancy to provide the system resiliency needed.

But where to apply redundancy? There are several options. You can create redundant mass storage, redundant systems (including their mass storage), even redundant networks (including all the systems and all their mass storage). You can create more than one copy of non-OS critical data so that if one copy dies, another copy is ready to go to keep the systems up and running. Redundancy is everywhere!

The Benefits of Redundancy

At first glance, it's easy to look at redundancy as nothing more than a backup of storage, systems, or even networks, but true redundancy is far more powerful. First is *fault tolerance*. With fault tolerance, the secondary storage, the system, and the network are online and ready to go. If something goes wrong, the data on the storage or the services provided by the system can have a minimal amount of disruption. Second, redundancy provides *high availability.* High availably means using redundancy in such a way as to ensure that certain levels of operational performance are balanced against risk. Third, you can work on one of your services offline with minimal impact to your customers, whether that's adding capacity or repairing a component. Let's look at the redundancy technologies that provide both fault tolerance and high availability.

RAID

Redundant array of inexpensive disks (RAID) is a fault tolerance technology that spans data across multiple hard disk drives or solid state drives within a server or workstation. This level of fault tolerance specifically addresses hard drive failure and balances the need for data redundancy with speed and performance. RAID uses multiple physical mass storage drives to create logical drives, usually making it transparent to users. Data is spanned across the different physical drives, along with metadata (usually parity information), so that if any one drive fails, the other drives in the RAID set can continue to provide data while the single drive is replaced.

 NOTE Many IT specialists prefer to describe RAID as "redundant array of *independent* disks," rather than the original *inexpensive*. You'll definitely see the terms out in the wild both ways. CompTIA goes with the original wording. Just remember RAID and you'll be fine on the exam.

There are several different RAID levels; which one you should use for a system depends upon different factors, including the number of available disks and the balance of total available space for storage, as well as the levels of speed and performance the system requires. RAID levels can be implemented in several ways. *Striping* typically means writing pieces of data equally across two physical disks. *Mirroring*, in contrast, completely duplicates data on each disk. Using more disks, you can include *parity* information, which enables data to be restored in the event of a single disk failure. You'll find combinations of all these. Figure 5-20 illustrates examples of different RAID levels using these techniques.

There are trade-offs for each of these different methods, which include total amount of storage space, speed, performance, and the number of disks required in the RAID array. Table 5-1 summarizes some of the different RAID levels and their details.

Figure 5-20
Examples of RAID configurations

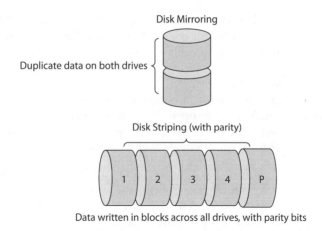

Disk Mirroring

Duplicate data on both drives

Disk Striping (with parity)

Data written in blocks across all drives, with parity bits

Storage Area Networks

A typical LAN has file servers that store data that is accessed via network stacks. It also has local storage that your system accesses via block-level controllers that access the drives.

A *storage area network (SAN)* is a network storage that enables you to access the shared folders by using block-level controls rather than the network stack. This gives SANs some unique capabilities, mainly on-the-fly volume creation/manipulation. On most systems,

RAID Level	Details	Minimum Number of Physical Drives Required
RAID 0	Disk striping; does not use mirroring or parity; provides for performance only with no redundancy.	2
RAID 1	Disk mirroring; all data is completely duplicated on both disks; uses no striping or parity but provides for full redundancy at the expense of the loss of half the total available disk space for duplication.	2
RAID 5	Disk striping with parity; parity information is spread across all disks evenly; $1/n$ of the total disk space available is used for parity.	3 to n
RAID 6	Disk striping with double distributed parity; this allows for failure of up to two drives.	4
RAID 1+0 (or sometimes seen as RAID 10)	Disk mirroring with striping; combines both RAID levels 0 and 1 for performance and redundancy; a stripe of two mirrored arrays.	4
RAID 0+1	Disk striping with mirroring; combines both RAID levels 0 and 1 for performance and redundancy; a mirror of two striped arrays.	4

Table 5-1 Summary of RAID Levels

if you want to add storage, you first get a storage device, configure it, mount it, and format it. On a SAN, you just tell the SAN controller to add another disk to your local system. You can create a new volume or you can mount an existing volume.

System Redundancy

RAID is certainly the go-to technology to provide fault tolerance for mass storage, but what about systems? What happens if the Web site sits only on one Web server and that server fails? Server redundant technologies such as multipath, NIC teaming, geographic dispersal, and virtualization provide both fault tolerance and high availability.

Multipath A *multipath* solution provides more than one way to access storage. A RAID 1 implementation with two controllers, one for each drive, is the traditional multipath solution (called *disk duplexing*, as you might recall from CompTIA A+ studies). More than one connection to a SAN is also a typical implementation of multipath.

NIC Teaming Network interface cards rarely fail, but when one does, the system with the bad NIC is offline until the NIC is replaced. *Network interface card (NIC) teaming* addresses this issue by using two or more NICs on a single system that act as though they are a single NIC with one MAC address and one IP addresses. Not only does NIC teaming increase throughput (sort of), but if one NIC fails, the other continues to work (Figure 5-21).

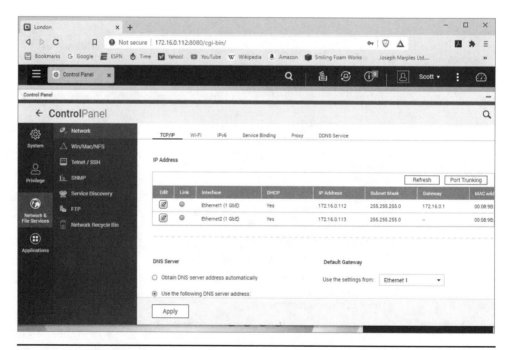

Figure 5-21 File server with NIC teaming

NOTE NIC teaming doesn't suddenly turn two Gigabit Ethernet NICs into 2-Gbps throughput for a system, although that's a common misconception. Moving one large file still tops out at 1 Gbps. Where you'll see better performance is when moving multiple files at the same time. The additional NIC or NICs essentially offer additional 1-Gbps lanes for traffic.

Geographic Dispersal   The gold standard for system redundancy is to make perfect copies of the same system and spread them apart geographically, then use the Internet to keep the copies identical. *Geographic dispersal* protects from natural disasters and widespread Internet disruption. You can set up your own dispersed servers, but virtualization services make it easy.

Virtualization/Cloud Services   For decades we used real servers in real locations (on-premises), but those days are over. Nothing beats virtualization, especially cloud-based services, for giving you all the benefits of redundancy, especially high availability, without outrageous cost and time. First, virtualization solutions are incredibly scalable. Let's say you develop a new Web app and launch it on a single Amazon S3 server, and suddenly your product is a huge hit (and the single server is swamped). Virtualization services like Amazon S3 make it easy to spin up more copies of your server (although you can do this locally—on *prem*, as they say—as well). Add as many copies as you want and need!

 EXAM TIP   Expect a question on the CompTIA Security+ exam that explores *on-premises vs. cloud* in terms of redundancy, high availability, and scalability.

Virtualization also makes geographic dispersal easy to achieve. Is your new Web site huge in Japan? Just tell Amazon to spin up some new servers over in Japan so your customers in Tokyo get the same speed and response as your US users (Figure 5-22).

The other amazing high-availability power of virtualization comes from elasticity. Going back to the Web app idea, some Web apps have cycles of high and low demand (tickets sales, sports broadcasts, etc.). These cases require *scalability* both in terms of

Figure 5-22   Virtualization makes geographic dispersal easy.

expanding and contracting on an as-needed basis, better known as *elasticity*. All virtualization providers have simple features to add or remove server instances automatically based on predetermined load values.

 NOTE Industry uses the term *template* to describe a server purchase. For example, you might order a certain tier of stuff. "I want a medium cluster with a blue level of security and redundancy." That's the template. Once you get it, you take a snapshot of it and can rebuild it at any time. So sweet!

Diversity

Security people have a tendency to stick with single technologies, crypto, and controls from preferred vendors. Why not? We know they work, we know how to use them, and we know how to fix them. The danger with such a lack of diversity is the possibility that all systems have the same vulnerability and can be taken out en masse.

When organizations rely on multiple redundant technologies, vendors, cryptographic systems, and security controls, that *diversity* provides cybersecurity resilience. If a single technology fails, a vendor disappears, the crypto system is cracked, or security controls change and conflict, an organization that employs multiple systems through diversity can quickly pivot and implement fixes.

Diversity takes more work, sure. Security and network people need to master multiple systems, vendor relations multiply with more than one vendor, and so on. But diversity enhances cybersecurity resilience.

Module 5-4: Securing Hardware

This module covers the following CompTIA Security+ objectives:

- **1.2 Given a scenario, analyze potential indicators to determine the type of attack**
- **2.5 Given a scenario, implement cybersecurity resilience**
- **2.7 Explain the importance of physical security controls**
- **3.2 Given a scenario, implement host or application security solutions**
- **3.3 Given a scenario, implement secure network designs**
- **3.8 Given a scenario, implement authentication and authorization solutions**

Many years ago, an overly cocky security tech friend presented a challenge to me. He said that he had secured a server system so perfectly that no unauthorized person could access the data, and he challenged me to try. Accepting the challenge, I didn't waste a moment trying to attack the system remotely. Instead, I simply put on some work clothes to look like a maintenance man, went to the location, and used my social engineering skills to gain entry. Once inside, I found the server and yanked out every hard drive. With plenty of time and completely nonsecure hardware, it was just a matter of cracking a Windows login and ... success!

There's a strong lesson here for any security person. Physical possession of mass storage—or complete systems that hold the mass storage devices—is every attacker's dream. Granted, getting to the data might be a challenge, but every pawn shop, every classified advertising medium, and every law enforcement office in the USA is filled with stolen systems. If an attacker can get to the physical system, no firewall, no network login, no wireless access point is going to prevent him from eventually getting to the precious data.

Secure hardware presents the last line of defense for these types of attacks. Virtually every piece of hardware that runs an Intel- or ARM-based CPU comes prepackaged with powerful tools to lock down a system to secure individual computers from physical attacks.

This module starts with a discussion of a few of the nasty types of physical attacks on systems. The module then covers many of the technologies used to protect systems from attacks, both intentional and unintentional. We'll finish with more specific options for securing boot integrity.

Physical Attacks

If a threat actor is allowed to get physical access to a system, even for the shortest of moments, there are plenty of interesting tools the threat actor may physically connect to the system to gather all kinds of information about the system, the users, and even the network.

Malicious USB Cable/Drives

Any unused USB port on a system is a huge vulnerability. A bad actor can easily plug in a Bluetooth adapter and instantly use his or her own Bluetooth keyboard. Figure 5-23 shows one of my favorite tools, a HAK5 USB Rubber Ducky. I just plug it into any USB port and it starts sending preconfigured commands, such as capturing keystrokes and delivering a payload to compromise the system.

The downside to a *malicious flash drive* is that someone is going to notice it eventually. That's why my good friends down at HAK5 make a similar tool that looks like a cable! HAK5's O.MG cables can plug between any two USB devices: smartphone to desktop, smartphone to power charger, desktop to USB device (such as an external drive or keyboard). While still working as any USB cable should, the O.MG steals any information it can based on how it is connected (Figure 5-24). The O.MG exemplifies a *malicious Universal Serial Bus (USB) cable* as defined in the CompTIA Security+ objectives.

 NOTE   HAK5.org makes awesome tools for testing systems, part of the field of pentesting. Check them out at https://shop.hak5.org.

I recommend disabling every unused USB port, usually leaving only one open in front of the system, thus easily observed. See the following sections for more options.

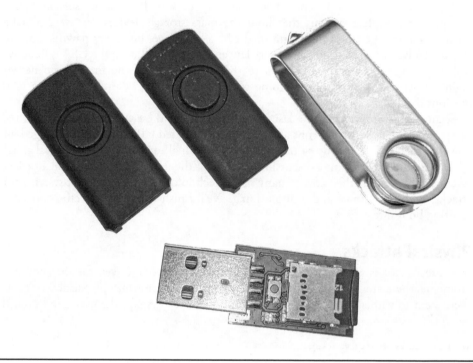

Figure 5-23 HAK5 USB Rubber Ducky

Figure 5-24
HAK5 O.MG cable
(Image: Berkah,
Getty Images)

EXAM TIP Look for an exam question on controlling removable media. The correct answer to the question likely will be related to disabling USB ports or, more specifically, not allowing access to USB ports to malicious actors.

Attacking Cards

Attackers love to copy and clone our plastic cards—credit cards, loyalty cards, office issued IDs … anything on a card is fair game to the right bad actor. The main weakness to any form of plastic card is the magnetic stripe on the back. The information on those stripes is easily read by a card scanner and can then be placed on another card. We call this *card cloning*.

So how do the bad guys read our cards? By using card skimmers. These devices sit surreptitiously on top of the card readers at ATMs, vending machines, gasoline pumps—wherever users insert cards—and read the stripe, a process called *skimming*. Card skimmers also usually come with cameras to capture users typing in a PIN code, a ZIP code, or a CVV code as well. Figure 5-25 shows an ATM skimmer.

Some security tools, in particular the EMV card format (the cards with the little chip), make skimming and cloning a lot harder than it used to be, but the many countries that have yet to fully adopt the EMV standards (such as the United States) are still happy hunting grounds for skimmers and cloners.

Securing the Systems

The first thing on any security person's list when new hardware comes in is to do what can be done to secure the systems. These steps are always carried out when new systems arrive and are brought online. Well, if not carried out, then at least considered!

Theft Prevention

All new equipment is given an inventory tag and tracked by installation location. Portable devices are issued to specific individuals who are solely authorized to use them and hold

Figure 5-25
ATM skimmer
(Image:
Chalongrat
Chuvaree /
EyeEm, Getty
Images)

some degree of responsibility for keeping them secure. Static devices are often secured when possible.

You can stop theft with some good physical security. First, almost all desktop and server system cases come with *anti-intrusion alarms*. If anyone opens the case, the system sets off an audible alarm.

Second, get a *cable lock*, particularly if you place a laptop in a tempting location for thieves. All laptops come with a reinforced cable lock port. You should consider Kensington Computer Products Group (www.kensington.com) for a variety of excellent cable locking systems.

Finally, don't forget a screen filter. *Screen filters* are excellent tools to narrow the field of vision. This prevents shoulder surfers from observing the content of your screen.

Securing Physical Ports

As previously mentioned, an unused USB port is a huge vulnerability. Account for every port on a system. USB ports are everywhere! Many monitors/displays have handy USB ports. Most printers and multifunction devices (MFDs) have USB ports. Even many home routers have USB ports. Those are the most important ones to turn off because you rarely observe them.

If at all possible, turn off all unneeded ports. If a port cannot be turned off, physically block it. Certain devices such as ports on portable devices need those ports working, so it's common to install *USB data blockers*, devices that you insert into a USB port that deny any data flow into the port, while still providing power for charging smartphones and such. See Figure 5-26. With a USB data blocker installed, devices like the previously discussed HAK5 tools won't work.

Securing Power

Good power is critical. All the locks, guards, and firewalls mean nothing if your systems don't have reliable, clean electrical sources. Let's consider what an organization can do to secure the power it has and needs.

 EXAM TIP   All this electrical stuff is more in the realm of data centers and distribution frames that power lots of servers and networking devices. Most of this equipment would make no sense in a home or office.

Dual Supply   Many higher-end devices support *dual power supplies*. These aren't complicated: if one power supply goes out, the other takes over. The only trick to dual power supplies is to make sure you buy a product that supports them and also make sure that product comes with two power supplies.

Figure 5-26
USB data blocker

Figure 5-27 Power generator (Image: Westend61, Getty Images)

Uninterruptible Power Supply An *uninterruptible power supply (UPS)* uses a small battery (often the same type used in motorcycles) as a backup power source if the power ever sags or goes out completely. It's very common to place a UPS at the bottom of an equipment rack, powering all the devices on the rack with quality, dependable power. A UPS is designed to power a system for a few minutes to enable an orderly shutdown.

Generator If you need to ensure that a system has uninterrupted power for an extended period of time after a power failure, you need to consider an onsite *generator* as a source of backup electricity. Generators are expensive, but if you need real backup power, this is your only choice. Most generators run on either natural gas or diesel (Figure 5-27).

Managed Power Distribution Units Great. You have a rack full of equipment and that equipment needs power. You have a UPS at the bottom of your rack, but now you need to distribute the power coming from your UPS to the devices. Plus you need to ensure that you have sufficient outlets for all the gear on the rack. That's where a *power distribution unit (PDU)* comes into play. At the simplest end a simple power strip is a PDU, but if you're going to distribute power, why not use a *managed PDU* that can monitor power usage, send alarms, and so forth?

Securing Boot Integrity

IT professionals need to plan for many contingencies so that users have secure computers with which to work. At the system level, for example, they must assure the security of individual system components by securing the supply chain. Second, they must implement technologies that will protect data in the event of theft or unauthorized physical access to systems. This section explores these aspects of physical security:

- Using TCG technologies
- Using TPM for boot security
- Using disk encryption
- Incorporating HSMs

Using TCG Technologies

The IT industry knew back in the mid-1990s that ensuring cross-platform technology security was going to take a lot of big companies working together, so AMD, Hewlett-Packard, IBM, Intel, and Microsoft got together and formed an organization now called the *Trusted Computing Group (TCG)*. Over the years, TCG has included roughly 100 of the most important hardware and operating system manufacturers (Figure 5-28).

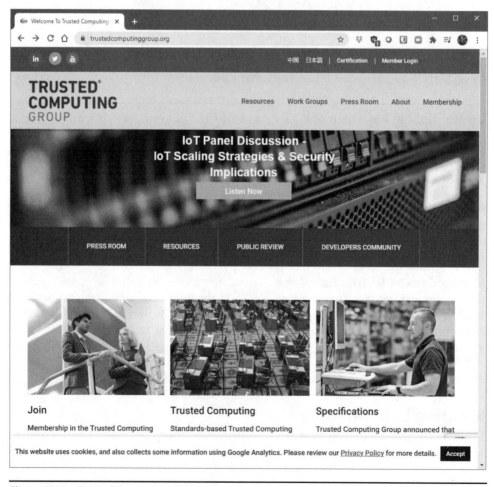

Figure 5-28 Trusted Computing Group

TCG is solely responsible for all the most popular technologies that, when used collectively, make your system very secure. Let's look at those technologies and see how they work.

Using TPM for Boot Security

Most modern computers ship with a chip called a *Trusted Platform Module (TPM)* (see Figure 5-29) that works with system firmware—UEFI in current PCs, for example—to provide a baseline level of security and trust. The operating system relies on this *hardware root of trust* to check for low-level changes at bootup. These changes can happen from malware, for example. Depending on the system, any tampering could lead to automatic loading of a last known-good system or a system stop.

 EXAM TIP Modern personal computers rely on Unified Extensible Firmware Interface (UEFI) for firmware, as you'll recall from your CompTIA A+ studies. Look for a question on the CompTIA Security+ exam that points to *boot security/Unified Extensible Firmware Interface (UEFI)* as the preferred method for assuring *boot integrity*.

This boot-level security, called generically *secure boot*, can also work with more centrally controlled systems. During the boot process, the TPM and UEFI generate reports about the process and can send those reports to a remote system, like a central authentication server. This process is called *boot attestation*. A typical scenario would describe analyzing the reports or reporting process involving TPM as an example of *authentication management*.

With Windows 10, Microsoft added another tool called *Measured Boot* that interacts with UEFI and TPM over a network to verify the integrity of the boot files. This architecture blocks malware such as rootkits.

 EXAM TIP Windows 8 and later feature Secure Boot to take advantage of TPM and UEFI to provide boot attestation. The Linux folks tend to use the open-source Opal Storage Specification.

Figure 5-29
TPM chip

Using Disk Encryption

Security professionals use various forms of disk encryption to protect *data at rest (DAR)*, files and folders stored on mass storage and not in transit/motion or in processing (active use). Disk encryption has been around in one shape or another for a long time and certainly predates TPM chips, but the presence of TPM provides a powerful tool for encrypting drives. Every operating system supports *full disk encryption (FDE)*, which typically means every part of a drive is encrypted except the boot sector. The FDE tool that comes with Windows Pro versions is called *BitLocker*. To encrypt a drive with BitLocker, you must have a motherboard with a TPM chip and you must have TPM enabled in UEFI (Figure 5-30).

 EXAM TIP Expect a question (or an answer) on the CompTIA Security+ exam that equates disk encryption as a method or part of the process of *hardening an operating system*. So think beyond securing data here to seeing solutions for a whole system.

You can go even more secure with disk encryption by using a *self-encrypting drive (SED)* that automatically encrypts and decrypts all data on the drive. From the outside, a SED looks exactly like any other drive. It works on both traditional hard disk drives (HDDs) and solid state drives (SSDs). A SED often comes with extra features, such as instantaneous drive wiping, that high-security folks really enjoy.

 EXAM TIP The Trusted Computing Group publishes the specifications for the Opal Storage Specification that enables SED for Linux as well as Windows.

Figure 5-30 BitLocker in Windows

Incorporating Hardware Security Modules

The many processes that take advantage of asymmetric key storage, authentication, encryption/decryption, and other functions can often swamp general-purpose CPUs and operating systems. For Web servers, automated teller machines, or other applications that perform an unusually high amount of key handling, it's usually a good idea to offload this work to other hardware. A *hardware security module (HSM)* is any type of hardware that's designed to do this work.

An HSM might look like a *network appliance*, supporting one or more servers; it might be a USB device; or like Figure 5-31, it might look like a PCIe card you install on a system. When cryptography is slowing down a server's response time, an HSM, with its optimized processors designed to handle cryptographic functions hundreds of times faster than an equivalent general-purpose CPU, will speed up key handling dramatically. HSMs are expensive, but when time is of the essence, HSMs are the way to go.

 EXAM TIP   A typical scenario would describe deploying HSMs as an example of *authentication management*.

 NOTE   You can use an HSM for secure boot (which is why it's placed here in the book). Often this manifests with a combination of flash media, system on a chip (SoC) systems, and certificates. The process is well beyond this discussion, but worth noting.

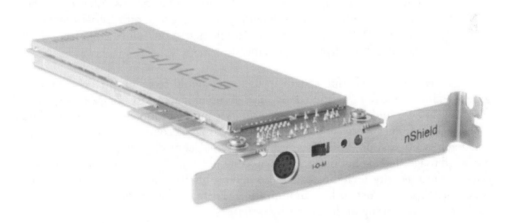

Figure 5-31   HSM PCIe card

Module 5-5: Securing Endpoints

This module covers the following CompTIA Security+ objectives:

- **1.6 Explain the security concerns associated with various types of vulnerabilities**
- **2.1 Explain the importance of security concepts in an enterprise environment**
- **3.2 Given a scenario, implement host or application security solutions**

The previous module discussed several tools to secure hardware and made more than one reference to securing operating systems and applications. This module carries the story forward, focusing on applying well-known security controls to design the right *endpoint protection*, for both operating systems and applications.

Hardening Operating Systems

Hardening an operating system means several things, but mostly it's about configuring the operating system and setting security options appropriately. Security professionals should adhere to the golden rule for hardening:

If you don't need it, remove it. If you can't remove it, turn it off.

Although all operating systems provide methods and interfaces for *secure configurations*, we're not going to focus on one specific operating system in this module. Instead, we'll focus on several configuration settings that should be considered regardless of operating system.

 NOTE The federal government and various organizations publish guidelines on specific settings for hardening systems. Check out the Department of Defense (DoD) Security Technical Implementation Guides (STIGs) as a great example: https://public.cyber.mil/stigs/.

Regardless of the operating system in use, you should focus on privilege levels and groups (administrative users and regular user accounts); access to storage media, shared files, and folders; and rights to change system settings. Additional settings you should evaluate include encryption and authentication settings, account settings such as lockout and login configuration, and password settings that control strength and complexity, password usage, and expiration time. You also should consider other system settings that directly affect security, including user rights and the ability to affect certain aspects of the system itself, such as network communication. These configuration settings contribute to the overall hardening of the operating system.

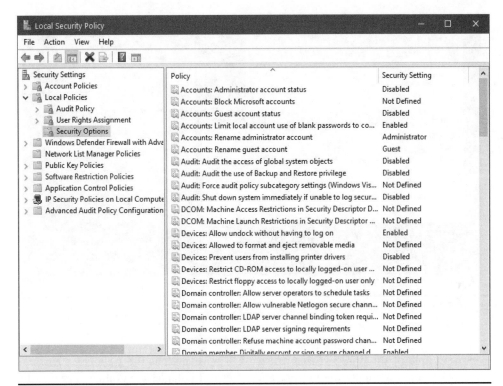

Figure 5-32   Security options in Windows 10

Figure 5-32 shows a sample of some of the different options that you can configure for security in Windows. Figure 5-33 shows other options that you can configure in a Linux operating system.

 EXAM TIP   You might see a question about endpoint security solutions that explicitly state the need to harden the Windows *Registry*, the central database in Windows for configuration of just about everything. For the most part, applying hardening techniques discussed in this module will lock down access to the Registry to only those accounts that need to access it—administrators, in short—and provide more than adequate security.

Trusted Operating System

A *trusted operating system* is a specialized version of an operating system, created and configured for high-security environments. It may require very specific hardware to run on. Trusted operating systems are also evaluated by a strict set of criteria and are usually used in environments such as the US Department of Defense and other government agencies, where multilevel security requirements are in place.

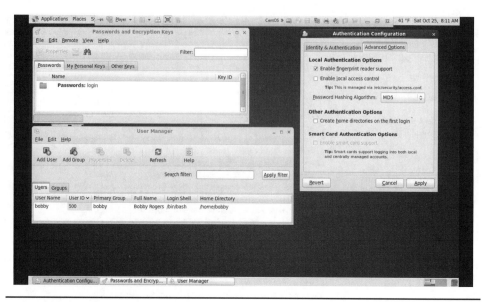

Figure 5-33 Security options in Linux

An example of the criteria that a trusted OS must meet is the *Common Criteria*, a set of standards that operating systems and other technologies are evaluated against for security. A lot of national governments worked together to create the Common Criteria, including the United States, the United Kingdom, Canada, Germany, France, the Netherlands, and more.

Trusted operating systems have very restrictive configuration settings and are hardened beyond the level needed for normal business operations in typical security environments. Examples of trusted operating systems include Trusted Solaris, SE Linux, and Trusted AIX. Some operating systems, such as Windows 10 and Windows Server, have been certified as trusted operating systems.

Host-Based Firewalls and Intrusion Detection

In addition to setting up security configurations on a host, you need to protect the host from a variety of network-based threats. Network-based firewalls and network-based intrusion detection/prevention systems—covered in detail in Chapter 6—work to protect the entire network from malicious traffic.

Host-based versions of these devices are usually software-based, installed on the host as an application. Their purpose is to filter traffic coming into the host from the network, based upon rules that inspect the traffic and make decisions about whether to allow or deny it into the host in accordance with those rules:

- A *host-based firewall*, like the excellent Windows Defender Firewall, blocks unwanted access based on port numbers and other criteria.

- A *host-based intrusion detection system (HIDS)* serves to detect patterns of malicious traffic, such as those that may target certain protocols or services that appear to cause excessive amounts of traffic, or other types of intrusion.

- A *host-based intrusion prevention system (HIPS)* actively scans incoming packets and blocks potentially harmful ones aggressively.

Host-based firewalls, HIDS, and HIPS may be included in the operating system, but they can also be independent applications installed on the host. You should carefully configure them to allow into the host only the traffic necessary for the host to perform its function. You should also baseline them to the normal types of network traffic that the host may experience. You should update host-based firewalls/HIDS/HIPS with new attack signatures as needed and tune them occasionally as the network environment changes to ensure that they fulfill their role in protecting the host from malicious traffic, while permitting traffic the users need to do their jobs. Figure 5-34 shows a side-by-side example of Windows and Linux firewalls.

NOTE In real-world implementations of host-based security measures, weigh the overall security posture of the device in question. Yes, you can lock down a resource completely, protecting it from attackers. But will this impede the effective use of that device? Balance is important.

Figure 5-34 Comparison of Windows and Linux firewalls

Disabling Open Ports and Services

Almost every host runs services that it doesn't need. In addition to wasting processing power and resources, a host that runs unnecessary services poses security risks. Services can be vulnerable to attacks for a variety of reasons, including unchecked privilege use, accessing sensitive resources, and so on. Adding unnecessary services to a host increases the vulnerabilities present on that host, widening the attack surface someone might use to launch an attack on the host.

Disable any unnecessary services or open ports as a basic hardening principle. If you have a public-facing Web server, for example, don't run any services that offer avenues of attack into the host or, worse, into the internal network. A public-facing Web server shouldn't run e-mail, DHCP, DNS, and so on. Internal hosts have the same issues; workstations don't need to run FTP servers or any other service that the user doesn't explicitly need to perform his or her job functions.

You should take the time to inventory all the different services that users, workstations, servers, and other devices need to perform their functions, and turn off any that aren't required. Often, when a device is first installed, it runs many unnecessary services by default; often these do not get disabled. Administrators should disable or uninstall those services, or at least configure them to run more securely. This involves restricting any unnecessary access to resources on the host or network, as well as following the principle of least privilege and configuring those services to run with limited-privilege accounts.

Application Security

Often, security administrators identify software that is harmful to computers or the organization for various reasons. In some cases, software may contain malicious code; in other cases, the organization may want to allow the use of certain applications, such as chat programs, file sharing programs, and video games (Figure 5-35). You can restrict access to these applications in several different ways, one of which is blacklisting. *Blacklisting* (or

Figure 5-35
But I need to play CounterStrike!

configuring a *block list/deny list*) involves an administrator adding an undesirable piece of software or an application to a list on a content filtering device, in Active Directory group policy, or on another type of mechanism, so that users are not allowed to download, install, or execute these applications. This keeps certain applications off the host. Applications may be blacklisted by default until an administrator has decided on whether to allow them to be used on the host or the network.

Whitelisting (or configuring an *allow list*) works similarly to blacklisting, except that a whitelist contains applications that are allowed on the network or that are okay to install and use on hosts. A whitelist would be useful in an environment where, by default, applications are not allowed unless approved by an administrator. This ensures that only certain applications can be installed and executed on the host. It also may help ensure that applications are denied by default until they are checked for malicious code or other undesirable characteristics before they are added to the whitelist.

 EXAM TIP On the CompTIA Security+ 601 exam, you might see the more neutral terms "block list/deny list" and "allow list" rather than the traditional terms "blacklisting" and "whitelisting." CompTIA replaced the traditional terminology with the new terminology in version 2 of the 601 exam objectives.

Applications and software can be restricted using several different criteria. You could restrict software based upon its publisher, whether you trust that publisher, or by file executable. You could also further restrict software by controlling whether certain file types can be executed or used on the host. You could use these criteria in a whitelist or a blacklist.

Figure 5-36 shows an example of how Windows can do very basic whitelisting and blacklisting using different criteria in the security settings on the local machine. When using blacklisting in a larger infrastructure—using Active Directory, for example—you have many more options to choose from.

Open Permissions

Most operating systems and devices default these days to requiring at least some minimal form of identification and authentication at login. Windows 10, for example, makes it very difficult to set up an account with no password requirement. Earlier versions of Windows weren't quite as strict, so people who wanted no-frills logins left their systems open to easy attacks. About the only places you'll find *open permissions* are kiosks at conventions and trade shows that enable users to access the Internet easily. As you should also know, don't use those systems to access any systems that require any personal account information. Don't log into Facebook from the trade show floor, in other words!

 EXAM TIP For the CompTIA Security+ exam, keep in mind that open permissions equates to no security at all for any accessible system.

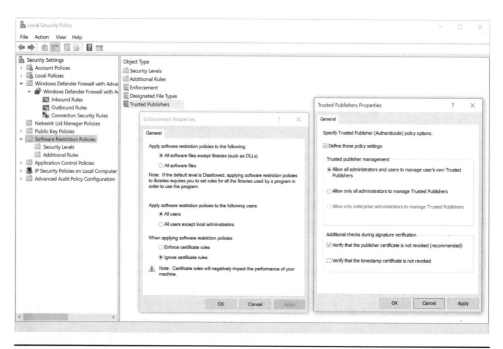

Figure 5-36   Application control in Windows

Disabling Default Accounts/Passwords

Out-of-the-box, operating systems often include default accounts with blank passwords or passwords that don't meet the organization's complexity requirements. Some of these default accounts may not even be necessary for the normal day-to-day operation of the host. A good example of such an account is the Windows default guest account (disabled by default in Windows 10). Linux operating systems are also vulnerable to this issue. A default Linux installation includes many accounts, all of which you should examine to determine whether they are necessary for the day-to-day operation of the host, and then disable or delete any that aren't necessary.

 EXAM TIP   Expect a question or two on the CompTIA Security+ exam that explores *default settings* or default accounts as examples of vulnerabilities caused by *weak configurations*. Some operating systems enable setup with *unsecure root accounts*, such as a local administrator with no password, which, as you should suspect, would be a bad thing!

Patch Management

Operating system vendors release patches and security updates to address issues such as unforeseen vulnerabilities. For the most part today, operating systems *auto-update*, meaning they seek out and download patches from their manufacturers automatically, although in some cases this must be done manually. This process is called *patch management*. In a home environment, it's probably okay for hosts to download and install patches automatically on a regular basis. In an enterprise environment, however, a more formalized patch management process should be in place that closely relates to configuration and change management.

 EXAM TIP   *Legacy platforms*, such as Windows 7 don't get security updates. No patches equates to increasing vulnerabilities, because bad guys like to keep looking for them. Do yourself and your users a solid and move away from legacy platforms as quickly as you can.

In a robust patch management process, administrators review patches for their applicability in the enterprise environment before installing them. Admins should research a new patch or update to discover what functionality it fixes or what security vulnerabilities it addresses. Admins should then look at the hosts in their environment to see if the patch applies to any of them. If they determine that the patch is needed, they should install it on test systems first to see if it causes issues with security or functionality. If it does cause significant issues, the organization may have to determine whether it will accept the risk of breaking functionality or security by installing the new patch, or will accept the risk incurred by not installing the patch and correcting any problems or issues the patch is intended to solve. If there are no significant issues, then the admins should follow the organization's formal procedure or process for installing the patch on the systems within the environment. Typically, this is done automatically through centralized *patch management tools* (software), but in some cases, manual intervention may be required and the admins may have to install the patch individually on each host in the enterprise.

In addition, admins should run a vulnerability scanner on the host both before and after installing the patch to ensure that it addresses the problem as intended. They also should document patches installed on production systems, so that if there is a problem that they don't notice immediately, they can check the patch installation process to determine if the patch was a factor in the issue.

 EXAM TIP   Improper or weak patch management can lead to vulnerabilities that bad people can and will exploit. IT managers should update everything properly, including firmware, operating systems (OS), and applications. That includes *third-party updates* as well, especially any custom software applications or utilities used by the organization.

Anti-malware

Anti-malware has come a long way from the early antivirus programs we used back in the 1990s. These first tools were drive scanners, using signatures to look for known viruses and doing their best to clean them out of systems. As time progressed, more features came online such as e-mail scanners, HTTP scanners, and RAM scanners. It wasn't uncommon for a single anti-malware tool to possess five or six different scanning types.

EXAM TIP Look for exam questions specifically addressing the output from *antivirus* software. Just substitute anti-malware software and you'll see the obvious answer.

Today's anti-malware tools include *point scanners*—often called real-time scanners—that provide real-time scanning of all incoming data, looking for malware signatures. Point scanners don't care about the type of data. They look for malware signatures in e-mail and Web browsers. Whatever application you use, a good point scanner will find and stop the malware before it infects your system (Figure 5-37).

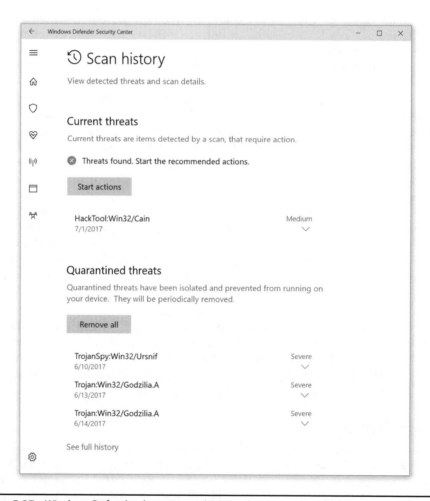

Figure 5-37 Windows Defender detecting malware

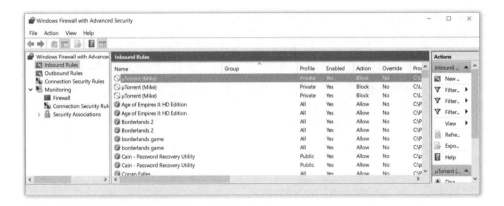

Figure 5-38 DEP settings in Windows 10

Data Execution Prevention

In the early 2000s, a series of worms attacked the Internet, infecting memory areas with buffer overflows and propagating themselves by attempting to contact random IP addresses. These worms were relatively easy to detect, but their ability to execute code in areas of memory normally used only for data storage proved to be a bit of a problem. To stop these types of attacks, Intel and AMD implemented a CPU feature called the No eXecute (NX) bit. All operating systems were updated to support the NX bit. In Microsoft Windows, NX bit support is called Data Execution Prevention (DEP). The generic term for this is *executable space protection*. I'll use DEP in this explanation for ease of use (and what you might see on the CompTIA Security+ exam).

EXAM TIP The CompTIA Security+ 601 objectives do *not* mention the NX bit or DEP, except to include the latter in the standard acronym list. It's doubtful you'll get tested on something that's been an enabled standard for nearly two decades.

DEP is on by default on every Windows operating system. Be aware that you can disable it in the system setup utility. Assuming DEP is enabled in firmware, there's always a place to check it in your operating system. Figure 5-38 shows DEP in Windows 10.

NOTE DEP should always be on, quietly protecting systems from buffer overflows. The need to turn off DEP is rare.

File Integrity Monitors

If malware is to be persistent, it must find a place to hide in mass storage. One popular strategy of malware is to create its own place to hide by replacing otherwise perfectly good files, both executable and data files, with refactored versions (Figure 5-39).

Figure 5-39
Which is the
real one?

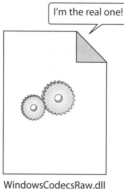
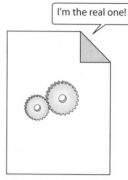

WindowsCodecsRaw.dll   WindowsCodecsRaw.dll

To defeat these bad actors, use a file integrity monitor as part of an anti-malware routine. As the name implies, a *file integrity monitor* makes sure the right files are in the right place. Most file integrity monitoring starts with a hash of the file itself, but may also add several other options:

- File date/time
- Version number (if executable)
- Digital signature
- Metadata (modify date)

By recording these values at installation of the operating system or application, a file integrity checker can verify without a doubt that the files being checked are the right ones.

 NOTE See Chapter 8 for more details on fully featured *file integrity monitoring (FIM)* systems that scale up to handle enterprise networks.

Data Loss Prevention

If your data is precious, you might want to add some *data loss prevention (DLP)* tools to the individual servers storing that data. Most DLP solutions are designed not only to keep your data's integrity at 100 percent but also to do several other jobs. Some DLP packages verify backups exist and are in good order. Some DLP packages monitor if data is being moved or copied (they call this data in transit/motion). Some DLP packages provide removable media control—called *USB blocking*—to prevent local copies being created. DLP works in all sorts of appliances, from enterprise routers to cloud-based services.

You'll find DLP employed in mail gateways, protecting e-mail messages and delivery. The mail gateway might employ DLP along with a spam filter to proactively delete known unsolicited messages and with encryption features for secure e-mail. (See also Chapter 11 for more discussion on secure protocols.)

Figure 5-40
Shredded
computers

Module 5-6: System Recycling

This module covers the following CompTIA Security+ objective:

- **4.1** **Given a scenario, use the appropriate tool to assess organizational security**

There comes a time when hard-working individual systems must say farewell. Technology becomes dated, upgrading is impossible or not cost-effective, feature sets are lacking, or a massive hardware failure (like a smoked motherboard) makes a repair simply not worth the cost in money and time. The process of disposing of systems is called *system recycling*.

There are two different ways to recycle. First, take a complete system to a scrapper that shreds the system—plastic, metal, everything—and recycles the core materials (Figure 5-40).

Alternatively, system recycling means to give the computer to someone else who needs it. Charitable organizations, schools, and private individuals badly need computers and will gratefully accept even somewhat dated systems.

In either case, the great issue for IT professionals is to ensure that none of the data on the soon-to-be-recycled mass storage devices survives. This process, called *data sanitization*, takes on several forms and steps, but a handy publication that provides helpful guidance is NIST Special Publication (SP) 800-88 Revision 1, *Guidelines for Media Sanitization* (Figure 5-41).

NIST SP 800-88 Rev. 1 breaks data sanitization into three main methods: clear, purge, and destroy. Each of these methods ensures the data on mass storage won't leave the infrastructure, but the methods vary in terms of security, convenience, and cost.

Clear

Clear means to tell the device through user commands inherent to the mass storage device to sanitize the data. One example of a clear would be to send commands to a hard drive to erase data. Clearing isn't, however, just a simple erase. It must eliminate data

NIST Special Publication 800-88
Revision 1

Guidelines for Media Sanitization

Richard Kissel
Andrew Regenscheid
Matthew Scholl
Kevin Stine

This publication is available free of charge from:
http://dx.doi.org/10.6028/NIST.SP.800-88r1

Figure 5-41   NIST SP 800-88, Revision 1

from the mass storage device in such a way as to ensure the data cannot be read again, even if forensic tools are used to try to recover the data.

The biggest question marks when it comes to clearing mass storage are HDDs and SSDs. The built-in erase/delete, format, and partition commands from any operating system generally do not remove data. True removal requires disk wiping utilities that overwrite the data on the entire drive. Figure 5-42 shows the interface of a highly regarded clearing/wiping tool, Parted Magic (https://partedmagic.com).

There's an old wives' tale that claims (depending on who you hear this story from) that you must overwrite data six or seven or nine times before the underlying data cannot be recovered forensically. In response to this, SP 800-88 Rev. 1 says the following:

> For storage devices containing *magnetic* media, a single overwrite pass with a fixed pattern such as binary zeros typically hinders recovery of data even if state of the art laboratory techniques are applied to attempt to retrieve the data.

For the overly paranoid, or for those whose employers require you to be so, however, the US Department of Defense wiping standard, DoD 5220.22-M, performs many overwrites. It should be noted that even the US DoD no longer requires this standard for data sanitization.

Figure 5-42 Parted Magic

NOTE A general rule on clear: if the device is an appliance (a router, a smartphone, a multipurpose printer), a factory reset will often sufficiently clear the device. This isn't a guarantee, and it's always a good idea to refer to the manufacturer directly.

Purge

Purge means to use anything other than an internal command to sanitize the data on the media. Probably the best example of purging is *degaussing* magnetic media. Degaussing means to expose the media to very powerful magnetic fields. Degaussing is 100 percent effective on HDDs, but is useless with SDDs as they do not store data magnetically. Degaussing machines are expensive, so most organizations that need to degauss take advantage of third-party solutions. Figure 5-43 shows the Web page of a company that specializes in data destruction, including degaussing.

Figure 5-43 Data Killers degaussing service Web page

Unfortunately, degaussing also destroys the media. Once an HDD is degaussed, the drive is destroyed. But not all purging is destructive. One potential alternative that might be available is *cryptographic erase (CE)*. If by chance you have something on mass storage that is encrypted with an asymmetric key, you can render the data undecipherable by eliminating the key pair, or at least the public key.

Destroy

Destroy quite literally means the physical destruction of the media. Secure data destruction methods depend on the media, but here are the four common techniques.

- **Burning**   Flammable media isn't as common as it used to be, but burning is still available for disks and tapes.

- **Pulping**   Exclusively for paper, pulping dissolves and cooks the paper, creating new paper.

- **Shredding**   Shredding means two different things. You can use shredders to chop up paper (or cards or tapes or optical media) into tiny pieces. If you're talking about hard drives, the proper term is pulverizing (see next).

- **Pulverizing**   Pulverizing mechanically rips apart the media or data storage. There are some excellent YouTube videos on this topic—assuming you like watching hard drives shredded into thousands of tiny pieces!

Questions

1. Rick logs into a public system as Guest and guesses correctly on a simple password to gain administrative access to the machine. What sort of attack surface does this represent?

   A. Angle plane

   B. Privilege escalation

   C. Service vector

   D. Zero-day

2. John receives a driver-signing error for a specific DLL file in his Windows system. This a classic symptom of what sort of attack?

   A. ARP poisoning

   B. MAC spoofing

   C. Refactoring

   D. Shimming

3. Samantha recommended new systems for a group of developers at remote locations. Each system is identical, with high-end processing components. For storage, she needs a solution that provides storage redundancy and performance.

She goes with RAID for each system, selecting four drives. Each user can lose up to two drives and not lose data. What RAID did she select?

A. RAID 0

B. RAID 1

C. RAID 5

D. RAID 6

4. The Trusted Computing Group introduced the idea of the _____, an integrated circuit chip that enables secure computing.

A. TCP

B. TPM

C. EMP

D. EMI

5. John's home system has automatic updates from Microsoft, yet at his office, his organization has a more formal method of updating systems called _____.

A. Automatic updates

B. Patch management

C. TOS

D. Allow listing

6. What sort of malware requires the user to pay to remove the malware?

A. Trojan horse

B. Keylogger

C. Adware

D. Ransomware

7. Marisol notices a small dongle between her USB keyboard and her system. Which of the following is most likely?

A. She is using an inline encryption device.

B. She has a TPM.

C. Someone has installed a keylogger.

D. Someone has installed a logic bomb.

8. Degaussing is associated with which form of data sanitization?

A. Clear

B. Purge

C. Destroy

D. Recycle

9. Jake gets a call from a user complaining about things seeming "squished" on the screen. Upon further review, Jake determines that the Edge browser on the user's laptop has a lot of nonstandard toolbars taking up part of the screen, thus making it harder to see Web pages and images at agreeable sizes. What sort of malware has infected the user's computer?

   A. PUP

   B. Ransomware

   C. Trojan horse

   D. Worm

10. Erin needs to implement a solution to provide redundancy of network connections for a critical server. What should she implement?

    A. Multipath

    B. NIC teaming

    C. RAID

    D. Virtualization

Answers

1. **B.** Privilege escalation scenarios have the bad guy increasing the scope of what he can do once authenticated to a system.

2. **C.** A refactoring attack tries to replace a device driver with a file that will add some sort of malicious payload.

3. **D.** A RAID 6 array requires at least four drives, but can lose up to two drives and still not lose data.

4. **B.** Trusted Platform Module (TPM) chips store a unique 2048-bit RSA key pair for security purposes.

5. **B.** Patch management describes the process used to keep systems updated in the enterprise.

6. **D.** Ransomware demands payment to restore files.

7. **C.** A random USB dongle can be a malicious device, such as a keylogger.

8. **B.** Although a degausser essentially renders a hard drive unusable, it falls into the category of purge.

9. **A.** Jake's user clearly has one or more potentially undesirable programs installed!

10. **B.** Erin should install and configure a second network interface connection in NIC teaming to provide redundancy of network connection.

6

The Basic LAN

Mesh, smesh. Just point me to the bus.

—Anonymous Luddite

Most computing devices interact within a TCP/IP broadcast domain, a *local area network (LAN)*, a crazy mélange of devices, from PCs to printers to smartphones to switches to thermostats to refrigerators. Securing each computing device requires attention and specific tools and technologies, as you learned in Chapter 5. Networks bring an extra layer of complexity and attack surfaces and, as you undoubtedly suspect, a whole new set of tools for security. This chapter explores securing a LAN in five modules:

- Layer 2 LAN Attacks
- Organizing LANs
- Implementing Secure Network Designs
- Virtual Private Networks
- Network-Based Intrusion Detection/Prevention

Module 6-1: Layer 2 LAN Attacks

This module covers the following CompTIA Security+ objective:

- **1.4 Given a scenario, analyze potential indicators associated with network attacks**

LANs offer great attack surfaces. This module explores Layer 2 (Data Link in the OSI seven-layer model) attacks, such as ARP poisoning, on-path attacks, MAC flooding, and MAC cloning. Why worry about Layer 3, Layer 4, or even Layer 7 for that matter, when you can attack way down the network stack? Let's check them out.

NOTE That question was a joke and a segue. Security professionals *definitely need to worry* about attack surfaces up and down the OSI layers. We'll get to other attacks shortly.

ARP Poisoning

Most every network in existence is Ethernet, and every network interface card (NIC) on an Ethernet network has a media access control (MAC) address. For one computer to send an IP packet to another computer on an Ethernet network, the IP packet must sit inside an Ethernet frame. An Ethernet frame consists of both a destination MAC address and a source MAC address. The sending system needs both the destination host's IP address and the destination host's MAC address. But what if the sending system knows the destination IP address but doesn't know the destination MAC address? In that case the sending system performs an *Address Resolution Protocol (ARP) broadcast* to determine the MAC address for that host.

Typically, when a system wants to send an IP packet, it broadcasts an ARP request that looks something like Figure 6-1.

The system then caches the ARP discovery for a minute or two. In Windows you can type the **arp -a** command at the command line to see the cached ARP addresses. In the following example, dynamic addresses are the temporary addresses that must be renewed with new ARP commands every few minutes. Static addresses are permanent and do not require new ARP updates.

```
C:\Users\Michaelm>arp -a
Interface: 172.18.13.117 --- 0x10
  Internet Address        Physical Address      Type
  172.18.13.1             d4-b2-7a-03-26-4d     dynamic
  172.18.13.102           a8-a1-59-06-08-82     dynamic
  172.18.13.107           16-07-f2-c0-44-89     dynamic
  172.18.13.255           ff-ff-ff-ff-ff-ff     static
  224.0.0.22              01-00-5e-00-00-16     static
  224.0.0.251             01-00-5e-00-00-fb     static
  224.0.0.252             01-00-5e-00-00-fc     static
  239.255.255.250         01-00-5e-7f-ff-fa     static
  255.255.255.255         ff-ff-ff-ff-ff-ff     static
```

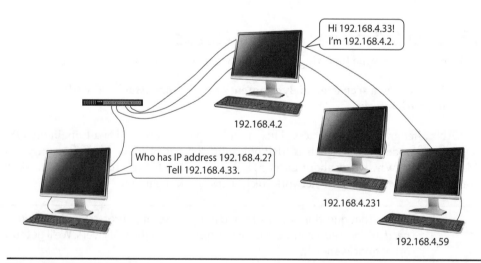

Figure 6-1 Typical ARP request

Figure 6-2 ARP spoofing in action

Note that most of the 172.18.13.*x* addresses in this example are other systems on the network that use dynamic IP addressing. The broadcast addresses 172.18.13.255 and 255.255.255.255 are static. Most of the other addresses are for multicast addresses.

So ARP's job is to resolve MAC addresses based on IP addresses using systems that broadcast requests and then update their ARP caches with the responses from other computers. But ARP has no security. Any computer can respond to an ARP request, even if that computer is an evil actor (Figure 6-2).

Any time an attacking system pretends to be another system in any way—by faking an IP address, a URL, or an e-mail address—it is *spoofing*. A system that responds with another system's MAC address via ARP requests is *ARP spoofing*. On the other hand, if some system gives false ARP information to another system, this poisons the victim system's ARP cache. The attacking system performs *ARP poisoning*. Figure 6-3 explores the differences.

Figure 6-3
ARP spoofing vs.
ARP poisoning

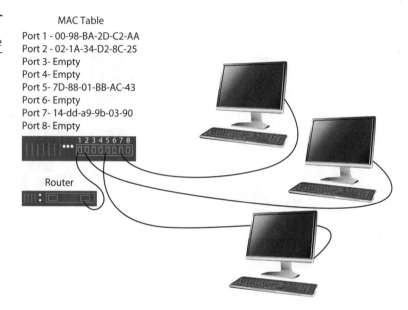

Figure 6-4
Switch MAC table

MAC Table
Port 1 - 00-98-BA-2D-C2-AA
Port 2 - 02-1A-34-D2-8C-25
Port 3- Empty
Port 4- Empty
Port 5- 7D-88-01-BB-AC-43
Port 6- Empty
Port 7- 14-dd-a9-9b-03-90
Port 8- Empty

Router

ARP poisoning doesn't stop with a single attacking system going after another system's ARP cache! Remember that every LAN has a Layer 2 switch that interconnects all the LAN devices. This switch keeps a listing of the MAC addresses to all connected systems (Figure 6-4).

An ARP poisoning program can confuse the switch by sending ARP commands directly to the switch, redirecting traffic to the attacking system. In Figure 6-5, the attacker impersonates a legitimate system.

ARP poisoning software can send false ARP commands. What havoc can this provoke? Two common types of attack use ARP spoofing/ARP poisoning: man-in-the-middle attacks and MAC flooding.

Man-in-the-Middle Attacks

Let's assume that you, the *evil actor*, have used your "Mission: Impossible" skills and infiltrated an office. You're sitting next to an RJ-45 connection on the target LAN. Your goal, should you choose to go further, is to get user J. Bond's user names and passwords for, well, just about everything he does online. To intercept his Web activity, for example, you set up an ARP poisoner to tell the switch that the ARP poisoner is now the router, thereby fooling the switch to send all the data from J. Bond's system directly to your system. You don't want J. Bond to get wise to you, so after all of his data comes into your system, you keep a copy but at the same time make sure the traffic goes on to the router and does whatever he wanted it to do. Your ARP poisoning system is now *in the middle* between J. Bond's computer and the Web server he is trying to connect to (Figure 6-6). You have now created a classic *man-in-the-middle (MITM) attack*! Excellent work, evil actor! Muwhawhawhaw!

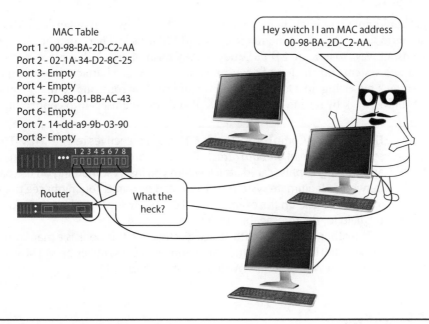

Figure 6-5 ARP poisoning the switch

 NOTE Apologies to the reader here. The primary author of this chapter—not naming names, but his initials are *MM*—can't keep his movie franchises straight, not even for one *million* dollars. – SJ

Figure 6-6 MITM J. Bond's system

You should note two items here. First, this isn't the only way to do an MITM attack. This scenario uses ARP poisoning to create an MITM attack. There are hundreds, if not thousands, of ways to execute MITM attacks. Any form of attack that places something between two systems for the job of acquiring data is an MITM attack. You could do an MITM attack by setting up a fake e-mail server and stealing someone's e-mail. You could do an MITM attack by setting up a rogue WAP and tricking users into connecting to it.

EXAM TIP The CompTIA Security+ 601 exam objectives refer to an MITM attack as a form of *on-path attack*. This is a more general term that can apply to any sophisticated attack where you insert something on the path between a legitimate system and a trusted resource. You might see the term "on-path attack" on the exam, but will definitely see "man-in-the-middle" in the field for the foreseeable future.

The other type of on-path attack discussed in this book is a man-in-the-browser (MITB) attack. As the name implies, it's essentially an MITM attack directed at Web browsers. We'll get to it in Chapter 11.

MAC Flooding

Switches filter traffic based on MAC addresses, very quickly establishing and maintaining a table—called a *content addressable memory (CAM)* table—that contains all the MAC addresses of the hosts connected to it. Traffic goes into the switch and then only to the specific recipient listed in the frame (Figure 6-7). If a switch does not know the intended

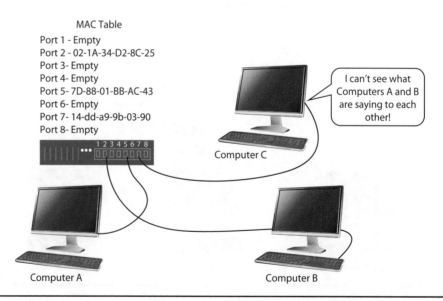

Figure 6-7 A properly running switch

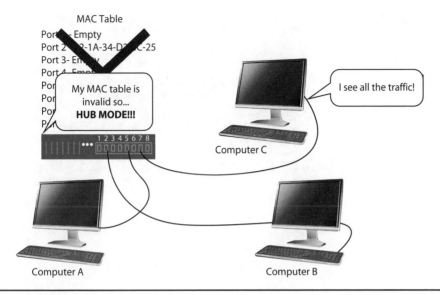

Figure 6-8 MAC flooding

recipient of a frame, the switch will broadcast that frame to all the connected devices, behaving much like an ancient hub. This is typical during the initial connection of a new device to the network, for example, until the switch's CAM table updates.

Attackers can take advantage of this aspect of switches through *media access control (MAC) flooding attacks*, sending many frames with "new" source MAC addresses, seeking to overwhelm the limited capacity of the CAM table (Figure 6-8). Using an ARP poisoner, for example, an attacker can broadcast hundreds of invalid ARP commands every few seconds. Once filled, the switch will flip to broadcast mode for LAN traffic.

Not only does MAC flooding force switches to broadcast all traffic, it's also a great way to open up an ARP poisoning attack. Once the switch goes into "hub mode" (my term, not an industry term), it will quickly send out a flurry of ARPs to try to rebuild the CAM table. This is a terrific opportunity for an ARP poisoner to send ARPs that tell the switch it is another system.

MAC Cloning

An attacker can use *MAC cloning*—changing the MAC address of a device to match the MAC address of another device—to gain illicit access to the network. MAC cloning is a legitimate and fairly common action. Figure 6-9 shows how to change the MAC address of a NIC in Windows using the NIC's properties.

Unlike ARP poisoning, MAC cloning is a permanent setting. The trick to making MAC cloning work as an attack is to remove or disable the device that originally had the MAC address. You can't have two devices with the same MAC address on a LAN for more than a few moments, as that will confuse the switch as well as other systems and will force a huge number of new ARPs as the network tries to figure out what's happening.

Figure 6-9
Changing the
MAC address in
Windows

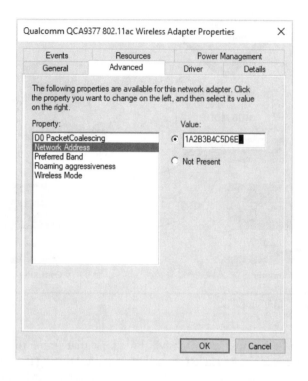

Many switches use a scheme called *port security* to protect against MAC cloning attacks. One of the more important features of port security is maintaining an inventory of every MAC address of allowed systems on the switch. Better switches do not allow a system with a MAC address that isn't listed in the MAC address inventory to access the network. They literally turn off the port where the offending system connects. Attackers will attempt to avoid this by using a system with a known MAC address.

NOTE MAC cloning has legitimate uses as well. It's common to change the MAC address of a small office/home office (SOHO) router issued by an ISP to the MAC address of the previous router to speed up installation of the new router.

Wireless access points commonly have a MAC setting that functions similarly to port security. The WAP stops systems that aren't "on the list" from authorizing to the SSID.

Module 6-2: Organizing LANs

This module covers the following CompTIA Security+ objectives:

- **2.1 Explain the importance of security concepts in an enterprise environment**
- **2.5 Given a scenario, implement cybersecurity resilience**
- **2.7 Explain the importance of physical security controls**
- **3.3 Given a scenario, implement secure network designs**

Figure 6-10
This is more
than a CompTIA
Network+ review.

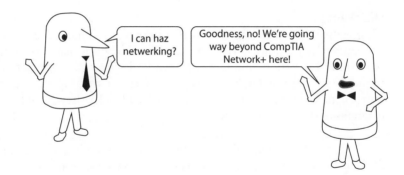

This module reviews local area network (LAN) technologies, including devices, architectures, and secure networking principles. Although the book has already briefly discussed secure network protocols, this section takes an in-depth look at network security, discussing network devices and how to configure them securely, the design elements that go into a secure network, and different security methods and technologies that help make up secure network administration.

Network security is an extremely important part of security in general, so reach back into your mind for all the knowledge and experience you've gained from CompTIA Network+ studies, as well as real-life experience. Also understand that this module is not a CompTIA Network+ exam review, although it discusses topics that may serve as a reminder of those studies. This module focuses on the *security* aspects of networking (Figure 6-10).

We'll specifically touch on three aspects of secure network design here: configuration management, network segmentation, and load balancing.

Configuration Management

Configuration management (CM) in general refers to how an organization keeps track of everything that affects its network, including the hardware in place, operating system versions and ordering, policies implemented, physical placement and layout of systems, and much more. CM directly relates to disaster recovery, which we'll cover in more detail in Chapter 13. If you know precisely the systems and software in place, you can more effectively deal with breaches, failures, software glitches, and so on.

This module touches on a few specific examples to include in the detailed documentation required for good CM, such as diagrams, standard naming conventions, IP schema, and baseline configuration. Just keep in mind that the topic goes way beyond CompTIA Security+ and into enterprise networking design, administration, and security.

NOTE   Other, more specialized certifications test much more deeply on CM topics, such as the ITIL certification from AXELOS.

Diagrams

Thorough and detailed *diagrams* map out the physical hardware of the network, including connectivity among devices, make and model of devices, operating system and version, firmware version, and so on. Network diagrams should function in layers, similar to the classic anatomy books with simple bones, arteries, organs, and more all on colored transparencies (Figure 6-11). Figures 6-12 and 6-13 show simple and more complex diagrams of the same network.

NOTE When it comes to network diagrams, learn Microsoft Visio, the industry-standard tool. Get it as soon as you can and start practicing.

Standard Naming Conventions

All documentation should use *standard naming conventions*—standard for your organization, at least—so network administrators and security professionals can glance at something labeled FS3-E4 and differentiate it from FS3-W7 easily. (C'mon, file server 3 on floor 4 in the East building in the campus area network versus file server 3 on floor 7 in the West building, right?) This standardization applies to every network asset, including system identification and network IDs. Standard naming conventions enable new team members to get up to speed quickly and avoid rookie mistakes that would cause problems for the organization.

Figure 6-11

Classic anatomy overlay (Image: ilbusca, Getty Images)

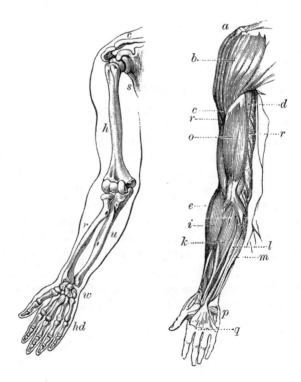

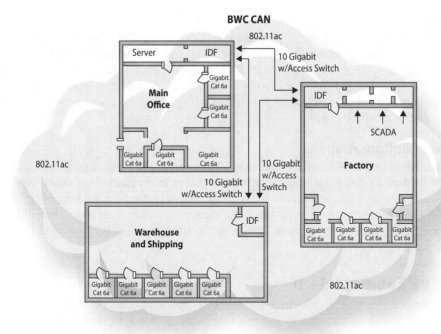

Figure 6-12 Diagram of the Bayland Widgets' campus area network

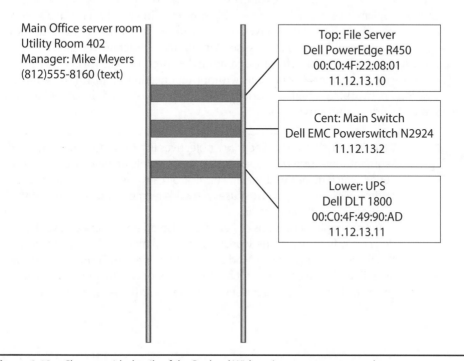

Figure 6-13 Closeup with details of the Bayland Widgets' campus area network

IP Schema

Part of good configuration management means implementing IPv4 addresses in a logical and consistent manner—the *Internet Protocol (IP) schema*. In one common IP schema, for example, the main router is set to x.x.x.1. Switches get range x.x.x.2–10, printers get range x.x.x.11–16, and workstations get all the rest. Most networks organize the first or last useable address in their subnet for the default gateway. Consistency and explicit documentation are the keys here.

Baseline Configuration

Once you have the network set up, run tests to determine the baseline performance of the network based on the baseline configuration you've implemented. In other words, CM means knowing how each part of the network *should* perform so it becomes rapidly apparent when something doesn't perform as expected. We'll see more about baselining in Chapter 13, but keep it in your head that it's an integral part of effective configuration management.

Network Segmentation

A good, secure network architecture organizes components into physical or logical groupings, enabling better security for the enterprise. *Network segmentation* generally means partitioning a single enterprise network into two or more subnetworks using either switches (at Layer 2) or routers (at Layer 3). Layer 2 switches use VLAN capabilities to turn single broadcast domains into multiple broadcast domains. Layer 3 routers split the enterprise into separate network IDs. Network-based firewalls work at this level; we can also implement screened subnets. This splitting either at Layer 2 or Layer 3 for different functions of the network gives us tremendous control over the data moving among systems and enables us to address security in many different ways.

Network segmentation also refers to separating the enterprise network both within (to reduce overhead and general traffic) and without (connecting to an ISP or some other organization's network). We'll glance briefly at the terminology and documentation that refers to these other connectivity points.

 EXAM TIP The CompTIA Security+ objectives list Zero Trust under network segmentation. *Zero Trust* operates on the principle of "never trust, always verify," which means exclude any traffic from anyone until you can prove that traffic is legitimate. Zero Trust uses network segmentation as some of the methods for excluding traffic.

Typical implementations of Zero Trust also operate at Layer 7, so they don't really fit the classic network segmentation models of Layers 2 and 3. You'll see the term again in Module 6-3 under "Internet Connection Firewalls." Keep in mind the concept as it relates to network segmentation, though, so you can properly parse questions on the CompTIA Security+ exam.

VLANs

You know that the defining characteristics of a LAN are that hosts are on the same subnet; that they communicate with each other without the need to be routed; and that they use hardware (MAC) addresses to identify each other during communications. Better switches can segment a network logically into two or more distinct and separate networks by implementing *virtual local area network (VLAN)* technology. A VLAN doesn't depend upon the physical layout of the network; it doesn't matter if the hosts are physically sitting next to each other or are located several buildings apart. A VLAN creates a logical network in which to assign hosts.

Once a host is assigned to a VLAN, it follows LAN conventions, as if it were physically a part of a LAN. You create VLANs on switches by configuring the switches to establish and recognize VLANs with certain characteristics. These characteristics include an IP subnet and VLAN membership. VLAN membership can be based on the switch port the host is plugged into (called a *port-based VLAN*); it can also be based on the MAC address of the client (a *MAC-based VLAN*). You could also have a *protocol-based VLAN*, which would ensure that any client with an IP address on a subnet would be assigned to a VLAN by default. You can assign different hosts to different VLANs, even if they plug into the same switch and sit right next to each other.

 EXAM TIP   Implementation of VLANs falls squarely in the CompTIA Network+ certification bailiwick. CompTIA Security+ cares that you know VLANs enhance network security through network segmentation.

Since VLANs operate with the same characteristics as normal LANs, broadcasts are not passed between them. In fact, it's necessary to route traffic between VLANs. You could use a traditional router for this, or, more often, you could configure the switch to route between VLANs (called *inter-VLAN routing*). If VLANs need to access networks that aren't controlled by the switch, the traffic must pass through a traditional router. Figure 6-14 illustrates an example VLAN setup.

VLANs contribute to security because they enable administrators to separate hosts from each other, usually based upon sensitivity. In other words, you can assign sensitive hosts to a VLAN and control which other hosts access them through the VLAN. Since VLANs are logical (and software-based), you can control other aspects of them from a security perspective. You can control what types of traffic can enter or exit the VLAN, and you can restrict access to hosts on that VLAN via a single policy. You can also provide for increased network performance by using VLANs to eliminate broadcast domains, the same as you would with a traditional router.

Network-Based Firewalls

A network-based firewall, like the host-based firewall discussed in Chapter 5, filters IP traffic based on rulesets known generically as *access control lists (ACLs)*. A network-based firewall manifests as a specialized hardware device (commonly but not exclusively a router), a type of *network appliance*.

Figure 6-14
VLANs on a
switch

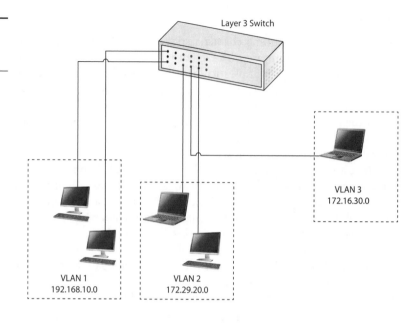

Layer 3 Switch

VLAN 3
172.16.30.0

VLAN 1
192.168.10.0

VLAN 2
172.29.20.0

> **NOTE** Given that routers interconnect LANs, adding firewall features to a
> router is a natural combination.

Network-based firewalls typically protect entire network segments. Traditionally, firewalls were thought of in terms of separating only public networks from private networks;
but modern security theory also emphasizes the use of firewalls in an internal network
to separate sensitive network segments from other internal networks. Firewalls can filter
traffic based upon a wide variety of criteria, including port, protocol, network service,
time of day, source or destination host, and even users or entire domains. More advanced
firewalls can also do deep-level traffic inspection, so even traffic that meets rules allowing
it to pass through the firewall could be denied due to the content of its traffic.

> **NOTE** Module 6-3 goes into specific types of network-based firewalls.

Screened Subnets

The best way to connect a LAN to the Internet is to use a firewall-capable router to act
as the interconnect between the LAN and an ISP. While simple LANs handle this nicely,
a network that includes public servers must have a more complex topology that protects
Internet systems but still enables less-protected access for public servers. To do this, create
a *screened subnet*—also known as a *demilitarized zone (DMZ)*—a LAN, separate from the

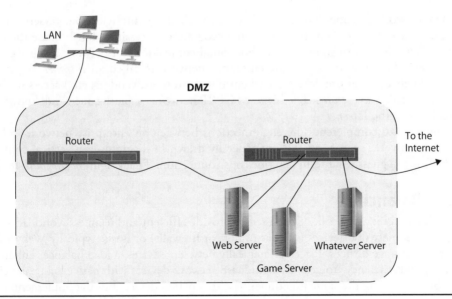

Figure 6-15   A screened subnet (DMZ)

internal LANs that contain workstations and private servers. The DMZ connects to the Internet via a lightly firewalled router, and an internal network connects to the DMZ via a much more aggressively firewalled router (Figure 6-15).

 EXAM TIP   The third iteration of the CompTIA Security+ 601 objectives changed the traditional term "demilitarized zone (DMZ)" to "screened subnet." You might see the latter term on the exam, so don't miss the question. You'll only see DMZ in the real world for the next few years—assuming the politically correct term catches on at all, so be prepared for that as well.

A lot of modern networks that employ a screened subnet use a specialized network appliance called a *jump server* that enables secure management of devices within the DMZ. The typical jump server enables logging and auditing and provides a single management point for user accounts.

Interconnecting Within and Without

Even relatively simple enterprise networks—like the Bayland Widgets' CAN illustrated earlier in this module—have multiple connections among servers within the network and, of course, connections to the outside world as well. Internal server-to-server communication can add a lot of overhead to a network if not managed properly. Proper network segmentation can reduce overall traffic by putting a server-to-server connection in a unique VLAN, for example, or separating the servers with routers.

The network documentation folks have long called the internal server-to-server connection *east-west traffic*, not because of any geographic necessities, but because the network diagrams tend to show them as horizontal connections. A network using VLANs or routers that's essentially a single enterprise network is called an *intranet*. A private TCP/IP network that provides external entities (customers, vendors, etc.) access to their intranet is called an *extranet*. The biggest TCP/IP network of all, the one we all know and love, is called the *Internet*.

And just for completeness here, connections between an enterprise network and an external network, such as an ISP, are generally drawn in diagrams as a vertical connection. Can you guess what term describes this connection? That's right, *north-south traffic*.

Load Balancing

A *load balancer* is a network device used to provide efficient and seamless workload sharing between network devices (such as routers or firewalls) or hosts, typically Web or file servers or storage devices. Placed strategically between devices, a load balancer enhances security and efficiency. You can also purchase network devices with native load balancing capability allowing the same functionality with a paired device, but the implementation is more complicated. As you might suspect from the name, load balancers provide *load balancing* to the network. Implement load balancers in a scenario where you need to enhance *cybersecurity resilience*.

High-Availability Clusters

A load balancer contributes to security by providing for high availability. If a server goes down, the load balancer can transparently and immediately provide for availability by transferring network and resource requests to an identically configured backup server. This is considered *persistence* in networking, meaning the network resources are always available. An *active/passive* high-availability cluster like this has one server active and the second passive, acting as a failover or backup.

 NOTE A cluster in this use is a group of servers that work together to provide a service, such as a Web site, Web service, or database.

In an *active/active* high-availability cluster, the load-balanced services perform the same functions at the same time, but with different transactions. As an example, two load-balanced Web servers would respond to different users' browser requests. The load balancer manages the traffic and requests going to each of the members of the service or device cluster for which it is responsible. This helps provide for efficiency, eliminates delays or latency, and provides for system and data availability if a member of the cluster is unable to fulfill requests or requires maintenance.

Scheduling

Load balancers may use several different criteria to determine scheduling—that is, which device gets a particular request. A load balancer may base its decisions on network traffic conditions, for example; it may use a turn-based system (otherwise known as a *round-robin* type of system); or it can send traffic based on available resources on the target systems in more advanced products. It is important to note that Web sites and applications need to maintain *session affinity* across load-balanced resources. If there are two Web servers behind a load balancer and a user's initial session is sent to Web server A, for example, the affinity between that user and the application thread active on Web server A must be maintained. Otherwise, the user's experience on the Web site would not be consistent—Web server A would have some of the information and Web server B would have other parts, resulting in a useless session, broken shopping cart, and so on.

A load balancer receives traffic for other devices or services via a *virtual IP address*. In a simple application, one Web server would receive and process all user sessions. In the preceding Web site example, both Web servers have individual IP addresses and both need to receive and process network traffic. To enable this, all the traffic is sent to a virtual IP address that is hosted on the load balancer, which forwards the relevant traffic to each resource behind it. This address is labeled "virtual" because it only exists for the purpose of routing traffic, and it is assigned to a device that already has a hardware-relevant IP address. A load balancer in an enterprise environment could host hundreds of virtual IP addresses for different applications.

EXAM TIP The use of virtualization—with virtual servers and systems—requires the same high degree of diligence with security as is required for physical machines and networks. The concepts and implementations of segmentation and isolation apply to virtualized networks just as much as to physical networks.

Module 6-3: Implementing Secure Network Designs

This module covers the following CompTIA Security+ objectives:

- **2.1** Explain the importance of security concepts in an enterprise environment
- **3.2** Given a scenario, implement host or application security solutions
- **3.3** Given a scenario, implement secure network designs

NOTE Wireless networks also need security and are an important part of just about every network out there. Wireless security gets its own discussion in Chapter 7.

Securing the LAN

To have a LAN you must have at least one switch. A perfectly functional LAN consists of nothing more than a single host and a single dumb switch, although in all but the smallest LANs you'll usually see two or more managed switches, creating the broadcast domain that defines a LAN. Most installations use rack-mounted switches with professionally installed structured cabling (Figure 6-16).

Figure 6-16
Switches in a rack

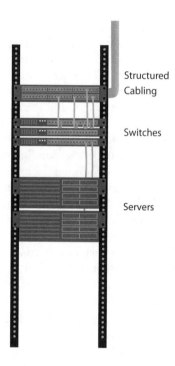

Structured
Cabling

Switches

Servers

Traditionally, a switch filters and forwards Ethernet frames, memorizing the MAC addresses of all the connected hosts and then creating point-to-point connections for all unicast traffic while at the same time remaining completely capable of supporting broadcasts.

 EXAM TIP The CompTIA Security+ objectives remind readers of an important secure network design and implementation tip, securely accessing servers for configuration. Typically, we access servers through *in-band management* software, such as VNC or SSH. The server operating system and software enable that access.

With *out-of-band management*, in contrast, the network administrator can access the server even if the server isn't running, directly interfacing with the firmware of the server. You might recall a common out-of-band management feature from your CompTIA Network+ studies, *lights-out management (LOM)*. Expect a question on secure network design that features out-of-band management.

Port Security

Bad actors love access to a network's switch. Access to a switch opens vulnerabilities to attacks. ARP spoofers steal the MAC addresses of legitimate systems, enabling man-in-the-middle/on-path attacks. Denial-of-service attacks can flood a switch with confusing

Figure 6-17 Just give me one port, just one…

MAC information. An attacker can plug in a rogue DHCP server, knocking systems off the network. They can start sending out IPv6 neighbor discovery packets, telling the hosts that the attacking system is their gateway and redirecting traffic (Figure 6-17).

Switch ports require security to protect against these attacks. Flood guards and loop prevention are a few of the features you'll see in all better switches. Keep in mind that port security is applied to individual ports.

Broadcast Storm Prevention Attackers use *traffic floods* primarily to conduct denial-of-service attacks on networks and hosts, since many hosts and network devices don't always react very favorably to excessive amounts of traffic or malformed traffic. Because flooding is a routine tactic of attackers, most modern network devices (and even some hosts) have flood protection built into their operating systems. These *flood guards* or *broadcast storm prevention* features work by detecting excessive traffic (by volume, as well as by rate of speed) and take steps to block the traffic or even turn off the offending port, so that the host doesn't have to process it. Most security devices, such as intrusion detection systems, firewalls, and robust network devices like better switches, have flood guards built in.

NOTE Flood guards protect against DoS attacks by limiting the number of new MAC addresses accepted.

Another common feature on better switches is called *media access control (MAC) filtering* (or *persistent MAC* or *sticky MAC addressing*). In many networks, a tech plugs a host into a port and the host stays there for years. The network administrator configures the switch port for that host to accept frames from only that MAC address, preventing bad actors from unplugging the host and plugging in their evil system.

Many enterprise-level switches come with a feature known as *Dynamic Host Configuration Protocol (DHCP) snooping*. With a DHCP snooping–capable switch, the switch is either automatically or manually given the IP addresses of the DHCP servers on your

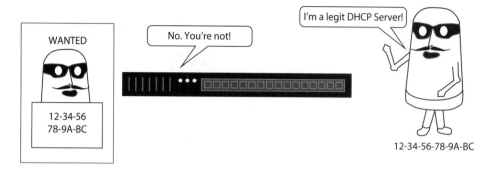

Figure 6-18   Trusted DHCP server

network. If any device other than the DHCP servers with the known IP addresses tries to send DHCP information, the server will automatically turn off its associated port (Figure 6-18).

Loop Prevention   Some floods happen just from misconfiguration. If two or more pathways connect two switches, for example, this creates a loop, which then causes a broadcast storm—a type of flood (Figure 6-19). All but the simplest switches implement some kind of *loop prevention*, such as the *Spanning Tree Protocol (STP)*.

STP is almost always enabled in the switch's configuration. When turned on, STP switches send out *Bridge Protocol Data Unit (BPDU) guard* frames every two seconds, quickly stopping loops by automatically turning off one of the ports that's supporting the loop (Figure 6-20).

Network Access Control   *Network access control (NAC)* provides network protection and security by prohibiting hosts from connecting to the organization's infrastructure unless they meet certain criteria. A NAC device provides an entry point or gateway into the network, typically for remote or mobile clients. This device checks the health and security settings of the client—a *host health check*—against a specified set of criteria before allowing it to access the network. For example, a NAC device could check the client for the latest antivirus signatures, the latest security updates, and other

Figure 6-19
Loops are bad.

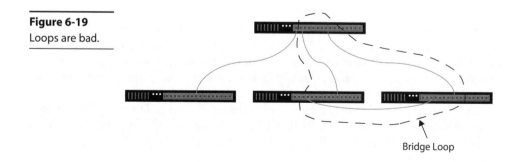

Figure 6-20
STP to the rescue!

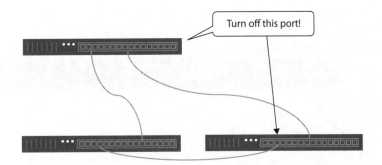

security configuration items. If the client does not meet these requirements, the NAC device does not allow the client to connect to the network. Additionally, the NAC device might be able to update the client dynamically or reconfigure certain options so that the client could proceed with authentication and connection to the infrastructure. NAC could also be used to authenticate devices, allowing only authorized devices to connect. Normally, a NAC device would be placed on a secure segment within a DMZ network.

NOTE Most networks that use NAC adopt a security position called Zero Trust (described in Module 6-2). No device is trusted *at all* until it passes a health check.

NAC supports devices using agents or runs agentless. *Agent-based NAC* tracks many features of potentially inbound devices, such as software versions and so on. The agent-based approach enables very fine control over allowing a device to connect to the network. The criteria used for an agent-based approach can be *permanent* or *dissolvable*. The former means the device that wants access to the network must have some software loaded—that software stays loaded. A dissolvable agent system runs something once on the device and admits or denies access; the software is then deleted.

Agentless NAC (such as one based on Windows Active Directory) would apply group policy rules to enforce the controls that an agent-based NAC device would do directly.

Internet Connection Firewalls

We've covered firewalls twice so far in this book, first for individual hosts, then as a tool to segment networks. Let's move back to firewalls one more time, this time to the place that most folks think about when they hear the word firewall: the default gateway.

Systems *inside* a LAN get their messages *out* of their LAN via a *default gateway*. The default gateway connects directly (or indirectly through in-house routers) to an ISP, which in turn connects to a router higher up on the Internet. Given the position of the default gateway at the edge of the network, it is a natural location to place a firewall to protect the local network. Network-based firewalls manifest in many ways, but the most common is at the default gateway, which includes a bevy of firewall features (Figure 6-21).

Figure 6-21   Typical gateway

 EXAM TIP   Given the setup of most networks these days, the default gateway often also acts as a *network address translation (NAT)* gateway, enabling many internal devices to use private IP addresses and access the Internet through a single public IP address. You'll recall how NAT works from CompTIA Network+. For CompTIA Security+, think of scenarios using NAT as a typical implementation of secure network designs.

This firewall manifests in many ways. SOHO environments see firewalling software added to the router directly. Larger networks require a different solution. As with so many other network components, firewalls can be software-based or dedicated hardware boxes. They come as open-source software or as proprietary software.

EXAM TIP Look for comparison questions on the CompTIA Security+ exam that explore hardware vs. software firewalls and open-source vs. proprietary firewall software solutions.

The primary function of any firewall is to inspect incoming IP packets and block the packets that could potentially hurt the hosts on the LAN. To do this, today's firewalls have three very different methods: *stateless*, *stateful*, and *application-based*. The more advanced firewalls —called *next-generation firewalls*—combine multiple methods.

Stateless Firewalls

A *stateless* firewall looks at every incoming packet individually without considering anything else that might be taking place (ergo *stateless*). Stateless firewalls, also called packet filters, are the oldest type of firewall. If you're going to have a firewall inspecting every packet, you must have some form of checklist that the firewall uses to determine whether a packet should be blocked. This is the router's access control list (ACL). The ACL for an Internet gateway firewall is a unique tool that defines what makes a packet good or bad.

A stateless firewall's ACL can only define aspects of an IP packet to filter. A typical ACL would include these aspects:

- **IP address** Block specific incoming/outgoing, destination/source IP addresses or complete network IDs

- **Port number** Block specific incoming/outgoing, destination/source port numbers or ranges of port numbers

- **Time/date** Block based on time of day, day of week

A stateless firewall makes it easy to combine filters to create surprisingly sophisticated ACL rules. You can set up a basic home firewall, for example, to keep your child's desktop system from accessing any Web pages (ports 80 and 443) between the hours of 10 P.M. and 6 A.M. on school nights. Figure 6-22 shows the ACL interface for a home router with a built-in firewall.

One feature of all ACLs is the idea of *implicit deny*. Implicit deny means that by default there is no access unless the ACL specifically allows it. For example, every firewall's ACL denies all incoming IP packets unless a particular packet is a response from a request initiated by one of the hosts on your LAN.

Stateless firewalls are simple and work well in many situations, but fail miserably where inspecting and blocking without consideration of the state isn't helpful. Consider a simple FTP session, run in the classic active mode:

1. A host inside the LAN (1.2.3.4) initiates a connection to an outside FTP server (2.3.4.5) using destination port 21 and, for this example, a source port of 12,345.

2. The firewall notes that an internal host has initiated an outgoing connection on port 21.

3. The FTP server responds to 1.2.3.4, port 12,345 with source IP address 2.3.4.5 and source port 21. The firewall recognizes this incoming connection as a response and does not block it.

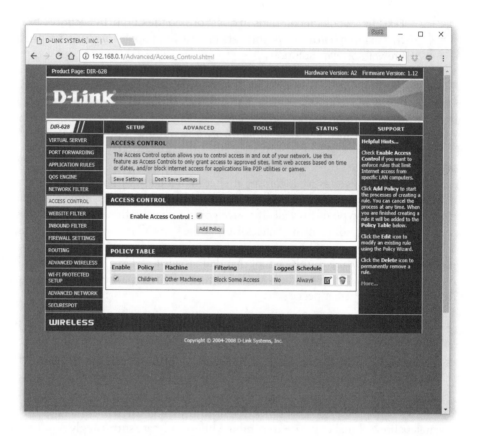

Figure 6-22   Firewall ACL interface

4. The FTP server initiates a data connection to 1.2.3.4, port 12,345 with source address IP 2.3.4.5 and source port 20.

5. The firewall does not recognize this incoming connection and, because of implicit deny, blocks the connection.

Stateless firewalls were such a problem for FTP that the FTP protocol was redesigned to use a second, passive mode. Passive mode only uses port 21.

Just as you can harden a switch against bad actors spoofing a legitimate system's MAC addresses, you can protect against IP address spoofing with a firewall. Helping to prevent IP address spoofing on our networks is one area where stateless firewalls still do a great job. Routers can use several *antispoofing* techniques. A very popular one is to have a router query its DHCP server for legitimate systems on the network. Every initial packet going out is cross-checked against the DHCP server's IP address list.

Stateful Firewalls

A *stateful* firewall understands the procedures and processes of different Internet protocols and filters any form of communication that is outside of proper procedures. A stateful firewall understands several functions expected in normal TCP and UDP communication and uses that intelligence to inspect the state of that connection. Stateful firewalls collect several packets in a connection and look at them as a state to determine if the communication meets correct protocol steps. One great example is how a stateful firewall can monitor a TCP connection. Every TCP connection starts with three messages, known as TCP's three-way handshake:

1. The initiating system sends a SYN message, requesting a TCP connection.

2. The responding system sends a SYN/ACK message, informing the initiating system it is ready to start a connection.

3. The initiating system sends an ACK message, acknowledging the responding system.

Figure 6-23 shows a Wireshark capture of a three-way handshake.

Let's say we have a stateful firewall protecting a Web server. It allows the incoming SYN connection from an unknown Web browser (a firewall protecting a public-facing server must allow incoming connections), but it stores a copy of the incoming packet in a table. It also allows the outgoing SYN/ACK packet from its server and keeps a copy of

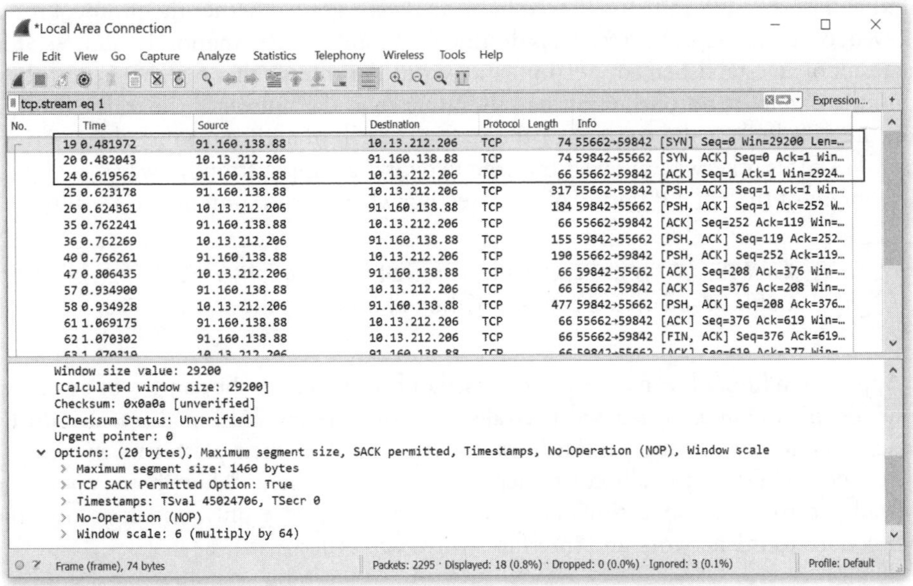

Figure 6-23   TCP three-way handshake

that as well. When the Web browser responds with a proper ACK message, the firewall sees this as a good connection and continues to keep the connection open. If the Web browser does anything that makes the stateful firewall think the connection is outside of the protocol, on the other hand, it will block the connection for a certain amount of time.

Stateful firewalls don't have ACLs. They come from the manufacturer with all the state-smarts they're ever going to have. For most stateless firewalls, it's simply a matter of turning them on or off to enable or disable firewall duties.

NOTE   Very advanced stateless firewalls (from companies like Cisco or Juniper) may have a few *filters* (don't call them ACLs) for their stateless firewalls, but those are outside the scope of the CompTIA Security+ exam.

Application Firewall

An *application* firewall has deep understanding of both the stateful and stateless aspects of a specific application (HTTP is by far the most common type of application firewall) and can filter any traffic for that application that could threaten it. Application firewalls can be thought of in two different contexts. In the first, an application firewall is an *appliance*—a box—or network device that works at all seven layers of the OSI model and can inspect data within protocols.

Think of a situation in which HTTP traffic is filtered in a firewall. In an ordinary stateful firewall, the traffic is filtered based upon an established connection from an internal host. HTTP traffic is allowed in or out based upon whether the protocol itself is allowed, over which port the traffic is destined, its source or destination IP address, if it is the result of an established connection, and so on. This means that filtering is done based upon the *characteristics* of the traffic itself, rather than the *content* of the traffic. Application firewalls look at the content of the traffic as well, in addition to its characteristics. So, if HTTP is otherwise allowed into the network, an application firewall also looks at the content of the HTTP traffic, often detecting whether the content itself is allowed.

EXAM TIP   A typical application firewall acts as a *content/URL filter*, blocking traffic based on the content of the traffic and on the source URL.

Application firewalls can be network-based or host-based; in the context of our discussions for this module, host-based firewalls are more relevant. Although most industrial static hosts do not use application firewalls specifically on their platforms, some of the more modern hosts, especially consumer devices, do have them. A host-based application firewall controls the applications and services on that device only, and it secures their connections to the network and interfaces with each other.

NOTE   Application firewalls are often referred to as Layer 7 firewalls because OSI Layer 7 is also known as the Application layer.

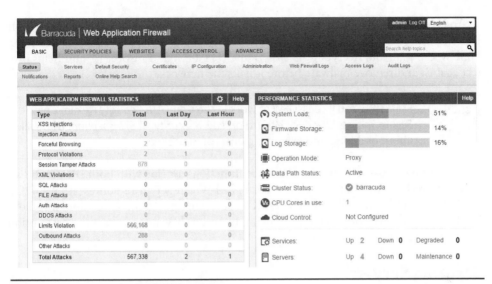

Figure 6-24 Barracuda cloud WAF settings

Given the huge number of Web applications living in the cloud, just about every manufacturer of application firewalls for Web apps—appropriately named *Web application firewalls (WAFs)*—also provides cloud-based virtual appliances (Figure 6-24).

EXAM TIP Look for questions on the CompTIA Security+ exam that compare firewall implementations, from appliance vs. host-based vs. virtual. Appliance assumes a dedicated hardware box; host-based relies on software running on a workstation; virtual has software running in a virtual machine to handle the firewall duties.

In a way, we can separate application firewalls from stateless and stateful firewalls in terms of their primary job. Application firewalls are designed to protect public-facing servers providing specific applications, so we can call them *application-based firewalls*. Stateless and stateful firewalls mainly protect LANs from the many evils that come from the Internet, so we can call them *network-based firewalls*. If you don't have a public Web application server or an e-mail server (or a few other applications), you have no need for this type of firewall.

Next-Generation Firewalls

A *next-generation firewall (NGFW)* functions at multiple layers of the OSI model to tackle traffic no traditional firewall can filter alone. A Layer 3 firewall can filter packets based on IP addresses, for example. A Layer 5 firewall can filter based on port numbers. Layer 7 firewalls understand different application protocols and can filter on the contents of the application data. An NGFW handles all of this and more.

An NGFW implements all sorts of traffic inspection policies at all layers. These include Ethernet rules (Layers 1 and 2), NAT rules (Layer 3), and HTTPS rules (Layer 7). An NGFW can grab and decrypt SSL/TLS traffic (HTTPS) and inspect it. This helps protect against and remove malware before it nails the network.

 EXAM TIP You'll see NGFW at work in the CompTIA Security+ exam doing *Secure Sockets Layer (SSL)/Transport Layer Security (TLS) inspection.* That's all about grabbing and examining encrypted packets.

As you might suspect, NGFW appliances function just fine with both IPv4 and IPv6 networks, or both for that matter. A typical NGFW can get an IP address from DHCP or DCHCv6 and play well with stateless IPv6 auto-configuration. When thinking about implications of IPv6 for a network, moving to an NGFW might make the best option for future-proofing your security.

Securing Servers

Anyone providing a server that offers any service to the public Internet has a big security job ahead of them, and the CompTIA Security+ exam objectives reflect the importance of this effort with many security topics covering what it takes to protect servers. In fact, all of Chapter 8 goes into detail on what's needed to protect different Internet services, such as Web and e-mail.

Before we start lighting up Web or e-mail servers, there's a lot we can do to place them in a safe place in which they can operate quickly and safely. We can choose from among many specialized security appliances to add to any network that supports one or more Internet servers, regardless of what type of Internet service they provide, to provide security.

Proxy Servers

The Internet is filled with servers and the clients that access them. In many situations, we find it helpful to put a box between the client and the server for certain applications. These boxes accept incoming requests from clients and forward those requests to servers. Equally, these boxes accept responses from servers and then forward them to the clients. These boxes are known as *proxy servers* or often just *proxies.*

 EXAM TIP Proxies work at the application level. There are Web proxies, e-mail proxies, FTP proxies, and so forth. Multipurpose proxies support multiple applications.

Proxies come in one of two forms: forward or reverse. A *forward proxy* is known to the client system, often in the same LAN, taking the requests from the client, maybe doing something with the request, and then forwarding the request to the server just like any other client (Figure 6-25).

Forward proxies are popular in organizations such as schools where the network administrators need to apply security controls to Internet access. A forward Web proxy

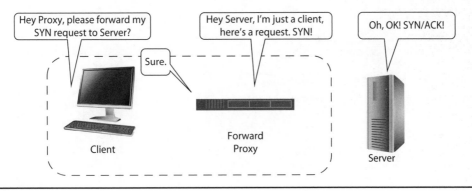

Figure 6-25 Forward proxy

almost always includes a strong firewall to check outgoing requests for blocked URLs, time-of-day restrictions, and anything else that needs be monitored to support the security policies of the organization.

A *reverse proxy* is used to protect servers. Reverse proxies are usually inside the same LAN as the servers. They always contain an application firewall to check the incoming requests for attack vectors and then pass the good requests to the server (Figure 6-26).

Proxies work at the application level, so traditionally a system's application must be configured to use a proxy. If a client is to use a forward Web proxy, then every Web browser on every client is configured to use it. Figure 6-27 shows the proxy settings in a Web browser.

All this configuration is a pain, especially if you have a thousand users all using different Web browsers. So why not let your router simply inspect all the data going out on the application's port numbers and simply redirect those packets to your proxy? That's the idea behind a *transparent proxy*. Most forward proxies support a transparent mode to do just this.

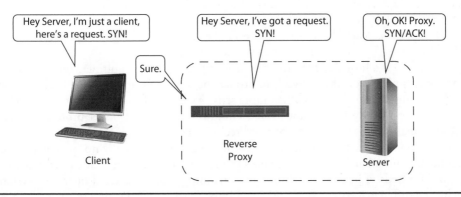

Figure 6-26 Reverse proxy

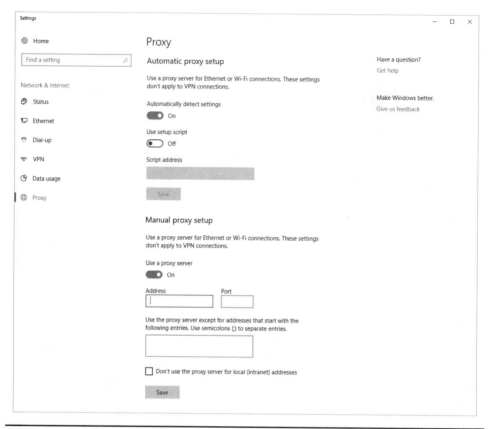

Figure 6-27   Web proxy settings

Deception and Disruption

Network security professionals and network administrators can set up systems to entice and lure would-be attackers into traps. These *deception and disruption* systems are so very sweet: honeyfiles, honeypots, and honeynets. And then there's the DNS sinkhole, a related technology. Let's take a look.

A *honeyfile* baits attackers to access it on a file server. The file name "passwords" could trigger an alarm when anyone accesses the honeyfile.

A *honeypot* is a host designed to be compromised, so it has multiple vulnerabilities. A honeypot is placed on the network to attract the attention of malicious hackers, hopefully drawing them away from other, more sensitive hosts. If an attacker victimizes a honeypot, you can study his methods and techniques to help you better protect the actual network against those same methods and techniques.

Honeypots can be boxes that are misconfigured or intentionally not patched, or they can be prebuilt virtual machines. There's even software out there that can emulate dozens or hundreds of hosts at the same time, spanning several different operating systems, including different versions of Windows, Linux, macOS, UNIX, and so on.

A *honeynet*, as you might guess, is an entire network of honeypots on their own network segment, used to get a hacker bogged down in a decoy network while the administrator locks down and secures the sensitive network and records and tracks the actions of the hacker.

Network deception techniques such as these can use fake assets, fake data, and fake telemetry (like server load, availability, memory consumption), all to gather intelligence on hacker techniques and sophistication.

A *DNS sinkhole* acts as a DNS server (or a DNS forwarder) for a LAN. The DNS sinkhole contains a list of known domains associated with malware, ad networks, and other forms of undesirable code. When a host on the LAN requests a DNS resolution, the DNS sinkhole compares the request to the list of known negative sites and, if there is a match, responds with a blank or null IP address. The effect of a working DNS sinkhole is the blocking of almost every advertisement for every system on the LAN with almost no negative performance impact on the LAN.

Module 6-4: Virtual Private Networks

This module covers the following CompTIA Security+ objectives:

- **3.1   Given a scenario, implement secure protocols**
- **3.3   Given a scenario, implement secure network designs**

A *virtual private network (VPN)* uses the public Internet as a direct connection between a single computer and a faraway LAN or between two faraway LANs. This is not a remote desktop connection or a terminal or a Web page connection. A VPN puts a single system or a separate LAN on the same broadcast domain, the same Layer 2 connection, just as if the faraway system plugged directly into the LAN's switch.

A successful VPN connection gives your remote system an IP address on your LAN. You can print from the remote system to your LAN's printers. You can see all the shared folders on other computers on the LAN. You are there. Well, at least your Ethernet frames are there.

VPNs are incredibly powerful for remote single users or remote networks that need to get to a LAN's internal servers. VPNs are a well-established technology and are easy to implement. Most enterprise environments have VPN access for employees and, in some cases, vendors. SOHO environments can use VPNs as well. My home network, for example, is configured to let me access my home network from anywhere on the Internet.

Given the popularity of VPNs and given the fact that they enable people to move potentially sensitive data securely across the wide-open Internet, VPNs are a very attractive target for the CompTIA Security+ exam. This module dives into VPNs, first describing how they work and then looking at the many protocol choices available for setting up a VPN.

EXAM TIP   Expect several questions on VPN scenarios on the CompTIA Security+ exam. In essence, a VPN boils down to making a secure connection to access remote resources as if they were local resources. Implement secure protocols (like IPsec) to make the VPN connections and thus implement secure network designs.

How VPNs Work

To make a faraway computer manifest as a local computer on your LAN, you need to do several actions. First, you need to connect to the other network over the Internet. That means you need a system with a public IP address that accepts VPN connections. Second, you need to create a second network connection that uses the Internet connection you've established to allow you to send LAN traffic over the Internet. Third, you should encode your data to keep private whatever files, print jobs, or other information you send to the faraway LAN.

VPNs work in one of two different ways. You can connect a single system to an existing LAN in what is called *remote access*, or you can connect two complete LANs in *site-to-site*. Figure 6-28 shows the two options.

To make a connection, at least one system must have a VPN server, more commonly called a *VPN concentrator*, designed to accept remote connections from either a single system (for remote access) or another VPN concentrator (for site-to-site). A VPN concentrator is often special VPN software installed on edge routers, or it may be VPN server software installed on a system inside your network. In either case, one system connects to the VPN server and makes a connection (Figure 6-29).

VPN connections require tunneling or embedding of IP traffic inside other packets. The VPN to VPN connection gets made, in other words, and then the true traffic happens inside the secure connection. The VPN concentrators continually insert the local

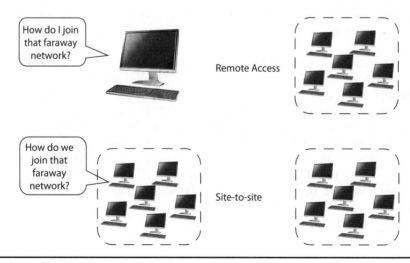

Figure 6-28   Remote access vs. site-to-site

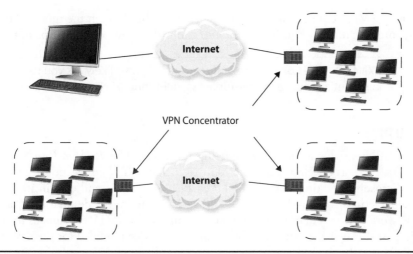

Figure 6-29   VPN concentrators added

traffic in Internet packets and send them through the tunnel; or they receive incoming Internet packets, strip away the outer IP information, and send the remaining frame to the local network (Figure 6-30).

 EXAM TIP   Site-to-site VPN concentrators generally never disconnect. We call these *always-on VPNs*.

One early problem with VPNs was that once you connected to a LAN, that was your only connection. Your IP address and default gateway were on that LAN; you used that LAN's DHCP and DNS servers. That meant if your computer was connected to a VPN and opened a Web browser, your computer went through the VPN connection and then went back out and used the Internet connection on your LAN. This is called a *full tunnel* and is a terrible way to get to the Internet. Current VPN technologies enable you

Figure 6-30
VPN tunnel on
one endpoint

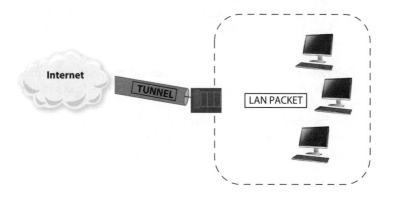

to configure a VPN connection to send only LAN traffic through the tunnel. All other traffic ignores the tunnel. This is a *split tunnel* and is the most common type of tunnel.

 EXAM TIP The CompTIA Security+ exam will most likely ask you to differentiate between split-tunnel vs. full-tunnel VPN connections.

Early VPNs

The first VPNs used one of two competing protocols. The *Point-to-Point Tunneling Protocol (PPTP)* was developed by Microsoft to include VPN connection technologies within Microsoft operating systems. PPTP enables a client to send data in it, much as you would a letter in an envelope. The PPTP packet contains the destination IP address of the network you are attempting to connect to. Inside this PPTP envelope is the traffic that will pass through the external VPN connection device intended for the destination network. This traffic would not be secure using PPTP alone; Microsoft uses its proprietary Microsoft Point-to-Point Encryption (MPPE) protocol to secure traffic traveling over PPTP. PPTP uses TCP port 1723. It's rarely seen over VPN connections these days, as most modern VPNs use some form of IPsec or SSL/TLS VPNs, described later.

Layer 2 Tunneling Protocol (L2TP) was developed jointly by Microsoft and Cisco, but it has become an Internet standard. Microsoft contributed aspects of its PPTP, while Cisco used its proprietary Layer 2 Forwarding (L2F) protocol. Like PPTP, L2TP is only an encapsulation protocol, simply providing transport services and protecting data through untrusted networks (such as the Internet) to get it to a destination network. L2TP still sees some adoption but is also fading to IPsec and SSL/TLS VPNs.

IPsec VPNs

Internet Protocol Security (IPsec) is a security protocol that works at the Network layer of the OSI model. IPsec was developed to provide security services (authentication and encryption) for IP traffic, since IP does not have any built-in native security protections. Three major protocols make up IPsec: AH, ESP, and ISAKMP.

 NOTE CompTIA lists IPsec with an uppercase S, *IPSec*. That's not accurate and never has been, but CompTIA uses the incorrect casing on every certification objective (not just Security+) that references IPsec.

The *Authentication Header (AH)* protocol provides authentication and integrity services for IP traffic. AH can be used on the entire IP packet, including the header and data payload.

The *Encapsulating Security Payload (ESP)* protocol takes care of encryption services. ESP can provide protection for the entire IP packet, depending the IPsec mode used, transport or tunnel.

Encrypting the IP header can cause problems if routers and other devices can't read the header information, including the source and destination IP addresses. Between hosts on a network, the header information isn't usually required to be encrypted, so ESP doesn't have to be used. This is called IPsec's *transport mode*. In transport mode, header information is not encrypted so that hosts and network devices can read it. The data, on the other hand, can be encrypted to protect it, even within a LAN.

IPsec *tunnel mode* is used when IP traffic is encapsulated and sent outside of a LAN, across WAN links to other networks. This is what happens in VPN implementations that use IPsec. In tunnel mode, since the IP packet is encapsulated in a tunneling protocol (such as L2TP), all the information in the packet, including headers and data payload, can be encrypted. So, ESP is typically used only in tunnel mode.

The third IPsec protocol—*Internet Security Association and Key Management Protocol (ISAKMP)*—is used to negotiate a mutually acceptable level of authentication and encryption methods between two hosts. This acceptable level of security is called the *security association (SA)*. An SA between two hosts defines the encryption type and method, algorithms used, types of cryptographic keys and key strengths, and so on. The Internet Key Exchange (IKE) protocol—IKEv2 these days—is used in ISAKMP to negotiate the SA between hosts. IKE uses UDP port 500 to accomplish this.

While IPsec is usually seen in VPN implementations paired up with L2TP as its tunneling protocol, IPsec can be very effective in securing traffic within a LAN, particularly sensitive traffic between hosts that an organization wouldn't want to be intercepted and examined. IPsec offers a wide variety of choices for encryption algorithms and strengths and is very flexible in its configuration. You can choose to protect all traffic between certain hosts or protect only certain aspects of traffic, such as certain protocols or traffic that travels between certain ports.

TLS VPNs

The only serious competitor to IPsec VPNs is VPNs using the SSL/TLS protocol. This is the same SSL/TLS protocol used in secure Web pages. SSL/TLS VPN connections don't require special client software installed on the system that wants to connect to the remote network. That system uses only a Web browser and SSL/TLS security to make the VPN connection.

 EXAM TIP Sophos has a Unified Threat Management (UTM) system on Amazon Web Services (AWS) that enables you to log into AWS and get a list of predefined network services. The system requires an HTML5-compliant browser—so the latest Chrome, Firefox, or Safari work fine—but the catch is interesting: you can only access content remotely; you can't download content to your local machine. Sophos calls its service a VPN portal—and CompTIA includes *HTML5* VPN as a VPN option. Be aware that this exists for the exam.

Module 6-5: Network-Based Intrusion Detection/Prevention

This module covers the following CompTIA Security+ objectives:

- **3.2 Given a scenario, implement host or application security solutions**
- **3.3 Given a scenario, implement secure network designs**

Network-based intrusion detection systems (NIDSs) and *network-based intrusion prevention systems (NIPSs)* look at attacks coming into the network at large instead of into a host. Attacks could be in the form of malformed network traffic or excessive amounts of traffic that would easily exceed a host's threshold to handle effectively. An attack could also manifest as malicious content embedded in traffic or other forms of malware. Network intrusion handling also might look at massive DDoS conditions, such as those caused by botnet attacks. (More on this specific attack in Chapter 8.)

Detection vs. Prevention

One point of interest is the difference between a NIDS and a NIPS. A NIDS is a *passive* device and focuses on detection alone, making it a *detection control*. It detects network traffic issues and alerts an administrator to these issues, also logging the events in the process. A NIPS, in contrast, is an *active* (CompTIA Security+ uses the term *inline*) device and focuses not only on detecting network attacks but also on preventing them.

 EXAM TIP The CompTIA Security+ exam will most likely ask you to contrast inline vs. passive network-based intrusion systems. NIPS are inline; NIDS are passive.

In addition to performing the same functions as a NIDS, a NIPS also tries to prevent or stop attacks by taking a series of preconfigured actions, based upon the characteristics of the attack. A NIPS may dynamically block traffic from a certain source address or domain, for example, or block a certain port or protocol if it detects issues with it. A NIPS can take other actions as well, such as shunting traffic to other interfaces, initiating other security actions, tracing the attack back to its origin, and performing some analysis on the attack, but whether a particular NIPS can perform these actions depends on the feature set of that NIPS.

Detecting Attacks

Whether your goal is to detect and prevent attacks or solely to detect them, network-based intrusion tools need some method to detect attacks. In general, NIDS/NIPS solutions act very much like firewalls in that they inspect packets. Detection falls into four types: behavior, signature-based, rule, and heuristic.

NOTE Many NIDS/NIPS vendors' detection solutions perform combinations of these four types of detection.

Behavior/Anomaly

A *behavior-* or *anomaly-based* system detects attacks after comparing traffic with a baseline of patterns considered normal for the network. For this to work, the intrusion detection system must be installed and then given the opportunity to "learn" how the normal flow of traffic behaves over the network. This can take time, but once the NIDS/NIPS establishes a good baseline of normal network traffic, the system will detect any unusual or anomalous traffic patterns that don't fit into the normal network traffic patterns and issue alerts on them as potential attacks.

NOTE Anomaly-based systems rely on rules and heuristic methods to determine when behavior on the network differs from normal. See the upcoming "Rule" and "Heuristic" sections for more details.

Signature

A *signature-based* system, on the other hand, uses preconfigured signature files (similarly to how anti-malware applications work), which are stored in the NIPS/NIDS database. These signatures define certain attack patterns based upon known traffic characteristics. Like an anti-malware solution, a signature-based NIDS/NIPS must also have its signatures database updated frequently, since the security community records new attack patterns often. These updates will usually come through a subscription-based service from the NIDS/NIPS vendor, although some community or open-source signatures may be available as well.

Rule

A *rule-based* system uses preconfigured rules in a ruleset, much like a firewall, to detect possible attacks. For example, if the system detected an excessive (beyond a set number or threshold) number of ICMP packets directed at a destination IP address on the network, the system would activate a rule, send an alert to administrators, and, in the case of a NIPS, stop the attack. Obviously, an administrator could configure unique rules for the organization based on its network environment and historical attack experiences, but these types of systems are also usually included as part of either a signature- or behavior-based system.

Heuristic

Finally, a *heuristic* system combines the best of both anomaly-based and signature-based systems. It starts out with a database of attack signatures and adapts them to network traffic patterns. It learns how different attacks manifest themselves on the network in which it is installed and adjusts its detection algorithms to fit the combination of network traffic behavior and signatures.

Which Is Best?

There's no way to answer that question, and in fact, detection systems are evolving so quickly that even these four types, while sufficient for purposes of the CompTIA Security+ exam, are arguably too simple when applied to the most modern NIDS/NIPS solutions. Although there are advantages and disadvantages to both anomaly-based and signature-based systems, often, modern NIDS/NIPS are hybrid systems and may use both techniques.

NOTE Host-based IDS/IPS solutions are almost always signature-based products.

The big measurement for the quality of a NIDS/NIPS boils down to the solution's detection *analytics*, as in how accurately they parse data. The goal of a NIDS/NIPS is to detect attacks and, in the case of the NIPS, do something about them. The great issues are false positive and false negative rates. Too many false positives will give you heartburn as you continually jump up and down from alarms that mean nothing. A false negative is even worse, as that means your NIDS/NIPS fails to catch actual attacks. The secret is to adjust the sensitivity of the NIDS/NIPS to create the best balance possible.

EXAM TIP Look for an exam question about advanced persistent threats (APTs), such as a terrorist organization trying to hack into a government agency, and the tools used to stop these attacks. Better security appliances implement *unified threat management (UTM)*, marrying traditional firewalls with other security services, such as NIPS, load balancing, and more.

Configuring Network-Based IDS/IPS

In general, a NIDS/NIPS consists of many components. The core component of any IDS/IPS is the *sensor*, the device that monitors the packets, searching for problems. Given the nature of detection versus prevention, a NIPS sensor must be installed in-band to your network traffic, while a NIDS sensor, being passive, is normally installed out-of-band. In-band in this context means the sensor processes all the traffic flowing through the network in real time. An out-of-band sensor processes traffic, in contrast, but not in real time. Figure 6-31 shows two sensors installed in a DMZ as examples of in-band versus out-of-band installation.

All packets must go through in-band sensor devices. Out-of-band sensor devices need some form of network connection that enables them to see all the traffic. Just plugging it into a switch only allows the sensor to see traffic to and from the switch plus broadcast traffic. If you want an out-of-band device to grab packets, you need a network tap or a port mirror.

Figure 6-31
In-band and
out-of-band
installations

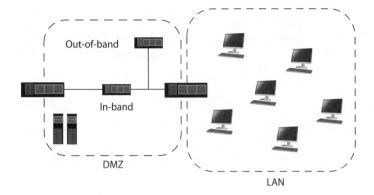

Network TAP

A *network TAP*—test access point—is a device that you can insert anywhere along a run to grab packets. The network TAP in Figure 6-32 works for 10/100/1000-BaseT Ethernet runs. You place this in the run (you'll need to run a few patches and cables for in/outs) and then add an out-of-band sensor to the right-hand side.

Port Mirroring

A *port mirror* (also called a Switched Port Analyzer, or SPAN, in Cisco devices) is a special port on a managed switch configurable to listen for all data going in and out of the switch. Unlike a network TAP, *port mirroring* is convenient and easily changed to reflect any changes in your NIDS/NIPS monitoring strategy. Port mirroring solutions are very handy when you want to monitor more than one VLAN at a time.

Be careful about terminology here. Some folks refer to port mirroring as copying the data from a *single* switch port to a monitoring port, while referring to *port spanning* as grouping *multiple* ports (or all of them) to a monitor port.

Figure 6-32   Garland Technology Network TAP P1GCCB (Photo courtesy of Garland Technology, www.garlandtechnology.com)

EXAM TIP For some reason, objective 3.3 on the CompTIA Security+ exam blurs some terms, calling a network TAP a *port tap*, for example, and SPAN under port mirroring, *port spanning*. Don't get confused between a TAP and a SPAN.

UTM

Many vendors sell single-box solutions to handle routing, firewalling, proxy, anti-malware, and NIPS. These *unified threat management (UTM)* boxes are excellent for several situations (especially when you have a single Internet access and no public-facing server). One area in which UTM thrives is monitoring: with only a single appliance to query, it's easy to get the information you need. Yet if you have a more complex NIDS/NIPS setup, monitoring the NIDS/NIPS gets a bit more complex.

Monitoring NIDS/NIPS

A newly installed NIDS/NIPS is only as good as the organization around it that handles the monitoring. Even the most automated NIPS needs a surprisingly high degree of monitoring, making sure humans react to attacks and remediate as needed. When you find yourself in a situation where this much monitoring takes place, you'll find *security information and event management (SIEM)*. We've already discussed SIEM broadly back in Chapter 4, but now that we have a specific job to do, let's revisit SIEM. This time we'll plug in a few parts of a typical SIEM installation for aggregation and correlation.

Collecting Data

When it comes to SIEM, it's all about *aggregation*: collecting data from disparate sources and organizing the data into a single format. Any device within a SIEM system that collects data is called a *collector* or an *aggregator*. In a simpler NIPS setup with three sensors, it's common to have a single server that acts as a collector, querying the sensors for data in real time.

Correlation

The next part of SIEM that fits nicely into NIDS/NIPS is correlation. *Correlation* is the logic that looks at data from disparate sources and can make determinations about events taking place on your network. (Note that a correlation engine could be in-band or out-of-band, depending on the placement of the NIDS/NIPS.)

In its simplest form, a correlation engine might query a log, see that the same event is logged from three different sources, and eliminate duplicates (*event deduplication*). A correlation engine uses the event of time constantly, so it's critical that all devices have *time synchronization* for correlation engines. A well-correlated log will have common fields for which we can configure the NIPS system for *automated alerts and triggers*. Finally, it's critical that all logs are archived.

Endpoint Detection and Response

Several security manufacturers have taken a further step in integrating security solutions to their advanced network appliances. Firewalls provide classic endpoint protection, blocking traffic from getting to a user's system, for example, or blocking attackers from accessing network resources. NIPSs actively monitor traffic that could pose a threat and act decisively to stop that activity.

Very sophisticated systems called *endpoint detection and response (EDR)* essentially combine an NGFW with a NIPS on steroids to provide end-to-end monitoring, analysis, response to threat, *and forensics* for additional research. Full EDR systems have rolled out since 2017 and will undoubtedly gain market share, at least at the high-end enterprise level.

Questions

1. Which network device enables sharing among multiple servers to provide security and efficiency?

   A. Load balancer

   B. Proxy server

   C. Screened subnet

   D. VPN

2. Which network device is used to send traffic to different physical networks, based upon logical addressing?

   A. Router

   B. Switch

   C. Load balancer

   D. Firewall

3. Which type of device is used to provide network protection and security by preventing hosts from connecting to the organization's infrastructure unless they meet certain criteria?

   A. Switch

   B. NAT device

   C. Firewall

   D. NAC device

4. All of the following characteristics describe VLANs, *except*:

   A. VLANs require routing between them.

   B. VLANs separate hosts into logical networks.

   C. VLANs can be used to apply security policies and filtering to different segments.

   D. VLANs allow any host plugged into the switch to become a member of the virtual segment.

5. Which of the following would be needed to block excessive traffic from a particular protocol?

   A. Broadcast storm prevention

   B. Loop protection

   C. ACL

   D. 802.1X

6. Which of the following describes a network appliance that intercepts user or host requests and then makes those requests to other hosts or networks on behalf of the user?

   A. Proxy

   B. Firewall

   C. NIDS

   D. NIPS

7. Alix sets up a firewall for her organization that inspects traffic at Layers 2, 3, and 7. What type of firewall did she most likely install?

   A. Application

   B. NGFW

   C. Stateful

   D. Stateless

8. A NIPS is considered a _____ type of control.

   A. detective

   B. preventive

   C. network

   D. host

9. Which of the following terms refers to a combination of multifunction security devices?

   A. NIDS/NIPS

   B. Application firewall

   C. Web security gateway

   D. Unified threat management

10. Which of the following does an application firewall focus on for traffic filtering?

    A. Traffic content

    B. Protocol and port

    C. Source or destination IP address

    D. Domain name

Answers

1. **A.** A load balancer enables sharing among multiple servers to provide security and efficiency.

2. **A.** A router is used to send traffic to different physical networks, based upon logical addressing.

3. **D.** A network access control (NAC) device is used to provide network protection and security by preventing hosts from connecting to the organization's infrastructure unless they meet certain criteria.

4. **D.** VLANs do not allow any hosts plugged into the switch to automatically become a member of the virtual segment; membership is based upon switch port, MAC address, or IP address.

5. **A.** A broadcast storm prevention implementation, such as a flood guard, is used to block excessive traffic from a particular protocol.

6. **A.** A proxy is a network appliance that intercepts user or host requests and then makes those requests to other hosts or networks on behalf of the user.

7. **B.** A next-generation firewall works at multiple layers of the OSI model.

8. **B.** A network-based intrusion prevention system (NIPS) is considered a preventive type of control.

9. **D.** Unified threat management (UTM) refers to a combination of multifunction security devices.

10. **A.** An application firewall focuses on traffic content for filtering, rather than on traffic characteristics.

Securing Wireless LANs

It's all about sound. It's that simple. Wireless is wireless, and it's digital. Hopefully somewhere along the line somebody will add more ones to the zeros. When digital first started, I swear I could hear the gap between the ones and the zeros.

—Eddie Van Halen

Modern networks incorporate wireless networks using the 802.11 standard, Wi-Fi, enabling laptops, tablets, and smartphones to connect to the wired resources, such as file servers and printers. Wireless networks, however, represent a broad attack surface that, if not secured properly, provides excellent opportunities for attackers to access those same resources. Thus, a key component of network security is to lock down wireless networks sufficiently to keep out attackers yet still enable authorized users to access network resources easily. This involves installing and configuring wireless security settings, such as cryptographic and authentication protocols, to secure the 802.11 wireless network, as described in this chapter. This chapter explores topics in securing wireless LANs in three modules:

- Networking with 802.11
- Attacking 802.11
- Securing 802.11

Module 7-1: Networking with 802.11

This module covers the following CompTIA Security+ objectives:

- **3.4 Given a scenario, install and configure wireless security settings**
- **3.8 Given a scenario, implement authentication and authorization solutions**

A reader posed this question: "If you could pick one attack surface to try first to penetrate a network, what would it be?" Perhaps not surprisingly at this point in the book, my answer was "Go for the Wi-Fi!" From the day 802.11 first rolled out in the very late 1990s, the 802.11 standard has shown several vulnerabilities, from the well-documented WEP and WPS exploits to more sophisticated attacks such as the TLS handshake.

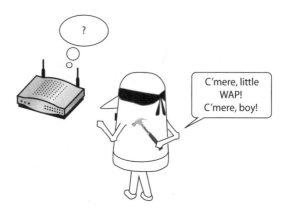

Figure 7-1
Wireless systems
provide a
tempting attack
surface.

An astute security professional, capable of properly configuring good-quality wireless access points (WAPs), should have no problem making an 802.11 network relatively secure. Unfortunately, very few people have that capability, and that's why wireless provides a tempting attack surface (Figure 7-1).

It is impossible to understand how to attack 802.11 or how to secure it without a solid understanding of 802.11. For that reason, this module explores two threads. We'll start with an overview of 802.11 security protocols (and some non-802.11 protocols that 802.11 uses). We'll then tour 802.11 authentication methods, including advanced authentications that only the most secure wireless networks implement.

NOTE I assume you know the essentials about 802.11 networks from studying CompTIA A+ or Network+ (or equivalent wireless network training) before tackling CompTIA Security+. If that's not the case, check out one of my *All-in-One* or *Passport* books on the subject.

Wireless Cryptographic Protocols

When wireless networking was first adopted in the consumer and business markets, no secure wireless protocols were available to prevent eavesdropping and traffic interception. As people became more security conscious, they realized that they needed encryption and authentication protection on wireless networks, as they had on wired networks. Even though the wireless medium is different, security was still a necessity. This resulted in the development of several *cryptographic protocols*—protocols meant to ensure security via encryption and cryptography, with varying degrees of effectiveness, which have been implemented in wireless networks over the years.

As technologies have improved, these wireless cryptographic protocols have improved as well, including newer and more secure methods of authenticating devices and encrypting traffic. In the next few sections, we'll discuss the different wireless security protocols, their advantages and disadvantages, and how you should implement them in your wireless network.

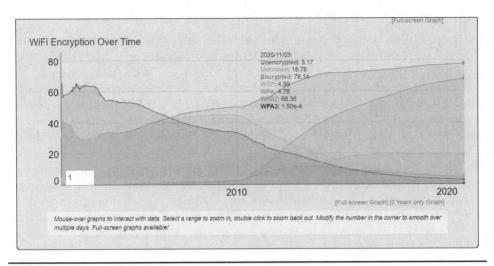

Figure 7-2 WEP is still out there (source: https://wigle.net/stats).

The Legacy of WEP

Wired Equivalent Privacy (WEP), the first security iteration of 802.11, used a shared password encryption scheme that within a few years was discovered to be mathematically crackable. The primary reason for this weakness came from poor key usage with the RC4 encryption. Today's WEP cracking tools will extract a WEP key in just a few minutes.

 NOTE To be fair to the original Wi-Fi developers, they didn't intend WEP as an encryption protocol. WEP was intended to provide wireless users the same level of security they could expect from a wired network (hence the name).

You'd think that, knowing WEP is so easily cracked for so long, no one would use WEP, correct? Wrong. According to Wigle.net, the popular 802.11 database, around 5 percent of all 802.11 networks use WEP encryption as I type this, although the number is slowly dropping (Figure 7-2).

RC4

Rivest Cipher version 4 (RC4) was built into WEP as its encryption protocol and was very efficient because, as a streaming protocol, it rapidly encrypts 1 bit (rather than entire blocks) of plaintext at a time. It uses a wide range of key sizes, from 40-bit to 2048-bit keys.

RC4 alone is not necessarily a weak protocol and is found in other secure protocol implementations beyond WEP. WEP poorly implemented the RC4 protocol, however, adding to the already numerous security flaws found in its design. For this reason, as well as the issues involved with small initialization vectors (IVs), small key size, and static key repetition, never use WEP in modern wireless networks.

WPA

When the wireless industry (specifically, the Wi-Fi Alliance) recognized the inherent security flaws in WEP, they realized they needed to do something very quickly to stem the growing problem of unsecured wireless networks using WEP. Simultaneously, the Institute of Electrical and Electronics Engineers (IEEE) began developing a new security protocol standard for wireless networks, known as 802.11i, but the standard was delayed for various reasons. The Wi-Fi Alliance implemented what was really a stopgap measure in the interim to replace WEP. The result was *Wi-Fi Protected Access (WPA)*, introduced in 2003.

WPA has several advantages over WEP, including the use of dynamic keys and larger key sizes. WPA, also unlike WEP, requires either no authentication (what some manufacturers call *open* mode), authentication to a RADIUS server (Enterprise Mode – WPA-ENT), or the use of a *pre-shared key (PSK)*. Originally conceived for personal or small business infrastructure networks, the PSK setup is called *WPA-Personal* (sometimes referred to as WPA-PSK) and can be used to authenticate wireless client devices and wireless access points mutually. *WPA-Enterprise*, robust but complex and hard to use, was developed for larger infrastructures and requires the use of the 802.1X authentication protocol, which we will cover a bit later in the module. Figure 7-3 shows the various protocol options found on wireless routers.

WPA uses the *Temporal Key Integrity Protocol (TKIP)* for generating encryption keys. TKIP makes it possible to use dynamic keys, which are generated on a per-packet basis. This means the keys are not repeated for different transmissions, but require a different encryption key on each individual packet. TKIP, combined with an improved implementation of the same RC4 stream cipher that WEP uses, provides WPA encryption. TKIP enables backward-compatibility with legacy WEP, uses 128-bit keys, and uses a 48-bit initialization vector.

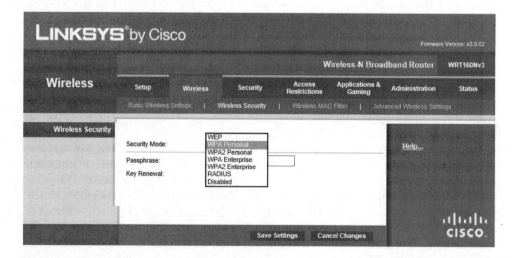

Figure 7-3   Wireless protocol choices on a wireless network

The 802.11i task group came up with a very clever patch for WEP in WPA with TKIP, but it was a patch built on the bones of WEP. Within a very short while, researchers showed ways to exploit the underlying WEP structures. WPA remained very difficult to crack for many years, but the full 802.11i standard needed to be implemented.

WPA2

Wi-Fi Protected Access 2 (WPA2) is the name of the first official implementation of the 802.11i wireless security protocol standard developed by the IEEE. It offers several improvements over the original WPA, such as replacing TKIP with AES, a 128-bit symmetric block cipher that's much more robust but is backward-compatible due to its inclusion of TKIP in its protocol suite. Like WPA, WPA2 also has two different implementations: *WPA2-Personal* (using a pre-shared key) and *WPA2-Enterprise*, which work the same way as they do in WPA.

A WPA/WPA2 passphrase can be from 8 to 63 case-sensitive ASCII characters, or 64 hexadecimal characters. Now, this passphrase is not the actual WPA/WPA2 key; the passphrase is used to generate the 256-bit pre-shared key that must be entered into all wireless devices on the same wireless network. Note that this is different from the way WEP implements its passwords; the WPA/WPA2 passphrase is not the key itself.

 EXAM TIP   Remember that WPA uses TKIP; WPA2 uses AES.

AES

The *Advanced Encryption Standard (AES)*—which you read about back in Module 2-3—is used by a wide variety of encryption applications. It was adopted as the official encryption standard for the United States by the National Institute of Standards and Technology (NIST), after an open competition with several different competing algorithms. AES uses the Rijndael encryption algorithm and is considered much stronger than previous symmetric algorithms used in wireless networking, such as RC4.

AES is the encryption algorithm used in WPA2 and uses a particular process, or *mode*, within WPA2 to encrypt traffic. This mode is called the *Counter Mode Cipher Block Chaining Message Authentication Code Protocol*, which CompTIA shortens to *Counter-mode/CBC-MAC Protocol (CCMP)*. CCMP uses a 128-bit key and 128-bit block size (since it is a *block* symmetric cipher, as opposed to the *streaming* RC4 symmetric cipher used in WEP and WPA), as well as 48-bit initialization vectors. The larger IV sizes help prevent replay attacks from being conducted against WPA2 (see "Replay Attacks," later in the chapter).

 NOTE   Wireless devices often have an encryption setting that lets you choose between AES, TKIP, and mixed mode. In *mixed mode*, both AES and TKIP are supported. It is not recommended.

WPA3

WPA2 has served the 802.11 industry since 2004, more than a lifetime in the IT industry. In this time frame WPA2 has started to show some weaknesses that enable skilled bad actors to break into wireless networks. One of the biggest weaknesses of WPA2 is the pre-shared key. Anyone in possession of the single PSK can give it to others and they can use it to access the network. Worse, there are a number of attacks—in particular the infamous KRACK on-path (MITM) attack—that work on any WPA2 network. By the middle aughts, it was clearly time to improve on WPA2 with the next generation of 802.11 security. The Wi-Fi Alliance released the replacement for WPA2, called *Wi-Fi Protected Access 3 (WPA3)*, in 2018.

WPA3 brings many improvements over WPA2. Most notably, *Simultaneous Authentication of Equals (SAE)* replaces PSK—at least for encryption. If you set up an "open" SSID with a WPA3-capable WAP, SAE automatically forces every WPA3-capable device connecting to that WAP to use a Diffie-Hellman–style authentication/encryption process. In other words, the day of the unencrypted wireless connection no longer exists in WPA3.

 EXAM TIP Look for a comparative question on the CompTIA Security+ exam that explores pre-shared key (PSK) vs. enterprise vs. open. This applies primarily to WPA2, not WPA3, but *PSK* means using personal mode, *enterprise* means connecting to a RADIUS server, and *open* means having no security at all (i.e., open season on your network).

WPS

You can fairly easily join to a wireless network any system that has a screen and input method (keyboard, mouse, or touch screen). Joining a system, such as a printer, that lacks a screen and input device is much harder. In many cases they require separate setup programs or painfully complex configurations through tiny text screens and pressing up and down buttons through entire alphanumeric strings to type in passwords.

Recognizing the popularity of wireless devices in non-enterprise networks, the Wi-Fi Alliance introduced *Wi-Fi Protected Setup (WPS)* in 2006. The goal of WPS is to enable anyone to join a WPS-capable device to a WPS-enabled wireless network just by pressing two buttons. Press the button on the WAP (Figure 7-4), then press the button on the device you want to join to the network; your device connects to the SSID and takes on the WAP's WPA2 encryption. Neat!

Alternatively, every WPS-enabled WAP comes with a fixed eight-digit PIN code to allow devices without a WPS button (like a laptop) to connect to the WAP. You press the button on the router and then enter the router's PIN code as the SSID's password. Unfortunately, the eight-digit code has two problems. First, only seven of the eight digits are used (the eighth digit is only a checksum). Additionally, the seven digits are confirmed in two groups: the first three values, then the last four. This means it only takes about 11,000 guesses to crack a WPA PIN code. Yipe!

Figure 7-4
Typical WPS
button on home
router

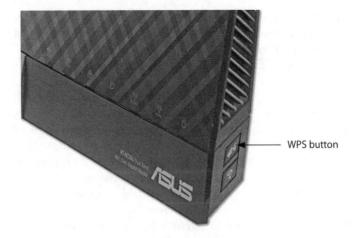

WPS button

So What Do We Use?

If you install an 802.11 network, the Wi-Fi Alliance states that you must use either WPA2-ENT or WPA2-PSK with a robust password. On all my PSK networks I make a point to use a 15- to 20-character password. Here's one of my favorites (please don't hack me): *ioncelivedinsedalia*.

Wireless Authentication Protocols

We've spent some time discussing wireless encryption, as well as wireless authentication, between a simple wireless client and its access point. Most of the discussion has been very general and could apply to small home wireless networks, small business networks, and even, to a degree, large enterprise-level wireless networks. Now let's take a moment to talk about the enterprise side of wireless networking, which usually involves more complex authentication methods and may involve using a wireless network to connect into a larger corporate wired network. We'll talk about different authentication methods and protocols that are primarily used in enterprise infrastructures, particularly when using the more advanced features of WPA and WPA2.

EXAM TIP Authentication protocols, as the name suggests, authenticate users to a network. Cryptographic protocols provide security mechanisms, such as encryption. Secure networks, wireless as well as wired, require use of both types of protocols.

802.1X

802.1X is an IEEE standard, just like the 802.3 Ethernet standards and 802.11 wireless networking standards. The great thing is that, while 802.1X is probably encountered most often on corporate wireless networks as the preferred form of authentication and access management control, it is not a wireless standard at all and can be used in wired networks as well. This actually makes it easier for wireless and wired networks to interoperate, since they can use the same authentication methods and can connect to each other quite easily. 802.1X is called a *port-based* access control method and can use a wide variety of different security protocols. In that respect, it's more of a security authentication framework than a protocol itself, since it allows various protocols to be used for authentication.

802.1X uses some interesting terms you may need to be familiar with for the exam. First, a wireless client device is known as a *supplicant* in an 802.1X environment. A wireless access point that uses 802.1X authentication methods is called the *authenticator*, and the source providing the authentication services to the wireless network is called the *authentication server*. 802.1X is interoperable with a number of remote access services and protocols, such as RADIUS and TACACS+, as well as centralized authentication databases such as Active Directory. This enables wireless clients to authenticate to traditional infrastructures using these different types of services.

802.1X can use several different types of authentication protocols, such as EAP, EAP-TLS, EAP-TTLS, PEAP, LEAP, and EAP-FAST. Let's check out this string of acronyms now.

EAP

Like the 802.1X authentication protocol, the *Extensible Authentication Protocol (EAP)* isn't so much a protocol as a security framework that provides for varied authentication methods. Many different protocols fit into the EAP framework, and that's really why it was devised in the first place. EAP recognizes that there are several different authentication methods, including certificate-based authentication and other multifactor authentication methods, such as smart cards and so on. EAP can still allow the traditional user name/password combination of authentication as well. EAP also allows for mutual authentication between devices as well as directory-based authentication services.

There are several different variations of EAP, some older, and some more suitable for use than others. These include EAP-TLS, EAP-TTLS, PEAP, and EAP-FAST (plus others you won't see on the exam). Let's cover the EAP versions mentioned in the CompTIA Security+ exam objective.

EAP-TLS

EAP Transport Layer Security (EAP-TLS) was for years the primary EAP variation used on high-security wireless networks. As the name implies, EAP-TLS uses the same TLS protocol used on secure Web pages. EAP-TLS requires both a server-side certificate and a client-side certificate (client-side certificates are rarely used on Web pages, but the TLS protocol certainly supports their use).

Client-side certificates are an administrative headache because every laptop, smartphone, tablet, or printer on the network must have a unique certificate. Losing a device requires disassociating the missing device's certificate to ensure security. If you want the ultimate in 802.11 authentication security, however, EAP-TLS is the way to go.

EAP-TTLS

EAP Tunneled Transport Layer Security (EAP-TTLS) may share a similar-sounding acronym to EAP-TLS, but it is a completely different EAP variation (Figure 7-5). EAP-TTLS

Figure 7-5
Configuring
802.1X on
a Windows
wireless client

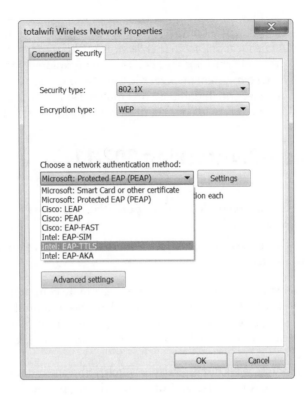

goes beyond the TLS protocol, adding a tunnel to provide better security. EAP-TTLS only requires a server-side certificate. EAP-TTLS is considered to be functionally equivalent to PEAP (see next).

PEAP

Protected Extensible Authentication Protocol (PEAP), another version that uses TLS, addressed problems with EAP and was developed as an open protocol by several vendors, such as Microsoft, RSA, and Cisco. PEAP is similar to EAP-TLS and requires a digital certificate on the server side of a connection to create a secure TLS tunnel. There are different versions of PEAP, depending upon the implementation and operating system, but all typically use digital certificates or smart cards for authentication.

LEAP and EAP-FAST

Lightweight Extensible Authentication Protocol (LEAP) is a proprietary protocol developed by Cisco and was used in their wireless LAN devices for authentication. LEAP uses dynamic WEP keys and provides for mutual authentication between wireless clients and a centralized RADIUS server. LEAP requires wireless clients to reauthenticate periodically, and when they do, they must use a new WEP key.

Cisco has replaced LEAP with *EAP-FAST* (for *Flexible Authentication via Secure Tunneling*), which addresses LEAP's security issues. EAP-FAST is lightweight but uses TLS tunnels to add security during authentication.

EXAM TIP The CompTIA Security+ objectives refer to a *Remote Authentication Dial-in User Service (RADIUS) Federation* authentication protocol, which mashes two terms you explored back in Chapter 3. A *federated* system involves the use of a common authentication system and credentials database that multiple entities use and share. A RADIUS federation could connect those systems wirelessly using RADIUS servers.

Module 7-2: Attacking 802.11

This module covers the following CompTIA Security+ objectives:

- **1.3   Given a scenario, analyze potential indicators associated with application attacks**
- **1.4   Given a scenario, analyze potential indicators associated with network attacks**

Attacks on wireless networks have never been more common than they are today, but why? Given that 802.11 wireless networks have been around for more than 20 years, you'd think by now we'd be better at securing them. Truth is, we are better, but the bad guys have gotten better as well. Plus, the wireless footprint keeps expanding. Wireless is everywhere.

In this module, we'll discuss various wireless threats and attacks that can be carried out against wireless networks and unsecure wireless protocols (such as the surprisingly still relevant WEPCrack). This module will discuss the attacks at length, so that by the next module, you'll be ready to learn the various ways you can harden wireless access points and networks against these types of attacks. We'll also glance at the other wireless standard, Bluetooth, at the tail end to examine attacks along that vector.

If you want to do some attacking (of the ethical variety, of course!), the first thing you'll need are some tools. There are many tools out there to attack 802.11, but in general you'll need three separate items:

- A good survey/stumbler tool to locate wireless networks and obtain detailed information
- Some kind of tool to start grabbing wireless packets
- Some type of attack tool that analyzes the data you've collected and grabs the passwords, keys, credentials, or whatever you want to grab

With those concepts in mind, let's turn to the specific toys in the attacker's toolbox. You'll see these on the CompTIA Security+ exam and, hopefully, use them for good in the real world.

Wireless Survey/Stumbler

To attack a wireless network, you first need to find one to attack. To do this, you use wireless survey/stumbler utilities. There are many such tools. Even the wireless client

Figure 7-6
Wi-Fi analyzer on
Android

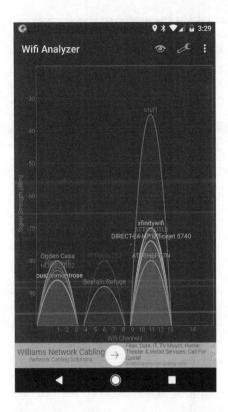

built into your operating system easily locates the wireless networks and will tell you the channel and encryption type. That's OK for users, but if you want to attack, you need a more serious survey tool. You need a survey tool like a *Wi-Fi analyzer* that not only sees the wireless network but also grabs critical information such as GPS location, WAP MAC address, detailed encryption type, WPS enabled, and so on. Figure 7-6 shows an Android Wi-Fi analyzer I use.

Packet Capture

Once you've found a target, you then need to start grabbing packets. To do this, you'll need some form of packet-capture tool that grabs wireless packets and gives you some control as to what packets you want to grab. Again, you have choices, but Airodump-ng—one of the many powerful tools that are part of the Aircrack-ng wireless suite, is very common and well supported (Figure 7-7).

Attack Tools

The entire goal of attacking wireless networks is to gather information. Every attack requires some type of utility that helps you do whatever you want to do. Do you want to crack WPS? There's a tool for that. Want to crack WEP? There's a tool for that. Want to intercept credentials? There's yet another tool for that.

```
Home - PuTTY                                                                   _ □ ×

 CH  5 ][ Elapsed: 2 mins ][ 2010-05-03 22:03 ][ enabled AP selection

 BSSID               PWR  Beacons    #Data, #/s  CH  MB   ENC  CIPHER AUTH ESSID

 00:18:39:83:00:3F   -53     512      1497    0   5  11   WPA  TKIP   PSK  Merdorp
 00:12:BF:1F:08:57   -61     451        19    0   6  54 . OPN              Philips WiFi
 00:12:BF:06:18:77   -64     384         0    0   6  54 . WEP  WEP        Philips WiFi
 00:1F:9F:A2:E2:2A   -72     398         5    0   1  54e  OPN             SpeedTouchAC3DF
 00:12:BF:3D:06:F6   -77      21         0    0   6  54 . OPN             Philips WiFi

 BSSID               STATION           PWR   Rate    Lost  Packets  Probes

 (not associated)    00:18:DE:AB:4A:1F  -73   0 - 1     0        4  Philips WiFi
 00:18:39:83:00:3F   00:1E:4C:AD:4E:F0  -43  11 -11     0     1647  Merdorp
 00:18:39:83:00:3F   00:13:02:13:9D:1A  -50  11 - 1     0      110  Merdorp
 00:12:BF:1F:08:57   00:15:AF:30:E3:4D  -62  36 -18     0       25
 00:12:BF:3D:06:F6   00:1E:4C:03:9E:46  -70   0 - 1     0       49
```

Figure 7-7   Selecting a specific WAP with Airodump-ng

The problem with any attack tool is that none of these tools are *intuitive*; you can't just throw your average script kiddie in front of one of these tools and expect results. The tools are not necessarily difficult to use, but they aren't so simple that you can plug and chug.

With that understanding in mind, there are some pretty great tools out there for wireless attacks. As a starting point, check out the previously mentioned Aircrack-ng, a suite of tools that handles several popular attacks, concentrating on WEP and WPA cracking.

 CAUTION   Please, please, please note that using hacking and cracking tools can land you in jail. That's *not a joke*. You can attack your personal systems all you want, of course. That's how to gain skills. But you need a signed agreement before you turn your newly minted mad hacking skills against an organization. Without that agreement, you risk committing a felony, and that, as we say in the business, is a *bad thing*.

Rogue Access Point

A *rogue access point* can indicate a potential wireless network attack, because it features an unauthorized WAP within a secure network that attracts people to connect to it. A rogue AP can be benign, for example, where a network user sets up a WAP to provide better signal strength in his or her area. As an attack, though, a malicious person deliberately places a rogue AP with the intent to monitor all of the connected victims' network traffic. In both cases, the rogue AP enables connectivity to the legitimate network. The malicious kind seeks information.

Hackers use several techniques to set up rogue APs. In a basic attack, the attacker uses an AP configured for very weak or nonexistent authentication. This makes the victim think that it's an open or free Internet AP.

NOTE Different parts of the wireless industry use either *AP* or *WAP* to describe a wireless access point. You'll see this throughout industry literature and hear it in discussions. The CompTIA Security+ 601 objectives refer to WAPs in one section and rogue access point in another, for example, where the "wireless" part is implied. The same applies to AP—the acronym implies wireless.

Often a rogue AP will broadcast a very strong signal so that users think it's the best free Internet access point compared to several others. Rogue APs work very well where there are several APs already transmitting, such as areas within range of businesses or establishments that offer free wireless access to their customers.

In another variation of this attack—called an *evil twin* attack—a hacker sets up a rogue AP that broadcasts the same (or very similar) Service Set Identifier (SSID), which appears as the wireless network's name to ordinary users. Often, however, the evil twin does not use the same security level as the legitimate AP, making it easier to connect to the evil twin. Unsuspecting users connect to this AP, thinking that it's one to which they normally should connect. Once connected to the evil twin's network, the attacker can intercept the user's network traffic through the evil twin, including user names, passwords, and any other traffic passed over the AP.

The evil twin attacker can gain user credentials that may also be used on other wireless networks, allowing the attacker to connect to the legitimate APs and begin an attack on those networks. The hacker may even further connect this rogue AP to the Internet, so the user never suspects that she is connected to the rogue AP.

Figure 7-8 shows an example of how an evil twin wireless network also appears with a legitimate one. Notice that the two are named similarly but are not configured the same in terms of required security.

Jamming

Occasionally, a wireless network can experience interference from another wireless device, which can occur, for example, when two wireless access points use adjacent frequencies or channels. Interference can interrupt and interfere with wireless network transmission and reception. For the most part, this interference is unintentional. *Jamming* is a form of intentional interference on wireless networks, designed as a denial-of-service (DoS) attack. This type of attack overpowers the signals of a legitimate wireless access point, typically using a rogue AP with its transmit power set to very high levels. Attackers can use other electronic devices as well to create interference, or jamming, in wireless networks, including specialized devices easily acquired from the Internet or put together by hobbyists.

Jammers are also commonly used to help evil twin attacks. By jamming a legitimate WAP's channel, all clients will automatically try to go to the evil twin (Figure 7-9). Even

Figure 7-8
An evil twin
rogue wireless
access point is
named similarly
to a legitimate
network AP.

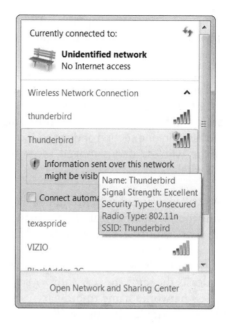

Currently connected to:

Unidentified network
No Internet access

Wireless Network Connection ⌃

thunderbird

Thunderbird

ⓘ Information sent over this network
might be visib| Name: Thunderbird
| Signal Strength: Excellent
☐ Connect autom| Security Type: Unsecured
| Radio Type: 802.11n
texaspride | SSID: Thunderbird

VIZIO

BlackAdder 2G

Open Network and Sharing Center

if your legitimate WAP tries to switch to another channel, a good jammer tracks the channel changes and continues to jam.

The only way to prevent jamming and interference is to look proactively for sources of wireless signals that are not coming from the corporate wireless network. The sources are usually in the same frequency range and may come from malicious wireless clients or rogue wireless access points.

NOTE Legally owning a jammer requires appropriate permission and licensing. In many countries even owning a jammer is illegal.

Figure 7-9
Jammer working
with an evil twin

Jam channel 6 with
Wi-Fi jammer

Legit WAP on channel 6
SSID: Thunderbird

Evil Twin WAP on channel 1
SSID: Thunderbird

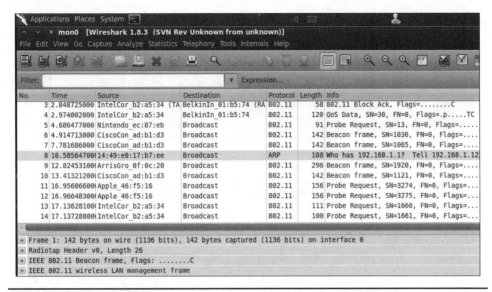

Figure 7-10 Packet sniffing a wireless network

Packet Sniffing

Just as with wired networks, attackers can sniff wireless networks for unencrypted data to capture and analyze, although the techniques and tools required differ. Usually, an attacker has to have a special wireless network card that can intercept packets and inject traffic on to the network. The attacker usually also must have a special driver for the network card, if he is using the Windows operating system, or he must put a network card into what's called *monitor* or *promiscuous* mode in Linux. Once the attacker has his equipment set up, it's simply a matter of using the sniffing software of choice, such as Wireshark, for example. Figure 7-10 shows a Wireshark capture of a packet sniffing session conducted on a wireless network.

NOTE All wireless sniffer tools require a special wireless NIC driver.

Deauthentication Attack

Encrypted wireless communication, as you might suspect, does not enable an attacker to run simple tools to capture data and glean important or sensitive information. That's the point of encryption, right? An attacker can grab beacon frames and management traffic and a bunch of encrypted traffic he can't read.

The 802.11 frames that make the initial connection between a WAP and a wireless client offer a unique attack vector. These standard management frames enable a client to connect, then establish credentials and so forth so that encrypted communication can happen happily.

```
root@bt:~# aireplay-ng -0 10 -a $AP -c $CLIENT mon0
20:08:52  Waiting for beacon frame (BSSID: 00:23:69:C1:E8:95) on channel 3
20:08:53  Sending 64 directed DeAuth. STMAC: [00:22:43:80:45:FB] [ 0|64 ACKs]
20:08:54  Sending 64 directed DeAuth. STMAC: [00:22:43:80:45:FB] [ 0|63 ACKs]
20:08:55  Sending 64 directed DeAuth. STMAC: [00:22:43:80:45:FB] [ 0|63 ACKs]
20:08:55  Sending 64 directed DeAuth. STMAC: [00:22:43:80:45:FB] [ 0|64 ACKs]
20:08:56  Sending 64 directed DeAuth. STMAC: [00:22:43:80:45:FB] [ 0|63 ACKs]
20:08:57  Sending 64 directed DeAuth. STMAC: [00:22:43:80:45:FB] [ 0|64 ACKs]
20:08:57  Sending 64 directed DeAuth. STMAC: [00:22:43:80:45:FB] [ 0|61 ACKs]
20:08:58  Sending 64 directed DeAuth. STMAC: [00:22:43:80:45:FB] [ 0|64 ACKs]
20:08:59  Sending 64 directed DeAuth. STMAC: [00:22:43:80:45:FB] [ 0|62 ACKs]
20:08:59  Sending 64 directed DeAuth. STMAC: [00:22:43:80:45:FB] [ 0|61 ACKs]
root@bt:~#
```

Figure 7-11 Conducting a deauthentication attack against a wireless client and its AP

In a *deauthentication attack*, a malicious actor sends a deauthentication frame to the WAP with a spoofed MAC address—picked up by simple sniffers in the clear from traffic between the WAP and the intended target client. The WAP dutifully disconnects the client (or *station*, as the Wi-Fi folks like to say). The client will then automatically try to reconnect—associate—with the WAP. What happens after this DoS attack ("I deny you access to the WAP!") depends on the bad guy's intent.

The client could unsuspectingly connect with an evil twin WAP and the bad guy could use various attacks—man-in-the-middle attack, brute-force attack, and so on—to get the client's password. Once the attacker has the password in hand, it's game over for the client. The bad guy could just be a jerk, doing a DoS for some sick laughs. Regardless of the subsequent actions, the deauthorization attack starts the process.

Figure 7-11 shows an example of a deauthentication attack, conducted using the aireplay-ng command in the Aircrack-ng tool suite. This tool is popularly found on Linux-based systems, particularly security distributions.

 EXAM TIP You'll hear the term *disassociation attack* as a form of deauthentication attack.

Near-Field Communication

Near-field communication (NFC) enables devices to send very low-power radio signals to each other by using a special chip implanted in the device. NFC requires that the devices be extremely close—like within four inches—to each other. NFC can be used for a wide variety of consumer and business applications, including quick payments with NFC-enabled smartphones and cash registers, parking meters, and other really cool and convenient transactions. NFC uses *radio-frequency identification (RFID)* technologies and, unfortunately, is vulnerable to several types of attacks. These attacks include eavesdropping by another NFC device, man-in-the-middle attacks, and relay attacks (relaying modified information back and forth from the victim's device, pretending to be the victim). Many WPS-enabled devices (see "WPS Attacks" later in this module) also use NFC, making wireless hacking of WPS-enabled networks easy.

Figure 7-12 A replay attack starts with a man-in-the-middle.

Replay Attacks

In a *replay attack*, data, particularly credentials such as user names and passwords, is intercepted and replayed back on the network to an unsuspecting host. The goal of the replay attack is to retransmit those credentials back to a host, effectively allowing the attacker to impersonate the victim. Credentials or other data passed in clear text is most vulnerable to replay attack, although certain versions of weak encryption algorithms can also be vulnerable to these types of attacks. Even if the attacker can't read the victim's credentials due to encryption, weak authentication methods may allow retransmitted credentials to be used to authenticate to a host. Note that this type of attack isn't unique to wireless networks; wired networks also suffer from replay attacks (Figure 7-12).

Strong encryption methods help defend against this type of attack. Another defense against this attack is through the use of *timestamping*, which limits the use of the credentials to a very narrow time period. The use of the Kerberos authentication protocol in Windows Active Directory networks, which makes heavy use of time stamps, counters replay attacks. Still another way of defending against this type of attack is for the originating host to digitally sign the traffic it sends. This assures the receiving host that the credentials or other data it receives is authentic.

 EXAM TIP The CompTIA Security+ objectives categorize a replay attack as a type of *application attack*. Others that fall into this category are DLL injections and privilege escalation attacks that you saw back in Chapter 5. You'll see many more in Chapter 11.

WEP/WPA Attacks

Like any streaming encryption, RC4 needs initialization vectors (IVs) to seed its encryption methods for protecting wireless traffic. Unfortunately, the IVs in WEP are considered weak, in that they are only 24 bits in length. This short length guarantees that WEP must repeat the IVs frequently, meaning that after sniffing a few million packets, an attacker can crack the WEP key mathematically (an *IV attack*). Today a number of off-the-shelf tools (such as the freeware Aircrack-ng) make cracking any WEP-encrypted SSID easy.

WPA has its weaknesses. It uses RC4 encryption, and cracking methods were developed to crack WPA—although it is much harder to crack WPA than WEP.

Although both WPA and WPA2 are very strong wireless security protocols, if your SSID uses a pre-shared key with a weak passphrase, they are both easily cracked, since the four-way handshakes they use to negotiate a connection between devices contain the WPA/WPA2 encryption key. This four-way handshake can be intercepted after a deauthentication attack forces a wireless client and AP to reestablish their connection and reauthenticate with each other. Once intercepted, a weak key can be cracked using standard dictionary or brute-force attacks, again using tools such as Aircrack-ng.

WPS Attacks

A WPS-enabled wireless router can connect to another WPS device (wireless printers are the most common) through a number of different methods. These methods all use a WPS personal identification number (PIN), which is enabled simply by pushing a button on the wireless router and the device. This PIN is used as the network's secure WPA key. This WPS PIN is susceptible to brute-force attacks.

 EXAM TIP The CompTIA Security+ exam might query you about an attack used in older Microsoft networks. A *pass the hash* attack takes advantage of weak points in the NT LAN Manager (NTLM) and LANMAN protocols. If the attacker has the hash of a user's password, the attacker can skip any kind of brute-force attack and use the hashed password to access the network. Modern Windows systems mitigate against this sort of attack, though the best defense is to not allow network administrators to log in to suspect systems and thus expose their passwords.

Wireless Peripherals

Wireless peripherals such as wireless keyboards and wireless mice are common and convenient, freeing us from messy cables and allowing more freedom of configuration. The problem with wireless peripherals is that they typically use Bluetooth as the wireless connection. Although Bluetooth is a mature and secure technology, an improperly configured Bluetooth peripheral is easy to hack. Let's take a moment and talk about the two old but still valid Bluetooth attacks, bluejacking and bluesnarfing.

 NOTE Bluetooth is not Wi-Fi, but a different wireless standard that you'll recall from CompTIA A+ or CompTIA Network+ studies.

Bluejacking

Although becoming rarer these days, Bluetooth attacks happen. In the early days of Bluetooth, protocols did not have adequate security measures built in, and devices by default allowed themselves to connect with any Bluetooth device that requested it. This enabled attackers to connect their Bluetooth device surreptitiously with an unsuspecting person's device and steal information from it, such as contacts and other personal information. These attacks are becoming rare because the Bluetooth protocol has evolved over time, and now more security measures are built into the protocol by default. Additionally, most Bluetooth devices have to undergo a type of authentication with each other, called *pairing*, which makes intercepting traffic between them more difficult. Another factor contributing to the rarity of these types of attacks is that Bluetooth has a very limited range: an attacker would have to be within around 35 feet of the victim to conduct the attack successfully.

Legacy devices still in use, however, as well as new devices improperly configured for security, are susceptible to Bluetooth attacks. One of the classic attacks on Bluetooth is called *bluejacking*. Bluejacking involves sending data to a target device, such as a smartphone, usually in the form of unsolicited text messages. Although mostly harmless, bluejacking can be annoying at best and constitutes harassment at worst. Bluejacking does not involve removing data from the device.

Bluesnarfing

Bluesnarfing is yet another classic Bluetooth attack, in which the attacker steals data from the target device by connecting to an unsuspecting user's device. Bluesnarfing can be used to get contacts, e-mails, text messages, pictures, videos, and other sensitive data. Once again, this type of attack is very rare these days, since most vendors have fixed vulnerabilities in their device operating systems and because of upgrades to the protocol itself.

You can stop both bluejacking and bluesnarfing attacks easily by making sure you don't leave your device in discoverable mode to prevent anyone from pairing to your device.

Module 7-3: Securing 802.11

This module covers the following CompTIA Security+ objective:

- **3.4   Given a scenario, install and configure wireless security settings**

Despite what you might think after reading the many scary stories from the previous module, it's not difficult to create a robust and secure 802.11 wireless network. This module discusses a number of installation considerations, security features, and administration tools to make a Wi-Fi network as secure as possible.

Installation Considerations

Network design that incorporates wireless connectivity offers choices these days in the type of access points to use, site surveys, and WAP placement. Let's start with installing WAPs.

Fat vs. Thin Access Points

An organization's choice of which technology to employ to provide wireless connectivity depends on several factors, including the location and complexity of its primary office network and the design philosophy and needs of individual enterprise offices. You'll hear the terms fat and thin access points to describe various APs, and we'll look at those in detail next. Terms aside, the choice boils down to where you want to manage the security on the network.

A *fat AP* has all the bells and whistles, including a management console where you can configure typical security controls, such as access control lists (ACLs), allow and block lists, encryption, and so on. A fat or *thick* AP is also called a *controller-based AP*. You manage each fat AP individually or, in the case of some vendors, manage all APs by sending them instructions from a global console to enact locally. A *thin AP* typically just acts as a repeater, taking the wireless signal and pushing it to a managed access control (AC) switch that handles encryption and other security. A thin AP is referred to as a *standalone AP*.

Here's an example of how design philosophy, location, and complexity dictate which technology to employ. A standalone satellite office in Brazil might need a fat AP to handle the wireless needs of its ten users and provide connectivity back to the home office. A building with multiple floors and hundreds of users might rely on one awesome switch (plus a redundant backup) to control dozens of thin access points.

Site Surveys

In a *site survey*, a network tech makes a technical assessment of the area in which a wireless network will be installed and operating. Usually, the tech performs a site survey before installing the wireless network, although sometimes it might be performed periodically when looking at network performance or before expanding the wireless network to accommodate new access points or additional capacity.

Site surveys help technical personnel understand the different issues that may be present in an area where the wireless network will be operational. These issues may affect considerations such as area coverage, network growth, access point and antenna placement, required power levels, and even network capacity (level of usage of the wireless network).

 NOTE Security professionals in the field of penetration testing love fake site surveys. People simply ignore folks walking around with a clipboard and survey uniforms.... This is social engineering—manipulating people to get into systems—at its finest. Chapter 12 covers social engineering techniques in detail.

Some of these issues include proximity to potential interference sources, channel overlaps from other SSIDs in the area, environmental and physical considerations (physical obstacles that may limit wireless signals, such as buildings, for example), and, of course, potential security issues (public areas where war driving may happen, for instance).

A *Wi-Fi analyzer* tool will scan an area for existing wireless networks, providing essential information for assessing an area for potential problems or obstacles when planning an installation of a Wi-Fi network. Figure 7-13 illustrates some of the data collected during a survey when using a Wi-Fi analyzer tool, in this case inSSIDer from Meta-Geek (www.metageek.com). A quick scan of a local area shows many networks, including named and hidden; the signal strength relative to the position of the scanning device in

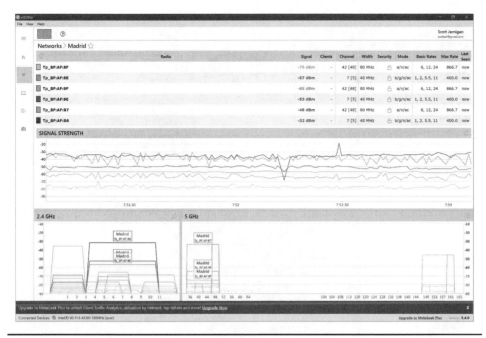

Figure 7-13   Viewing the Wi-Fi spectrum when performing a site survey

decibels (lower number is stronger); number of radios, the security level, such as WPA, WEP, WPA2, open; and mode, such as 802.11b/g for the open network and 802.11a/b/g/n/ac/ax for one of the locked down networks. Additionally, the screenshot shows the Madrid network selected so you can see the channels in use graphically in the lower third of the screen—3 and 11 in the 2.4 GHz band; 34, 46, and 50 in the 5 GHz band.

 EXAM TIP   Wi-Fi networks use radio-frequency spectrums or bands split into channels, which you might recall from your CompTIA Network+ studies. The 2.4 GHz band has a fairly small number of channels, several of which overlap. Excessive traffic on overlapping channels—even with separate SSIDs— can cause problems. This is sometimes referred to as *adjacent-channel interference*, which the CompTIA Security+ objectives shorten to *channel overlaps*.

When conducting a site survey, a technician measures potential coverage distances, identifies obstacles that may block wireless signals, and performs various tests to determine optimal placement of antennas and access points. The technician will usually map out the area and identify potential sources of interference, such as power cabling, cell towers, or other radio-frequency interference (RFI)–producing sources. Technicians also should plan for capacity, meaning that they need to know how many users will connect to the wireless network at any given time and what types of data or applications they will use over the wireless network.

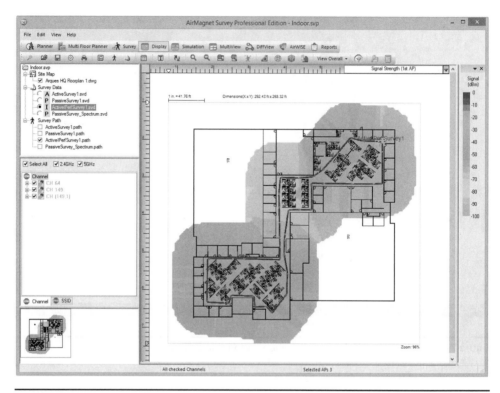

Figure 7-14 AirMagnet Survey Pro

There are plenty of tools to support a wireless survey, like AirMagnet Survey Pro (Figure 7-14). All good survey utilities share some common ways to report their findings. One of the most powerful reports that they generate is called a heat map. A *heat map* is nothing more than a graphical representation of the radio-frequency (RF) sources on a site, using different colors to represent the intensity of the signal. Figure 7-15 shows a sample heat map. Some companies take heat map tech to the minute, showing the precise location of User Joe in the building based on his network traffic. This can be a great tool.

Although this might not seem like a security consideration, remember that availability of data is directly tied to security (remember the CIA triad: confidentiality, accountability, integrity). After completing the site survey, the technician usually provides recommendations to managers and the team that will install or expand the wireless network, so they can configure it optimally for both performance and security.

WAP Placement

Wireless access point (WAP) placement matters not only in making sure that people can get a strong enough signal to access the wireless network, but also for security reasons. A WAP with a standard omnidirectional antenna located too close to an outer wall of a facility makes the wireless signal easier to pick up outside the facility, which makes

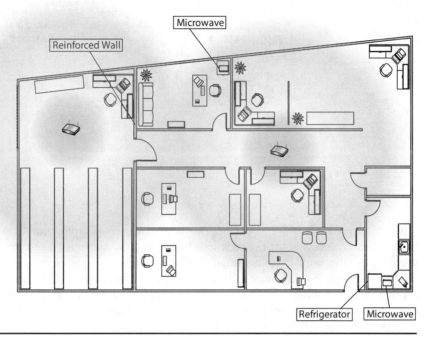

Figure 7-15   Site survey with heat map

it easier for bad actors to pick up the wireless signal and attempt to hack the network. Ideally, both for performance and security reasons, centralize WAP placement within a facility; in other words, place WAPs with omnidirectional antennas centrally throughout different areas of the facility so that they can adequately span all areas of coverage within a facility, without being too close to exterior walls or the roof whenever possible.

Place a WAP with a directional antenna, in contrast, so that the signal points to the area of desired coverage. Placing such a WAP on the inside of an outer wall, pointed into the interior, can provide excellent coverage with little chance of signal spillage.

Wireless Configuration

A good layout of enterprise-level WAPs, properly placed and using the right antennas, is a great start for any wireless network. Now it's time to take advantage of the many 802.11 features to protect your network.

Controller and Access Point Security

No wireless network has any hope of security without serious consideration of *controller and access point security*. Start with the basics in a SOHO network and replace default passwords for any wireless access point to something much more secure. Also, if possible, change any factory-configured SSID passwords. (See Figure 7-16.) Don't use the same password on every WAP. Finally, be sure to restrict physical access to the WAP.

Figure 7-16
Factory passwords are well known.

Once you get beyond a SOHO network, as you'll recall from your CompTIA Network+ studies, access point management becomes more centralized. A typical medium-sized organization, for example, might deploy a dozen *managed access points* across their offices that require a *controller* to handle setup, configuration, and security. You secure access to the controller software the same way you secure access to any critical application, through proper account management, as in making sure only the appropriate user accounts can access the controller software. When you scale up further—think campus area network (CAN) here with 100+ APs—many organizations use dedicated hardware AP controllers to configure access point security. Secure access to the AP controllers just as you would any mission-critical network appliance, through limiting physical access as well as proper account management.

SSID Broadcasting

The SSID is the wireless network name. This name is usually broadcast out to let wireless clients know that it exists. Nontechnical users rely on SSID broadcasting to locate and connect to networks. The SSID has absolutely nothing to do with security.

Early in the wireless revolution, standard security practices held that to secure a wireless network, you should keep the SSID from broadcasting; this was a practice called *SSID hiding* or *cloaking*. This practice prevented casual wireless snooping and was meant to keep unauthorized people from connecting to a wireless network. The theory was that if they couldn't see the network name, they couldn't connect to it.

These days, most wireless network clients can pick up all the nearby wireless networks, even if they have cloaked SSIDs, as you can see in the Wi-Fi analyzer scan in Figure 7-13, above. And you can easily install software on a wireless client that can tell you what the wireless SSID is, simply because wireless clients can also broadcast SSID information out. Even if people can't see the network name, they will see that an unknown wireless network does exist. Then a determined hacker can connect to it.

In addition to cloaking SSIDs, some security administrators also recommend renaming the SSIDs from the default wireless access point name that is usually broadcast when you first install an access point. This may be a good idea to help users connect to the correct network, but from a security perspective it isn't effective and may actually confuse users, causing them not to be able to connect to a wireless network.

 EXAM TIP An SSID has *nothing* to do with security. It's just the network name for a Wi-Fi network.

MAC Filtering

Remember that the MAC address is burned into every single network card manufactured, including wireless network cards, and these addresses are used the same way. The MAC address is a 12-digit hexadecimal number that identifies the manufacturer of the card and the individual card itself. Because it can identify the individual network card, and by extension the client, some administrators filter wireless network access by the MAC address of the client. Most wireless access points have the ability to do MAC filtering, as you'll recall from Chapter 6, either allowing or denying a particular MAC address (and the host that has the MAC address) on the network.

MAC filtering is frequently used as a security measure, since it can deny access to wireless network cards that are listed in a table on the access point. However, you should know that it's quite simple to spoof a MAC address, so, like SSID cloaking, this isn't an effective security measure and should not be used by itself to protect a wireless network.

The other part about MAC filtering is that if you use it as a security measure (in conjunction with other more secure measures, hopefully), you should configure MAC filtering to *allow* certain MAC addresses only, rather than attempt to *deny* certain MAC addresses. This is simply because you can deny only what you know about; of course, it's difficult to deny a MAC address that you don't know exists. So MAC address filtering should be used on a default deny basis (deny all), with only a few addresses as exceptions. Figure 7-17 shows my home WAP's MAC filtering settings.

Power Level Controls

You may be tempted to think that boosting the power on your wireless access point gives you better performance and enables your clients to connect to your network with a stronger signal. You'd be right about that, except for a couple of things. The first thing is that raising the power levels on your WAP beyond a specified level may be illegal in certain areas. Most WAPs have preset power levels, usually a balance between what's legally acceptable in its intended region and performance requirements. It isn't too difficult to download nonstandard firmware or software that allows you to change those power levels, however, sometimes beyond the legal limit allowed in your area. The second thing is that the higher power levels on your WAPs can adversely affect the security on your network. This is because the more powerful the signal, the farther out that signal will transmit. So, in addition to all of your authorized clients being able to see the wireless network, get a really good signal, and connect to it, unauthorized people (read: hackers or people looking for free Internet connectivity) will also be able to do the same thing.

In addition to limiting omnidirectional-antenna WAP placement to centralized areas within your facility, you should reduce antenna power levels on those WAPs to the lowest

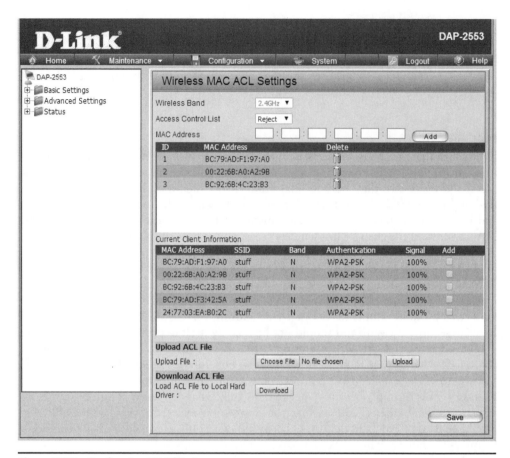

Figure 7-17 Configuring MAC filtering

acceptable point at which users can still receive a strong signal from the network. This prevents the signal from leaving your facility as much as possible. You may even have to lower the power levels and simply provide more access points throughout the facility to keep the signals confined to the immediate area as a sort of trade-off. It's probably not realistic to think that you're going to be able to limit stray signals fully, but limiting them to as short a distance as possible outside your facility can help your security posture, since any would-be hacker may have to get unacceptably close to your building to hack into or connect to your network.

Captive Portals

Many organizations set up Wi-Fi networks so clients default to a captive portal when logging in. A *captive portal* is a Web page that prompts clients to enter proper credentials to gain further access to the network (Figure 7-18). This enables the organization to control

Figure 7-18 Mike's captive portal

or limit access to clients accessing from an acceptable location and with proper authentication. You'll see captive portals used in many hotels, for example, as a way to provide paying guests access to the Internet via Wi-Fi and stopping freeloaders from getting in and leaching bandwidth.

Captive portals provide a secure method for authenticating a wireless client in a couple of ways. First, it may be impractical to share a pre-shared key or device certificate with everyone who is authorized to use the wireless network (think airport customers or hotel guests, for example), but the wireless network may still require some sort of authentication. A captive portal setup allows a wireless client to connect to the wireless network and reach only a single Web site, where the users must authenticate to the wireless network before they can use it any further.

A business may provide wireless access for its external partners or customers rather than allowing them to use its interior corporate wireless network. The captive portal would help serve such a function in this case. It enables authentication and can assist in accounting for wireless network access that has been paid for by a customer. For authorized employees connecting to a corporate network, a captive portal can also serve as a type of network access control (see Chapter 6 for more details on NAC), since an otherwise authorized wireless device may have to use certain protocols or have certain requirements present to connect to the network (patches, antivirus signatures, and so on).

Security Posture Assessment

Part of a network professional's job is to use tools to assess the security posture of a network. With wireless networks, that means to run assessment tools to probe the network, looking for any errors in implementation or any weaknesses.

The cool part for you is that you already know the assessment tools—you used them to attack wireless networks in Module 7-2! Use Aircrack-ng, Wireshark, and any number of Wi-Fi analyzers and wireless scanners/crackers to probe wireless networks.

Organizations often hire third parties to assess a network security posture. Many companies have created in-house groups dedicated to performing and maintaining posture assessments.

Questions

1. Erin is tasked to design a wireless network for the new wing of her office, which consists of two large rooms with cubicles. Her budget allows for two high-end WAPs that support WEP, WPA, WPA2, or WPA3 or four medium-end WAPs that support WEP, WPA, or WPA2. In such a scenario, which option will provide the best security?

   A. Install the two high-end WAPs enabled for WPA2 to provide the best coverage and security.

   B. Install the two high-end WAPs enabled for WPA3 to provide the best coverage and security.

   C. Install the four medium-end WAPs enabled for WPA to provide the best coverage and security.

   D. Install the four medium-end WAPs enabled for WPA2 to provide the best coverage and security.

2. Ellen gets a call from a local café she provides tech support to, complaining that some users on older devices can't connect to the newly upgraded WAP (but they could connect to the previous WAP). What could be the problem?

   A. She set up the WAP to use WPA and TKIP.

   B. She set up the WAP to use WPA2 and only AES.

   C. She set up the WAP to use mixed mode.

   D. She set up the WAP in open mode.

3. Which Cisco authentication protocol provides the best wireless security?

   A. 802.1X

   B. EAP-TLS

   C. EAP-FAST

   D. LEAP

4. Jane runs a coffee shop that shares walls with two other businesses. She wants to install a Wi-Fi network for her clients, but wants to make sure she's neither sharing the network with the other businesses nor interfering with their wireless

networks. She has the option of installing one or more 802.11ac WAPs with omnidirectional antennas. What's her best option in this scenario?

   A. Jane should install one WAP in the center of her establishment.

   B. Jane should install one WAP in the center of her establishment and then reduce the power level.

   C. Jane should install one WAP in the center of her establishment and then increase the power level.

   D. Jane should install two WAPs, one on either wall, and point the antennas to the center of her establishment.

5. Andre wants to hack a Wi-Fi network (for learning purposes!). Which type of tool would enable him to find the wireless signals to start the attack?

   A. Wireless survey

   B. Packet capture

   C. WEP cracking

   D. WPA cracking

6. Which of the following can happen if an attacker sets the power levels on a rogue access point to overpower the wireless transmissions of a legitimate access point?

   A. Jamming

   B. Beaconing

   C. Deauthentication

   D. Spoofing

7. Jaime was working on a term paper at the local café and noticed that her connection to the WAP kept dropping. Her system would reconnect rapidly, but the behavior was odd. Which of the following kind of attack would most likely create this scenario?

   A. Bluejacking

   B. Deauthorization attack

   C. Jamming

   D. Replay attack

8. Which of the following technologies requires that two devices be within four inches of each other in order to communicate?

   A. 802.11i

   B. WPA

   C. Bluetooth

   D. NFC

9. Ezra has been tasked to provide for a hotel a Wi-Fi solution that enables hotel staff to control who can access the wireless resources. The solution should include both location and login authentication. What might accomplish those goals?

   A. Captive portal

   B. Disable SSID broadcast

   C. MAC filtering block list

   D. MAC filtering allow list

10. Which of the following options will provide a graphical representation of the wireless signals—including their strength—in a site survey?

    A. Bluesnarfing

    B. Captive portal

    C. Heat map

    D. RFID map

Answers

1. **B.** WPA3 completely trumps earlier Wi-Fi encryption standards in terms of security.

2. **B.** Most likely, Ellen set up the WAP to allow only traffic encrypted with WPA2 and only AES. Although it will reduce security, changing the WAP to mixed mode would provide support for older Wi-Fi clients.

3. **C.** Of the two Cisco authentication protocols listed here, EAP-FAST offers way better security (through TLS) than LEAP (WEP and RC4).

4. **B.** It'll require some experimentation, but reducing the power level for a centered WAP should make the signal available only for her customers. Such a setup reduces signal bleed into other spaces.

5. **A.** Starting with a wireless survey or stumbler tool would enable Andre to find the signals he wants to capture. He could follow up with a packet capture tool, like Airodump-ng, and then hammer the packets for content with an attack tool.

6. **A.** Jamming, intentional interference on a wireless network to cause denial of service, can occur if an attacker sets the power levels on a rogue access point to overpower the wireless transmissions of a legitimate access point.

7. **B.** Although you could make an argument for a jamming type of attack, this is most likely a deauthorization attack, kicking Jaime's system off the WAP in hopes that it would connect to an evil twin WAP.

8. **D.** Near-field communication (NFC) requires that two devices be within four inches of each other in order to communicate.

9. **A.** Creating a captive portal would provide the desired solution, especially the login authentication.

10. **C.** A heat map provides a graphical representation of the wireless networks—and their relative signal strengths—in an area.

Securing Public Servers

With Cloud Computing, it is no longer a question of If,
but rather When and How.

—Ludmila Morozova-Bussva

The world accesses public servers—resources on the Internet—to live and prosper in the global economy. IT security professionals must secure public servers or the world will simply *fail*. (Dramatic enough intro to this chapter? It's good stuff, so read on!)

This chapter explores how security professionals deal with public servers, emphasizing cloud computing, in four modules:

- Attacking and Defending Public Servers
- Virtualization Security
- Cloud Deployment
- Securing the Cloud

Module 8-1: Attacking and Defending Public Servers

This module covers the following CompTIA Security+ objectives:

- **1.4 Given a scenario, analyze potential indicators associated with network attacks**
- **2.2 Summarize virtualization and cloud computing concepts**
- **3.3 Given a scenario, implement secure network designs**

Anytime you connect a server to the Internet, you expose that server to all the evils and troubles lurking out there. The fact that anyone can at least attempt to connect to your server gives bad actors with access to a DNS name or IP address a lovely attack surface, thus giving them the opportunity to try to do something nefarious to your server.

This module first describes a distributed denial-of-service attack and then discusses some of the tools used to secure public-facing servers and mitigate the effect of these attacks.

Distributed Denial-of-Service

If a bad actor wants to disrupt your organization's normal operations, one of the most disruptive actions they can attempt is to make one of your Internet-connected servers stop working so that server can no longer provide essential resources. There are plenty of ways to attempt this, but for the most part security professionals have learned from experience how to stop the vast majority of attacks, with one exception.

A *distributed denial-of-service (DDoS)* attack is when many systems send requests to a server with the goal of swamping the server with clients so that it responds too slowly for legitimate users or, in some cases, causes the server to reboot/lockup/fail in some way (Figure 8-1). The attack can stop a specific *application* (such as a Web server) or drop an entire *network* if successful. DDoS attacks on *operational technology (OT)* sites such as power plants that might be running on older systems can prove particularly disruptive and devastating.

 NOTE   A *denial-of-service (DoS) attack* involves one system sending lots of requests to a single server. A DDoS attack is when hundreds, if not thousands, of systems send requests to a single server.

So how do we get lots of systems to work together to attack a specific server? Why, malware of course! A bad actor might send hundreds of thousands of e-mail messages to infect as many systems as possible. The zombie computers may run for months with malware that doesn't affect the systems . . . until it's time to attack!

The problem with this simple DDoS attack is the fact that most servers are designed to handle a huge number of requests per second. To make the server work harder, attackers

Figure 8-1
The basic DDoS

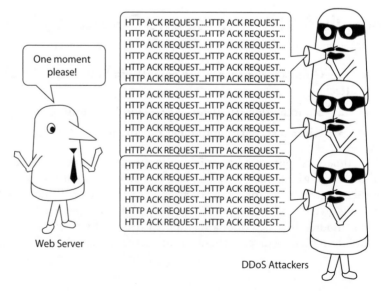

Web Server

DDoS Attackers

not only send lots of requests, they do things to the requests so the server has to spend relatively large amounts of time per request to deal with them. Here are a few ways an attack can do this:

- Send lots of UDP packets to random port numbers on the server, making it respond to them with errors
- Use lots of bogus IP addresses, forcing the server to wait for a response from a client that doesn't exist
- Send intentionally mangled requests, forcing the server to try to read them and hopefully timeout (Figure 8-2)
- Send lots of requests without ever responding
- Send lots of requests but respond just slow enough that the server keeps the connection
- Take advantage of some weakness in the server software to make bad things happen

Keep in mind that each of these ways is just a strategy. There are many methods that are useful in DDoS attacks.

DDoS attacks plague networks today. As quickly as certain forms of attacks are discovered and stopped, bad actors only need to make subtle changes as they discover new weaknesses and then repeat the same types of attacks. Protecting public-facing servers from DDoS starts with making server configuration secure.

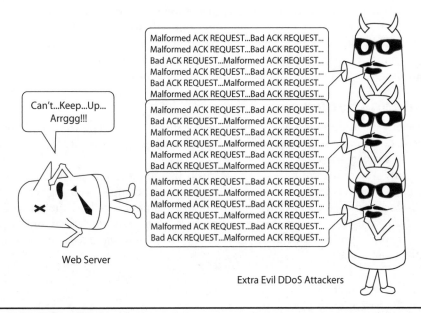

Figure 8-2 Making DDoS harder

Route Security

Routers enable networks to interconnect. Network engineers focus on *secure network design* principles with routers to ensure the information that enables that interconnectivity stays safe and uncorrupted. The details of the routing tables matter.

A lot of this you'll remember from your CompTIA Network+ (or equivalent) studies, that every routing protocol—RIPv2, BGP, EIGRP, OSPF—supports route authentication. Neighbor authentication, for example, makes certain that routers know which neighbor to trust and accept only reliable routing information. Protections such as this prevent bad routes from getting into routing tables and stop naughty information, like malformed packets, from messing up routing.

Implementation of route security measures goes well outside the scope of CompTIA Security+. But you need to know that ensuring route security is an essential part of network design.

Quality of Service

The *quality of service (QoS)* router feature enables you to control the bandwidth of different protocols coming through a router. With QoS you can assign a minimum or a maximum bandwidth set either as a percentage of the router's total bandwidth or as a set speed (MB/sec, for example).

The QoS feature makes sure that certain protocols never max out the router and ensure that critical protocols always have adequate bandwidth. Figure 8-3 shows a typical implementation of QoS that sets the maximum any application on the network can grab, thus making sure other applications have bandwidth too.

QoS is also a relatively handy way to provide some security to your router. Let's say that you want to enable SFTP on your router but only to occasionally update a single small file. This will never take much bandwidth, correct? So why not give SFTP only a tiny amount of bandwidth just in case a bad actor wants to try to use it to do a lot of downloading? It won't stop them, but it will slow them down dramatically.

Monitoring Services

It's generally a bad thing if a public-facing server stops serving. The server's administrators need to know as soon as possible if any issue arises that prevents the server from serving on a timely basis.

The only way to determine a server's status is by monitoring the server. Monitoring might be as simple as trying to log onto the server or as complex as using remote tools to query logs and events and comparing them to baselines to see how the server is performing. *File integrity monitors*, for example, check for baseline deviations and can alert administrators of problems. Basically, any *file integrity monitoring (FIM)* needs to answer these three questions:

- Is the system up?
- Is the system too busy?
- Are strange things happening?

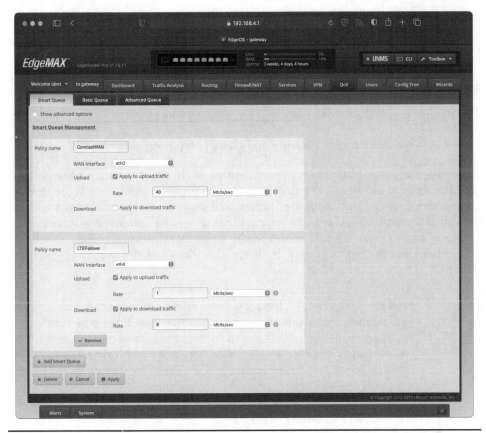

Figure 8-3   Smart Queue Management QoS on a Ubiqiti EdgeMAX router

System monitoring is a thankless job but a necessary one. Any competent administrator should have little difficulty setting up a monitoring system, but start adding more servers (and more servers requiring 24/7 monitoring), and the workload becomes unrealistic for all but the largest of organizations.

Luckily, moving your servers to the cloud gives administrators access to organizations who will take over the monitoring of your servers for a (relatively) small monthly cost. You give these monitoring services access to your server, usually by giving them an account on the server or by installing a software "agent" on your servers, and they'll happily take over all the mundane monitoring for you.

 NOTE   Monitoring services are most common on the cloud, but they're perfectly capable of monitoring on-premises servers as well.

Companies that provide security monitoring services are one example of *managed security service providers (MSSPs)*, a subset of *managed service providers (MSPs)*. An MSP is an organization that provides some form of IT service for a fee. MSPs provide backup, infrastructure, and storage services. If you have a need for any type of IT service, there's an MSP out there for you! An MSSP is nothing more than an MSP that concentrates on IT security, such as a monitoring service.

Module 8-2: Virtualization Security

This module covers the following CompTIA Security+ objective:

- **2.2   Summarize virtualization and cloud computing concepts**

Virtualization dominates today's computing world. If you're accessing a Web app on the Internet, you are almost certainly accessing a virtual machine. If you use iCloud, Dropbox, or Google Drive, your files, photos, and songs are stored on virtual machines. Even within most LANs, the Windows and Linux servers are commonly virtualized.

This module covers virtualization and the many security issues involved with virtualization. Security features span both virtualization and the cloud, as you'll see (Figure 8-4).

EXAM TIP   The CompTIA Security+ exam might ask you to compare various virtualization and cloud services, noting the location of these services. Pay attention in this module and the next to the differences between *on-premises vs. off-premises* (also called *hosted* or *cloud*), primarily about who's responsible for maintenance and service. (On-premises means you have to do the work; off-premises means you don't. Hosted services have techs who don't work directly for you; cloud abstracts the whole thing away and you just don't worry about it.)

You probably have an idea of what virtualization involves. You may have learned about only part of it, however, or perhaps you have been peripherally involved in setting up a virtual environment. Maybe you've put together a test lab on a single PC and run a few virtual machines on it, or perhaps you've designed and architected an entire virtualized environment for a large organization. In any case, you'll need to be familiar with several important concepts for the exam, so we're going to cover them here. These concepts include virtualization architecture, containers, virtualization risks, and virtualization for security.

Figure 8-4
Cloud and
virtualization are
closely related

Virtualization Architecture

In the basic sense, *virtualization* means to run an entire instance of an operating system on a host physical machine. The *virtual machine (VM)*, or *guest*, exists as a file in an application. Applications known as *hypervisors* create and use these files to initiate a VM. When the VM is turned on, the hypervisor acts as a mediator between the host operating system and the guest operating system, providing access to both physical and logical resources. These resources could include sound cards, network connections, hard drives, USB drives, and any other peripherals that a physical machine could use.

 EXAM TIP Oddly, CompTIA dropped hypervisor from the Security+ objectives when going from SY0-501 to SY0-601. We assure you that any discussion of virtual machines in the real world includes hypervisors. Don't be surprised to see the term in questions on your exam.

As far as the virtual machine is concerned, it doesn't "know" that it is not a physical machine; it functions as if it were a completely solid physical device. That means that it behaves as a physical device and can run applications, service user requests, make network connections, and so on. You can use VMs as file servers, user workstations, DNS servers, Web servers, and almost anything else that a physical machine can do. Unfortunately, this also means VMs have the same weaknesses as physical devices, and they must be secured and hardened against attack.

You can run almost any operating system as a VM—Windows, Linux, UNIX, BSD, and (to a lesser extent) macOS. Even the Android operating systems used in mobile devices can be run as a VM. The host machine, on the other hand, can also run various operating systems, including Windows, Linux, or macOS. The real requirement is that a compatible application must create and run VMs on a particular host operating system. That brings us to the discussion of hypervisors.

There are two types of hypervisors: Type 1 and Type 2 (Figure 8-5). A *Type 1 hypervisor* is a limited-function, stripped-down operating system in its own right. It runs the host machine and serves to provide the single functionality of managing the VMs installed on it. These types of hypervisors are usually called *bare-metal* (or sometimes *native*) hypervisors, because they provide a very limited functionality and only boot up the physical machine and handle resource access from the VMs. Several popular Type 1 hypervisors are available; some of them are even free to use. Microsoft has a Windows-based hypervisor (Hyper-V); the Linux community has a lot, such as Kernel-based Virtual Machine (KVM). Commercial hypervisors are also available, such as those developed by VMware.

 NOTE You'll see Roman numerals used by some sources for the hypervisor types, so Type I and Type II.

For the most part, Type 1 hypervisors are usually installed and then run in "headless" mode, meaning that they don't require a user to sit down at a keyboard console or monitor. They are usually managed remotely through a Web browser on a workstation

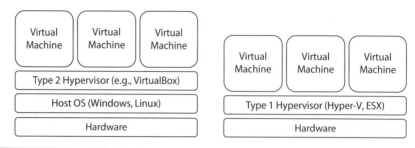

Figure 8-5 Type 1 and Type 2 hypervisors

after their network connectivity has been set up. Figure 8-6 shows an example of how VMware's ESXi server, a popular bare-metal hypervisor, is accessed and managed remotely via a browser (Apple Safari, in this case). Rarely, an administrator might have to sit at a console at the host server to perform configuration tasks that can't be done remotely.

A *Type 2 hypervisor* is an application that runs on top of a host operating system. You may have used a hypervisor product such as VMware Workstation, Oracle VirtualBox, or Parallels for macOS. These are Type 2 hypervisors that can be used to create and manage

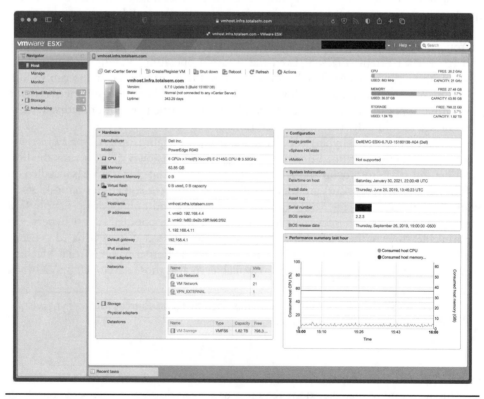

Figure 8-6 Accessing an ESXi server through the Safari Web browser

a limited number of virtual machines. Usually these types of hypervisors are used in small environments to create and test different aspects of virtualization. For larger production environments used in businesses, Type 1 hypervisors are normally used and are typically installed on very powerful, robust physical hardware. Figure 8-7 shows the user interface of VirtualBox, a popular free hypervisor application produced by Oracle.

Virtual machines can also have unique network architectures. They can use multiple network configuration options, depending upon the type of host system they are installed on. You can configure a network connection that is directly connected to the outside network through the host machine's network interface card, and the VM receives its IP addressing information from the outside network. This is called *bridging*. A VM could also receive its IP addressing information directly from the hypervisor installed on the host. In this regard, the hypervisor acts as a Dynamic Host Configuration Protocol (DHCP) server and provides private IP addressing (through network address translation, or NAT) to the *virtual host*—the VMs within the host machine. The host would then act as the default network gateway for any VMs installed on it.

You can set up a virtualized network within the host so that only virtual hosts can communicate with it and each other. In other words, they can't contact the outside world through the virtual network unless the host is configured to allow it. You can

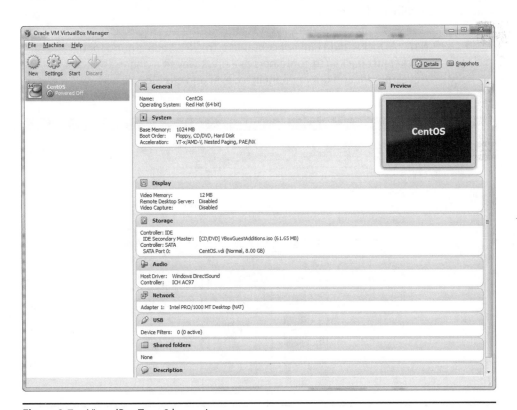

Figure 8-7 VirtualBox Type 2 hypervisor

configure the network portion of the virtual environment in several different ways, based upon how you want VMs to communicate with the outside network, the host, and each other.

Containers

VMs are great. VMs enable you to use the wildly powerful hardware of modern computers to create full operating system environments that you enable or disable at will. The OSes run applications. They network. They are, for all intents and purposes, unique computing machines. A VM requires an operating system, a license for that OS, configuration, security, and so on. But what if your network needs are simpler?

Containers offer a related experience to a VM, except that they include only the essentials of a network application—what you might think of as a server, plus programming that enables that application to run on any OS and network with other systems. Putting applications into containers—called *application cells* in some systems—enables software developers and distributors to spin up any number of copies of their functioning applications for testing purposes and more. When done right, containers enable application spin-up to happen almost instantly and make it much easier and simpler for network admins to manage servers. *Docker* provides the most common platform, or management system, for containers (Figure 8-8).

 NOTE Docker didn't invent containers; they've been around for decades. Docker just packaged containers as a great way to manage application development and deployment in a clever and easy-to-use way.

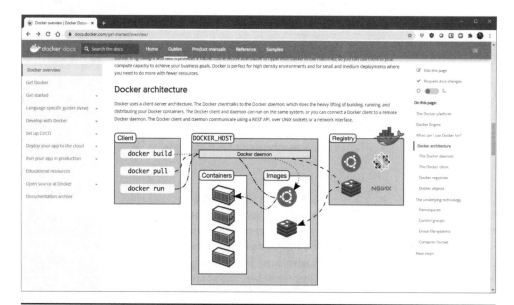

Figure 8-8 Docker architecture

Virtualization Risks

Of course, even beneficial technologies like virtualization have inherent risks. Virtualization is the solution to many problems, such as scalability, hardware production, and even security in some respects, but it also has risks. For example, with virtualization, single points of failure for host machines are risks, because if the host machine becomes unavailable, loses connectivity, or encounters a serious hardware error, all the virtual machines that reside on it are also lost. In addition, because multiple VMs may be running on a host, and some may have several services running on them, this adds to the attack surface of the host. All the services that the VMs run communicate with the outside world and the network, so they all represent different attack vectors as well. These represent a threat not only to each VM but also overall to the host.

Yet another risk involves redundancy and availability. Although virtualization helps in ensuring redundancy and availability, failure on the part of administrators to take advantage of these features could result in the loss of critical data if a VM fails and it has not been backed up or otherwise preserved. Security could also be considered at risk with VMs because complacent administrators often mistakenly think that securing the host machine is enough, and sometimes they forget to secure the VMs as well. So don't be surprised when you encounter a fairly secure host machine that has VMs running on it that have blank passwords or default security configurations. Remember that almost any risk that a physical machine can incur can also be incurred on a VM. You should take the same security measures on VMs that you take on a physical machine.

VM Sprawl

Once you have a hypervisor up and running, authorized users can easily whip up new VMs anytime they wish; that creates a problem called VM sprawl. *VM sprawl* is the out-of-control creation of VMs outside your security control. Your marketing department spins up a new Web server for a job fair; the engineering department makes a VM to test some new software they're thinking about buying; the IT department adds extra servers to run, as they say, stuff.

VM sprawl is a huge problem without a simple answer other than good monitoring. Network administrators need to implement policies or practices for *VM sprawl avoidance*. Every hypervisor has authentication tools to limit who can make VMs. Use those tools. Make clear policies that prohibit users from building their own hypervisors or, even worse, buying their own cloud VMs! Other than that, your job is to maintain good inventory of all existing VMs and to perform ongoing monitoring to look for new VMs that shouldn't be there.

VM Escape

VM escape takes place when a user inside a VM finds a way to break out (escape) the VM and somehow get into the underlying hypervisor/host operating system. Network security people need to know the problem and implement, as much as possible, *VM escape protection*.

On the good side, VM escape exploits terrify the IT world and, once detected, are very quickly patched. On the downside, there is no anti-VM escape tool. Hopefully, you'll have intrusion detection or intrusion prevention tools to mitigate the attack, like any other attack. As mentioned earlier, VMs need all the same security tools used on physical systems.

Hardening Virtual Machines

Locking down and securing virtual machines is not much different from doing the same to physical hosts. All the security considerations for physical hosts also apply to VMs. They require frequent patching and updating; they require locking down configuration settings; they need secure account settings; and when setting up users, you should follow the principle of least privilege. One nice thing about a VM is that once you have hardened the configuration as needed, you can always use it as a baseline and replicate it multiple times, so that each VM you create starts out with that hardened baseline and requires only recent patches or configuration changes. This makes it much easier to deploy VMs on a large-scale basis.

VMs require network connectivity to ensure that patches get updated in a timely manner. You also need to make sure that you install anti-malware on the VMs, since, like all networked hosts, they are susceptible to malware from Web sites, malicious files, and so forth. They should all also have host-based firewalls or multipurpose packages that take care of firewall, anti-malware, and intrusion detection software.

In addition to the normal things that you would do to secure physical hosts, VMs lend themselves to some other security measures. When not active, VMs are simply files located in storage, and as such they can be protected through permissions, encryption, and separation, the same as you would protect any other types of sensitive data files. They can also be copied and stored securely on secure media. Also like physical machines, VMs should be backed up periodically to ensure availability, as discussed next.

Snapshots and Backups

Like physical machines, virtual machines also need to be backed up from time to time. VMs have some advantages, however, in that they are native files located on a file system of some sort, so you can treat them like files for backup purposes. You could perform file backups to network-based or offline storage, and you could also encrypt these files when they're backed up. You can also restore these files at will if a VM fails or becomes inaccessible. And you can use them to create additional duplicate VMs for redundancy purposes.

You can also perform snapshots on VMs. A *snapshot* is a point-in-time backup of the current system state of the VM. This means the VM would back up and preserve any applications in use, user data, or other configuration details specific to that system's state at that moment. You could take a snapshot of a VM before installing a new application or a critical patch, for example, and save the snapshot so that if the patch or software caused a functionality or security issue, the snapshot could be restored, enabling you to revert to the state the VM was in before the installation. You can use incremental sets of snapshots or combine them with traditional backup methods to maintain highly focused, comprehensive system state backups for availability.

Using Virtualization for Security

Virtual environments can provide stable, segregated environments in which to test applications, software, and even malicious code. Virtualization can also contribute to system and data availability by maintaining multiple redundant copies of identical virtual machines. In the next few sections, we'll go into a bit more detail on how virtualization contributes to the overall security posture in the organization.

Patch Compatibility

You already know that you should test patches before applying them to production environments. This is because sometimes patches have unforeseen negative effects on production hosts, which can quickly take down critical operations. One thing that a virtual environment can give you is a complete test environment that mirrors the production environment. You can copy a physical machine and create an identically configured VM out of it. You can use this to your advantage by creating an almost exact replica of your physical environment in the virtual world, and test your patches, configuration changes, and updates in this test environment before you apply them to the physical machine. This helps avoid unintentional issues when you apply patches to production machines. It also provides you an opportunity to see where issues may exist and determine ways to correct them before the patch goes into production.

Host Availability and Elasticity

Virtual environments offer organizations real flexibility in the use of their infrastructure for both availability and elasticity. Virtualization supports *availability* in that you can almost instantly duplicate production hosts (whether physical or virtual) in a virtual environment, adding redundant capabilities for availability purposes or assets for use when existing hosts aren't enough. You can copy physical machines and convert them to virtual machines and, because VMs are merely files, you can copy and reinstantiate them as new additional VMs (with a few basic configuration changes, of course).

Virtualization provides *elasticity*, meaning you can expand, duplicate, reconfigure, repurpose, and reuse resources in the environment (in this case, virtual hosts) on the fly, as the need for them arises or shrinks. This provides an organization flexibility in its use of resources, saving physical machines and reallocating, activating, and deactivating hosts as needed in dynamic-use situations. Virtual machines can be provisioned, configured, and stored in advance for just such instances.

Virtualization applies to networking components as well, enabling rapid scalability and adaptability of networks of VMs. *Software-defined networking (SDN)* enables centralization of portions of the routing and switching (such as creating and maintaining routing tables), which can then be rapidly pushed to routers and switches that only handle the packets and frames. Current SDN boxes employ security features that can rapidly respond automatically to attacks such as DDoS attacks.

Security Control Testing

Virtualization enables security professionals to test various security controls on virtual hosts, either before implementing them in production or as changes to the production environment occur. You can configure different controls to test effectiveness and functionality, to ensure that the appropriate control is implemented correctly for the environment. This can help confirm whether a new security patch will break an application; whether a configuration change is effective in reducing a vulnerability; whether a change to an operating system's function or configuration breaks its security baseline; and whether a target host is configured as securely as you need it to be for vulnerability and penetration-testing purposes.

Sandboxing

Sandboxing provides an enclosed environment in which to run potentially dangerous applications, or even malware, to determine the effect they would have on the environment. Often, security professionals need to see the effects of an application or software on a host to determine how it interacts with the system and the network. This can help them identify potential issues with untrusted software, such as executables and scripts. Sandboxing allows you to test potentially harmful software in a controlled, isolated environment, without the possibility of affecting other hosts or allowing unwanted communication to the network. Virtualization provides sandboxing capabilities by giving you the option of running an isolated virtual host for that purpose.

Module 8-3: Cloud Deployment

This module covers the following CompTIA Security+ objectives:

- **2.2 Summarize virtualization and cloud computing concepts**
- **2.4 Summarize authentication and authorization design concepts**
- **3.6 Given a scenario, apply cybersecurity solutions to the cloud**

It didn't take very long after the introduction of virtualization for some clever people to realize something simple yet amazing. They could build a big server farm in a central location, fill it with servers, load a VM hypervisor on each of those servers, and add a (relatively) easy-to-use, Web-based interface so that thousands of paying customers could create and manage their own VMs. That's the core of what cloud computing is all about.

Cloud computing simply means to move computers, or at least some aspect of those local computers, to a location only identified with an IP address or a DNS name. Think of cloud computing just as you would any other service you pay for—such as water, electricity, cable, phone, Internet, and so on—except that now you're paying for computing as a service. Those computing services run the full gamut, from processing power, storage, applications, and more.

 NOTE Cloud computing isn't just for the public Internet. You'll see private clouds as well later in this module.

Cloud computing got its name from the many network architectural diagrams, such as the one shown in Figure 8-9, where the Internet is portrayed as a cartoonish cloud figure, meaning it's abstracted from the rest of your network beyond your perimeter and Internet service delivery point.

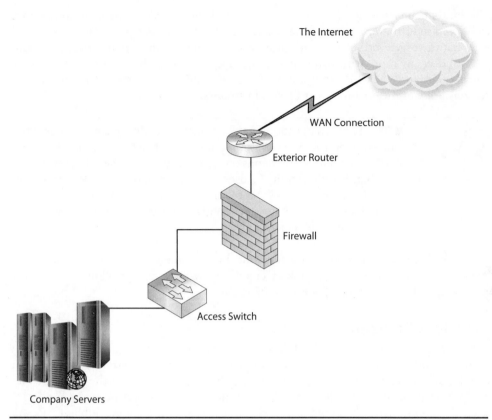

Figure 8-9   The cloud

Cloud computing offers many advantages, because it removes all the responsibility and overhead for maintaining data storage and processing in your computer, or even on your premises, and hands it over to a cloud service provider. A *cloud service provider (CSP)* essentially is a third party that owns a data center full of virtual servers, with multiple fast connections to the Internet. The CSP installs different types of operating systems and applications on its servers so that it can provide different services to customers via the Internet.

Interestingly, with the shift of responsibility over mundane aspects of computing, like hardware maintenance, operating system updates, application patches, and updates from on-premises administrators to the CSP, the overall responsibility for authentication and authorization remains in the hands of local administrators. In a typical small office, for example, the local admin runs a Microsoft Active Directory domain and handles user accounts, groups, permissions, and so forth. Scaling up to a medium or larger organization, teams will handle the various aspects of Active Directory, but it's essentially the same.

Moving to the cloud with software as a service (SaaS) offerings such as Microsoft 365 just shifts the security structure from local Active Directory to Azure Active Directory.

The local or enterprise administrators continue to handle user accounts, groups, permissions, and so forth, but they're Azure Active Directory accounts, groups, etc.

What the organization's administrators gain by going to the cloud is that they don't have to deal any more with maintenance and upgrades of hardware, operating systems, and applications. The CSP handles all that. Authentication and authorization remain the responsibility of the organization's IT administrators.

EXAM TIP   Expect a question on the CompTIA Security+ exam that compares or contrasts cloud vs. on-premises requirements. In a nutshell, cloud deployments put fewer demands on local hardware, but higher demand on network bandwidth; security focuses on cloud solutions (see Module 8-4 for specifics). On-premises networks require more local hardware firepower and a lot more local expertise from techs and administrators. And the differences are about responsibility for security.

As you'll see in the next several sections of this module, cloud service providers can offer all types of services. Let's look at cloud deployment models, cloud architecture models, and then wrap with "Cloud Growing Pains."

Let's Talk Amazon

Before we go any further, we have to take a moment to recognize the king of all cloud service providers: Amazon Web Services (Figure 8-10). Amazon certainly didn't invent cloud computing, but Amazon was the first public CSP that made the idea of cloud computing popular and widespread. Using innovative ideas and deep economies of scale, AWS dominates the cloud and stands as the one of the largest public CSPs. All hail AWS!

Over the years AWS has seen many superb competitors enter the cloud marketplace: Google Cloud, Microsoft Azure, and IBM Cloud, just to name a few. Although the organizations backing these competitors are also very large, Amazon was the first to market,

Figure 8-10
AWS is the king
of the cloud
service providers

and as the cloud leader AWS created many terms that are common lexicon for the cloud industry. The CompTIA Security+ exam leans heavily on some of these terms, so you need to know them. Let's dive right in with regions, zones, compute, storage, and network.

Regions

AWS divides the globe into over 20 regions. By default, your location is based on your physical location, but you may add regions (for extra cost) when you need wider coverage. The following are a few sample AWS regions:

- **us-west-1**   US West (Northern California)
- **us-west-2**   US West (Oregon)
- **af-south-1**   Africa (Cape Town)

Zones

AWS divides regions into multiple availability *zones* to provide even more geographic separation to get your application even closer to end users. Here are some examples of AWS zones, part of the us-west-1 region used in the United States:

- **us-west-2-lax-1a**   US West (Los Angeles)
- **us-west-2-lax-1b**   US West (Los Angeles)

Amazon Product Categories

When AWS first opened, it basically offered a single product: public-facing virtual machines that you could configure and run individually. You want two VMs? Great! Just spin up a second one! You want more? Go nuts! Over time, AWS has invented (or copied) so many more products beyond this single system that Amazon was compelled to invent an organization for these product categories, which initially consisted of three categories: Compute, Storage, and Network. As you can see in Figure 8-11, the categories have gotten a lot more granular since then.

 EXAM TIP   AWS uses the terms *Compute*, *Storage*, and *Network*. Know them, as they are objectives on the CompTIA Security+ exam.

Compute Products   Any product that has to do with computation is a *Compute* product. AWS's Amazon Elastic Compute Cloud (Amazon EC2) is the compute product you use to create VMs (AWS calls an individual VM an *instance*). Need to run containers on the cloud without spinning up your own instance? Then try Amazon Elastic Container Service (Amazon ECS).

Storage Products   AWS Compute products generally come with just enough storage to boot your OS and that's about it. If you need more data storage, you're going to want an AWS *Storage* product; the secret here is knowing what you need to store. Looking for general-purpose storage, the equivalent of adding an extra drive to the system? You want Amazon Simple Storage Service (Amazon S3). Want a cheap backup solution?

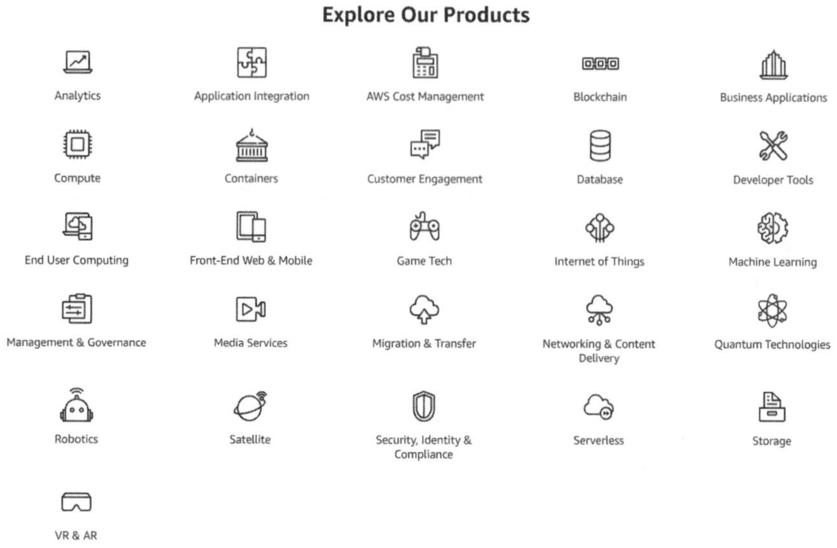

Explore Our Products

Analytics	Application Integration	AWS Cost Management	Blockchain	Business Applications
Compute	Containers	Customer Engagement	Database	Developer Tools
End User Computing	Front-End Web & Mobile	Game Tech	Internet of Things	Machine Learning
Management & Governance	Media Services	Migration & Transfer	Networking & Content Delivery	Quantum Technologies
Robotics	Satellite	Security, Identity & Compliance	Serverless	Storage
VR & AR				

Figure 8-11   AWS main product page (https://aws.amazon.com/products)

Try AWS Backup. Got a huge FTP/SFTP/FTPS site and want to move it all to AWS? Then you need the AWS Transfer Family.

Network Products   If you can move individual systems up to the cloud, then why not move a network up there as well? Any AWS product that provides or supports networking on the cloud goes into the *Network* product line. If you have multiple instances on the cloud, why not tie them together with a virtual network? That's Amazon Virtual Private Cloud (Amazon VPC). On AWS, never call your virtual network a virtual network—call it your VPC if you want other techs to understand you. Would you like your on-premises servers to talk easily to your VPC? Then grab AWS Transit Gateway.

Get Used to AWS Terms!

If you want to get into cloud security, if you want to pass the CompTIA Security+ exam, you need to get comfortable with these terms that AWS has introduced. The cloud industry may be over ten years old, but it continues to grow in terms of size and services. This is in no way a complete list of *AWSisms*, but this will get you started—and most importantly through the CompTIA Security+ exam.

NOTE   These terms are now standard across the cloud industry, but AWS invented them.

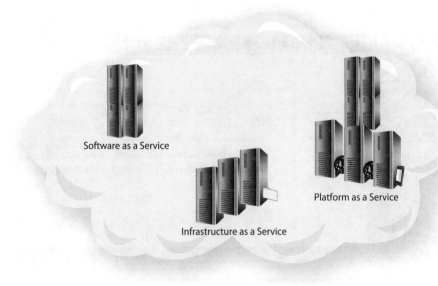

Figure 8-12   A notional cloud service architecture

Cloud Deployment Models

There's not really a one-size-fits-all *cloud deployment model*—online services that people can rent or buy. The next few sections explore several types of cloud services offered by *cloud service providers*. Some of these services are simplistic, such as data storage, for example, but others are very complex and can supplement or even replace parts of enterprise-wide infrastructures. Many of these types of services are *scalable*, meaning that anyone from home users, to small businesses, to large corporations can make use of them. We'll discuss these services from a business perspective, of course, but similar principles apply, whether a business is a small-office/home-office type of setup or a large corporate enterprise that spans several geographical locations. In Figure 8-12, you can see an example of how cloud services might be organized.

Software as a Service

With *software as a service (SaaS)*, customers run software that's stored in the cloud (almost always on a virtualized server) and used via a Web URL or, in some cases, a client program stored on a local system. SaaS is wildly popular today. Voice over IP (VoIP) services such as Skype and Google Voice provide voice/video communication. *Cloud storage* solutions such as Dropbox and Microsoft OneDrive provide terabytes of storage for files; by definition, that storage resides outside the physical network. Even traditional office applications are now available via SaaS. Microsoft offers Office as an SaaS solution via Microsoft Office 365 (Figure 8-13).

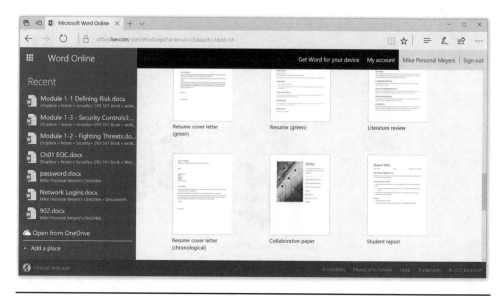

Figure 8-13 We wrote this textbook entirely with Office 365

SaaS offers several advantages to businesses. First, software licensing costs less via the cloud. The software licensing may be subscription-based, so an organization may purchase licenses based upon numbers of users or concurrent connections. Second, an organization can avoid the legal ramifications of software piracy, since an application on the cloud can't be easily copied and transferred from computer to computer or taken home by employees. In fact, the organization doesn't have to store or manage any media at all, because the software is stored and used in the cloud, with the exception of occasional small components downloaded to a user's workstation.

Security as a service (SECaaS) is a subset of SaaS that focuses only on bundling security solutions. As you might imagine, the security solutions offered run the gamut of every security solution you would implement on premises, such as security assessments, vulnerability scanning, and so on.

Infrastructure as a Service

Infrastructure as a service (IaaS) goes beyond posting simple software applications in the cloud. IaaS provides entire machines, such as Windows or Linux hosts, for example, for remote connection and use. Of course, these aren't physical machines; they are virtual machines hosted by a CSP's infrastructure. Users simply connect to them via the Remote Desktop Protocol (RDP) or another secure remote connection protocol and use them as they would any other computer. Users can run applications installed on the virtual machine, create content, process data, and perform any other typical tasks they would perform on a physical machine. An example of IaaS is Amazon EC2; Figure 8-14 shows the EC2 interface for creating a new VM (AWS calls VMs *instances*).

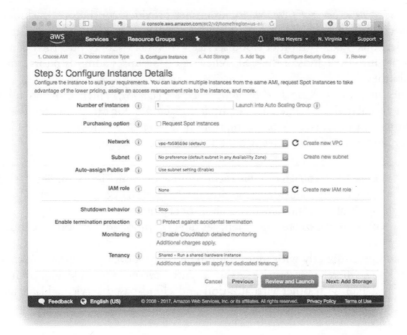

Figure 8-14   Interface for Amazon EC2

Usually, however, IaaS implementations provide servers rather than workstations; most businesses that leverage an IaaS provider do so for server VMs. The advantage of having virtual servers through an IaaS provider is that the business doesn't have to provision, manage, or maintain huge server farms or data centers—all that's done for them by the provider. The provider handles patches, updates, configuration, and so on. Additionally, licensing for servers provided through an IaaS contract is usually far more streamlined, and cheaper.

Platform as a Service

Platform as a service (PaaS) offers a business a computing platform—such as a Web application server or database server, for example—that it can use to provide services both internally and to customers on the Internet. Many online storefronts use this model to conduct business, rather than hosting on their own premises the physical servers, Web sites, databases, and applications. Again, the advantages of using this type of service are cost savings, no requirement to build and maintain the infrastructure on site, and the guarantee of around-the-clock availability—plus, the PaaS provider takes care of the patching and configuration work.

Anything as a Service

The big three—SaaS, IaaS, and PaaS—get a lot of attention, but today anyone can develop virtually (pardon the pun) any type of resource, software, or application that anyone might need. With *anything as a service (XaaS)* your choices are vast.

Monitoring as a Service (MaaS), for example, provides continuous tracking of the health of online services used by an organization, such as systems, instances, networks, and applications. Like with other cloud services, this XaaS variety puts the maintenance and security into the hands of the CSP, relieving on-premises administrators from those responsibilities.

Another interesting XaaS is *desktop as a service (DaaS)*, which provides users with their own virtual desktops. Their actual physical machines don't really matter: they can be full desktops, thin clients, tablets, or smartphones. No matter where users are located or what they have at hand, they have instant access to their desktop.

EXAM TIP   You'll recall *thin clients* from your CompTIA A+ studies, essentially a keyboard, mouse, and monitor that access an operating system, applications, and data remotely. Expect a question on the CompTIA Security+ exam that explores thin clients as direct components of cloud computing.

DaaS competes directly with more traditional Citrix-developed *virtual desktop infrastructure (VDI)*, where an enterprise sets up a central server to provide desktop interfaces for users. Just like with other virtualization and cloud-based services, DaaS takes the managing of hardware and software out of the hands of local IT staff, freeing them up for other tasks.

NOTE   The CompTIA Security+ acronym list includes *Virtual Desktop Environment (VDE)*, but that's not all that common a usage. VDE *usually* stands for *Virtual Distributed Ethernet*, a networking virtualization technology used in Linux. *Neither* use of VDE is synonymous with VDI.

Cloud Architecture Models

Although we stated that cloud environments are operated primarily by large companies with huge data centers, this isn't always the case. In fact, an increasing number of clouds are popping up that follow a few different architecture models. These include private clouds, public clouds, and a few other models we'll briefly go over. Any of these various cloud architectures may be used, depending on the organization's specific needs and its reliance on third-party providers or its requirements to keep computing resources in house.

Private Cloud

In a *private cloud*, as you might expect, one party uses the cloud environment—the infrastructure, network devices, connections, and servers. A private cloud doesn't necessarily mean that the infrastructure also resides physically within the business's own data center on its physical premises. It could certainly be that way (military organizations and very large corporations often host their own private cloud, for example), but a private cloud can also be hosted by a third-party provider as a contracted service. Regardless of where the environment is hosted, a private cloud is for the use of the business that's paying for it—it's not for public or shared use. It can still host the same types of services described earlier.

A private cloud may cost the organization a bit more if it's hosted within a data center it owns and operates, but this cost is usually absorbed by the cost of operating the data center itself. An organization can save a bit of money if a third-party provider operates the data center for the organization, however. Another advantage of a private cloud, other than exclusive use, is that the organization may be able to exert more control over data security and availability levels.

NOTE One of the challenges to private clouds is the connection between a private cloud service provider and on-premises systems. Companies like AWS provide an interface called a *transit gateway* that gives any system a simple way to connect to your cloud. In most cases the connection is via a VPN.

Public Cloud

A *public cloud* is usually operated by a third-party provider that sells or rents "pieces" of the cloud to different entities, such as small businesses or large corporations, to use as they need. These services and the "size" of the piece of cloud an organization gets may be scalable, based on the customer's needs. Customers usually don't get direct connections to the provider, as they might in a private cloud model; the connections are typically made over the customers' existing Internet connections. Several business models are used for these types of clouds, including subscription models, pay-per-use, and so on. Unlike a private cloud, the security and availability levels are pretty much standardized by the provider and offered as part of the contract; organizations purchasing those services may not have any control over those terms. Examples of public cloud service providers include offerings from Amazon Web Services (AWS), Google Cloud Storage, and the Microsoft Cloud.

Community Cloud

A *community cloud* is made up of infrastructures from several different entities, which may be CSPs, business partners, and so on. In this structure, common services are offered to all participants in the community cloud, to one degree or another. An example of a community cloud is one that is shared among universities or educational institutions. Each institution provides a piece of infrastructure, and the cloud may include third-party providers as well, to form a cloud shared by all.

Hybrid Cloud

A *hybrid cloud* is any combination of the cloud models described previously. You could have public/private hybrids, private/community hybrids, and so on. A hybrid might be used because all parties need common cloud services (common application or Web platforms, for instance, on linked or connected Web sites), while maintaining their own private or community clouds for other purposes. Hybrid clouds could be constructed in many different ways, using third-party providers, private or shared data centers, and so on, as well as different types of connections (direct, Internet-only, and so on). Figure 8-15 sums up the relationships between the different cloud types.

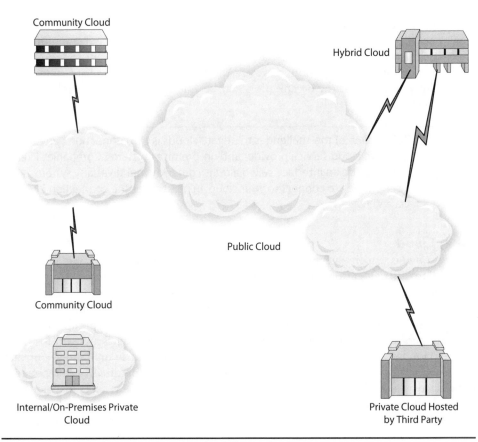

Figure 8-15   The relationships between the different cloud types

EXAM TIP   Over time, an organization can find itself in a situation where it's using services from multiple providers—IaaS here, PaaS there, XaaS everywhere. This self-evolving mess only gets more complicated with hybrid clouds that include third-party access to their services (or vice versa). *Services integration* is a type of propriety solution offered by companies to streamline, organize, and simplify (as much as possible) a wide-ranging array of services into a single source.

There's no set definition for services integration. Solutions are customized to fit an organization's specific components and vendor solutions. You might find the term *service integration and management (SIAM)* used instead of services integration as well.

Cloud Growing Pains

The explosive growth in cloud computing has led to some issues where a one-size-fits-all solution doesn't work efficiently for an organization, specifically in terms of latency and scalability. Several solutions fine-tune cloud-based networks to address these issues.

Latency

A standard cloud computing system moves the processing of data from the local network to the cloud servers. That simplifies the needs of the local network and optimizes the processing—that's the ideal. The downside of cloud-based processing is that it induces latency. Data has to flow to the cloud, get processed, and then get pushed back to devices.

A lot of devices and systems handle this latency without problems. But an increasing number of smart devices—phones, tablets, Internet of Things (IoT) devices, surveillance systems, and so forth—need low-latency processing of immediate data. Two related options—fog computing and edge computing—address the latency issue.

In essence, the buzz-sounding solutions of fog computing and edge computing push some of the processing in a cloud network back to the local network. *Fog computing* devices do a lot of local processing before syncing to the cloud so that, for example, you know quickly when someone's ringing your smart doorbell. *Edge computing* adds local processing and data storage, sometimes with dedicated processing stations. If this sounds familiar, it's because that's the way networks worked before the cloud phenomenon! It's as if providers pushed everyone to cloud solutions and then had to dial it back to address latency issues, and they could use cool new marketing terms.

Scalability

Scalability in cloud networks means giving organizations flexibility to grow on demand. Two options help address this issue efficiently, microservices and serverless architecture.

Microservices/API More sophisticated Web applications are complex beasts, requiring teams of programmers and potentially services all working together to make these applications do what they do. To that end, there's motivation to split up and delegate the work needed to make a Web app work. That's where microservices and APIs come into play.

Consider a typical Web app that includes merchant functions for purchases and inventory and a user logon function for special pages. Instead of making the Web app monolithic (one big pile o' code), we can separate the application into free-standing *microservices*—programming sections—that support the application as a whole. One microservice might handle user logins, another the inventory database, and so forth. These microservices might be written in-house, provided by third parties, or even treated like an XaaS.

Complementing microservices are *application programming interfaces (APIs)*, the interfaces that enable different programs or different parts of a program to access another's code. APIs aren't new, but in this context APIs mean the interfaces that different parties use to access Web applications.

Employing microservices (and APIs to make connections) means developers can focus on the parts of an application under demand, rather than try to make everything scale up. If the database is getting slammed and needs updating, the programmers can focus on the microservices that address the database needs and not have to worry about the unaffected parts. This increases scalability efficiently.

Serverless Architecture Classically in the cloud there is some amount of work placed on administrators to set up servers. In a typical cloud service—let's consider IaaS for this example—the cloud service requires you to configure a server and then use that server as, well, a server. Even with PaaS, you still need to configure a server and make sure it's running whatever essential service.

In a *serverless architecture*, the CSP offers services directly to end users. This usually manifests as functions or software downloaded as needed for provider services such as storage or messaging. Serverless solutions such as AWS Lambda merely require your endpoints to "point" toward a domain name for those services.

 NOTE Serverless architecture isn't truly serverless. It's just that you aren't required to set up a server. Your CSP provides services directly to your endpoints.

Module 8-4: Securing the Cloud

This module covers the following CompTIA Security+ objectives:

- **1.2 Given a scenario, analyze potential indicators to determine the type of attack**
- **1.6 Explain the security concerns associated with various types of vulnerabilities**
- **2.2 Summarize virtualization and cloud computing concepts**
- **3.6 Given a scenario, apply cybersecurity solutions to the cloud**

Replacing on-premises networks with cloud-based networks presents a security challenge. In the first place, many vulnerabilities and attacks don't really change very much between cloud and on-premises. On the other hand, cloud infrastructures bring up a number of interesting security controls and capabilities that work differently than on-premises. Let's look at some of these.

 EXAM TIP Look for questions on the CompTIA Security+ exam that compare *cloud-based vs. on-premises attacks* and *cloud-based vs. on-premises vulnerabilities*. The physical component of on-premises vulnerabilities and attacks doesn't apply to cloud-based vulnerabilities and attacks. All of the network-specific vulnerabilities and attacks to exploit those vulnerabilities apply to cloud-based and on-premises networks.

Cloud Security Controls

Cloud security controls address the unique features of cloud computing to mitigate several security issues. This section first explores zones as a cloud security control and various security controls for storage, network, and compute cloud services. We'll finish with a nod to SDN/SDV and cloud native controls.

Zones

Zones are the bread and butter of AWS cloud security controls. Zones usually come in pairs. Zones are real-time copies of each other, providing extremely *high availability across zones* as well as making *integration and auditing* easier. There's not much to add here from a security standpoint.

 NOTE Other cloud service providers use the concept of zones. Microsoft Azure has regions that subdivide into zones, for example. Regardless of the specific label used by CSPs, the idea is to provide high availability so customer downtime or lag is reduced to as near zero as possible.

Storage

Nothing does mass storage like the cloud! From databases accessed millions of times per second to long-term archival materials, cloud storage is wonderfully convenient. For example, simply placing mass storage on the cloud instantly takes care of mundane items such as backup because all of your data is stored in zones, providing automatic *replication* and *high availability*.

Cloud storage services require permissions just like any resource. File servers need permissions. Mail servers need permissions. You get the idea. Cloud service providers—let's just say AWS, as Amazon invented this term—call their permissions *resource policies*. A *policy* is an object in AWS that defines the *permissions* to an identity or resource. AWS defines two types of resource policies: identity-based policies and resource-based policies. Identity-based policies are assigned to users, groups, or roles. Resource-based policies are attached to a resource.

Given the fact that the cloud is always a remote connection, *encryption* is essential. Encryption is generally an easy thing to implement given that everything we might ever want to do application-wise has a secure protocol. The challenge with encryption in cloud solutions isn't the actual encryption *per se*; it's the storage and administration of all the passwords, keys, certificates, RSA tokens, and other secret stuff needed to keep all these encryptions working.

A *secrets management* solution takes all those secrets away from the apps that traditionally store them and locks them away in a separate database, giving administrators a one-stop-shop location to manage the secrets without affecting the application that needs them.

Network

Many small cloud customers tend to build a single-server system on the cloud, accessing the system as needed to keep it running properly. As customer needs increase, it's very common to create multiple systems and connect them into *virtual networks*, all residing on the cloud.

The most important concept about virtual networks is that they work exactly like an on-premises network. IP assignment (static or DHCP), DNS, subnetting, firewalls, and similar issues all apply to a virtual network—it's simply a matter of figuring out how your CSP offers the tools necessary to make these configurations.

AWS calls a virtual network a virtual private cloud (VPC). But what happens if you want public-facing servers on your AWS cloud? No problem. Just make separate subnets and make one of those subnets public! That's right, with AWS you make a virtual private cloud and then make part (or all) of the VPC public.

EXAM TIP Expect a question on the CompTIA Security+ exam that asks you to compare options or solutions for public and private subnets.

The actual steps of *segmentation* of a network vary among CSPs, but the process is similar. First, define network IDs. Second, connect separate network IDs using virtual routers, adding firewalls as needed.

API Inspection and Integration Odds are good that if your organization were to develop a Web application, that application would use some form of API to connect to other applications. APIs do so much of the heavy lifting today interconnecting applications. These other applications might be as simple as tools to share some database information; or they may connect two apps to enable single sign-on.

If you're going to use an API with a Web application, consider two items. First, how does the application perform API integration? In other words, how does the application connect to another application's API (or vice versa)? Second, how does the application perform API inspection to ensure that only the correct data moves between the apps?

A cloud app provider creates one or more APIs to enable access to its products. Various cloud security providers such as Microsoft Cloud App Security work with that cloud app provider to optimize interaction with the APIs, which includes API inspection for account information, audit trails, app permissions, and so on. Ensuring secure access between APIs enables functional use of Web applications.

Firewalls in the Cloud Cloud networks need all the same protections from external attackers that any on-premises network needs. Where an on-premises firewall protects physical networks, *cloud firewalls* protect cloud networks.

EXAM TIP With AWS cloud networks you can create (up to five) *security groups* with each VPC that act as a virtual firewall for the instance. They control inbound and outbound traffic and can each have different rules for handling traffic.

There are several firewall considerations in a cloud environment. First, what does your cloud network *need for segmentation*? For small operations, a Web application firewall in front of a single instance may be all you need (Figure 8-16). Maybe in a larger situation you would place an edge firewall in front of multiple servers. Larger still and you might need multiple *next-generation firewalls (NGFWs)* segmenting many subnets at multiple Open Systems Interconnection (OSI) layers.

Cloud service providers can offer firewalling at one or more OSI layers, depending on the needs of the organization. They can make Layer 3 firewalls available for specific purposes, for example, and Layer 4 for others, plus NGFW solutions for overall security. A key factor for an organization needing firewalling isn't capability, *per se*, but *cost*.

A CSP may offer many types of firewalls, but not for free! CSPs use a metered pricing system, charging by the gigabits/month. These prices are usually inexpensive relative to the overall cost of your cloud . . . until they are not. An aggressive DDoS attack, for

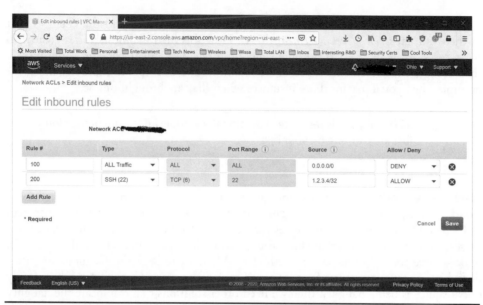

Figure 8-16   Traditional firewall configuration in AWS

example, can increase your monthly *firewall as a service (FWaaS)* costs by a factor of tens of thousands.

NOTE   All cloud service providers offer some form of "How much am I spending and why" reporting/alarms. Take advantage to avoid costly surprises!

Compute

Securing compute components means focusing on immediate, active processing. That means securing VPC endpoints, dynamic resource allocation, software-defined visibility, instance awareness, and container security (plus security groups, discussed previously).

VPC Endpoint   When CSPs offer XaaS, you need some method to enable your cloud to connect to these services. In the AWS world, your VPC needs a connection to that service. Instead of wasting potentially valuable IP addresses, virtual routers, and such, AWS creates a private IP address to the service you choose—called a *virtual private cloud (VPC) endpoint*—and your VPC just . . . connects to it.

Dynamic Resource Allocation   It's not hard for a CSP to adjust resources allocated to a customer based on need. Some examples of resources are CPU and memory bandwidth, storage capacity and speed, network connection, and number of instances of the server (there are many more). The challenge is how to do this dynamically, to adjust the resource allocation to the customer so that the utilization is as close to 100 percent as possible.

Dynamic resource allocation is agreed upon between the CSP and the client as part of their mutual *service-level agreement (SLA)*. How this SLA manifests varies greatly. In most cases, even the SLA is automatically adjusted by a client clicking some button that changes the agreement. If you agree to allow your CSP to add more instances, for example, then you'll pay for those instances when they are brought online.

NOTE Dynamic resource allocation is a wonderful feature of the cloud—just keep an eye on your bill!

Instance Awareness   It's very common for an organization to run many instances of cloud services. For example, an organization might be running hundreds of instances of Google Drive—corporate instances that are shared by users; individual instances for personal use; and instances shared by groups within the organization. Firewalls, NGFWs, SDV—these tools do not have a method to differentiate between instances, i.e., they don't have *instance awareness*. Sure, they can turn off access to Google Drive, but if only one instance is being naughty, then we need other solutions that can locate the naughty instances causing problems and shut them down without killing everything.

NOTE   Netskope (https://netskope.com)—and other companies—offers solution for protection and prevention among cloud instances that lack instance awareness.

Container Security   Containers are the way to go in the world of application development due to their convenience, tiny footprint, and ease of use, but they come with their own security issues. The best way to consider those issues is to think of any container as three distinct components. First is the underlying operating system, second is the container software, and last is the application running inside the container.

The underlying OS isn't anything special in terms of security requirements other than your awareness that the usual security applied to a host might affect the container itself. Never patch an OS without first investigating anything that might affect the security of the container software. Also monitor file permissions and user accounts that might provide unauthorized access to the container software.

Container applications like Docker and Kubernetes have their own access control lists (ACLs) to the application as well as the images they store. Careful auditing and monitoring are required, especially in environments where many hands are working on the same product. Take advantage of the container application's role-based controls as well as segmentation of the application into separate images as needed. Also make sure any container software updates do not affect your images.

Last, consider the security of your images. It's common to use signed images to verify image integrity. Never add third-party files to your image without careful inspection.

Software-Defined Visibility

Monitoring a complex network can easily become messy. IDS/IPS, firewalls, and SIEM setups aren't nearly as static in a cloud as they are in a classic on-premises network. In particular, software-defined networking (SDN) setups make it challenging to monitor cloud networks using classical tools.

Enter *software-defined visibility (SDV)*. By applying software (called APIs in this area) to every (or at least most) devices on the network—including end nodes—any part of the network is now visible to your defensive tools. Any device can detect and respond to an attack. SDV all but removes potential blind spots on your network. Most SDV solutions are proprietary and only seen on larger, more secure networks.

Cloud Native Controls vs. Third-Party Solutions

AWS provides a huge number of amazing controls built into the AWS space. These hundreds of controls, created by and offered by AWS, are known collectively as *native controls* (Figure 8-17). AWS, like all other CSPs, however, gives third parties access to AWS VPCs via APIs. This has created an entire industry of third parties that provide solutions for thousands of niche situations.

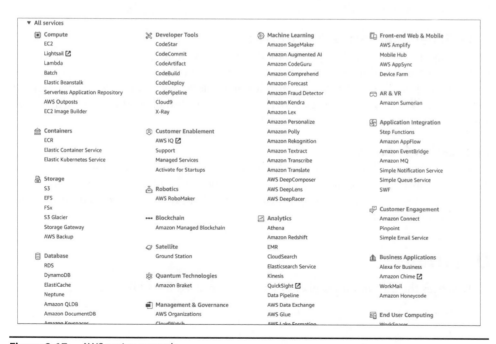

Figure 8-17   AWS native controls

Unique Cloud Security Solutions

The cloud introduced not only a whole new class of security controls but many security solutions as well. Let's look at three here:

- CASB
- SWG
- Application security

Cloud Access Security Broker

Cloud access security broker (CASB) refers to a service that manifests as a layer of software between a cloud application and an enterprise or organization, designed to provide security. Most commonly, the major cloud organizations—like Google, Amazon, Microsoft, and so on—have invested heavily in automated controls implemented through APIs. You can rely on these companies for proper security.

A *proxy-based CASB*, in contrast, relies on a third party's software in between the cloud service provider and an organization or enterprise that uses those services. Proxy-based services inject more security problems rather than reduce security risks. The proxy-based services seem to have briefly appeared but flamed out. If you get asked about CASBs on the exam, focus on the API-based models.

Next-Generation Secure Web Gateway

As quickly as cloud-based applications develop new solutions to address previously unconsidered vulnerabilities, new issues come into focus, requiring yet another class of security solutions. Arguably the newest solution is the *next-generation secure web gateway (SWG)*. An SWG stands between a Web application and all of the services that Web application uses.

Application Security

Chapter 11 covers a lot about secure Web development, but the term *application security* is so cloud-centric that it warrants a mention here. Cloud applications need a lot of security in development and during runtime. Tools that provide that form of security are under the umbrella of application security.

Questions

1. What's the minimum number of computers needed for a DDoS attack?

   A. 1

   B. 2

   C. 10

   D. 1000

2. What is a company that provides security monitoring for a fee called?

   A. IaaS

   B. MSP

   C. MttF

   D. Security broker

3. Virtual machines must have a _____ in which to run.

   A. bare metal

   B. container

   C. database

   D. hypervisor

4. Docker is a popular management system for what sort of product?

   A. Containers

   B. Security

   C. Shoes

   D. VMs

5. The accounting department built their own hypervisor and added four virtual machines without letting anyone know. This is an example of what virtualization issue?

   A. Hypervisor

   B. Unauthorized zone

   C. VM escape

   D. VM sprawl

6. John's cloud service provider enables him to set up virtual machines. He can add any operating system he wants. This is an example of which type of service?

   A. IaaS

   B. PaaS

   C. SaaS

   D. XaaS

7. Total Seminars deploys both a public cloud and a private cloud. What kind of cloud solution do they have?

   A. Community cloud

   B. Hybrid cloud

   C. Private cloud

   D. Trusted cloud

8. AWS divides the world into more than 20 _____.

    A. cubits

    B. regions

    C. sectors

    D. zones

9. A(n) _____ solution takes secrets away from apps that traditionally store them and locks them away in a separate database.

    A. BitLocker

    B. Internet key exchange

    C. password vault

    D. secrets management

10. Bill's company provides every employee with personalized storage space. His cloud service provider gives him a tool called _____ that enables him to shut down any individual instance if there's a problem.

    A. instance awareness

    B. NGFW

    C. SWG

    D. VPC endpoint

Answers

    1. B. A distributed denial-of-service attack needs two or more computers to carry out its attack.

    2. B. A managed service provider provides security monitoring for a fee.

    3. D. VMs rely on a hypervisor to run.

    4. A. Docker is a popular management system for containers.

    5. D. Unauthorized creation of VMs in an organization is an example of VM sprawl.

    6. A. An infrastructure as a service enables deployment of full systems running a variety of operating systems.

    7. B. A hybrid cloud combines different types of cloud solutions.

    8. B. Amazon Web Services divides the world into 20+ regions to enhance efficiency.

    9. D. A secrets management solution takes secrets away from apps that traditionally store them.

    10. A. Instance awareness tools enable quick and effective control over instances.

Securing Dedicated Systems

*Hey, Scott! Let's combine embedded, specialized, and mobile systems
into the same chapter! What could go wrong?*

—Mike Meyers

What makes embedded systems, specialized systems, and mobile systems sufficiently similar to cover them in a single chapter? That's a valid question, considering they run on a wide array of operating systems—from Windows, Linux, and macOS to Android, iOS, and customized single-platform OSes—and have a variety of uses, including single-purpose devices (e.g., an Internet-connected refrigerator), specific-purpose devices (e.g., a home automation hub), and multipurpose devices (e.g., a smartphone or tablet). So what's the connection?

Every one of these devices, which we dub dedicated systems, comes from the factory as complete and unchangeable computing hardware. When you buy a fitness watch, for example, you buy a sophisticated computing device, but one that you can't upgrade or change. When you buy a new Apple iPad with 64 GB of storage, 64 GB of storage is all you'll ever get with that machine. The CPU will never change. The RAM will never change.

 EXAM TIP *Dedicated systems* is a term we coined and *not* one you'll see on the CompTIA Security+ exam.

That unchanging hardware coupled with changeable firmware or software presents unique challenges in security. These devices are part of your network, interconnected with general-purpose computing devices (like a Windows PC or a Linux server), and absolutely must be part of your overall security posture. Not securing them puts everything else in your system at risk.

This chapter explores securing dedicated systems in four modules:

- Embedded, Specialized, and Mobile Systems
- Connecting to Dedicated Systems
- Security Constraints for Dedicated Systems
- Implementing Secure Mobile Solutions

Module 9-1: Embedded, Specialized, and Mobile Systems

This module covers the following CompTIA Security+ objectives:

- **2.6   Explain the security implications of embedded and specialized systems**
- **3.5   Given a scenario, implement secure mobile solutions**

Embedded, specialized, and mobile systems power a huge portion of modern computing tasks, and they come in a variety seemingly as diverse as the fish in the sea. This section touches on the dedicated systems you'll encounter on the CompTIA Security+ exam:

- Embedded systems
- SCADA/ICS
- Internet of Things
- Specialized systems
- Mobile systems

Embedded Systems

The definition of *embedded system* is a moving target depending on the author. For some in the IT industry, the term "embedded system" refers to any computing component packaged as a discrete part of a larger package. A network interface chip soldered onto a motherboard, for example, could be considered an embedded system. It's a processor. It has discrete functions that enable the larger system to accomplish things. This broad definition encompasses thousands of other examples, such as a point-of-sale system at a supermarket checkout, which handles local tasks (taking credit card information) but depends on a larger system (the store's network infrastructure) to complete transactions. As these examples suggest, such a broad definition of embedded system is too unwieldy to be practical.

CompTIA uses the term *embedded system* more narrowly to describe discrete hardware components that make up portions of systems. Specifically, the 601 objectives describe embedded systems as those running a Raspberry Pi, a field-programmable gate array processor, or an Arduino. Let's look at all three examples.

Figure 9-1 Raspberry Pi SoC (Image: Future Publishing / Contributor, Getty Images)

Raspberry Pi

The *Raspberry Pi* powers an array of embedded devices and systems, most notably the DNS Pi-hole and custom industrial control solutions. The Raspberry Pi exemplifies the *system on chip (SoC)* design concept, where all the processing components reside on a single circuit board—that includes CPU, RAM, system BIOS, Ethernet networking, and Wi-Fi networking; plus connectivity points for peripherals such as a keyboard, mouse, and monitor. Figure 9-1 shows a Raspberry Pi 3b.

NOTE A *DNS Pi-hole* uses a Raspberry Pi at the outer edge of a network, with the DNS server running special software to block any extra links on Web sites that display ads. Implementing a Pi-hole will transform your computing experience without sacrificing network performance. Goodbye, ads! Check out the Dave Rush Pi features on the TotalSeminarsChannel channel on YouTube for the scoop.

The Raspberry Pi models can run various Linux distros, including Ubuntu, Kali Linux, and the dedicated Raspberry OS. As such, you can use a Pi as a standalone multipurpose computer that replaces a Windows or macOS desktop (and apply all the standard security measures for desktop systems). But the Pi's small size and very small price have made it a favorite component in embedded systems, from manufacturing to industrial sensor controls. Zaro's Family Bakery in New York City, for example, employs a Pi along with wireless sensors to monitor temperatures in the bakery's freezers. This frees employees from physically checking temps and thus adds efficiency to their operations.

From a security standpoint, Raspberry Pi systems act, smell, and taste like a typical desktop system, just writ small. The typical Pi can plug into standard peripherals—keyboard, mouse, monitor—and connect to wired and wireless networks. The Linux operating systems that run Pis require the same security considerations of desktop Linux computers, with secure passwords, accounts, and so on. Physical access to a Pi presents the same danger as physical access to a PC or Mac.

Field-Programmable Gate Array

Embedded systems that require flexibility in processing capabilities use *field-programmable gate array (FPGA)* computers that, as the name suggests, you can reprogram to optimize for various tasks. An FPGA does not have a fixed CPU, like the Raspberry Pi, but rather has integrated circuits (ICs) that developers can redefine as needed. You'll see FPGAs used in vehicular systems, such as airplanes and automobiles, where switching hardware to make changes would be prohibitively expensive. Reprogramming the hardware for updates or corrections makes more sense.

Embedded systems running on an FPGA tend to run a *real-time operating system (RTOS)*, such as Windows Embedded Compact (Figure 9-2). An RTOS is designed to respond in real time to inputs. An RTOS is critical for anti-lock brakes, safety stops, and so forth.

Figure 9-2
Windows
Embedded
Compact

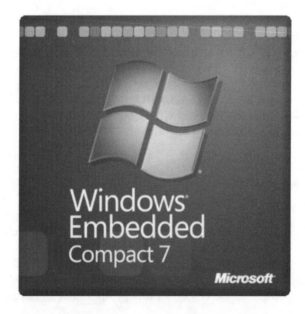

Figure 9-3
Arduino board
with breadboard

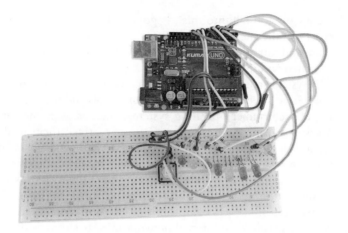

From a security standpoint, keeping the firmware up to date to work through bugs helps. Plus, limiting physical access to control ports or connections minimizes the potential for an attacker to damage your systems.

Arduino

Circuit boards and microcontrollers made by the *Arduino* company enable embedded systems used in motion detection, robotics, thermostats, drones, diagnostic systems, and more. Arduino products are open source and programmable using the programming languages C and C++. Open source combined with low cost, approachable programming and many connection options have made the Arduino boards the go-to devices at both the professional and enthusiast level for embedded devices. Figure 9-3 shows a typical Arduino system with an attached breadboard (for extending the capabilities of the board, in this case, for music).

You might think that "open source" and "approachable" would make embedded systems with Arduino at the heart susceptible to hacking, but it's usually the other way around. A lot of people use Arduino systems to power their hacking of other systems!

Arduino systems have security concerns. Physical access, like with FPGA systems, presents a clear danger. The limited memory on Arduino-based systems leaves them vulnerable to buffer overflow and heap attacks. The systems often connect automatically to the nearest access point when the default connection fails, again providing an opportunity for mischief. As with all computing systems, assume Arduinos need careful thought and preparation for security.

SCADA/ICS

Supervisory control and data acquisition (SCADA) systems are used in industrial applications, such as energy utilities (electric plants, nuclear power plants), production facilities (for logistics and control of manufacturing systems, for example), sewage treatment centers, and other specialized applications. *Heating, ventilation, and air conditioning*

(HVAC) controls also fall into this category and are often automated and connected to the Internet or other networks to monitor and control environmental elements such as temperature and humidity in a facility. You'll often hear the term *industrial control system (ICS)* associated with SCADA.

SCADA systems are more and more often being connected to the Internet, and often in an unprotected state. They run TCP/IP protocols and use embedded versions of some of the popular consumer operating systems, such as Windows or Linux. This makes SCADA systems prime targets for hackers, who attack them to damage critical infrastructure, launch denial-of-service (DoS) attacks, and generally create mischief and outright harm. Since SCADA systems often connect to very critical systems, it's not too hard to imagine a hacker attacking and gaining control of these systems and seriously affecting power, water, and other utilities and services on a massive scale. There have even been reported instances of hackers compromising SCADA systems and launching attacks on an organization's traditional internal network infrastructure through them.

One such attack allegedly carried out by the United States and Israel—the *Stuxnet* worm attack, code-named "Olympic Games"—blasted through Iranian industrial processes for refining nuclear material. No one on any side will confirm anything—hello international espionage and sabotage—but the attack destroyed upwards of 1000 nuclear centrifuges, putting a serious dent in Iran's nuclear enrichment capabilities.

Methods of mitigating these types of attacks include the traditional ones, such as encryption, authentication, and patch management. In the case of many of these systems, infrastructure controls, such as intrusion detection systems (IDSs) and firewall devices, should also be implemented. One other method that should be examined is the complete separation of these networks and their devices from public networks, such as the Internet, a form of *air gap*. (See Chapter 10 for the scoop on air gaps.)

Internet of Things

The term *Internet of Things (IoT)* describes the many computing devices (other than PCs, routers, and servers) that connect through the Internet, which is about as broad a definition as it gets. IoT often refers to smaller helper devices, such as lightbulbs you can turn on or off remotely, but it also applies to heating and cooling systems (*facility automation* tools), *smart devices* like a refrigerator that can tell you how much milk is left, diapers that inform you when junior needs a change, and so on.

You'll find a lot of devices marketed as part of the Internet of Things, such as *wearables* like the Fitbit fitness watch (Figure 9-4). Wearables have *sensors* for things like heart rate and number of steps taken; better ones have location tracking systems. The highest-end wearable devices, like the Apple iWatch, function as an alternative or extension of a smartphone, enabling text messaging, music, and more, all connected through the Internet via the cellular networks.

Some devices that might seem an odd fit fall into the IoT category, such as *multifunction devices (MFDs)* that combine printers, scanners, and copiers into one machine and then add Internet capabilities. You can print to MFDs from a variety of devices, including smartphones like the Apple iPhone via AirPrint, plus scan and send PDF files directly to Internet or e-mail destinations.

Figure 9-4   Fitbit IoT watch (Image: Smith Collection/Gado / Contributor, Getty Images)

 EXAM TIP   The CompTIA Security+ 601 exam objectives refer to multifunction devices as *multifunction printers (MFPs)*, so be prepared for either term on the exam.

IoT device manufacturers use a wide variety of different operating systems for their devices. The big players have their own operating systems, such as Android Things (Google), Windows IoT (Microsoft), and Amazon FreeRTOS (Amazon). Plus there are at least a dozen open-source operating systems, many based on a Linux core, such as Snappy (Ubuntu), or on the C programming language, such as TinyOS.

As you might imagine, with such incredible diversity of hardware and operating systems, combined with the dizzyingly efficient wireless networking capabilities, IoT security is a nightmare.

Additionally, what IoT devices have in common from a security standpoint are *weak default* settings. Most manufacturers of IoT devices in the consumer sphere, for example, err on the side of ease of use for the consumer rather than rigorous security for the power user or IT security specialist. Fine-tuning options such as connectivity and notification settings can go a long way toward adding worthwhile security to IoT devices.

Specialized Systems

Both CompTIA and many writers throw up their hands at the rest of the dedicated systems, calling them simply *specialized systems*. A specialized system offers all the hallmarks of other dedicated systems, such as relying on an SoC or using an RTOS. The specialized systems that you'll run into most commonly fall into several categories:

- Medical systems
- In-vehicle computing systems
- Smart meters
- Surveillance systems
- Voice over IP

Medical Systems

The push to smaller and increasingly powerful computing devices that can connect to the Internet has revolutionized some *medical systems*. People with irregular heartbeats have benefitted from pulses from an electronic device called a pacemaker for decades. The pacemaker simply stabilizes the heartbeat, granting the wearer generally a much longer lifespan. For 50+ years, pacemakers were (relatively) simple devices, implanted in patients and replaced periodically as their batteries depleted. Spin to today.

IoT pacemakers not only provide stimulus to regularize the heartbeat but also transmit over the Internet so doctors and technicians can monitor the patient's heart and the current level of battery power. IoT pacemakers eliminate the guesswork of when to replace or recharge a traditional pacemaker, yet another example of a breakthrough in medicine made possible through IT. See Figure 9-5.

Other *Internet of Medical Things (IoMT)* devices—both wearable and implanted—monitor all sorts of things, from general vital signs to specific things like glucose levels in diabetic patients. The IoMT field continues to grow, combining medical systems with phenomenal technology advances.

The inherent security risks involved with IoMT devices cannot be dismissed. Any device that connects to a network has vulnerabilities and the potential for hacking. A hacked medical lifesaving device could have deadly consequences. So far in the field attacks have been theoretical. There's hope for humanity?

NOTE As soon as you venture into the medical field, take into consideration the *Health Insurance Portability and Accountability Act of 1996 (HIPAA)* discussed way back in Chapter 1. HIPAA stipulates rules governing personal/private medical information that security professionals absolutely need to account for in the planning and deployment of systems.

Figure 9-5
IoT pacemaker
shown in X-ray
(Image: Trout55,
Getty Images)

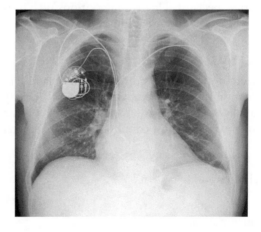

Figure 9-6
Connected automotive computing system (Image: mbbirdy, Getty Images)

In-Vehicle Computing Systems

Automobile manufacturers have incorporated computing devices into their products for decades. Adding connectivity to the global network was but a matter of getting systems and electronics in place. The consumer market demands automobiles with built-in systems that provide navigational functions, entertainment functions, and even access to the Internet (Figure 9-6). Automobile manufacturers want to cater to consumers by including all of these great features, as well as the ability to access vehicle health information via network connections. These network connections may include Bluetooth, Wi-Fi, or even, in some cases, cellular connectivity.

NOTE Although *not* included in the CompTIA Security+ exam, not surprisingly *vehicle-to-vehicle (V2V)* communications have standards, notably the *IEEE 1609 Wireless Access in Vehicular Environments (WAVE)* protocol stack. Also related are *vehicular ad hoc networks (VANETs)*, connectivity options for on-the-fly interconnectivity among automobiles. These technologies, protocols, and standards have been around for years, but the push to self-driving cars seems to furthering the cause.

Again, V2V and VANET are not on the CompTIA Security+ 601 exam, but where there are interoperable wireless computer systems, you'll find vulnerabilities that require careful consideration by IT security professionals.

So if computers are now being built into automobiles or added in as aftermarket devices, what are the security ramifications? And how do you secure in-vehicle computer systems? Will it become necessary to install a firewall in your car?

And it's not just automobiles that have computing systems. Aircraft of all sorts, both manned and unmanned, have increasingly sophisticated computing systems, many connected to extended networks and the Internet. Your next *unmanned aerial vehicle (UAV)*—that's a *drone*, for all you normal folks—guaranteed will have multiple *embedded camera systems*, high-end wireless networking capabilities, and an SoC to run them all (Figure 9-7).

Figure 9-7
DJI drone with one SoC to rule them all! (Image: ROBYN BECK / Contributor, Getty Images)

From a security perspective, in-vehicle computing systems have some of the same common vulnerabilities that other systems have, which may include network security issues, such as the vulnerabilities inherent to Bluetooth, Wi-Fi, and cellular technologies. There are also issues involving firmware and patch updates to the systems. Many of these systems have USB or SD card ports, for example, to upload firmware updates or play media content on the devices. Perhaps someday someone will develop a virus or other type of malware that could be injected into these types of systems via a removable media device.

Other security issues may be only the speculative fantasies of geeks, such as a hacker taking over your car and driving it while you're going down the road or conducting a DoS attack on your engine or transmission, resulting in the car coming to a complete halt on the Autobahn. However remote these possibilities may be, they may not be too far down the road (pun intended). In short, vehicular computing systems are a new frontier, for both security professionals and hackers. Although traditional security methods and controls will probably work to a large degree, other methods will have to be developed to ensure that these types of static hosts are well protected from malicious users and attacks.

Smart Meters

Smart meters rely on cellular and wireless networks to communicate to consumers and utility companies real-time information about power usage, usually electricity, but also natural gas or water. A smart meter can alert when something spikes unexpectedly—such as water usage, indicating a possible water main break that starts wastefully dumping liters of water—and help consumers and providers optimize power usage. Figure 9-8 shows a smart meter that records and reports on the electricity usage at my house.

Surveillance Systems

Consumer use of *surveillance systems* has exploded with the advent of phenomenal camera technologies, SoC capabilities, and cellular and Wi-Fi connectivity. Grainy footage of people trying to penetrate government facilities back in the day has evolved into

Figure 9-8
Smart meter

gloriously high-definition footage and audio of people stealing packages from your front porch. The wireless Ring doorbell at my front door (Figure 9-9), for example, enables me to interact in real time with people at the door, regardless of whether I'm in the house or across the planet (Figure 9-10).

The security implications and considerations with modern IoT surveillance systems run from paranoia to downright scary. Ring devices, for example, interface with Amazon

Figure 9-9   Ring doorbell (Image: Chip Somodevilla / Staff, Getty Images)

Figure 9-10
Ring app

Alexa home infotainment devices to send your security footage to "the cloud." Nothing stops "the cloud" from sharing your footage with local law enforcement or companies that can monetize the information in some other way. Other device manufacturers have been accused of sending personal information gathered from their devices secretly to other nation states.

EXAM TIP Surveillance systems are a good example of *point-to-multipoint* communication, where the base station interacts with multiple wireless nodes (the cameras). The nodes don't communicate with each other, but rather all report back to the base.

Voice over IP

Office telephone systems used to have their own dedicated wiring and devices, all functioning on the antique POTS signaling standards. Telephone connections centered on a PBX block and used Cat 1 cabling with RJ-11 jacks (Figure 9-11).

It became increasingly obvious that installing dual cable runs (Cat 1 and Cat 5) in new buildings late last century was a waste because Cat 5 could do the work of either cabling standard. Eventually developers came up with *Voice over IP (VoIP)*, a way to do telephony over TCP/IP networks, with no need to use ancient technology. Many (most?) enterprises today have ditched the old PBX telephone systems for modern VoIP systems.

Figure 9-11
RJ-45 and RJ-11
jacks (Image:
pablohart, Getty
Images)

This is all stuff you should remember from CompTIA Network+ or even CompTIA A+ training, so I doubt we're telling you something new here. The real question for CompTIA Security+ is what security implications VoIP systems pose.

You need to secure VoIP communications just like you would any other IP network. Typical VoIP attacks include denial of service, spoofing telephone numbers, and just harassment.

Mobile Systems

The term *mobile systems* refers to all of the general computing devices not tethered to a cable, such as laptop computers (running Windows, macOS, Linux, or Chrome), tablets (running iOS or Android), and smartphones (also iOS or Android). Figure 9-12 shows a Microsoft Surface portable computer running Windows 10.

Mobile systems, as general-purpose devices, function similarly to other *Internet of Computing (IoC)* devices (workstations, servers, routers) and have similar security issues and solutions. Keep the OS and apps updated. Keep the firmware updated to ward off attacks. Manage the devices with firewalls and other standard security options.

Mobile systems differ from the wired IoC devices in connectivity, on the other hand, which we'll look at next, and in mobile-specific security issues (in Module 9-4). We'll also explore problematic areas when introducing mobile devices to the enterprise.

Figure 9-12
Microsoft Surface (and yes, I have a ping pong table in my dining room . . . Don't judge!)

Module 9-2: Connecting to Dedicated Systems

This module covers the following CompTIA Security+ objectives:

- **2.6   Explain the security implications of embedded and specialized systems**
- **3.5   Given a scenario, implement secure mobile solutions**

Dedicated systems rely on many of the same technologies to enable communication among devices. This module first explores the security implications in common technologies shared among the devices and then looks at low-power technologies exclusive to IoT devices.

 NOTE   This module assumes you have CompTIA Network+ knowledge of how these various technologies work. If you need a refresher, check out the excellent *CompTIA Network+ Certification All-in-One Exam Guide* by yours truly.

To put all of the communication technologies in context, this module offers several examples based on the following hypothetical scenario. The Bayland Widgets Corporation (BWC) main campus has several buildings connected via fiber-optic cabling and Ethernet. (The details of those connections are unimportant for this discussion; we're just setting the stage.) One of the buildings houses the factory that builds BWC's world-famous widgets. A SCADA system—including processors, control modules, sensors, actuator arms, robotics, etc.—controls the production machines. The main office building has employees, naturally, and a diverse collection of IoC and IoT devices. These devices include standard workstations and servers, plus many portable computers, tablets, smartphones, wearables, and so on. Plus, the entire campus has a surveillance system comprising cameras and control units, all of which feed back to the security center.

The menagerie of devices introduces a plethora of device communication types, all of which have security implications. Let's look first at communication technologies prevalent in most of the devices, then turn to specific IoT communication technologies.

Common Communication Technologies

Many devices in the BWC campus connect with common technologies. These include cellular networks, 802.11 Wi-Fi, Bluetooth, NFC, and infrared.

Cellular

Current *cellular networks* rely on either 4G or 5G technologies connecting cells (geographical areas) via various radio frequencies. Cellular radio towers with base transceiver stations enable the networks to cover enormous areas.

4G networks provide excellent coverage using the 450- to 3800-MHz bands, enabling download speeds at up to 300 Mbps and upload speeds of 75 Mbps. *5G* networks operate at three distinct bands: Low-band, Mid-band, and High-band. The higher the band, the faster the connection speed, but the shorter the range. 5G devices connect automatically at the fastest speed available at range.

Most cellular devices also use a *subscriber identity module (SIM) card* (Figure 9-13) that stores identity (hence the name) and enables authentication between the device and mobile carriers. All sorts of devices use SIM cards, from smartphones to cameras to wearable IoT devices.

NOTE SIM cards can be hacked, especially in older devices. The CompTIA 601 objectives don't mention SimJacker, but the attack exploits a common software installed on SIM cards from virtually every manufacturer, called S@T Browser. The fix? Upgrade to a device that uses a current SIM card without that vulnerability.

The BWC campus has several cellular towers nearby, providing Internet connectivity (and thus interconnectivity) with a ton of employee devices. Every employee has a smartphone, for example, and many have tablets with cellular connection capabilities.

Cellular voice and data services these days offer very robust security. Direct sniffing of these networks is difficult at best (assuming you're using a late-generation 4G/LTE or 5G phone). Carriers will quickly detect and act on any attempts to emulate a cell tower, for example, which could lead to serious legal ramifications for the bad actor.

An attacker has the best potential for success attacking cellular by avoiding cellular altogether. The switch point for devices between cellular and Wi-Fi provides an excellent attack surface because Wi-Fi offers much weaker security than cellular.

Finally, privacy issues should concern users and IT security folks when working with cellular. Turning off geolocation services—where the cellular provider can track your whereabouts at all times—can enhance privacy, although you'll lose useful functionality. Getting directions from Siri or from Google Maps goes right out the window, because geolocation services access the *Global Positioning System (GPS)* satellite network to show where you are in relation to other places.

Figure 9-13
Typical SIM
card (Image:
Thomas Trutschel
/ Contributor,
Getty Images)

Wi-Fi/Bluetooth

Chapter 7 covered *Wi-Fi* in detail and *Bluetooth* a bit more lightly. Every wireless security aspect covered previously applies to mobile and IoT devices, but they add a few more problems. One of the most challenging issues in Wi-Fi comes from stored profiles. Mobile devices can grab standardized hotspot SSIDs pushed out by ISPs such as "xfinitywifi" or "attwifi," and some will in turn become mobile hotspots that seem very similar to the initial hotspot (Figure 9-14).

You can enhance or upgrade some dedicated devices by adding the latest generation Wi-Fi or Bluetooth card via a *universal serial bus (USB)* port. Conversely, some users might try to skirt air gap rules (where their devices should not connect with other devices) by plugging in a USB cellular device. These shouldn't be common variances, but they might show up on a Security+ exam in your near future.

 EXAM TIP Bluetooth is an example of *point-to-point* communication, from one device to another device.

BWC has a mesh Wi-Fi network throughout the campus, providing both interior and exterior space connectivity for mobile devices. For security, the IT department implements WPA3 encryption throughout, though also providing access using WPA2 for older devices during the transition year. The mixed encryption system isn't ideal, but it's good enough.

Figure 9-14
Author's Xfinity
hotspot

Near-Field Communication

Many mobile devices use *near-field communication (NFC)*, just like you read about in Module 7-2, for quick payments and such. NFC uses *radio-frequency identification (RFID)* technologies to enable communication with unpowered electronic tags on an unlicensed ISM radio-frequency band (13.56 MHz). All the security issues for NFC apply to its use in mobile devices.

While NFC contains basic encryption, the technology relies on the short distances (within four inches) and quick communication to provide security. Modern payment services that use NFC, such as Apple Pay, add their own security protocols as well to ensure safety of personal information.

NOTE   Android embraces NFC heavily. Apple typically uses NFC only for the Apple Pay app, although Apple is slowly opening iOS to more NFC options.

Infrared

One of your authors loves his Android phones if for no other reason than only Androids (and not all of them) come with an *infrared (IR)* transmitter—enabling connectivity via light waves—known generically as an *infrared blaster*. IR blasters can emulate any IR remote control, turning any Android into a universal remote. Since these devices only transmit simple remote-control commands, there is no risk to your mobile device. The risk is that any IR blaster can quickly take complete control of any device designed to receive those commands, making the Android the bad actor. The only real defense is to block the IR receivers.

NOTE   The other author eschews Android, fully embracing the Apple iOS ecosystem. He's clearly the more cultured of the two, even if it means not being able to hijack the hotel lobby television.

IoT-Specific Communication Technologies

IoT developers use communication technologies created specifically for low-powered IoT devices. There are quite a few proprietary and open-source technologies in use. Four common ones are Narrowband IoT, Bluetooth Low Energy, Zigbee, and ANT.

Narrowband IoT

Developers use the Narrowband Internet of Things (NB-IoT) technology for high connection density IoT deployment, specifically with an eye to maximizing battery life and minimizing costs. Narrowband means NB-IoT uses only a single radio frequency—200 KHz. The goal with NB-IoT is to provide good coverage and devices that don't need recharging for years.

EXAM TIP Part of the underlying physical layer of NB-IoT can rely on devices that use *baseband radio processors* that manage radio functions from multiple devices. Sounds like a circular definition, but you might see the term on the exam.

Bluetooth Low Energy

The inexpensive devices that employ the *Bluetooth Low Energy (BLE)* networking technology consume very little electricity, yet have a range similar to their big brother Bluetooth. BLE devices are not compatible with Bluetooth, but the technology is part of the Bluetooth 4.0 and Bluetooth 5 standards. Like Bluetooth, BLE creates a personal area network (PAN) for devices interconnecting. Every major mobile and desktop OS supports BLE. BLE devices range from security to home entertainment to medical.

Zigbee

Devices and systems that rely on the *Zigbee* communication protocols offer ad hoc personal area networks that use very low-power radios. This low-bandwidth solution works perfectly for things like medical device data collection and home automation. Zigbee is an open standard, so adoption by manufacturers is increasing.

BWC has implemented centrally monitored Zigbee systems in its new buildings to control lighting, window blinds, access control, and climate control. The cost savings provided by the smart IoT systems compared to the older dumb systems in the original buildings will most likely lead to systems upgrades in the near future. Old might be quaint or picturesque, but energy efficiency helps everyone.

ANT

ANT is a low-speed, low-power networking technology. Wi-Fi and Bluetooth are powerful wireless tools, but both of these technologies require rather chatty, relatively power-hungry devices. Bluetooth isn't nearly as power hungry or as fast as Wi-Fi, but when you have very small devices such as heart rate monitors, even Bluetooth uses too much power.

Garmin introduced the proprietary ANT protocol around 2007 for low-power sensors that don't send a lot of data and that often go for extended periods of time without transferring data (like your author's heart rate monitor that's used at most once a week). The latest version of ANT is called ANT+. ANT/ANT+ is a superb protocol that's incredibly low powered and has enough bandwidth for many devices. ANT is encrypted with AES, so hacking isn't an issue (yet). The only downside to ANT/ANT+ is that Apple devices lack an ANT radio. In that case you'd need an ANT/ANT+ USB dongle to talk to an ANT device (Figure 9-15).

EXAM TIP You *won't* be tested on ANT or ANT+ on the CompTIA Security+ exam. We've included the technology here as useful real-world information.

Figure 9-15
ANT USB dongle

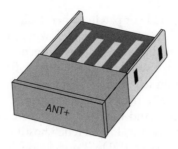

Module 9-3: Security Constraints for Dedicated Systems

This module covers the following CompTIA Security+ objectives:

- **2.6 Explain the security implications of embedded and specialized systems**
- **2.8 Summarize the basics of cryptographic concepts**

IT security specialists need a solid understanding of the security constraints and concerns for embedded systems, IoT systems, and specialized systems to help clients secure their networks. This section explores hardware, programming, and connectivity.

Hardware

Embedded and specialized systems come in an astonishing variety, but they have one feature in common: the static nature of their hardware. When you buy a device built around an SoC, for example, you can't change or upgrade the core computing capabilities of the device. (That's the *compute* portion of devices, in industry jargon.) You can certainly add all kinds of additional features to a Raspberry Pi, but the core CPU, RAM, and connection options don't change.

That static nature also applies to the security built into the device by the manufacturer, especially when dealing with IoT devices. Competition in the market drives manufacturers to reduce costs or provide *low-cost* devices for consumers. This often means serious resource constraints to favor price over security. Further, manufacturers release devices into the market with the assumption that they're "place and forget" devices for consumers; in other words, once set up, consumers will assume they're done configuring or messing with the devices. This leads to a lot of problems, especially when dealing with the flip side of hardware, software.

Programming

Dedicated systems—especially IoT—have glaring security weaknesses because of the nature of the systems. Consumers have deployed billions of IoT devices; manufacturers have chosen low cost and ease of use over security. Many IoT devices have very specialized operating systems based in read-only memory (ROM) of some sort that requires user interaction to upgrade or patch. Other dedicated devices rely on light Linux distros that may not have all the security locked down. I'm not exaggerating the problem here.

A group of undergraduate students at Rutgers University in the United States developed the *Mirai* botnet, a simple and ingenious software program that did a blanket scan for open Telnet ports on IoT devices over a wide geographic area. Mirai targeted the IoT devices and automatically tried 61 user name and password combinations to build an enormous botnet army. And then the Mirai developers attacked. In September 2016, Mirai was successfully used against a French hosting company that provided tools to stop distributed denial-of-service (DDoS) attacks on Minecraft servers. You read that correctly. "Anna-Senpai," the leader of the Mirai developers, was a serious Minecraft player. And he led a DDoS attack against a company specializing in anti-DDoS protection.

 NOTE Anna-Senpai's real name is Paras Jha. His cohorts were Josiah White and Dalton Norman. All of them were just supersmart college students trying out a new technology. They served a lot of hours of community service after confessing to the FBI and, presumably, are deep in the white hat security world now.

Unfortunately for the world, after the first successful Mirai botnet attack, the developers released the Mirai source code online. The next serious attack happened a month later against Dyn, Inc., which was a major provider of DNS services in the United States (subsequently acquired by Oracle). This attack caused some major players on the Internet to go dark for a few hours, including Twitter, Reddit, and Spotify. And the Mirai source code is still out there, getting modified and refined. The risk is real.

Updating the programming that secures dedicated systems offers the best route to security. Let's look at obstacles to updating and then paths to updating.

Inability to Patch

Dedicated systems often don't lend themselves to automatic updates. This constraint could be caused by several factors:

- Some of these dedicated systems are not always connected to the Internet—a network constraint. In the case of SCADA systems or medical devices, for example, there may be no way to connect them to the Internet without incurring a security risk.

- The vendor may not have included an automated update process with the device. Some devices may require the download of a patch, an image, or a piece of firmware that has to be manually installed on the device using a very specific process, often resulting in rebooting the device into a special maintenance mode.

- The data sensitivity of the systems in question might be so high that the organization can't perform automatic updates or connect them to the Internet for classification reasons. For example, some US government systems, particularly those of a classified nature, cannot be connected to the Internet.

For these reasons, manual updates may be required for some static dedicated systems. If you have the ability to automate device updates, then obviously you should use that method as much as possible, since it ensures that updates are applied in the most efficient way possible. On the other hand, manual updates can give you the opportunity to test patches and other software updates before applying them to a production system. Often, you can download updates manually, test them in a test environment that mirrors your production systems, and then apply them to the production systems only after you are sure that they will cause no ill effects. You should also record manual updates, so that you can trace any issues that arise from them back to a particular patch or update.

Firmware Version Control

Many devices running dedicated systems get firmware updates. Remember that firmware is typically applied as updates to programming in the chips on the hardware portion of the system, rather than as patches to the operating system or application software. Firmware updates can fix issues with both the operating system and hardware on a device, as well as provide for security patches. Firmware updates can also add new features to a device. For personal devices, firmware version control may not be a big issue; often if the user experiences any issues with the device after the firmware has been updated, the user can reverse the update process and regress to an earlier version rather easily. In an enterprise environment, however, it's extremely important to maintain version control on firmware updates, because a firmware update may cause issues with production software or devices that the organization needs to fulfill its business purposes.

As I mentioned previously when discussing manual updates, you should first test firmware updates in an appropriate environment, and then apply them to production devices only after you have confirmed that they cause no ill effects. You also should record firmware versions in a central database. Read the documentation accompanying the firmware updates to learn about any known issues with other software or hardware used by the organization.

Connectivity

Dedicated systems for the most part connect to other computing devices. Systems running multipurpose operating systems like Linux and hooked up with Ethernet or 802.11 Wi-Fi generally use the standard protocols used for connectivity with IoC devices. Moving over to IoT device connectivity, on the other hand, brings up a lot of security issues in communication and cryptography.

Low-powered IoT devices rely on *low-power protocols*, such as Zigbee, Bluetooth Low Energy (BLE), and IPv6 over Low-Power Wireless Personal Area Networks (6LoW-PAN), that enable connectivity over a short *range* (compared to 802.11 Wi-Fi). (You read about Zigbee and BLE in Module 9-2.) Low-powered IoT devices rely on *lightweight cryptographic algorithms* that don't offer as much security as heavier ones—because they need to function using much lower computing power. Worse, because of their static nature, the IoT devices cannot upgrade to more secure protocols in the future. And the previously mentioned "place and forget" nature of IoT means consumers won't even think about upgrading with more secure components down the road.

Most IoT devices rely on simple password-based authentication methods, though the process and security involved vary tremendously. There is no universal authentication protocol for IoT, but rather a multitude of frameworks, all constrained by the relatively limited processing power of IoT devices. Some ecosystems from the big players, like Amazon and Google, use the same authentication as their desktop applications, but smaller players that create light bulbs, refrigerators, and so on? Their devices rely on simple passwords.

Compounding the security issues with IoT devices is the implied trust among devices within a network space. *Implied trust* traditionally refers to all the networked computers inside an enterprise or single building. You trust that employees won't hack each other or do malicious things. You protect against outside threats, but not inside. (This is rapidly changing, as we'll discuss in a moment.)

In the context of consumer IoT devices, implied trust refers to the trust consumers have in device vendors. Consider the scenario of a consumer purchasing a series of home automation devices to control lighting, heating and cooling, security, and so on. Assuming that the consumer purchases from a single vendor, such as Google or Amazon, the consumer implicitly trusts the vendor to provide security in two areas. First, inside the home, the consumer implicitly trusts that the vendor has made its devices interoperable and secure. Second, beyond the home, the consumer implicitly trusts that the vendor has a secure cloud to support all the cloud features of its devices.

In practice, this trust model breaks down swiftly because consumers mix and match IoT devices from different vendors all the time. These heterogenous vendor devices often don't communicate well together straight out of the box. What is the typical consumer's solution? Lower the security settings that stop the devices from talking amongst themselves. This, as we say in the business, is a *bad thing*. And at the consumer level, all the security issues outlined previously remain the unfortunate current state of affairs.

At the enterprise level, in contrast, a lot of companies have adopted (or are in the process of adopting) the National Institute for Standards and Technologies (NIST) *zero trust architecture (ZTA)* guidelines that recommend organizations require proper authentication and authorization in all interactions with assets. In other words, ZTA throws out the implicit trust model and insists on secure connections within as well as without the enterprise. In practice it means that Joe's iPad should not connect to any network shares without proper authentication, even though Joe has been a loyal employee for 22 years.

 NOTE   See NIST Special Publication 800-207, *Zero Trust Architecture*, for more on ZTA.

Module 9-4: Implementing Secure Mobile Solutions

This module covers the following CompTIA Security+ objectives:

- **3.5   Given a scenario, implement secure mobile solutions**
- **3.7   Given a scenario, implement identity and account management controls**

When so-called "smart" devices entered the consumer market, they were all the rage because, beyond traditional voice communications, they enabled users to communicate with friends, family, and associates nearly simultaneously in several new ways, by using social media sites, sharing photos and videos, using text and chat messages, and so on. They also became the ubiquitous computing platform, replacing traditional desktops and laptops to a large degree, enabling users to play games, manage their finances, dictate short documents, and perform other tasks. The problem was, however, that users expected to see the same cool, wide-ranging functions on their work computers as well, but the business world hadn't caught up with the mobile device app explosion. As a result, many users started bringing their devices to work, most of the time without management approval, and doing company work on them. Figure 9-16 shows examples of some of the personal mobile devices that wander into the office.

That's all changed now, of course, as businesses rapidly adopted mobile devices into their infrastructures. Businesses issue smartphones and tablets to employees, provide for their communications links and Internet services, and allow employees to use these devices to perform work functions—and, in some cases, even do some of their personal stuff on them.

Unfortunately, any new technology or change in the business infrastructure introduces new security issues. Sometimes organizations are in such a hurry to implement new technology that they overlook security issues, and their main focus is on how much stuff the technology or device can do. In other words, the focus is on the functionality of the device or technology rather than on security. With the infiltration of mobile devices into the business world, however, developers and engineers, business managers, and even users to a certain degree have worked to make use of mobile devices more secure.

Figure 9-16 Personal mobile devices that tend to show up at work (photo courtesy of Sarah McNeill Photography, used with permission)

The next few sections explore some of the security features that mobile devices offer and how to integrate them into the corporate infrastructure and networks. We'll do this in six sections:

- Mobile device management
- Deployment models
- Inventory control and asset tracking
- Application management and security
- Encryption and authentication
- Enforcement and monitoring for device security

Mobile Device Management

Mobile device management (MDM) is a process in the business infrastructure in which the company can bring mobile devices under the umbrella of the company's existing end-user device management for traditional desktops and laptops. MDM enables a company to manage all the devices that connect to the company's network centrally—not just the devices tied to a desk that don't exit the building in someone's pocket. Many considerations go into MDM, including the wide variety of vendors, platforms, operating systems, applications, features, and even telecom providers for these devices. Unless the business standardizes on one vendor or platform, it may find that managing all of these different devices is challenging.

Essentially, through MDM, a business can manage a mobile device using the same technologies and methods used for traditional desktops, and with the same level of control. Figure 9-17 shows an example of a basic MDM software user interface.

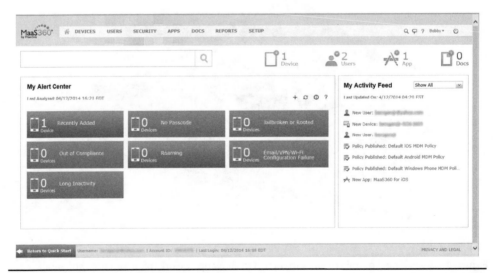

Figure 9-17   Basic MDM software

Subsets or related technologies to MDM include MicroSD hardware security modules, unified endpoint management, and Security Enhanced Linux for Android. Let's explore these technologies.

MicroSD Hardware Security Module

The *MicroSD hardware security module (HSM)* works specifically with Android-based smartphones and tablets to provide robust encryption and security via a microSD smart card. The smart card includes public key encryption, public key authentication, and crazy levels of encryption, including 256-bit AES, 521-bit ECC, and 4096-bit RSA. Add a MicroSD HSM card to devices in your enterprise to enhance security.

 NOTE We covered HSM in general way back in Module 5-4. Check out that section to refresh your memory if necessary.

Unified Endpoint Management

Unified Endpoint Management (UEM) tools take MDM to the next level, providing the enterprise with centralized control over all endpoints, including mobile devices (smartphones, tablets, laptops) and IoT devices such as wireless MFDs (introduced in Module 9-1) and wearables.

 EXAM TIP UEM products currently seem to be as much about marketing as about technology, but expect a question about the awesome control offered by UEM for the enterprise on the CompTIA Security+ exam.

Security Enhanced Linux for Android

Increasingly, Android-based devices rely on a mandatory access control (MAC) mechanism to provide security called *Security Enhanced Linux (SELinux)*. SELinux gives security experts security policies that govern all aspects of deployed Android devices, such as operations, objects, and processes. This granular security enhances the traditional security in Android devices which was based on discretionary access control (DAC). DAC worked well enough in the beginning, but malicious or faulty apps could leak data; DAC permissions lacked subtleties or granularity to work well in some situations; and root or superuser accounts could run all sorts of setuid programs or system daemons with no control. SELinux for Android—or *SEAndroid*, in CompTIA speak—provides a serious security upgrade over DAC.

Deployment Models

The *deployment model* with mobile devices specifies how employees get a mobile device in their hands. The deployment model defines issues such as whether the corporation provides devices to employees or employees bring their own devices. The deployment model defines aspects of mobile device management.

Corporate-Owned, Business Only

A *corporate-owned, business only (COBO)* deployment model means that the organization issues mobile devices to employees and holds ownership of the devices, the maintenance of the devices, and the applications and the data on the devices.

Bring Your Own Device

Everyone already has a smartphone, and *bring your own device (BYOD)* deployment means to have employees bring their own devices and use them for business purposes. This brings up a number of security issues, as BYOD compels employees to offer some amount of control of their personal systems to the organization.

Choose Your Own Device

With the *choose your own device (CYOD)* deployment model the organization offers a selection of mobile devices from which employees can choose. Either employees buy the devices outright or the organization owns the device and offers employees an attractive rental for the duration of their employment. In either case, the organization has complete control over the mobile device (although employees may install personal apps).

Corporate-Owned, Personally Enabled

Similar to COBO, with the *corporate-owned, personally enabled (COPE)* deployment model the organization issues a mobile device, but unlike COBO, employees are allowed to install a specific number of preapproved (white-listed) apps for their personal use.

Containerization

BYOD, CYOD, and COPE all share a common problem: how can we separate the organization's applications and data from the employee's applications and data on the same device? Every mobile operating system supports containers to address this issue. A *container* is nothing more than a virtual operating system just as a virtual machine is virtual hardware. Using *containerization* enables the organization to create a separate operating system on the mobile device, completely separating the employee's applications and data from the organization's.

Figure 9-18 shows one example of containerization offered on an Android system. Note that there are two Contacts, two Calendars, and two Play Store apps. Using containerization enables this feature.

Containerization normally relies on *storage segmentation*, the practice of partitioning off storage areas in the device, usually to provide separate areas for company or sensitive data and personal data. Through storage segmentation, it's possible to impose different access controls on specific types of data. Figure 9-19 describes the concepts of sandboxing (which you read about in Module 8-2) and containerization. Storage segmentation can be imposed on the device's built-in storage area or on removable media as well.

Virtual Desktop Infrastructure

If an organization wants to avoid the issue of device ownership altogether, it can get around the problem completely by offering a *virtual desktop infrastructure (VDI)*, which

Figure 9-18
Containerization on an Android-based mobile device

you also read about in Module 8-3. With a VDI, every employee has a virtual machine running on a server owned by the organization. The employee may access this machine via any device running any operating system and is presented a virtual desktop with the applications the employee needs.

Figure 9-19
Containerization used to separate apps and data from each other

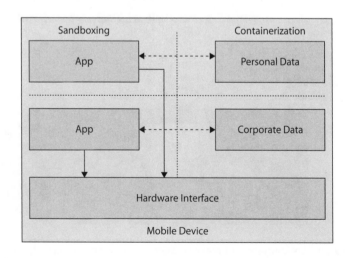

Inventory Control and Asset Tracking

One of the great things about using mobile devices in the enterprise is that employees can use them anywhere. Unfortunately, however, that means that the devices don't always reside on the company property. They walk off with the user, so the company often doesn't know exactly where they are and what they're being used for, or even who's using them. As with traditional desktops, *inventory control* is important with mobile devices, perhaps more important, since they are portable. Several technologies make it easier to manage mobile devices, even when they are off the company campus.

We will discuss many of these technologies later when we get into device-specific security methods, but for now understand that companies can't implement any of them well unless they are part of an overall MDM infrastructure. MDM enables centralized control of devices, including inventory control, so IT management always knows the location of devices and, in many cases, knows which authorized users have control over them. Since mobile devices tend to talk to the MDM infrastructure often, IT management can have an almost 100 percent real-time inventory of mobile devices via the MDM software. Of course, the traditional method of having a user bring the device to the office to scan it with a barcode reader can also make sure that IT management knows the device is safely checked in or out.

Along with inventory control, asset tracking is important. *Asset tracking* means knowing the location of devices at all times, who has them, and how they are being used. Asset tracking can be provided through the MDM infrastructure as well as via the device—through features such as GPS and other location-based services, as well as software agents that can be placed on the devices when they come under management control. Combined with strong security policies applied to mobile devices through MDM, asset tracking can provide visibility into what's happening with these devices at all times. Figure 9-20 illustrates how location services can show the exact location of a device.

Figure 9-20 Location services make it easier to track mobile device assets.

Device Access Control

Yet another management goal of business when integrating mobile devices into its networks is to control what data, systems, and resources the mobile devices connect to and access—*device access control*. As with any other device or user, the goal is to make sure that people using mobile devices can access only the data and systems they need to do their job and no more. Your organization can and should definitely use traditional access controls, which include restrictive rights, permissions, and privileges. You can implement these controls at the resource level, such as assigning permissions to a folder or file, but you can also implement them at the network level. For example, modern mobile devices can use strong authentication mechanisms, such as certificate-based authentication, which you can integrate with your network's directory services, such as Active Directory. This can prevent an unauthorized user from stealing a mobile device and attempting to connect to your network and access your resources. Other traditional methods of access control that you can use in conjunction with mobile devices include firewalls, network access control devices, and so on.

On the flip side of device access control, in addition to the desire to control access to network resources within the business perimeter, most administrators also want to control what a device can access and do when it leaves the company network. This can be harder to control since the device is no longer under the physical or logical control of the company. It may connect to unsecure home or hotel networks, for example, or to unsecure free Wi-Fi networks that have no required authentication or encryption. These are challenges when trying to control devices remotely and control what they can access offsite. Fortunately, administrators can apply MDM security policies to devices to control access to certain content (*content management*), applications, and Internet sites. These policies prevent users from doing things or accessing content that's prohibited by the company. Figure 9-21 illustrates how this works.

Geotagging

Geotagging is the process of including in a file, such as a picture or video file, metadata that contains the location information of the device when the file was created or processed. For example, people often take pictures and geotag them with location information, which might include the GPS coordinates, time and date stamps, and other types of information, to include a description of an event. Geotagging is useful from several perspectives in the corporate environment. An investigator conducting a forensic analysis of a device, for example, could look at geotag information in the file metadata to try to determine patterns of where the device has been and how it has been used. Geotagging also may serve a purpose in verifying the time, date, and location of an employee who performs a certain action, which may be required for compliance or policy reasons.

 NOTE The CompTIA Security+ exam objectives use the term *GPS tagging* for *geotagging*. These terms are synonymous.

The use of geotagging in tracking employees and their activities must be carefully considered, however, in environments where users are allowed to process corporate data on their own personal devices. As with all personal data, geotagging can give away information

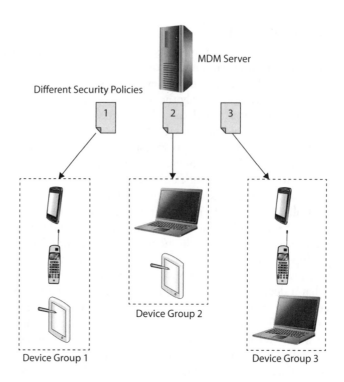

Figure 9-21
MDM can push security configuration and policies to all mobile devices in the enterprise.

MDM Server

Different Security Policies

Device Group 1

Device Group 2

Device Group 3

that an employee might not want the company to have, especially if it involves information of a personal nature. We'll discuss that scenario later in the module. As with all the other issues discussed here, geotagging should be addressed in policy documents.

Remote Management

Remote management is the key to protecting data in the corporate infrastructure. As mentioned, once the device leaves company property, it's difficult to control—that is, unless the company has installed and configured remote management capabilities. This requires admins to configure the MDM software properly, as well as the settings on the device itself. Remote management enables a business to reach out and touch the device virtually to monitor its location and use, as well as to protect data in the event the device is lost or stolen. You need to be aware of a few different remote management functions for the Security+ exam, as well as for use on the job.

Geolocation uses the GPS feature of the mobile device to locate it. Figure 9-22 shows the Google device manager (called Find My Device) locating the author's phone as he watches the Houston Astros instead of working on this book.

Remote wiping (or *remote wipe*) is a capability you should use in the event a device is lost or stolen and is not likely to be recovered. In this scenario, the MDM software would enable you to send commands to the device that will completely wipe its storage areas, erasing sensitive data, configuration, and so on. Wiping the device could effectively render it useless, or at least reset it back to factory conditions.

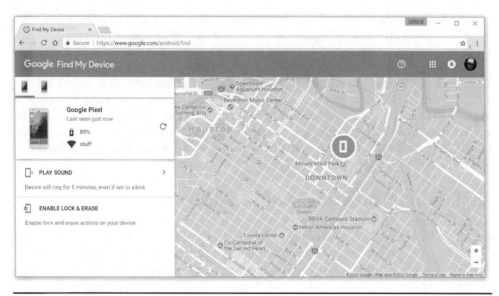

Figure 9-22   Google device manager

Remote control is another security feature that you can enable on the device through MDM software. You can use this feature to take over the device if a user can't figure out how to do something, of course, but a more useful security feature might be to take control of the device to prevent its misuse or to extract data from it before it's wiped. You can also remotely unlock a device using this feature if the user has forgotten a passcode and doesn't want to keep typing it in and risk wiping the device after several incorrect entries.

Onboarding/Offboarding

Managing mobile devices starts with the processes the organization uses in onboarding and offboarding mobile devices. *Onboarding* encompasses all of the processes used to introduce a new mobile device into the network and assign it to the user. This includes *provisioning* the device to ensure that the device has the right settings to access the mobile service provider or telecom provider, as well as installing all of the company-approved applications on the device. Provisioning also entails making sure the right user permissions and accesses are installed on the device, such as user names and passwords, digital certificates, and so on. The point of onboarding and provisioning a device is to make sure that the device is fully functional so that a user can use it to process company data.

Offboarding, as you might guess, is almost the exact opposite of onboarding and provisioning. During *offboarding*, IT management collects the device from the user and takes away access to the network with this device. In an orderly offboarding process, user data is removed from the device and, if applicable, returned to the user. Corporate data is also removed from the device and stored or disposed of as appropriate.

The device might be decommissioned completely, removing it from inventory and disposing of it, in the case of legacy devices or devices that no longer function properly. If the device is not disposed of, it might be reused within the enterprise and issued to another user; in that event it would go through the onboarding and provisioning process again (although it may not require as much in terms of device activation and so on).

If the device has been collected from the user based upon a violation of policy or the law, the device might also be subject to forensic analysis and examination, as well as retention of any personal and corporate data on the device. In any event, a process should be established within the organization for both onboarding and offboarding mobile devices securely.

Application Management and Security

Application management means that the organization determines what applications can be installed and used on the mobile device, as well as where it gets those applications from. The organization can impose technical policies on devices that prohibit them from downloading applications from certain app stores, for example, and restrict them to downloading applications only from the internal company app repository or a specific vendor or platform app store.

Application management also means exercising control over what apps can do on the device, as well as what data they can access. For example, an organization can use certain methods to prevent a user's personal app from accessing any corporate data stored on the device. These methods may include restricting copy and paste operations, restricting a user's personal e-mail app from accessing the corporate e-mail's contacts list, and other controls. Application control can be imposed on the device using different technical policies, as well as tight control over user rights and privileges on the device. Other methods, such as sandboxing and containerization (discussed earlier in this module), can be used to separate applications and data from each other so that no interaction is possible between them.

Application Security

The organization should exert some sort of control over the security of the applications themselves, simply because there may be security and interoperability issues with all the different apps on mobile devices. This is dubbed *application management*. Some of these applications may not work well with company-approved enterprise applications, and some of these apps may not store, process, or transmit sensitive data securely. The organization may want to control which types of apps can be installed and used on mobile devices, using either MDM or *mobile application management (MAM)* technologies. The company may also want to set up its own app store, rather than allowing users to download apps from a vendor's app store. An admin can use *push notifications* to get services to devices, defining what apps are included (rather than relying on users to check for and download important apps or updates).

Application Whitelisting

In *application whitelisting*, the organization allows only certain trusted applications to be installed on mobile devices. The organization may exclude certain applications due to security, interoperability, or licensing issues. Applications acceptable in the organization might include secure e-mail applications, file transfer applications, and productivity applications. Whitelisting enables the organization to include accepted applications in policy configuration files that are sent to and maintained on the mobile device. These policies may prevent a user from downloading and using unapproved apps or from using certain vendor app stores. Often, secure configuration files for these apps are also included for an app when the device is provisioned.

 EXAM TIP The CompTIA Security+ 601 exam objectives replaced the term *whitelisting* with *allow list* in objective 3.2 and *application approved list* in objective 4.4. You will most likely see the commonly used term— whitelisting—on both the exam and certainly in the real world, but be prepared if CompTIA updates their question pool to see the newer terms.

Encryption and Authentication

Using encryption on mobile devices can protect data while it is stored on the device or during transmission from the device back to the corporate network through untrusted networks, such as the Internet. Mobile devices can make use of encryption in various ways, including encrypting both internal and removable storage and providing encryption for secure data exchange during file transfer and e-mail, for example. The key point about encryption is that, although most mobile devices support current encryption standards, the different levels of encryption, including algorithm and strength, as well as encryption negotiation methods, must be configured identically on both the device and the endpoint, such as a server or network device. If the two devices don't have compatible encryption methods configured, neither will be able to send or receive information securely. In some cases, using different encryption methods may prevent them from communicating at all.

Authentication

You'll remember from earlier discussions that the first step in the authentication process is for the user to identify herself, either through a user name and password combination or through some other form of multifactor authentication, such as a smart card and PIN, biometric thumbprint, and so on. Once the user has identified herself, the authentication process verifies and validates the user against a database of credentials. The user is authenticated only when the system can confirm that she is, in fact, the user who presented the identification to the system and no one else.

Mobile devices use the same types of authentication systems and technologies that traditional desktops and server systems use. The catch is that they must be compatible with existing authentication systems, such as user name and passwords (including length and complexity requirements), PIN codes, biometrics, and digital certificates. MDM concepts and principles require a password or PIN or both. Regardless of the authentication method used, mobile devices must support the different standards and protocols used in an enterprise authentication system. Supporting the authentication process is the process of managing a user's credentials, including user name, password, and even the cryptographic keys associated with digital identities. These topics are covered next.

EXAM TIP Expect a question on the CompTIA Security+ exam for which the correct answer indicates proper MDM policies requiring passwords and PINs along with biometrics to greatly enhance mobile device security.

Credential and Key Management

Credential management involves all of the processes and technologies involved with provisioning and maintaining user accounts and credentials. This usually includes account provisioning, creating secure passwords for users, and ensuring that passwords are managed throughout their life cycle (including password changes, compromise, and so on). Credential management also may involve issuing and managing digital identities, which are commonly associated with digital certificates and cryptographic keys.

Key management refers to the ability of the organization to manage cryptographic keys—the digital certificates and keys that people use to authenticate to corporate systems. The organization could use these digital certificates for e-mail authentication, digital signatures, and encryption, and to ensure data integrity within the organization. Key management involves managing the life cycle of cryptographic keys from their creation through their destruction, and all of the use that occurs with them in between. An organization must issue digital identities securely to users by confirming their identities, setting them up for the proper usage, installing them on mobile devices, and troubleshooting any issues with them. Between the events of key creation and destruction, cryptographic keys may also be subject to reissue, suspension, revocation, and renewal. All of these processes require that the organization have a stable certificate management process installed, even before the introduction of mobile devices into the business environment. The organization may install digital identities on mobile devices to enable secure access of corporate e-mail and other sensitive resources. Because of the mobile nature of these devices and the possibility of device loss or theft, it's also very important for the organization to have the processes in place to suspend or revoke cryptographic keys quickly and their associated digital identities if needed.

Context-Aware Authentication

User names, passwords, certificates, and other authentication schemes require tremendous overhead to maintain these security frameworks. *Context-aware authentication* adds extra power to the authenticating tool that enables it to look at the context of the entity authentication. The context may include the user name, the MAC address of the device used to connect, what resources they are attempting to access, time of day, even their location. Context-aware authentication software can make authentication with mobile devices much easier and more secure.

Enforcement and Monitoring for Device Security

Now that we've talked about a few of the main security goals from a corporate perspective, let's talk about some of the methods for enforcement and monitoring of device-specific security measures that can help ensure the protection of sensitive data. Some of these measures are already included on the device and can be quite effective when used by themselves, and others are effective only when integrated into the corporate MDM infrastructure. All measures can protect the device and its data from unauthorized access and loss.

Rooting/Jailbreaking

Every mobile device comes from the factory with root access protected from the user. This is an important aspect of all mobile operating systems, as reserving root access enables the creator of the OS to update software, provide containerization, and impede a number of security vulnerabilities that giving root access would allow. When a user *roots* an Android system or *jailbreaks* an iOS system, they take root access. Any good MDM software can detect this during onboarding or during ongoing monitoring to let the organization know if this takes place.

One of the main reasons people root/jailbreak their mobile device is to install applications from third-party app stores that will not work as desired without root access (plenty of third-party apps run on non-rooted or non-jailbroken phones as well). Whether you root/jailbreak or not, third-party app stores are outside the control of Apple and Google and do not provide any security. Figure 9-23 shows one third-party store for Android apps, F-Droid.

Figure 9-23

F-Droid

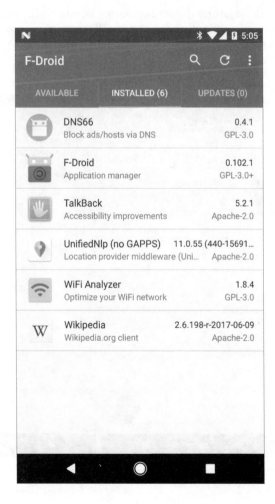

EXAM TIP The CompTIA Security+ 601 objectives use the older term, *application stores*, rather than *app stores*. Expect to see a question on *third-party application stores* on the exam. They mean app stores.

Sideloading

The standard Android installation file type is the APK file. Normally, APK files are downloaded automatically from Web stores and installed. However, it is possible to copy an APK file from a thumb drive, an SSD drive, or even across the network or Bluetooth and install the APK file without any interference from a Web store. This is called *sideloading* (Figure 9-24). Sideloading is risky because there are no safeties on the installation media. Aside from agreements with employees not to sideload, there's no foolproof current mechanism to enforce or monitor a prohibition.

Firmware

Every mobile device stores the core operating system on firmware. Like any firmware these days, you can update that firmware to install *custom firmware*. Normally, we only update firmware when the OS maker has carefully tested the update and then automatically

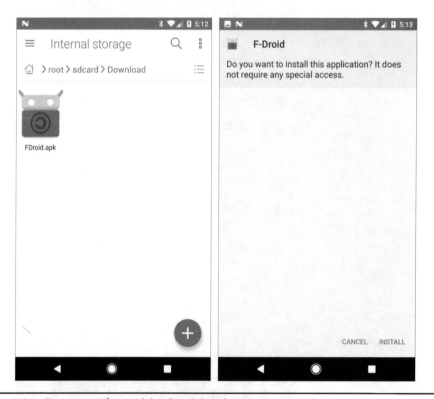

Figure 9-24 Two screens from sideloading F-Droid app

performs the update. Also, make sure the mobile device has plenty of charge and is connected via USB or Wi-Fi when you update firmware. You should disable the capability to update via cellular, called an *over-the-air (OTA) update* or *firmware OTA update*. This is usually a simple setting on the device or an MDM policy setting.

It's very common to install custom firmware—called ROM, for read-only memory—on an Android device, especially if it's an older phone that is no longer updated. These custom ROMs are handy but will void warranties and wreak havoc with any installed apps, and thus should never be installed unless there's a very specific reason.

Carrier Unlocking

A carrier may lock a phone so that the phone will only accept SIM chips from that carrier. With *carrier unlocking*, an unlocked phone can accept a SIM chip from any carrier. For years, unlocking was nearly impossible to accomplish, but today in most countries carriers are required by law to unlock a phone when requested. That's great for private users, but an organization may not want users to unlock their phones and perhaps install apps that break corporate security.

Texting/Voice Monitoring

Texting via *Short Message Service (SMS)*, *Multimedia Message Service (MMS)*, or *Rich Communication Services (RCS)* is ubiquitous for everyone who uses a smartphone, but an organization may want to monitor texting to ensure users aren't blowing through their plan limits. SMS sends essentially just text and doesn't require much overhead. MMS and RCS, on the other hand, can incorporate multimedia objects—audio and video recordings—within the text messages and thus use a lot more resources.

USB OTG

All smart devices connect directly or indirectly to USB. Normally, the device acts as a USB client, enabling a system to connect to a desktop, for example, to transfer a file. Almost all Android phones also have *USB On-The-Go (OTG)*. USB OTG–capable devices automatically turn into hosts when plugged into USB client devices like thumb drives or even mice. You can turn off USB OTG to prevent users from copying data off their system just by plugging in a thumb drive (Figure 9-25).

Wi-Fi Direct/Ad Hoc

In most cases, mobile devices use Wi-Fi by connecting to a WAP broadcasting an SSID, just like a portable computer. This is known as *infrastructure mode*; all the traffic goes through the WAP, even if your device communicates with another device on the same SSID. With *Wi-Fi Direct*, enabled devices can connect directly to each other if in range, much like Bluetooth devices can pair. There's generally a PIN code to share and the devices automatically negotiate to see which one will be the soft access point, or soft AP. Wi-Fi Direct is available on most Android devices and in Apple devices (branded as AirDrop and AirPlay).

Another traditional method for connecting wireless devices is *ad hoc mode*, where devices connect in a mesh network as a group of peers. There's no WAP involved.

Figure 9-25
USB OTG

 NOTE When you make direct connections among devices through Wi-Fi Direct or ad hoc mode, bypassing any centralized node, you effectively bypass any monitoring of the traffic among those devices.

Finally, *mobile ad hoc networks (MANETs)* are a form of wireless ad hoc mode used for on-the-fly communication. Every mobile device becomes a router, moving traffic to other stations nearby. You can find MANETs in use in many applications, such as mobile military communications, vehicular networks, and more, where there is need for connection that requires no radio or cellular tower. MANETs are just off the CompTIA radar for the current Security+ exam, but expect to interact with them a lot in an IT security career going forward.

Tethering/Mobile Hotspot

All mobile operating systems have the tethering feature. *Tethering* means to have a mobile device sharing its cellular connection with another system via USB. *Mobile hotspot* is the ability for a mobile device to share its cellular connection as a WAP via Wi-Fi. These are handy features, but they can be expensive to use and expose a system to bad actors. Turning off these features is a common security control.

Payment Methods

Digital wallet payment systems enable payment for goods and services via smartphone or other computing device without the need for physical transfers of money. As of this writing, there are several well-funded digital wallet offerings, including Android Pay, Apple Pay, and PayPal. If an organization authorizes a specific payment method, the organization should monitor usage of that service.

Screen Lock and Device Lockout

A *screen lock* enables a user to lock access manually to the device from anyone, unless the person inputs the correct passcode or PIN. While the screen lock is engaged, the device may have only very limited functions, including the ability to make an emergency phone call or advance tracks if some sort of media file is playing on the device. In any event, more advanced operations and data access are prevented while the screen lock is engaged.

In addition to being manually engaged by the user, screens can be configured to be locked after a certain amount of inactivity on the device—three minutes, for example. This prevents unauthorized access to the device if the user lays it down or someone grabs it while the user is still logged in.

Device lockout occurs when the device prevents someone from accessing it because the person has incorrectly entered the password or PIN too many times. If this is a valid user and he has simply forgotten his passcode, lockout features can take different actions. First, the user might simply be locked out of the device for a specified period of time, giving him enough time to contact the company and either obtain the correct passcode or have an administrator remotely unlock the device. Lockouts can also be more drastic, such as wiping the device after a certain number of incorrect passcode entries. More advanced features may include having a device remotely contact the administrator if it has been locked out.

Full Device Encryption

Full device encryption protects all the data on a mobile device. With this security feature, the storage device itself, such as the device's internal hard drive, is fully encrypted and can't be used unless it's decrypted when the device is powered up. In some cases, you could set full device encryption to require a passcode or passphrase on startup, before the user even logs on. In other cases, you could also make sure that the device storage can't be accessed periodically, even while it's on, without the user reauthenticating occasionally.

 NOTE Some FDE systems include remote wipe features. This gives IT security the capability to disable a lost or stolen mobile device, hopefully before any data is accessed or company resources are compromised.

GPS Services

All mobile devices have certain built-in technologies and functions to help determine their precise location and provide location-based services to the users. Most rely on or access the *Global Positioning System (GPS)*, the satellite-based system owned and operated by the US government.

In addition to typical user services, such as finding the nearest restaurant or gas station, location-based services using GPS can assist network administrators in managing mobile devices in the enterprise in several different ways. First, they can use GPS to help maintain an accurate location fix on the device. This might be necessary if the organization wants to ensure that devices are used only in certain areas or tracked by location. These same services can also be used to help the network administrator maintain a fix on the device if it gets lost or stolen.

Another use of GPS and location-based services is to ensure that the device remains on company property, a practice called *geofencing*. Geofencing ensures that a mobile device stays within a preset perimeter established by the administrator, using MDM software. If the device leaves the company property or gets beyond this perimeter, it will send an alert to the administrator. In addition to GPS, mobile devices can also use Wi-Fi networks to ascertain their location information, although this isn't as accurate.

External Media

Most mobile devices made today can accept different types of removable media, such as Secure Digital (SD) cards or their smaller counterparts, mini- and micro-SD cards. These *external media* cards are used to store additional data to help prevent using up all of the device's primary storage. In the enterprise, removable storage media can be used in different ways. First, through MDM policy, removable storage media could be used to store all of the user's personal data to keep it separate from corporate data. This way, when the device is returned to the network administrator, all she has to do is remove the SD card that contains the personal data. A business can also do the exact opposite and allow only corporate data to be stored on the removable media. That way, when the device leaves the company property, the removable media could be stored on site, reducing the risk of data loss when the device is out of the company's physical control. In either situation, data could be encrypted on the removable media, so that if it's removed from the device, it can't be accessed.

Disabling Unused Features

From your experience in securing user desktops in the organization, you probably already know that one of the best security practices you can use is to disable any unused features, services, ports, protocols, and so on, because doing so reduces the computer's attack surface. For example, if the user is only typing e-mails, surfing the Web, and so forth, he probably has no need for applications or services on the box that might allow him to perform administrative actions on the network. Likewise, the server running the company's Web page probably doesn't need to have e-mail services running on it. In any case, the same is true with mobile devices.

Depending largely on what the business's security policy states, users may not need to have certain services running on their mobile devices. They also may not need to use some of the native apps that come on some mobile devices, such as smartphones. This might include third-party or free e-mail programs, chat programs, games, and so on. Through MDM policy, as well as MAM, you can limit what applications and services a user can access and use on a mobile device. Of course, this may not make you very popular with the employees in the company, but it will go a long way toward helping to secure mobile devices that connect to your network.

Onboard Camera and Video Concerns

The use of onboard cameras and video is another interesting security issue in the corporate environment. Since almost all mobile devices have some sort of built-in camera or video recorder, this can be an issue in the corporate environment with regard to using the device in sensitive areas or processing sensitive corporate information on the device. It can also be a privacy issue, in that people have the right to choose whether to be photographed or filmed in certain settings. With smartphone video capabilities being fairly ubiquitous, many employees, especially in sensitive areas, would not want to find out, for example, that they are now the subject of a viral YouTube video! The company definitely would not want to discover that sensitive areas have been recorded. In some highly sensitive data processing areas, companies prohibit cameras of any type, meaning that smartphones, tablets, or other items the user might normally use to process company data on are excluded from the areas in question.

The use of cameras and video recorders of any type, including those on mobile devices, should be addressed in security policies to set rules on where and how they may be used, or even banning their use in certain areas and situations. The policy may simply require that they be turned off within the company property or certain secure areas, or it may prohibit mobile devices with cameras from being brought into certain areas at all. Policy may also further state that any employee taking unauthorized pictures or videos of any persons or areas may be subject to having their device confiscated and their video or pictures deleted from the device.

Audio Recordings

Mobile devices have *recording microphones* as well as video options, so enforcement and monitoring options must take these into consideration as well. A device in a pocket or pack can capture conversations that could do damage to an organization.

Questions

1. Which of the following are examples of embedded systems? (Choose two.)

   A. Arduino

   B. ASUS desktop

   C. Raspberry Pi

   D. Laser printer

2. Which of the following would be a benefit of a smart meter?

   A. Determine electrical usage over a month

   B. Alert in case of electrical spikes

   C. Enable the utility company to control electrical usage

   D. Can be used instead of a breaker in case of overusage

3. NFC uses _____ technology to transmit data.

   A. infrared

   B. laser

   C. radio

   D. sonic

4. Which of the following is an IoT-specific communication technology?

   A. 802.11

   B. Buc-ee's

   C. Ethernet

   D. Zigbee

5. Which of the following could be a security issue unique to embedded systems?

   A. Drive capacity

   B. Patching

   C. RAM upgrades

   D. Wattage requirements

6. MicroSD HSM works specifically with _____.

   A. Android

   B. iOS

   C. macOS

   D. Windows

7. Which of the following deployment models requires that employees provide their own smartphone?

   A. BYOD

   B. COBO

   C. CYOD

   D. COPE

8. The process of adding GPS information into a photograph is called _____.

   A. geoduck

   B. geolocation

   C. geotagging

   D. geotracing

9. The process of making your phone able to use any carrier's SIM card is called _____.

   A. blocking

   B. carrier unlocking

   C. rooting

   D. sideloading

10. What is the difference between tethering and a mobile hotspot?

   A. Tethering uses Bluetooth, while a mobile hotspot uses Wi-Fi.

   B. Tethering uses Wi-Fi, while a mobile hotspot uses Bluetooth.

   C. Tethering uses USB, while a mobile hotspot uses Wi-Fi.

   D. There is no difference.

Answers

1. A, C. Definitions for embedded systems vary, but for the CompTIA Security+ exam, go with Arduino and Raspberry Pi devices (along with FPGA).

2. B. Smart meters track electrical usage and can alert the consumer or utility company about any unusual spike in usage.

3. A. Near-field communication uses radio technology for close proximity data transmission.

4. D. Of the technologies (and retail giant) listed here, only Zigbee is uniquely for IoT devices.

5. B. It's vitally important to patch embedded systems to enhance security.

6. A. MicroSD hardware security modules work specifically with Android devices.

7. A. The bring your own device model enables or requires employees to provide their own mobile devices, such as smartphones, rather than use company-issued devices.

8. C. You can add GPS information to photos, videos, and more through the geotagging process.

9. B. Carrier unlocking (or just unlocking) enables a smartphone to use any carrier's SIM card.

10. C. Tethering connects a mobile device to a desktop via USB. A mobile hotspot enables network connectivity for other devices via Wi-Fi.

CHAPTER 10

Physical Security

*The third-person narrator, instead of being omniscient,
is like a constantly running surveillance tape.*

—Andrew Vachss

Your facilities require security. We've spent a lot of ink in this book discussing network security, but straight-up physical security also matters to security professionals. This chapter explores aspects of facility security in two modules:

- Physical Security Controls
- Environmental Controls

Let's get to them!

 NOTE CompTIA (inexplicably) included "screened subnet (previously known as demilitarized zone)" under *physical* security controls. You read about screened subnets way back in Chapter 6, where they fit nicely under network segmentation.)

Module 10-1: Physical Security Controls

This module covers the following CompTIA Security+ objective:

- **2.7 Explain the importance of physical security controls**

Perimeter security and physical security help protect data, systems, and networks and provide for personnel safety. As an information security professional, you need to know how perimeter controls and physical controls protect your systems and people. This module explores perimeter controls and physical controls from both the safety and protection standpoints. We'll start with passive systems, then look at alert systems, and finish up with manned defensive systems.

Passive Defensive Systems and Perimeter Controls

Passive defensive systems or *physical controls* regulate physical access to information systems and areas and protect the people who work in the facility housing the systems in those areas. Physical access controls help protect systems and people from threats such as theft, intruders, and unauthorized access. Physical controls have both security and safety considerations.

Perimeter controls surround a facility or a sensitive area to prevent unauthorized personnel from entering those areas. They also protect the authorized people who are allowed to enter those areas. Perimeter controls, the first line of defense at a facility, include gates, guards, and other physical security measures. Perimeter controls have both a security value and a safety value, and in the next few sections, we'll discuss both of those aspects.

Fencing

Fencing—a straight-up physical barrier—deters unwanted and unauthorized visitors (Figure 10-1). Fencing is often used at facilities that require higher security than a simple lock on the door. Fencing can intimidate trespassers or attackers, particularly tall fencing with barbed wire strung across the top. Fencing can cost a lot, but it serves several purposes.

First, fencing establishes specific entry and exit points around the facility. It establishes an area between outer entry points and inner entry points, creating a buffer zone to provide distance between the facility entrance and the public area. A well-lit buffer zone makes it more difficult for a trespasser or thief to get from the fence to the facility without being seen. Second, a fence can artificially create entry points in specific areas around the facility. In other words, someone can't simply walk up to the side of the building and try to enter through a window; they first must pass through a central entry gate to get in. When the fence is built, the entry gate can be placed wherever it makes sense for more easily controlled access; it doesn't necessarily have to be at the front door of the building.

Figure 10-1
Barrier fence at a secure facility (Image: Robert Brook, Getty Images)

Figure 10-2
A high-security
fence

When planning facility security, you should consider several characteristics of fencing. The first is height. Depending upon the desired security level, a short fence (about four feet high) might be okay to keep out the general public and curious trespassers. Higher fencing, possibly seven or eight feet high, can deter even very athletic and determined people. Barbed wire strung across the top of the fence provides a little extra incentive for people to decide that breaking into your facility is not worth the trouble. Fencing should be in good repair, not rusty, firmly in place in the ground to prevent someone from digging under it, and secured with concrete whenever possible.

Another consideration is the fence's wire gauge. The gauge of the wires that make chain-link fence, for example, is important to fence strength. Fences come in various wire gauges, but a good gauge for secure fencing is 11, 9, or 6 gauge. Six gauge is the thickest fencing wire and provides the strongest fence. Gauge size directly affects how easily an intruder may cut through the fence. Mesh size is also a characteristic to consider. Mesh size refers to the size of the holes between the wire mesh. Smaller mesh sizes are much better for security than larger mesh sizes, because the smaller holes make it more difficult to climb the fence. Figure 10-2 shows an example of a high-security fence.

Barricades

Barricades are physical security devices that can block unauthorized personnel from entering an area. Barricades are often used in the area surrounding a facility to keep vehicles from getting too close to a building, for example. They can also be used inside a facility to control the flow of people through secure areas.

Figure 10-3
Common
bollards

Barricades can be made out of various materials, including concrete and metal. They are usually constructed to delay a determined intruder long enough for security and other response personnel to neutralize any threats posed by the intruder. *Bollards*—concrete or metal posts—are examples of barricades that might be placed outside of a facility around drive-through areas, parking lots, and even sidewalks. Figure 10-3 shows an example of bollards. Bollards impede vehicular traffic but do not deter foot traffic.

Signage

Signage—words on plates of metal, wood, or plastic—helps deter unwanted visitors. *Signs* can warn intruders away from restricted areas and instruct authorized personnel to follow the proper security and safety procedures. Signs can direct personnel during an evacuation to the correct exit points, warn personnel about potential safety hazards in the facility, or help them find proper safety or fire suppression equipment. In short, the value of signs cannot be understated, because they may be required to help deter unauthorized activities or intruders but can also help protect the safety of the people who work in the facility. In some cases, signage throughout a facility may be required by laws or safety regulations to prevent the organization from being involved in liability issues.

Signs should follow national and international standards for symbols and colors, especially those that mark hazardous conditions. New employees should be briefed regarding the signs, as periodically all employees should be updated. Signs should be placed in well-lit areas and should not be obstructed by large objects. Figure 10-4 shows how a well-placed sign can help protect both personnel and equipment from unauthorized access and harm.

Lighting

Lighting is another critical aspect of perimeter security. During evening or dark hours, lighting can help ensure that trespassers, attackers, and thieves are deterred from venturing

Figure 10-4
Signage that
protects people
and equipment

out into open areas when trying to approach a facility or harm its personnel. Lighting can be placed at various points along the perimeter fence, at least at distances that allow the outer edges of the areas of light projected from poles to overlap with each other (usually no more than about 20 or 25 feet apart for tall poles, or about 8 to 10 feet apart for shorter ones). Lighting should also be placed at gates, at door entrances, along sidewalks, and in foyers or entryways. Emergency lighting should be in place throughout a facility in the event of a power outage (Figure 10-5).

Some lights may be controlled differently than others, depending upon their location and security needs. For example, fence perimeter lighting may be programmed with a timer to come on at certain hours only, such as from dusk till dawn. Such fencing is naturally lit by daylight during daytime hours, and fencing is usually placed in easy-to-see areas. Other types of lighting make use of motion sensors that turn lights on only when someone approaches an area. Still other types of lighting may be lit when an alarm or intrusion detection system (IDS) is triggered.

Figure 10-5
Emergency light
(Image: benoitb,
Getty Images)

Figure 10-6
Complex (for
its day) lock
(Image: Ozcan
MALKOCER,
Getty Images)

Locks

Locks are physical security controls that can help keep unauthorized persons from entering doorways, secure areas, and perimeters. Depending on where the locks are placed and what other security measures are in place, locks can be simple and inexpensive or very complex (Figure 10-6). Although most locks can keep casual intruders out, they really serve only to delay a determined intruder for a certain amount of time and rely on multiple other physical controls to assist in keeping an intruder out. *Delay factor* is sometimes a consideration in choosing a lock for a particular use.

Among the different *lock types* are physical (or mechanical) locks and electronic locks. Most *physical locks* use ordinary keys and can be purchased from a hardware store. Combination locks, which require a numerical combination or PIN code to unlock them, and locks built into the door or other type of entrance (such as a gate, vault, or safe) are also popular hardware locks. Each has advantages and disadvantages, depending on the level of security you require. Each also has different variations. Ordinary padlocks, referred to as *warded locks*, may appear to be strong, but they can easily be cut or picked (Figure 10-7).

NOTE Some physical locks, called *device locks*, are used to lock down items that are easily stolen, such as laptops. Some mobile devices have a special slot to facilitate this type of lock.

Figure 10-7
Broken padlock
(Image:
Tom Kelley /
Contributor,
Getty Images)

Figure 10-8
Electronic
lock (Image:
krisanapong
detraphiphat,
Getty Images)

Electronic locks are more sophisticated and may use various protection mechanisms. Usually, an electronic lock uses a PIN code and may be known as a *cipher lock*. Electronic locks usually have their mechanisms protected by metal containers or embedded into walls (Figure 10-8). They may be programmable, offering configurable options, such as the ability to program in separate PINs for different people, a lockout threshold for the number of incorrect PIN entries, a lockout delay, and so on. They also may be tied to other security measures, such as *smart cards* or *badges*—physical authentication devices—and *biometric* mechanisms—such as fingerprint readers.

Secure Areas

Buildings offer passive security features through the design of entry points, special secure rooms, and secure components. These include mantraps, vaults, protected cabling systems, and air gaps.

Access Control Vestibules (Mantraps) *Mantraps* guide and control individuals physically as they enter or exit a facility. A mantrap is a small room or compartment, with two doors that are individually locked, usually electronically. One individual at a time enters the mantrap, and the entry door is locked.

 EXAM TIP CompTIA uses the nonstandard term *access control vestibule* to refer to mantrap-designed rooms. Although the non-gendered term should be used, you're unlikely to hear it in common speech for many years. Be prepared for either term on the CompTIA Security+ exam.

A mantrap usually has some type of authentication station in the room, or even a one-way glass window so that a guard can observe the individual and confirm his or her identity, or ensure that the visitor doesn't possess any unauthorized weapons or items. (We'll talk more specifically about guards later in this module.) The individual may have to use biometrics or a smart card and PIN to authenticate themselves at the station. If the individual is properly authenticated, the exit doors open and allow the person to enter into the secure area.

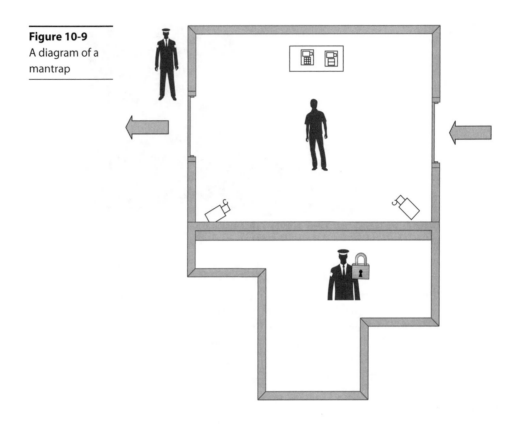

Figure 10-9
A diagram of a mantrap

If the individual is not authenticated, or the guard suspects an issue with the person, he or she can be detained in the mantrap until the proper authorities or security personnel can be summoned to help secure the person.

Mantraps are normally used in highly secure facilities, such as data centers, where positive authentication of personnel is of critical importance. Mantraps also are used to prevent tailgating, making it virtually impossible. Mantraps may also use additional security features, such as video cameras, body scanners, metal detectors, and even scales to compare weights when a person enters and exits a facility. This last measure might be employed to ensure that individuals are not stealing items from the facility on exit. Figure 10-9 shows a diagram of a mantrap.

Vaults and Safes   Some organizations have specially designed rooms or room components to house particularly important company possessions. A *vault* you've likely seen in every cops and robbers movie. A giant metal door with a super-complicated lock protects the contents of a thick-walled room (Figure 10-10). (That's where we store our gold bullion, by the way.) More commonly, most organizations have a designated safe, a smaller version of a vault for storing valuables, such as secure passwords and important papers (Figure 10-11).

Figure 10-10
Classic vault
(Image: Peter
Dazeley, Getty
Images)

Protected Cabling Distribution   Physical security also involves protecting equipment and systems, but it wouldn't be very effective if the cables that connected the systems were damaged or cut. The systems wouldn't be able to communicate, rendering them as ineffective as if someone had destroyed or damaged them.

Protecting physical cabling is as much about facility design as anything else. The facility should be designed so that physical cabling is run outside of normal traffic areas, through ducts in the walls or ceiling. The end connection points of the cabling should be physically protected from unauthorized access, by placing termination points such as switches in locked closets, and protecting end-user device connection points in offices and other rooms from unauthorized access.

In addition to physical security design, protecting cabling involves other possible measures, including using shielded cabling to prevent eavesdropping (or using fiber cable); configuring systems to send alarms when a connection is lost, possibly indicating a cut or damaged cable; and even using technical or logical controls that prevent unauthorized devices from connecting to end-user cable connection points, such as network outlets, by controlling port access.

Figure 10-11
A safe (Image:
imaginima, Getty
Images)

Air Gap   Passive security methods also include network design, such as providing physical separation between secure and nonsecure networks, an *air gap*. A highly secure facility, for example, would have interconnected internal systems to enable people to get work done, but have an Internet-connected system in a reception area for visitors to use. That system would in no way connect with any of the secure systems.

Active Alert Systems

Most organizations employ some form or forms of active alert systems to provide warning in case of attempted intrusion past the passive systems in place. These include many types of alarms to alert people in case of intrusion. Sensors enable detection.

Alarms

Physical *alarm systems* and *intrusion detection systems* are a must in any physical security program. Alarm systems can be loud and obnoxious, such as fire or tornado alarms, but they can also be silent alarms that sound or activate only at a guard station. Silent alarms alert security personnel without alerting an intruder that he or she has been discovered, giving security personnel time to reach and subdue the intruder. Alarm systems can be activated by any number of factors, including manually by personnel, by opening alarmed doors, and even by motion sensors in an area.

Motion Detection Sensors

Motion detection involves sensing the presence of a person in an area using different types of sensors. Motion detection sensors might use invisible light beams that are emitted from photoelectric sensors in a room; breaking the light beams would trigger the alarm. The beams could be lasers or infrared detection devices. Or the sensor could monitor environmental factors such as *temperature*, humidity *(moisture detection)*, and air pressure, so that an individual entering that area would change those factors and cause the temperature to rise a few degrees or the air pressure or flow to change slightly. These almost imperceptible changes to the environment might indicate unauthorized personnel in the area and trigger an alarm.

Yet another type of motion sensor uses plates in the floor that detect weights or pressure on the plates; individuals stepping on one of these plates would trigger an alarm. Keep in mind that motion sensors and some other advanced types of physical intrusion detection systems are typically used only in highly secure areas, although commercial- and private-grade motion sensors can be used in small businesses and homes.

Noise Detection Sensors

Noise detection sensors pick up unusual sound levels and are used in very specific security settings, such as hospitals. The systems are calibrated or baselined for a typical night, for example, and then can detect when an unusual noise happens. Staff can be alerted and sent to investigate. Noise detection sensors used to be more common as part of regular intrusion detection systems, but now fill very specialized niches.

Figure 10-12
A proximity
badge reader

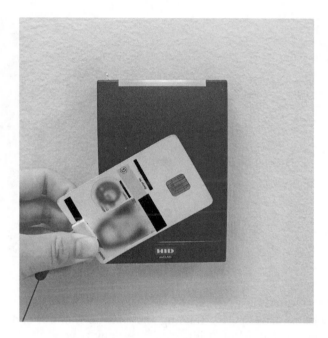

Proximity Readers

A *proximity reader* device is used to help authenticate personnel entering or exiting a facility. The person places a *smart card* or other access device near the sensor so it can be read via RFID or another passive wireless technology. The reader receives information from the card regarding the individual's identity. The individual may further authenticate by using a PIN or biometric method, such as a thumbprint scan, retinal scan, or voiceprint.

In addition to proximity readers, full-contact readers are also available for a facility to use. These readers require that a smart card or other device actually touch the reader or be swiped into the reader a certain way so that it can read a barcode or other type of coding on the card. Full-contact readers normally don't require any kind of passive wireless radio signals. For more efficient and economic use, the same smart cards used to authenticate people physically can also be used to authenticate individuals to information systems, enabling a sort of one-stop physical single sign-on capability. Figure 10-12 shows an example of a proximity badge reader.

Manned Defensive Systems

Once you have passive and active defensive systems and devices in place, the next line of defense brings in intelligent actors—traditionally people, but the times they are a-changing. The security personnel actively monitor many different types of devices, such as cameras, televisions, and drones. Let's look at the people first, then turn to the devices.

Figure 10-13
People are
important!
(Image:
fatihhoca, Getty
Images)

Security Guards

Security guards have specific training and skills to monitor and maintain facility security (Figure 10-13). Most facilities that have any type of physical security have guards, and despite all of the new advances in technologies that might one day eliminate them, human guards will likely be a cornerstone of facility security for years to come.

Guards in the *reception* area of a building manage people in real time. They can actively review people who step up to the entryway and, again, actively allow or deny access to the facility. They can and should log in and out every single visitor on a *visitor log*. A typical secure facility I teach in, for example, screens my entry into the parking area, then again into the vestibule/waiting room; requires surrender of my driver's license; and requires a sign-in with time stamp. I go through a scanner, as does my laptop bag and personal items. And an armed person escorts me to and from my classroom. That's standard procedure.

EXAM TIP Expect a question on the CompTIA Security+ exam that addresses *two-person integrity/control*. In a general sense, *two-person integrity (TPI)* simply means that you have two guards in the same space at all times, so one guard can't mess up (inadvertently or on purpose) without the other guard catching the problem. Specifically, TPI refers to the nuclear weapons controls in the United States; again, so one person can't make a catastrophic mistake. It's a failsafe mechanism.

Note that TPI in practice is often used in communication rooms, classified material handling, and other places. It's not just about human guards.

Guards offer several advantages over electronic physical controls. First, guards are human beings and can make the split-second decisions that are sometimes needed in fast-moving security, safety, or emergency events. Second, a well-trained guard force can provide vast, intelligent coverage of all physical security areas within a facility. If guards have solid, comprehensive security procedures they execute on a timely basis, they can help eliminate the huge majority of physical security problems. Guards are required to be conscientious, observant, well-trained, and even a little bit suspicious and paranoid to do their jobs well.

The disadvantages of using guards don't outweigh the advantages, but you should understand them all the same. First, guards require resources, such as specialized equipment, training, and even monetary resources (whether contracted out or as part of the organization's own internal security force). Maintaining a guard force can be quite expensive and has challenges that are typical to maintaining human resources, such as pay, benefits, disciplinary problems, promotions, and so forth.

Guards are human beings, like any other employee, and some have the same weaknesses that any other employee would have, regardless of specialized security training. Human beings miss things sometimes, they aren't always as observant as they should be, and sometimes they fail to follow security procedures properly. They can also be subject to social engineering attacks (discussed in a later module).

All-in-all, however, guards provide an effective set of security controls that are considered deterrent, preventive, detective, corrective, compensating, and recovery, all at the same time. They can also be assisted by other types of physical security controls, including alarms, surveillance devices, and intrusion detection systems.

Robot Sentries

The increasingly sophisticated artificial intelligence features of computer systems combined with brilliantly engineered mechanical systems will usher in the use of *robot sentries* (Figure 10-14) perhaps by the time you're reading these words. The *Internet of Things (IoT)* wireless connectivity and the amazing advances in super-tiny *system on a chip (SoC)* computing mean the era of human-only guards is done. While the first devices

Figure 10-14 The robot sentries probably won't be surfing on a smartphone . . . . (Image: Donald Iain Smith, Getty Images)

(announced by companies like Switch) look more like traffic cones with wheels than *Terminator*-style humanoids, look for increasing integration of human and robotic guards and sentries in the near future.

Video Surveillance and CCTVs

Closed-circuit television systems (CCTVs) can be placed throughout a facility. CCTVs use cameras to record surveillance video and transmit it to a central monitoring station, which enables guards to extend their view of the facility (Figure 10-15).

CCTV systems detect and watch intruders in areas where guards can't be all the time. Some considerations with CCTV devices include whether the device will be used indoors or outdoors. Outdoor environmental factors such as temperature, wind, rain, and so on can affect how well certain CCTV devices work. The size of the area under CCTV surveillance is also a consideration, in that the field of view (how large an area the camera can "see") for different CCTVs varies. The amount of light in an area is also a consideration when you install CCTVs in an area, since more light provides a better picture of the area. Some CCTVs are specifically designed for use in poorly lit or dark areas.

 EXAM TIP Hiding or obscuring CCTV cameras helps enhance the security of a network. This *industrial camouflage* potentially causes attackers to miss the fact that cameras are rolling, thus minimizing the attackers' ability to avoid visual or auditory capture.

CCTV systems should be integrated with other physical security systems, such as alarms, motion detectors, and so on, and should be directly integrated with the central

Figure 10-15
Monitoring the camera feeds (Image: Monty Rakusen, Getty Images)

monitoring console used by physical security personnel. They should also enable security professionals to view areas in real time and record events to media for later review. Recording systems should automatically kick in with *motion recognition* hardware detecting movement, thus capturing anything larger than a squirrel that enters a camera's field of view. CCTVs should also date and time stamp those recordings so that a realistic time frame of events can be reconstructed if needed.

 EXAM TIP Speaking of squirrels . . . some security camera software employs *object detection* algorithms, meaning the software can provide an alert when detecting something out of the ordinary. The movement of a squirrel or bird wouldn't trigger anything, for example, but an unauthorized drone would. You might get a question on the CompTIA Security+ exam on object detection. Don't miss it!

There is some speculation as to which is better—a human guard or a video surveillance system. Human guards can make quick decisions and perform a wide variety of security functions, but they can't be everywhere at once and they can miss things. Additionally, a guard's memory may or may not be reliable when trying to determine exactly what happened during an incident. Video surveillance systems, on the other hand, can be placed wherever you need them, can provide real-time surveillance of areas, and can record video for later playback and review.

Any speculation over which to use isn't really worthwhile, though; a good layered physical security system should use both guards and video surveillance systems to provide comprehensive coverage of a facility. Video surveillance systems can be used to extend the eyes and ears of guards into places where they can't be all the time. Guards can quickly be dispatched to any areas that video surveillance picks up any potential security issues and can effectively mitigate those issues. Guards and video surveillance systems complement each other and should be used together. Facilities security managers shouldn't need to make the choice between guards or video surveillance because of budget or resource restrictions; they should simply use both.

Drones

Small, remotely controlled flying surveillance vehicles—*drones*—form increasingly useful tools for security professionals to patrol areas (Figure 10-16). Drones offer the benefits of mobility and quiet operation, ~~plus pinpoint accuracy with remote laser targeting systems. . .~~ err . . . . Actively monitoring security personnel can spot threats and contact the appropriate authorities.

Modern drones feature excellent surveillance features, from high-definition cameras (4K is common today) to superb processing power and battery life. Drones provide low-cost perimeter patrols, access to difficult-to-reach areas, and much more. Drones can both record video and send that data back to their control center in real time. The unmanned aerial vehicle (UAV) market and usefulness will just keep going up as technology improves and prices decrease.

Figure 10-16 Unmanned aerial vehicle (UAV), a.k.a. a drone

Module 10-2: Environmental Controls

This module covers the following CompTIA Security+ objective:

- **2.7 Explain the importance of physical security controls**

As a security professional, the environment that your systems are housed in affects their security in at least one very important way: availability. Remember in the introduction to the book where we discussed the CIA triad, which consists of confidentiality, integrity, and availability? *Availability* is one of the key concerns for security professionals, and both environmental security and physical security directly affect system availability for your users.

This module explores modifying and managing interference, fire suppression, HVAC controls (including temperature and humidity), hot and cold aisles, and environmental monitoring. You need to know how these things affect the availability of systems, both for the CompTIA Security+ exam and, more importantly, as an IT security professional.

EMI and RFI Shielding

Electromagnetic interference (EMI) and *radio-frequency interference (RFI)* are two types of electrical interference that can cause issues with the electrical power that flows into your systems. Either can result from power entering your facility or supplying your systems that is not considered "clean" power. In other words, it's incoming power that has electrical interference and voltage fluctuations (sometimes referred to as *line noise*). These two types of interference can cause issues with power that could affect your systems, causing them occasionally to freeze, reboot arbitrarily, or do other weird things.

All kinds of sources can create EMI, including lightning, electrical motors or generators, and even fluorescent lighting installed too close to power or data cables.

Figure 10-17
Shielded
Ethernet cable

An organization that plans to move into a new or renovated building can address some of these issues in advance with good facility design, but you don't always get that luxury if you've moved into an existing facility that has these problems. And even if you can spend a lot of money, you can't always tear apart walls or ceilings and rip out and rerun cabling, any more than you can control the type of power the power company supplies to your facility. You have some options, however, to help prevent and minimize EMI.

First, use specially shielded Ethernet cable (Figure 10-17) that can prevent outside interference from causing line noise. This type of cable reduces the amount of EMI in both data and power cabling. It can allow cleaner data transmissions, as well as cleaner power, to get to your systems. (Or, better still, use fiber-optic cable in place of copper. Optical signals laugh at EMI.)

Second, use power conditioners, uninterruptible power supplies (UPSs), and other devices that clean up power before it gets to your systems, ensuring consistent and constant clean power delivered to your computer equipment. These special devices are also known as *voltage regulators* or *line conditioners*. Most modern data centers have this type of equipment, as well as robust power cabling and construction, so that they can deliver clean power to equipment.

EXAM TIP   Better data centers offer *Faraday cages* for sensitive equipment, which are devices that prevent RFI or EMI from damaging contents stored. Faraday cages are named for the English scientist—Michael Faraday—who created the design way back in the 19th century.

Fire Suppression

Fire is a serious issue that can affect the safety of personnel as well as that of equipment and facilities. To protect against fires, you first should know how to prevent them, then how to detect them, and finally how to suppress them when they do occur. Prevention is your best insurance policy against fire damage; make sure that the workspace is free of combustible materials and that all hazards that could cause a fire are minimized as much as possible. Prevention also means educating people on the different causes of fires and how *they* can help prevent them.

Absent prevention, detecting a fire is also important. Quick detection means that you can save lives and prevent damage to facilities and equipment. Detection methods

Figure 10-18
Smoke detector
installation
(Image: JGI, Getty
Images)

include heat, smoke, light, and gas detection. Simple smoke detectors (Figure 10-18) located throughout the facility will help, but you also may need more advanced detection systems in large operations or data centers.

Some detectors are smoke activated, others are heat activated. You also may need to install temperature sensors throughout areas that are hard to see or reach, where there may be a lot of equipment that heats up easily, or where there are major power outlets or connections. Photoelectric devices detect changes in light intensity, so they can detect smoke or intense light from flames. Other types of fire detection equipment include devices that can detect hazardous fumes or gases that may result from fires burning plastics and other noxious materials.

There are four basic classes of fire, and each has its own preferred method of suppression. (See the upcoming Table 10-1.) Because fire reacts differently to different materials, there are some suppression methods you would not want to use with certain fires. For example, you would not want to spray water on an electrical fire because of electrical shock hazards. You also would not want to spray water on a flammable liquid fire, because it can cause a fire to spread uncontrollably.

Although some data centers have sprinkler or sophisticated water suppression systems (wet and dry pipe, and deluge systems) to put out large fires, water can pose several disadvantages. First, as mentioned in the case with electrical fires or flammable liquids, this can actually cause the fire to be worse or can cause other hazards. Second, even if water

Figure 10-19
Fire? I've got
this! (Image:
John M Lund
Photography Inc,
Getty Images)

can put out the fire, it's likely going to damage electrical equipment, furniture, and facilities, especially if it's a large amount of water dumped onto a huge fire.

Most modern data centers these days have foam fire suppression systems, such as FM-200 or another approved chemical foam. This type of system not only is very effective for putting out large fires but is also typically safe for humans and equipment. It may be a real pain to clean up the mess afterward, though! Fortunately, if the fire is caught early enough, it can be extinguished with ordinary handheld fire extinguishers that should be located throughout the facility (by law). See Figure 10-19.

It's best to use the type of fire extinguishers that are appropriate for the type of fire you have. Table 10-1 lists the different classes of fires, their characteristics, and the different materials that are in the appropriate fire extinguishers for those types.

NOTE For those of you who are CompTIA A+ or Network+ certified: Do these fire extinguisher examples sound familiar? They should, because they are on all three exams.

Class	Type	Contains
A	Combustibles (wood, paper)	Foam, water
B	Liquids (gasoline, oil)	CO_2, foam, powder
C	Electrical (electronic equipment)	CO_2
D	Combustible metals (sodium, magnesium)	Powder

Table 10-1 Types of Fires and Appropriate Fire Extinguishers

HVAC

Heating, ventilation, and air conditioning (HVAC) systems ensure that the environments that humans work in, and that equipment functions in, are kept comfortable, at the right temperature and well ventilated, and that the air quality in them is at a consistently good level. These systems are an important part of any business, to be sure, but they are that much more important in an operations or data center that has a lot of hot equipment and requires controlled temperature and humidity levels. Most large data centers may even have their own dedicated HVAC systems that are separate from the rest of the facility, since computing equipment tends to draw a lot of power and requires very sensitive, specialized equipment to keep it within an acceptable range. Most HVAC controls are automated and can be controlled from a centralized facility, such as a physical plant or operator console.

Temperature and Humidity Controls

As part of the HVAC system within a facility, temperature and humidity controls are of critical importance in a data center (Figure 10-20). Most people find that data centers are cooler than they find comfortable, so it's not unusual to see people dressed in sweaters or light jackets inside of a data center, even on a hot August day in Alabama or Texas. This is because equipment tends to heat up a great deal during its normal operation, and when you have a great deal of equipment crammed into what may be a small room, the temperature can rapidly increase. To that end, temperature controls are designed to keep room temperatures cool. In addition to breaking down and simply not operating properly, overheated equipment can also be permanently damaged and can occasionally start fires.

Humidity, the amount of moisture in the air, is also an issue in data centers, regardless of the season. If the weather or climate is dry, the air contains less moisture, and this can

Figure 10-20
HVAC unit
(Image: Mikael
Vaisanen, Getty
Images)

cause a lot of static electricity. Static electricity in a data center is a bad thing, because if two components touch, or if a person touches a piece of sensitive electronic equipment, static electricity can damage that equipment. On the other hand, in high humidity areas or seasons, there's more moisture in the air, which can adversely affect electrical equipment. Moisture can cause condensation, which means that water can drip into electrical components, damaging them or causing them to short out and possibly start a fire. Either way, too much humidity or not enough humidity is a bad thing for computing equipment.

A device that monitors humidity in a data center is called a *hygrometer* or, if it can measure both temperature and humidity at the same time, a *hygrothermograph*. Like automated temperature controls and other HVAC equipment, these devices can be centrally monitored through a remote console and alert operators whenever the temperature or humidity changes from certain levels. HVAC controls can be automatically or remotely adjusted based upon information received from these monitors.

EXAM TIP You do *not* need to know the terms *hygrometer* or *hygrothermograph* for any CompTIA exam!

Hot and Cold Aisles

The concept of *hot and cold aisles* relates to designing the layout of data centers intelligently and efficiently. In this type of setup, aisles of equipment racks are set up such that there are alternating hot and cold aisles, enabling cooler air to be blown into equipment as hotter air is pulled away from them. This involves not only arranging equipment in certain ways by aisle (usually with the different pieces of equipment in the different aisles facing each other) but also using ventilation and air ducts appropriately within these hot and cold aisles, both in the floors and ceiling. Figure 10-21 illustrates how hot and cold aisles work.

Figure 10-21
An example of hot and cold aisles

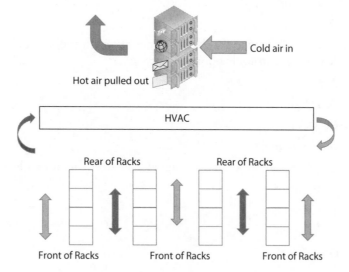

Environmental Monitoring

Even if all of the controls we've discussed so far in this module are installed and working, monitoring the environmental controls is still very important, because things can occasionally happen—equipment can break, power cabling can go bad, HVAC systems can fail, humans can fiddle with temperature and humidity controls, and so on. *Environmental monitoring* ensures that systems maintain a constant state of ideal temperature, humidity, and power. Environmental monitoring is also used to detect smoke and heat that would indicate the early stages of a fire, and it is a very effective preventive control in this aspect.

Environmental monitoring can be part of your network facility monitoring systems; you can place environmental sensors throughout a facility that automatically report their status to operator consoles on the same systems that help you monitor other aspects of the network, such as device status, throughput, bandwidth, network traffic, and so on.

Questions

1. What kind of device impedes vehicle intrusion but does not inhibit foot traffic?

   A. Bollard

   B. Camera

   C. CCTV

   D. Fencing

2. What kind of device directs people away from secure systems and warns against dangerous areas?

   A. Alarms

   B. CCTV

   C. Fencing

   D. Signage

3. All of the following are characteristics of fencing you should consider when deploying it around your facility, *except*:

   A. Gauge

   B. Height

   C. Mesh

   D. Fire rating

4. Which type of lock relies on human characteristics for authentication?

   A. Biometric

   B. Cybernetic

   C. Electronic

   D. Physical

5. Joan wants to install a physical intrusion detection system around her building that would send an alert if someone jumped the fence. What should she install?

A. Drone

B. Moisture detection

C. Motion detection

D. Object detection

6. Jose wants to enhance the overall effectiveness of the camera network employed on the perimeter of his building. What should he do to reduce the possibility that attackers can avoid or bypass his devices?

A. Add signage that misdirects the attackers.

B. Increase the number of CCTV devices.

C. Add motion detection sensors.

D. Use industrial camouflage.

7. Edwin wants to secure access to a building on his campus that houses an HVAC system. Which solution would cost the *least* while still providing security?

A. Biometric door lock

B. Electronic door lock

C. Physical door lock

D. Motion detection CCTV system

8. What device would protect sensitive devices from RFI or EMI?

A. Air gap

B. Faraday cage

C. UPS

D. Vault

9. Your manager wants you to make sure that enough fire extinguishers are available in the data center to take care of possible electrical fires. Which class of fire extinguishers should be used in the data center?

A. Class A

B. Class B

C. Class C

D. Class D

10. Heating, ventilation, and air conditioning (HVAC) systems control all of the following environmental factors in a data center, *except*:

    A. Power

    B. Temperature

    C. Humidity

    D. Air filtration

Answers

1. **A.** A bollard—more than one, of course—prevents vehicles from getting too close to buildings. Unlike fencing, though, people can walk on by.

2. **D.** You can make an argument that fencing helps people make appropriate decisions, but the better answer here is signage. Signage can caution, warn, and inform people.

3. **D.** Fire rating is not a consideration when deploying fencing, since fences are not designed to prevent or suppress the spread of fires.

4. **A.** Biometric locks key on—pun intended— characteristics of humans, such as fingerprints or retinal scans.

5. **C.** Motion detection sensors will pick up unauthorized fence jumpers more quickly and easily than the other device or sensor types listed here.

6. **D.** Use industrial camouflage to hide or obscure the cameras so attackers don't know their evil deeds are being recorded.

7. **C.** Of these options, a simple physical lock is the least expensive solution.

8. **B.** A Faraday cage offers crazy levels of protection from RFI, EMI, and EMP. A thick enough vault might do the trick too, but it's not the best answer here.

9. **C.** Class C fire extinguishers are the appropriate type used in electrical fires.

10. **A.** Power is not controlled by HVAC systems.

CHAPTER 11

Secure Protocols and Applications

Knowing is not enough; we must apply. Willing is not enough; we must do.

—Johann Wolfgang von Goethe

To get two hosts to communicate securely requires addressing numerous factors. What authentication should they use? What encryption? How do they initiate the secure communication? How is it terminated? What happens if something doesn't work as expected?

Any competent programmer can write her own secure methods to deal with these questions, but that's a silly waste of time. Implementing secure, standardized, well-tested, and well-known protocols is a quick and easy solution to address all of these questions.

Secure protocols give huge benefits. First, with a standardized secure protocol, programmers may write code that's guaranteed to work with other systems using the same protocol. Second, a secure protocol is well-tested by thousands of third parties, giving everyone involved with that protocol confidence in its security. Third, a well-known protocol is constantly under review and being improved, ensuring that the protocol continues to stay secure.

The applications that use secure protocols as well as the development process to create those applications present huge security issues. Applications (and in this case we're talking mainly about Web applications) are subject to the majority of the well-known attacks you can read about in the news. To that end this chapter takes a dive into the types of attacks sustained by Web applications and closes with the processes used by developers to best ensure their applications are secure.

This chapter explores secure protocols and applications in five modules:

- Secure Internet Protocols
- Secure Web and E-mail
- Web Application Attacks
- Application Security
- Certificates in Security

Module 11-1: Secure Internet Protocols

This module covers the following CompTIA Security+ objectives:

- **1.4   Given a scenario, analyze potential indicators associated with network attacks**
- **1.6   Explain the security concerns associated with various types of vulnerabilities**
- **3.1   Given a scenario, implement secure protocols**
- **3.3   Given a scenario, implement secure network designs**

The Fathers of the Internet (any *The IT Crowd* fans out there?) never designed the TCP/IP stack for security. No one thought to add security to the TCP or UDP applications that ran on the Internet. Why should they? Back then most people assumed the Internet would never get beyond a few thousand computers and no one thought that the Internet would one day be a platform for e-commerce or contain personal or private information. Over time security was added, but almost every application initially came out with a completely non-secure version, requiring a later redesign to add security.

 EXAM TIP   One of the most common TCP/IP protocols, DHCP, appears only obliquely on the secure protocols list on the exam. Cisco implements a feature in IOS called *DHCP Secured IP Address Assignment*. This combats DHCP spoofing attacks and its best use case is in *network address allocation* attack scenarios. You first ran into these types of attacks way back in Chapter 5, on ARP spoofing.

DHCP is the most common way to allocate network addresses to clients. Securing DHCP thus helps protect networks. You won't be tested on the specific IOS feature mentioned here, but should know that such tools exist.

The problem is that all of these non-secure protocols still work perfectly, albeit not securely. You can install them, but the inherent weak configurations of such—CompTIA calls them *unsecure protocols*—open your network to attack. Security professionals must recognize situations where they need to replace non-secure protocols with their secure equivalents.

This module tours six secure versions of Internet applications that initially came out as non-secure:

- DNSSEC
- SNMP
- SSH
- FTPS
- SFTP
- SRTP

The CompTIA Security+ exam doesn't expect you to have expertise in these secure protocols, but it does expect you to have a basic understanding of them, their general use, their port numbers, and situations where they are appropriate.

 EXAM TIP One of the non-secure protocols without a secure counterpoint is the Network Time Protocol (NTP). NTP *doesn't* appear in the CompTIA Security+ exam objectives directly, but it certainly does indirectly. A use-case scenario where NTP is relevant is in *time synchronization*. In an attack or accident that causes NTP to fail or hiccup so that time in a network is out of sync, the most common result is that users can't log into the network.

DNS Security

The *Domain Name System (DNS)* resolves Internet names to IP addresses. So, for example, when you type in www.google.com, DNS resolves the Internet name to the IP address that your computer and other networking devices along the way need to connect you to that site. DNS consists of clients (hosts that need to get name resolution services) and servers (used to provide name translation services).

Without going too far back into CompTIA Network+ territory, remember that DNS uses *authoritative* servers that host DNS *zones*, which are the domain namespaces of the organization and its subdomains and hosts. Authoritative servers for a DNS domain can be primary or secondary servers. Primary servers host the writable copy of the zone file and replicate it to the secondary servers. A *zone file* is a mapping of host names to IP addresses and is used to make the name-to-IP address translation.

 NOTE The *hosts* file on every personal computer can hard-code DNS information. Messing around with the file, as you'll recall from CompTIA Network+, enables great pranks on children and coworkers, but a malicious actor with access to a hosts file can do some damage.

Hosts make DNS queries to servers, and responses can come from authoritative servers or caching servers. Caching servers retain in their own memory caches the name resolution responses they have received to queries they have previously made to other DNS servers. Caching servers may not necessarily host DNS zones of their own; they may merely make requests on behalf of hosts and cache the responses they receive for future requests. DNS as a protocol uses TCP port 53, as well as UDP port 53, and is an Application layer protocol. TCP is used for zone transfers between primary and secondary servers, while UDP is used for queries and responses between hosts and servers.

 EXAM TIP Watch for use cases on the exam where DNS servers are under attack. DNSSEC eliminates almost all forms of direct attacks on DNS servers.

DNS cache poisoning is the most common attack against DNS servers. If an attacker can target a DNS server to query an evil DNS server instead of the correct one, the evil

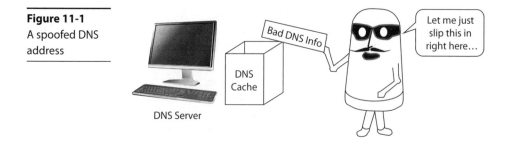

Figure 11-1
A spoofed DNS
address

server can in turn tell the target DNS server spoofed DNS information (Figure 11-1). The DNS server will cache that spoofed information, spreading it to hosts and possibly other DNS servers.

 EXAM TIP The CompTIA Security+ exam objectives refer to DNS cache poisoning as simply *DNS poisoning*. Expect to see the shortened term on the exam.

To prevent cache poisoning and implement secure network designs for DNS, the typical use-case scenario is to switch to *Domain Name System Security Extensions (DNS-SEC)* for *domain name resolution* (resolving domain names to IP addresses). DNSSEC takes advantage of DNS's tree-like structure to digitally sign every zone file for (eventually) every domain in the DNS hierarchy. The DNS root as well as all top-level domains (.COM, .EDU, etc.) and hundreds of thousands of other DNS servers now use DNSSEC.

 EXAM TIP DNSSEC uses port 53 just like regular DNS.

DNSSEC implements additional resource record types to DNS. Resource record signature (RRSIG) types, for example, hold the DNSSEC signature for a specific record, which DNS resolvers can use to verify a public key, stored in a DNSKEY record. A next secure record (NSEC) enables DNS resolvers to check the next record name in a zone. A next secure record version 3 (NSEC3) enables DNS resolvers to verify hash values stored, thus showing record names that don't exist as records.

SNMP

Simple Network Management Protocol, version 3 (SNMPv3), mentioned back in Chapter 4, is the basis for many network management tools. SNMP uses *SNMP agents*, installed by default on most network devices, that respond to queries (*gets*) from SNMP manager programs. Agents can also be configured to send *traps*, asynchronous communication from agents to managers (Figure 11-2).

SNMPv1 and SNMPv2 lacked any form of security beyond a password transmitted in the clear. Anyone who could intercept the conversation between agent and managers

Figure 11-2
SNMP gets and
traps

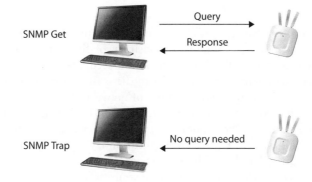

could read critical data information. SNMPv3 is identical to SNMPv2 but adds robust and flexible encryption. The modern use-case scenario for securely monitoring *routing and switching* is to use SNMPv3.

 EXAM TIP All versions of SNMP use UDP ports 161 and 162.

SNMPv3 support is very common on all enterprise network devices. In any use case where you want direct monitoring of routers, switches, wireless access points, or individual computers, SNMPv3 is the protocol you need.

SSH

Telnet enables connection with a remote system wherein you can send commands, an essential tool since the beginning of the Internet. One of the most important goals of the Internet was to create a remote terminal connection to far-flung systems. Unfortunately, Telnet has no security other than a simple user name and password transmitted in the clear. A series of attacks on networks in the late 1980s and early 1990s—not only on Telnet but equally on unsecured FTP sites (see "FTP," next)—showed the need for secure protocols.

The *Secure Shell (SSH)* protocol was invented as a direct replacement for Telnet and other non-secure remote terminal programs. Plus, in a bit of foresight that over time has proven to be utterly amazing, SSH was designed to run in a tunneling mode, enabling any other application to run within an encrypted SSH tunnel. When connecting to a remote site that you want to access like a local site, use SSH rather than Telnet. That's the best use-case scenario for *secure remote access*.

 EXAM TIP SSH uses TCP port 22.

FTP

The *File Transfer Protocol (FTP)* enables users to upload and download files to and from an FTP server, which contains a repository of files set up by an organization for its users or customers. FTP is inherently a non-secure protocol, simply because it does not encrypt any data sent or received. All traffic is unencrypted, so it is subject to interception by a malicious entity with the use of network sniffers. FTP has no built-in security mechanisms; it does have a form of weak authentication that can be used, but again, even the authentication traffic is not encrypted or otherwise protected, so credentials are subject to sniffing as well. FTP is an Application layer protocol and uses two TCP ports to function, ports 20 and 21. These ports are for data and control commands, respectively.

Modern systems require much more security, so a typical use case scenario involving file transfer means substituting FTP for one of its more secure relatives. These protocols are FTPS and SFTP.

FTPS

File Transfer Protocol, Secure (FTPS) is a secure version of FTP that can be used over a Secure Sockets Layer (SSL) or Transport Layer Security (TLS) secure session connection. (See the "SSL" and "TLS" sections in Module 11-2 for details on the protocols.) Adding SSL or TLS enables users to perform FTP file transfers securely, using built-in encryption and authentication mechanisms (usually involving public and private keys). Unlike other applications that use SSL or TLS, FTPS uses TCP port 990.

SFTP

Applications that use *SSH File Transfer Protocol (SFTP)* encrypt an FTP session via an SSH tunnel. More common than FTPS, SFTP (also known as SSH-FTP) uses SSH, so it protects data through encryption and authentication services. It functions similarly to normal FTP, but all data is encrypted through an SSH tunnel running on port 22, so it can't be easily intercepted or read.

SFTP is *not* the same thing as regular FTP or FTPS, so don't confuse them. SFTP does not use SSL or TLS at all. Additionally, there is yet another way you could use SSH: like other non-secure protocols, such as Telnet and HTTP, you could send regular non-secure FTP through an SSH tunnel. Note that when used in this manner, it is not the same thing as SFTP.

Confused yet? Table 11-1 helps to clarify it for you by breaking down the different file copy and transfer protocols.

Protocol	Security Method	Notes
FTP	None	Ordinary file transfer with no security built in. Uses TCP ports 20 and 21.
FTPS	FTP over SSL	Uses SSL's built-in encryption and authentication methods. Uses TCP port 990.
SFTP	Secure file transfer utility included in SSH suite	Ideal for transferring files on a more permanent basis. Uses SSH and TCP port 22.

Table 11-1   Various Ways to Copy and Transfer Files Securely and Non-securely

SRTP

Real-time Transport Protocol (RTP) is a critical component of almost every form of telephony over IP, such as Voice over IP (VoIP). Like so many protocols before it, RTP has no real security, making interception of voice calls easy and forcing many VoIP application vendors (Skype is a great example) to create their own proprietary encryptions.

Unlike the time frame between so many unsecure protocols and their secure versions, just a few years later the industry adopted *Secure Real-time Transport Protocol (SRTP)*, an extension to RTP that uses the same port as RTP (by default UDP 5004, although this is easily and often changed). SRTP adds a few headers to support encryption and message integrity.

The massive growth of video and audio across the Internet and the need to secure them creates a number of use cases where existing *voice and video* solutions using RTP need to switch to SRTP. While the exact switching method varies from solution to solution, in many cases little more than a patch and a few updates are all that's needed to make non-secure voice and video well secured.

Module 11-2: Secure Web and E-mail

This module covers the following CompTIA Security+ objectives:

- **1.4   Given a scenario, analyze potential indicators associated with network attacks**
- **3.1   Given a scenario, implement secure protocols**

Web applications have displaced many of the more traditional TCP/IP applications. In the past if you wanted to transfer a file to another person, for example, you would probably use FTP. FTP is still popular, but for many file transfer scenarios, cloud-storage Web apps such as Google Drive, iCloud, or Dropbox are very popular.

E-mail, perhaps the most traditional of traditional TCP/IP applications, has spent the last few years moving from non-secure to highly secure in response to attacks. While most users no longer use e-mail applications for e-mail (instead using Gmail, Yahoo!, or other Web-based e-mail services), the protocols unique to e-mail continue to soldier on in far more secure ways than in years before.

There's no doubt the predominance of the Web motivates the industry to ensure good security for HTTP. There are also plenty of powerful protocols to secure e-mail from prying eyes. This module looks at the protocols used to secure both Web and e-mail applications. It examines in more detail terms bandied about since almost the beginning of this book, such as TLS, to clarify how these secure protocols help keep Web pages, Web apps, and e-mail secure.

HTTP

The *Hypertext Transfer Protocol (HTTP)* enables users to access Web resources on the Internet. Hosts can use HTTP requests to send and receive Hypertext Markup Language (HTML) documents as well as other Internet content from Web applications.

HTTP is not a secure protocol by itself. All content sent over an HTTP request and response is unencrypted—that is, it is sent in plaintext, which can be easily intercepted and read by anyone, including malicious hackers. Sending sensitive data over ordinary HTTP can be very non-secure. One solution to this issue was developed by sending HTTP traffic over more secure protocols, in particular TLS (see the upcoming "TLS" section).

HTTPS

Hypertext Transfer Protocol over SSL/TLS (HTTPS) sends normal HTTP traffic over an encrypted SSL or TLS connection. SSL and TLS can be used to send almost any protocol, though, providing security services for that traffic. A typical use-case scenario for substituting HTTPS for HTTP is when a client wants a Web store that can handle secure monetary transactions. HTTPS is essential for e-commerce. Another use-case scenario is with *subscription services*, such as Microsoft Office 365. All the big software as a service (SaaS) providers use HTTPS by default to secure authentication. HTTP uses TCP port 80, and HTTPS uses TCP port 443, the port used by SSL and TLS.

 EXAM TIP Both HTTP and HTTPS reside at the Application layer in the OSI model. Also, CompTIA defines HTTPS as *Hypertext Transfer Protocol Secure* in the Acronyms list of the CompTIA Security+ 601 objectives. Almost for sure you'll only see HTTPS and not the spelled-out version(s) of the protocol name, but be on the lookout just in case.

SSL

The *Secure Sockets Layer (SSL)* protocol provides both encryption and authentication services between hosts during data transmission. For encryption services, it encrypts the entire session between two hosts in an SSL tunnel. Any traffic that is sent between the hosts during that session is encrypted and protected from unauthorized interception. For authentication, SSL normally uses digital certificates to authenticate a server to a client. However, SSL also supports mutual authentication where both the host and client exchange certificates.

 NOTE SSL is rarely used to secure Web sites, but it's still around for other applications such as FTPS.

TLS

SSL has been vulnerable to an increasing number of attacks due mainly to vulnerabilities to downgrade attacks, allowing attackers to take advantage of weaker algorithms. Because of the weaknesses in cryptographic algorithms used in various versions of SSL, the *Transport Layer Security (TLS)* protocol was developed to replace SSL a while back, and has now all but completely replaced SSL for secure Web pages. Currently, all modern operating systems, browsers, and Web-based applications support TLS.

From a functional standpoint, SSL and TLS are very similar. In fact, while TLS has supplanted SSL, it's very common to see references to SSL/TLS, especially when discussing aspects where the two protocols are virtually identical. SSL/TLS uses TCP port 443 for backward compatibility with SSL-based technologies.

TLS secures sensitive data transferred during Web sessions. In addition to providing secure session services for Web traffic, TLS is used to protect other protocols that require secure sessions such as SFTP.

SSL/TLS Handshake

TLS connections require a back-and-forth interaction between client and server—called the *SSL/TLS handshake*—to establish identity and authentication. If a client wants to create a secure HTTPS connection with a server, the client first creates an HTTP connection. It then begins the SSL/TLS handshake to establish that connection. Here's a somewhat simplified overview of the steps:

1. Client hello

2. Server hello

3. Key exchange

4. Finish

Client Hello   The client, already connected to the server via HTTP, initiates the HTTPS connection with an SSL/TLS *hello* message. This message informs the server that the client wants to connect via HTTPS and describes the types of key exchange the client supports. Figure 11-3 shows part of the client hello captured in Wireshark.

Every cipher suite defines everything needed in the key exchange on a single line. Inspecting one of these suites in detail, the following line informs the server of a single cipher suite the client can perform:

```
Cipher Suite: TLS_ECDHE_ECDSA_WITH_AES_128_GCM_SHA256 (0xc02b)
```

A single cipher suite contains very specific combinations of authentication/key exchange, encryption, and integrity protocols.

The preceding line indicates that the client can perform the following:

- **TLS_ECDHE_ECDSA**   This is the authentication method, Elliptic-curve Diffie-Hellman Ephemeral key exchange using the Elliptic-curve Digital Signature Algorithm.

- **AES_128_GCM**   This is the encryption, AES-128 as the block cipher using GCM mode.

- **SHA256**   This is the integrity protocol, SHA-256 HMAC for the authentication hash.

Server Hello   The server reads the client hello, choosing a cipher suite from the list. It then responds with the cipher suite it chose plus any information to begin the key exchange. Figure 11-4 shows part of the server hello message captured in Wireshark, declaring the cipher suite and also beginning the key exchange.

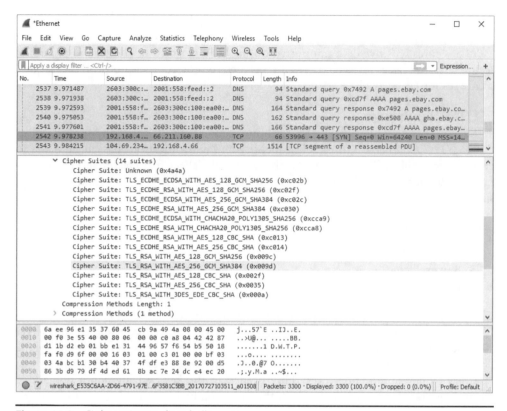

Figure 11-3　Cipher suites in client hello message

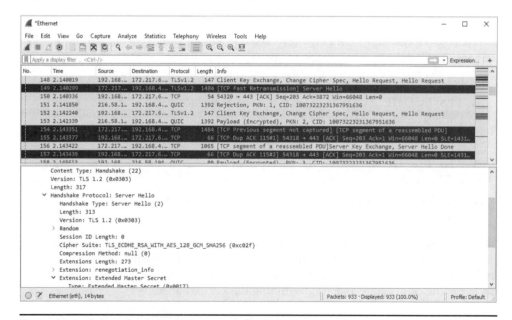

Figure 11-4　Selected cipher suite in server hello message

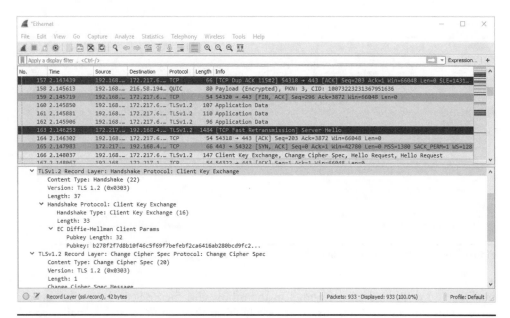

Figure 11-5   Key exchange (in this case, Diffie-Hellman) and change cipher spec in a single TLS packet

Key Exchange   From this point, there are several message options depending on the cipher suite. Two common commands are key exchange and change cipher spec. *Key exchange* handles any part of the key exchange process, and *change cipher spec* handles any adjustments to the exchange process. TLS can pack multiple TLS commands into a single TLS packet to speed things up. It's not uncommon to see a single TLS packet, as shown in Figure 11-5.

Finish   Once the client and the server are satisfied that the key exchange has worked, the SSL/TLS tunnel is now established. Both sides signify setup is complete with finish messages. Figure 11-6 shows a server sending a *finish* command (Wireshark calls them Hello Done). Also notice the encrypted packets below the finish command.

 EXAM TIP   The SSL/TLS handshake is one of the more computational demanding aspects of implementing this level of security. Device manufacturers have developed hardware appliances—called *SSL/TLS accelerators*—that take the handshake burden off the systems.

E-mail

Whether you use a Web client or a more traditional client, e-mail is an important Internet application. E-mail uses specific protocols, and you must understand how they work (and of course know the port numbers).

POP3

The *Post Office Protocol version 3 (POP3)* is an e-mail client protocol used to receive e-mail through client applications. Client applications that use POP3 access the user's

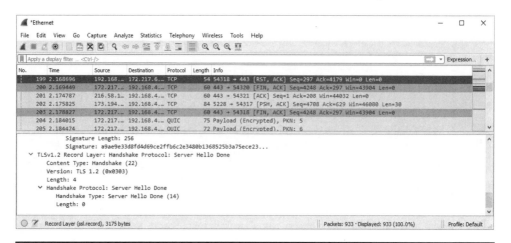

Figure 11-6 Finish command (Hello Done) followed by encrypted packets

mailbox and download all the e-mail in the inbox, and then delete the mail from the server. This can confuse some users, especially when they log in to their e-mail account from different clients and find that their e-mail has "disappeared." POP3 allows only one connection at a time to the user's inbox.

 EXAM TIP   POP3 uses TCP port 110.

IMAP4

The *Internet Message Access Protocol version 4 (IMAP4)* is also a client e-mail protocol, although it is in more widespread use these days than POP3. IMAP4, which uses TCP port 143 by default, can connect to an organizational or Web-based e-mail server and download client e-mail messages. It differs from POP3 in that you can have multiple connections to the server from multiple user clients, and e-mail isn't automatically deleted from the server. Like POP3, IMAP4 is also a non-secure protocol.

 EXAM TIP   IMAP4 uses TCP port 143.

SMTP

Simple Mail Transfer Protocol (SMTP) is the server-side e-mail protocol used to send e-mail messages from an organization's e-mail server. SMTP is an Application layer protocol that uses TCP port 25. Like some of the older protocols discussed in this module, SMTP has no built-in security mechanisms. It provides no authentication between hosts or for users, and it relies on external authentication mechanisms such as Lightweight Directory Access Protocol (LDAP)–based directory systems for authentication.

Besides being a non-secure protocol, SMTP is also vulnerable to various attacks. SMTP is vulnerable to an *SMTP relay attack*, where a malicious person can connect to the SMTP server and send e-mail from it, spoofing the organization's users and e-mail addresses. This attack can be prevented by configuring the SMTP server not to allow unauthenticated connections and by disallowing SMTP relay.

EXAM TIP You'll recall LDAP from way back in Chapter 3 as the protocol used to assist in allowing already authenticated users to browse and locate objects in a distributed network database. The CompTIA Security+ objectives mention *LDAP over SSL (LDAPS)* as one of the secure protocols. While this is technically true, LDAPS was deprecated right along with LDAPv2 way back in 2003. LDAPv3 uses extensions that make use of secure protocols such as TLS to provide security today.

You might see an exam question that posits a use-case scenario about *directory services* that would substitute *Secure LDAP* or LDAPS for LDAP; choose that answer if it seems obvious. In reality today, current versions of LDAP provide secure extensions.

Securing E-mail

For decades, none of the big three e-mail protocols—POP3, IMAP, or SMTP—had any form of encryption. Everything you did, including sending your user name and password, was in the clear. Well, over time e-mail servers weathered millions of unique attacks, wreaking havoc with spam, phishing, and far worse.

These attacks got so bad that many organizations developed blacklists of known evil IP addresses and domains, sometimes even blocking legitimate domain e-mail messages. We now have *domain reputation* and IP reputation sites that anyone may access, giving those domains that find themselves on the *naughty domains* blacklist a tool to restore their reputation.

EXAM TIP As noted previously, the CompTIA Security+ 601 objectives have swapped out the traditional term "blacklist" for "block list/deny list." You'll definitely hear the former term in normal tech person conversation and see that in all the literature. You might see the latter term on your exam.

To give encryption to the POP3, IMAP, and SMTP protocols, the Internet folks added SSL/TLS and let your e-mail run through the encrypted tunnel, just as HTTP runs through an SSL/TLS tunnel.

Three secure versions of the previously non-secure mail protocols go by a few names, but most commonly you'll see them as *POP3 over SSL/TLS (POP3S), IMAP over SSL/ TLS (IMAPS),* and *SMTP Secure (SMTPS)*. Let's stick with those. Each of these secure e-mail protocols uses a unique port number as follows:

- POP3S uses port 995.
- Secure IMAPS uses port 993.
- Secure SMTPS uses port 465.

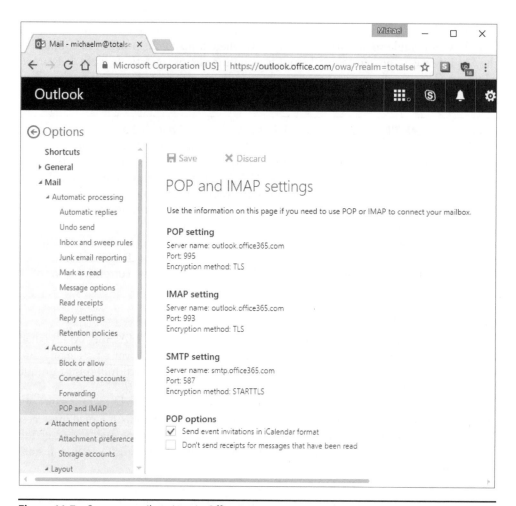

Figure 11-7   Secure e-mail settings in Office 365

All e-mail servers support secure e-mail protocols. In typical use-case scenarios, you configure a secure e-mail protocol simply by adding a certificate to the e-mail server and setting up the secure ports. On the client side, you need to configure each e-mail account to use secure e-mail protocols. Figure 11-7 shows my e-mail account settings in Office 365.

Wait a minute! Note that the SMTP server in Figure 11-7 uses port 587 instead of 465. This is an older version of SMTP Secure called STARTTLS. STARTTLS is functionally equivalent to SMTPS, but uses port 587 instead of port 465.

MIME, S/MIME

Multipurpose Internet Mail Extensions (MIME) is the protocol built into every e-mail client that enables users to make e-mail attachments. MIME works by converting the attached file to text, using headers so that the receiving e-mail client can then convert the text files back into the original file type. MIME's ability to attach files created an opportunity for users to use their own e-mail security protocols, even if their e-mail servers didn't use secure POP3, IMAP, or SMTP. Secure e-mail protocols only work if you have an e-mail server configured to support them. In most cases, users have no control over their servers and must use e-mail servers that still use non-secure POP3/IMAP/SMTP. In these cases, user can take control of their e-mail security using Secure/Multipurpose Internet Mail Extensions (S/MIME). S/MIME was developed from MIME, but took the concept a step further, as S/MIME enables individual e-mail clients to attach personal certificates and digital signatures to e-mail messages just like any other MIME attachment. Using these attachments, S/MIME enables users to encrypt e-mail messages to each other.

Module 11-3: Web Application Attacks

This module covers the following CompTIA Security+ objectives:

- **1.1   Compare and contrast different types of social engineering techniques**
- **1.3   Given a scenario, analyze potential indicators associated with application attacks**
- **1.4   Given a scenario, analyze potential indicators associated with network attacks**
- **1.6   Explain the security concerns associated with various types of vulnerabilities**

Given the popularity of Web apps on the Internet today, they are easily the single most generic target for all kinds of attacks. The biggest challenge to Web application attacks is the public nature of the Web. As an Internet-facing server, a Web app is subject to all the types of attacks already discussed in the book (plus a few more); as an application, it's subject to attacks unique to applications.

This module covers the many types of attacks that bad actors tend to use against Web applications. We've previously covered a number of these attacks in more generic ways (attacking the network, attacking individual hosts, attacking servers), so this module concentrates on how these attacks affect Web applications. We'll start with injection attacks, then discuss hijacking and related attacks, and finish with a diverse group of other types of attacks.

Injection Attacks

In its basic form, an *injection attack* inserts—*injects*—additional code or malicious content into a site, typically using an opening provided through user input. *User input* could come from a field on a form or via one of several methods for posting content back to the Web server. Injecting data into a user input field works because of a lack of input validation. *Input validation* should occur when the Web application receives a user input request, and it means that the Web application has been programmed to check and restrict user input to a valid range of responses. For instance, input validation would check for, and prevent, a user entering alphabetic text data into a field that requires numerical values. Lack of input validation allows a malicious user to circumvent the expected data in the field and add or embed data that might be used to get a different response from the application or server.

Several different types of content can be injected into a Web application, including SQL statements, operating system commands, LDAP commands, and XML. Each of these types of injectable content takes certain actions to cause specific reactions from the Web application and server. Attackers can use these injection attacks to gain unauthorized access to data, execute commands on the Web server itself, and set up the server for further attacks. We'll cover some of these injection attacks in the next few sections.

 NOTE You first saw injection attacks way back in Chapter 5, with *DLL injections*. Similar techniques apply to the injection attacks listed in this chapter.

Command Injection

Command injection is a technique with which a malicious user could append or embed commands into a user input request and cause either retrieval of information from the system or command execution on the host itself. The malicious user could include application-specific commands, such as database commands, operating system commands, and even commands that can affect the network, such as those needed to connect to a shared network resource. Most command injection attacks are tailored to the operating system or application used on the server, but some generic commands, especially those embedded in URLs, can affect a variety of systems in different ways.

For example, let's say you have a URL that looks like this:

```
http://confidential/cgi-bin/appscript.pl?doc=secret.txt
```

You could alter that URL by appending a pipe symbol on the end, along with a command, like so:

```
http://confidential/cgi-bin/appscript.pl?doc=/bin/ls|
```

On a Linux-based system, this embedded command would execute a directory listing on the target computer. The PERL script that executes on the server as part of the normal application (appscript.pl) would allow a command to be executed on the host also, since it can pipe the command to the shell.

SQL Injection

Database programmers use *Structured Query Language (SQL)* to create and manipulate database structures as well as the data that resides in those structures. Most relational databases use some variation of SQL to manage their data structures (such as tables, views, and so on). With the wide availability of databases residing as part of a back-end tier for Internet-facing Web applications, attacks on those databases and their structures are commonplace.

Many of these attacks use SQL to attack a database, through vulnerabilities in the Web application, usually in user input fields. For example, if you had an application that asked for a user name and e-mail address on a form, an attacker could attempt to manipulate this user input to include SQL commands as part of the input. This is called *SQL injection*

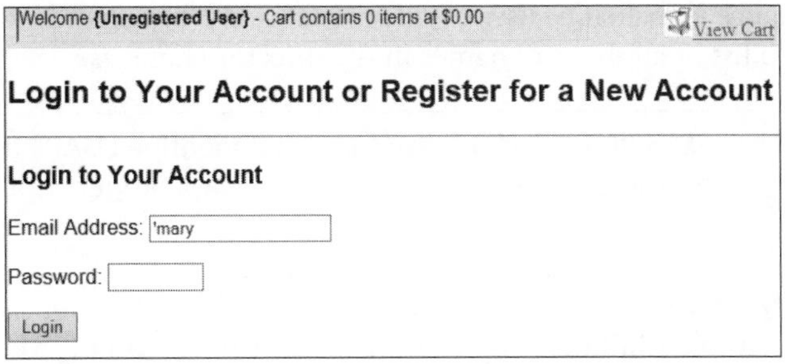

Figure 11-8

An SQL injection attack

(SQLi), because it sends SQL input (normally in the form of SQL database manipulation commands) to the database. The results returned to the user could be responses to those commands, including responses that give up important data to the user. Putting in '1'='1 rather than a user name, for example, forces the database to select all users rather than a specific user (a classic SQL injection attack).

Figures 11-8 and 11-9 show examples of a simple SQL injection used in a Web login form and the resulting response from the credentials file, which shows data the user isn't authorized to see.

LDAP Injection

The Lightweight Directory Access Protocol (LDAP) is used in distributed directory service structures that contain network, user, and computer information. LDAP is used to query the directory services database in order to locate network-based resources. The most popular examples of distributed directory service are Microsoft Active Directory, OpenLDAP, and NetIQ eDirectory. They are all based on the X.500 Directory Services standard and use LDAP to provide standard communication services between directory-based objects.

LDAP injection can be performed on any directory services database that has not been secured; its purpose, like other forms of injection, is to get data from the directory database that a user would otherwise be unauthorized to obtain. Some Web applications use directory services databases to perform their intended functions (service authentication or data lookups, for example). LDAP injection involves embedding LDAP query commands into routine Web application requests and getting data back in response.

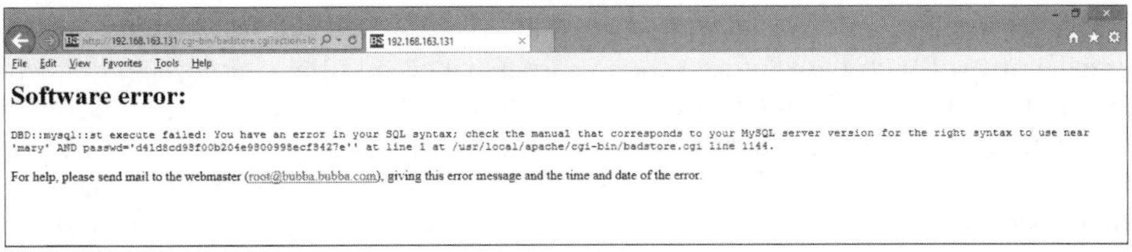

Figure 11-9   The result of the SQL injection

For instance, a malicious user could embed LDAP commands into an input request and retrieve a list of all the user names in the directory database.

 EXAM TIP Watch for use cases that mention LDAP attacks. The best defense for these (on the exam) is almost always proper application of LDAPS.

XML Injection

The Extensible Markup Language (XML) is similar to HTML and other markup languages. It provides a standards-based way to encode documents for consistent, unified presentation and formatting. It is often used to format data elements from database applications that are viewed through Web applications. *XML injection*, similar to the other types of injection attacks discussed here, sends malicious XML content to a Web application, taking advantage of any lack of input validation and XML parsing.

The challenge to XML injections is that they literally fit into any type of attack. One possible example would be an attacker injecting a large dollar value into a known XML field called credit balance. It is important to harden Web pages against these types of attacks.

Hijacking and Related Attacks

Any Web session has control tokens used to track the status of the session at any given moment. A token might be a cookie tracking the contents of a shopping cart, for example, or it might be some JavaScript variable tracking your character's location in a Web-based game. Whatever and wherever your session tokens might live, any form of attack that attempts to manipulate these tokens in a way that attacks the mechanism of your Web site is known generically as a *session hijacking attack*.

Cross-Site Scripting

Cross-site scripting (XSS) attacks can affect both hosts and Web applications. An XSS attack comes in the form of malicious script content injected into a vulnerable Web site, usually one that the client browser trusts. Because content from a trusted site often has elevated access to a browser or its components, the malicious content could be sent to a client and have these elevated privileges as well. From there, it can access sensitive information on the client, including content and session cookie information. This information could contain user credentials as well as financial information (in the form of credit card or bank account numbers), for example.

XSS attacks are very common; in fact, these types of attacks are estimated to be a large majority of Web-based attacks today, surpassing even buffer overflows in frequency (see "Buffer Overflow," later in the chapter). Many Web sites are vulnerable to XSS attacks, usually through malformed HTML requests or via active content and scripting languages such as Java, JavaScript, ActiveX, Visual Basic Script (VBScript), Flash, and others. Although there are many variations of XSS attacks, Figure 11-10 illustrates one way that a simple XSS attack could work.

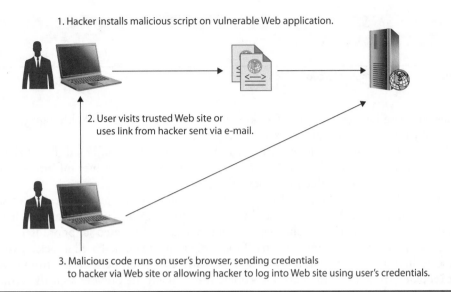

1. Hacker installs malicious script on vulnerable Web application.

2. User visits trusted Web site or uses link from hacker sent via e-mail.

3. Malicious code runs on user's browser, sending credentials to hacker via Web site or allowing hacker to log into Web site using user's credentials.

Figure 11-10   A simple XSS attack

Cross-Site Request Forgery

Cross-site request forgery (XSRF) attacks attempt to steal authentication information from session cookies during a user's current browsing session. The user is normally tricked into visiting a malicious Web site through redirection or phishing, and the malicious Web site executes code that attempts to steal the authentication information and impersonate the user. Note that this attack requires that the user already be authenticated to the secure site, so that their session credentials are stored in the browser.

Server-side Request Forgery

Most Web servers interface with some kind of back-end database for one reason or another. The most common way for a Web server to talk to the database server is with HTTP calls/requests. These are safe, as the Web server is permanently logged into that database server using operating system–level security (like a domain logon). If an attacker sees these requests it does them no good, because they're not logged in. If an attacker can forge an HTTP request to get the Web server to query somewhere else, like, for example, the \Users\Admin folder in Windows or the /bin folder in Linux, then they might gain access to critical information such as logons. This attack is called a *server-side request forgery*.

Cookies

Cookies are small text files stored on a browser that contain information about the Web sites you visit. In some cases, cookies are used to retain user preferences for the site, but cookies can contain sensitive information, such as user credentials or financial data (credit card information, for example) as well. These last types of cookies are *session cookies*, since they are (supposedly) not persistent and expire for each session and must be

Figure 11-11 Example of a cookie file

renewed for subsequent sessions. Cookies are stored as text files, and although they are not easily human readable, they are not encrypted.

Web sites that use the Adobe Flash player for certain content offer a different type of cookie called a *local shared object* or *flash cookie*. Flash cookies store user information and can be a security concern due to privacy issues.

Attacks that take advantage of cookies usually come in the form of stealing session cookies from a user's Web browser and using the session information contained therein to authenticate as the user. Cookies can be collected via a Web-based script or intercepted during a traffic capture using a sniffer. Protecting against cookie-based attacks involves using techniques such as enforcing new session authentication periodically from a Web site, cookie expiration, and control of cookie use through the browser security settings. Figure 11-11 shows an example of a basic cookie text file.

NOTE A *zombie cookie* is a particularly nefarious type of cookie that re-creates itself from an external source outside the cookie storage area.

Man-in-the-Browser

Man-in-the-middle (MITM) attacks are common and popular attack vectors for Web applications. One popular variant called *man-in-the-browser* is a client-side attack, initiated by the user inadvertently running a Trojan horse on his or her system. This Trojan horse in turn grabs communication between the client and the server, silently sending whatever data the attacker wants to a third location while still seemingly working perfectly to the user.

EXAM TIP Although common parlance uses *man-in-the-middle* and *man-in-the-browser* to describe these attacks, CompTIA has shifted the language to non-binary. So you might see these attacks referred to as *on-path attacks*. This language shift makes logical sense, because the attackers put themselves in the *path* of information flow, and thus can capture precious information.

More commonly in the literature these days you'll see "person" substituted for "man" when shifting to inclusive language, so *person-in-the-browser (PITB)* or *person-in-the-middle (PITM)*. You *won't* see PITB or PITM on the Security+ exam.

Clickjacking

Clickjacking is an older form of attack where a malicious/compromised Web site places invisible controls on a page, giving users the impression they are clicking some safe item that actually is an active control for something malicious.

One of the more common forms of clickjacking comes from an HTML data structure called an iFrame. An *iFrame* is basically a Web page within a Web page, complete with its own controls and applications.

Session Replay

A *session replay* is a man-in-the-middle attack where the bad actor intercepts a session in progress and replays it to the Web server in an attempt to get access to the Web application. Session replay attacks, particularly the infamous FireFox Firesheep extension back in 2010, motivated the entire industry to switch from HTTP to exclusively HTTPS for all public Web pages. HTTPS makes session replays much more difficult.

 NOTE Replay attacks are well covered in Module 7-2.

Header Manipulation

As part of normal communications with Web applications, the Web application and the browser exchange request and response messages so the client can access content in the Web application. These HTTP requests and responses have headers that contain information such as commands, directives, and so on. A *header manipulation* attack modifies these headers so they contain malicious information, such as harmful commands and scripts. When the client receives these manipulated headers, the client often executes these commands, resulting in malicious actions occurring on the client. Beyond executing simple commands, manipulating HTTP headers can allow an attacker to carry out other attacks, such as cross-site scripting, session hijacking, cookie stealing, and injection attacks. A mitigation for this type of attack is to configure Web application servers to ignore client-side headers, since they are usually the source of header manipulation.

Other Web Application Attacks

Other attacks can be executed against a server hosting a Web application. These don't necessarily require injection, although often they are carried out through an injection attack. Some of these attacks might yield only information about the system that a hacker could use to formulate an attack, such as Web server version or directory structure, but other attacks can result in direct unauthorized access to sensitive data. Some attacks can even allow the attacker to run privileged commands or arbitrary code on a host. We'll discuss some of these attacks in this section, including DNS attacks, directory traversal, overflow attacks, add-ons, and zero-day attacks.

DNS Attacks

One of the best ways to wreak havoc on a Web application is to mess with its associated DNS. Users rely on DNS to get to specific Web apps. By attacking DNS, bad actors can prevent users from even getting to the Web app itself. Let's consider some forms of DNS attack.

Domain Hijacking *Domain hijacking* means to take control of a legitimate domain registration in some way that the actual owner does not desire. DNS registration procedures today are quite robust, making domain hijacking tricky in most cases. However, in some cases hijacking still takes place. Organizations generally have a domain registrar such as GoDaddy (www.godaddy.com). If the user is attacked by some form of man-in-the-middle (a.k.a. on-path) attack, the user might send the password to that account to a bad actor. Often a DNS domain comes with an e-mail account that allows a bad actor to access the registration. Domain hijacking is correctable, but remediation sometimes takes days, if not weeks, which is plenty of time for a Web app to lose its customer base.

URL Redirection A *Universal Resource Locator (URL) redirection* attack dupes a viewer, usually of an e-mail message, into clicking a URL that looks like a legit site but redirects them to a scam site. URL redirections are part of every phishing e-mail.

Secure Sockets Layer (SSL) Stripping *SSL stripping* is a man-in-the-middle attack to get users to connect to an HTTP Web site when they mean to go to an HTTPS Web site. Discovered around 2010, an SSL stripping attack detects a legitimate HTTPS request from a client, strips away the HTTPS data, and redirects the user to a look-alike site, hoping the user will enter a user name and password. You can protect against SSL stripping by configuring a Web browser to treat any non-secure Web page as a security risk.

DNS Amplification *DNS amplification* is a form of distributed denial-of-service (DDoS) attack that attacks a Web application's DNS server instead of the Web app itself. DNS amplification attacks work in various ways, but the goal is to confuse legitimate DNS servers by sending spoofed/malformed DNS queries in some way to amplify what's normally a simple, single DNS query into hundreds of queries.

 EXAM TIP DNSSEC is useless against DNS amplification. A DDoS attack with DNS requests is directed at public DNS servers and therefore doesn't support DNSSEC.

Typosquatting/URL Hijacking Most Internet users have made a typo while entering a URL and suddenly discovered themselves on a completely different Web site than the one they intended. Con artists and scammers have bought up many domains that differ just slightly from a legitimate site, preferably with a spelling that people commonly mistake. That's called *typosquatting*. A user might type www.aamazon.com and think he or she is headed to the commercial giant, Amazon, but then end up at some sleazy or dangerous site. The big companies buy up the typo-prone domain names, but smaller sites are vulnerable.

Another method of typosquatting—also called *URL hijacking*—involves registering the same domain name as a legitimate company, but with a different top-level domain. For example, rather than legitcompany.com, the hijacker might register legitcompany.biz. The alternate Web site might mimic the legitimate site in the hopes of getting personal or financial information from unsuspecting users.

Directory Traversal

Directory traversal is an attack in which the entire directory of a Web site and its server are examined with the intent of locating files of interest to the attacker. These could include nonpublic files that contain sensitive information; or configuration or content files that an attacker may alter to gain information to launch further attacks on the system or network. Directory traversal attacks are conducted by entering different directory levels into a URL or user input field, causing the Web application to change directories and sometimes display the contents of a directory. You can prevent this attack through user input validation, as well as by restricting the URL from displaying directory names in the Web application. Additionally, at the operating system level, you can secure files and directories with the proper access permissions to prevent unauthorized users from being able to read files or list directory contents.

Buffer Overflow

A *buffer overflow* is a condition by which an attacker, through malicious input or an automated exploit, sends unexpected input into a program, usually into its memory registers or buffers. The unexpected input could be a different data type than expected or an abnormally large amount of data that crashes a buffer when it can hold only a finite amount of data. A buffer overflow condition exceeds the limits of the application and is used to cause error conditions that may result in denial-of-service for the application or server, unexpected access to sensitive data, the ability to run administrative commands or utilities on the host, or even the the ability to execute arbitrary code on the host. You can prevent buffer overflows through secure coding practices, including input valida-tion, data type and length restrictions, error-handling routines, and bounds checking for memory allocation. (See Module 11-4 for the details on secure coding practices.)

Arbitrary Code Execution or Remote Code Execution

Malicious hackers can execute commands, scripts, applets, and other types of programs on a host that enable them to run whatever type of code they wish. They can perpetrate these *arbitrary code execution* attacks through injection, malware, or any number of other attack vectors. *Remote code execution* is a variation of this type of attack that can often be run after an attacker gains a remote shell to a host. The effectiveness of both of these types of attacks is enhanced if the attacker has gained elevated privileges on the host.

Zero-Day Attacks

Very often, hackers (and security professionals) discover previously unknown vulnerabili-ties for operating systems, applications, and other software or code, what are called *zero-day vulnerabilities*. Occasionally, not even the vendor knows that the software includes an exploitable vulnerability, so they may not have a patch or fix for it immediately. A *zero-day attack* exploits those vulnerabilities.

Since there are no known patches or mitigations for the attack, the hackers are free to exploit these vulnerabilities without fear of having them mitigated or, in some cases, even discovered. Zero-day vulnerabilities usually have some sort of available mitigation or fix within a few days or weeks, but that's more than enough time for a hacker to take advantage of any associated vulnerabilities.

Module 11-4: Application Security

This module covers the following CompTIA Security+ objectives:

- **1.6 Explain the security concerns associated with various types of vulnerabilities**
- **2.1 Explain the importance of security concepts in an enterprise environment**
- **2.2 Summarize virtualization and cloud computing concepts**
- **2.3 Summarize secure application development, deployment, and automation concepts**
- **3.2 Given a scenario, implement host or application security solutions**

In the earlier days of security, most of the focus was on securing networks. As time passed, the focus turned to securing operating systems. Eventually, as more vulnerabilities were discovered in applications (both traditional client/server and Web applications), more of an emphasis was placed on application security. *Application security* not only means hardening an application, much like you would a network device, operating system, or host, but also means considering security throughout the software design and development processes.

Application security begins with the process of developing well-hardened applications written from the ground up to resist attacks. But it doesn't end there. The developers of a great Web app understand that changes will take place, that performance, feature, and security goals are continually defined and redefined, making security a part of the ongoing evolution of the life of a Web application.

This module explores the life cycle of a Web application and the security involved at each step. The software creation *environment* follows five distinct points:

1. **Development:** Creating the new code
2. **Test:** Verifying the code works as specified
3. **Staging:** Positioning the final code in as close to the real world as possible
4. **Production:** Running the code in the real world
5. **Quality assurance:** Following up once the code is live

 NOTE The CompTIA Security+ exam doesn't test on programming skills, merely the aspects of applications that relate to IT security.

Development

Developing any but the simplest Web applications requires a vast amount of organization and planning. Any Web app starts with a vision, but to bring that vision to fruition, developers must define a huge number of very specific requirements and goals and then fulfill them on a timely basis. The result of these requirements and goals often manifests as a *baseline*, a minimum set of performance values that define a certain aspect of what the application must do.

Resource vs. Security Constraints

A big part of applying security to application development is the ongoing battle of resources versus security constraints. Developers must constantly assess their resources against the burden of adding security, all the while trying to find the best balance between the two. More security adds hardware, bandwidth, and maintenance costs.

Scalability and Elasticity Considerations

One big challenge to consider when developing new secure code is to prepare for changes in demand. *Scalability* means meeting changes in demand over longer time frames. Think of the natural growth in popularity of your product. Scale considerations may mean issues such as bringing on more systems, or dispersing systems geographically (thank goodness for the cloud, eh?). *Elasticity* addresses the ups and downs of demand. If you sell holiday decorations, for example, you often have much more business around holidays than after a holiday. In that case the cloud once again makes life easy, as all cloud providers have products that directly address elasticity.

Choosing the Proper Tools

The days of writing code from scratch in a text editor are long gone for any type of serious software development. Today we use development tools that help us write clean, error-free, and secure code. One example is a *software development kit (SDK)*, a combination of documentation, development environment, and premade code (known as *libraries*) for common tasks and for interfacing with other software via an *application programming interface (API)* and tutorials. Platform developers such as Microsoft and Google provide SDKs to help folks develop software for their platforms. If you want to make an Android app, you'll probably grab a copy of Android Studio. If you're making Windows applications that use the Microsoft .NET framework, you get the .NET Framework SDK. Pretty much every platform has at least one SDK. Platforms like Android have many to choose from.

 NOTE There is no industry standard for what goes into an SDK. Every SDK is unique in what it provides.

You must consider *licensing* when choosing an SDK. SDKs come with licensing (proprietary or free) and you cannot mix license types. This isn't that big of a problem if you stick to libraries provided by the SDK. This can be a huge issue if you decide to use third-party libraries. Always check those licenses!

Security is always a consideration during development, and SDK security is no exception. APIs are the language that allows different applications to communicate, but the libraries that do the talking come with the SDK. There are some significant *API considerations*. We just mentioned licensing but there's always a chance that you may run into malicious code (especially in third-party libraries) or poorly written code that exposes personally identifiable information (PII). Fortunately, there are tools to help you avoid these issues; we'll discuss them later in this module.

Finally, using any resources not developed in-house adds risk. *Outsourced code development,* by definition, means you increase third-party risks because your organization doesn't maintain 100 percent control over the code. Organizations use third-party code, such as outlined earlier, all the time. Factoring in the security implications is an important consideration.

Platform

Understanding how applications function presents two challenges. First, what type of code is the application running and where does this code exist? Second, two systems are involved, a server and a client. Since the application is code, it must be running on one of those two systems, but which one? It's not necessarily clear where the application runs. Answering these two questions defines what is called the application's *platform.*

Executable or Runtime?   The classic application is an executable file that runs on a local computer. A programmer writes the executable file in some form of programming language such as C++ within some form of integrated development environment (IDE) like the one shown in Figure 11-12. When complete, the programmer runs the code through a compiler to create the executable file.

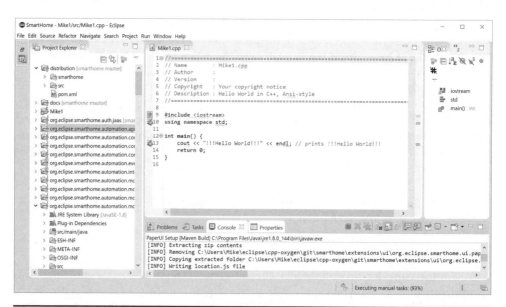

Figure 11-12   Eclipse IDE

Executable code works well on a standalone system, and a local computer's executable programs easily access a remote computer's data, but standardized application protocols like HTTP add complexities that make executable files fall short. When a program is compiled, the resulting executable file is for a specific operating system. When you send an HTML file from a server to a client's Web browser, however, there are too many variables: What Web browser is the client running? What operating system? What is the client's screen resolution?

This problem is avoided by running applications using *runtime* or *interpreted code*, specifically designed to work with Web browsers. There are many languages used; today Python and JavaScript are the most common.

Unlike executable code, interpreted code isn't compiled. Interpreted code isn't designed for a specific operating system. Interpreted code is never as fast as compiled code, but it's flexible, and on the Web that's a huge benefit over executable code.

Server or Client Side?   So where does the interpreted code run? You have two choices here. In one case you run the code on the server, building a new Web page for the client and then sending that page to the client. The client then sends traditional HTTP commands back to the server, which reads that data and creates another Web page. The alternative is to run the code on the client. In this case the browser must know how to download the script and then run it. The Web server in most cases acts like little more than a database.

JavaScript is the dominant server-side interpreted language. All browsers run JavaScript by default. All browsers can turn off running scripts, although turning off JavaScript will make most Web sites functionless (Figure 11-13).

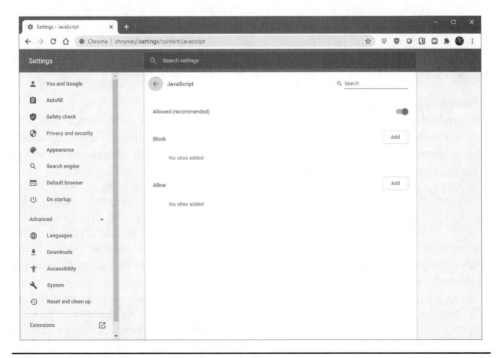

Figure 11-13   Enable/disable options for JavaScript in Chrome browser

NOTE In general, a server-side platform is more secure than a client-side platform, but client-side is generally faster.

Software Diversity

When developing compiled programs into binary executable files, programmers make every copy of that application an identical copy. To make executables most robust against attacks, an organization may choose to use a special *compiler* that creates different binary executables every time. Sure, the executables all do the same thing, but by making each executable unique, it's harder for attackers to identify the program by file size, hash, and so forth.

Secure Baseline

While any application may have hundreds of baselines, a *secure baseline* defines the core of what the developers must do to make the application secure. In a way, you could look at the secure baseline more like the application's security controls.

Benchmarks/Secure Configuration Guides

An application is only as secure as the hardware, operating system, and network infrastructure devices on which it resides. Earlier chapters stressed the need for good benchmarks and configurations, but it's always a good idea to double-check everything your application needs. Verify security at this point before an application is working. Keep in mind that there are plenty of *platform/vendor-specific guides* to help. Always start with a good *general-purpose guide* (this book is a great resource), but also realize every Web server software, every operating system, every application server, and certainly every network infrastructure device has clear secure configuration guides to help administrators harden every part of the platform your applications need. Use them.

Offloading Encryption

It's standard to run Web applications on top of HTTPS for good security. The Web server that the Web application runs on has all it needs to support HTTPS, but that is on top of any and all processing of the Web app itself. If the Web application has a large adoption, it's easy to overwhelm a single Web server.

There's plenty a developer can do to reduce workload. Adding more servers and load balancing, as described back in Chapter 6, for example, is very common. Another job that's easily taken off a server's plate is handing encryption/decryption by implementing *crypto service providers* or *crypto modules*. Crypto service providers and crypto modules do the same job: handling all forms of encryption requested by one or more systems. They can be software built into the system or hardware software modules connected to the system.

The only real difference between crypto service providers and crypto modules are where they are implemented. Crypto service providers are more Windows-centric, while crypto modules are more open source. Both can handle virtually any cryptographic algorithm, so an important part of the implementation of these devices is *algorithm selection*. Given that Web servers lean heavily on TLS, it's important to select a crypto device that supports PKI exchange (Diffie-Hellman, RSA, and Elliptic-curve algorithms) as well as AES for symmetric encryption.

Secure Coding Techniques

Whether the platform is client side or server side, good development practices require thinking about security from the moment the application is first considered. The CompTIA Security+ exam objectives mention several specific *secure coding techniques*, all of which are well known and commonly used on all Web applications.

 EXAM TIP You might see the term *secure coding practices* as a synonym for *secure coding techniques* on the CompTIA Security+ exam.

Input Validation The previous module described injection attacks that use manipulated inputs to do malicious things to Web applications as well as the system running the Web apps. Common types of these attacks include command insertion, cross-site scripting, buffer overflows, and SQL injection.

Proper input validation helps prevent these types of attack. If a Web application asks for a last name, the chances that someone has a crazy last name like this one are pretty slim:

```
\esc format C: /y
```

If the characters \, :, or / appear in the last name input, a Web app with proper input validation will reject that data. Alternatively, the Web app can sanitize the input. *Sanitizing* means to allow all data but strip out any questionable characters.

 NOTE Do yourself a favor and look up this famous Web comic: https://xkcd .com/327/.

Input validation varies dramatically when comparing server-side versus client-side platforms. In classic server-side applications, the code executes on the server and the server handles most, if not all, validation. As you might guess, client-side applications execute code on the client and the client has to handle the validation.

 EXAM TIP Look for a question on the exam that asks about server-side versus client-side execution and validation. This essentially asks which machine is doing the work.

Error Handling Despite all the testing done to prevent bugs, every application has bugs that cause errors. All Web servers or database backends have default error screens that

Server Error in '/database/users.table' Application.

lastname.customer.preview attempted divide by zero.

Description: An unhandled exception occurred during the execution of the current user request. Please review the state table for more information about this error.

Exception Details: SystemDivideByZeroException: Attempted to divide by zero

Source Error:

Figure 11-14   Web server default error screen

Oooops!

Looks like there's an error with the database. Please retry now.
If the error persists contact support: mike@notarealdomain.com

Figure 11-15   Good error-handling example. (Yes, that's me, dressed up like Henry VIII.)

give bad actors a lot of information to help them crack a Web application. Figure 11-14 shows an example of a default error screen from Microsoft IIS Web server. Note the great information (for attackers) placed on the screen.

Proper error handling isn't going to stop all errors, but it will prevent errors from appearing on the user interface for easy viewing by attackers. Figure 11-15 shows an example of a better error-handling page.

NOTE   There are well-established procedures to perform good error handling. One great resource is the Open Web Application Security Project (OWASP). Check it out at www.owasp.org.

Normalization   *Normalization* is a database term meaning to store and organize data so that it exists in one form only. For example, a user database has the three tables shown in Figure 11-16.

Notice how the StudentID and CourseID fields are used for indexing (think of an index field as a sorting tool). That's great, but also notice how the CourseName and Instructor fields are repeated in two tables. This is unnecessary and not good normalization.

In this simple example, only a few fields are repeated in a database. Now imagine a Web app that takes data from thousands of users in multiple tables, all with their own complex fields. Failure to normalize exposes databases to excess size, potential logic errors, and overall inefficiency.

Stored Procedures   Most Web apps count on some form of database backend to handle the storage and manipulation of whatever data the apps need. These databases come in standardized formats that usually respond to SQL queries. SQL is a powerful language, and bad actors who know SQL well can wreak havoc on an ill-prepared database.

Figure 11-16
Poor
normalization in
a database

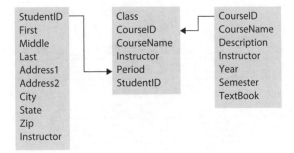

Stored procedures harden Web apps. A stored procedure is a piece of code, custom written by the developers of the app and stored in the database. These stored procedures only respond to a specific query format defined by the developer. Stored procedures make it much harder for bad actors to use common SQL queries to access a database.

Data Exposure/Encryption   Any Web app is going to have data moving between the server and the client. Additionally, in some cases a Web app might need to store some data locally on the client for certain amounts of time (like an online Security+ practice suite at https://hub.totalsem.com). Every Web app should take advantage of HTTPS to protect the data in transit/motion, but HTTPS is useless once the data gets to the client or the server. In these cases, exposed data that needs hiding—maybe a database, maybe a simple temporary data structure, or in some cases even the local code itself—must be encrypted.

All the popular interpreted programming languages provide access to different encryption tools, based on well-understood and strong cryptographic algorithms, such as AES. Trying to write homemade encryption is never a good idea.

The nature of interpreted code is that the system must read it as quickly as possible, making encryption a less-than-attractive option. There are ways to *obfuscate* or *camouflage* code, on the other hand, so that it's extremely difficult to read. Figure 11-17 shows a form of obfuscation used with JavaScript called *minifying*. Minified code is stripped of everything but the core code itself.

Database Tokenization   It's up to the developers to determine which fields in which database tables need to be tokenized. They must also make sure that the tokenization isn't broken in other indexed tables the database may use.

Database Salting   If your database stores passwords, odds are good you will store the password's hash value. But rainbow tables are powerful attack tools, so you'll need to introduce some sort of salting mechanism to the plaintext password before you hash it. It's the developer's job to make this determination and to ensure the salting mechanism isn't in any way visible to an attacker.

Database Hashing   IT security professionals use hashes with databases in two ways. First, they hash a static database (one that isn't being updated) to ensure that it hasn't been altered. Second, they use hashing to find a data record without relying on indexing, something you'll see employed in very large databases.

Figure 11-17 Minified JavaScript

Code Reuse

The phrase *don't reinvent the wheel* is a popular mantra in application development. Every language is filled with prewritten subroutines, objects, and tools, all generally packaged into *software libraries* to handle almost anything a new Web app might need. These software libraries might be free to use, or they might cost 20 percent (or some other percentage) of the entire budget for the application. In every case, though, reusing someone else's code—*code reuse*—adds security, saves money, and reduces development time.

NOTE Code reuse isn't limited to software libraries used by the Web app. It might be pieces of code used by the underlying Web server, the operating system, or even firmware/machine language in the hardware.

The downside to code reuse is that bad actors know that Web apps rely on it. These libraries must run in memory to work for the app. Bad actors know they're running and try to get access to this code and can cause lots of trouble if they do get access. Over the years, attacks have appeared that exploit the reused code, exposing previously unknown vulnerabilities. The IT industry's response to these attacks varies from the no-execute (NX) bit, built into every CPU, to specialized tools designed to hide, disable, or scramble the reused code.

Dead Code   *Dead code* is programming that's part of the finished application but doesn't do anything. Dead code is to programming as typos are to writing: writers try to avoid them, but they hippen. On the surface, there's no real security risk to dead code. Dead code adds compilation/interpretation time, makes the code bigger than it needs to be, and might confuse the next programmer reading the code, but none of these will get your system hacked. Use static analyzers to eliminate dead code. (See the upcoming section "Static Code Analysis" for the details.)

Memory Management   Web apps are programs, and programs must run in either the server's or the client's memory. Many attacks—buffer overflow and code reuse, for example—work by accessing a system's memory in some unauthorized fashion. Therefore, talking about memory as an attack vector isn't useful as much as talking about the more detailed attacks. The CompTIA Security+ exam objectives mention *memory management* as a secure coding technique, but it's part of the discussion of specific attacks.

Web-Specific Techniques   Secure cookies and Hypertext Transfer Protocol (HTTP) headers add security to Web applications. *Secure cookies* have a special "secure" attribute that tells the system to never send unless it has a secure connection. *HTTP headers* come with every Web page and give the browser critical information. HTTP headers are susceptible to cross-site scripting attacks, however, so to defend headers, most Web solutions employ features such as content security policy to thwart requests from unauthorized URLs.

Code Quality and Testing

Once an application has been written, or at least a functional part of the application is complete, it's time to move out of development and into *testing*, also often called *debugging*. At this stage, the application is tested for *code quality*—proper logic, efficiency, and response time. Testing is also the perfect place to verify security. There are many tools available for the programming team to use for debugging, and the CompTIA Security+ exam objectives specifically name a few of them.

This testing should not be confused with the real-time tools provided by most programming languages. Most languages provide a programming tool known as an *integrated development environment (IDE)*. An IDE supports code writing through real-time features that continually check the source code, as the programmer is writing the code, for items such as proper syntax. These features, while handy, can't check source code for logic errors or security problems. Instead, either a static or a dynamic analysis must be used.

 EXAM TIP   The first test of any code starts with a *manual code review*, usually by the coder who just wrote the code. This is normally done within the development environment.

Static Code Analysis

Static code analysis is a debugging process where the source code is read but the code is not run. All applications use some form of *static code analyzer*, and most IDEs have one built in to the IDE itself. But programmers aren't limited to just the one in the IDE. Dozens of great static code analyzers are available; they tend to specialize in specific languages and packages. They are self-standing—they are plug-ins to IDEs. Pretty much, there are always three or four static code analyzers that are appropriate for any one situation.

 NOTE Most programmers agree that it's good practice to run more than one static code analyzer on a single project.

Static code analyzers are important, but they don't run the code; they're limited to looking solely at the static code. If you want to put the code through the wringer, you need to move to dynamic code analysis.

Dynamic Code Analysis

Dynamic code analysis is the process of checking an application, or at least a piece of an application, by running the code and observing the logic, inputs, interface, and memory management. Unlike static code analysis, a proper dynamic code analysis is far more manual; most, if not all, of the application's functionality is tested. Dynamic analysis tools tend to work with tools such as memory trackers that give the testers a real-time vision of what the application is doing in memory to detect buffer overflow and code reuse weaknesses.

Input testing, or *fuzzing*, is one of the most important tests done dynamically. Fuzzing means to enter unexpected data into the Web app's input fields to see how the app reacts. Fuzzing can use simple random data (sometimes called *monkey fuzzing*) or it can use intentionally dangerous injection commands, such as entering \[drop table]:user into a last name field.

Automation/Scripting

You'd be hard-pressed to find an active Web application that isn't in a state of continuous development as programmers come up with ways to make the application better or faster or more feature rich. So how does an organization test that application to ensure no weaknesses appear in the code? The secret is automation or scripting.

Automated testing uses special testing software that works with scripts commonly written by the programmers (or perhaps the quality assurance team) to create *automated courses of action* for the deployment process. These steps may happen weekly, daily, or, as CompTIA wants to discuss, continuously.

- **Continuous monitoring** Automated processes that monitor the functioning Web application itself.
- **Continuous validation** Tests to verify the code is running as expected.

- **Continuous integration**   Processes to verify different parts of the application software are working together properly.

- **Continuous delivery**   Automated tools to deploy the latest version to a customer.

- **Continuous deployment**   The process that makes continuous delivery happen.

 EXAM TIP   You'll see these topics outlined (continuous monitoring, continuous validation, and so on) on the CompTIA Security+ exam as examples of *automation/scripting* in secure application development.

Many development environments use a series of servers in the development process. These may include *development servers* where the programmers write and save their code. *Testing servers* test the product. *Trial servers* enable users to explore the application to look for feature issues. *Production servers* send the product to real users. These steps are automated, and while rarely truly continuous, as the Security+ objective states, they certainly can be daily or as needed.

Staging

Staging moves the code from the developers' computers onto servers, bringing the product closer to deployment, but with controls to do critical testing. *Non-functional testing* tests everything outside the primary function of the code. This includes security testing and performance testing. *Black-box testing* separates the tester from the source code. The tester inserts inputs and checks the outputs, looking for weaknesses or flaws. Staging often employs *sandboxing*, the use of virtual machines (VMs) to enable aggressive testing of the application without risking any problems with the rest of the network.

Production

There's a point where the testing is done and it's time to pull the trigger and get that Web application online and running. This is an exciting time for the developers of the Web application, because their product is finally exposed to the public Internet. This is where all the security issues discussed in this book come into play, such as firewalls, DMZs, load balancing, and intrusion detection/prevention.

The process of moving an application from the development environment to the production environment is called *provisioning*. The process of removing an application from the production environment is called *deprovisioning*.

One important part of the provisioning process, and almost always the last step before the application is uploaded to a server, is code signing. *Code signing* means to sign an individual executable/interpreted code digitally so that users have confidence the code they run is the actual code from the developer. Figure 11-18 shows an example of a warning sign from a Windows 10 system, notifying the user that the executable code is not known to Windows as an approved developer.

Figure 11-18
Windows
unknown
certificate
warning

Windows protected your PC

Windows Defender SmartScreen prevented an unrecognized app from
starting. Running this app might put your PC at risk.
More info

Don't run

Quality Assurance

Quality assurance (QA) defines the processes used to ensure that the production code
meets customer requirements while staying as close to error-free as possible. Two items
to note here. First, just because quality assurance is at the end of the five-part application
development process, it's really everywhere in the process. Second, QA is different from
the earlier mentioned code quality. Code quality is a big part of the quality assurance process, but it's not the only part. A good QA program includes user training, test standards,
and good organization of quality testing personnel and processes.

Getting Organized

Using the five-step application lifespan defined by the CompTIA Security+ objectives is
convenient, but it's also an outrageous oversimplification, making application development look like a linear process. The reality is that any Web application, even a simple
in-house application, is a complex process that's never linear. Let's look at four *development life cycle models*: waterfall, DevOps, Secure DevOps, and Agile.

Waterfall Model

Starting as far back as the mid-1970s, software development used a linear process known
as the *waterfall* model. Like a waterfall, each step of software development had a start
and an end, which then led down to the next step. Figure 11-19 shows the steps placed
in a waterfall pattern.

Figure 11-19
A waterfall model

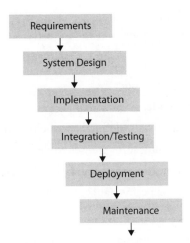

DevOps

The waterfall model neglects the reality of application development and lifespan in the real world. The reason an application exists is to do some type of job, to be operational. The correct goal of development is to work closely with operations to ensure the application is effective, efficient, secure, up to date, and available. *DevOps*, a grammatically poor but fun-sounding combination of the words "development" and "operations," defines steps that show how the lifespan of an application is more cyclical than linear. A popular way to describe DevOps is the DevOps toolchain, as shown in Figure 11-20.

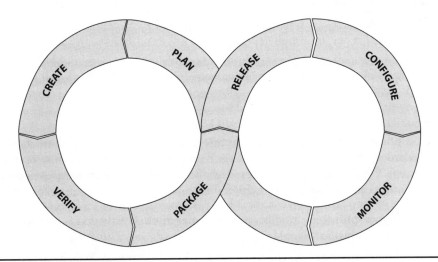

Figure 11-20   DevOps toolchain

The CompTIA Security+ exam is not going to test on these steps. These steps are well known and understood throughout the industry, so you should know them too.

1. **Plan.** What is needed? Requirements.

2. **Create.** Develop the code.

3. **Verify.** Test the code.

4. **Package.** Get approvals, define how the product is released.

5. **Release.** Provisioning software, schedules.

6. **Configure.** Application storage, application configuration.

7. **Monitor.** Monitor performance, security, end-user experience.

Secure DevOps

Secure DevOps means to integrate security tightly into the DevOps toolchain. Security fits into almost every point of the DevOps cycle in what is known as *continuous integration*, but a few important areas are as follows:

- Run *security automation tools* to speed up security testing and eliminate human error. Automation is very popular for many aspects of security testing, such as fuzzing.

- Add strict *change management and version controls* to ensure faults aren't introduced into the application.

- Introduce *security concerns and requirements* at the planning stage to ensure strong security integration.

- *Integrity measurement* shows the honesty, morality, and quality of the application.

- *Baselining* defines security objectives that the application must meet.

- *Immutable systems* are systems that once deployed are never upgraded, changed, or patched. They are simply replaced. This is easy to do in a VM environment.

- *Infrastructure as code (IaC)* means to use preset definition files as opposed to manual configurations to set up servers. IaC prevents accidental vulnerabilities due to flawed server configurations.

Agile

From the moment the waterfall model was first formalized, a number of alternate models were forwarded, all with limited success. Years ago, representatives from these alternative models came together and generated the "Manifesto for Agile Software Development," which espouses the following 12 principles (http://agilemanifesto.org/principles.html):

1. Our highest priority is to satisfy the customer through early and continuous delivery of valuable software.

2. Welcome changing requirements, even late in development. Agile processes harness change for the customer's competitive advantage.

3. Deliver working software frequently, from a couple of weeks to a couple of months, with a preference to the shorter timescale.

4. Business people and developers must work together daily throughout the project.

5. Build projects around motivated individuals. Give them the environment and support they need, and trust them to get the job done.

6. The most efficient and effective method of conveying information to and within a development team is face-to-face conversation.

7. Working software is the primary measure of progress.

8. Agile processes promote sustainable development. The sponsors, developers, and users should be able to maintain a constant pace indefinitely.

9. Continuous attention to technical excellence and good design enhances agility.

10. Simplicity—the art of maximizing the amount of work not done—is essential.

11. The best architectures, requirements, and designs emerge from self-organizing teams.

12. At regular intervals, the team reflects on how to become more effective, then tunes and adjusts its behavior accordingly.

This manifesto didn't define a development model as much as it did a philosophy that stands on these 12 principles.

From this manifesto, a number of different development frameworks have been developed. A complete coverage of even one of the Agile frameworks is far outside the scope of CompTIA Security+, but let's take a moment to consider one framework called Scrum.

 NOTE The word Scrum comes from the rugby scrum.

A *Scrum* is a process framework, a series of actions members of a development team need to do to keep software development moving as quickly and efficiently as possible. For example, every day every developer participates in a roughly 15-minute daily Scrum Meeting. In this meeting, every member of the team tells the other members several things:

- What they've done since the last daily Scrum Meeting.
- What they plan to have done by the next daily Scrum Meeting.
- Any issues or problems that need to be resolved to keep them moving forward.

Many development teams manifest Agile in their organizations using Scrum principles. Scrum has a proven track record and a rich, complex methodology as well as its own set of certifications.

Module 11-5: Certificates in Security

This module covers the following CompTIA Security+ objective:

- **3.9   Given a scenario, implement public key infrastructure**

Application security using public key infrastructure (PKI)–based digital certificates is a common tool used in many applications. While digital certificates using PKI was discussed way back in Chapter 2, the practical process of implementing certificates in a production environment creates an opportunity for interesting scenarios that address the steps (and missteps) that take place with certificates.

This module breaks the process of implementing a certificate into several sections. First, the module reviews the concepts and components of certificates, then moves into a discussion of PKI, as presented in Chapter 2, along with a few additional components. The next sections explore online and offline certificate issues and present a PKI scenario. The next two sections detail all the major types of certificates and cover certificate formats; that is, how certificates manifest on systems. The final section explores key escrow.

Certificate Concepts and Components

Asymmetric encryption works through the orderly exchange of public keys. Sending a public key from one host to another is fraught with security issues. Digital certificates combat these security issues. A digital certificate is a preset data format that contains, at an absolute minimum, a public key plus a digital signature generated by the sending body.

The *X.509 standard* defines specific items that must be part of any certificate for use on the Internet. The X.509 standard requires that these data items are identified using X.509 standard *object identifiers (OIDs)*, strings of numbers separated by periods. Figure 11-21 shows some examples of OIDs: Code Signing and Windows Hardware Driver Verification. Other settings in Figure 11-21 seem to lack OIDs. They're there, but the Windows certificate viewer doesn't show them.

 NOTE   OIDs are used in places other than certificates. Check out www.oid-info.com for exhaustive discussions on the uses of OID in technology.

PKI Concepts

For a certificate to provide the necessary security, it must contain a digital signature from a third party. A certificate that lacks a third-party signature is called a *self-signed certificate*. So where does this third-party signature come from? Well, it must come from an organization that has its own certificate that can apply a signature to a certificate trusted by both the sender of the certificate and the receiver (Figure 11-22).

Figure 11-21
OIDs in a
certificate

In this case, both Bob and Marisol trust Janet's signature, but who signs Janet's certificate? Janet signs her own certificate, creating a self-signed certificate (Figure 11-23).

As more users come into play, this structure grows. In this example, Julie stays at the top of the trust tree, but more people join directly to Julie; others may trust Bob or Marisol (Figure 11-24), creating what's known as a tree-shaped chain-of-trust model. Janet at the top becomes the *root certificate*. Bob and Marisol are called *intermediate certificates* and the rest are individual *user certificates*.

The process of getting a certificate isn't a user making her own and then somehow having a third party fill in a blank line of the certificate. Rather, the user requests a trusted person or entity to make the certificate. A user generates a *certificate signing request (CSR)* and sends the CSR as part of an application for a new certificate. The third party uses the CSR to make a digital certificate and sends the new certificate to the user.

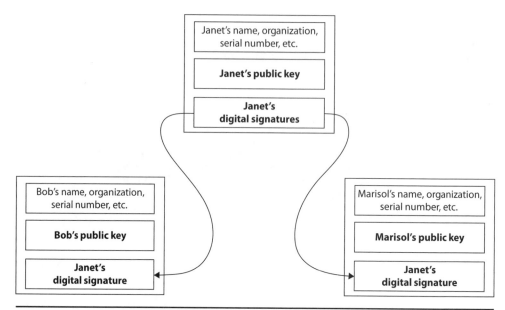

Figure 11-22   Bob and Marisol trust Janet's signature.

So what does Janet as the root get out of all this? Unless Janet makes some form of (probably financial) demand from those who trust her certificate, nothing except trust. The same problem exists for the intermediate certificates. Trust is valuable, and people and organizations happily pay for the confidence of good trust.

NOTE   For a single certificate, there is a specific path of trusts from a user certificate up to the root certificate. This is called a *certificate chain* and, as you might imagine, the process is called *certificate chaining*.

Figure 11-23
Janet's self-
signed certificate

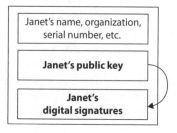

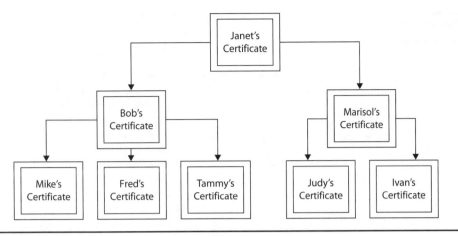

Figure 11-24 Tree-shaped chain-of-trust model

This trust model is the cornerstone of PKI, the primary method by which certificates are trusted on the Internet. PKI consists primarily of the following entities:

- **Certificate authority (CA)** Any organization that issues digital certificates and that also has a self-signed root certificate (also called a *trust anchor*) accessible on the public Internet (although there's an issue with this, as you'll see shortly).

- **Subordinate CA** Organizations or entities to which CAs delegate the day-to-day issuance of certificates on behalf of the CA. In more complicated structures, you'll see *intermediate CAs* between the CA and subordinate CAs. These CAs issue intermediate certificates that handle the day-to-day security of the trust chain.

- **End entity certificates** The certificates issued by CAs or intermediate CAs used by secure servers to initiate secure sessions.

The PKI model used by the Internet consists of several certificate authorities, each creating their own separate tree-shaped chain-of-trust model, as shown in Figure 11-25.

Online vs. Offline CA

The root certificate for a CA is an incredibly important certificate. Nevertheless, the nature of PKI means that the root certificate must be online, visible on the public Internet. Should this certificate be compromised in any way, the CA's entire PKI becomes useless. Many CAs take their trust anchor offline, using only their subordinate CAs for the day-to-day work. They bring the root certificates online only to issue new subordinate CAs, then take the root back offline.

Figure 11-25
PKI trust model

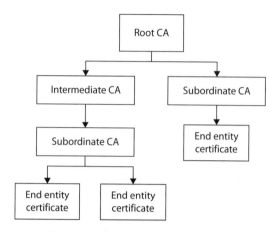

It's easy to see the PKI certificate chain in action by looking at the certificate store on any host. Figure 11-26 shows the Windows certificate store, displaying the certificate chain (Windows calls it the certification path) on its own tab in the dialog box.

Figure 11-26
Certificate chain (a.k.a. the *path*) in Windows

PKI TLS Scenario

To see how these certificates work together, consider a basic scenario where a person wants to access a TLS-secured Web site using a Web browser.

1. During the TLS handshake, the Web server sends a copy of its entire certificate chain (end certificate, intermediates, and root) to the Web browser.

2. The Web browser stores copies of the root and intermediate certificates locally. Starting with the root certificate, the Web browser marches down through the chain, carefully checking each certificate.

3. Part of this check includes running Certificate Revocation List (CRL) and Online Certificate Status Protocol (OCSP). Refer back to Chapter 2 for details on these two important concepts.

4. Many Web servers speed up the OCSP process by using OCSP stapling. *Stapling* means to send a premade OCSP response automatically with every certificate in the chain. Web browsers designed to use OCSP stapling will use this premade response.

5. Assuming the certificate chain is correct, the Web browser accepts the certificates and the TLS handshake continues. If there's a problem—a *certificate issue*—the browser stops the handshake and gives an error, displaying some form of information to give the user a clue as to the problem (Figure 11-27).

Figure 11-27
Certificate error
in Chrome on
Android

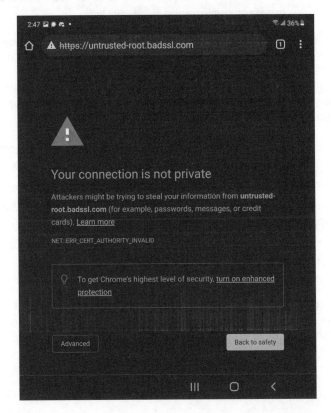

Types of Certificates

It's common for those interested in X.509 certificates to explore HTTPS using TLS as the first exposure to certificates, but it's equally important to know that many applications beyond HTTPS use X.509 certificates. You'll even find variations among HTTPS certificates.

HTTPS Certificate Types

With a new entity, such as an individual who wants to set up his or her own secure Web server, the issuing CA must trust that entity. So how does a CA determine whether it should trust that entity? When PKI was first established, there was no ruleset that defined how a CA should ascertain a potential entity's trustworthiness prior to issuing a certificate. Over time, a few extensions were added to certificates that defined different levels of trust. The CompTIA Security+ exam covers domain validation and extended validation certificate types.

Domain Validation Certificates   *Domain validation (DV)* certificates are the lowest level of SSL certificates. CAs issue DV certificates to the domain admin contact in the public record associated with a domain name. DV certificates are cheap (or even free) and the process is automatic, making for very quickly issued certificates.

The problem with DV certificates is that they are susceptible to phishing and man-in-the-middle attacks. There's no verification check that the DNS name matches the organization, nor is the organization itself checked.

Extended Validation Certificates   An *extended validation (EV)* certificate differs from a DV certificate, requiring a more rigorous process of verifying the applicant. The CA/Browser Forum (www.cabforum.org), a voluntary group of CAs and browser developers, maintains clear guidelines for their members to use to verify entities for EV certificates.

The steps for obtaining an EV certificate vary by organization type, but for a private organization to get an EV certificate, the following must happen:

1. Verify the organization is properly formed (incorporated, private).

2. Verify some form of registration of the organization (such as its Dun & Bradstreet rating).

3. Verify the organization's formal legal name against the name used on the EV application.

4. Verify the name and address of the organization or the name and address of a registered agent for the applying entity.

CAs have the right to add to this list of requirements.

EV certificates aren't required, but as the public continues to be aware of the extra trust involved with sites using EV certificates, any e-commerce site or other sensitive data services should move to EV certificates for the extra security and trust.

Figure 11-28 Two certificates for two different URLs on the same domain

Wildcard Certificates

HTTP certificates typically are issued to specific URLs. For example, my company has one certificate for the www.totalsem.com Web site and a second certificate for our portal, hub.totalsem.com. We purchased the two certificates at different times and from different CAs (Figure 11-28).

Wildcard certificates apply to a whole domain, rather than a specific URL. If we were to purchase a wildcard certificate for totalsem.com, every subdomain we create would use that certificate. This sounds great, right? We would need to purchase a single certificate to secure www.totalsem.com and hub.totalsem.com, two subdomains of totalsem.com.

The danger comes from rogue servers. Suppose Janet (our fictional employee) creates a custom server for some purpose that's outside the company purview, such as a game server or a torrent mirror. The wildcard certificate would apply to counterstrike.totalsem .com or torrents.totalsem.com just like it would to the legitimate company URLs.

There are legitimate places to use a wildcard certificate. An internal network where trust is less an issue is one example. Another example is when an organization is in complete control of its own CA, such as Google (Figure 11-29).

Subject Alternative Name (SAN) extensions to X.509 enable certificates that support more than one specific domain name. SAN certificates—as they're marketed—list the domains they support. Figure 11-30 shows a SAN certificate detail.

Pinning

There are scenarios where a bad actor might try to take over a CA and quickly update the entire PKI for that CA, generating perfectly legal (chain-wise) certificates. To combat this, a technique called *HTTP Public Key Pinning (HPKP)* is used. HPKP uses *pins*, which are simply stored hashes of the public key that the host machines can compare against to verify that the public key inside the certificate is the same as anticipated.

EXAM TIP *Pinning* in the context of HPKP means the server lists a set of public key hashes. HPKP has been deprecated as of this writing, but you might see the term on the CompTIA Security+ 601 exam.

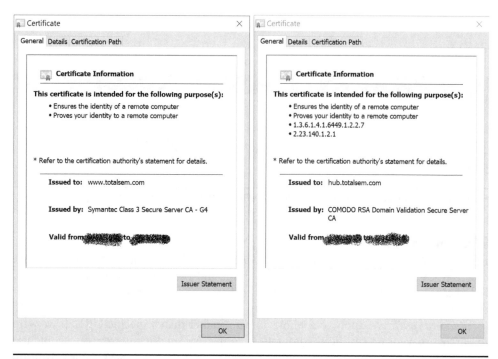

Figure 11-29   Google is big enough to use wildcards publicly.

Other Certificates

X.509 digital certificates were designed from the beginning to support any application that needed a safe, trustable model for public key exchange. Granted, SSL/TLS handshakes are certainly the most popular single use of them, but there are plenty more. Here's a list of other popular formats for certificate use:

- E-mail
- Code signing
- Machine/computer
- User

E-mail   Traditional e-mail has no encryption, making all e-mail easily read by man-in-the-middle (a.k.a. on-path) attacks. E-mail certificates aren't used for authentication as in HTTP, but are used with S/MIME to generate encrypted e-mail. To use S/MIME, discussed earlier in this chapter, each e-mail account needs its own key pair. To encrypt e-mail messages, two e-mail users must first exchange public keys. The public keys are exchanged via e-mail certificates.

S/MIME e-mail certificates have lost a lot of popularity due to the growing popularity of secure SNMP/POP3/IMAP protocols. In these cases, SSL/TLS certificates are installed on e-mail servers just as SSL/TLS certificates are installed on Web servers.

Figure 11-30
SAN certificate
that includes
wildcards

The one benefit to S/MIME is that individual users have complete control over their e-mail encryption. Modern versions do not provide point-to-point encryption, as e-mail is only encrypted from server to server.

Web-based e-mail services (such as Gmail) provide end-to-end encryption. They use HTTPS exclusively.

EXAM TIP Be ready for scenarios on the CompTIA Security+ exam that challenge administrators for certain e-mail situations. Normally, e-mail uses unencrypted credentials/clear text for exchanging messages. A user that needs encrypted, secure e-mail communication must use S/MIME.

Code Signing   *Code signing* verifies that an executable file is in good order via digital signatures. Application developers create key pairs, sign the code by encrypting a hash with the private key, and then distribute the code. Assuming users have the certificate from the developer, they can use the public key to verify the digital signature. Like e-mail, code signing uses PKI extensively (Figure 11-31).

Figure 11-31
Code signing
certificate

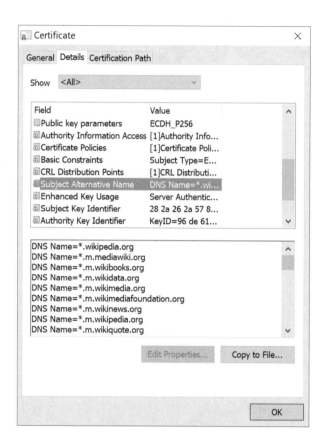

Machine/Computer   Assigning a certificate to individual computers isn't too common, but there are places where this is used. Very high-security, enterprise-level 802.11 wireless networks using EAP-TTLS security can assign a *machine* certificate to every system. Figure 11-32 shows the configuration of EAP-TTLS on a Windows system.

 NOTE   Chapter 7 covered EAP-TTLS in detail.

User   *User* certificates are used in unique circumstances where some application needs good security applied to individual users. On Windows systems that support Encrypting File System (EFS), each user on an individual host receives a certificate when the user activates EFS.

Certificate Formats

Certificates contain quite a bit of data that needs organization in terms of storage. A certificate sitting on a hard drive manifests as a file. Over the years a number of file formats have been developed. In general, these many formats can be organized by certain criteria.

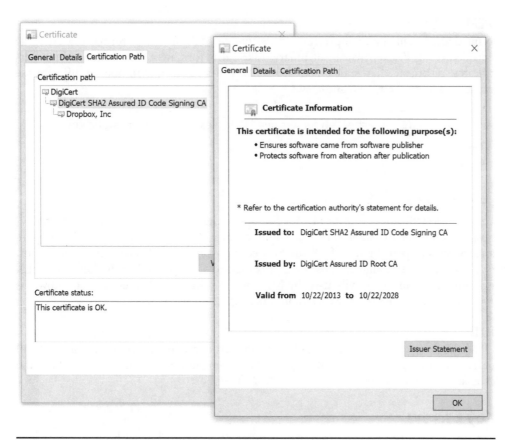

Figure 11-32 Configuring EAP-TTLS on a wireless network

First, is the data encoded in binary format or in Base64 text? Second, what's being stored in the single file? Does the file format store just a single certificate, a completed certificate chain, or a full key pair?

There is no benefit of one format versus another. It's simply a matter of what type of certificate information is needed, what type of encryption is needed, and what a platform requires.

NOTE There are tools to convert most certificate formats into other formats.

DER

Distinguished Encoding Rules (DER) is an early and complex binary format for storing pretty much anything desired in terms of certificates. DER is binary, storing single certificates, certificate chains, or private keys. A DER format uses either a .der or .cer extension. This type of format is often used with Java applications.

PEM

Named after a failed e-mail project, *Privacy Enhanced Mail (PEM)* format is a DER file encoded using Base64 instead of binary. Like DER format, it may contain single certificates, certificate chains, or private keys. PEM files come in a number of different file extensions: .pem, .crt, .cer, and .key.

NOTE Apache Web servers need PEM files to store their certificates.

PFX/PKCS#12

Leaving a certificate in the form of a file opens the file itself to risk from theft. *Personal Information Exchange (PFX)* files fully encrypt all the data in the file and require a password to open them. A PFX file may contain single certificates, certificate chains, or private keys, although in most cases it is used to store public/private key pairs. PFX is a binary file and is heavily used by Microsoft products. PFX files are also known as *PKCS#12*. These files use the extension .pfx or .p12.

P7B

Of all the format types, a *P7B* file only contains certificates or certificate chains. P7B will never contain a private key. P7B files use Base64 encoding and almost always have the extension .p7b. P7B files are also known as *PKCS#7*.

Key Escrow

Private keys tend to be forgotten in certificate discussions, but without a private key, a certificate is useless. Any protocol that uses the idea of a server handing out public keys also means that the server in question must carefully and securely store a private key as well.

Loss of a private key can be disastrous, yet it happens more than one might think. There are plenty of scenarios where a hard drive fails, wiping out or corrupting a private key, rendering a server useless.

Key escrow is the process of an organization storing a copy of a server (or servers) key pairs for safety in a place where a third party might have access to them in case of a serious mishap.

Questions

1. Cache poisoning is directed against which of the following servers?

    A. DHCP

    B. Web

    C. Domain controller

    D. DNS

2. Which of the following are secure FTP protocols? (Choose two.)

    A. SSL

    B. FTPS

    C. SFTP

    D. TFTP

    E. SSH

3. The four-step process that initiates an SSL/TLS session is called a(n) _____.

    A. initialization

    B. authentication

    C. handshake

    D. connection

4. Encrypted IMAP uses which TCP port number?

    A. 995

    B. 993

    C. 465

    D. 587

5. Scott receives an e-mail from Mike with a digital signature attachment. Mike is probably using which of the following protocols?

    A. Secure SMTP

    B. SFTP

    C. TFTP

    D. S/MIME

6. Inserting unexpected text into a URL is what form of attack?

    A. Command injection

    B. SQL injection

    C. LDAP injection

    D. XML injection

7. What kind of attack manipulates a token on an established Web session?

    A. Buffer overflow

    B. LDAP injection

    C. Cross-site scripting

    D. Clickjacking

8. A new attack that is previously unknown to the security world is called a
_____ attack.

   A. birthday

   B. header manipulation

   C. proto-malware

   D. zero-day

9. Which of the following is a minimum set of performance values that define a
certain aspect of what the application must do?

   A. Requirements

   B. Agile

   C. Model

   D. Baseline

10. Scrum is a _____ based on the Agile philosophy.

   A. timing system

   B. DevOps cycle

   C. process framework

   D. manifesto

Answers

1. **D.** Cache poisoning attacks DNS servers.

2. **B, C.** The two secure FTP protocols are File Transfer Protocol, Secure (FTPS)
   and SSH File Transfer Protocol (SFTP).

3. **C.** The four-step process that initiates an SSL/TLS session is called a handshake.

4. **B.** Encrypted IMAP uses TCP port number 993.

5. **D.** E-mail attachments of all sorts use MIME; the secure version is S/MIME.

6. **A.** A command injection attack inserts unexpected text into a URL.

7. **C.** A cross-site scripting (XSS) attack manipulates a token on an established
   Web session.

8. **D.** A zero-day attack pounces on a previously unknown vulnerability in software
   or operating systems.

9. **D.** A baseline documents a minimum set of performance values that define aspects
   of an application.

10. **C.** A Scrum is a process framework based on the Agile program development
    philosophy.

Testing Infrastructure

Those are my principles, and if you don't like them . . . well I have others.

—Groucho Marx

Any infrastructure has vulnerabilities, whether in software flaws, network configuration choices, or employee foibles. Good, security-conscious organizations not only need to understand the ways attackers can gain access to their infrastructure but also need to test infrastructure thoroughly for any weakness.

This chapter explores these themes in five modules:

- Vulnerability Impact
- Social Engineering
- Artificial Intelligence
- Security Assessment
- Assessment Tools

Module 12-1: Vulnerability Impact

This module covers the following CompTIA Security+ objectives:

- **1.6   Explain the security concerns associated with various types of vulnerabilities**
- **2.6   Explain the security implications of embedded and specialized systems**
- **5.3   Explain the importance of policies to organizational security**

Testing infrastructure is a broad concept that involves just about every topic previously covered in this book. A big part of testing infrastructure involves understanding the impact of many common vulnerabilities. This module covers these vulnerabilities and discusses the impact of an attack against them.

This module groups vulnerabilities into three types: device/hardware, configuration, and management/design. As you read, keep in mind that while these three headings are not in the CompTIA Security+ exam objectives, the individual vulnerabilities most certainly are.

NOTE For some reason the CompTIA objectives list a few items, such as zero-day, as vulnerabilities even though they are clearly threats. In the spirit of completeness, I've included them here.

Device/Hardware Vulnerabilities

As you've seen throughout the book, the individual boxes/things—home automation, switches, routers, smartphones, desktops, and so forth—have many vulnerabilities. Here are the ones specifically mentioned on the CompTIA Security+ exam objectives:

- Embedded systems
- End-of-life systems
- Lack of vendor support
- System sprawl/undocumented assets

Embedded Systems

Embedded systems—which we covered way back in Chapter 9—suffer from some specific vulnerabilities. The main goals of attacks against embedded systems are to take over the systems, prevent the systems from operating, or steal the data coming in and out of the embedded systems. The impact of unsecured vulnerabilities is potentially massive, from complete loss of resources relying on the system, to sensitive data loss. The ICS/SCADA industries, heavy users of embedded systems, understand the impact of an attack that could literally take down manufacturing systems or, possibly the worst-case scenario, cause the shutdown or destruction of rail systems and power grids.

End-of-Life Systems

End-of-life systems—like that essential Windows 7 computer that you're finally able to retire—have one serious vulnerability in that they may store sensitive data. Data sanitization processes prevent the impact of these vulnerabilities by eliminating the data before the system passes out of the organization's hands and into recycling.

Lack of Vendor Support

All systems need some amount of vendor support. Vendors provide repair/replacement. Vendors provide firmware/software patches. Vendors usually provide some online user forums to give end users a place to discuss configuration and security. *Lack of vendor support* denies users the capability to address these important issues, creating serious vulnerabilities. The impact of these vulnerabilities is vast but includes potential system takeovers and data theft due to unpatched systems. When Microsoft stopped supporting and patching Windows 7 in January 2020, for example, the security flaws in the OS didn't go away. People who continue to use Windows 7 become increasingly vulnerable to hacking. Lack of vendor support is almost always a motivation to stop using equipment and move to another vendor.

System Sprawl/Undocumented Assets

When an organization acquires any form of system, physical or virtual, in an unordered, uncontrolled, or unprotected fashion, that system will not benefit from the protection that organized IT security provides to the infrastructure as a whole. The acquisition of undocumented assets is called *system sprawl*, which either sounds quaint or like a bad 1980s horror flick. The impact of these types of systems can be devastating to an organization, enabling bad actors to take control of those systems, and potentially to control the entire infrastructure. Some of the most horrifying incidents in the history of IT security—such as an organization having every server in its internal network wiped clean—came from a vulnerable system, outside the control or even knowledge of the security group that's attacked by bad actors.

Configuration Vulnerabilities

Every device that uses an IP address needs some amount of configuration. Almost every chapter thus far has discussed configuration, from routers to WAPs to IoT, but the CompTIA Security+ exam will test you on the impact of common vulnerabilities. A few of these vulnerabilities should ring familiar to you, but again, this module is all about the impact:

- Default settings
- Misconfiguration/weak configuration
- Improperly configured accounts
- Improper certificate and key management

Default Settings

If a device comes with firmware, it will have default settings. Default settings or configurations are nice in that they often enable a device to work well for unsophisticated users. Classic factory defaults include user name/passwords, SSIDs, IP addresses, and DHCP servers. The downside to default settings is that pretty much anyone with even basic knowledge of your devices may gain instant control. Entire Web sites are dedicated to default user names and passwords (Figure 12-1).

The impact of such vulnerabilities varies depending on the type of device. Taking control of a home router may give a bad actor access to your personal data. Taking control of a WAP might give a bad actor access to anyone's data who accesses that WAP's SSID. Internet access might be stopped, although most attackers will prefer to not be so obvious.

Misconfiguration/Weak Configuration

Default settings might be unique to firmware-based devices, but misconfiguration or weak configurations cover just about every type of hardware and software in existence. *Misconfigurations* include enabling services or functions that leave a system vulnerable to an attack, such as leaving on FTP support for a Web server (Figure 12-2). Note that

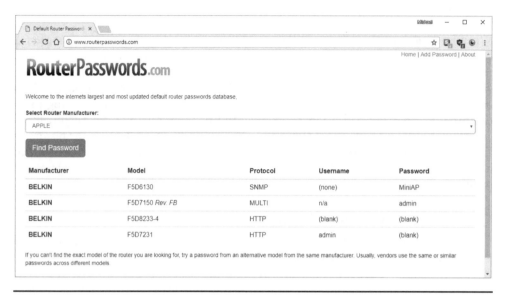

Figure 12-1 Typical user name/password site

most devices have services and functions enabled by default. You need to disable anything unneeded.

Weak configurations, as the name implies, fail to take advantage of the full strength
offered by a system or software. Two great examples here are weak passwords and
weak encryption. Once again using a Web server as an example, it's far too easy to

Figure 12-2 Do you really want FTP on this Web site?

provide support for older, weaker encryptions such as SSL when TLS is the way to go these days.

 NOTE You read a lot about weak configurations back in Chapter 5, such as open permissions, unsecure root accounts, weak encryption, default settings, errors, and open ports and services. Chapter 11 brushed on unsecure protocols. This module ties up the loose ends!

Improperly Configured Accounts

Almost everything has some form of account, and there are plenty of ways to configure accounts improperly. Default user names and passwords are typical examples, but this can go much deeper. Leaving guest or anonymous accounts active on server applications gives bad actors an easy entrée into a system, with the resulting impact being whatever evil they decide to do. Improperly configured operating system or file system accounts potentially could impact the system by giving unintentionally elevated privileges to otherwise normal users, exposing sensitive data to those who otherwise would not have access.

Improper Certificate and Key Management

The most important aspect of certificate and key management is protection of your private keys. Giving a bad actor access to a private key stops the power of asymmetric encryption, leaving the application open to the impact of spoofing and data theft. Every operating system does a great job protecting certificates, so it's usually up to the admins and users to make silly mistakes. One of the most classic mistakes is exporting copies of certificates or keys outside the protected data store, as shown in Figure 12-3.

Figure 12-3
Exported certificate sitting on a Windows Desktop. Not smart!

Management/Design Vulnerabilities

Some vulnerabilities aren't as technical as the ones mentioned thus far. These are what we call management/design vulnerabilities. The following four specifically listed vulnerabilities cover broader issues—one might be tempted to call these *all the rest*:

- Untrained users
- Vulnerable business processes
- Architecture/design weaknesses
- New threats/zero-day attacks

Untrained Users

There are few issues that scare a security professional more than untrained users. Without proper training, users will unwittingly wreak havoc on your infrastructure from the inside. Every IT person has plenty of stories of users unintentionally

- Installing their own home routers in the organization
- Wiping out entire hard drives with one command
- Shutting down gateway routers
- Giving away user names and passwords over the phone
- Copying sensitive data to thumb drives
- Making Facebook posts of their system information

The impact of untrained users spans the gamut of nightmares: data loss, data theft, loss of reputation, business opportunity, even legal issues. Failure to train users properly is simply not an acceptable situation for any organization.

Vulnerable Business Processes

Almost hand in hand with untrained users are vulnerable business processes. Back in Chapter 1, you learned that the concept of business impact analysis includes the recognition of critical business processes. Failure to secure vulnerable business processes impacts the bottom line of the organization, preventing the organization from doing its job. This would include financial loss and loss of reputation.

Architecture/Design Weaknesses

Any IT infrastructure has some amount of complexity. As the organization grows, that complexity increases exponentially. It's easy to insert design weaknesses inadvertently into your organization IT and security architecture. The impact of those weaknesses is that they open unanticipated vulnerabilities to bad actors. The best way to avoid these weaknesses is solid initial design, good change management, plenty of ongoing vulnerability assessments, and occasional penetration testing.

New Threats/Zero-Day Attacks

A *zero-day* attack is a previously unknown attack that hasn't been analyzed for mitigation. The impact of a zero-day varies by the type of vulnerability the attack exposes. Remember that zero-day means no one has analyzed it (and by extension made any defense). That doesn't mean, however, that your existing defenses can't detect and in many cases slow down or even mitigate the attacks at least to an extent. Good patching, good layered defense, good monitoring for indicators of compromise (IoC), and staying on top of the happenings in the security world are your only defense against a previously unknown attack.

 NOTE   Effective response to a zero-day attack also requires no panic-driven fixes that might cause more damage than the attack! Rely on your existing defenses to mitigate the initial attack and apply fixes as appropriate for full protection.

Module 12-2: Social Engineering

This module covers the following CompTIA Security+ objective:

- **1.1   Compare and contrast different types of social engineering techniques**

You've learned about the technical aspects of security, and you've seen how you can use technical measures, such as firewalls, encryption, strong authentication, and so forth, to secure data and systems. But what about the people who use and interact with the systems and data within the organization? What technical measures can you use to secure the system from human security issues? Is there a patch for being human? This module shifts gears and discusses the human element, focusing on human beings as a security weakness.

In this module, we'll look at the types of attacks that can take place when an attacker finds and exploits vulnerabilities in the "wetware"—the human being (Figure 12-4). We'll also examine why these types of attacks are so effective.

Figure 12-4
Wetware is
a common
term in social
engineering.

Earlier in the book, we looked at some of the different types of technical attacks that can be perpetrated against a system or network. This module explores attacks against people. *Social engineering* essentially means that an attacker or malicious person attempts to exploit human weaknesses to gain information about a network, a system, or even an entire organization.

Human beings need to be social; we interact well with each other as a species, for the most part, and most human beings need that interaction. We want to be liked and to be helpful, we respect and fear authority, and so on. In some cases, our emotions, needs, desires, and opinions can be used against us by a malicious person who is adept at manipulating and influencing people. The next sections explore the goals and the principles of social engineering attacks and examine some of these attacks in depth, including how they are executed.

Social Engineering Goals

So, what are the goals of social engineering? What does social engineering achieve that other forms of attack may not achieve as well or at all? While social engineering works for all kinds of attacks, the CompTIA Security+ objectives list *23!* separate types of social engineering techniques. We've boiled them down into five very specific goals:

- Reconnaissance
- Credential harvesting
- Identity fraud
- Monetary theft
- Influence campaigns

Reconnaissance

Every proper attack on an organization begins with *reconnaissance* to feel out an enterprise's attack surface for potential weak spots. Social engineering is almost always a first step (along with passive scanning and researching social media) towards any attack. If an attacker initially obtains insider credentials using social media, further reconnaissance is much easier. Various social engineering techniques, as you'll see, enable the attacker to gain access, often physical access, to an organization. Once inside, the reconnaissance can continue with information gathering of many types.

Credential Harvesting

Social engineering attacks often focus on gathering essential information, such as identification and authentication credentials pertaining to members of an organization. Such *credential harvesting* attempts to obtain the credentials of one or more persons inside an organization. Credential harvesting is extremely common in social engineering, and you'll see this goal played out through many techniques we'll discuss here. A credential attack may be just a reconnaissance tool, as just mentioned, or it might be an end in and of itself as a tool for any other type of attack.

Identity Fraud

Identity fraud is the use of another person's name, address, Social Security number, credit card number, and other personally identifiable information (PII) for personal gain. *Identity theft* is the process of gaining the personal information in order to commit identity fraud. Identity fraud is a huge problem today—so bad that you probably either have personally been a victim of identity fraud or know someone who has.

Identity theft takes on many forms: a skimming machine on an ATM, an illicit e-mail purportedly from your bank directing you to a fake Web site to get you to log into your account, or an unsolicited SMS message telling you that you've won a prize.

Identity fraud as a goal differs somewhat from credential harvesting and the techniques used differ as well. The former steals PII to pretend to be that person; the latter uses identification and authentication information to access an organization's resources in general.

Monetary Theft

A fourth goal of social engineering is simply theft, not of secrets or intellectual property, but straight up money. Several of the social engineering attacks discussed next seek to gain the precise information to parlay into financial gain. Here's an example.

Most business-to-business billing is done with credit. One company receives a product or service from another company. The supplier then submits an invoice—a time stamped bill—specifying the goods or services rendered and the time period (usually 30 days) within which to submit payment.

An *invoice scam* takes place when an attacker discovers that a company does business with a particular vendor. The attacker submits a fake invoice that mimics that vendor's invoice in all respects except the payment destination, which is an address or account controlled by the attacker. Many social engineering techniques enable gathering of the specific information needed to pull off this kind of scam.

Influence Campaigns

Organizations with political agendas have been seeking to sway others to their way of thinking for centuries using available news options, such as town criers, newspapers, radio, television, and social media. While there's nothing inherently wrong with informing people with facts, there's a moral issue to spreading inaccurate, emotional, and fear-mongering information to foment dissent (Figure 12-5).

The popularity of the Internet has taken influence campaigns to a whole new level. Using *social media*, bad actors, from individuals to state actors, issue propaganda, pushing disinformation to far more people than newspapers, phone canvassing, or e-mail messages could ever have dreamed.

Nations—*state actors*—may use influence campaigns as part of hybrid warfare. *Hybrid warfare* means to use influence campaigns, such as "winning hearts and minds" strategies, as part of conventional warfare.

Influence campaigns rely on information, both for sources and targets. Attackers can use social engineering techniques to gather this information.

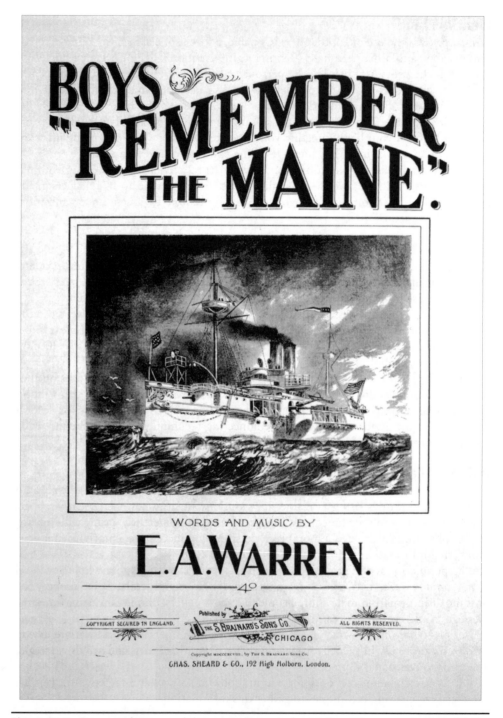

Figure 12-5 Propaganda song and slogan used as part of a disinformation campaign to justify the Spanish-American War of 1898 (Image: Sheridan Libraries/Levy/Gado / Contributor Getty Images)

Principles

Social engineering attacks are both very common and very effective. In fact, most network intrusions geared toward a particular enterprise start with some form of social engineering attack. There are hundreds of variations of social engineering attacks: maybe someone pretending to be someone else on a phone call; perhaps an e-mail message asking for your user name and password. We'll talk about the types of attacks in the next section, but before we do, ponder these questions. What are the principles of social engineering? What are the *reasons for effectiveness* of social engineering attacks? In other words, what makes social engineering work so well?

Humans are a social species, with an innate desire to help their fellow humans. Humans want to be part of a group, to work collectively, to be a part of the team. Social engineers use those traits to *elicit information* people wouldn't normally share with others. Social engineers will initiate contact with potential targets by impersonation or prepending dangerous information with seemingly legitimate correspondence, all with one goal—for the attacked to give them information.

So what are these principles so highly touted by CompTIA? They're clearly listed in the Security+ objectives. No, CompTIA didn't invent these principles, and no, they are not some kind of industry standard, but they've been around for years, and CompTIA has picked the following seven.

 EXAM TIP There's a lot of overlap in these principles of social engineering. Remember this when you see a related question on the exam, as it may have more than one correct answer. And focus on social engineering as many ways of *eliciting information* from people.

Authority

Social engineers who design attacks that leverage the *authority* principle take advantage of two reactions most people have to authoritative sources, such as bosses, VIPs, and so on: respect and fear. People respect people in authority and sometimes even fear them, because interactions with them reveal that they are in a position of authority for a reason; they may have power over us, such as the power to fire us or give us raises, for instance. We also respect positions of authority because we're typically taught that tendency as we grow up, and we experience it when we enter the workforce. Because of our fear of and respect for authority, we sometimes bend over backward to do what we're being asked to do by an authority figure, regardless of how we feel about it. Sometimes we act out of fear of the authority figure, and sometimes we want to impress important people with our knowledge, helpfulness, willingness to do our jobs, and so on. Attackers make use of these tendencies to convince us that we are *required* to take these actions by virtue of the position of authority they are impersonating.

Intimidation

Intimidation can go hand-in-hand with the fear of authority. Of course, a target can feel intimidated by an authority figure he fears, but it doesn't necessarily have to be an authority figure. An attacker can pretend to be a loud, boisterous jerk who threatens the target with all manner of bad results if he doesn't get his way, for example. The attacker may pretend to be an irate customer who threatens to complain about the target's actions to his boss or another real authority figure.

This kind of behavior typically intimidates people and can even cause them to want the attacker and their issues to "go away," so the victim is willing to do whatever it takes to satisfy the attacker's request as soon as possible. For example, consider a social engineer who calls the helpdesk and demands that her password be reset. She may yell and scream and threaten to talk to the helpdesk person's boss about his incompetence or lack of willingness to help if the helpdesk technician doesn't reset the password. A lot of new and inexperienced technicians fold to that type of intimidation; usually it's the better-trained and more experienced techs who know how to stay calm and handle difficult people and can thwart an attacker's use of intimidation as a social engineering technique.

Consensus

Social engineers who design attacks based on the *consensus* principle tend to be a little bit nicer, more understanding, and more sympathetic to the needs of the target. He attempts to find common ground with the target, such as a shared background, likes and dislikes, hobbies, or even opinions. He also may try to reason with a type of twisted common sense to get the target to agree that what he's asking for makes perfect sense, building a consensus with the victim and making the victim think his way, so to speak. Or, the social engineer will convince the target that everyone else is doing an action, so that action must be fine for the target to do too. Since people normally like to be agreed with, like to be accepted, and like to find common ground with people, they're more amenable to these types of attack. Additionally, everyone wants to think that they have "common sense," so they're more apt to break rules that don't seem to make sense if the attacker can simply get them to agree.

These types of attack may take a little bit more of an effort on the part of the attacker, simply because he has to do his homework and understand the target a bit better before he approaches and engages a target. The attacker might drop a few familiar names; this gives the victim confidence that the attacker is legitimate, since he knows someone who the target knows.

Here's an example: In a military setting, an attacker calls a helpdesk employee. The attacker presents the helpdesk technician with this scenario:

> I'm General Johnson's aide, Captain Smith. Can you believe this guy is asking *me* to have his password reset? It's incredible that he's so lazy he can't do it himself. What a guy…. But you know how it is to get an order from a general, right? You just do what you gotta do, even though it might be *technically* against the rules, you know? Can you help me out?

This attack could be effective on many levels. First, the attacker is dropping names the technician may be familiar with, so the technician may be slightly intimidated. Second, the attacker is attempting to build rapport with the technician by pretending to be just an ordinary person trying to do his job. Third, the attacker willingly admits to the technician that he's asking the technician to break the rules, but he's hoping the technician will feel sorry for him and do so anyway because he's just following orders.

Scarcity

Scarcity is another tactic used in social engineering. Scarcity refers to offering the victim or target something that they really want, something that may be otherwise difficult to obtain. It may be something intangible, such as a promotion, a new position, or some other type of incentive. It also may be something very tangible, such as an object or something else the target wants. For example, the social engineer could offer the target courtside basketball tickets if the target will reset a password over the phone rather than requiring the "user" (the social engineer) to present identification in person. The scarce item may be something as simple as an exotic coffee, or concert tickets, or something the target may not think is important enough to question. The attacker may use the scarce item as a kind of a "thank you" for doing a favor, thus continuing to build a good relationship with the victim.

Urgency

An attacker may use *urgency* to get a victim to perform an action or provide information quickly, without being able to think about it clearly or confirm that the attacker really needs the information or is authorized to request the action. You may have heard of an attacker pretending to be an administrative assistant, calling on behalf of his boss, who is out of town and has locked her user account. The admin assistant urgently begs or otherwise pressures the target to unlock the account or change the password without confirmation from the user. There's usually some contrived story about how the user can't be contacted by phone or is currently on a plane and can't verify the request herself. The fake admin assistant may insist that he will get into trouble with the boss, or the boss has a critical meeting with a very important customer and needs immediate access to the account once her plane lands. All this false pretext conveys a sense of urgency designed to pressure the target into performing the desired action or even giving the attacker information. Combined with a person's natural desire to help someone in need, especially in an urgent or critical situation, this technique is often quite effective.

EXAM TIP Urgency attacks work really well during penetration testing, where good guys probe a network on purpose to discover any vulnerabilities. See Module 13-3 for much more on penetration testing.

Familiarity/Liking

People like to be liked. That's a simple fact of human existence. So, people respond positively to people who like them or take the time to get to know them. Developing a bond with a social engineering target can help the attacker better persuade and influence the target into giving him what he wants in terms of information or having the target perform certain actions for him. For example, let's say that the target works in a secure area that houses some cool technology or scientific experiments. The attacker establishes a familiar and friendly relationship with the victim and bolsters her ego, making her feel good about the relationship. The attacker then casually asks the victim to let him into the restricted area so he can see some of the cool stuff that goes on there. After a bit of pressure and cajoling, the target may give in and sneak the attacker into the restricted area when no one's looking, thinking that it won't hurt if they are there together, and it's only for a few minutes. It likely wouldn't take an attacker long to install a hardware keystroke logger, a listening device, a small hidden camera, or even a wireless sniffer unobtrusively, once the target gets him into the restricted area.

Trust

Trust is yet another factor in successful social engineering attacks. Humans have a propensity to trust, especially when they feel that trust has been earned and when they feel trusted likewise. Social engineers know this and seek to establish different levels of trust between themselves and their victims, based upon the circumstances, their goals, and the level of rapport they can establish with the target. The attacker may need only a very low level of trust for some purposes, but may require a deep level of trust for others. The more an attacker needs from a target, the more trust they must establish with the victim. Often, these types of trust relationships can take weeks or even months to develop and involve using many of the techniques we've described previously to establish the relationship, develop a bond, and create trust between the attacker and the target. The attacker also may make the victim feel trusted as well, which can strengthen and hasten the trust relationship.

It's interesting to note that in most successful social engineering attacks, more than a single factor or technique is used; it's likely that none of these techniques would be very effective alone. Attackers can create complex situations involving multiple approaches to a target and use methods that establish trust, sway their victim's opinion and actions, and generally manipulate the victim. Of course, it really all depends upon the situation. Some social engineering attacks may involve only a brief interaction with a target that lasts only a few minutes and involves very simple attack methods. A simple attack, again, may be used to gain access to a more important person or put the attacker in a better situation to leverage a larger, more complex attack.

Types of Attacks

Let's explore several different types of social engineering attacks, including the basic types that you'll see on the Security+ exam. These attacks can range from the very simple to the very complex, and they may involve complicated scenarios or even multiple avenues of approach. You can probably use your imagination to come up with a dozen or more types of attacks or methods that a malicious social engineer would use to get what he wanted.

 EXAM TIP Many social engineering attacks involve *data exfiltration*, getting data off a computer without permission. An attacker can accomplish this in person, such as by gaining physical access to a system, inserting a thumb drive, and copying files. Data exfiltration can also happen through malware or social engineering, such as tricking an employee into providing confidential information to the "auditor." It's a catchy buzzword for theft.

Spam

Spam is unsolicited e-mail, usually advertising for some product or service. It's challenging to call most spam "social engineering" unless you're the type who thinks any form of advertising is inherently social engineering. The problem is that a small percentage of spam is truly evil in that these nefarious spams are really trying to steal from you or your organization. Keep this in mind as we define these "evil" spam types in this section.

Phishing

A *phishing* attack involves something that poses as a trusted source but attempts to deliver a malicious payload or gather personal or sensitive information from an individual, such as a Social Security number, driver's license number, credit card information, bank accounts, user names, and passwords. The attack typically involves an e-mail message sent to a user claiming that the user needs to connect to or log onto a site (with the link provided, of course) to verify an account or other such pretext. The user clicks the link in the e-mail and is directed to a site that looks convincingly genuine, and may even mirror a real site. The phishing attack can take many forms at this point. The link might download malicious software that runs a ransomware attack, encrypting files or drives and then demanding money to decrypt the files. The link might have extra information at the beginning—*prepending*—that adds an unexpected payload to the link. Alternatively, the unsuspecting user might input her credentials or information as the e-mail requests, not knowing that instead of passing on this information in a secure way to a legitimate site, she is simply handing it over to an attacker.

Phishing attacks have become increasingly sophisticated over the years; early phishing e-mails could be spotted as obvious frauds because they came from unknown or obfuscated domains, used broken wording or incorrect spelling and grammar in the message, and redirected the user to a site that was obviously not a legitimate business site. Nowadays, phishing attacks are executed with much more sophistication and precision; they often are very professional and convincing in their wording, use spoofed or similar-sounding domain names, and redirect users to professional-looking Web sites that may even provide some sort of fake functionality. Figure 12-6 shows an example of a phishing e-mail attack.

Figure 12-6

A phishing e-mail

Figure 12-7   Gophish in action

Note that phishing is different from pharming; in a phishing attack, the user is directed to a fake site through a link embedded in an e-mail. In a *pharming* attack, the user is redirected to a fake site through some other means, such as malware on the computer, host file poisoning, or redirection from a DNS server that has been compromised. The end results can be the same, however; if a user is redirected to a fake site through a pharming attack, the user's system may be attacked or the user may be enticed to input sensitive information into the site, which is then collected by the attacker.

As you'll recall from way back in Module 1-7, phishing is such a big issue that many companies use phishing campaign/simulation software to help train employees to recognize and avoid phishing attacks. Figure 12-7 shows an example of the open-source Gophish simulator tool.

Spear Phishing

In another variation of phishing attacks, *spear phishing*, the social engineer targets the phishing e-mail specifically toward an individual or associated group (think "the accounting department of company X"), instead of being generic enough to target many people at once. In the spear phishing e-mail, the attacker will often use information that can be linked to the victims, such as personal information the attacker has already gathered by some other means. Examples might include the last four digits of victims' credit card numbers or Social Security numbers, or partial date of birth. This lends credibility to the attack and makes it easier to persuade the victims that the e-mail is genuine. Another common spear phishing tactic is to spoof a known sender; for example, if Bob frequently receives PDF reports from Alice, a savvy attacker could spoof an e-mail to Bob from Alice containing a malicious attachment, and Bob would likely not think twice about opening it.

Figure 12-8
A smishing SMS

Whaling

Whaling is a variant of phishing, where the social engineer sends the phishing e-mail to a high-value target instead of the masses. Usually, whaling attacks target senior executives and others in important positions. (Whaling, as in attacks trying to land the biggest fish possible. I know, I know. Whales are not fish. Just go with it.) These types of attacks involve much higher stakes, because senior personnel in the organization have information that may be considered more critical and of higher value to an attacker. Like phishing, whaling attacks can deliver a malicious payload or gather sensitive information.

Smishing

A *smishing* attack is a phishing attack that uses SMS texts instead of e-mail. These are often cleverly designed to look like common texts received from vendors. Figure 12-8 is a sample received by your author.

EXAM TIP Don't confuse smishing with *spam over instant messaging (SPIM)*, which is spam received over instant messaging instead of e-mail.

Vishing

Vishing is yet another variant of phishing attacks that is often perpetrated via Voice over IP (VoIP) telephone networks. Vishing can be quite effective because it may use prerecorded messages and spoofed telephone numbers to convince a target that the message is legitimate. The attack may advise victims to go to a Web URL to correct or verify their information, or even to call a number, where the attacker will impersonate someone who has the authority to collect the information and "help" the victim.

Pretexting

A *pretexting* attack has the same goal as a phishing attack—gain knowledge and entry—but differs in that it creates a plausible scenario for the target to grant the desired information. For example, an attacker may call an employee, state that she is from the HR department, and provide the pretext that she is clarifying records and needs personal information from the employee.. Create some worthy story that gullible people will fall for and you've got a perfect pretexting attack.

Social engineers commonly use e-mail to deliver pretexting attacks. I regularly get e-mail messages from "legitimate" sources—using official logos and everything—that ask me to log into my PayPal or US Postal Service account. Helpfully, they have a link in case I've "forgotten" my password. Analyzing the specific links reveals that clicking the password reset link takes me to some sketchy site. The pretext is great, though, and can fool the gullible.

Shoulder Surfing

Shoulder surfing, an attack that is often undetected by the victim, involves the attacker inconspicuously looking over the victim's shoulder at her computer screen to see what she is typing or viewing. This type of attack is usually one of opportunity; the attacker simply waits for the right moment to walk by the victim and look at what she is doing, or he invents a reason to engage the victim in conversation while he glances at the screen. Modern technology enables shoulder surfing with a smartphone camera from across a room. Proximity is a relative term.

The attacker can use shoulder surfing to steal user credentials, account numbers, and other sensitive information, although usually it's only in small amounts due to the brief and unpredictable nature of the attack. Users can thwart these attacks simply by being cautious with overly curious passersby. Figure 12-9 shows how simple—and productive— shoulder surfing can be for an attacker.

Dumpster Diving

Often, organizations throw away papers, optical discs, and other types of materials they no longer need. These materials can contain sensitive information. A person with malicious intent can access that trash to try to gather information to use in an attack against the organization; an action with a cute name, dumpster diving.

Dumpster diving can help a social engineer gather all kinds of information about an organization from discarded company directories, organizational charts, server and

Figure 12-9
Shoulder surfing yields good results!

Figure 12-10
Finding treasure
in a dumpster

operating system manuals, contract documents, financial records, and other items. For example, if the company throws away a bunch of user manuals on an older version of Microsoft SQL Server, an attacker might assume that the company recently upgraded to the newest version, and that might give him an idea about what vulnerabilities the new version could have. Company directories and organizational charts can give an attacker insight into who works where, how important he or she is, and who works for whom, along with personal information, such as cell phone numbers and e-mail addresses. Attackers can use all this information to prepare and execute a social engineering attack on the organization's personnel.

Dumpster diving attacks are reasonably easy to prevent; the organization can simply screen its trash and make sure that it shreds or recycles sensitive documents and media. The organization must train employees to dispose of anything containing potentially sensitive information securely and not simply throw it into the dumpster. Additionally, the organization might want to install CCTVs or fences around its dumpsters and trash areas. In Figure 12-10, you can see an example of valuable information an attacker might find when dumpster diving.

Tailgating

In a typical *tailgating* social engineering attack, a bad actor follows an authorized person through a security checkpoint or door to gain access to unauthorized areas. Or it could involve a little bit of creativity: the intruder, with arms full, could ask for help opening a door to get in. Social engineers have also been known to ride in wheelchairs, walk on crutches, or otherwise appear to be disadvantaged and unable to open a door or get through a security checkpoint without assistance. To mitigate vulnerabilities associated with tailgating, an organization should require positive identification and authentication using access badges and accounting for every single individual who comes through a checkpoint. Many organizations use *mantraps*, or *access control vestibules*, like you read about back in Chapter 10, to protect against tailgating.

Impersonation

An impersonator masquerades as a valid network user, perhaps someone with higher privileges or status in the organization than the victim. The social engineer impersonates a valid user over e-mail, telephone, or social media and convinces the victim that he works in the organization. This technique is effective only if the target doesn't personally know the user being impersonated. The victim may have heard of the impersonated user during business or may have seen his name on an organizational chart.

Impersonation also encompasses the scenario of an attacker pretending to be a delivery person, utility company employee, custodian, etc. Someone typically "invisible" to other employees can slip right through to gain physical access to the organization.

 EXAM TIP   Sometimes an intruder can actually be a valid network user. A disgruntled employee can do some serious damage to your network and systems. Troubleshooting insider threat scenarios requires careful monitoring of logs and reports, especially looking for patterns of company security policy violations.

Hoax

We've all probably received the e-mails stating that little Timmy is dying of a serious disease and wants his e-mail forwarded to 10,000 people, or that Bill Gates is giving away his fortune and you can receive a part of it if you forward the e-mail to 10 of your friends. You've probably also seen e-mails asking you to provide bank account information so that a deposed prince or forgotten relative can deposit millions of dollars into your bank account to save their fortune. These are hoax e-mails, and they usually merely waste the recipients' time, increase e-mail traffic in the organization, and cause a nuisance. A *hoax* is a lie or false story that leads one or more people to believe something is true that is very much not true.

Occasionally, hoaxes can be used to carry out serious, sophisticated attacks. For example, a chain e-mail hoax could also have a virus attached to it, and by forwarding it to 10 friends, you are, in fact, spreading the virus. A hoax could also be used to track who the recipient knows; some chain e-mails ask the receiver to forward the mail to several friends as well as the original sender. This would enable an attacker to gain information regarding the victim's associates, as well as their e-mail addresses.

Hoaxes aren't confined to e-mail; hoaxers can use fake Web sites, social media sites, and even telephone calls to perpetrate a hoax. Their goal may be to get donations, spread a fake story, or even simply see how many people will fall for it. As with most other social engineering attacks, an organization's best defense against hoaxes is a good security education and training program for users.

Watering Hole Attack

Attackers have another tool that targets groups who would normally ignore or resist a spear phishing attack. In a *watering hole attack*, the bad actor researches the Web-usage patterns of a group, such as a company or department, to find a Web site that the group commonly visits and evidently trusts (analogous to a watering hole that antelope frequent, unaware of the lions hiding in the bushes). The attacker then infects that site.

The group continues to access the infected Web site, blissfully unaware that their computers have been infected. The bad actor then steals information in typical malware-attack fashion.

Module 12-3: Artificial Intelligence

This module covers the following CompTIA Security+ objective:

- **1.2   Given a scenario, analyze potential indicators to determine the type of attack**

Harnessing the power of computers to compromise security in computer-based networks, a long-time trope in science fiction stories, has rolled into reality today. Brilliant computers can mine data and attack systems. Brilliant systems can defend against all sorts of attacks. And brilliant programmers can attack the brilliant computers and systems because they understand how they work. This section explores artificial intelligence in IT security in four sections:

- Understanding artificial intelligence
- Machine learning essentials
- Big data and OSINT
- Adversarial artificial intelligence

Understanding Artificial Intelligence

A computer with *artificial intelligence (AI)* not only can do things that humans can do but can do them independently of humans directing the computer to do them. AI is all over the place these days. Facial recognition enabling you to log into your smartphone automatically? AI. Alexa or Siri responding to your voice when you ask for a song or directions? AI. Capturing and painstakingly analyzing every TCP/IP packet that flows into and out of your network and then both alerting security professionals of a breach and taking action to stop that breach in real time? AI on steroids. Let's put AI in the context of analyzing potential indicators of an attack, or more specifically, how bad actors can use AI to attack our systems. The first step in this bigger picture is machine learning.

Machine Learning Essentials

Computers with *machine learning (ML)* capabilities can improve their responses based on new information. Their programming can take input and change output over time to incorporate new data. Google's Gmail employs machine learning by filtering your messages into various groups, from Inbox to Spam. Five new messages from your buddy Sam talking about the latest Arsenal game continue to show up in your Inbox, but five new messages asking you to log into PayPal, all with similar language, get flagged and eventually tossed into your Spam folder. The algorithms running Gmail are sophisticated enough to recognize new patterns and then "learn" to treat these new messages differently. ML capabilities directly relate to AI and especially to AI attacking systems.

Combining AI and ML can—and does—provide robust system defenses against cyberattacks. If your intrusion prevention system can detect and process potential threats—even those previously unknown—what attacker could get through? Game over! (Unfortunately not, but read on.)

OSINT

Knowledge. It's out there, waiting to be gathered, processed, and put to use in your adversaries' nefarious schemes. A talented researcher—Grace, in this case, pictured in Figure 12-11—could use her *natural intelligence* to sift through social media postings, articles, Twitter feeds, news stories, and other open sources to gather enough knowledge to create a viable attack surface. Recall from Chapter 9 the world-famous Bayland Widgets Corporation (BWC), for example. Over the past decade, BWC has had 1000+ employees, interacted with 100+ companies, and been a featured organization in a dozen news articles. Our big-brain researcher could painstakingly track down the accounts for those employees and companies on LinkedIn, Facebook, Twitter, and more, culling any useful information. She could also run Google searches for every name to see any postings or connections.

 NOTE   Figure 12-11 is a photograph of Grace Hopper, famed computer scientist and US Navy rear admiral, taken in 1944. Dr. Hopper (Ph.D. in mathematics from Yale) was a pioneer in computer programming, changing the paradigm from solely using machine language to coding in English with a translator—now called a compiler—that led to the development of the COBOL language, still widely used today.

Doing such manual research would take a lot of time and effort for a single brilliant researcher or even a group of talented researchers. If only we could devise some machine to automatically search all these sources and . . . Oh, right. Enter AI, ML, and OSINT.

Figure 12-11
Our brilliant researcher at work (Image: Bettmann / Contributor, Getty Images)

Using AI and ML, programmers have created computing systems that can rapidly search and sort through open-source resources on the Internet. The AI algorithms can pick out useful material with ML algorithms refining and teaching the AI how to do it more efficiently on the fly. The resulting *open-source intelligence (OSINT)* can give the potential attacker one or more plausible attack surfaces in a comparably super-short time.

Adversarial Artificial Intelligence

Graceland Gadgets Corporation wants to gather information on Bayland Widget's latest mechanical masterpiece to do a little industrial espionage, as it were. GGC spins up its computers to gather OSINT on BWC and, once it has a suitable attack surface, unleashes the hounds on BWC's internal network resources. If GGC's programmers know what sort of AI or ML algorithms BWC's IPS uses, they can salt in deliberately misleading terms or fuzz to mess with the defender's AI. They can disguise their packets as harmless traffic. In CompTIA speak, they could insert *tainted training data for machine learning*, thus disrupting the defense. This process of deliberate deception to penetrate AI defenses is called *adversarial artificial intelligence* or *adversarial machine learning*, depending on which aspect of the AI is being attacked.

This spy versus spy action takes another twist. How can the BWC security team prevent this type of attack? They can stop the attackers from discovering the algorithms the BWC IPS AI defense system uses! Protecting the security of machine learning algorithms is an important defense in cybersecurity.

Module 12-4: Security Assessment

This module covers the following CompTIA Security+ objectives:

- **1.7   Summarize the techniques used in security assessments**
- **1.8   Explain the techniques used in penetration testing**
- **4.3   Given an incident, utilize appropriate data sources to support an investigation**

By this point, you've learned how to defend your systems and networks and the information that's processed on them. Assuming you've implemented all of the security methods you've learned about, you might be tempted to say that your systems and network are fairly secure. But suppose someone posed the question, "How do you know they're secure?" How can you measure the level of security you've implemented on your systems? Is it enough? You'll get answers to these questions by performing security assessments on your infrastructure. In this module, you'll learn a few things about assessing security as well as some security tools and techniques you can use to test security on your network.

During a security assessment, you'll determine whether the security controls in place are adequate and will stand up to attacks or any other negative event that might cause a loss of data or systems. To do this, you have to take an offensive posture. This means using tools and techniques on your network that will help you see exactly how secure it really is. We'll talk about several different types of assessments, including threat hunting, vulnerability scans, and penetration testing.

Before we get into the meat of this module, here's a word of caution: The tools and techniques we'll discuss are meant to be used for good purposes only. I'm not trying to train you to be malicious hackers or to compromise systems, but it's important that you understand how some of the same tools and techniques that hackers use can be used to test security on systems that you own and manage. In other words, use your Jedi powers for good, not evil!

Threat Hunting

No matter how strong your defenses, undetected cyberattacks will hit your enterprise. To counter these, your organization should have a threat hunting program in place. *Threat hunting* is an active process of locating cyberattacks and mitigating them as they are discovered.

Acquiring and implementing knowledge of security threats enables an organization to counter cyberattacks. Numerous sources provide information about cutting-edge attacks and security threats. This section explores intelligence fusion, threat feeds, and advisories and bulletins.

Intelligence Fusion

The terrorist attack on the United States on September 11, 2001 (9/11) illustrated (among many things) the need for sharing among the many federal and local agencies involved in intelligence gathering. Various agencies had some information about the impending terrorist attacks, but the culture of inclusiveness meant little cross-agency sharing and thus a catastrophic failure in overall intelligence to predict and stop the terrorist attack.

The United States and other countries developed *fusion centers* to address this problem, organizations designed to promote the sharing of intelligence among state and federal agencies. From their original anti-terrorism design, fusion centers have expanded into the world of IT security as well. There are close to 80 fusion centers in the United States alone.

In IT, the concept of *intelligence fusion* means to combine threat intelligence from multiple sources. Fusion centers are part of the puzzle pieces, but so are open-source intelligence (OSINT) discussed previously, threat feeds (next), and advisories and bulletins.

Threat Feeds

Threat feeds are sources, usually private, that report on different aspects of IT security. It's a real challenge to keep up with what's happening in security given the huge number of blogs, Web sites, videos, podcasts, and such. To make your life easier, most threat reporting sources output their information using *Really Simple Syndication (RSS)* feeds. RSS feeds have been around forever, but they're especially popular for IT security folks (Figure 12-12).

Everyone has different interests and areas when it comes to security. The feeds you choose to follow will change as your knowledge and specialties change. That's normal.

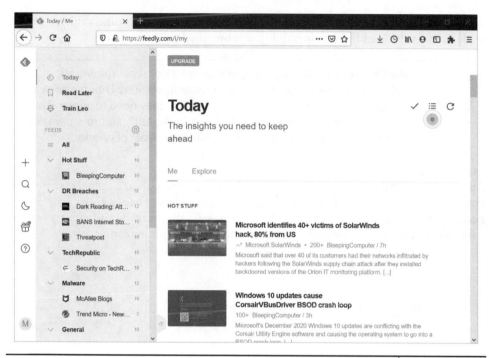

Figure 12-12 Author's RSS feeds

Advisories and Bulletins

Advisories and bulletins are announcements made by organizations providing security issues or information about their products. The primary difference between threat feeds and advisories/bulletins is that the former provide general intelligence about the threat landscape, whereas the latter provide threat intelligence about a specific vulnerability in a particular hardware or software product. Advisories are not periodicals.

EXAM TIP The CompTIA Security+ 601 objectives list *maneuver* as a characteristic of cyberthreat hunting methods, but that doesn't seem to be a term of art. Security experts certainly move from one threat hunting technique to another to optimize the action.

Vulnerability Scans

You and your organization expend a lot of time and resources to protect your infrastructure. How do you know your protections are effective or sufficient? How do you know that you haven't left any exposed vulnerabilities? The way to answer these questions is to run a *vulnerability scan*, a process, using specialized software, to inspect a system to identify lack of security controls, weak security controls, and common misconfigurations. Vulnerability scans are passive because no actual exploits are attempted on potential vulnerabilities. In other words, a vulnerability scan will identify a vulnerability, not what exploits might be used if the vulnerability was breached.

 EXAM TIP Vulnerability scanning identifies lack of security controls, weak security controls, and common misconfigurations. IT pros review the *vulnerability scan output* to determine whether they need to implement any new security controls, strengthen existing security controls, or make configuration changes and, if so, determine the order of priority.

Scan Targets

Any enterprise's IT resources are complicated, so don't think there's a single type of vulnerability scan. Different parts of an enterprise have different needs, so security professionals tend to separate the scans into different types. Tailor scans for different aspects of a specific enterprise. The following are common targets of vulnerability scans:

- Operating systems
- Applications
- Web applications
- Network
- Cloud services

Regardless of the aspect of the enterprise being checked, vulnerability scanners share some common functions. First, they inspect. Inspection varies dramatically depending on the type of scanning taking place. An operating system vulnerability scanner may look at running processes, while a *Web application* vulnerability scan might watch incoming HTTP requests. Inspection is usually the longest part of a vulnerability scan.

Vulnerability scans also consist of a *configuration review*. Exactly what is considered to be part of the configuration to review depends on the type of vulnerability scan. A *network* scan would certainly consider the ACL in a network firewall, while an *application* scan might include any configuration files or settings for that application.

All vulnerability scanners take advantage of any log files pertinent to the type of scan, performing a *log review*, an inspection of logs, not only looking for events indicating potential vulnerabilities but scanning the log files themselves for vulnerabilities. A log review can explore logs for changes made by unauthorized users, for example.

Scanning Processes

There's a vulnerability scanner for every job. There are also a number of popular "do a lot of different vulnerability scanning" tools out there. One great example is SolarWinds Network Configuration Manager (Figure 12-13).

If you look closely at Figure 12-13 you'll notice part of the report generated on the screen includes references to the *Common Vulnerabilities and Exposures (CVE)* database. Many vulnerability scanners use the CVE or the *Common Vulnerability Scoring System (CVSS)* to help look for these known vulnerabilities as well as using them as a reporting tool.

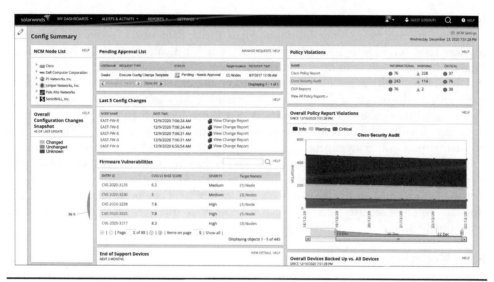

Figure 12-13 SolarWinds Network Configuration Manager

The open-source CVSS provides scores based on various metrics, such as the ease or impact of a specific exploit. The 0–10 scale ramps up in severity, so a difficult-to-implement, low impact exploit would get a low number, whereas an easy-to-implement, devastating exploit would push toward a 10. The scoring enables an organization to prioritize fixes needed according to the possible impact of the vulnerability.

TIP All vulnerability scanners are continually updated with CVE/CVSS data.

Vulnerability scanning software can be non-intrusive or intrusive, depending upon how it's configured. *Non-intrusive* scans are set to provide a cursory look at a system, preventing the scanner from affecting the performance of the system being scanned. An *intrusive* scan, on the other hand, performs in-depth checking on potential vulnerabilities and in some cases can cause a system to crash or reboot, affecting availability for its users. In addition to configuring the level of intrusiveness for a scan, most scanning programs allow you to perform a credentialed scan versus a non-credentialed one. A *credentialed scan* uses known valid authentication and gives you much more information, because you can access more information and configuration details about a system when logged in with valid privileged credentials than you can access if you are not logged in. A *non-credentialed scan* might be used when you have no knowledge of any system accounts.

False Positives

When you examine the results of a vulnerability scan to determine the effectiveness of your security controls, pay attention to false positives and false negatives. A *false positive* occurs when a tool finds a vulnerability that doesn't exist. For example, I've seen a popular assessment tool find vulnerabilities associated with Microsoft's Internet Information Services (IIS) on a Linux box, which is pretty much ridiculous since IIS won't run on Linux! Of course, this is an off-the-wall example of a false positive.

Often, false positives are not so easy to detect and can be quite subtle. You may have to investigate the details of the findings to determine if it's an actual vulnerability.

The good thing about a false positive is that it can be a relief to find that you really don't have a vulnerability even if the scanner detects one. The bad thing about a false positive is that you may expend resources, such as time and money, on correcting a vulnerability that doesn't really exist, before you determine it's a false positive. That's why it's a good idea to analyze each vulnerability and get confirmation from another tool or method before you assume that you have a vulnerability. False positives can create more work for you as a security person, which reduces your effectiveness in managing other, real vulnerabilities.

False Negatives

A false negative, on the other hand, can be a very serious issue. A *false negative* occurs when your tool doesn't detect a vulnerability that in fact exists. A false negative also occurs when a process or system allows unauthorized access, for example, where it should not.

False negatives happen. They're caused by issues such as IPS scanner plug-ins not being kept up to date, or log file settings that ignore problems they shouldn't ignore. The potential for false negatives is another reason to use multiple tools when you perform security scanning on your systems. This is also a very good reason for performing in-depth penetration tests. A penetration test can locate vulnerabilities that ordinary vulnerability scanning may not detect, since experienced penetration testers know to try various tools and techniques on different types of systems that may allow them to compromise a system.

Penetration Testing

Penetration testing (often shortened to *pen testing*), as opposed to vulnerability scanning, actually exploits weaknesses on a system. Although vulnerability scanning presents the possibilities regarding how a threat could be exploited, the results of a vulnerability scan are purely theoretical to a large degree. A vulnerability scanner doesn't tell you whether a threat could actually exploit any particular weakness, just that the possibility is there. Penetration testing, on the other hand, goes a step further. In addition to identifying vulnerabilities on the system, a penetration test can verify that a threat exists and that it actually could, in fact, exploit a given vulnerability.

 EXAM TIP If confronted with a question about pen testing versus vulnerability scanning on the CompTIA Security+ exam, keep in mind that pen testing exploits weaknesses, whereas vulnerability scanning only reveals possible weaknesses.

During a penetration test, *ethical hackers* (proud term for people who possess hacking knowledge and skills, but use their Jedi powers only for good and with the permission and support of their targets) attempt to bypass security controls by actively testing them and exploiting any identified vulnerabilities. IT pros who do pen testing are commonly referred to as *pentesters*.

 EXAM TIP   The CompTIA Security+ 601 objectives use the term *authorized hackers* to describe ethical hackers more specifically as legitimate actors on the correct side of the law.

Penetration Testing Types

You should be aware of a couple of different types of penetration tests. First, there's the *black box* test, in which an ethical hacker performs a penetration test on the system with no prior knowledge whatsoever about how the system is designed and architected, what defenses it may have, or any other characteristics about the system or network. The tester will have to perform footprinting and reconnaissance activities on the network to find out how it's connected and what its defenses are, as well as its weaknesses, just the same as a malicious hacker would do. Note that this type of testing is also referred to as *blind testing*.

 EXAM TIP   Look for the term *unknown environment testing* on the CompTIA Security+ exam. That's synonymous with *black box testing*.

The next type of penetration test is called a *gray box* test. In this type of test, the ethical hacker may have some limited knowledge of the network or systems, gained from the organization that wants the test. The ethical hacker may have an IP address range, for example, or a simple network diagram, or even a listing of the operating systems they will find on a network. Beyond this, though, they have no knowledge of any vulnerabilities in the system. A gray box test simulates an insider attack, someone who would have some knowledge of systems already. What sort of potential damage could an insider do? The gray box approach analyzes this aspect of network security.

 EXAM TIP   Look for the term *partially known environment testing* on the CompTIA Security+ exam. That's synonymous with *gray box testing*.

At the other end of the spectrum is a *white box* test. In a white box test, the penetration tester has full knowledge of the network and access to network diagrams, detailed information about hosts and services on the network, and even previous vulnerability scans that may show weaknesses in systems.

 EXAM TIP   Look for the term *known environment testing* on the CompTIA Security+ exam. That's synonymous with *white box testing*.

Which type of penetration test the organization should choose depends on how much time (and money) it wants to spend on the tester getting information about the network versus actually trying to exploit the vulnerabilities. There may be value to having the tester start with no knowledge and trying to find out what they can, so that the organization can determine how much information a malicious hacker could actually get. On the flip side of that argument, the goal may be to exploit vulnerabilities versus trying to gain information about the system, so a full white box test can save time and money and enable the tester to focus on that important part of the assessment.

Rules of Engagement

Any penetration test needs to define what can and can't be done by all participants in the pen test exercise. This is the goal of the *rules of engagement (RoE)*, a written document, reviewed and agreed upon by all teams in the exercise, that defines what types of attacks are allowed as well as what and where the teams may attack. Microsoft keeps a great example of an RoE here: https://www.microsoft.com/en-us/msrc/pentest-rules-of-engagement.

There's more documentation to a pen test than an RoE! Penetration testing *requires permission* from the organization being tested and must occur during a time frame the organization approves. Penetration testing without permission means breaking the law and going to jail if caught! Ethical hackers obtain physical, written permission in the form of penetration testing documentation, such as a standardized authorization form from the Open Web Application Security Project (OWASP). OWASP provides (among other things) vendor-neutral forms in use throughout the IT industry for risk assessment to protect the companies that provide pen tests and other tests. OWASP has vulnerability testing authorization documentation, for example, to provide cover for vulnerability testers.

Pen Test Exercise Types

Penetration tests are treated as an exercise between two teams. The *red team* is tasked with the job of performing the penetration testing. They're the ones we more typically think of as the hacker types who use clever attacks and tools to get into other folks' networks. Red teams emulate potential attacker techniques. But the red team is only part of the pen test exercise. Every good pen test also includes a *blue team*, the insider team, the defender if you will. Any good pen test isn't just the red team against your infrastructure. Just as in a real-world attack, your inside folks, your blue team, would work actively to mitigate any attack—even one taking place in real time.

There are two more teams that may appear in a pen test exercise. First is the *white team*, the judges of the exercise. They verify RoE is respected. They may score the pen test (if scoring is an option) as well as act as observers of the exercise. Second is the *purple team* that acts as an intermediary between the red team and the blue team, providing communication and feedback throughout the exercise, to make sure that both teams grow from the experience and recognize lessons learned from the exercise.

 EXAM TIP Different organizations define the purple pen test team differently. A common variation from what we describe here, for example, defines a purple team as a combination of a red team and a blue team, functioning as both attacker and defender to understand the security state of an organization. Be prepared for either definition of a purple team on the CompTIA Security+ exam.

Be aware that there is no law, tradition, or expectation that every pen test has all these different color teams. A basic pen test may only have a red team, thus known as a *red-team exercise*. In some cases the blue team is just the security staff of the target organization. A purple team may not be needed when the red and blue teams are working together productively.

 EXAM TIP Don't confuse the terms "black box," "white box," and "gray box" with other terms you may hear that describe the hacker. A *black hat* hacker, for example, is a malicious hacker who uses her knowledge and skills to compromise systems. A *gray hat* hacker is known to use her skills for both good and evil at times, and a *white hat* hacker is usually a penetration testing professional or *ethical hacker*. Regardless of intent, without permission a hacker is just a criminal.

Reconnaissance

The penetration testing process starts with information gathering, or what the pen test folks call reconnaissance. With *passive reconnaissance*, the *intent* is to keep the targeted company from detecting the information-gathering techniques. While almost nothing is *completely* undetectable, the pentester uses tools and techniques that make detection of activity difficult. Passive reconnaissance avoids the risk of discovery by the target organization's personnel.

The Internet is stuffed with public, *open-source intelligence (OSINT)* that anyone may access—if they know where to look. OSINT includes easy and obvious sources such as social media but also includes interesting sites such as WhatsMyName (https://whatsmyname.app) that search for usernames on thousands of sites (Figure 12-14).

Figure 12-14 Search for author's user name in WhatsMyName

Playing in the world of OSINT is both completely legal and terrifying in the amount of information it provides. Check out the OSINT Framework (https://osintframework .com/) for a great place to get started in your exploration of OSINT.

With *active reconnaissance*, on the other hand, the pentester employs a broader range of tools, such as network mapping, port scanning, and more. Active reconnaissance puts the pentester at greater risk of discovery, but this needs to happen as part of the testing process. (See "Banner Grabbing" later in this module for a good example of active reconnaissance techniques.)

The pentester performs attacks on the system to see if he or she can compromise the system, steal data, conduct denial-of-service attacks, and so on. Through penetration testing, a security professional can determine whether weaknesses can be exploited way before a malicious hacker tries.

 EXAM TIP *Footprinting* is the process of collecting as much information as possible about your target network and is the first step of any reconnaissance.

You can use the results from penetration tests to determine how better to protect the system by mitigating the vulnerabilities that the tester was able to exploit. In some cases, you don't have to waste your time or resources mitigating vulnerabilities that actually might not be so easily exploitable in the real world. Of course, you shouldn't necessarily ignore these vulnerabilities, but you may be able to lower the risk incurred from them and spend your money and other resources on vulnerabilities that are exploitable and that may in fact be high-risk items.

Wireless networks, especially 802.11 Wi-Fi networks, are by nature publicly accessible, as it's impossible to stop radio waves short of very expensive shielding. Knowing this, it's not illegal to inspect 802.11 packets flying through the air, and all good pentesters take advantage of this by *war driving*: searching for wireless networks for passive reconnaissance.

 EXAM TIP All of the war *whatevers* discussed here were popular 20+ years ago and are most certainly *not* a thing now . . . except on the CompTIA Security+ exam. Know what they were for the exam and then never speak of them again.

Traditional war driving consists of an automobile, a laptop running good war driving software (Netstumbler and Kismet are two classics), and a powerful antenna. As the car drives through a location, it picks up SSID information and logs it into the software, storing GPS information along with the SSID name, type, and strength.

War driving implies driving in a car, but there are plenty of other options for gathering information. *War cycling* on a bicycle, *war walking* when on foot, or *war flying* when using an airplane, drone, or unmanned aerial vehicle (UAV) can all yield effective snooping results.

Figure 12-15 The penetration testing process

Pen Testing Strategies

Penetration testing can go very deep into an organization's systems. Post-reconnaissance, a pentester might start the attack by using social engineering techniques (e.g., posing as a trusted vendor) to get a user inside an organization to access a Web site for a security patch. The pentester controls that Web site and runs software that captures information about the system used to download the patch. After that *initial exploitation*, the pentester might install a backdoor entrance into the compromised system to gain *persistence*—perpetual access to the company network.

As another option, the pentester could access the compromised system and, through *privilege escalation*, run software tools that require administrator or root privilege. One such use of escalation of privilege is called a *pivot*, or *pivoting*, by which software tools discover previously hidden networks connected to the compromised system. Or, the pivot can happen along a new pathway, hidden or not. I can get to Bob's desktop, for example, and then pivot to a connected router. Armed with this new knowledge, the pentester can waltz deeper into the organization, exposing more and more weaknesses. Figure 12-15 shows the generic process of penetration testing.

Banner Grabbing

Banner grabbing is a technique that you can use to footprint a system and the services that run on it. For example, you could run the `telnet` command and connect to a certain Web server on TCP port 80, and in some cases, you might receive an error message that tells you the type of Web server software running on the box, its version, and other juicy information about it that might help you plan an attack against it. Banner grabbing is kind of a hit-or-miss technique, however, because a lot of modern network-based software by default is protected against giving up information about itself. Other software can be manually configured not to give up information, but oftentimes the administrator has not bothered to configure it this way. Other services, such as file shares, FTP servers, DNS and other network services, and even particular operating systems are vulnerable to different banner grabbing techniques. Figure 12-16 shows an example of banner grabbing.

Lateral Movement

Once a pentester has gained a foothold into a system, it's time to exploit that foothold. Sometimes the foothold (let's say, for example, access to a basic user account on a Windows system) isn't sufficient to get to the pentester's goal. In these cases the pentester makes a *lateral movement* by performing some action in another direction (perhaps starting a service) in hopes of gaining deeper access.

Figure 12-16
Banner grabbing
from a Web
server

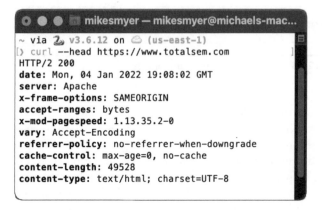

```
  ● ● ●    🖥 mikesmyer — mikesmyer@michaels-mac...
  ~ via  v3.6.12 on  (us-east-1)
  ] curl --head https://www.totalsem.com
  HTTP/2 200
  date: Mon, 04 Jan 2022 19:08:02 GMT
  server: Apache
  x-frame-options: SAMEORIGIN
  accept-ranges: bytes
  x-mod-pagespeed: 1.13.35.2-0
  vary: Accept-Encoding
  referrer-policy: no-referrer-when-downgrade
  cache-control: max-age=0, no-cache
  content-length: 49528
  content-type: text/html; charset=UTF-8
```

Cleanup

Pen testing can leave quite a mess behind in an attacked system in the form of accounts with different privileges, folders/files created by the pentester, registry changes, log file entries . . . this list of messes goes on and on. A good pentester makes a point to clean up the system after the attack. This process has one very important function: to hide the fact that the system was compromised.

Often the cleanup is what alerts the security staff something is amiss. Cleanup is an art as much as it is a skill, and sometimes the best cleanup is to burn the system down (or at least the logs anyway). Wiping out a system is proof *someone* was there, just not proof *you* were the one.

Bug Bounty

There's no such thing as flawless software or firmware. Equally true is the fact that people will eventually stumble across the bugs and vulnerabilities. Finally, it's probably a good idea for developers to motivate the people who stumble across these bugs to inform them so they can patch/update as needed. Knowing this, software developers generally offer some form of *bug bounty*, an offer of payment to anyone who discovers and reports bugs/vulnerabilities in their code.

Organizations that are serious about the security of their systems hire penetration testing firms. If the ethical hackers can get in, then so can the bad guys. You need to assess the security of networks and systems for which you are responsible.

Module 12-5: Assessment Tools

This module covers the following CompTIA Security+ objective:

• **4.1 Given a scenario, use the appropriate tool to assess organizational security**

We've discussed various methods of conducting security assessments and penetration tests; now it's time to talk about some of the tools used to perform these assessments.

Keep in mind that most of these tools are like a double-edged sword. They can be used for good purposes, by ethical security professionals, to maintain the security of their systems and networks. Or they can be used by malicious individuals to steal data, conduct denial-of-service attacks, hack into systems, and perform all sorts of other kinds of malicious mischief.

This module explores *network reconnaissance and discovery tools*. That's a fancy way to describe tools that enable security professionals (on both sides of the legal divide) to probe and explore networks to assess the security levels of an organization.

Protocol Analyzer

A *protocol analyzer*, as you'll recall from way back in Chapter 4, processes data scanned by a packet sniffer. A sniffer collects network traffic, throughout the OSI levels, regardless of port, protocol, or service (provided it's one that the sniffer can understand). Packet sniffers are the programs that capture and store frames. Two popular packet sniffers are *libpcap* in Linux or *WinPcap* on Windows systems. These packet sniffers are usually installed along with the protocol or packet analyzer.

The protocol analyzer such as Wireshark examines the captured data to determine different characteristics about the traffic to troubleshoot network connectivity problems. You can also use a sniffer to intercept and collect traffic so that you can examine it for security issues with a packet analyzer. For example, you could intercept traffic on the network to see if any unauthorized FTP servers are connected to the infrastructure. You could look for FTP traffic, determine the source IP address, and track down the unauthorized box and yank it from the network.

A malicious person, on the other hand, could use a sniffer to intercept traffic in hopes of capturing plaintext information, such as passwords, personal or confidential information, and so on. You can use encryption as one protection against a malicious person using a sniffer to gather information. Sniffers can still capture encrypted traffic, but since the traffic can't easily be decrypted, the malicious hacker gets to see only garbage, unless he employs other, more sophisticated methods to decrypt the traffic.

You can use sniffers and protocol analyzers on either wired or wireless networks, provided the device has a supported wired or wireless network card that can be used to capture the traffic. Wireshark is probably the most popular protocol analyzer software among security professionals and hackers, because it works great and it's free. Wireshark is available for both Windows and Linux platforms. A screenshot of Wireshark in action is shown in Figure 12-17.

Network Scanner

A *network scanner* is a tool used to send specially constructed network traffic to the host to get it to reply in a specific manner. Because of the way the TCP/IP stack is implemented on various hosts, the replies that the host returns can indicate what the operating system is, what ports and services it is using, and whether it is susceptible to certain types of network-based attacks. As you'll recall from Chapter 4, Nmap is probably the most commonly used

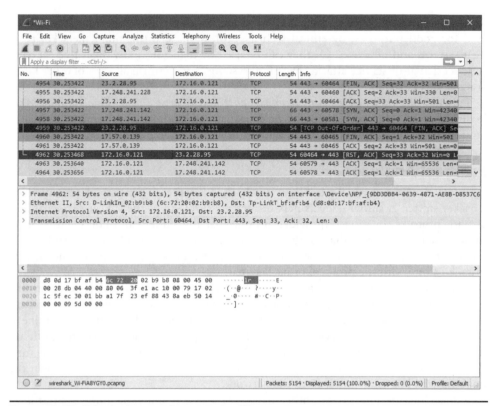

Figure 12-17   Wireshark, a popular network sniffer

network scanner, and it is available for almost any OS you can imagine. Security folks use Nmap to detect non-secure hosts on the network so they can fix them, while evil hackers use it to try to find attack vectors in vulnerable hosts. Nmap comes in both command-line and GUI flavors. Figure 12-18 shows output from the command-line version.

Figure 12-18
Results from the
Nmap network
scanner

```
Nmap scan report for 192.168.163.128
Host is up (0.00093s latency).
Not shown: 992 filtered ports
PORT       STATE SERVICE
135/tcp    open  msrpc
139/tcp    open  netbios-ssn
445/tcp    open  microsoft-ds
554/tcp    open  rtsp
2869/tcp   open  icslap
3306/tcp   open  mysql
5357/tcp   open  wsdapi
10243/tcp open  unknown
MAC Address: 00:0C:29:A5:76:55 (VMware)

Nmap scan report for 192.168.163.143
Host is up (0.00057s latency).
Not shown: 999 closed ports
PORT    STATE SERVICE
80/tcp open  http
```

Vulnerability Scanner

A *vulnerability scanner* is software used to determine vulnerabilities on a host. The scanner can gather information about a computer, including what ports and services it is running, which software it has installed, including the operating system and its version, what patches are installed, and even vulnerabilities that exist on the computer. A network-based vulnerability scanner, such as the popular *Nessus* scanner, can send specifically crafted network traffic to a host to elicit certain responses from that host. The responses from the computer can show vulnerabilities that might allow an attacker to compromise the host over the network, such as using unsecure protocols, weak encryption, open file shares, and so forth.

A security professional can use a vulnerability scanner to discover weaknesses in the hosts on the network and fix those vulnerabilities, so hackers can't take advantage of them. A malicious person, on the other hand, can use a vulnerability scanner to determine how best to attack a host or network. Figure 12-19 shows an example of Nessus, one of the most popular vulnerability scanners.

NOTE Nessus used to be the go-to tool for vulnerability scanners, but is now a wildly expensive program from Tenable Solutions. You'll find many organizations that continue to use Nessus, but if you want a great vulnerability scanner at a great price (free), try *OpenVAS* (https://www.openvas.org/).

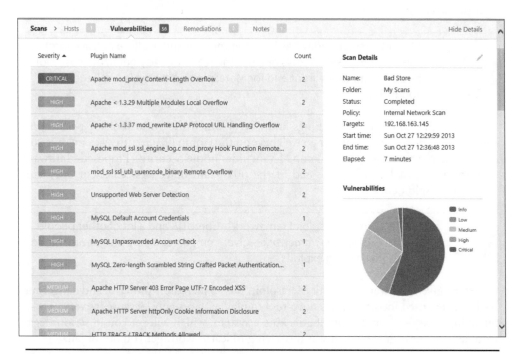

Figure 12-19 The Nessus vulnerability scanner

Configuration Compliance Scanner

The flip side of a vulnerability scanner is a *configuration compliance scanner*, a tool that scans critical systems to see if they meet the compliance standards set by IT security professionals in an organization. A good scanner, like Nessus discussed in the prior section, can check for and report on systems out of compliance on any number of issues, such as password length minimums, permission issues, and much more. (Nessus is both a vulnerability scanner and a configuration compliance scanner.)

Checks are based on standard audit files for systems that IT security folks customize to fit the needs of their organization. If your company uses primarily Cisco systems for routers, switches, and other appliances, you could download the Cisco-specific Configuration Audit Policies file from www.tenable.com, add it to your Nessus scanner, and run it to check systems. (Tenable is the company that produces Nessus.) Tenable has literally hundreds of audit files tailored to specific systems that you can and should customize further.

Penetration Testing with Metasploit

Imagine if a group of superbly skilled security experts got together, pooled their knowledge about every possible way to hack into systems and networks, and then *published that information on the Web*. Sounds scary and crazy, right? That's the team behind *Metasploit*, a platform for penetration testing by the good guys. As the Metasploit folks tell it, the bad guys already know this stuff. Legit companies need to know it too to arm themselves against the enemy.

 NOTE Metasploit today has free (community) and wildly expensive (pro) tools. The professional tools get into the realm of crazy good, but cost a lot. The best community front end for Metasploit right now is Armitage. (Google it!)

Metasploit can do amazing things and is very much the go-to tool for pen testing today. The functions and features go well beyond the CompTIA Security+ exam, but you should explore this tool, which CompTIA includes in the Security+ Proposed Hardware and Software List located at the end of the 601 exam objectives. Check it out here: https://metasploit.com.

 EXAM TIP The Metasploit Framework—CompTIA and a lot of other people call it an *exploitation framework*—gives companies a very programmable set of tools for creating exploits.

Let me give you a warning about Metasploit. It is an incredibly powerful and dangerous toolset when used incorrectly. It's not a tool to play with casually, because it's very easy—terrifyingly easy—to find yourself attacking a system, which will get you in serious legal trouble. Be forewarned here: "I was just trying to learn" won't get you out of jail.

Specific Tools Mentioned by CompTIA

We've mentioned a number of tools in this section, but the CompTIA Security+ objectives list even more. These are all well-known tools, but they don't fit easily under any of the assessment tool types already discussed. Most, if not all, of these tools are available in the *Kali Linux* distro, also included in CompTIA's Security+ Proposed Hardware and Software List along with Metasploit.

hping

The *hping* port scanner can do much more than scan ports. Start with the ping command and give it tons of extra abilities, such as sending out just about any kind of TCP, UDP, or ICMP packet, or enable the tool to receive packets from your targets—that's hping. The current version of hping is hping3. The following hping command sends a simple ICMP flood attack to the IP address 192.168.1.1:

```
hping3 –icmp  -S 192.168.1.1 -p 80 –flood
```

netcat

netcat (run with the command nc) that you saw back in Chapter 4 is one of those tools that's so flexible that it's hard to say what all it can do. netcat can open any port on a local system, in essence making that system act like a sandbox. netcat is a fine port scanner as well as a fine port redirector. If you need to do something with a port or an IP address, netcat can help. The following command tells netcat to scan ports 8000 to 8200 on target 192.168.1.1:

```
nc -z -v 192.168.1.1 8000-8200
```

cURL

The Linux terminal tool *cURL* enables virtually any form of file transfer. cURL supports the following protocols for file transfer: HTTP, FTP, IMAP4, POP3, SCP, SFTP, SMTP, TFTP, Telnet, and LDAP. Here's an example of using cURL to download a file using FTP:

```
curl -o mike.zip ftp://speedtest.tele2.net/10GB.zip
```

theHarvester

theHarvester is a program designed to search OSINT for information about domains, with an emphasis on e-mail messages. theHarvester is very good at finding where domain e-mail messages are used. theHarvester uses many different sources and puts a search into a simple command-line tool. The following command tells theHarvester to search for the use of totalsem.com using all sources, but to stop at 5000 results:

```
theharvester -d totalsem.com -l 5000 -b all
```

Sn1per

Sn1per is a pen testing reconnaissance framework and automated attack tool. It's a framework in that it works with other popular tools like Nmap and Metasploit to gather information about the target. Sn1per is an incredibly powerful tool and one all good pentesters know and use. The following command tells Sn1per to perform reconnaissance on a target using only Web protocols:

```
sniper -t www.cheftbrown.com -re -m
```

scanless

If you run a port scan from a local system, it's easy for people to trace the scan back to you. *scanless* is a Python 3 command-line utility and library for using Web sites that can perform port scans on your behalf. The following command runs scanless against a single target using all scanners:

```
scanless -v 192.168.1.1 -s all
```

dnsenum

dnsenum finds all the DNS servers for a specific domain, an action called *enumeration*. Enumeration is an important step for many types of pen testing, and dnsenum is the tool to use. The following dnsenum command will enumerate the target domain:

```
dnsenum --noreverse cheftbrown.com
```

Cuckoo Sandbox

Cuckoo Sandbox is a malware analyzer. You run Cuckoo with a suspicious file, and the program will analyze it for malware. Cuckoo Sandbox is very powerful, but very easy to use. It's constantly updated for new forms of malware and is often more aware than many anti-malware tools.

tcpreplay

The pcap file type is the standard way to store and analyze packet captures. IT security pros lean heavily on analyzing packet captures to understand attacks. tcpreplay enables you to edit and replay pcap files out to your network. Here is a typical use:

```
scott@kali:~/Desktop$ sudo tcpreplay -i eth3 -t -K -loop 250 mikehack.pcap
```

(And no, I didn't really hack Mike's system, capturing packets for later analysis . . . as far as he knows.)

Interpreting Security Assessment Tool Results

Once you run all of your cool security tools against the system or network, you'll be tempted to plunge right in and start exploiting all the different vulnerabilities you find, or at least you'll want to begin to remediate them by changing configurations, installing patches, and throwing money and resources at the system. One word of caution about this, however: You can't always rely solely on the results of tool findings as a basis for your security and remediation strategy. Different tools interpret findings from different systems, well, differently. Some tools may find a vulnerability and indicate that it's a very high risk, while others may find the same vulnerability a low or medium risk. Some tools may not even find the vulnerabilities that other tools identified. For that reason alone, it's a good idea to use several tools and look at the findings from a holistic approach.

Because of inconsistencies and tool findings, and because they don't give the entire picture of how systems and networks are set up, you have to consider tool findings in addition to other factors when you analyze the results. For example, the tool may tell you that you have ports open on a system that may be high risk, but the tool doesn't know that you have an application or a valid business process that requires those ports to be open. You may have mitigated the risk of those open ports in a different way, such as by isolating the system on a restricted network, locking down application permissions, installing network security devices to protect the system, and so forth. So, even though a tool finding may indicate that the vulnerability is a high risk, you've mitigated that risk down to a lower level through other means, using other compensating security controls. This is part of an entire risk assessment, analysis, and mitigation strategy.

Questions

1. Which of the following vulnerabilities can be avoided with data sanitization?

    A. Embedded systems

    B. End-of-life systems

    C. Lack of vendor support

    D. System sprawl

2. Which of the following attacks is conducted by trying to get a view of sensitive information on a user's screen?

    A. Dumpster diving

    B. Tailgating

    C. Eavesdropping

    D. Shoulder surfing

3. You are a security administrator in a company, and a user has just forwarded a suspicious e-mail to you that directs the user to click a link to a banking Web site and enter their credentials to verify the account. What type of social engineering attack is being attempted?

    A. Phishing

    B. Vishing

    C. Man-in-the middle

    D. E-mail hoax

4. An attacker calls an administrative assistant and tells him that she is the new executive assistant for the company senior vice president. She claims the VP is traveling, and she needs access to certain sensitive files in a file share. The attacker tries to bully the admin assistant into giving her permissions to the file share

by threatening to have him fired if he doesn't oblige. Which two characteristics of human behavior is the attacker trying to take advantage of in this attack? (Choose two.)

A. Trust

B. Fear of authority

C. Social proof

D. Respect for authority

5. A person calls and tells you that he has locked his account because he forgot his remote access password. He tells you that he doesn't have time to come down to your desk and positively identify himself because he is offsite at a customer facility and must present an important briefing to the customer within the next few minutes. He insists that he needs his remote access password changed immediately, but promises to come and see you after he returns to the office to verify his identity. What kind of social engineering tactic is being used in this attack?

A. Authority

B. Familiarity

C. Intimidation

D. Urgency

6. The IT security director for Bayland Widgets Corporation sets up a scenario to test the effectiveness of the organization's security programs. He assigns Mary to lead the red team and John to lead the blue team. Which role does each team play in the exercise?

A. The red team emulates techniques used by attackers. The blue team emulates the organization's defenses.

B. The red team emulates the organization's defenses. The blue team emulates techniques used by attackers.

C. The red team and blue team combine into the purple team, acting as both attackers and defenders.

D. The red team emulates techniques used by attackers. The blue team makes certain that the red and white teams follow the rules of engagement.

7. Which of the following types of assessments actually exploits weaknesses found in a system?

A. Code review

B. Architecture review

C. Vulnerability test

D. Penetration test

8. You are performing a penetration test and are given only some basic information on the target system, including its IP address range and a basic network diagram. What type of penetration test is this considered to be?

   A. Gray box test

   B. Black box test

   C. White box test

   D. Double-blind test

9. A security testing tool that does not interfere with the operation of the system or network at all is considered:

   A. Active

   B. Passive

   C. Less accurate

   D. Easily detectable

10. Which of the following is considered a dangerous type of finding because it can actually mean that a potential security vulnerability goes undetected?

    A. False positive

    B. False negative

    C. False flag

    D. False scan

Answers

1. **B.** Eliminating data on end-of-life systems avoids vulnerabilities to sensitive data.

2. **D.** Shoulder surfing is an attack in which the perpetrator tries to view sensitive information on a user's screen.

3. **A.** A phishing attack is conducted by sending an e-mail to an unsuspecting user to get the user to click a link in the e-mail and enter sensitive information, such as credentials or other personal information, into the site.

4. **B, D.** The attacker is taking advantage of the human tendency to fear and respect authority figures.

5. **D.** The attacker is trying to use a tactic involving urgency of need to get the remote access password reset without having his identity verified.

6. **A.** The red team emulates techniques used by attackers. The blue team handles the organization's defense.

7. **D.** A penetration test is designed to exploit any vulnerabilities found in a system.

8. **A.** A gray box test is one in which the tester is given only limited information on the target network.

9. **B.** A passive tool does not interfere with the operation or performance of the system or network.

10. **B.** A false negative can mean that an actual vulnerability goes undetected.

Dealing with Incidents

How strange that nature does not knock, and yet does not intrude!

—Emily Dickinson

Bad things happen, even to the most security-conscious organizations. As an IT security professional, you need to know how to respond to negative events. This chapter explores responses to incidents ranging from the minor (like a system crash) to the major (natural disaster wiping out the company HQ) in three modules:

- Incident Response
- Digital Forensics
- Continuity of Operations and Disaster Recovery

Module 13-1: Incident Response

This module covers the following CompTIA Security+ objectives:

- **1.7 Summarize the techniques used in security assessments**
- **2.1 Explain the importance of security concepts in an enterprise environment**
- **4.2 Summarize the importance of policies, processes, and procedures for incident response**
- **4.4 Given an incident, apply mitigation techniques or controls to secure an environment**

Most organizations can't afford to wonder *if* an incident will ever happen to them; they need to wonder *when*, because negative events or incidents will happen to every organization at some point. Incident response is not something that a business can simply ignore until an incident occurs. An incident response program requires careful planning in advance.

This module explores the basics of incident response, including planning, preparing, and executing a solid response. The module also discusses mitigation and recovery from incidents and how to minimize the damage from a negative event by separating affected systems from unaffected systems.

EXAM TIP CompTIA Security+ objective 2.1 mentions *response and recovery controls* as a security concept. We couldn't agree more! In fact, you should *read this entire chapter* to see many examples of response and recovery controls.

Incident Response Concepts

Several critical concepts are involved with setting up and executing an *incident response plan*, a set of documents and procedures that specify policies and essential personnel roles to deal with an attack or system failure. Some of these concepts involve planning and management functions, such as developing policy, allocating resources, staffing an incident response team, using exercises and drills, and making sure that everyone is trained regarding their responsibilities. Other concepts involve putting the plan into motion and executing it when the incident occurs.

For purposes of our discussion of incident response, an *incident* is a negative event that adversely affects the organization, its data and systems, its people, and its overall ability to perform mission or business functions. An incident could be a malicious hacking attack from the outside. It could be an insider threat, such as when an employee steals proprietary data and sells it to a competitor; or it could be a natural disaster such as a fire or flood. This module focuses on incidents in general; Module 10-3 provides a more detailed discussion about business continuity and disaster recovery.

Risk Mitigation Strategies

This module and the two that follow emphasize what you have learned so far about risk management principles. Risk management balances cost against strategies to reduce threats and the impact of attacks. Incident management and response supports a risk management program by ensuring that the organization can address an incident quickly when it occurs, reducing the damage to the organization and systems. By having an active incident response program, you can control, investigate, and conclude a damaging event more quickly. This reduces risk and enables the organization to deal better with a variety of threats.

Incident Management

An incident response can seem like madness, but you should pay attention to a method for that madness. The National Institute of Standards and Technology (NIST) has provided a very good incident response methodology in its Special Publication (SP) 800-61, Revision 2, *Computer Security Incident Handling Guide*, which you can use in your organization. It covers the key areas of incident response, including preparation, detection and analysis, containment, and so on. The incident response life cycle that NIST offers is illustrated in Figure 13-1. We'll discuss much of this methodology in this module.

Incident management is about having all the proper management buy-in, policies, and commitment of resources to the incident response program. This starts at the top of the organization, when senior managers and executives set the incident management response policy. The policy should direct the establishment of an incident response program, to

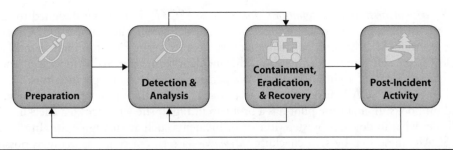

Figure 13-1   NIST's incident response life cycle (from NIST SP 800-61, Rev. 2)

include building an incident response team, establishing response time frames, defining different levels of incidents, and so on. The policy should also include the appointment of someone who has the overall responsibility for the program.

After senior leadership establishes the policy, the person with overall responsibility for the program selects staff for the incident response team, ensures they receive training, and purchases any equipment the team requires. The team then develops incident response procedures and prepares the organization to respond to the inevitable negative events that will eventually occur.

The incident response plan, which is more detailed than the policy itself, outlines the procedures involved with responding to the different types of incidents. The plan should contain information about the different levels and types of incidents, how to respond to them, who will be called, when an incident will be elevated to additional levels of management, and the general chain of events that must happen to contain the incident.

The security team should review all of the incident response policy and planning documentation on a periodic basis to ensure that it remains current and factors in any new changes to the operating or business environment. Many organizations review this documentation at least annually; in businesses where the operational environment and other factors frequently change, this review should occur more often.

For many organizations in the United States, incident response policy review means reviewing the NIST incident response controls that they *must* use. You can check the NIST controls wrapped up in a nice package here:

https://nvd.nist.gov/800-53/Rev4/family/Incident%20Response

An organization should also exercise its incident response plans occasionally to make sure that those folks who have responsibilities and duties related to a response know what to do. Testing these plans and running proper *exercises* can also help to ensure that all the right equipment is in place and that all the response processes work the way they should. Many of these items will be covered in the following sections.

Security Orchestration, Automation, and Response

Network protection tools such as security information and event management (SIEM) provide all kinds of amazing tools to detect potential incidents. These tools are so good that it's challenging today for security professionals to stay on top of these incidents without being overwhelmed.

Security orchestration, automation, and response (SOAR) is a toolset designed to assist security professionals to react to incidents with intelligence and automation. Consider this example: SIEM is great at telling you someone's logging on too many times, and SOAR is the software that learns about this incident from your SIEM tools and sends a message to the user, asking him if he is the person doing the bad login attempts.

So how does SOAR automate? Two important parts of this automation are playbooks and runbooks. If an airline pilot has a problem in flight, she will turn to a checklist that tells her what to do, step-by-step, in case of incidents such as an engine fire. In the case of SOAR, these step-by-step checklist *playbooks*—a series of steps, as many as possible automated—address a potential incident. Similarly, *runbooks* include conditional steps that define whether or not a certain step is taken. SOAR offers mitigation techniques and assistance to secure an environment in the face of an incident.

Incident Response Procedures

All the planning to get an incident response plan in shape focuses on procedures that the organization will follow when an incident happens. A good set of well-written procedures will help the response go like clockwork; conversely, poor or nonexistent procedures will have everyone running around with their hair on fire wondering what to do and wasting valuable time. The incident response team can write procedures to a very detailed degree or very broadly, depending upon the activities that must occur when a response is initiated.

When writing the procedures, the team should seek input from the same people who will have to do the job during the actual response. For example, if the incident response plan dictates that a server be restored from a backup in case of a hacking attack, the people who must perform that task during an emergency should help write those procedures to ensure that they can perform those tasks well. In any case, the organization should make sure that these procedures are well circulated to the right people and reviewed for accuracy and completeness. In the next few sections, we'll discuss procedures developed and used during preparation, as well as when the incident response plan is executed.

Preparation

Preparation is one of the most critical parts of incident response. If you are the person assigned overall responsibility for implementing the incident response program, you must make sure all the right equipment is in place, all the right people are assigned to critical positions, and all those people are trained on what to do *before* the incident occurs. You also need to have a good checklist of procedures that the team can use to respond quickly to and contain an incident. Good preparation also includes having a solid incident response plan that has been tested to make sure that an actual response flows as it should.

Staffing Staffing the incident response team with qualified people is critical; if, during an incident, people don't have the training or the experience required to carry out the response, it will probably not go very well. Consider staffing the team with people who have experience in several different areas. Of course, you'll want technical people who have experience in networking, server administration, security, and so on. It helps if these people have worked in different areas during their careers so they can perform multiple tasks. You also need people who have expertise in areas such as incident response, business continuity, forensics, and disaster recovery, since your incidents may span different types of events and levels of response.

Outside of the technical team, you may choose to include representatives from a variety of areas within the organization, including HR, accounting, public relations, and so on. Management personnel will also need to be on the team to coordinate the entire response. The same people who are responsible for planning the incident response strategy and providing input to the policy and procedures are likely going to be some of the same people who respond to an incident. It makes for a more effective response if this is the case, since those responders have the experience in developing the incident response program from the beginning and will be intimately familiar with how it is set up and how it should be executed.

In addition, the team will have to be trained on all their incident response tasks and responsibilities. Although some of these responsibilities may mirror their daily job activities, some of their response tasks may be outside of their daily routines. One other aspect of staffing your incident response team is that some of your team members, in the event of an actual incident, may come from outside of the organization and could include members of law enforcement, your Internet service provider, software and equipment vendors, and so on. You'll have to plan carefully how and when to integrate these outside participants into your team.

 EXAM TIP The US federal government uses the term *Computer Incident Response Team (CIRT)* to describe the IT security professionals who act first to implement an incident response plan in the event of a problem. This is also a term you'll see on the CompTIA Security+ exam. The generic term is the one used in this chapter, *incident response team*. Also known as *Computer Security Incident Response Team (CSIRT)*, just in case you desperately needed to memorize yet another term today.

All these people, from the leaders of the incident response team to the representatives of various divisions, from upper management to outside participants, are *stakeholders*—meaning they have a vested interest in what happens to your organization. Major clients of the organization are also stakeholders. All have a stake in the success and well-being of the organization. You should consider *stakeholder management* before, during, and after an incident. The key concept here is to keep stakeholders informed. Let them know about your preparations. Engage them during an incident. Keeping stakeholders in the dark during an attack does two things: robs you of potential insight or ideas they might have and opens you to the criticism that better leadership would have made a huge difference in mitigating the effects of an incident. Make stakeholders part of the recovery process because they have a vested interest in the organization's health.

Finally, the incident response team leaders need to keep a level head and demand it in others. Sometimes folks—especially higher management types—tend to freak out during an incident; that freak-out can result in responses and actions that are worse than the incident itself. *Before* the team even starts, the team lead needs to have spent plenty of time making sure the upper management and stakeholders trust what he or she is doing. Otherwise, the response can be worse than the attack, especially if it turns out to be a false positive!

Understanding Cyberattacks Cyberattacks pose grave risks to organizations—which we've long recognized—and nation states. The US Department of Defense added cyberspace back in 2011 to air, sea, land, and space as the fifth warfare domain. To address defense in cyberspace, the DoD turned to attack frameworks.

An *attack framework*, as the name implies, is a structure that defines the tactics, techniques, and procedures (TTPs) of typical attacks on a network. The CompTIA Security+ lists three popular frameworks to consider when preparing for incident response: MITRE ATT&CK, the Cyber Kill Chain, and the Diamond Model of Intrusion Analysis.

MITRE ATT&CK is probably the most popular and complex of the three frameworks. ATT&CK not only defines the steps of an attack but also defines plenty of TTPs used to achieve these steps. Figure 13-2 shows a small part of the MITRE ATT&CK Matrix from https://attack.mitre.org.

The *Cyber Kill Chain* attack framework concentrates on seven linear steps that take place during a cyberattack. Instead of considering techniques used in each step, Cyber Kill Chain uses the idea of *countermeasures* to give security professionals ideas to consider to counter an attack (see Figure 13-3).

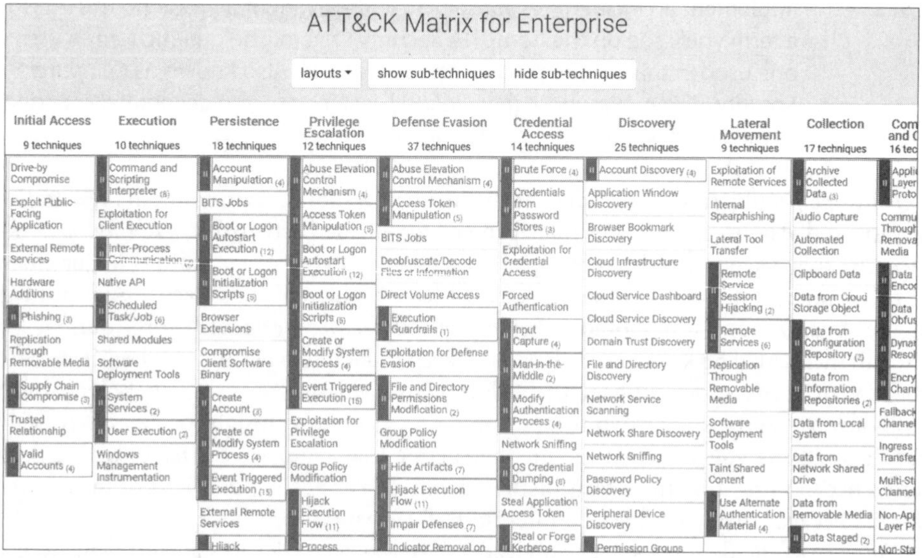

Figure 13-2 Detail of MITRE ATT&CK Matrix (https://attack.mitre.org)

Figure 13-3
Cyber Kill Chain

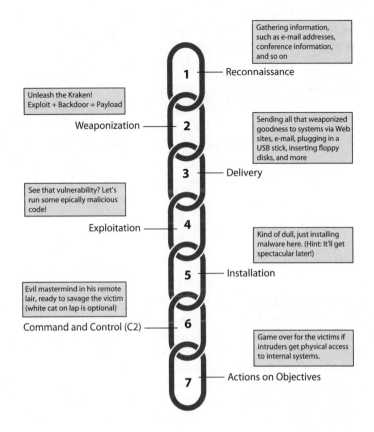

Gathering information, such as e-mail addresses, conference information, and so on

1 — Reconnaissance

Unleash the Kraken! Exploit + Backdoor = Payload

Weaponization — 2

Sending all that weaponized goodness to systems via Web sites, e-mail, plugging in a USB stick, inserting floppy disks, and more

3 — Delivery

See that vulnerability? Let's run some epically malicious code!

Exploitation — 4

Kind of dull, just installing malware here. (Hint: It'll get spectacular later!)

5 — Installation

Evil mastermind in his remote lair, ready to savage the victim (white cat on lap is optional)

Command and Control (C2) — 6

Game over for the victims if intruders get physical access to internal systems.

7 — Actions on Objectives

The *Diamond Model of Intrusion Analysis* is very different from either of the previously mentioned attack frameworks. Instead of a matrix or a list of events, the Diamond model uses a diamond shape, such as shown in Figure 13-4. The vertices of the diamond represent the major players in an intrusion event. Meta-features are lesser players.

Individual attacks manifest as paths along the diamond, making it an interesting tool to show features such as pivoting—a concept that's difficult to show using the other two frameworks. Figure 13-5 is an example from the original whitepaper describing pivots taking place from an initial malware attack.

IT security professionals don't have to choose a single framework to use to understand attacks and know how best to stop them. The MITRE ATT&CK framework is certainly the most popular, but IT professionals often refer to the other two frameworks as a matter of learning and understanding cyberattacks.

Communication Plan   Incident response preparation must include a detailed *communication plan* that outlines how every member of the team can interact with each other during an incident. The communication plan takes into account the chain of command, the decision makers, the backup decision makers who need to step up if a primary decision maker is unavailable, and so on. The plan details the methods and technologies required to maintain proper communication even if the power is out and the Internet is down.

Figure 13-4
Diamond Model
of Intrusion
Analysis

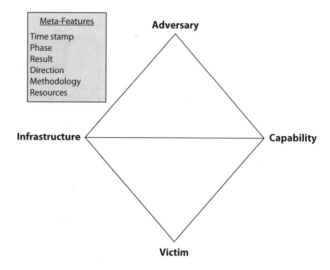

The communication plan includes methods for contacting and providing information to regulatory authorities. A breach that involves customer personal information, for example, requires immediate reporting in most states. The communication plan must outline the avenues for that reporting. Team members need clear guidance on handling PII, PHI, and other protected information during an event. You'll want to protect team members from accidentally getting in trouble when they are just trying to do their jobs and securing attacked resources. Finally, securing communication lines is incredibly important. An attacker who can monitor internal communication can easily avoid your defense.

Developing a Response Strategy   A *response strategy* dictates how the organization will respond to different incidents. Some incidents, such as hacking attacks, require a

Figure 13-5
Diamond Model
pivoting

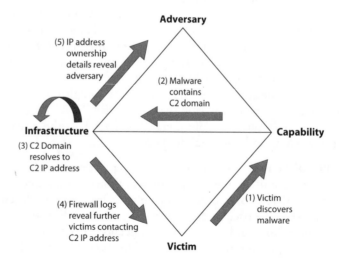

level of response and possibly a unique response team. The sequence of response for incidents may also differ from those for other types of incidents, and the level of seriousness of an incident will factor into the response strategy. For example, if a piece of malware infects a single PC, it may be considered less serious and more easily contained than a worm that infects the entire network, so the level of response may be different.

The business's response strategy takes all of this into account. The strategy should define the various types of events that can occur, their levels of impact, and the measured responses that should be taken when they occur. The strategy should have *documented incident types* and *category definitions* that cover anything conceivable that could go wrong. The strategy should also indicate which *roles and responsibilities* are needed for each type of incident and which skill sets will be needed for the incident response team members. The plan must outline procedures for *reporting requirements* and *escalation* when problems go beyond the capabilities of a team member.

If all of this sounds a lot like the risk assessment and analysis processes, it's because incident response, like many of the other things we will talk about over the next few modules, is part of the overall risk management strategy for the organization. Your incident response strategy can be defined as part of the policy document, or as a separate attachment that goes into more detail regarding how the organization will respond to the various incidents that will occur.

Putting It All Together   Once you have put together an incident response policy, staffed the team, and developed a strategy for responding to incidents, your organization must commit resources (time, money, equipment, facilities, and so on) to the program. This includes time for training the incident response team members as well as exercising the incident response plan. You'll need to acquire the appropriate equipment and supplies for the response, such as computers, forensic imagers, software, and so on. The organization should also set aside a workspace within the facility where the team can meet, organize, and manage the response. This can be a dedicated workspace or a space where they would normally work in the data center or on the operations floor. Either way, the organization needs to make provisions such that in the event of an incident, priority is given to the incident response team so that they can deal with the issue quickly and efficiently.

Exercises and Testing

The organization should exercise and test the plans periodically—at least annually—to refresh everyone's memory on what to do during an incident or disaster, and as part of regularly scheduled training. When you test incident response plans, you can often discover things that were forgotten or weren't adequately considered. In this respect, testing your plans can help you improve them and consider any possible scenarios that could occur. Document all testing for both recordkeeping and improvement. Now let's discuss the different types of exercises and tests.

Documentation Reviews   The *documentation review* is the simplest form of test. In this type of test, the incident response plan and associated documents are reviewed by relevant personnel, including managers, recovery team members, and anyone else who may have responsibilities directly affecting the plans. The team may review the plans in a group setting or by simply passing them along from team member to team member, who review them in turn. They should review the plans periodically, such as on an annual or semiannual basis, or at least when there are significant changes to the plans or the operating environment. During these reviews, they should check the plans for currentness, effectiveness, resource allocation, and general common sense. They should document these formal reviews for historical record purposes and as part of compliance with governance (including corporate and legal requirements).

Tabletop Exercises   A *tabletop exercise* is a type of group review, sometimes literally conducted around the conference room table. In a tabletop exercise, there's a little bit more involvement compared to documentation review by the key players, including managers, team members, and other critical personnel who have incident response duties. During the exercise, the group may be presented with scenarios in which they will be directed to respond accordingly. The response can be verbal or written; typically, no actual recovery operations are conducted during a tabletop exercise. These types of exercises are useful in that they allow everyone involved to step through the incident response processes and may help to point out deficiencies in the plans. They are also useful training tools and serve to help team members become more familiar with and accustomed to their roles within the plan.

Walkthrough Tests   A step above the tabletop exercise is the *walkthrough test*. In a walkthrough test, there's usually more involvement by relevant team members, and they may go through the motions of fulfilling their responsibilities and conducting the activities required during an actual incident or disaster. This test may be conducted partially in a conference room or entirely out in the actual operations areas of the business. Normally this test does not involve shutting down systems or performing actual recovery operations. Team members may simulate response activities as much as possible without conducting them.

A walkthrough test can help point out logistical or practical issues not previously considered around a conference room table, such as the need to move heavy equipment (and maintain nearby the appropriate gear and tools to do so). This type of exercise is also useful as both a training tool and a way to ensure that the plan works as it should.

Full Tests and Disaster Recovery Exercises   At some point, the organization may conduct a full-scale test of its incident response plans. In these types of exercises, all personnel are usually involved and may conduct activities as they would during a real incident. A full test may involve shutting down systems to simulate their loss, recovering backup data to alternate systems, and activating alternate processing sites. It may also involve parallel processing using both production and backup systems. These types of *simulations* are the most involved and will likely take away some significant time from actual production activities. They should not, however, be permitted to impose unnecessary risk on the business by shutting down and recovering actual production systems during the exercises, as that may lead to an actual incident or real downtime. Since these simulations normally require extensive resources, such as people, equipment, and so on, they are typically conducted infrequently.

Incident Response Process

If you've ever been a bystander or an observer when an incident has occurred in an organization, you've probably seen a wide range of reactions when the event kicks off. In a well-organized *incident response process*, people quickly and efficiently perform their tasks without panicking, but with a sense of urgency. They have all the equipment and supplies they need to do their jobs, and the incident response process flows smoothly. At the other extreme, people run around with their hair on fire, wondering what to do, and not having a clear sense of direction. They may have to look for equipment to execute the response and may wind up taking production equipment offline to respond to an incident in another area of the business. Usually, however, an organization's response falls somewhere in the middle of the spectrum. As described in the previous section, *preparation* is important; it gives the organization a greater potential for success during an incident response.

 EXAM TIP CompTIA Security+ includes preparation as part of the incident response process, though for many organizations that is a step prior to action. The incident response process on the exam has six steps—preparation, identification, containment, eradication, recovery, and lessons learned.

Most of what we've discussed up to this point involves the preparation phase of the NIST incident response life cycle. Executing your incident response involves the next two phases of that same life cycle: detection and analysis, as well as containment, eradication, and recovery. Detection involves understanding your infrastructure and environment and being able to discover indications that an incident has occurred. You can detect an incident in different ways, such as through automated intrusion detection systems, antivirus software, and logging alerts. Other incidents may be detected only through manual audits of different events, logs, and procedures.

Incident analysis involves looking at all the potential incidents that you discover to determine which are actual incidents and which are false positives. That can be a full-time job and may require dedicated staff. Because the organization is constantly generating computer and network logs and other data, it can be a challenge to stay ahead of the curve and examine the most recent data to determine whether the organization has suffered a negative incident such as a hacking attack. Some incidents are easy to detect, such as a serious malware attack, a Web defacement, or denial-of-service attack. Other incidents won't be so easy to see and may occur over long periods of time instead of during a workday or in a short time span. Event analysis and correlation is the subject of a much broader conversation than included in this module, but you should understand that analysis is the first step in determining whether you've experienced an incident.

The goal of incident analysis is to determine exactly what has happened. This includes answering such questions as these: Who is the victim? Who is the perpetrator? What systems or data does the incident affect? Where did the incident occur (on one machine, for example, or from the external network)? When did it occur? Exactly how did it occur? How does it impact the business? Some of these questions can be answered only through an in-depth forensic analysis, which is the subject of the next module. Analysis should tell you exactly what's happened and what you're facing, so you can respond appropriately in the next phase of the life cycle, which is concerned with containing an incident.

The next phase (*containment*, *eradication*, and *recovery*, per NIST) involves stopping the incident, eradicating its effects, and recovering from the incident. For serious incidents, you can afford to spend only a short amount of time on analysis, and you may need to focus more on containing the incident to prevent further damage to the business and its infrastructure. During this phase, the incident response team is activated, and even if the cause of the incident and its details aren't known at the time, the team works to contain it and stop the damage.

If the incident is a network attack, for example, the team may need to take a drastic measure such as unplugging the organization from the Internet or shutting down certain services within the business. If it's a malware attack, the team should focus on containing the malware to the smallest number of systems possible and preventing its spread. If data is being extracted from the network, then containing it would mean stopping that data from leaving the network by shutting down a system or blocking traffic at the perimeter of the network, for example. In any case, the incident response strategy and procedures should dictate exactly how the organization should go about containing the incident and eradicating its effects.

NOTE We outline the clear steps in the incident response process here, which flow beautifully from step to step … in print. In the real word, the steps can blur heavily depending on the circumstances. If analysis and recovery don't quite work right, for example, eradication efforts will be hampered. Be prepared for multiple shades of gray along each step border.

Keep in mind that while this phase is going on, the organization should make every effort to preserve evidence of the incident for later analysis and action. This includes preserving log files, properly handling forensic evidence on systems, and so on. Preserving evidence is also a focus of Module 13-2.

Recovering from an incident involves getting the systems, data, and processes that depend on them back into operation. Depending on the nature of the incident, this may be easier said than done, since critical systems may be damaged or may need to be kept offline for the duration of the recovery, and these systems may be subject to evidence collection after an incident. Module 13-3 explores recovery processes after a disaster.

First Responder Procedures *First response* is a critical phase of the incident response plan, simply because during the first few minutes or hours of an incident several things can happen that affect how well the organization is able to contain and recover from the event. First response is also critical in the preservation of evidence. We'll discuss first responder procedures from a general perspective, as they apply to most incidents and negative events. The first responder's overall duties should be to secure the scene (if necessary), determine the scope of the incident, try to determine the seriousness and impact of the incident, and start the notification process for the incident management and response team.

The first response may not be initially executed by members of the incident response team; an incident may be detected and responded to by the personnel or operators on duty at the time the incident occurs. If an incident is very serious, the response may not be able to wait until the response team is activated and called in. Because of this, all personnel should have some measure of training in responding to an incident, whether that training involves simply activating the team and notifying the appropriate personnel, or securing the scene, preserving evidence, stopping an attack, and so on. The level of response should allow the team to be notified and activated in time to prevent or minimize damage to the organization's infrastructure.

At the same time, however, the first responder should make every effort to preserve valuable evidence that investigators will need to analyze the incident. For example, if a workstation is being attacked over the network, the first responder may need to unplug that workstation from the network, but keep it up and running so that investigators can collect and analyze information regarding network connections, running processes, and so on. In some cases, it may even be desirable to allow the attack to continue so that investigators can collect data and use it to identify the attacker and how they got into the network in the first place. Management should discuss and make decisions regarding those actions in advance, before the incident occurs, and set forth criteria that dictates if and when certain actions will be executed by first responders, based upon the seriousness of the event. It's important that your procedures are detailed enough that these personnel who are less trained can execute the initial steps in an orderly fashion with a minimum of panic. Write down the procedures and make sure everyone knows where the procedures are located!

Incident Identification   A first response also involves *incident identification*, trying to determine the scope of the event, identify what kind of event it is, and determine the impact. The scope of an incident would include, for example, whether the incident is confined to one workstation, involves only one group of users, or affects the entire network. If you can isolate the event to specific sections of a network, you can hopefully mitigate the effects. Isolation accompanies identification closely. Determining the type of event—malware, a physical security breach, and so on—can help with isolation and lead to mitigation efforts. Finally, the impact of the incident may be difficult to determine at first, so this may be the initial best guess on the part of the first responder. However, it may be better to overestimate the impact to the organization than to underestimate it to prevent serious damage to the infrastructure. The incident response team may find that a questionnaire or checklist is valuable in helping a first responder quickly determine the scope and impact of the incident.

Escalation and Notification   The other key piece of the first responder's actions is to notify management immediately so the incident response team can be activated and called in. The first responder should be prepared to provide as much information as possible to the incident response team lead so that this person can start the appropriate response measures as soon as he or she arrives. Documenting any actions taken along with any observations or events about the incident are other tasks for the first responder.

Once the team has been notified, the first incident response lead on the scene should determine whether the incident should be *escalated* to upper management, or even outside the organization, such as to the organization's Internet service provider or law enforcement. If outside expertise is required, the event may have to be escalated even further. The level of seriousness of the event, as well as the scope of the event, will determine how it's escalated. For example, if an incident such as a hacking attack affects the organization and its internal network, but could also spread to the Internet, another organization, or an upstream provider, the incident should be escalated as quickly as possible. Once again, the organization's incident management strategy and policy should dictate different levels of impact and how they are escalated based upon predetermined criteria.

Incident Containment   The incident response team should also work on *containment* to try to limit the effects of the incident in impact and scope. For example, in the event of a malware attack, the team should try to stop the connections between the infected workstations and servers and the rest of the network to prevent the malware from spreading. In the event of a denial-of-service attack, the team could isolate the network segment under attack from the outside network, such as by quarantining the device or devices, removing it/them from the network, and even shutting it/them down completely.

Well-implemented network *segmentation* through the use of VLANs can go a long way toward effective containment. If accounting is on a separate VLAN from sales, for example, and a sales computer gets hit with malware, an administrator can quickly drop the inter-VLAN routing between accounting and sales remotely, effectively stopping any possibility of the former getting compromised by the latter. This is arguably even faster than running to a network switch and pulling a few cables!

Quarantining a device or system is designed to prevent an incident from spreading beyond that device or system to the rest of the infrastructure. It may mean unplugging the device from the network, or even dynamically switching it to an isolated network segment or virtual LAN. Reasons for quarantining a device include a malware attack, denial-of-service or other form of network attack, or even prohibited use by an insider. If a device is removed from the network, it may remain powered on so that valuable evidence can be collected from it, and then the device can be shut down and stored while the incident is being investigated. In any case, it should not be allowed back on the network until it has been sanitized and reimaged to prevent recurrence of the attack or spread of any malicious software.

Data Breach   These days, a data breach is one of the most commonly occurring security incidents you'll see plastered across the news. A *data breach* is the result of another security incident, whether it's an attack by hackers, a careless or malicious insider, or even an accident involving faulty processes or procedures. Regardless of the cause, data breaches should be responded to above and beyond the security incident that caused them. An organization will naturally respond to a hacking attack or malicious insider with routine response patterns that include intrusion detection systems, system hardening measures, and so on. The organization also must respond to the result of some of these incidents—the data breach itself—in unique ways.

A data breach normally involves data of a sensitive or protected nature, and most often involves data belonging to or concerning an entity outside the organizational business. If the breach is confined only to organizationally owned proprietary or sensitive data, then the organization takes the hit for the loss alone in the form of lost business, revenue, or just sheer embarrassment. If the breach encompasses data concerning individuals or organizations outside the business, it's a much more serious issue and could involve not only loss of business revenue but also legal sanctions and criminal punishment.

Normally, the types of data involved in a serious breach include protected health information (PHI) under the Health Insurance Portability and Accountability Act (HIPAA), personal financial information, and even personally identifiable information (PII) that could include names, dates of birth, addresses, Social Security numbers, and so on. An example of a breach that had multiple types of data was the Sony breach in late 2014. In addition to proprietary data (including actual movies), personal data regarding Sony employees was included in the breach. Along with potential fines and other liability issues, the company lost valuable intellectual property, as well as the confidence and goodwill of its stakeholders. In the long run, this may be more damaging than the sheer dollar value of the financial losses.

An organization's response to a data breach goes beyond the technical aspects of isolating network segments, removing malware, tightening down systems, and so on, although those technical measures are also included, of course. The organization may also have to respond to a data breach by informing the subjects of the data compromised, such as individuals or companies, as well as other entities, such as law enforcement. It may also have to inform regulatory organizations such as the US Office for Civil Rights, in the event of a PHI breach, or the Securities and Exchange Commission if financial data has been lost. Law enforcement agencies, such as the Federal Bureau of Investigation and other appropriate entities, may require notification about a data breach. Both state and federal laws dictate how an organization must respond to a data breach, what steps it must take to prevent further damage, and even how it must compensate the victims. Obviously, all this will involve not only upper management and the incident response team, but the organization's legal personnel and its public relations team, since the breach will likely be plastered all over the news. The organization should ensure that it has both a technical and a management incident response strategy in place to deal with data breaches.

Damage and Loss Control   The damage from an incident is not always easy to determine. Damage includes technical damage to systems (such as malware infection), data loss, equipment damage or theft, and other direct impacts. Damage can also include costs related to containment of an incident, as well as costs of eradicating the cause and repairing damage to the infrastructure. These costs might be incurred in terms of labor dollars for response personnel, as well as equipment and software needed not only to clean up the incident but also to mitigate its effects and prevent it from occurring again.

Damage can also include the intangible aspects of an incident, such as damage to public and consumer confidence in the organization and reputation in the marketplace. If proprietary or sensitive data is lost, the damage could include loss of business and revenue and the inability to compete in the marketplace. Additional damage can come in the form of legal or criminal proceedings against the organization that may result in heavy fines, imprisonment, or even shutting down the business.

Controlling and minimizing the damage and loss from an incident involves taking all the proactive security measures we've discussed throughout this book up until this point. These include all the administrative, technical, and operational measures used to secure an organization's infrastructure and data. Securing people, systems, and equipment are all key to controlling and minimizing damage and loss.

Post-Incident Activity

How an organization deals with an incident after it has been discovered, analyzed, investigated, contained, and eradicated is just as important as a response process. The organization must figure out how to learn from the event and use what it has learned not only to prevent the incident from occurring again but also to determine how to deal with such events more effectively in the future. The organization should develop a post-incident strategy that includes collecting all the data regarding how the incident occurred, what steps it could have taken to prevent it, how effective the response was, and what it could have done better. All this information can be used to prevent and mitigate future negative events.

Mitigation Steps Some of the mitigation steps that an organization should take include a proactive look at the threats and vulnerabilities on the network. This goes back to risk assessment and analysis and may mean that the initial assessment was either incomplete or too narrow in scope. The post-response to an incident should cause the organization to go back and examine its risk management process. Once it has examined threats and vulnerabilities, the organization should essentially beef up its risk management program by taking additional measures toward preventing and mitigating the types of incidents it just experienced. Management should look at putting additional resources toward controls that would have prevented the incident in the first place, as well as improving its incident response detection and response capabilities. This may mean spending additional money for equipment and supplies and providing additional training for incident response team members. In any event, the organization should look for deficiencies in its risk management processes and day-to-day business operations that could have contributed to the incident and the level of response.

Lessons Learned Part of responding to an incident involves taking the *lessons learned* to heart and using them toward preventing future incidents and responding to them in a more effective way. The organization should examine the circumstances leading up to the incident in detail, making note of deficiencies and how to correct them, as well as the response to the incident, to improve the incident detection, analysis, containment, and eradication processes. These lessons learned should be documented as part of the overall final incident report and incorporated into the organization's existing policies, processes, and procedures.

Reporting There are several aspects of reporting during an incident response. During the response effort, the incident response team should report progress on the response and anything discovered about the nature of the incident to management, along with any outside agencies that require the information, such as law enforcement, for example. There should probably be at least a daily briefing for management (and law enforcement, if applicable) on the progress of the response, the damage to the infrastructure, and how the damage is being contained and eradicated.

After the response, the incident response team should submit a final report that details the entire incident from start to finish, the different activities performed as part of the response, the root causes of the incident and how it could have been prevented, any damage to the business or infrastructure, and recommendations for future actions. The report may include a cost breakdown of labor, equipment, and any other supplies needed to respond adequately to the incident. It may also include any deficiencies that were noted during the response, particularly in personnel, training, or other resources. In addition to the report that goes to management, compliance requirements may necessitate that a report be submitted to law enforcement, a regulatory agency, or even to other outside entities (particularly in the case of a data breach). This report may include some of the same information as the internal management report, as well as additional information that may be required for legal or compliance purposes. The organization should also make sure that anyone requiring copies of the incident response reports gets them, but it should also take measures to protect any sensitive or proprietary information contained in them.

 NOTE The NIST incident response controls reference details as nitty-gritty as reporting. They include things like ensuring notification to supply chain folks, adding automated tools to the reporting mix, and more.

Recovery/Reconstitution   Recovery operations, as well as getting the business processes back into operation, are covered more in depth in Module 13-3. However, it's important that after an incident the business processes and systems be brought back up to normal functionality as soon as possible to prevent further negative impact on the business. This may involve restoring data from backups, reinstalling servers or network devices, patching systems, and even installing new equipment. All the recovery operations will probably be focused on the damage that was done during the incident and involve recovering those systems and data damaged by the event.

Retention Policies   There's a better than average chance that a successful incident is going to cause some serious problems for your enterprise, possibly moving that incident into forensics, continuity of operations, and disaster recovery. As you move into those areas, well covered in the rest of this chapter, you'll see that *retention policies*—like you read about way back in Chapter 1—should specify saving records of anything that might manifest as documentation or evidence. The challenge here is that it's important to keep these ideas in mind at the very beginning of an incident (even if the last item on your mind is retention).

Scenarios: Mitigation During and After an Incident

Well, there sure has been a *lot* of discussion in this book covering different forms of mitigation procedures, and hopefully you've developed some ideas on the processes involved with incident response. To that end, the CompTIA Security+ provides some interesting objectives that challenge your ability to recognize the application of mitigation techniques or controls for very specific scenarios. Let's cover some of those right here.

NOTE In case you skipped Chapters 9 or 12, the scenarios that follow deal with two rival corporations, the Bayland Widgets Corporation (BWC) and the Graceland Gadgets Corporation (GGC). Both have medium-sized campuses that featured in previous scenarios. The scenarios here are about malware and industrial espionage. Get ready to rumble!

Bad Malware Attack

Most of the systems in the accounting department at Bayland Widgets Corporation (BWC) are suddenly running very slowly. In addition, those systems' host-based firewalls are sending alarms to the SIEM system, all warning of a malware attack.

This is happening right now. There are no other such warnings anywhere else on the network, so this possible malware attack hasn't spread beyond the accounting department's systems. It's time to do some *containment* of this outbreak!

But first, take a deep breath. Identify that this is actually a malware attack and not something much more mundane, like the effects of a rollout of new accounting software that has bugs that drain systems. The incident response team needs to clarify the culprit before shutting down an entire subnet (which will cause BWC to lose money). If the incident response team confirms that the firewalls have identified a true malware attack, put the incident response plan into action.

Start by *isolating* the outbreak. If this were a single system, or perhaps a few systems, some quick unplugging would do the trick. But in this case, the systems of the entire accounting department are involved. The clever BWC IT people have the accounting department on its own VLAN so they can just unplug the trunk off the switch—or better yet just shut off that VLAN connection completely to *segment* the VLAN from the rest of the network.

With the accounting network segmented from the rest of your network, it's time to do some malware mitigation, and that means continue to keep the infected systems isolated from the clean systems in the accounting department. As each system is cleaned, you can place them back online.

Bad Application

Genie, the deputy head of IT security at BWC, starts hearing some disturbing rumors of employees gaming at lunch and on breaks on company computers. Gaming isn't an issue, *per se*, because even the company president gleefully frags along with his employees. The problem is the *specific* game that's all the rage, a game developed in a decidedly foreign land (New Jersey) and suspected of being malware in disguise.

When Genie investigates the game, sure enough, users have okayed opening an assortment of unusual ports and, in some cases, opened those ports on the out-facing routers so the "game will run better," as one system administrator confessed. (It was Tom, but no one is pointing fingers.)

It's time for an intervention. Genie is the IT security pro who will *reconfigure the endpoint security solutions* and *implement configuration changes* to save BWC from a hostile takeover by the New Jersey–based Graceland Gadgets Corporation.

NOTE   Although this section is presented as a tongue-in-cheek scenario, the principles behind the mitigation techniques and controls are deadly serious. Pay attention to the substance here.

Approve or Deny?   On a big-picture scale, Genie needs to configure the network to approve or deny specific applications. She could publish an *application approved list* to all employees, *whitelisting* apps they can put on their workstations or mobile devices. Genie could monitor compliance and caution (or write up) anyone who failed to comply with policy. That method—whitelisting—absolutely applies in many circumstances.

On the other hand, Genie could add an *application block list* or *deny list* to prevent anyone from installing a forbidden app. This *blacklisting* might receive some backlash from the employees but would certainly stop the GGC app from running on endpoints—workstations and mobile devices, in this case—right now. That seems to be the logical solution. The next step is implementing this mitigation technique or control to blacklist efficiently/effectively.

Configuration Changes   Genie begins the mitigation process, stopping the GGC app from being installed on more machines and, perhaps more importantly, stopping the secret malicious payload in the GGC app from propagating to more computers on the BWC network. She needs to quarantine and then configure a whole bunch of devices to stop the hostile takeover.

Genie can *quarantine* areas of the network, just like you read about earlier in the module, by unplugging a VLAN or taking it offline. The beauty of segmentation in a LAN environment is containment of problems is much easier to achieve.

Configuration changes involve a whole lot of variations and interfaces, simply because the modern enterprise computing environment has a wide variety of devices and connectivity options. The basic protection unit in a network—a firewall—has to be configured with rules that apply to wired connections and wireless connections. *Firewall rules* can allow or block specific traffic and specific applications. Other network security devices can be set up to police specific types of traffic or traffic from specific Web sites; in other words, they can act as a *content filter/URL filter*.

EXAM TIP   On a meta level, networking security devices can filter for any kind of PII flowing through e-mail or chat, such as Social Security numbers, and block those messages. You might see such a scenario as an example of *data loss prevention (DLP)* that you read about in Module 5-5.

You read about *mobile device management (MDM)* back in Module 9-4 in gory detail, so there's not too much to add here. Genie uses MDM configuration methods to block the GGC app from any company-issued smartphone or tablet.

EXAM TIP Our scenario shatters on the rocks of one last mitigation technique mentioned in CompTIA Security+ objective 4.4, which is *update or revoke certificates*. You know about certificates and even revocation from way back in Module 2-7. Genie could, in theory, block any local system or server from accepting a certificate on a GGC server and revoke any certificates already accepted. That would certainly mitigate against further attacks/invasions from the GGC. Yes, we know, that's stretching the scenario past breaking. Just don't miss the question on the exam!

Module 13-2: Digital Forensics

This module covers the following CompTIA Security+ objectives:

- **2.8 Summarize the basics of cryptographic concepts**
- **4.1 Given a scenario, use the appropriate tool to assess organizational security**
- **4.5 Explain the key aspects of digital forensics**

Digital forensics is a forensics specialty that focuses on gathering, recovering, investigating, and documenting evidence from various digital sources, including computers, networks, storage media, mobile devices, and more. Anything with ones and zeros is fair game.

Digital forensics was once a very small niche in the information security world. Over time, however, as computer-related crime and misuse have increased, it has become more important. Today, forensics is its own discipline within IT security. Digital forensics, like its medical and criminal counterparts, is a very exacting science. It requires strong skills and knowledge in a wide variety of areas, including operating systems, networking, information security, and even law. The procedures used in digital forensics must be very exacting and precise for the results to be useful and admissible in a court of law. Even in private or corporate investigations, the digital forensics investigator should always assume that the case may eventually go to court, so each case should be approached with a high level of investigative standards.

In this module, we'll discuss digital forensics concepts, procedures, and methods. We'll cover how to obtain and handle digital evidence as well as perform analysis on the evidence to be presented to law enforcement or corporate management. First, let's review some important digital forensics concepts.

Digital Forensics Concepts

A digital forensics professional, like other security professionals, requires a variety of general and specific skills. The digital forensics investigator may see primarily Windows boxes in the course of her work, becoming adept at working on those operating systems. Likewise, Linux aficionados will be more comfortable working on those types of hosts. Forensic work primarily with computers is a subcategory called *computer forensics*. Networking gurus will also be more comfortable working with *network forensics* cases. Regardless of skills, expertise, and preferred areas in forensics, all investigators should be familiar with some fundamental concepts that apply to any type of case and any type of system. These concepts relate to collecting and handling evidence, as well as maintaining legal and ethical integrity of the investigation.

Impartiality and the Acquisition of Evidence

Many digital forensics investigators work for law enforcement or government agencies. Investigators also work for corporations, businesses, lawyers, and so on. Regardless of whom the investigator works for, the investigator's goal should always be to obtain, handle, and analyze evidence impartially. Even when working for law enforcement, the investigator should always seek to gather any evidence related to an incident or crime, even if that evidence is *exculpatory* in nature and may prove the innocence of a suspect. An investigator who only seeks to prove the guilt (looking for *inculpatory* evidence) of a suspect in an investigation cannot render a fair and impartial analysis of the evidence. All digital evidence, regardless of whether it points to innocence or guilt, must be treated with equal care when it is collected and analyzed.

Documentation/Evidence

The technical mechanics of handling evidence, such as use of the chain of custody, for example, will be discussed a bit later in the module, but for now you should know that handling evidence is a very critical aspect of conducting a forensic investigation. A forensics investigator is responsible for the following:

- Carefully controlling and monitoring evidence, including precise *documentation* of the circumstances under which it is collected, handled, stored, transferred, and disposed of

- Protecting electronic evidence such as system components—mass storage drives, workstations, media, and so on—by storing it in anti-static bags when possible

- Inventorying and labeling all evidence per the requirements of the investigating agency, with the investigator's name, date, item inventory number, and other pertinent information on all *tags* (Figure 13-6)

- Photographing or producing video of systems and evidence in their original, undisturbed state whenever possible before moving them or interacting with them

- Performing integrity checking mechanisms, such as hashing, on digital evidence whenever possible to ensure that it has not been tampered with or otherwise altered

- Establishing and maintaining the chain of custody throughout the life of the evidence and the investigation

- Creating accurate and exhaustive *reports* on every aspect of the operation to provide essential accounting information

 EXAM TIP Expect a question on e-discovery on the CompTIA Security+ exam. *E-discovery* is the collection of data for litigation or investigations where the data is in digital or electronic format rather than paper, hard-copy photographs, etc. The digital data often includes typical things accompanying computer files, such as time and date of creation and editing, for example.

Figure 13-6
Tagged evidence
(Image: STAN
HONDA / Staff,
Getty Images)

All digital forensic investigations should be approached from the perspective that they may ultimately end up in a court of law and be subject to legal rules for collecting, maintaining, analyzing, and introducing evidence into a court. In the United States, the Federal Rules of Evidence (FRE) prescribe the conditions under which computer-based evidence, such as files, logs, and so forth, may be entered into evidence for a criminal case. And the Federal Rules of Civil Procedure (FRCP) dictate how digital evidence may be presented in a noncriminal case. These two sources of rules should be reviewed and understood very well by digital forensics investigators.

Evidence takes many forms in legality and admissibility. *Best evidence* is usually original evidence, such as *real evidence* (physical objects) and *direct evidence* (usually in the form of testimony regarding events that were personally witnessed by someone). *Circumstantial evidence* tends to support a conclusion but does not absolutely prove it. Evidence that attempts to reconstruct an event in question is known as *demonstrative evidence*, which can be in the form of charts, graphs, drawings, and so forth, used to help non-technical people, such as the members of a jury, understand an event. Evidence that directly supports or proves a definitive assertion could be considered *documentary evidence*.

Digital evidence is difficult to categorize in these terms, but is typically considered documentary evidence, since it could be documents, log files, images, and so forth. One key item about the *admissibility* of digital evidence in a legal proceeding is that it must be generated during normal business. In other words, log files can be considered admissible because the computer generates them as part of its normal operation. On the other hand, data created and entered into a computer by human beings is typically considered inadmissible, since it is subjective and not trustworthy.

Since 2006, the FRCP have required organizations to place all forms of relevant information, both electronic and physical, under *legal hold* if they reasonably anticipate litigation or government investigation in any form. That means that the company must stop typical cycling procedures that would result in the deletion of records, drives, or other sources that save electronic data.

Data Volatility

In terms of the technical aspect of data collection, the investigator should pay special attention to the *order of volatility*, because digital evidence is very fragile and can be easily altered or destroyed. The investigator should always approach the collection process with this in mind and should attempt to collect the most volatile data first as the highest priority. The investigator will use different methods, tools, and techniques to collect different types of digital evidence, such as the contents of RAM, files from hard drives, log files from a firewall, and so on. A good digital forensics investigator will have a complete kit of tools and equipment necessary to collect evidence from a wide variety of sources. The key aspect, however, is collecting the most perishable data first.

 EXAM TIP   The specific forensics tools discussed later in this module (such as FTK Imager, dd, memdump, and Autopsy) enable you to *assess organizational security*, according to the CompTIA Security+ objectives. We already covered many of the assessment tools commonly associated with organizational security (such as traceroute, Nmap, and netstat) way back in Chapter 4. We also already discussed the pentesting tools lumped into this category (such as cURL, theHarvester, and Nessus) with the rest of pentesting, in Module 12-4.

Order of Volatility

Best practices offered in the digital forensics world, developed from law enforcement procedures, computer security practices, and other sources, dictate a certain order of collection of data by a digital forensics investigator. Obviously, the investigator should collect the most perishable data first, including data from a "live" collection involving a computer that is still powered on and may have data residing in memory or on the screen. As the order of volatility progresses, the investigator should collect data that is less and less volatile, such as that stored on a hard disk that isn't currently in use or powered on. The next few sections discuss the specific order of volatility and perishability of data and how it is collected from each source.

RAM   *System random-access memory (RAM)* is one of the most volatile locations of digital evidence you'll encounter as a digital forensics investigator. Because the contents of RAM are subject to change constantly, and because it can be wiped out whenever the computer's power is turned off, it is a high priority during evidence collection. You'll have to worry about collecting the contents of RAM if the system is powered on and running. This type of collection is called a *live response* and requires special tools and techniques to collect the contents while disturbing the data in RAM as little as possible. Digital evidence located in RAM includes running processes, network connections, active applications, active user data, and so on. It's also possible that encryption keys and passwords may exist in RAM in an unencrypted state, so they can be gathered as well during a live response.

Several tools can dump the entire contents of RAM into a file, and other tools can be used to gather information selectively on running processes and connections as well. These tools may dump this information into a text file or other type of database for further analysis. Both techniques should be used to collect as much perishable data as possible.

Hard Disk and Solid State Drives   Standard mass storage drives, such as *hard disk drives (HDDs)* and *solid state drives (SSDs)*, located within the machine are certainly the most valuable source of digital evidence, but they are lower down the list in order of volatility, since they do not lose their data when powered off or removed from the machine. An HDD or SSD does not have to be examined using live response techniques; it should be removed from the computer after it has been powered down and then analyzed later. We'll discuss the techniques used to gather information from mass storage drives and ensure its integrity later in the module.

NOTE   For some reason, the CompTIA Security+ 601 exam objectives only talk about "disk" for data acquisition targets, as in HDDs, not SSDs. Because solid state drives will be the most common system drives sooner rather than later, we've included them in the discussion here.

Other Media and Sources of Digital Evidence   Most other types of media that offer a more permanent type of storage than system RAM can be examined after the machine has been powered down, inventoried, and taken to a laboratory. These types of media are also usually removable, such as optical discs, SD cards, and USB devices. This typically makes them the least volatile data, but no less important in the process of collection and analysis. As mentioned, you should inventory them and start a chain of custody to protect their integrity.

System Sources of Evidence   There are many sources of evidence within computing systems aside from the overall mass storage image. Let's look at swap files, operating system files, firmware, snapshots, cache, and artifacts.

- **Swap file**   All modern operating systems use a portion of mass storage for temporary placement of items in RAM, called the *swap file* (*pagefile.sys* in Windows). You'll recall this from your CompTIA A+ studies. Information in the swap file changes as the user opens and closes programs and data files. The key takeaway here is that when you capture a system in a frozen moment of time, the last contents in the swap file remain on the mass storage device.

- **OS files**   Analyzing operating system files for changes—malicious or otherwise—inconsistent with the developer norms can lead to interesting clues and information about usage. Even something as simple as the text hosts file— where you can add DNS entries to redirect at the host level—with a couple of choice additions can lead to more information.

- **Firmware**   As you'll recall from previous studies (like earlier in this book or from CompTIA A+), firmware is the underlying programming in computing devices that either is the operating system or starts an operating system, like Microsoft Windows. Firmware is stored in nonvolatile memory (NVRAM) and usually gets updated rarely after arriving from the manufacturer. The programming can be modified, which in a PC, you'd update the motherboard firmware to support a new CPU, for example. Inserting malicious code into firmware after the fact is possible, such as the TrickBot malware that either bricks firmware, inserts ransomware, or spreads across connected vulnerable devices. Compared with regular malware attacks, firmware attacks are rare.

- **Snapshots** Snapshots (full images) of virtual machines can provide a wealth of information. Each snapshot captures the state of the VM at a specific time. If the user employed VMs in witting (attacks) or unwitting (as part of a botnet) schemes, for example, some of the data might be beautifully preserved in a VM snapshot. Having a set of VM snapshots can yield almost as much vital information as capturing that number of full systems.

EXAM TIP *Snapshots* can also mean something as simple as taking a screen snap/capture. Refer to the context of the question to determine which way you should go for the answer.

- **Cache** Every OS and most computing devices provide modest amounts of storage—called a *cache*—for portions of code, data, links, and so forth that the computer uses regularly. That cached information can sometimes be recovered and analyzed, again leading to clues for future forensic exploration.

- **Artifacts** HDDs don't store data in perfect rows and columns of 1's and 0's, unlike the illustrations we use to explain data storage in simpler books, like those focused on CompTIA ITF+ or CompTIA A+. Storage, deletion, rewriting blocks . . . it's a slightly messy process. In fact, you can take an HDD full of data and overwrite all that data and still leave findable traces of data behind, called *artifacts*. Don't tell the bad guys this, but running special software (discussed shortly) can find artifacts and compare them with portions of code from known-illegal objects and make matches that stand up in court as evidence.

EXAM TIP Security professionals use the term *artifacts* to have a couple of meanings. The use here as *recoverable data on wiped drives* is used by a lot of forensics teams in various US government agencies. An alternative definition uses the term artifacts in a more general, English sense, to mean *small pieces of evidence that you have to capture right away* through snapshots, screen capture image programs, and so on. Be prepared on the CompTIA Security+ exam to go with either definition.

External Sources of Evidence The many devices that make up personal mobile computing—smartphones, tablets, laptops, wearables—and devices connected elsewhere in a LAN or WLAN can yield all sorts of forensic information for examiners. The log files of location services can help track the movements of the bearers of mobile devices, not just to say, "Bill was at this take-out joint at 1 AM on Thursday," but also how fast he was going to get from point A to point B and what route he took. Figure 13-7 shows a screenshot from a fitness app (Strava) on my smartphone. It clearly shows an early morning

Figure 13-7
Strava
recording of the
whereabouts
of one of the
authors

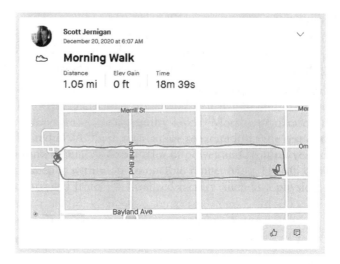

walk (because of the time stamp and pace), a stop at a convenience store (all the squiggles on the far left), and then a walk back down a different street to the starting point. Date, time, distance, route, all recorded.

Wireless networks make it easy to hide devices that connect to the wireless LAN. Tracking network settings and connections and documenting locations and connection points can help you discover hidden nodes. A fairly recent raid by a US government agency on a suspected trafficker of illegal images, for example, yielded the usual desktop and mobile systems. After bagging and tagging and all that, the agents did one last thorough sweep of the network. Lo and behold, some device was still hitting the wireless access point. It turned out to be the main file server, operated headlessly/remotely via Wi-Fi, completely hidden behind a solid wall. Bingo! Evidence captured, bad guys busted, and the world is a better place.

On-Premises vs. Cloud

The prevalence of cloud computing as part of the go-to aspects of modern networks adds another dimension to forensics. An organization has control over or access to every aspect of local resources, or *on-premises resources*. If a security breach occurs, all the standard forensics methodologies that you're reading about in this module apply.

The *cloud service provider (CSP)* controls its own resources and access to those resources. You can't just barge into your CSP's office and demand control over a forensic investigation into a breach that occurred at the CSP! You need to have agreements in place ahead of time, such as a *right-to-audit* clause in the contract between your organization and the CSP that outlines precisely that—in the case of a breach, your forensics team can investigate.

In addition to agreements between an organization and a CSP, regulatory, jurisdictional, and legal considerations also come into play when dealing with on-premises versus cloud forensic situations. Every organization is governed by *regulatory* provisions—regulations and laws, such as the ones discussed several times previously in this book. If your organization works with government contracts, for example, and a breach occurs, expect government forensics teams to investigate. The fun part with the cloud is that holds true even if your data or services are in the cloud, hosted by the CSP.

Further, the location of the breach defines the *jurisdiction* of the investigating bodies. In the United States, if the breach affects interstate commerce, then it's clearly the jurisdiction of the federal government per the Commerce Clause in the Constitution. But what if it's a data breach at an Amazon AWS data center in Pocatello, Idaho, and your company is based in Houston, Texas? Idaho forensics investigators would have first shot because of the location of the breach.

Finally, *data breach notification laws* vary throughout the United States (and I assume other countries have similar variations). With a data breach that occurred at Bayland Widgets Corporation in Texas that exposed PII, for example, BWC must inform all affected customers immediately. (There are some exceptions for not impeding a criminal investigation, but the law is pretty clear.) In contrast, in a similar data breach exposing PII in Alabama, on the other hand, Gantt Gadgets has to inform affected people after an investigation only if the breach is likely to cause substantial harm. The precise wording of the two data breach notification laws makes their different approaches very clear:

- Texas: Any person or business that owns personal information, or licenses electronic personal data in the state of Texas, is required to immediately report a data breach as soon as it occurs.

- Alabama: Notification is required if, following a prompt and thorough investigation, it is deemed that the security breach is likely to cause substantial harm to the individuals affected. If, after a good faith investigation, it's determined that there is not likely a substantial risk of harm, notification is not required.

Critical Forensics Practices

When discussing basic forensics concepts, certain practices are common to all investigations regardless of operating system in use, nature of the investigation, and so on. These practices are critical to an investigation, and although they are very basic in nature, they can make or break an investigation and may make the difference between the successful prosecution or dismissal of the case due to faulty forensics procedures. The next few items we will discuss are critical practices you need to know both for the exam and as a real-life forensics investigator.

First Response

First response to an investigation is a critical step in the process that affects the entire investigation and its outcome. It's one part of the process that can't be redone right the second time; it must be done correctly the first time, from the beginning. Most organizations don't employ a full-time qualified and trained forensics investigator; they might have qualified people who have other primary duties in the security or IT administration departments, and those personnel will act as first (and sometimes only) responders to an incident requiring forensic skills. At minimum, they should be trained on what to do—and what *not* to do—during the initial response to a forensics incident, including how to secure the scene, and how to approach and identify potential evidence, collect it, and secure it using chain of custody.

Securing the scene is the first task and is certainly not least important; the first responder should make sure that only personnel necessary to the response and investigation be involved and have access to the scene. These may include representatives from the legal, HR, and security departments, as well as certain managers. You should be very careful, however, to make sure that the number of people aware of and involved in the response is kept to the absolute minimum. There will, of course, be people in the organization who sometimes overestimate their own importance and try to be involved in the investigation. This usually leads to difficulties in keeping the scene intact, investigating the case objectively, and being able to keep the investigation confidential.

NOTE Securing the scene sometimes takes subterfuge, such as using a ruse or note to get a suspected internal user away from his or her system and into a company breakroom. Investigators can swoop in quickly and secure the scene without interference.

During the initial response to an incident requiring a forensic investigation, the impulse is to begin immediately examining the system, plugging in disc imaging devices, and so on, but the first thing an investigator (or qualified responder) should do is photograph or take video of the scene. This is because the human memory is fallible and subjective, and establishing a legal case often requires proving exactly how a system was set up and running, to include its placement, devices plugged into it (and into which ports), and what was shown on the screen (if it's turned on) when the responder arrived.

After you (the investigator) have photographed the scene, you should begin to assess the situation. You'll need to determine in what state the computer is running. Is it powered off or on? Is a user logged in or logged out? What applications or processes are visible on the screen?

Based upon this, as well as the nature of the incident (for example, hacking attack, computer misuse, criminal investigation, and so on), you must decide whether to do a "live" response by collecting evidence with the computer up and running or to collect data after the machine is powered off, if it isn't already. A live response can get valuable data that is in RAM, such as running processes, network connections, active sessions, and so on, but you also risk tainting the evidence by collecting it, since a live response can change data, files, and their access times. A discussion on data volatility and the order of collection is presented earlier in the module.

In addition to deciding whether to perform a live response or not, you must also decide whether you should disconnect the system from the network. If the system is under attack, you must balance the desire to stop the attack and limit data loss with the possibility of gaining valuable information about the nature of the attack and the attacker. You'll make this decision based upon the critical nature of the data involved, the seriousness and impact of the attack, and the damage to the system and network.

NOTE The first response certainly can differ if there's a law enforcement issue involved. In the latter case, an internal team wouldn't likely be touching any evidence at all.

A first response must also include a comprehensive inventory of all evidence collected and seized by the investigator. As a first responder, you should inventory systems, peripherals, and media, as well as any other device or item deemed relevant to the investigation. You should record the inventory on a form that allows you to enter the type of hardware device, make, model, and serial number of any item seized as evidence. You should also establish a chain of custody at this point, the details of which are discussed next.

Chain of Custody and Securely Handling Evidence

Evidence is any item that can be used to substantiate or support your case and the investigation. To be used in most legal proceedings, evidence items should be reliable and not subjected to the possibility of alteration or modification in any way. There should also be the assurance that the evidence has been under positive control and in secure storage at all times. This last part is accomplished through the chain of custody process. *Chain of custody* begins when the evidence is initially seized or collected and establishes a continuous accounting of where the evidence is at all times, who has possessed it, what activities were performed on it, and the details of its storage, use, and transfer. This process helps to ensure the integrity of evidence and minimizes the possibility that it has been altered or tampered with. Chain of custody contributes to the admissibility and value of evidence in court.

In addition to the formal chain of custody process, evidence must be handled properly to make sure it does not get damaged, lost, tampered with, or stolen. Properly handling evidence includes storing it securely in locked cabinets or safes, storing it in a secure room that is restricted to certain personnel, conducting periodic inventories, documenting when evidence is removed or placed into storage, and documenting any analysis actions that take place with the evidence. Additionally, proper handling and storage requires taking into account considerations such as humidity, temperature, electrostatic discharge, and other environmental issues that inherently affect electronic devices and digital storage media.

NOTE You might get some resistance to following proper chain of custody practices, because to non-security people they may seem overly dramatic or rule-bound. *Persist.* You literally never know when an incident response investigation may turn up something that interests authorities .... Cover your posterior by following proper chain of custody practices in forensic investigations.

Timelines of Sequence of Events

Time is a critical element in a digital forensic investigation, in many ways. First, files on a computer are normally "stamped" by the operating system or file system with the system time and date to indicate when the file was modified, accessed, or created (referred to sometimes as the *MAC times*, or simply *time stamps*). Timestamping is an important consideration in a case, simply because it provides a record of when a suspect may have interacted with a file. Log files also use timestamping for events they record, such as login activity, file or folder access, use of privileges, and so forth. Even a forensics investigator's software used to collect and analyze evidence provides time stamps so that the activities the investigator performs can be tracked, verified, and used to provide confirmation of a sound analysis on the evidence.

The key to timestamping electronic data, such as files and logs, is time synchronization. On a network, hosts often get their time from a central source, such as a network time server or Internet-based time source running the Network Time Protocol (NTP) on UDP port 123. The hosts on the network, if set correctly, consider time zone differences between the local time zone and Universal Coordinated Time (UTC), which NTP normally uses. Still, it's a good idea to verify time zone settings and synchronization (as well as the use of NTP over manual time settings) when investigating to ensure that a host is getting the correct time, or at least to account for time differences between file MAC times, log time stamps, and other events relevant to the investigation. A good investigation needs to record the *time offset*, the difference between the time stamp and the time zone, usually GMT.

It's worth mentioning here that the use of time stamps isn't limited to electronic files, data, and records. The investigator should also manually use time stamps on written or paper logs, forms, and so on to help enforce the accountability and validation of manual activities during the investigation. This is especially important on the chain of custody forms, as well as interview records and other manually created records pertaining to the investigation.

Data Integrity and Preservation

Data integrity is a critical part of a digital forensics investigation. In addition to protecting physical evidence, such as removable media and hard drives, protecting the files on those types of media is just as important. Because digital evidence is subject to volatility and change, it's important to establish that the digital evidence collected remains unchanged throughout the course of the investigation, including the storage, analysis, and presentation of the evidence. Ensuring data integrity throughout the investigation is called *preservation*. At the file level, this is achieved by a process called *hashing*. Hashing uses cryptographic algorithms (known as hashing algorithms), which offer a way to represent digital evidence (primarily files) as a numerical value (or *sum*) known as a *hash*. MD5 and the SHA series of hashing algorithms (such as SHA-1, SHA-2, SHA-512, and so on) are the hashing algorithms primarily used for this purpose.

 EXAM TIP   A related but much lighter process than hashing creates a *checksum* of a document before sending, then compares the document using the same checksum upon receipt. This process catches accidental bit flips in data transmissions over networks.

The theory behind hashing is that if a hash (also called a message digest) is recorded for a file, any tiny change to the file will change the hash value. Even if one binary digit, or *bit* (a 1 or a 0), of a file changes, the measured hash value will change. This means

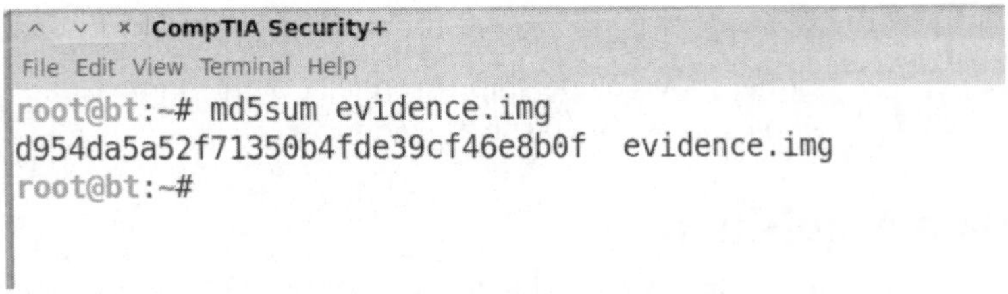

Figure 13-8
An MD5 hash generated for an evidence file in Linux

```
^  v  ×  CompTIA Security+
File  Edit  View  Terminal  Help
root@bt:~# md5sum evidence.img
d954da5a52f71350b4fde39cf46e8b0f  evidence.img
root@bt:~#
```

that if a hash value is taken for a piece of digital evidence, and later a hash value is taken again for the same evidence, they should exactly match unless the evidence has been tampered with or changed. This process ensures digital evidence integrity and can be used against individual files, folders, or even complete images of an entire hard drive or other digital storage media. Figure 13-8 shows an MD5 sum generated for a file in the Linux operating system.

EXAM TIP Hashing in forensics helps prove the integrity of data captured in an investigation. Part of the integrity process involves *non-repudiation*, where a person cannot deny that he or she took a specific action. The person's identity has been positively verified, and any actions that person takes are traced back to that identity.

Provenance

When someone brings in a painting for auction at the great auction houses, such as Sotheby's in London, questions inevitably arise. Is it stolen? Is it real? The seller needs to provide—or research needs to happen to determine—the provenance of the art. *Provenance* establishes the history of ownership of the art from the hand of the artist to each owner over time. Provenance can be proven through photographs, documentary evidence, markings on the art (although these can be altered over time), and so forth. Being able to show a photograph that depicts an artist with his work shown in the background, for example, to providing documentation or photos proving the seller's ancestors purchased the work from the artist and a will showing the seller inherited the work would provide adequate provenance that the seller was the rightful owner of a genuine Picasso.

NOTE There are many examples of twentieth-century (and later) artists photographed with their work, as described earlier. We were unable to get permission to print an example here, but do a Google Image search for "Picasso in his studio" and you'll see dozens of clear examples.

Provenance works similarly in digital forensics, designed to track data from the time of creation, the creator, changes over time, who had access to the data, and the current location(s). This historical trail can help investigators understand how data wound up in their case, who had it previously, and what changes were made.

EXAM TIP Provenance and chain of custody are very different things. The former shows ownership, essentially, of the original data. The latter tracks who handles data taken as evidence.

Data Acquisition

Once evidence has been seized, the investigator must go through another process to capture the evidence, generically called *data acquisition*. Earlier we mentioned the process of gathering or capturing evidence in order of volatility, starting with system RAM and moving on to hard drives and other removable storage media. This process also includes evidence beyond a single workstation, such as network servers and any device that stores processes, transmits, or receives data in most forms. Some special-purpose devices will require more unique methods of capturing evidence, including dumping logs and configuration files from network devices, copying database structures, and so on. Any form of digital data, such as a file, an application, or a network capture, should be captured as needed. In the next couple of sections, we'll discuss a few aspects of capturing types of digital evidence.

Capture Contents of RAM

Capturing the most volatile of all data sources—physical memory, or RAM—takes priority in the early response to an incident. You can use the *memdump* command-line tool in Linux to copy (or *dump*) the contents of RAM directly across a network, not changing anything. Connect to the remote system using netcat or openssl, then run memdump. You can analyze the data later. Sweet!

Capture a System Image

A *system image* is usually a file or series of files that contains the entire contents of a hard drive or other digital storage media (as opposed to a photographic or graphic image). You could, of course, perform a routine copy of all files and folders on a hard drive to another media. This would get *some* of the digital evidence located on the drive, but it wouldn't get areas of the drive that contain deleted files, metadata structures, and so on.

To get these crucial areas of the drive, you must go through a process known as *imaging* the drive. In the forensic imaging process, you're trying to get a bit-by-bit copy of the entire drive, to include hidden or system areas, slack space, file tables and other metadata, and so on, in addition to the files and directories that are normally visible to the user. Since routine copy processes don't typically capture all this data, you might use a forensic imaging program or even a special hardware device to capture an image from media.

Once you've obtained the system image, you should perform a hash on the image files to establish their integrity. You should also make a backup copy of the system image and perform your forensic analysis on the backup, rather than on your original image.

EXAM TIP Capture a system image and take hashes using SHA-1 or MD5 to verify the acquired disk image. Do this again during the investigation to make sure nothing changed on the image.

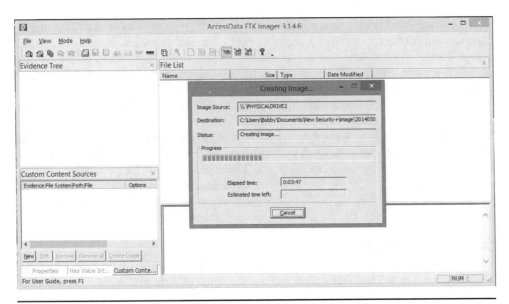

Figure 13-9   AccessData's FTK Imager capturing an image of a USB stick

Several forensics tools are available to capture system images, including commercial tools such as *FTK Imager* and its big brother, Access Data Forensic Toolkit (FTK), and the EnCase commercial software suite. These commercial tools usually offer a full range of system image and digital evidence analysis functions as well. Additionally, there are hardware imaging devices specifically designed for forensics use; these can capture system images from different types of media and create their hash values at the same time. Figure 13-9 shows an example of AccessData's FTK Imager capturing an image of a USB stick.

 EXAM TIP   The process in forensics for capturing every scrap of information, including hidden and deleted files, is called *recovery*.

The *dd* command-line tool in Linux and macOS enables you to make a system image with a few simple commands and make sure no data changes. Use dd in conjunction with MD5 to make an error-free disk image. The cool part is you can boot to a live media drive, like a USB thumb drive with Kali Linux installed, connect an external USB hard drive of sufficient capacity, and then run through your steps to create the hash and copy whichever drive you want to the external drive, all without touching anything internal to the system.

Capture Video

Digital forensic investigations should try to *capture video evidence*. If the video is in the form of a file that comes off the workstation in question, you should treat it as you would any other file by establishing its integrity via hashing and analyzing it for its evidentiary value. Video that comes out of a surveillance camera is of equal value as evidence, but it may be stored as a digital file on a removable media or even in a central storage area of a workstation or server. Although rare these days, video could also be stored on a type of videotape, or it may come in a proprietary file format, depending upon the manufacture of the surveillance camera and system.

In any case, the considerations for capturing video are like those for most other forms of evidence. It is seized the same way, accounted for, and handled using a chain of custody. If it's digital in nature or stored on tape or another type of media, it should be forensically copied, and the analysis performed on the copy. If it's a digital format, it should also be hashed for integrity purposes. The analysis should be performed only on a copy of the original evidence, like all digital evidence, and may require conversion to a popular video format if its native format is proprietary in nature. Literally dozens of file viewers and analysis tools can be used to examine captured video.

Capture Individual Files

When you need only an individual file, take a moment to create a hash of the file and then copy the file and hash to a separate location, such as a thumb drive. Keep another copy of the hash in another, secure location.

Data acquisition for individual files is rare but useful in specific situations. One time, I found several images attached to an e-mail message. Suspecting that these images were using *steganography*—the science of hiding information in other data—I went through the secure data acquisition process and sent them to a forensics lab for analysis. Sure enough, the images contained text files.

 NOTE *Steganography tools* enable you to encrypt data within image, video, and audio files. These tools also enable decryption of those files.

Network Traffic and Event Logs

Network traffic and *event logs*, as mentioned previously, are also viable forms of digital evidence as long as proof exists that the stored copies weren't manipulated. Logs can give insight as to the events that occurred on the network relating to network traffic that has occurred between hosts and servers, as well as between the internal network and the Internet. Most network devices log files in one of several common formats and store these files locally on the device or on a central storage device on the network. Log files are also used for event correlation. For instance, if you are tracking the actions of the user on a workstation who may have accessed prohibited content on the Internet, not only would you look at the files and logs on the workstation he used, but you'd also examine the event logs on network devices, such as proxy servers and firewalls, to correlate the user's actions and times to establish a working timeline of the events.

Log files capture network traffic that has already occurred, but they don't capture information about active network traffic. This is where a network sniffer, sometimes called a *protocol analyzer* (the term used by CompTIA), is useful. You can use a sniffer, which could be either hardware or software in nature, to capture ongoing network traffic and save it to a file for later analysis. You can also examine the capture in real time, so that you can see what's currently going on in the network. This may be useful if you are investigating an ongoing attack, for example, and are trying to determine how the attacker is getting into the network or what type of data he is trying to steal or damage. This type of capture also may help you if you are investigating a user who is performing prohibited or criminal actions on the network, and you want to catch her in the act. You should store and treat network traffic capture files as any other type of digital evidence. You should analyze only copies of the files, taken after you have created hash values for them to establish integrity.

NOTE   Refer back to Chapter 4 for the gory details on packet sniffers and protocol analyzers.

Witness Interviews

Part of data acquisition requires the forensics team to interview witnesses who may have information about the incident. The team records the witness interviews for later review. Seemingly unimportant details from one interview might mesh with details from other interviews to provide clues to solving the incident.

NOTE   It can get very hairy when you start involving witnesses, because people have the right to be silent when questioned by an officer of the law, but perhaps not when questioned by higher-ups in business. But the right to avoid self-incrimination certainly applies. Be careful.

Analyzing Evidence

Acquiring and capturing evidence in a forensically sound manner, in accordance with established procedures that will hold up in court, is a huge part of the forensic investigation. Sometimes first responders who are not otherwise trained in forensics procedures are the people who collect digital evidence, and they may have no further involvement in its further analysis. At other times, the same people who collect it will also analyze it, and they must be trained with skills beyond those required by first responders.

Analyzing digital evidence requires skills that include advanced knowledge of how hard drives and other storage media are constructed, file systems and bit-level construction of files and data, and so on. The forensics investigator also must know how encryption systems work and how a knowledgeable suspect may hide data in files.

Forensics investigators can use tools to help with data analysis, which are used to reassemble pieces of data into usable evidence that communicate what a suspect was doing, how, and sometimes even why. In fact, forensic analysis is used to establish an indisputable chain of events and actions against a timeline, for the purposes of proving or disproving a suspect's innocence or guilt. A forensic analysis should answer six questions about actions and events that took place on the system or network: who, what, where, when, why, and how.

Common Analysis Tasks

Regardless of type of data or system examined, a forensics investigator must know how to perform some common tasks. Forensically sound data collection is one of those tasks, as well as knowing how to forensically copy or image digital storage media.

A forensics investigator needs to know also how to perform analysis tasks, such as analyze files and file systems, look for hidden files, recover deleted or corrupt files, decrypt data that has been encrypted by a suspect, and reconstruct a timeline of events that occurred on the system or network. The investigator should know techniques for *data recovery* with mass storage devices deliberately wiped, such as software tools for peeling back file overwrites and scanning for the artifacts previously mentioned.

 EXAM TIP One of the go-to tools for data recovery in forensics is the Windows-based *WinHex* from X-Ways. Essentially a hex editor, WinHex can examine all sorts of drives (and more) for information at the granular level. For more details, check the source: https://x-ways.net/winhex.

A forensics investigator may also have to be an expert in hacking attacks, so that she can adequately analyze illegal penetrations into a system or network. Malware analysis is also a task a forensics investigator may occasionally perform, so being familiar with different types of malware and how they are constructed is also important.

 EXAM TIP A great (free!) tool for examining a system's Internet activities, browsing history, malware infections, and the like is *Autopsy*. This is a modular tool, meaning you can add capabilities as you need them, created by Basis Technology. Check out Autopsy at https://autopsy.com.

Big Data Analysis

Traditionally, most forensics investigations involve single systems or are limited to a single network and its hosts. As more and more data is generated and distributed across the Internet, investigators are increasingly finding that they are investigating cases that involve *big data*, or very large and complex data sets. Some of these data sets are stored in huge data centers, or even in the cloud, and could be spread out across several geographical sites and systems.

Performing data collection and analysis on big data is a huge task and will likely require teams of IT and forensics professionals if it involves large amounts of distributed data. The investigator will also collect and analyze smaller subsets of data related to the case at hand.

One advantage to big data is that it usually isn't volatile; it is usually backed up quite extensively so there is no fear of data loss. The biggest challenge in an investigation involving big data is to locate data relevant to a case and extract that data using specialized tools (database query tools) and analyzing the smaller data sets. Otherwise, evidence obtained from big data should be treated as any other forensics evidence: data extracted from a large data set should be copied, hashed, and analyzed using standard forensics tools. An extra effort on the part of the forensics investigator may be required to document carefully how data was extracted, under what circumstances, why it is relevant to the case, and how it was handled during analysis, for the benefit of the court.

 EXAM TIP The CompTIA Security+ exam objectives use the term *strategic intelligence/counterintelligence* to refer to an organization taking advantage of the information gathered in a forensic investigation to serve as knowledge to defend the organization from future attacks. In other words, organizations can and should salvage some useful intelligence from the otherwise negative event of a security breach.

Module 13-3: Continuity of Operations and Disaster Recovery

This module covers the following CompTIA Security+ objectives:

- **2.1** **Explain the importance of security concepts in an enterprise environment**
- **2.5** **Given a scenario, implement cybersecurity resilience**
- **4.2** **Summarize the importance of policies, processes, and procedures for incident response**
- **5.3** **Explain the importance of policies to organizational security**
- **5.4** **Summarize risk management processes and concepts**

Business continuity consists of the planning and processes that an organization undertakes to ensure that it survives and can function after a disaster or incident. This includes identifying critical processes, prioritizing systems and equipment, and determining the business impact if any of these processes or systems are unavailable to the organization for extended periods of time. Since this impact is closely related to risk analysis, the organization should perform this type of planning as part of, and in conjunction with, the organization's risk management processes.

Additionally, planning involves determining strategies to bring critical services, systems, and data back online after recovery so the organization can assume some level of operations. The organization must ensure that the preparation and logistics support is in place to bring these critical pieces back online. This module revisits the concepts of risk management covered in Chapter 1 and introduces contingency planning concepts. The module will conclude with key elements of disaster recovery plans and backup and restore plans and policies.

Risk Management Best Practices

Risk management factors into business continuity. A business must plan for and mitigate risk, after all, to survive and thrive another day. Chapter 1 detailed risk management concepts, such as infrastructure, security controls, risk management frameworks, and industry-standard frameworks and reference architectures. This section provides a refresher on risk assessment and then goes into detail on organizational policies. To enhance or maximize organizational security, the organization's policies include implementing robust change management procedures, change controls, and asset management.

 EXAM TIP Pay attention to the nuances of risk management in the questions. Module 1-2 covered risk in terms of frameworks and best practices, for example. This module hits broadly on risk management concepts.

Also, note that you'll see change management, change control, and asset management as *organizational policies* on the CompTIA Security+ exam.

Risk Assessment

A *risk assessment* encompasses the activities that focus on the collection of information (threats, assets, vulnerabilities, and impacts) and analysis of that information to determine the degree of damage and impact to a system or business from threats. Risk assessment also seeks to quantify items such as cost, downtime, and so on, and to determine how those items can be mitigated or reduced. A risk assessment in terms of business continuity focuses on what relevant threats to business operations exist and how they impact the business's ability to function after a negative event.

Site Risk Assessment

A *site risk assessment* focuses on one aspect of an overall organizational risk assessment, the facilities. What potential risk factors could impact operations? Is the area in which the site is located prone to floods, hurricanes, earthquakes, tornados, blizzards, or wildfires? What about people-based attack vectors, such as exposed (versus underground) wiring for electricity, Internet, and cellular?

Part of site risk assessment includes documenting specific areas at risk as single points of failure. Do all the servers in the company reside in a single server room? What kind of disruption would cutting electricity to that room or disabling HVAC (specifically the air conditioning part of HVAC) cause to the overall organization? (See "Removing Single Points of Failure" later in this chapter for a broader discussion.)

A site risk assessment includes maps, diagrams, and more, detailing every facility and potential risks involved. All of this information feeds directly into the bigger business impact analysis (covered in a later section, "Business Impact Analysis").

Change Management

An IT infrastructure is an ever-changing thing. Applications are updated, operating systems change, server configurations adjust; change is a tricky part of managing an infrastructure. Change needs to happen, but not at the cost of losing security. The process of creating change in your infrastructure in an organized, controlled, safe way is called *change management*.

Change management usually begins with a *change management team*. This team, consisting of people from throughout your organization, is tasked with the job of investigating, testing, and authorizing all but the simplest changes to your network.

Changes tend to be initiated at two levels: strategic-level changes, typically initiated by management and major in scope (for example, switching all the servers from Windows to Linux); and infrastructure-level changes, typically initiated by a department by making a request to the change management team. Let's go over what to expect when dealing with change management.

Initiating the Change   The first part of many change processes is a request from a part of the organization. Let's say you're in charge of IT security for an accounting department that includes dozens of accountants with dozens of PCs. A new version of their core accounting software has been released, and the change management team needs to manage the upgrade securely.

Changes start with a *change request*. Depending on the organization, this can be a highly official document or, for a smaller organization, nothing more than a detailed e-mail message. Whatever the case, the initiating person or group needs to document the reason for this change. A good change request will include the following:

- **Type of change**   Software and hardware changes are obviously part of this category, but this could also encompass issues like backup methods, work hours, network access, workflow changes, and so forth.

- **Configuration procedures**   What is it going to take to make this change happen? Who will help? How long will it take?

- **Rollback process**   If this change in some way makes such a negative impact that going back to how things were before the change is needed, what will it take to roll back to the previous configuration?

- **Potential impact**   How will this change impact the organization? Will it save time? Save money? Increase efficiency? Will it affect the perception of the organization?

- **Notification**   What steps will be taken to notify the organization about this change?

Dealing with the Change Management Team   With the change request in hand, it's time to get the change approved. Most organizations rely on a well-written change request form to get the details. The *approval process* usually consists of considering the issues listed in the change request, but also management approval and funding.

Making the Change Happen   Once your change is approved, the real work starts. Equipment, software, tools, and so forth must be purchased. Configuration teams need to be trained. The change committee must provide an adequate *maintenance window*: the time it will take to implement and thoroughly test the coming changes. As part of that process, the committee must *authorize downtime* for systems, departments, and so on. Likewise, the committee provides *notification of the change* to those people who will be affected, if possible, providing alternative workplaces or equipment.

Documenting the Change   The ongoing and last step of the change is *documentation*. All changes must be clearly documented, including but not limited to the following:

- Network configurations, such as server settings, router configurations, and so on
- Additions to the network, such as additional servers, switches, and so on
- Physical location changes, such as moved workstations, relocated switches, and so on

Change Control

Implementing *change control* enables an organization to plan for and upgrade equipment in an orderly, logical, and secure fashion. Change control governs every aspect of upgrades, from "proposal, justification, implementation, testing, review, and disposition of changes to the systems" to documentation of any system changes or modifications. Change control requires, as you might suspect, complete baselines of all current systems and then documentation of all changes to those baselines with upgrades or modifications.

As with most controls, a designated committee—in this case a configuration control board—has to review and approve any proposed changes. This board often includes representatives from organizations bringing in entirely new systems.

Finally, the configuration change control process requires auditing. Auditing includes before and after documentation, plus any auditing information that was produced or required during the update, upgrade, or modification of systems.

 NOTE   The quoted text in the first paragraph under "Change Control" came from the source of all configuration change control wisdom, NIST SP 800-53 (Rev. 4), CM-3, "Configuration Change Control." Check out the source here: https://nvd.nist.gov/800-53/Rev4/control/CM-3.

Asset Management

IT asset management (ITAM) systems connect many existing systems in an organization to create a single source for information about everything IT-related in that organization. The goal with ITAM is to enhance security by making available quickly information on assets such as location, model, operating system, vulnerabilities to known threats, physical security in place, and compliance with laws and regulations. The scope of ITAM is pretty huge, in other words!

The key here is that with an ITAM system in place, an organization can readily track IT assets throughout their lifespan, from acquisition to modification, from assignment to users, to upgrade needs and actual upgrades, and finally to destruction or recycling at end of life. ITAM monitors systems for hardware and software installations that aren't on the approved list (naughty, naughty!) and any new vulnerabilities that crop up, plus the updates and patches needed to address those vulnerabilities.

The specific components or assets included in an ITAM system vary among every organization. A medical organization will have different assets than an engineering firm, though with some overlap. Specific software and hardware devices would differ, but both organizations would have a lot of Windows or macOS workstations and mobile devices, such as tablets and smartphones. For a deep dive into one such ITAM system directed at financial services, check out the NIST *magnum opus* on the subject, NIST SP 1800-5, *IT Asset Management*: https://nvlpubs.nist.gov/nistpubs/SpecialPublications/NIST .SP.1800-5.pdf.

Contingency Planning and Resilience

Organizations conduct *contingency planning* to ensure the continued function and operation of the organization in the event of a disaster or serious incident. The goal is to create a *resilient* organization, one that can respond to risk, changes, disasters, and so on.

Contingency planning involves a defined process, and it essentially starts by identifying the business assets (including equipment, people, systems, data, and processes) and determining how critical they are to the function of the business. Contingency planning next examines these assets for degree of impact to the business in the event they are lost or nonfunctional during a disaster, and then prioritizes them for *order of restoration*. The impact on the business if critical assets and processes are lost could be financial or operational, or it could have other negative effects. In any case, contingency planning is designed to ensure that these assets are successfully and effectively recovered after a disaster so the business can continue operating.

The next few sections outline some of the key processes and activities involved with contingency planning. You can find a more detailed discussion on business continuity and disaster recovery planning in NIST SP 800-34, Rev. 1, *Contingency Planning Guide for Federal Information Systems*, which was written with government systems in mind but can be used by any business to aid in contingency planning efforts.

 NOTE Some authors and organizations use the term *business continuity planning (BCP)* rather than *contingency planning and resilience* to describe the overarching process for creating all the plans covered in this section (plus a lot more plans). The term BCP is common enough, so expect to see it in the field. We've opted in this edition to go with the NIST guidelines and use the term contingency planning and resilience for the overall field.

Business Impact Analysis

One of the first steps an organization must take in contingency planning is to conduct a *business impact analysis (BIA)* in which an organization identifies assets, determines their criticality to the organization and the impact if those assets are lost, and prioritizes them for restoration in the event of a disaster. If any of these steps sound familiar, it's because the BIA process closely mirrors parts of risk management.

The BIA is performed before other contingency planning steps, because the organization must know *what* it is protecting and how important those assets are to the business before it can plan on how to protect them. Once the organization has identified critical assets and their impacts, it can determine how best to protect them and how much resources it can afford to use to protect those assets, based upon differing threats and their likelihood of occurrence.

Identification of Critical Systems and Components

As part of the BIA process, the organization must identify critical systems and their components. Some of this depends upon the different points of view of the users and functional areas within the organization, so most functional areas in the organization should be represented when the BIA is performed. For example, both the human resources and accounting functions in the organization may each insist that their systems are more critical to the survival of the business than anyone else's. Likewise, the same might apply for engineering and production functions. This is one reason why top management should be involved in the BIA process, to provide objective decision-making capabilities as to which systems and components are critical, and in what priority they must be restored.

Which systems and components are designated as critical may depend upon several factors, including the criticality of the processes they support. For example, if the business's primary mission is online order fulfillment for different products, the business will likely deem the systems and components directly involved in that process (such as Web servers, database servers, financial transaction systems, and so on) more critical than other support systems, such as human resources and accounting systems. The business deems those other support systems important, but it may not necessarily depend upon them for survival, at least in the short term, and to get back up and running again.

The organization should define exactly what constitutes a critical system or component. The organization may develop different categorizations of criticality, based upon the business process supported. For example, a priority one asset may be deemed as the most critical type, directly supporting the primary business mission. A priority two asset may support secondary business functions or even a support system. The organization could also define criticality in terms of system function. For example, it may designate all primary systems supporting the business mission as a priority one and designate any backup or redundant systems as a priority two. Another such categorization may classify all Web servers as priority one, for instance. In any event, we can't overstate the importance of this part of the BIA process.

Removing Single Points of Failure

Without proper planning, or sometimes because of changes over time, an organization might discover it depends for critical function on a single specialized machine, person, or process, creating a *single point of failure*. If that essential entity fails, in other words, bad things happen. Smaller organizations can't necessarily avoid single points of failure, but organizations both small and large need to recognize those points and plan for the eventuality of failure. Let's look at a few examples.

Single points of failure include technologies and equipment such as a single server that processes a critical business function or a system that houses the only copy of a database. A single point of failure doesn't have to be technological, however. A person can also be a single point of failure. For example, suppose only one administrator has access to a piece of critical data or an encrypted file. If something happens to that administrator—she leaves the organization or becomes ill or dies—the organization will have lost access to that data or file. A process can also be a single point of failure. Without an alternative way of processing a financial transaction, for example, failure of the process involved means that the organization no longer has that capability.

During both the risk assessment and business impact analysis processes, an organization should identify single points of failure and eliminate them as efficiently as possible. The organization can accomplish this by purchasing more equipment (such as a backup server), appointing and training an alternate administrator to perform certain duties or have certain access in the event the primary administrator isn't available, and looking at processes critically for redundant capabilities.

In eliminating single points of failure, redundancy is a key concept. Organization management may be reluctant to include redundant equipment, personnel, or processes, as this offers no immediate return on investment (ROI) and can be costly, but they will usually be glad they made the investment the first time a (former) single point of failure fails. Redundancy is discussed a bit later in the module.

Functional Recovery Plans

The next step in contingency planning is to create a series of documents that cover every aspect of the organization, from personnel to equipment, facilities, recovery options, and more. Various organizations use these plans as interactive units or standalone structures. This section puts most of the plans under the umbrella term, business continuity plan, with the remainder under disaster recovery plans.

Business Continuity Plan

The purpose of business continuity planning is to produce a document, the *business continuity plan (BCP)*, which details disaster- and incident-related risks to critical systems, the impact if those systems are lost, and how best to preserve them. This document also specifies how to recover the organization after a disaster and continue business operations. The planning process that goes into producing the detailed plan involves personnel from the entire organization at all management and technical levels. It involves technical personnel, human resources personnel, facilities and security personnel, and representatives from almost every part of the organization. A formal BCP team should be established and mandated with certain goals and tasks. Producing comprehensive continuity and recovery documentation should be one of those tasks, as well as establishing the concrete policies, procedures, and processes necessary to react to an incident, recover from it, and re-establish business operations.

Continuity of Operations Planning
Although they are parts of the same process, *continuity of operations planning (COOP)* and disaster recovery planning are two separate activities with distinct goals. *Continuity of operations (COO)* ensures that the business is functioning and operating again in its primary business mission, while disaster recovery is more of an intermediate step between the actual disaster event and bringing the business back to an operational state. *Disaster recovery planning (DRP)* is concerned with the reaction and response to a disaster and is focused on saving lives, preventing injury, and preserving equipment, data, and facilities. DRP will be discussed a bit later in the module.

COOP ensures that the business has the appropriate systems, equipment, data, infrastructure, and, of course, people to resume and maintain operations. This means that considerations such as backups, spare equipment, alternate processing sites, spare

Figure 13-10
The relationship
between
continuity of
operations and
disaster recovery

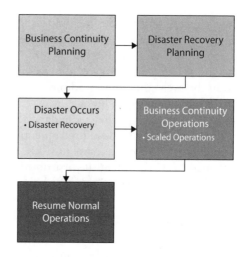

supplies, and so on, are equally important in keeping the business up and running. Figure 13-10 illustrates the relationship of business COO and disaster recovery processes and activities.

NOTE The result of *continuity of operations planning (COOP)* is to create a document, a *continuity of operations plan (COOP)*. Yes, the industry uses the same initialism for both the verb (planning) and the noun (plan). It's rampant, unfortunately. You'll see it shortly again with DRP (and see it frequently with BCP).

One potential fallacy in planning is the assumption that COO means that the business will be back in a fully operational state equal to what it was before the disaster, but this usually isn't the case. In a serious disaster, most businesses will likely recover to an operational state that is somewhat diminished from normal function and operations. This is something that the organization should consider and prepare for during the planning process. The organization should determine the acceptable level for COO and how to achieve that target level. The organization may need to acknowledge that assuming partial operations may be the appropriate step, particularly in the event of a widespread disaster that affects other organizations, public infrastructures, and so on. Even a 50 percent resumption of operations may be considerably better than none and may be even more than other businesses may be able to achieve in a widespread disaster. The organization should set a target COO level and plan on how to achieve that level.

Proper COOP should consider a lot of things aside from machines and locations. Such planning must include exercises for testing the plan; procedures for reporting—so called *after-action reports*; and failover systems that engage immediately in case of a sudden machine death. The COOP should detail alternate processing sites and alternate business practices. (These come up in detail later in the module.)

Disaster Recovery Plan

A *disaster recovery plan (DRP)* is mostly concerned with the practical and immediate activities following an event that include saving lives, preventing injury, salvaging equipment, relocating the physical business infrastructure to a recovery site, and so on. A DRP is often considered a subset of an overall business continuity plan. The major difference is that a BCP is concerned with planning and getting everything in place such that business functions can resume after a disaster, while a DRP is more about the recovery operations. Both are important, but each focus on different parts of the same overall process.

Backup and Restore Plans and Policies

One of the key areas in preparing for a disaster is backing up data to prevent data loss in case the business loses a server, or a disaster occurs and the business loses its entire data center. Because everything in security begins with policy, having a well-defined backup policy is an important start to being prepared for data loss in the event of a disaster.

The overall backup strategy should specify the frequency and types of backups, of course, but, beyond that, it should specify what data is to be backed up and how. An organization can use several different methods to back up data, and these should be specified in the policy. Policy should also dictate which functional area is responsible for data backups, as well as how quickly data must be restored. The policy may also indicate whether data backups should be stored offsite and, if so, how they should be transported, if they should be encrypted, and so on, to protect organizational data further. The policy will also specify who is responsible for data backups, such as the IT department or server management team, for example. During a disaster, certain key positions may be designated as responsible for backups and restorations, if the disaster response team is not organized in the same way as the normal business operations are.

Supporting the backup policy should be the actual plans and procedures that will be used to perform backups. Policy gives direction on *what* must be done and *why*, but not necessarily *how*. For example, a policy would state that all information regarding customer credit card data must be recoverable within two days of a disaster to meet customer expectations and cannot be accessed by the third-party data storage vendor to remain in compliance with Payment Card Industry Data Security Standard (PCI DSS) regulations. This is where plans and procedures come in. The plans and procedures would then specify details such as how both the flat files and the database information are backed up and which encryption method to use. Backup plans and procedures should further define how backups are performed, the methods used, and restoration options. Management will normally write policy (based upon input from the appropriate technical folks), and the people implementing the policy will usually write the plans and procedures.

These policies, plans, and procedures all support the overarching business continuity plan as well as any disaster recovery plans that must be implemented. Together, they ensure that the organization will be able to restore critical data in the event of a disaster or incident.

Backup Execution and Frequency

You can perform backups in several ways. There's no one right way; the choice of which methods to use depends upon several factors that the organization must consider. One of the most important factors is the criticality of data. In other words, how important is the data that must be backed up, and how quickly must it be restored to get the organization back up and running? Some backup methods can back up data more quickly than others but may restore data more slowly. Other methods back up data in certain increments based upon file archive bits. Any combination of these methods may be used for the optimum backup solution for the organization.

Backup frequency is another factor that the organization must determine. Data that rarely changes may need to be backed up monthly only. Daily transactional data, however, such as the type produced in financial or commercial transactions, may need to be backed up on a minute-by-minute basis, or even in near real-time, to ensure that the most current data is available and all-important transactions have processed. For example, if an earthquake suddenly hit and destroyed a company's primary e-commerce server, in a well-designed transactional backup system, the speed of recovery and failover is so lightning fast that a customer could click "Buy" and not even realize that the computer that registered the purchase was destroyed, because a new system came online 1000 miles away and recovered the customer's transaction without a visible slowdown. That is totally amazing!

Backup frequency is also related to criticality of data, as are the other backup considerations. If the organization has a low tolerance for losing data because of its criticality, it should increase the backup frequency. The tolerance for (and measurement of) the amount of data that an organization can afford to lose for any given time frame is discussed later in the module.

Backup Types

The type of backup needed by an organization varies almost as much as the organization varies from every other organization. The CompTIA Security+ objectives dump a lot of backup "things" under the "Backup Types" category, but we'll break them into more manageable chunks:

- Standard backup methods
- Backup media

Standard Backup Methods   There are four standard backup methods: full backups, incremental backups, differential backups, and snapshots. Let's briefly discuss each.

In a *full backup*, regardless of whether you back up a shared folder, a single hard drive, a RAID array, or an entire server, everything is included in the backup set. At the basic file system level, a full backup also *sets the archive bits* on files to indicate that the files have been backed up.

You can think of an archive bit as an on/off switch. If the archive bit is turned "on" (shown by a binary one in the file metadata), the file has been changed and requires a backup. If the archive bit is turned "off" (signified by a binary zero), the file has been backed up and the archive bit is said to have been "cleared."

Full backups clear archive bits to show that the files have been backed up recently. Any changes to any of the files result in the archive bits being turned back on for those files.

An organization may execute a full backup once weekly, for example, or even daily, as needed by the organization and depending upon the backup system it has available. Of course, the concept of archive bits applies only to files in the file system itself; it wouldn't necessarily apply to other types of data structures, such as database tables, for instance. However, other data structures may have similar metadata that indicates its backup or archive status.

 EXAM TIP Two other full backup types—*copy* and *image*—make a replica of a drive for storage elsewhere. Using commands such as dd in Linux, you can very easily capture a system image and place it elsewhere in the network, as you'll recall from Module 13-2. One important difference here between the standard full backup method and copy or image is that the latter two *do not* turn off the archive bit.

The *incremental backup* typically backs up only files that have changed since the last full backup. In other words, when an incremental backup runs, it backs up only the files that have the archive bits turned on. After it backs up those files, it turns off the archive bits. If a full backup is run, and then files subsequently change, an incremental backup backs up only those files. Because data can change daily, incremental backups should run daily as well. If there is a data loss on the backup source itself, apply this *restoration order*: first restore the full backup and then restore all following incremental backups in the order they were run. Figure 13-11 shows conceptually how a backup scheme involving incremental backups might work.

The *differential backup* also gets only a subset of the total data and is also based upon the archive bit setting. However, the major difference between a differential backup and an incremental backup is that the differential backup does not clear the archive bit—it leaves it turned on.

So, when you run a full backup and then data changes, you can run a differential backup and it will back up the data files that have the archive bits turned on. Since a differential backup does not clear the archive bit, the next differential backup that you

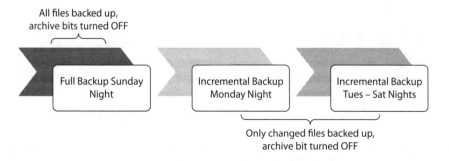

Figure 13-11 A backup scheme using full and incremental backups

run will not only back up that same data but will also add any additional files that have changed since the last differential (and full) backup. Differential backups, then, are cumulative.

Normally, the first differential backup that you run after a full backup may not take very long to execute, but each subsequent differential backup that you run takes increasingly longer to execute because it is backing up more data than the previous differential backup. One advantage to differential backups, however, is that if you must restore data, you restore the full backup first, followed by only the last differential backup to be executed. No other differential backup is necessary for the restoration order, since the last backup contains all the accumulated changed data. Figure 13-12 illustrates the concept of using a combination of full and differential backups.

A *snapshot* stores a version of an operating system (including applications) at a given moment in time. These are common for individual system backups, such as restore points in Windows and Time Machine backups in macOS. For servers and such, a snapshot as a backup refers to the powerful feature with virtual machines that enables you to save a version of a functional VM to restore very quickly if anything negative happens to the functional server. A company DNS server might run on a virtual machine, for example. If that server gets corrupted or compromised, rather than restoring it from backup, you could simply delete the image and load a clean snapshot.

To summarize restoration order differences, full backups must be run first and restored first. With incremental backups, first restore the full backup and then restore all incremental backups in the order they were executed. Incremental backups do not take very long to back up data, but because you must restore all of them, they can make restoration time a bit lengthy.

Differential backups, on the other hand, initially back up data quickly, but slowly take longer and longer to back up. However, when a differential backup is restored, only the last backup needs to be restored after the full backup. A typical scenario might involve an organization executing a full backup on a weekly basis, followed by daily incremental or differential backups. It's also possible to mix and match these types of backups, but that is usually dependent on the type of backup software and system used. Finally, use a snapshot to load clean VMs to replace corrupted or compromised images.

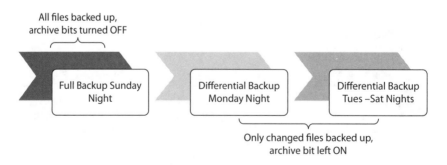

Figure 13-12 Using full and differential backups

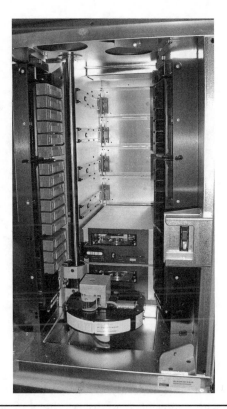

Figure 13-13   Small ADIC Scalar 100 tape library (photo by Aaron Kuhn from Hatfield, PA. https://creativecommons.org/licenses/by-sa/2.0/)

Backup Media: Tape   Preferred backup media has changed over the years because, *progress*. Traditionally, magnetic tape provided incredibly inexpensive storage with the offset of very slow (compared to any other storage media) restore times. Tape solutions—such as the ADIC Scalar 100 shown in Figure 13-13—coupled with incremental or differential backups, provided the low-cost, long-term backup solution for literally decades. A lot of cloud storage providers still use tape for archival backup, especially for records an organization probably won't need but must store for a set number of years to comply with government regulations.

Backup Media: External Enclosure   All local and network-based backup solutions today use hard disk drives as the basic storage unit. Hard drive systems can be directly connected external enclosures, NAS, SAN, or cloud-based.

An *external hard drive* backup system typically has one or more drives in an enclosure that plugs directly into a computer (Figure 13-14). This is a standard backup method that everybody should use. Get USB 3 or better if you can, but even USB 2 provides decent enough speed.

Figure 13-14
Seagate
external hard
drive (Image:
MacFormat
Magazine /
Contributor,
Getty Images)

Backup Media: NAS   Scaling up for active homes and small businesses, you can add storage devices to the wired or wireless network. A *network-attached storage (NAS)* system is a standalone box filled with removable hard drives. The NAS operating system enables remote access and monitoring and often a lot of other features handy for consumers, such as media centers and the like. Figure 13-15 shows a Drobo NAS. Figure 13-16 shows the Drobo NAS with the faceplate removed for easy access to the internal drives. NAS devices provide *file-based storage* of data. To LAN devices, in other words, accessing the NAS is precisely the same as accessing another computer's shared folder over a network.

Figure 13-15
Drobo NAS
(Image:
MacFormat
Magazine /
Contributor,
Getty Images)

Figure 13-16
Drobo NAS
with drives
revealed (Image:
MacFormat
Magazine /
Contributor,
Getty Images)

Backup Media: SAN   Scaling up to the enterprise requires a more scalable backup solution. A *storage area network (SAN)* typically combines multiple devices into a coherent block-storage space, then connects to hosts using blazingly fast Fibre Channel networking (Figure 13-17). The block storage enables a SAN to provide simultaneous high-speed access to multiple users, divide space in whatever way makes sense for the network, and even create what appears to be external hard drives connected to local machines. SANs are much more complicated and expensive than NASs but are pretty much the solution for enterprise on-premises backup and storage.

Backup Media: Cloud   The movement to back up in the cloud, harnessing concentrated storage power managed by someone else, has consumed IT, from individual users all the way up to the mightiest enterprises. Because it makes sense. Starting with creative and well-marketed leaders such as Carbonite, all the way up to the biggest

Figure 13-17
SAN from the
back side (Image:
picture alliance
/ Contributor,
Getty Images)

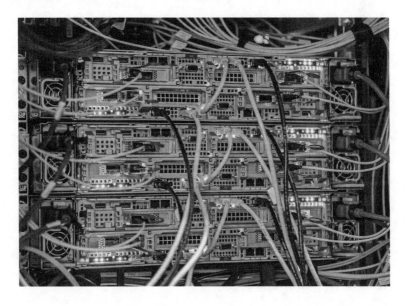

players in the world, such as Amazon and Google, cloud storage and backup offers security and dependability.

The early days of cloud storage stuttered because of throttled or not-quite-developed Internet connection speeds, especially upload speeds. Individuals and businesses just kept adding more local storage capacity and data and ISPs wouldn't or couldn't increase upload speeds. With the jump to symmetric fiber offering speeds upwards of 1 Gbps up/ down, cloud backup make perfect sense for just about everyone.

Providers such as Backblaze offer turnkey solutions at affordable prices. A typical SOHO environment with ten computers and a NAS, for example, can back up unlimited data with Backblaze for a song. Figure 13-18 (composite screenshot) shows pricing for a year at a mere $60 per computer and $98.25 for the SAN.

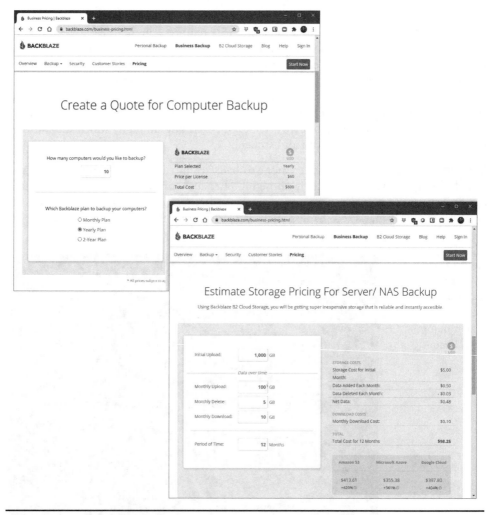

Figure 13-18 Backblaze pricing

Online vs. Offline Backups

The concept of *online versus offline backups* refers to the state of the data at the time of the backup. When dealing with a big database, for example, an *online backup* means the backup happens while the database is live and in use by however many numbers of simultaneous users. This has the advantage of not disrupting any use of the database. With SAP databases, logs keep track of changes and get backed up with the database.

With an *offline backup*, in contrast, the database is shut down. The process backs up a clean copy of the database files and, with SAP at least, stores no log files because no changes happen to the database during the backup.

The restoration process in the case of the database described reverses the process. The files are restored to the database from the offline backup, then the system is brought up for use. With online backup, the log files stored with the backup help guide the restoration process.

EXAM TIP A lot of authors equate the word "online" with "cloud" here and describe online versus offline as cloud versus on-premises or local. Because CompTIA includes distinct objectives for cloud, disk, offsite, etc., we think you'll be tested on the explanation given here. Be prepared to pivot in case the only possibly correct answer to an obvious cloud-as-right-answer question offers online, not cloud.

Geographical Considerations

As companies move to integrate with and take advantage of cloud computing, they must consider a lot of issues, including offsite storage, distance and location considerations, and legal implications such as data sovereignty.

Offsite Storage   Storing backup drives at a location distant from your primary organization provides essential security in the event of a disaster. My company is in Houston, Texas, for example, the land of rodeos and hurricanes. Keeping a backup of our critical data—financial information, intellectual property, and so on—in some storage facility that's not going to be affected by Hurricane [name] next year is essential. [Shakes fist at memory of cleanup after Hurricane Harvey!] The key for organizations is to determine how to keep that offsite backup as current as possible and secure as well. (See "Recovery Sites" later in this module for more details.)

Distance and Location Considerations   Although cloud access can seem instant for many users, the distance between your primary location and online services and storage can make a difference in recovery from disasters. See "Recovery Sites" for some examples. The location of offsite backups and services matters because of law and international jurisdictions. Plus, as in my Houston + hurricanes example, picking a site not prone to the same sorts of disasters your home site can experience is very important.

Legal Implications   Who owns the data you save offsite? What laws apply to both content and searchability? The term *data sovereignty* encompasses many of these legal issues, specifically meaning that data stored in a country is subject to the laws of that country.

What's legal in Pittsburgh might be legal in Paris, too, but wildly illegal in Istanbul. The location of your backup data and recovery sites can make a very big difference in how your data is treated.

Recovery Sites

Recovery sites are an important consideration for site resiliency in disaster recovery planning. Unfortunately, until they need such resiliency, your bosses may not understand the need for such a site. The reason for having *site resiliency* is to prepare for a disaster so that the business can operate if the primary site is compromised due to damage or destruction from a natural disaster, mass power outage, communications interruption, and so on. Even if your business primarily has an Internet storefront, it probably has a physical location that houses personnel, data, records, and business processes. Although the servers and infrastructure may be outsourced to a third party, the business's physical location may be rendered unusable during a disaster, and this alone may prevent the business from operating. Organizations should provide an alternate processing site.

You should know about three types of recovery sites to consider in disaster recovery planning. These are the three types you're likely to see on the CompTIA Security+ exam. The site type an organization chooses depends upon a variety of factors, including cost and expense, the ability to provision a recovery site, and the need to recover the business either very quickly or to have the luxury of being able to wait a longer amount of time before recovering the business to an alternate location.

The three types of recovery sites that you need to know about, in order of increasing cost and required infrastructure, are the cold site, the warm site, and the hot site.

Cold Site   The cold site is attractive to a lot of organizations simply because it's probably the cheapest of the three. A *cold site* is essentially empty floor space where you can set up business operations. The site may have no utilities connected and running at all, or it may have, at minimum, electricity and running water. It also may have heating and air conditioning, but will probably not have any communications connections, such as phone or Internet service. A cold site typically doesn't have any equipment or work areas set up—it's essentially just empty floor space waiting for the organization to move in if necessary.

The best thing about a cold site is that it's cheap. The worst thing about a cold site is that it's so bare in terms of what it provides that it will likely take a long time to move the business into it and set up operations. The organization should decide which is more important, cost or recovery time, and decide on whether a cold site is appropriate. An organization that uses a cold site may have the luxury of a great deal of time before it has to recover the business to normal processing levels.

If you've never encountered a cold site, it may be because they are rarer than warm or hot sites. Organizations that use them either never expect to need them, also have backup warm or hot sites and the cold site is just a second backup, or use a similar concept in establishing alternate processing sites. For example, suppose a small grocery store chain has four grocery stores and outsources its IT processes. A single desktop computer in one store contains all employee data and graphics for newspaper ads for the stores. If that computer goes down, weekly full backups could be sent over to another store; if a disaster hits, they can simply buy a new desktop and keep it in one of the other stores. This is like having a "cold" capability, but at a "hot" site, if that makes sense.

Warm Site   As Goldilocks thought, a warm site may turn out to be just right for an organization. A *warm site* is a little bit more expensive than a cold site, because it provides a little more than empty floor space. It will likely come with full utilities, including heat and air conditioning, electricity and running water, and perhaps even phone and Internet service already provided. A warm site could also come with some rudimentary workspaces set up, such as tables and chairs. An organization that uses a warm site will typically also install some basic equipment that it would need for processing, such as workstations and some servers—probably not enough to run the full operations, but enough at least to get started while recovering the rest of the business to the recovery site.

The organization may also install peripherals such as printers, scanners, and so on. Typically, this spare equipment likely wouldn't be updated with the latest operating systems, patches, applications, or even transactional data the business needs to get going again. But at least having all this equipment in place could cut down on the time it would take to recover the business to the recovery site and start processing again.

A warm site may be a little bit more expensive than a cold site, but it may also provide a happy medium between cost and recovery time. An organization that uses a warm site usually has a need to recover operations reasonably fast, but it doesn't have to do it immediately.

Hot Site   As you might've guessed, the hot site is the most expensive recovery site. A *hot site* offers a bigger bang for your buck, however, because a hot site has all the amenities—floor space, utilities, workspace, and fully mission-capable equipment—required to switch business processing from the primary site to the recovery site, with little interruption. This means that an organization can quickly resume operations after a disaster. All the equipment, applications, and data, including current backups and transaction data, are in place at the hot site, or at least they are readily available for restoration in the event of a disaster. This can be accomplished in several ways, including storing current backups at the recovery site, real-time transactional journaling, and sending live data to the recovery site frequently.

As mentioned, an organization must pay a heavy price in terms of cost and infrastructure for having a hot site available to the organization. But if the organization requires an almost immediate recovery back to full operations, the expense could be well justified. Many businesses would stand to lose a great deal of money by the hour or day if they could not restore processing quickly after a significant disaster. The bottom line is that the hot site can provide for almost immediate recovery, but at a greater cost.

One interesting note about hot (and even, to a degree, warm) sites is that because of big leaps in certain technologies, such as virtualization technologies, organizations are finding it much easier to establish and maintain these sites. Ten years ago, hardly anyone had a hot site, but they are much more common now because the equipment and space requirements for virtual machines are so much less, and because it's so easy to keep the hot site VMs looking just like the live sites by just creating snapshots, cloning, or using other technology built into the VM software.

 EXAM TIP An old trick to handling CompTIA recovery site questions is to remember the following: Hot sites are ready in hours, warm sites are ready in a day, and cold sites are ready in a week. This isn't exactly the case in the real world, but it will help on the exam.

So, how would an organization determine whether it needs a cold, warm, or hot site? Go back to the business impact analysis that was conducted during your business continuity planning. The BIA process helps your organization to determine its assets, to prioritize those assets, and to determine how losing them would impact the organization in terms of cost, productivity, and so on. This analysis leads to determining two other critical pieces of information that can help your organization decide what type of alternate processing site it may need: recovery time objective and recovery point objective, discussed next.

Recovery Time and Recovery Point Objectives

As part of the business continuity and disaster recovery planning process, your organization will need to determine two important factors that influence how quickly it must recover operations and how much data it can afford to lose during a disaster without preventing it from recovering. Normally, an organization would determine this during its business impact analysis. These factors are the recovery time objective (RTO) and the recovery point objective (RPO).

Recovery Time Objective The RTO is the maximum amount of time an organization can be down due to a disaster or an incident. It could be hours or days, depending on the organization's tolerance for downtime. RTO can be calculated several ways, including averaging several RTOs for given processes and systems; or it could be standardized as the shortest amount of downtime allowable for the most critical business processes or systems. It could also be calculated as a cumulative result of the minimum time necessary it takes to restore several critical systems back into operation (using a process called *critical path analysis*).

Recovery Point Objective The RPO is also measured in time, but in the context of data. It's the maximum amount of data that can be lost for the organization, after which the business cannot recover or would suffer significant loss. For example, in a near real-time transaction processing system, the RPO might be only a few minutes' worth of data that can afford to be lost. Another business may have a more tolerable level of data loss, and their RPO may be 24 hours' worth of data. RPO can be affected by several factors, including data criticality and the amount of data an organization creates or processes in a given time frame. In the first example, the organization may have high volumes of data that must be processed quickly, such as financial or inventory data. The second example may indicate a business whose data throughput, in terms of creation or processing, is low or less frequent.

In bringing back the importance of our discussion earlier on transactional backups, let's say that an organization's RPO is very small and they can afford to lose only a few minutes of data. But let's also say that they have been the victim of a hacking attack that may have started a few days earlier. Obviously, they can't just wipe out the last few days' worth of data without a significant (and probably serious) impact to operations. How could they maintain their RPO, yet track down faulty or changed data? By using transaction-based recovery and rolling back only certain records within the past few days of business, those that are suspect due to the hacking attack, that's how.

 NOTE The focus on *high availability* for systems (discussed way back in Chapter 5) means organizations should have technologies in place to make recovery very fast. Technologies such as *Nutanix* provide the capability to, with the flip of a switch, change literal, physical operations from one site to the next instantaneously. That's pretty sweet!

Questions

1. You are recommending personnel for incident response team lead positions. You have several candidates from which to choose and are recommending personnel based upon key characteristics. On which of the following characteristics should you base your recommendations? (Choose two.)

   A. Certifications

   B. Seniority

   C. Training

   D. Experience

2. Which of the following are considered part of executing an incident response? (Choose two.)

   A. Detection and analysis

   B. Preparation

   C. Containment and eradication

   D. Reporting

3. When you are collecting evidence at the scene of the crime, you should store electronic components in which type of containers?

   A. Plastic bags

   B. Paper bags

   C. Metal containers

   D. Anti-static bags

4. Which two United States evidence guidelines provide standards of submitting evidence into criminal and civil court cases? (Choose two.)

   A. Federal Rules of Evidence

   B. 4th Amendment of the US Constitution

   C. Federal Rules of Civil Procedure

   D. Electronic Communications Privacy Act

5. You are the first responder in a company to a potential computer incident involving an employee's workstation. What is the first step you should take when you arrive at the scene?

   A. Unplug the workstation.

   B. Secure the scene.

   C. Capture the contents of RAM.

   D. Inventory the workstation and its peripherals.

6. Which of the following should be immediately established when collecting electronic components as evidence?

   A. Authority over the investigation

   B. Guilt of the suspect

   C. Chain of custody

   D. Sequence of events and timeline

7. Which plan or steps should an organization take at the start of contingency planning to identify assets, determine criticality of assets and potential impact of loss of those assets, and restoration priorities?

   A. BCP

   B. BIA

   C. COOP

   D. DRP

8. Which plan is mostly concerned with the practical and immediate activities following an event that include saving lives, preventing injury, salvaging equipment, and relocating the physical business infrastructure to a recovery site?

   A. BCP

   B. BIA

   C. COOP

   D. DRP

9. Your business needs to be able to resume processing within 12 hours after a disaster. You are looking at recovery site options and decide that the site must have all utilities, redundant equipment, and daily data backups restored to the site. What type of recovery site have you decided to implement?

   A. Cold site

   B. Warm site

   C. Hot site

   D. Shared site

10. You are evaluating several possible solutions for alternate processing sites for your business. You decide that you can afford the expense of a warm site and balance it against the time it will take to set up and recover the business operations to the site. Which of the following are characteristics of a warm site? (Choose two.)

   A. Fully redundant equipment located at the site, loaded with the most current daily backups

   B. Some equipment located at the site to begin limited operations

   C. Heat, water, electricity, and communications in a standby mode

   D. No utilities

Answers

1. **C, D.** Training and experience are key characteristics to consider when recommending personnel for incident response team lead positions.

2. **A, C.** Detection, analysis, containment, and eradication are all steps performed when executing an incident response.

3. **D.** When collecting evidence at the scene of the crime, you should store electronic components in anti-static bags to prevent damage to them.

4. **A, C.** The Federal Rules of Evidence (FRE) and the Federal Rules of Civil Procedure (FRCP) are two standards that dictate how evidence should be introduced into criminal and civil courts, respectively.

5. **B.** Securing the scene is the first step a first responder should take in investigating a potential computer-related incident.

6. **C.** A chain of custody should be established immediately when collecting evidence from the scene of a crime.

7. **B.** Organizations should conduct a business impact analysis as a first step in contingency planning to identify assets, determine criticality of assets and the potential impact of loss of those assets, and restoration priorities.

8. **D.** A disaster recovery plan is mostly concerned with the practical and immediate activities following an event that include saving lives, preventing injury, salvaging equipment, and relocating the physical business infrastructure to a recovery site.

9. **C.** Given the desired time frame to recover the business operations and the level of equipment and support at the site the business needs, this would be a hot site.

10. **B, C.** A warm site is characterized by having heat, water, electricity, and communications, often in a standby mode, as well as having some equipment located at the site to begin limited operations during a recovery.

Exam Objective Map

Exam SY0-601

Exam SY0-601 Objectives	Chapter-Module	Page No.
1.0 Threats, Attacks, and Vulnerabilities		
1.1 Compare and contrast different types of social engineering techniques.		
Phishing	12-2	571
Smishing	12-2	573
Vishing	12-2	573
Spam	12-2	571
Spam over instant messaging (SPIM)	12-2	573
Spear phishing	12-2	572
Dumpster diving	12-2	574
Shoulder surfing	12-2	574
Pharming	12-2	572
Tailgating	12-2	575
Eliciting information	12-2	567
Whaling	12-2	573
Prepending	12-2	571
Identity fraud	12-2	565
Invoice scams	12-2	565
Credential harvesting	12-2	564
Reconnaissance	12-2	564
Hoax	12-2	576
Impersonation	12-2	576
Watering hole attack	12-2	576
Typosquatting	11-3	524
Pretexting	12-2	573

Exam SY0-601 Objectives	Chapter-Module	Page No.
Threat intelligent sources	1-1	5, 7–13
Open-source intelligence (OSINT)	1-1	5, 8
Closed/proprietary	1-1	13
Vulnerability databases	1-1	10
Public/private information-sharing centers	1-1	8
Dark web	1-1	8
Indicators of compromise	1-1	9
Automated Indicator Sharing (AIS)	1-1	8
Structured Threat Information eXpression (STIX)/ Trusted Automated eXchange of Intelligence Information (TAXII)	1-1	8
Predictive analysis	1-1	10
Threat maps	1-1	10
File/code repositories	1-1	10
Research sources	1-1	9, 13–15
Vendor websites	1-1	13
Vulnerability feeds	1-1	13
Conferences	1-1	13
Academic journals	1-1	13
Request for comments (RFC)	1-1	13
Local industry groups	1-1	13
Social media	1-1	14
Threat feeds	1-1	9
Adversary tactics, techniques, and procedures (TTP)	1-1	9
1.6 Explain the security concerns associated with various types of vulnerabilities.		
Cloud-based vs. on-premises vulnerabilities	8-4	426
Zero-day	12-1	525–526
Weak configurations	5-1, 5-5, 11-1, 12-1	272, 316, 504, 560
Open permissions	5-5	315
Unsecure root accounts	5-5	316
Errors	5-1	271
Weak encryption	5-1, 12-1	272, 560
Unsecure protocols	11-1	504
Default settings	5-5	316
Open ports and services	5-5	314

About the Online Content

This book comes complete with TotalTester Online customizable practice exam software with more than 200 practice exam questions and other book resources, including a selection of free online training videos from Mike Meyers, a selection of free online TotalSims simulations, and an online list of Mike Meyers' Cool Tools for CompTIA Security+.

System Requirements

The current and previous major versions of the following desktop browsers are recommended and supported: Chrome, Microsoft Edge, Firefox, and Safari. These browsers update frequently, and sometimes an update may cause compatibility issues with the TotalTester Online or other content hosted on the Training Hub. If you run into a problem using one of these browsers, please try using another until the problem is resolved.

Your Total Seminars Training Hub Account

To get access to the online content you will need to create an account on the Total Seminars Training Hub. Registration is free, and you will be able to track all your online content using your account. You may also opt in if you wish to receive marketing information from McGraw Hill or Total Seminars, but this is not required for you to gain access to the online content.

Privacy Notice

McGraw Hill values your privacy. Please be sure to read the Privacy Notice available during registration to see how the information you have provided will be used. You may view our Corporate Customer Privacy Policy by visiting the McGraw Hill Privacy Center. Visit the **mheducation.com** site and click **Privacy** at the bottom of the page.

Single User License Terms and Conditions

Online access to the digital content included with this book is governed by the McGraw Hill License Agreement outlined next. By using this digital content you agree to the terms of that license.

Access   To register and activate your Total Seminars Training Hub account, simply follow these easy steps.

1. Go to this URL: **hub.totalsem.com/mheclaim**

2. To register and create a new Training Hub account, enter your e-mail address, name, and password on the **Register** tab. No further personal information (such as credit card number) is required to create an account.

   If you already have a Total Seminars Training Hub account, enter your e-mail address and password on the **Log in** tab.

3. Enter your Product Key: `bq22-dzdg-fn7j`

4. Click to accept the user license terms.

5. For new users, click the **Register and Claim** button to create your account. For existing users, click the **Log in and Claim** button.

   You will be taken to the Training Hub and have access to the content for this book.

Duration of License   Access to your online content through the Total Seminars Training Hub will expire one year from the date the publisher declares the book out of print.

Your purchase of this McGraw Hill product, including its access code, through a retail store is subject to the refund policy of that store.

The Content is a copyrighted work of McGraw Hill, and McGraw Hill reserves all rights in and to the Content. The Work is © 2021 by McGraw Hill.

Restrictions on Transfer   The user is receiving only a limited right to use the Content for the user's own internal and personal use, dependent on purchase and continued ownership of this book. The user may not reproduce, forward, modify, create derivative works based upon, transmit, distribute, disseminate, sell, publish, or sublicense the Content or in any way commingle the Content with other third-party content without McGraw Hill's consent.

Limited Warranty   The McGraw Hill Content is provided on an "as is" basis. Neither McGraw Hill nor its licensors make any guarantees or warranties of any kind, either express or implied, including, but not limited to, implied warranties of merchantability or fitness for a particular purpose or use as to any McGraw Hill Content or the information therein or any warranties as to the accuracy, completeness, correctness, or results to be obtained from, accessing or using the McGraw Hill Content, or any material referenced in such Content or any information entered into licensee's product by users or other persons and/or any material available on or that can be accessed through the licensee's product (including via any hyperlink or otherwise) or as to non-infringement of third-party rights. Any warranties of any kind, whether express or implied, are disclaimed. Any material or data obtained through use of the McGraw Hill Content is at your own discretion and risk and user understands that it will be solely responsible for any resulting damage to its computer system or loss of data.

Neither McGraw Hill nor its licensors shall be liable to any subscriber or to any user or anyone else for any inaccuracy, delay, interruption in service, error or omission, regardless of cause, or for any damage resulting therefrom.

In no event will McGraw Hill or its licensors be liable for any indirect, special or consequential damages, including but not limited to, lost time, lost money, lost profits or good will, whether in contract, tort, strict liability or otherwise, and whether or not such damages are foreseen or unforeseen with respect to any use of the McGraw Hill Content.

TotalTester Online

TotalTester Online provides you with a simulation of the CompTIA Security+ exam. Exams can be taken in Practice Mode or Exam Mode. Practice Mode provides an assistance window with hints, references to the book, explanations of the correct and incorrect answers, and the option to check your answer as you take the test. Exam Mode provides a simulation of the actual exam. The number of questions, the types of questions, and the time allowed are intended to be an accurate representation of the exam environment. The option to customize your quiz allows you to create custom exams from selected domains or chapters, and you can further customize the number of questions and time allowed.

To take a test, follow the instructions provided in the previous section to register and activate your Total Seminars Training Hub account. When you register you will be taken to the Total Seminars Training Hub. From the Training Hub Home page, select **Mike Meyers' Security+ Guide, 3e (SY0-601)** from the Study drop-down menu at the top of the page, or from the list of Your Topics on the Home page. You can then select the TotalTester option to customize your quiz and begin testing yourself in Practice Mode or Exam Mode. All exams provide an overall grade and a grade broken down by domain.

Other Book Resources

The following sections detail the other resources available with your book. You can access these items by selecting the Resources tab, or by selecting **Mike Meyers' Security+ Guide, 3e (SY0-601)** from the Study drop-down menu at the top of the page or from the list of Your Topics on the Home page. The menu on the right side of the screen outlines all of the available resources.

Video Training from Mike Meyers

Video from the author provides detailed examples of key certification objectives. Navigate to the Resources tab and select **Videos for Mike Meyers' CompTIA Security+ Guide, 3e (SY0-601)** on the Resources tab menu. The link will take you to select CompTIA Security+ videos for exam SY0-601. You'll have access to free videos that cover a selection of chapters in the book, with an option to purchase Mike's complete video training series.

TotalSim Simulations

The free TotalSim simulations selected for this book are organized by chapter, and there are free simulations available for reviewing topics covered in the book with an option to purchase access to the full TotalSims for CompTIA Security+ exam SY0-601. You can access the TotalSims by navigating to the Resources tab and selecting **TotalSims for Mike Meyers' CompTIA Security+ Guide, 3e (SY0-601)**.

Mike's Cool Tools

Mike loves freeware and open-source networking tools. Most of the utilities can be downloaded from the Internet. Navigate to the Resources tab and select **Mike's Cool Tools for Mike Meyers' CompTIA Security+ Guide, 3e (SY0-601)**, which will open the Mike's Cool Tools page.

 CAUTION   Although all of the tools are "Mike Meyers Approved," there is no guarantee they will work for you. Read any and all documentation that comes with each utility before using that program.

Technical Support

For questions regarding the TotalTester, the Mike Meyers videos, TotalSims, Mike's Cool Tools, or operation of the Training Hub, visit **www.totalsem.com** or e-mail **support@totalsem.com**.

For questions regarding book content, visit **www.mheducation.com/customerservice**.

802.1X   A port-based authentication mechanism for networks; it usually requires authentication from the connecting client, and sometimes even the user. 802.1X is very often seen in enterprise wireless solutions, as well as hardwired Ethernet infrastructures.

802.11   *See* IEEE 802.11.

802.11i   A wireless standard that added security features; also known as *WPA2*.

AAA (authentication, authorization, and accounting)   *See* authentication, authorization, and accounting (AAA).

acceptable use policy (AUP)   Organizational policy that describes both acceptable and unacceptable actions when using organizational computing resources, as well as the consequences of unacceptable use.

access control   All-inclusive term that defines the degree of access granted to use a particular resource, data, systems, or facilities. That resource may be anything from a switch port, to permissions on a particular file, authentication methods, and even physical controls.

access control list (ACL)   A clearly defined list of permissions that specifies what actions an authenticated user may perform on a shared resource. Access control lists are used on objects, such as files and folders, as well as on network devices, such as routers.

access control vestibule   An entryway into a secure facility with two concurrently locked doors and a small space between them, providing one-way entry or exit. This is a security measure taken to prevent tailgating and provide positive authentication for individuals. Traditionally called a *mantrap*.

access log   A log generated on a device, or manually, that gives details of a particular access event, such as a user name or ID, time stamp, and the object or resource that was accessed.

access point (AP)   A network device that provides a connection point for hosts to enter the network; most often associated with wireless clients.

accountability   The practice of holding users accountable for their actions; it involves conclusively tying a user account to any action performed.

accounting   Keeping an historical record of what users do to shared resources.

Active Directory (AD)   Microsoft's centralized authentication and directory services infrastructure, implementing the Lightweight Directory Access Protocol. *See also* Lightweight Directory Access Protocol (LDAP).

active reconnaissance   An information gathering technique in penetration testing where the pentester uses tools and techniques that may or may not avoid detection, but put the attacker at risk of discovery (for example, injection of packets directly onto the wire or purposefully walking up to a locked door to attempt entry).

ad hoc mode   A wireless networking mode where each node is in direct contact with every other node in a decentralized free-for-all. Ad hoc mode is similar to the *mesh topology*.

administrator account   Credentials granted to a user that has complete power over the resource as well as the complete serving system. Windows calls this account *administrator*. In macOS and Linux/UNIX, this account is called *root*.

Advanced Encryption Standard (AES)   The official encryption standard for the US government; it is based upon the Rijndael encryption algorithm and uses key sizes of 128, 192, and 256 bits. It is a symmetric block algorithm, with 128-bit block sizes.

advanced persistent threat (APT)   When a threat actor gains control of a system and remains undetected for a long period of time, continually looking for new data to steal.

adversary tactics, techniques, and procedures (TTP)   The actions of threat actors to gain access to infrastructure. A *tactic* is the goal of the attacker. A *technique* is how the attacker implements that tactic. A *procedure* is precisely how the attacker performs the technique.

adware   A program or add-in downloaded from the Internet that monitors the types of Web sites you frequent and uses that information to generate targeted advertisements, usually pop-up windows.

AES   *See* Advanced Encryption Standard (AES).

Agile   A nonlinear software development life cycle model.

AI   *See* artificial intelligence (AI).

air gap   Typically, the act of physically separating a network from every other network. This can apply to virtually any resource, even individual systems.

Aircrack-ng   An open-source tool for penetration testing many aspects of wireless networks.

algorithm   A mathematical method used in the encryption process to convert plaintext into ciphertext.

allow action   The action of an access control that permits data or communication to pass through or to access a resource. Access control lists may use rules that allow or deny specific data or access to a resource. *See also* block action.

allow/block list The practice of allowing only specifically allowed programs, applications, executables, and files, from only allowed providers, into a network or system. Traditionally called *whitelisting*.

annualized loss expectancy (ALE) The expected loss of an asset determined over a period of one year. It is determined by calculating as follows: ALE = single loss expectancy (SLE) × annualized rate of occurrence (ARO).

annualized rate of occurrence (ARO) The number of times a negative event is expected to occur on a yearly basis.

ANT Low-speed, low-power proprietary networking technology used in some Garmin IoT devices; current version is *ANT+*.

anti-malware Software that attempts to block several types of software threats to a client, including viruses, Trojan horses, worms, and other unapproved software installation and execution.

antivirus Software that attempts to prevent viruses from installing or executing on a client. Some antivirus software may also attempt to remove the virus or eradicate the effects of a virus after an infection.

anything as a service (XaaS) Catch-all term for computing resources delivered via the cloud, rather than locally.

Apache HTTP Server Open-source Web server that runs primarily on Linux, but also on Windows and many UNIX-like platforms. Apache runs on a zillion Web servers (it surpassed 100 million way back in 2009). Competes for market share primarily with NGINX. *See also* NGINX.

API *See* application programming interface (API).

API attack Typically, a distributed denial-of-service (DDoS) attack that attempts to overload an API by sending traffic from multiple clients.

application aware Advanced feature of some stateful firewalls where the content of the data is inspected to ensure it comes from, or is destined for, an appropriate application. Application-aware firewalls look both deeply and more broadly to ensure that the data content and other aspects of the packet are appropriate to the data transfer being conducted. Packets that fall outside these awareness criteria are denied by the firewall.

application firewall A type of firewall that inspects network traffic to determine if the traffic should be allowed or not. Application firewalls go beyond firewalls that filter based on network protocol or port. *See also* application aware.

Application layer *See* Open Systems Interconnection (OSI) seven-layer model.

application log A type of log that details application-specific events, such as when an application opens or closes. Different types of application logs record different events.

application programming interface (API)   Software that enables programs or parts of programs to interact.

archive bit   An attribute of a file that shows whether the file has been backed up since the last change. Each time a file is opened, changed, or saved, the archive bit is turned on. Some types of backups turn off the archive bit to indicate that a good backup of the file exists on tape.

Arduino   Circuit boards and microcontrollers made by the *Arduino* company used as embedded systems in motion detection, robotics, thermostats, drones, diagnostic systems, and more.

armored virus   A very sophisticated type of virus that has built-in protections to evade detection from antivirus solutions. Some of these protections include encryption or the ability of the virus to change its characteristics.

arp   Command-line utility used to determine the MAC address that corresponds to a particular IP address.

ARP poisoning   A type of attack where the attacker attempts to associate a false hardware or MAC address to her machine to fool victim clients into communicating with that machine rather than a legitimate device. This is often associated with man-in-the-middle (a.k.a. on-path) attacks. Also called *ARP cache poisoning*.

ARP spoofing   System responding to an ARP request with another system's MAC address.

artificial intelligence (AI)   Computing devices capable of "learning," assessing new information, and changing actions to accommodate. In security terms, AI-capable systems can respond to new or altered threats with altered responses.

asset   Anything that the organization values or that is important to its mission. Assets can be tangible, such as data, equipment, facilities, and people, or intangible, such as reputation, customer satisfaction, and so on.

asset value (AV)   A value assigned to an asset; usually expressed in terms of dollars. Asset value is used in quantitative risk calculations.

asymmetric cryptography   A form of cryptography that uses two separate, but mathematically related, keys for encryption and decryption; also called *public key cryptography*.

attack   An action where a threat actor actively attempts to take advantage of a vulnerability.

attack framework   Structure that defines the tactics, techniques, and procedures (TTP) of typical attacks on a network. *See* Cyber Kill Chain, Diamond Model of Intrusion Analysis, and MITRE ATT&CK for widely used frameworks.

attack surface   All the vulnerabilities for a specific infrastructure item.

attack vector   Pathway to gain access to infrastructure.

attestation   Multifactor authentication option that assures that hardware or software behind the authentication factors matches the proper standards and protocols.

attribute-based access control (ABAC)   An access control model based upon identifying information about a resource, such as subject (like name, clearance, department) or object (data type, classification, color). Access to resources is granted or denied based on preset rules concerning those attributes.

auditing   The practice of recording events and analyzing them to detect negative events and determine patterns or trends. Auditing is usually performed through examination of manual and automatic logs.

authentication   The process that verifies the identity of the individual, an action traced to an individual or host, or traffic originating from a host. This process proves identity and is associated with non-repudiation.

authentication attributes   Use of different characteristics of identification to identify a user or validate his or her credentials. These include somewhere you are, something you can do, something you exhibit, or someone you know. Often combined with one or more authentication factors for multifactor authentication. *See also* authentication factors *and* multifactor authentication.

authentication, authorization, and accounting (AAA)   A security philosophy wherein a computer trying to connect to a network must first present some form of credential, have that credential verified, and then be subject to restrictive permissions within the network or on the resource.

authentication factors   Use of different characteristics of identification to identify a user and validate his or her credentials. These include knowledge (something you know), possession (something you have), and inherence (something you are). *See also* authentication attributes *and* multifactor authentication.

authentication server (AS)   A server that performs an authentication role at a network. In Kerberos realms, this is also the server that authenticates a user and provides a Ticket-Granting Ticket (TGT).

authorization   The step in the AAA philosophy during which a client's or user's rights or permissions are verified, based upon predetermined decisions. *See also* authentication, authorization, and accounting (AAA).

automation   The programming and sensing tools that enable compromised systems to use their non-persistence and redundancy to recover themselves with little or no human intervention.

availability   Ensuring that information and systems can be used for authorized purposes by authorized users whenever and however they need them.

back up   To save important data in a secondary location as a safety precaution against the loss of the primary data.

backdoor   A mechanism often built into a program or software application by its developers to facilitate quick and easy maintenance or to bypass security mechanisms.

banner grabbing   The act of causing a server or other resource to give up information about its configuration, including its running software, version, and other information that could potentially lead an attacker to discover an attack vector.

baseline   The state of a system when all required operating system software and applications, as well as configuration details, have been configured exactly according to a predetermined standard.

bash   Command-line processor in many Linux distributions; the default terminal interface or shell.

behavior-based system   A system that relies on an established pattern of behavior, typically through the establishment of a usage baseline, to detect unusual patterns, such as network attacks or misuse. *See also* heuristic system, network-based intrusion detection system (NIDS), *and* network-based intrusion prevention system (NIPS).

best evidence   The original evidence obtained in an investigation. It is usually the preferred evidence and consists of *real evidence*, which comprises physical objects, and *direct evidence*, which is direct testimony from witnesses.

big data   Large conglomerations of disparate data sets combined to create huge data warehouses.

biometric device   A device that scans fingerprints, retinas, or even the sound of the user's voice to provide a more secure (though not foolproof) replacement for both passwords and smart devices.

biometrics   Human physical characteristics that can be measured and saved to be compared as authentication in granting the user access to a network or resource. Common biometric factors used in access control include fingerprints, facial scans, retinal scans, voice pattern recognition, and others.

birthday attack   A cryptanalytic technique that focuses on hash function collisions and the probabilities of birthday problem mathematics formulae.

black box test (or blind box test)   A type of penetration test where the tester has no prior knowledge of the network they are targeting and must discover details about the network through testing methodologies, which include reconnaissance and footprinting. Also referred to as an *unknown environment test*.

black hat hacker   A hacker who uses his or her technical skills only for malicious purposes, usually with the goal of illegal access, data theft, or destruction. Also called an *unauthorized hacker*.

blacklisting   *See* block list/deny list.

block action   Deny access to a resource, via either a firewall, an access control server, or other secure gateway. *See also* allow action.

block cipher (or algorithm)   A cryptographic algorithm that works on defined lengths of blocks of text.

block list/deny list   The process of detailing that an application or data is explicitly not allowed on the network or host. Can include software, executables, disallowed Web sites, and even specific types of data. Traditionally called *blacklisting*.

blockchain   Decentralized, peer-to-peer system for secure interaction between buyer and seller; basis for Bitcoin and other cryptocurrencies.

Blowfish   A symmetric block algorithm invented by Bruce Schneier that uses 64-bit blocks, key sizes from 32 bits to 448 bits, and 16 rounds of encryption.

blue team   Defending group in a pentesting exercise.

bluejacking   A type of Bluetooth attack in which a malicious user connects to an unsuspecting victim's Bluetooth device and sends unsolicited data to it, such as messages or media.

bluesnarfing   A type of Bluetooth attack in which a malicious user connects to an unsuspecting victim's Bluetooth device and steals information from it, such as contact information.

Bluetooth   Wireless communication technology that enables devices to pair and exchange data. Commonly used to connect peripherals to computing devices (such as a small keyboard to a tablet).

Bluetooth Low Energy (BTE)   Networking technology designed for minimal electrical usage and used in some IoT devices; part of the Bluetooth 5 standard.

boot attestation   Secure boot feature that uses TPM and UEFI to generate reports to a remote system, such as a central authentication server.

bot   In this context, a computer remotely controlled by a malicious operator.

botnet   A group of computers under the remote control of one malicious operator, used to further attack other hosts.

bring your own device (BYOD)   Mobile device environment in which employees are allowed to use their personally owned devices to access, store, and process data belonging to the organization.

brute-force attack   A type of attack wherein every permutation of some form of data is tried in an attempt to discover protected information. Most commonly used for password cracking.

BTE   *See* Bluetooth Low Energy (BTE).

buffer overflow   Program error where temporary storage area fills and causes unpredictable results.

buffer overflow attack   A type of attack in which the amount of system memory specifically allocated to an application is overflowed with either too much or nonstandard data in an effort to cause the application to fail or be susceptible to arbitrary command execution.

bug bounty   Reward program for assistance by an organization for people to find flaws in their systems, especially in security, vulnerabilities, and exploits.

business continuity plan (BCP)   Document that details disaster- and incident-related risks to critical systems, the impact if those systems are lost, and how best to preserve them.

business continuity planning (BCP)   The process of ensuring that a business can continue at some level of operation immediately following a disaster.

business impact analysis (BIA)   A type of assessment in which a business identifies and prioritizes its assets, processes, and other critical types of operations so that it may be able to determine which of these must be recovered first and foremost after a disaster in order to ensure business continuity.

business partnership agreement (BPA)   An agreement that specifies what type of business partnership two entities will have; often this dictates other considerations, such as interconnection requirements and security.

BYOD   *See* bring your own device (BYOD).

CAC   *See* common access card (CAC).

captive portal   Web page that prompts clients to enter proper credentials to gain further access to the network.

capture the flag   Training technique that challenges security personnel to accomplish something on a remote system.

CASB   *See* cloud access security broker (CASB).

cat   Linux/UNIX terminal command that enables viewing and combining text files.

CCTV   *See* closed-circuit television (CCTV).

Center of Internet Security (CIS)   Nonprofit, nongovernmental organization that publishes the *CIS Benchmarks* framework used by many organizations for risk management.

centralized authentication   A method of authentication in which a single set of authentication policies and mechanisms is used in the organization and applies to all resources.

certificate An electronic file used for a variety of purposes, most commonly to verify the identity of a resource (such as a PC, user, or service). A digital certificate stores a public key with a digital signature, personal information about the resource (URL, e-mail address, phone numbers, whatever), and (commonly) a second digital signature from a trusted third party. (A *self-signed certificate* lacks a third-party signature.)

certificate authority (CA) An entity responsible for issuing and managing digital certificates throughout the certificate life cycle.

certificate revocation list (CRL) An electronic file, published by a certificate authority, that shows all certificates that have been revoked by that CA.

chain of custody A process used to track the collection, handling, and transfer of evidence.

Challenge Handshake Authentication Protocol (CHAP) A remote access authentication protocol in which the authenticating system challenges the remote client, which must provide the proper response, which is then compared by the authenticating server. If the server receives the answer it expects, the user is authenticated.

change management The process of initiating, approving, testing, implementing, and documenting significant changes to the infrastructure.

change request A formally documented request for a modification to some aspect of the network or computing environment.

chmod Linux/UNIX terminal command for changing file and directory permissions.

choose your own device (CYOD) Deployment model where an organization allows employees to select from several mobile devices.

cipher A representation of text on a character-by-character basis. Enciphering converts a character of plaintext to ciphertext, and deciphering converts a character of ciphertext to plaintext.

cipher mode Defined method that determines how a plaintext block is input and changed to produce ciphertext. Used in DES and other encryption standards. Examples include Electronic Code Book (ECB) mode, Cipher Block Chaining (CBC) mode, and more.

cipher suite Group of algorithms used to secure network connections.

ciphertext Plaintext that has been encrypted and converted to an unreadable format.

circumstantial evidence Evidence that cannot necessarily prove a conclusion, but does support it.

CIS *See* Center for Internet Security (CIS).

clean desk space policy A policy that requires employees to clear sensitive data out of work areas so that it is stored securely at the end of the workday.

clear text *See* plaintext.

clear text credentials User credentials that are sent over the network unencrypted, making them easily readable by anyone who could intercept them.

clickjacking An attack where a malicious/compromised Web site places invisible controls on a page, giving users the impression they are clicking some safe item that actually is an active control for something malicious.

client A computer program or host that uses the services of another computer program or host; software that extracts information from a server.

client-to-site A type of VPN connection where a single computer logs into a remote network and connects to a larger network as if it were internally on the network.

closed-circuit television (CCTV) A self-contained, closed system in which video cameras feed their signal to specific, dedicated monitors and storage devices.

cloud access security broker (CASB) Service that manifests as a layer of software between a cloud application and an enterprise or organization, designed to provide security.

cloud computing Moving some or all aspects of a local computer to a location only identified with an IP address or a DNS name.

cloud computing service A third-party service in which applications, and even services, are stored and executed by external resources, such as computing and storage infrastructure, usually not under control of the originating organization.

cloud service provider (CSP) Organization that sells Internet-based products, such as applications, storage, and networking.

clustering A way of combining separate physical resources, such as servers, so that they appear as one logical resource and are able to service client requests even if one member of the cluster becomes unavailable.

CM *See* configuration management (CM).

COBO *See* corporate-owned, business only (COBO).

code In cryptography, a representation of an entire phrase or sentence.

codebook A predefined dictionary that contains codes and the plaintext they represent.

cold site A bare location that consists of essentially floor space of a building, facilities, desks, toilets, parking, and everything that a business needs, except computing equipment or utilities.

collision The rare occurrence of two variable-length pieces of plaintext that, when hashed, produce identical message digests.

collision attack   Attempt to discover or find two inputs that produce identical hash values.

command and control (C2)   Protocols designed to enable servers to manage bots and botnets without human interaction.

command injection   A type of Web-based attack where additional commands are injected into a user-fillable field in the hopes of causing an error or security issue within the Web application.

common access card (CAC)   US Department of Defense (DoD)–issued PIV card for active duty military members, civilian employees, and contractors. *See also* personal identification verification (PIV) card.

Common Vulnerabilities and Exposures (CVE)   Database containing known cybersecurity weaknesses (vulnerabilities) or exploitable vectors used in cybersecurity.

community cloud   A cloud composed of infrastructures from several different entities, which may be cloud service providers, business partners, and so on. In this structure, common services are offered to all participants in the community cloud to one degree or another. Community clouds are usually paid for and used by several like organizations, such as colleges or hospitals.

compensating control   A security control that temporarily compensates for a weakness in another control.

competitive intelligence   The gathering of information about competitors, their customers, their business practices, and so on.

competitors   In a security sense, outside organizations that try to gain access to the same customers as the targeted company.

computer forensics   A subdiscipline of digital forensics focused on gathering, preserving, and presenting (in a court of law) evidence that is stored on a computer or embedded media. *See also* digital forensics.

confidentiality   The security goal of protecting information and systems from unauthorized access.

configuration compliance scanner   A tool that scans critical systems to see if they meet the compliance standards set by IT security professionals in an organization.

configuration management (CM)   A set of documents, policies, and procedures designed to help maintain and update the network infrastructure in a logical, orderly fashion.

connectionless   A type of communication characterized by sending packets that are not acknowledged by the destination host. UDP is an example of a connectionless protocol in the TCP/IP suite.

connectionless protocol A protocol that does not establish and verify a connection between the hosts before sending data; it just sends the data and assumes that it is received without error. This type of communication is faster than communication using connection-oriented protocols. UDP is an example of a connectionless protocol.

connection-oriented Network communication between two hosts that includes negotiation between the hosts to establish a communication session. Data segments are then transferred between hosts, with each segment being acknowledged before a subsequent segment can be sent. Orderly closure of the communication is conducted at the end of the data transfer or in the event of a communication failure. TCP is the only connection-oriented protocol in the TCP/IP suite.

connection-oriented protocol A protocol that establishes a connection between two hosts before transmitting data and verifies receipt before closing the connection between the hosts. TCP is an example of a connection-oriented protocol.

container Discrete software package component used in virtualization, notably Docker, to provide security without the overhead of a full virtual machine.

containerization The practice of separating different types of data in a system, typically used on mobile devices in which personal and corporate data are kept separated.

contingency planning The process of creating documents that set forth how to recover quickly from an incident as well as protect lives and equipment.

continuity of operations (COO) A plan that ensures business or government has the appropriate systems, equipment, data, infrastructure, and, of course, people to resume and maintain operations in the face of a catastrophic incident.

continuity of operations planning (COOP) Process to ensure that an organization has the appropriate systems, equipment, data, infrastructure, and, of course, people to resume and maintain operations in the face of a catastrophic incident.

continuous monitoring A proactive way of ensuring that the network administrator receives all logs and data points throughout the network from all network devices and all systems, on a constant basis, to detect security issues.

control A security measure designed to protect an asset or make up for its security weakness.

control risk Probability of loss resulting from the malfunction of internal control measures implemented to mitigate risks.

COO *See* continuity of operations (COO).

cookie A small piece of text that contains information about a Web browsing session; it is stored on a user's computer and is often used to enhance the Web browsing experience, although it can cause security issues if not properly controlled.

COOP *See* continuity of operations planning (COOP).

COPE *See* corporate-owned, personally enabled (COPE).

corporate-owned, business only (COBO) Deployment model where an organization issues and maintains control over mobile devices issued to employees.

corporate-owned, personally enabled (COPE) Deployment model where an organization issues and maintains control over mobile devices, but allows employees to install a variety of preapproved apps.

corrective control A type of security control that corrects an issue caused by an ineffective security control or security weakness. It is typically only temporary until a more permanent solution can be found.

credential harvesting Attack that obtains user name or identity of a person inside an organization.

credential management Processes and technologies for provisioning and maintaining user accounts and credentials.

criminal syndicate In a security sense, organization that uses extra-legal methods to gain access to resources. Also known as *organized crime*.

cross-site request forgery (XSRF) A type of session hijacking attack that attempts to steal authentication information from session cookies during a user's current browsing session.

cross-site scripting (XSS) A type of session hijacking attack in which malicious script content is injected into a vulnerable Web site, usually one that the client browser trusts.

cross-trust A system in a public key infrastructure (PKI) whereby organizations typically have their own certificate authorities and issuing servers. Organizations have their root CAs trust each other to further business partnership arrangements.

cryptanalysis The study of breaking encryption.

cryptography The science of hiding information.

cryptomalware Malicious software that uses some form of encryption to lock a user out of a system, often with a demand for payment—ransomware—to unlock the system.

cryptosystem The total of the methods, techniques, algorithms, and keys used in a cryptographic process or system.

Cuckoo Sandbox Malware analyzer.

cURL Linux terminal command that enables file transfer using a variety of protocols, from FTP to HTTP, IMAP4, POP3, Telnet, and LDAP (and more). Works without user interaction, so it's good for automated tasks.

CVE *See* Common Vulnerabilities and Exposures (CVE).

Cyber Kill Chain   Attack framework developed by Lockheed Martin that details the stages of a cyberattack, from reconnaissance all the way to the kill with exfiltration of data. Used by cybersecurity experts to prepare for cyberattacks.

Cyber Observable eXpression (CybOX)   Specification sponsored by the US Department of Homeland Security (DHS) for facilitating cybersecurity information sharing; provides standardized specifications for communicating about cybersecurity phenomenon and elements, from malware types to event logging.

CybOX   *See* Cyber Observable eXpression (CybOX).

CYOD   *See* choose your own device (CYOD).

DaaS   *See* desktop as a service (DaaS).

Dark Web   Internet sites that are inaccessible without using specific applications such as the Tor network, because search engines, like Google, do not index them. Often associated with criminal activity, but this is not universally accurate.

data at rest   The state of data while it is in storage and not being processed or transmitted. This applies to data stored on any computing device, from network storage servers to desktops to mobile devices.

Data Encryption Standard (DES)   Older encryption standard that used a 56-bit key and a 64-bit block size; based upon the Lucifer algorithm.

data exfiltration   Social engineering attack to extract data from a computing device without permission.

data in process   *See* data in use.

data in transit   The state of data during transmission or reception. Also called *data in motion*.

data in use   The state of data while it is being used, such as actively loaded into RAM and running processes. Also called *data in process*.

Data Link layer   *See* Open Systems Interconnection (OSI) seven-layer model.

data loss prevention (DLP)   The combination of technologies, processes, and procedures used to prevent the release and loss of sensitive organizational data to unauthorized entities.

data sensitivity   The level of protection data requires based upon its criticality and the need to keep it from unauthorized access or modification.

data sovereignty   Principle where laws of the country of origin of data apply to that data.

dd   Linux and macOS terminal command used to create full disk images.

dead code   Programming included in a product that doesn't do anything.

deauthentication attack   Denial-of-service (DoS) strike that disconnects a wireless host from a wireless access point (WAP), so that the victim is forced to reconnect and exchange the wireless key multiple times; an attacker can then perform an offline brute-force cracking of the password.

decentralized authentication   A method of authentication in which all hosts use their own authentication methods, databases, and policies to allow access to resources located on the host.

decryption   The process of converting ciphertext back into its original plaintext.

defense-in-depth   A concept that requires the use of multiple layers of security defenses and controls at various points, rather than relying on only a single control.

demilitarized zone (DMZ)   *See* screened subnet.

demonstrative evidence   Evidence that attempts to re-create an event in question.

denial-of-service (DoS) attack   An attack that floods a networked server with so many requests that it becomes overwhelmed and ceases to function, affecting availability. DoS attacks are designed to keep legitimate users from using their resources.

deployment model   Guidelines or plans specifying how employees receive a mobile device, such as BYOD, COBO, CYOD, or COPE.

deprovisioning   The process of removing an application from a production environment.

desktop as a service (DaaS)   Cloud-based service that provides users a full designated workstation experience (i.e., *their* desktop) from any device they use to connect.

detective control   A security control whose function is to detect illegal, unauthorized, or abnormal activities.

deterrent control   A security control designed to prevent someone from performing an unauthorized or illegal act. Deterrent controls rely on the fact that the user is aware that the control is in place.

DevOps   A cyclical software development life cycle model. *Secure DevOps* integrates security into the toolchain.

DH   *See* Diffie-Hellman (DH).

Diameter   A proposed replacement for the RADIUS remote access protocol.

Diamond Model of Intrusion Analysis   Attack framework that focuses on four aspects of a threat, namely adversary, victim, infrastructure, and capability. The model helps IT security professionals prepare for a cyberattack.

dictionary attack   A form of password cracking that relies on a text file—a dictionary file—that contains many common words and non-words used for passwords.

differential backup   A type of backup similar to an incremental backup in that it backs up the files that have been changed since the last backup. However, this type of backup does not change the state of the archive bit. This type of backup can be one of the slowest to perform but the fastest to restore.

Diffie-Hellman (DH)   An asymmetric key exchange protocol with several variations. It is used to negotiate a secret session key between two hosts and securely exchange that key using public key cryptography.

dig   *See* Domain Information Groper (DIG).

digital certificate   A digital file containing the details of a certificate, including an individual's identity, the certificate's purpose, and the issuing authority. It is usually signed by the entity that issued it.

digital forensics   The science of gathering, preserving, and presenting (in a court of law) evidence that is stored on any digital media.

digital signature   A message that is signed (encrypted) by an individual's private key, which can only be decrypted by the public key in the pair. This assures that the message could have been sent or signed only by that individual, since they are the only one in possession of the private key.

digital wallet   Cashless payment system for goods and services; used by smartphones and other mobile devices.

direct evidence   A type of best evidence, usually in the form of written or oral testimony, from people who actually witnessed an event.

directory traversal   A Web-based attack in which an attacker is able to browse different directories and their contents on the Web server, including those that would normally be restricted to authorized users. It is conducted by entering different directory levels into a URL or user input field, causing the Web application to change directories and sometimes display the contents of a directory.

disaster recovery   The process of reacting to an incident or disaster and recovering an organization, its personnel, and its systems to a functioning state.

disaster recovery plan (DRP)   Process to ensure safety of personnel and preservation of equipment, data, and facilities in the face of a catastrophic incident.

discretionary access control (DAC)   An authorization model based on the idea that there is an owner of a resource who may, at his or her discretion, assign access to that resource. DAC is considered much more flexible than mandatory access control (MAC).

distributed denial-of-service (DDoS) attack   A DoS attack that uses hundreds or thousands of computers under the control of a single operator to conduct a devastating attack against other hosts or networks.

DLL injection   Attack technique that places a malicious dynamic-link library (DLL) in address space intended for legitimate DLLs.

DMZ   *See* screened subnet.

DNS   *See* Domain Name System (DNS).

DNS amplification   A form of distributed denial-of-service (DDoS) attack that attacks a Web application's DNS server instead of the Web app itself.

DNS cache poisoning   Attack that enters spoofed or false DNS information to a DNS server so that the server returns incorrect information when queried.

DNS sinkhole   A specially designed Domain Name Service server for a network that contains and blocks a list of domains with known association with malware, ad networks, and other undesirable code. Blocks most forms of advertisement for all computers in the network.

DNSEnum   Tool for discovering DNS servers for a specific domain.

DNSSEC   *See* Domain Name System Security Extensions (DNSSEC).

documentary evidence   Evidence that directly supports or proves a definitive assertion; documentary evidence could be written or in the form of computer-generated data.

documentation   A collection of artifacts that supports a security assertion.

domain   A grouping of users, computers, and/or networks. In Microsoft networking, a domain is a group of computers and users that shares a common security accounts database and a common security policy. For the Internet, a domain is a group of computers that shares a common element in the computers' DNS hierarchical name.

domain controller   A Microsoft Windows Server system specifically configured to store user and server account information for its domain. Often abbreviated as "DC." Windows domain controllers store all account and security information in the *Active Directory* distributed directory service.

domain hijacking   Attack that takes control of a legitimate domain registration in some way that the actual owner does not desire.

Domain Information Groper (DIG)   Command-line tool in non-Windows systems used to diagnose DNS problems.

Domain Name System (DNS)   The service and protocol associated with resolving Internet Protocol addresses to human-recognizable domain names; DNS uses TCP and UDP ports 53.

Domain Name System Security Extensions (DNSSEC)   A suite of security extensions proposed and used by the US government and other entities that allows for secure DNS queries and zone transfers. DNSSEC provides the capability to authenticate DNS information from known and trusted servers.

domain validation (DV) certificate   Lowest level of Secure Sockets Layer (SSL) certificate issued by CAs; DVs have no verification check. *See also* extended validation (EV) certificate.

double-blind test   A type of penetration test in which neither the testers nor the defenders are aware of aspects of the test; testers have no knowledge of the network they are attacking, and defenders have no knowledge of the attack itself. This test serves to provide valuable information on both attack methods and vulnerabilities, as well as the ability of network defenders to detect and defend against network attacks.

downgrade attack   A legitimate request to a server to use a weak, deprecated algorithm that's easier to crack in hopes of then successfully getting keys, passwords, and so forth.

drone   *See* unmanned aerial vehicle (UAV).

DRP   *See* disaster recovery plan (DRP).

due care   Performing all actions an organization or person could reasonably be expected to perform in order to prevent or reduce potential harm.

due diligence   The act of fully investigating or researching potential issues and being completely aware of the ramifications.

dumpster diving   A nontechnical type of attack, classified as a social engineering attack, in which an attacker attempts to gain information about an organization by digging through its trash, hoping to find sensitive information.

Dynamic Host Configuration Protocol (DHCP)   Service and protocol responsible for automatically providing IP addressing information to network hosts; it uses UDP on ports 67 and 68.

EAP   *See* Extensible Authentication Protocol (EAP).

east-west traffic   Convention used to describe internal server-to-server connections in a LAN.

EDR   *See* endpoint detection and response (EDR).

electromagnetic interference (EMI)   A type of interference generated by any device or component that produces electrical or radio-frequency signals.

electromagnetic pulse (EMP)   The short release of electromagnetic radiation from a source, person-made (e.g., a nuclear bomb or a power line transformer exploding) or environmental (a lightning strike). If concentrated (i.e., the source producing the blast is strong enough), it can have adverse effects on electrical circuits and communications.

electronic discovery (e-discovery)   The legal process of requesting and providing any data generated through the computer forensics process.

ElGamal   Asymmetric algorithm used for both digital signatures and general encryption; based on Diffie-Hellman algorithms. It is also the basis for the US government's Digital Signature Algorithm (DSA).

elliptic-curve cryptography (ECC)   Asymmetric algorithm based upon mathematical problems involving the algebraic structure of elliptic curves over finite fields; suitable for use in small mobile devices because of the low computing power requirements.

embedded system   A complete computer system—CPU, RAM, storage, operating system, drivers, etc.—whose only job is to perform a specific function either by itself or as part of a larger system.

EMI   *See* electromagnetic interference (EMI).

encapsulation   The process of including encrypted data from one network, using encryption protocols such as IPsec, into a tunneling protocol, such as L2TP, for the purposes of sending it across an untrusted network.

encryption   The process of converting plaintext into ciphertext.

end of life (EOL)   Announcement by a manufacturer that they will no longer sell a particular product.

end of service life (EOSL)   Announcement by a manufacturer that they will no longer support a particular product.

endpoint detection and response (EDR)   Networking technologies that operate on multiple OSI layers, designed to protect endpoints from a variety of network threats.

enterprise information security architecture (EISA)   An analysis of existing security systems, encompassing industry-standard frameworks and regulatory compliance.

environmental monitoring   Using devices and sensors in telecommunications rooms to monitor humidity, temperature, and more.

EOL   *See* end of life (EOL).

EOSL   *See* end of service life (EOSL).

ephemeral key   A key that is generated for one immediate use only and is never used again.

ethical hacker   Typically, a security professional who uses his or her security knowledge and abilities only for lawful purposes, to include assessing the security of a system or network to identify vulnerabilities and exploits that can be corrected.

evil twin   An attack that lures people into logging into a rogue access point that looks similar to a legitimate access point.

exception   Unexpected input or result in an application.

executable virus   A virus that is literally an extension of an executable and is unable to exist by itself. Once an infected executable file is run, the virus loads into memory, adding copies of itself to other executables that are subsequently run.

expert witness   A person who has the knowledge and skill necessary to testify in court that forensics procedures and processes were sound and followed accurately and closely. Expert witnesses must be formally recognized by the court, through various means, including years of experience, certification, education, professional status, and so on. It's up to the court to decide if an expert witness is sufficient or not during the case, and if the court will accept their testimony. Expert witnesses normally have not witnessed the actual facts of the case; they merely testify as to the value of the evidence presented and its potential accuracy. *See also* witness.

exposure factor (EF)   The level of loss that an asset may experience during a negative event, usually expressed as a percentage. It is used in quantitative risk calculations.

extended validation (EV) certificate   A Secure Sockets Layer (SSL) certificate issued by CAs that includes a rigorous verification process. Considered much more secure than domain validation (DV) certificates.

Extensible Authentication Protocol (EAP)   A flexible, extensible authentication framework that is capable of using different security protocols and authentication methods. It is widely seen in both wireless and remote communications.

external firewall   A firewall that is placed on the external perimeter of a sensitive or private network and serves to filter undesirable traffic from an untrusted network to a trusted network.

fail safe   Failure condition that occurs during an emergency, in which security mechanisms fail to a safe mode rather than a secure mode. An example of this would be a secure door lock that fails and is kept unlocked during an emergency situation so personnel could evacuate a facility.

fail secure   Failure condition that occurs during an emergency, in which the security mechanisms fail to a secure mode rather than a safe mode. An example of this would be a secure door lock that is kept locked during an emergency, ensuring that valuable assets and data are protected.

false acceptance rate (FAR)   The level of errors that the system may generate indicating that unauthorized users are actually identified and authenticated as valid users in a biometric system.

false negative   A term used to describe the condition where it is believed there is no vulnerability, but, upon further investigation, there is in fact a valid vulnerability.

false positive   A term used to describe the condition where a vulnerability may be shown to exist, when, upon further investigation, there is no vulnerability.

false rejection rate (FRR)   The rate of errors caused from rejecting someone who is in fact an authorized user and should be authenticated. This is also known as a *type I error*.

Faraday cage   Device designed to stop RFI, EMI, and EMP from damaging sensitive equipment.

fault tolerance   The capability of any system to continue functioning after some part of the system has failed. RAID is an example of a hardware device that provides fault tolerance for hard drives.

federated system   A common authentication system shared by multiple separate entities that allows users to authenticate seamlessly among the different entities.

Fibre Channel (FC)   A self-contained, high-speed storage environment with its own storage arrays, cables, protocols, and switches. Fibre Channel is a critical part of storage area networking (SAN).

field-programmable gate array (FPGA)   Computer that can be reprogrammed to optimize for various tasks.

File Transfer Protocol (FTP)   An application-level protocol used to transfer files from one host to another. It is an unsecure protocol that does not encrypt its traffic, and it uses TCP ports 20 and 21.

File Transfer Protocol, Secure (FTPS)   A version of FTP made secure by tunneling it over a Secure Sockets Layer (SSL) or Transport Layer Security (TLS) connection. It uses TCP port 990 and should not be confused with either SFTP (which is a Secure Shell [SSH] implementation of FTP) or Secure FTP (which normally involves tunneling ordinary FTP traffic over an SSH connection).

fileless malware   Software designed to do harm to computer systems; uniquely resides only in active memory, not mass storage; also called *fileless virus*.

firewall   A device that restricts and filters traffic between two separate networks. Firewalls can be placed between the public Internet and a private network or between two internal networks of different sensitivities.

first responder   Any person who first notices, reports, or responds to an incident. The first responder's overall duties should be to secure the scene (if necessary), determine the scope of the incident, try to determine the seriousness and impact of the incident, and start the notification process for the incident management and response team.

flood guard   Mechanism that automatically stops or prevents network attacks, such as ICMP or SYN floods, by disconnecting the network when these attacks reach a specified threshold.

forensics report   A document that describes the details of gathering, securing, transporting, and investigating evidence.

FPGA   *See* field-programmable gate array (FPGA).

FTK Imager   Commercial software suite for analyzing system images and other digital evidence.

full backup   Captures all the data on a particular server, drive, or device and resets the archive bit to zero for all files, indicating that they have been backed up.

full disk encryption (FDE)   Software or hardware function that scrambles contents of an HDD or SSD to make them unreadable without proper authentication. This protects data at rest; access to the contents of the drive only happens if the user can enter credentials before the operating system boots (pre-boot authentication). BitLocker in Windows is one tool that provides FDE.

fusion center   Organization designed to promote the sharing of intelligence among US state and federal agencies.

fuzzing   A type of assessment whereby random data is inserted into an application in hopes of generating and discovering errors or security issues. Fuzzing is a type of dynamic analysis of software in development.

gamification   Training technique that relies on games to teach security to users.

GDPR   *See* General Data Protection Regulation (GDPR).

General Data Protection Regulation (GDPR)   European Union (EU) legal framework that specifies protections for personal data and information of EU citizens regardless of the location of that data or information.

geofencing   Practice where mobile devices are configured to alert the administrator if they are removed from a particular area, such as the business campus.

geolocation   Use of built-in GPS feature to locate a mobile device.

geotagging   Practice of ascertaining geolocation data from a device based upon characteristics of its phone calls, text messages, pictures, and video content. Called *GPS tagging* by CompTIA.

Global Positioning System (GPS)   Satellite-based system owned and operated by the US government to provide precise location and location-based services.

governance   Overarching rules and requirements applied to an organization that dictate how it conducts business, protects data, and obeys the law. Governance comes in the forms of laws, regulations, internal rules, and industry standards.

GPS   *See* Global Positioning System (GPS).

gray box test   Type of penetration test where the tester has some limited information regarding the target network, possibly including IP address space and other limited details about the target. Also called a *partially known environment test*.

gray hat hacker   A hacker who sometimes uses his or her abilities and knowledge for good purposes and other times for evil purposes. Mentioned as a *semi-authorized hacker* in some exam objectives.

grep   Linux/UNIX terminal command that enables more efficient search in a text file.

group   A collection of network users or computers that share similar characteristics and need similar permissions or security settings; groups are created to make administrative tasks more efficient.

group policy   A feature of Windows Active Directory that allows an administrator to apply policy settings to entire groups of computers and users within the domain. Generically, in the non-Windows context, group policy refers to a policy of managing users in a defined logical group, by functional, geographical, or security requirements.

Group Policy Object (GPO)   A set of configuration settings that enables network administrators to define multiple security configuration settings to very particular sets of users and computers within a Windows Active Directory domain.

guest   In terms of virtualization, an operating system running as a virtual machine inside a hypervisor.

guest network   A logically separated network that can contain or allow access to any resource the organization provides to unsecured hosts or unauthenticated users.

guidelines   Suggested methods of performing actions or securing data and systems. Guidelines are typically not mandatory, but offer general assistance and advice.

hacker   Term popularized by the media used to describe a person who breaks into computer systems and networks. Hackers can be categorized as white hat hackers (ethical hackers or security professionals), gray hat hackers (hackers who use their abilities for both good and evil purposes), and black hat hackers (malicious hackers). Mentioned in some exam objectives as *authorized hackers, semi-authorized hackers,* and *unauthorized hackers,* respectively.

hacktivist   A hacker and an activist. These threat actors have some form of agenda, often political or fueled by a sense of injustice.

hardening   Locking down the security configurations of hardware and software to a very secure or restrictive degree.

hardware security module (HSM)   A hardware device, sometimes physically separated from other devices, that provides security services, such as encryption and key management or storage.

hash   The fixed-length cryptographic sum that represents a variable-length piece of text. Also called a *message digest*.

Hash-based Message Authentication Code (HMAC)   System used in conjunction with a hashing algorithm and symmetric key in order to both authenticate and verify the integrity of a message.

Hash-based Message Authentication Code (HMAC)–based one-time password (HOTP)   A form of one-time password authentication that uses a hash value combined with a symmetric key.

hashing   The process of creating a fixed-length message digest that represents a variable-length piece of text.

head   Linux/UNIX terminal command that displays the first ten lines of a text file.

header manipulation   Process of injecting additional information into a URL or Web page header to cause a Web application to produce abnormal data or perform actions unintended by the developer.

Health Insurance Portability and Accountability Act (HIPAA)   US law enacted in 1996 to provide data privacy and security provisions for safeguarding medical information. *See also* protected health information (PHI).

heat map   Graphical representation of the radio-frequency (RF) sources on a site, using different colors to represent the intensity of the signal.

heating, ventilation, and air conditioning (HVAC)   Equipment involved in heating and cooling environments within a facility. These items include boilers, furnaces, air conditioners and ducts, plenums, and air passages, as well as their monitoring and control devices.

heuristic system   A system that "learns" network traffic and usage patterns by observing and recording normal behaviors.

hex (hexadecimal)   Symbols based on a numbering system of base 16 using ten digits and six letters to display the combinations of four binary digits, 0000 to 1111. Hex is represented by digits 0 through 9 and *A* through *F*, so that 09h (1001 in binary) has a value of 9, and 0Ah (1010 in binary) has a value of 10.

hierarchical trust   A system in a public key infrastructure (PKI) whereby intermediate certificate authorities trust the root certificate authority.

high availability (HA)   A term used to describe a system or network that must be kept at a significantly high and reliable level of availability for its users; typically measured as some form of a precise decimal percentage, such as 99.999 percent availability. It is the measure of the tolerance a business has for downtime with critical systems or processes.

HIPAA   *See* Health Insurance Portability and Accountability Act of 1996 (HIPAA).

hoax   A social engineering attack that uses a lie or false story to lead one or more people to believe something is true that is very much not true.

honeyfile   A file created by an administrator to attract computer hackers for tracking and analysis purposes.

honeynet   An entire network of honeypots on their own network segment, used to get a hacker bogged down in a decoy network while the administrator locks down and secures the sensitive network and records and tracks the actions of the hacker.

honeypot   A network host that an administrator sets up for the express purpose of attracting computer hackers, usually so that their attack methods can be recorded and analyzed.

host   A single device (usually a computer) on a TCP/IP network that has an IP address; any device that can be the source or destination of a data packet. Also, a computer running multiple virtualized operating systems.

host-based anti-malware   Anti-malware software that is installed on individual systems, as opposed to the network at large.

host-based firewall   A software firewall, such as Windows Firewall, that is installed on a host device to provide firewall services for just that machine.

host-based intrusion detection system (HIDS)   Software installed on a computer that can detect patterns of malicious traffic, such as those that may target certain protocols or services that appear to cause excessive amounts of traffic, or other types of intrusion.

host-based intrusion prevention system (HIPS)   Software installed on a computer that can stop malicious traffic, such as those that may target certain protocols or services.

hot and cold aisles   Design and layout of equipment racks in a data center such that hot air and cold air are alternately forced through the front and back of the aisles so that hot air is drawn away from equipment and cold air is pushed into equipment, assisting in maintaining the optimum operating temperature.

hot site   A complete backup facility to continue business operations. It is considered "hot" because it has all resources in place, including computers, network infrastructure, and current backups, so that operations can commence within hours or even minutes after a disaster renders the primary site nonoperational.

hotspot   Cellular connection used to access the Internet.

hping   Part of the Nmap system; tools for assessing and auditing firewalls and networks.

HVAC   *See* heating, ventilation, and air conditioning (HVAC).

hybrid cloud   A conglomeration of public and private cloud resources, connected to achieve some target result. There is no clear line that defines how much of a hybrid cloud infrastructure is private and how much is public.

hybrid cryptography   Using both symmetric and asymmetric cryptography together in order to make up for each type's disadvantages and leverage each type's advantages.

hygrometer (or hygrothermograph)   A device used to monitor and control environmental conditions, particularly humidity, within a data center or equipment room.

Hypertext Transfer Protocol over SSL/TLS (HTTPS)   A protocol to transfer hypertext data from a Web page to a client in a secure and encrypted fashion. Secure Sockets Layer (SSL) and Transport Layer Security (TLS) are used to establish a secure communication connection between hosts. All HTTP data sent through this encrypted communications tunnel is protected between client and server.

hypervisor (virtual machine monitor)   In virtualization, a layer of programming that creates, supports, and manages a virtual machine. A hypervisor can be either Type 1, which is a specialized operating system itself (also called *bare-metal hypervisor*), or Type 2, which is an application that resides on a host OS.

ICS   *See* industrial control system (ICS).

IDE   *See* integrated development environment (IDE).

identification   The act of presenting credentials to a system for authentication.

identity fraud   Use of another person's name, address, Social Security number, credit card number, etc., for personal gain.

identity management system (IMS)   Tool used to simplify secure access to multiple Internet-based services via single sign-on.

identity provider (IdP)   System or entity that enables authentication; facilitates single sign-on to cloud services, among other applications.

identity theft   Process of gaining personal information to commit *identity fraud*.

IdP   *See* identity provider (IdP).

IEEE 802.11   IEEE subcommittee that defined the standards for wireless communications in the 2.4- and 5.0-GHz frequency ranges.

ifconfig   A command-line utility for Linux servers and workstations that displays the current TCP/IP configuration of the machine, similar to ipconfig for Windows systems. The newer command-line utility, ip, is replacing ifconfig on most systems.

imaging   The process of creating an exact forensic duplicate of a storage media.

impact   The degree of harm to or effect on an asset or the organization when a threat exploits a vulnerability in the asset.

impersonation   The act of pretending to be someone else, or even another host, in order to wage an attack on a victim system, network, or person.

implicit deny   The process of denying access to network traffic, or actions, due to the fact that that access has not been explicitly allowed.

inbound traffic   Network traffic coming into the network.

incident response   Response and reaction to any potential negative events that take place within an organization. The incident response process is preparation, identification, containment, eradication, recovery, and lessons learned.

incident response plan   Set of documents and procedures that specify policies and essential personnel roles to deal with an attack or system failure.

incremental backup   Type of backup that backs up only the files that have been changed since the last full backup; this usually backs up only the files with the archive bits turned on. This type of backup also resets the archive bits to off.

indicator of compromise (IoC)   Artifact of an intrusion, such as a sudden increase in outgoing network traffic, malware signatures, strange changes in file permissions; used as key evidence collected in forensic investigations.

industrial control system (ICS)   A system that controls other systems, typically manufacturing or utility systems (versus end-user types of systems).

influence campaign   Use of media (e.g., print, television, Internet) to sway opinions of people.

Information Sharing and Analysis Centers (ISACs)   Government-sponsored organizations that collect and share cybersecurity threats with both public and private entities.

infrared (IR)   Connectivity or networking technology using light waves as a means for communicating data.

infrastructure   In IT risk management, refers to every aspect of an organization, from the organization itself to its computers, networks, employees, physical security, and sometimes third-party access.

infrastructure as a service (IaaS)   Cloud service that provides infrastructure, such as servers and network devices, to process, transfer, and store business data in a third-party environment. *See also* cloud computing service.

infrastructure mode   Mode in which wireless networks use one or more wireless access points to connect the wireless network nodes centrally. This configuration is similar to the *star topology* of a wired network.

inherent risk   Amount of risk in the absence of controls.

inheritance   A condition in which user permissions assigned to an object automatically flow from higher-level (parent) objects to lower-level (child) objects, such as folders and files.

initialization vector (IV) attack   A type of attack that focuses on the weakness of the initialization vector of a security key, such as a Wired Equivalent Privacy (WEP) key.

injection attack   A type of Web-based attack where additional characters, commands, or other data is injected into a user-fillable field or a URL in the hopes of causing an error or security issue within the Web application.

input validation   The mechanisms used to ensure that any input into a Web field form meets strict criteria.

insider threat   Potential for people within an organization who have access to resources to attack the organization.

integer overflow   Program error when a value greater than an integer variable causes an application to stop working.

integer overflow attack   A type of attack where input numerical information exceeds the bounds or ability of variables to process it. This attack may come in the form of numbers outside of a specified range or length.

integrated development environment (IDE)   A programming tool available in most programming languages that supports code writing through real-time features that continually check the source code, as the programmer is writing the code, for items such as proper syntax.

integrity   The goal of security that ensures that data has not been subjected to unauthorized change or modification.

interconnection service agreement (ISA)   An agreement between two parties, usually either two businesses or two providers, that specifies the terms of connecting their respective private network infrastructures.

internal connections   The connections between computers within the internal boundaries of a network.

internal network   A private LAN, with a unique network ID, that resides behind a router.

internal threats   Threats that originate from inside an organization or network. These threats could include malicious users, misuse of resources, and accidents or unintentional actions.

International Organization for Standardization (ISO)   Standard-setting body that produces many of the IT and industrial standards used throughout the world. Based in Geneva, Switzerland, ISO has representation from standards bodies from most countries on Earth.

Internet Control Message Protocol (ICMP)   A TCP/IP protocol used to handle many low-level functions such as error reporting. ICMP messages are usually request and response pairs such as echo requests and responses, router solicitations and responses, and traceroute requests and responses. There are also unsolicited "responses" (advertisements) that consist of single packets. ICMP messages are connectionless.

Internet Engineering Task Force (IETF)   An international organization that develops Internet standards, particularly those associated with the TCP/IP suite of protocols.

Internet Group Management Protocol (IGMP) A protocol that routers use to communicate with hosts to determine a "group" membership in order to determine which computers want to receive a multicast. Once a multicast has started, IGMP is responsible for maintaining the multicast and terminating it at completion.

Internet Message Access Protocol (IMAP) A client e-mail protocol that is an alternative to POP3. Currently in its fourth revision, IMAP4 retrieves e-mail from an e-mail server like POP3, but has a number of features that make it a more popular e-mail tool. IMAP4 enables users to create folders on the e-mail server, for example, and allows multiple clients to access a single mailbox. IMAP uses TCP port 143.

Internet of Computing (IoC) Devices connected to the Internet, such as desktop PCs, workstations, servers, and routers; traditional connected devices, as opposed to Internet of Things devices such as lightbulbs, thermostats, televisions, and so on.

Internet of Things (IoT) The idea that everyday objects could be capable of communicating with each other via the Internet. Although this capability certainly exists to an extent now, the future of this technology has much greater implications. Specialized devices connected to the Internet of Things are referred to as *static hosts*.

Internet Protocol (IP) A protocol in the TCP/IP suite that is responsible for logical addressing and routing packets to different subnetworks; IP resides at the Network layer of the OSI model.

Internet Protocol Security (IPsec) A Network layer encryption protocol that is used to encrypt data and transport it either internally between specified hosts (called *transport mode*) or externally between networks, over an unsecure method, using a tunneling protocol (called *tunnel mode*).

Internet Protocol version 4 (IPv4) Older version of the Internet Protocol in which addresses consist of four sets of numbers, each number being a value between 0 and 255, using a period to separate the numbers (often called *dotted decimal* format). No IPv4 address may be all 0's or all 255s. Examples of IPv4 addresses include 192.168.0.1 and 64.176.19.164.

Internet Protocol version 6 (IPv6) Newer version of the Internet Protocol in which addresses consist of eight sets of four hexadecimal numbers, each number being a value between 0000 and FFFF, using a colon to separate the numbers. No IP address may be all 0's or all FFFFs. An example of an IPv6 address is FEDC:BA98:7654:3210:0800:20 0C:00CF:1234.

Internet Small Computer System Interface (iSCSI) A protocol that enables the SCSI command set to be transported over a TCP/IP network from a client to an iSCSI-based storage system. iSCSI is popular with storage area network (SAN) systems.

intranet A private TCP/IP network inside a company or organization.

intrusion detection system (IDS) A system designed to detect network intrusions based upon traffic characteristics. *See also* network-based intrusion detection system (NIDS).

intrusion prevention system (IPS) A system that not only is responsible for detecting network attacks based upon certain traffic characteristics but also has the ability to prevent and stop the attacks upon detection. *See also* network-based intrusion prevention system (NIPS).

IoC *See* indicator of compromise (IoC) or Internet of Computing (IoC).

ip A command-line utility for Linux servers and workstations that displays the current TCP/IP configuration of the machine; similar to ipconfig for Windows systems.

IP address The numeric address of a computer connected to a TCP/IP network, such as the Internet. IPv4 addresses are 32 bits long, written as four octets of 8-bit binary. IPv6 addresses are 128 bits long, written as eight sets of four hexadecimal characters. IP addresses must be matched with a valid subnet mask, which identifies the part of the IP address that is the network ID and the part that is the host ID.

IP filtering A method of filtering or checking network traffic based on source and destination IP addresses.

IP spoofing An attack that replaces a legitimate IP address with another and fools the system to send data to that other IP address. The same type of attack directed to MAC addresses is *MAC spoofing*.

ipconfig A command-line utility for Windows that displays the current TCP/IP configuration of the machine; similar to UNIX/Linux's ifconfig.

IR *See* infrared (IR).

ISAC *See* Information Sharing and Analysis Centers (ISACs).

ISO *See* International Organization for Standardization (ISO).

jamming The act of causing intentional radio-frequency interference on a wireless network.

job rotation A personnel security concept that involves periodically moving employees to different job positions in order to facilitate training and prevent fraud or improper acts.

journalctl Linux log viewing tool.

Kerberos An authentication standard designed to allow different operating systems and applications to authenticate each other. Kerberos uses time stamps and a Ticket-Granting Service as mechanisms to provide authentication and access to different resources.

Kerckhoffs's principle   A cryptography principle that states that the algorithm should not be the secret part of the cryptographic process or method used; the principle states that the key should be the secret part of the cryptosystem.

key   A secret piece of information, such as a password, passphrase, or passcode, that is used along with an algorithm to convert plaintext and ciphertext; also called a *cryptovariable*.

Key Distribution Center (KDC)   A designated system in a Kerberos realm that generates keys and provides for authentication. In a Windows Active Directory domain, this function is typically performed by a domain controller.

key escrow   Practice of allowing a third party to maintain knowledge or copies of encryption or decryption keys.

key exchange   The process used to exchange keys between users who send a message and those who receive it. Keys can be exchanged in-band (using the same system that other communications use) or out-of-band (using an alternate means of communication to prevent interception of the key).

key length   Number of bits in a key; also referred to as *key size*.

key management   The process of generating, issuing, managing, revoking, and disposing of encryption and decryption keys throughout their life cycle.

key pair   Name for the two keys generated in asymmetric key cryptography systems. One key in the pair is always a private key, and one key is always a public key. The keys in a pair are not identical; however, they are mathematically related.

key stream   An input of random bits used with an algorithm and inserted into the encryption process, which assists in changing plaintext to ciphertext.

key stretching   Various efforts and processes used to strengthen otherwise weak keys, including multiple rounds of encryption and padding.

keylogger   Malware or physical device that records keystrokes.

LAN Manager (LANMAN)   An older, proprietary authentication protocol used in earlier versions of Microsoft Windows.

layer 2 switch   Any device that filters and forwards frames based on the MAC addresses of the sending and receiving machines. An ordinary "switch" is typically considered a layer 2 switch.

Layer 2 Tunneling Protocol (L2TP)   A VPN protocol developed from two proprietary protocols, Layer 2 Forwarding (L2F) by Cisco and Point-to-Point Tunneling Protocol (PPTP) from Microsoft. LT2P has no authentication or encryption, but uses IPsec to provide for its security mechanisms.

layer 3 switch A switch that also functions as a router, allowing routing between different logical subnets and eliminating broadcast domains.

legal hold Requirement for an organization anticipating litigation or government investigation to retain all electronic and physical records.

Lightweight Directory Access Protocol (LDAP) A protocol that is used in distributed directory services networks, such as Active Directory, to assist hosts in locating network resources. LDAP replaced the older X.500 directory services protocol and uses TCP port 389 by default. A secure version of LDAP, called LDAP over SSL (LDAPS), used TCP port 636; deprecated with LDAP version 2 (version 3 is the current version at the time of this writing).

Lightweight Directory Access Protocol (LDAP) injection An attack in which malicious LDAP queries and commands are injected into a Web site that has access to an LDAP database. The objective of the attack is to gain user information or even create objects, such as user accounts, in the database.

Lightweight Extensible Authentication Protocol (LEAP) A proprietary version of EAP used almost exclusively by Cisco wireless products. LEAP uses MS-CHAP authentication between a wireless client and a RADIUS server.

likelihood The level of possibility of a negative event, such as a threat, exploiting a vulnerability. Also phrased as *likelihood of occurrence*.

Linux The popular open-source operating system, derived from UNIX, that has a command-line interface as well as many different graphical user interface options.

live boot media Operating system installed and playable on removable media, such as an optical disc or flash media drive, such that you can boot to the media and have a complete, functioning system without touching mass storage installed in that system.

load balancing The process of taking several servers and making them appear to network users as a single server, balancing the workload of processing and supporting heavy bandwidth needs.

local user account A user account that is unique to a single host or system and stored in the local system's files.

log file An audit trail produced automatically from the system, or manually by a human being. Log files contain information about system events, security events, and various types of performance information.

log management The process of providing proper security and maintenance for log files to ensure they are protected from unauthorized access or modification. Log management can be centralized (managed across all devices in the enterprise) or decentralized (managed on a per-host basis).

logger Linux/UNIX terminal command that enables adding text to log files manually.

logic bomb A malicious script planted in a system or network, designed to perform an adverse action, such as deleting sensitive data or rendering a system inoperable. Logic bombs are not malware per se and are usually intended to execute at a certain time or after a given set of actions or circumstances occurs.

logical address A network address that is assigned automatically by the DHCP service or manually by an administrator (unlike a physical address that is burned into the network interface card [NIC]).

MAC (media access control) address Unique 48-bit address assigned to each network card. IEEE assigns blocks of possible addresses to various NIC manufacturers to help ensure that each address is unique. The Data Link layer of the OSI seven-layer model uses MAC addresses to locate machines.

MAC address filtering A method of limiting access to a wireless network based on the physical addresses of wireless network interface cards (NICs). Also called *MAC limiting*.

MAC cloning Deliberately changing a MAC address to match the MAC address of another device.

MAC flooding Attack that uses ARP poisoning to send many frames to overwhelm a switch. *See also* ARP poisoning.

MAC time In the field of computer forensics, the time stamp metadata contained in a file that indicates when the file was modified, accessed, or created (MAC).

machine learning (ML) Capability of computing that enables a device to improve responses based on new information without human intervention.

macro A specially written collection of application-level commands that can be programmed to perform the same functions as a virus. Malicious macros normally automatically start when the application is run and execute malicious actions.

malicious user A user who consciously attempts to access, steal, or damage resources.

malware Any program or code (e.g., macro, script, virus, Trojan, worm, or spyware) designed to perform malicious actions on a system.

managed security service provider (MSSP) Company that provides real-time system monitoring, often based in the cloud.

managerial controls Security steps or rules that that apply organization-wide, such as periodic password updates.

mandatory access control (MAC) A security model in which every resource is assigned a label that defines its security level. If the user lacks the security level assigned to a resource, the user cannot get access to that resource. MAC is typically found only in highly secure systems.

mandatory vacations   A personnel security concept that requires employees to take vacations so that their actions while holding a particular position can be extensively investigated and audited while they are absent.

man-in-the-browser (MITB) attack   *See* on-path attack.

man-in-the-middle (MITM) attack   *See* on-path attack.

mantrap   *See* access control vestibule.

mean time between failures (MTBF)   A numerical estimate for a piece of hardware or equipment that indicates how much time likely will pass between major failures of that hardware or equipment.

mean time to failure (MTTF)   A numerical estimate for a piece of hardware or equipment that indicates the length of time the hardware or equipment is expected to last in operation before it needs to be replaced.

mean time to repair (MTTR)   A numerical estimate for a piece of hardware or equipment that indicates the likely time between the point a component fails and the time it can be recovered, either through repair or replacement. Also referred to as *mean time to recovery*.

Measured Boot   Windows 10 feature that interacts with UEFI and TPM to verify boot file integrity over a network.

measurement systems analysis (MSA)   Testing methodologies for assessing the accuracy of third-party contributions to an organization.

memdump   Linux tool for copying information in RAM directly across a network with no changes; used in forensics.

memorandum of understanding (MOU)   A document that defines an agreement between two parties in situations where a legal contract is not necessary or appropriate, such as where both parties work for the same overall organization.

memory leak   Program error where a single process begins to ask for more and more memory from the system without ever releasing memory.

message digest   *See* hash.

Message Digest 5 (MD5)   Hashing algorithm used to compute fixed-length message digests of variable-length pieces of texts, developed by Ron Rivest. It generates a 128-bit hash that is 32 hexadecimal characters long. Although MD5 is still widely used, it has been deprecated due to the potential for collisions, and is currently considered unsuitable for modern hashing applications.

MITRE ATT&CK   Set of standards or definitions—a *framework*—that enables IT security professionals to prepare for cybersecurity attacks; developed by the MITRE Corporation.

ML   *See* machine learning (ML).

mobile application management (MAM) Management structure and technologies used to centrally manage which types of apps can be installed and used on mobile devices.

mobile device forensics A subdiscipline of digital forensics focused on gathering, preserving, and presenting (in a court of law) evidence that is stored on mobile devices, such as smart phones and tablets. *See also* digital forensics.

mobile device management (MDM) The management structure and technologies used to centrally manage all aspects of mobile devices for an organization.

modes of operation *See* cipher mode.

MSA *See* measurement systems analysis (MSA).

MS-CHAP Microsoft's variation of the CHAP protocol that uses a slightly more advanced encryption protocol. MS-CHAPv2 is most often seen in earlier versions of Windows.

MSSP *See* managed security service provider (MSSP).

multifactor authentication A form of authentication where a user must use two or more factors to prove his or her identity.

multiperson control A form of control in which a sensitive task requires more than one person to perform it; this practice prevents collusion, fraud, and unauthorized access. Alternatively referred to as *two-person integrity/control*.

Multipurpose Internet Mail Extensions (MIME) Protocol built into every e-mail client that enables users to make e-mail attachments.

NAC *See* network access control (NAC).

National Institute of Standards and Technologies (NIST) Part of the US Department of Commerce; creates publications that designate specifications for an enormous variety of product categories.

near-field communications (NFC) A technology recently implemented in mobile devices that enables the devices to communicate with each other within very close proximity or when touching each other. NFC is becoming popular in commercial device payment systems and file exchange applications.

need-to-know The requirement that an individual must have a valid reason, based upon their job or position, for accessing systems or data.

Nessus A popular and extremely comprehensive vulnerability testing tool. Previously an open-source tool, it has now become a widely used enterprise-level commercial product developed by Tenable, Inc.

NetBIOS An older application programming interface that provides services to the Session layer of the OSI model. It stands for Network Basic Input/Output System and was primarily used in earlier versions of Windows to transition to using full TCP/IP protocols.

netcat (nc)   An extremely versatile Linux command-line utility that reads and writes data across TCP/IP connections; can be used as a tunneling protocol, a scanner, and an advanced hacking tool. It's frequently nicknamed the *Swiss Army knife of hacking tools.*

NetFlow   Cisco proprietary tool that provides real-time information about IP traffic in a network.

netstat   A universal command-line utility used to examine the TCP/IP connections open on a given host.

network access control (NAC)   Methods and technologies used to impose security and configuration settings on a device before it is allowed into the corporate network. NAC is usually implemented through a hardware device or associated technologies.

network access policy   A set of rules that defines who can access the network, how it can be accessed, and what resources in the network can be used.

network address translation (NAT)   A method used by various network and security devices to translate an organization's public IP addresses to its private IP address space.

network as a service (NaaS)   A cloud service that provides various infrastructure services to businesses, including network, server, and security services. *See also* cloud computing service.

network forensics   A subdiscipline of digital forensics focused on gathering, preserving, and presenting (in a court of law) evidence in computer network traffic. *See also* digital forensics.

network scanner   A program that probes ports on a remote system, logging the state of the scanned ports and assisting in determining whether a port has a vulnerability that can be exploited.

network segmentation   Partitioning a single network into two or more subnetworks using either switches or routers.

Network Time Protocol (NTP)   A protocol that is used to contact authoritative time servers in order to establish a synchronized time source within the network.

network-attached storage (NAS)   A dedicated file server that has its own file system and typically uses hardware and software designed for serving and storing files.

network-based firewall   A network-based device that filters traffic coming into and out of the network, based upon different characteristics. Firewalls use rulesets that dictate what type of traffic is allowed and what type will be blocked or denied.

network-based intrusion detection system (NIDS)   A system that detects network attacks based upon certain traffic characteristics. *See also* intrusion detection system (IDS).

network-based intrusion prevention system (NIPS) A system that not only is responsible for detecting network attacks based upon certain traffic characteristics but also has the ability to prevent and stop the attacks upon detection. *See also* intrusion prevention system (IPS).

next-generation firewall (NGFW) Software or network appliance that filters traffic on multiple OSI layers.

NGFW *See* next-generation firewall (NGFW).

NGINX Open-source, fast, and efficient Web server designed specifically to outperform Apache HTTP Server. Used for high availability, load balancing, reverse proxy, and more, NGINX (pronounced "engine X") zoomed past previously popular Web servers like Microsoft Internet Information Services (IIS) to match or surpass Apache in use. *See also* Apache HTTP Server.

NIST *See* National Institute of Standards and Technologies (NIST).

NIST Federal Information Processing Standards (FIPS) Publication 199 *Standards for Security Categorization of Federal Information and Information Systems*; publication considered the *de facto* framework for IT data classification.

NIST SP 800-122 *Guide to Protecting the Confidentiality of Personally Identifiable Information (PII)*; publication outlining many examples of PII.

NIST SP 800-30, Rev. 1 *Guide for Conducting Risk Assessments*, foundational risk assessment guide for organizations.

NIST SP 800-88, Rev. 1 *Guidelines for Media Sanitization*; publication outlining secure data destruction policies and procedures.

Nmap A network utility designed to scan a network and create a map. Frequently used as a vulnerability scanner.

nonce An arbitrary value, usually created by the application or operating system storing passwords, added to the end of a password before it is hashed to prevent replay attacks.

non-disclosure agreement (NDA) A legal document that prohibits the signer from disclosing any company secrets learned as a part of his or her job.

non-persistence A method to bring a system back quickly to its pre-attack state without needing a fixed set of hardware, OS, or configuration. Used to enhance resiliency.

non-repudiation The process of ensuring that a person or entity cannot deny that they took an action, such as sending a message.

NoSQL A type of database that is typically used in big data applications but does not necessarily rely on Structured Query Language to create or retrieve data. The lack of a standardized structure makes NoSQL difficult to secure.

nslookup   A once-handy tool that advanced techs used to query the functions of DNS servers. Most public DNS servers now ignore all but the most basic nslookup queries.

NT LAN Manager (NTLM)/NTLM v2   Replacement for Microsoft's earlier LAN Manager authentication protocol; version 2 can still be found on Windows systems, and is typically only used when the system is not part of a domain or cannot use Kerberos for authentication purposes. Both are very unsecure protocols.

NTFS permissions   Specific resource permissions found in Windows-based networks.

OAuth   Standard that enables users to access Web sites using credentials from other Web services, such as Amazon or Google, without compromising or sharing those credentials.

obfuscate   Goal of encryption, which is to make plaintext unreadable, to look like a jumble of data.

offboarding   The process of orderly separating an employee from the organization, including termination letter, exit interview, return of all company equipment, and transfer of knowledge for subsequent hires.

onboarding   The process of giving a new hire the knowledge and skills he or she needs to do the job, while at the same time defining the behaviors expected of the new hire within the corporate culture.

one-time password (OTP)   A system-generated password that is used to authenticate for one session only. Examples include token-based authentication and the type of authentication used for personal e-mail accounts through mobile devices.

Online Certificate Status Protocol (OCSP)   A security protocol used by an organization to publish the revocation status of digital certificates in an electronic certificate revocation list (CRL).

on-path attack   Attack in which a third party surreptitiously inserts themselves into a network conversation between two hosts and covertly intercepts traffic thought to be only between those other people. Traditionally called a *man-in-the-middle (MITM) attack* or *man-in-the-browser (MITB) attack*.

Open Systems Interconnection (OSI) seven-layer model   An architecture model based on the OSI protocol suite that defines and standardizes the flow of data between computers. The following lists the seven layers:

- **Layer 1**   The *Physical layer* defines hardware connections and turns binary into physical pulses (electrical or light). Repeaters and hubs operate at the Physical layer.

- **Layer 2**   The *Data Link layer* identifies devices on the Physical layer. MAC addresses are part of the Data Link layer. Bridges operate at the Data Link layer.

- **Layer 3**   The *Network layer* moves packets between computers on different networks. Routers operate at the Network layer. IP and IPX operate at the Network layer.

- **Layer 4** The *Transport layer* breaks data down into manageable chunks. TCP, UDP, SPX, and NetBEUI operate at the Transport layer.

- **Layer 5** The *Session layer* manages connections between machines. NetBIOS and Sockets operate at the Session layer.

- **Layer 6** The *Presentation layer*, which can also manage data encryption, hides the differences among various types of computer systems.

- **Layer 7** The *Application layer* provides tools for programs to use to access the network (and the lower layers). HTTP, FTP, SMTP, and POP3 are all examples of protocols that operate at the Application layer.

Open Web Application Security Project (OWASP) Resources for protections against Web application attacks; published by the *de facto* standards body for secure Web-application development, the OWASP Foundation.

OpenID Authentication protocol that enables users to log into Web sites using credentials established with other services, such as Google or Amazon.

open-source intelligence (OSINT) Information from media (newspapers, television), public government reports, professional and academic publications, social media and other Internet-based sources, and so forth.

operational controls Security steps or rules that apply to a single unit in an organization and deal with how things get done. For example, reset a PC controller daily.

order of data volatility The order in which data should be obtained from a system during a forensic investigation, based on its perishability. The order of data collection and volatility is typically the contents of RAM first, which includes running processes and open network connections, and then more traditional permanent storage devices, such as hard drives, CDs, DVDs, and removable media.

organized crime In a security sense, organization that uses extra-legal methods to gain access to resources. Also known as *criminal syndicate*.

OSINT *See* open-source intelligence (OSINT).

outbound traffic Packets leaving the network from within it.

out-of-band management Capability of network administrators to access a server via firmware, bypassing the server operating system.

OWASP *See* Open Web Application Security Project (OWASP).

packet filtering A mechanism that filters (examines) any incoming or outgoing network traffic from a particular IP address or range of IP addresses to see if the traffic matches specific rules and then allows or denies the traffic based upon those rules. Also known as *IP filtering*.

packet sniffer *See* protocol analyzer.

pass the hash   Very old attack that takes advantage of weak points in the NT LAN Manager (NTLM) and LANMAN protocols. Modern operating systems do not have this vulnerability.

passive reconnaissance   An information gathering technique in penetration testing where the pentester uses tools and techniques that make detection of activity difficult. The information is gathered without the target's knowledge and usually consists of open, available, and legal-to-acquire sources.

password   A series of secret characters that enables a user to gain access to a system or resource.

Password Authentication Protocol (PAP)   An older form of authentication protocol that sends all information in clear text by default.

password cracker   Type of tool used by bad actors to read ciphertext or hashes and try to extract a plaintext key or password; also called *password recovery tool*.

password spraying attack   Attack applying a few common passwords to many accounts in an organization.

password vault   Application that stores passwords for many sites.

patch management   Process of updating—automatically or manually—programming that makes a computing device function securely. Windows Update, an automatic feature of Microsoft Windows, is a typical example.

pathping   Windows command combining a traceroute followed by a ping to determine connectivity.

Payment Card Industry Data Security Standard (PCI DSS)   Standard that should be adopted by everyone who processes credit card transactions; provides for a dozen highly detailed security controls to mitigate credit card fraud.

PCI DSS   *See* Payment Card Industry Data Security Standard (PCI DSS).

penetration testing   A controlled, authorized attempt to intrude into a network or system and exploit any found vulnerabilities in order to improve the security of the system.

perfect forward secrecy (PFS)   Concept of cryptography in which any key generated by another key cannot be used to reverse-engineer the process and discover the original key.

perimeter   The outer boundaries of a network, usually delineated by external security and traffic devices, such as routers, firewalls, demilitarized zones, and so on.

permissions   Sets of attributes that network administrators assign to users and groups to define what they can do to resources.

personal identification number (PIN)   A numerical password or passcode commonly used with ATMs and smart cards.

personal identification verification (PIV) card   A type of smart card commonly used in two-factor authentication schemes. It may contain electronic chips storing personal digital certificates, and it serves to identify a user and grant access to various resources.

personally identifiable information (PII)   Information that is unique to an individual and may serve to identify that individual. Examples include (but are not limited to) Social Security numbers, bank account numbers, names and addresses, and birthdates.

personnel management policy   Defines the way a user works within the organization, including standard operating procedures, mandatory vacations, job rotation, and more.

pharming   A social engineering technique to redirect a user to a fake site through some means, such as malware on the computer, host file poisoning, or redirection from a DNS server that has been compromised.

phishing   A social engineering technique where the attacker poses as a trusted source in order to obtain sensitive information; this attack is typically carried out via e-mail and fake Web sites.

phishing campaign   Organizational security testing technique that uses controlled phishing attacks to determine user awareness levels.

physical address   An address burned into a ROM chip on a network interface card. A MAC address is an example of a physical or hardware address.

physical control   A type of control that covers physical and operational security measures. Examples include guards, gates, cipher locked doors, fences, evacuation procedures, and so on.

ping (Packet Internet Groper)   A small network message sent by a computer to check for the presence and response of another system. A ping uses ICMP packets. *See also* Internet Control Message Protocol (ICMP).

ping -6   A switch for the Windows version of ping that specifies that the host under test has an IPv6 address.

ping6   Linux command-line utility specifically designed to ping hosts with an IPv6 address.

PIV card   *See* personal identification verification (PIV) card.

plaintext   Ordinary human- or machine-readable unencrypted text.

platform   Specific type of hardware and software environment that supports various computer systems. Examples of different platforms include operating systems, such as Microsoft Windows and macOS, and hardware platforms, such as Intel and the older PowerPC platforms.

platform as a service (PaaS)   A cloud-based service that provides hardware, operating system, and development platforms for its users. *See also* cloud computing service.

Point-to-Point Protocol (PPP)   An older protocol used to connect remote hosts to networks, typically via a modem connection.

Point-to-Point Tunneling Protocol (PPTP)   A Microsoft protocol that works with PPP to provide a secure data link between computers using encryption.

polyalphabetic substitution cipher   A type of cipher that uses multiple alphabets to substitute individual characters for other characters.

polymorphic malware   A type of malware that is designed to change characteristics, including signatures, making it harder to detect by anti-malware solutions.

port (logical connection)   In TCP/IP, a 16-bit number between 0 and 65535 assigned to a particular TCP/IP process or application. For example, Web servers use port 80 (HTTP) to transfer Web pages to clients. The first 1024 ports are called *well-known ports*. They have been pre-assigned and generally refer to TCP/IP processes and applications that have been around for a long time.

port address translation (PAT)   A common implementation of network address translation (NAT) where the internal client's source port is kept in a table and used in the translation process. When external communications are returned for that client, the device handling NAT knows the intended client.

port authentication   A function of many advanced networking devices that authenticates a connecting device at the point of connection. IEEE 802.1X is an example of a port authentication method.

port blocking   Preventing the passage of any TCP segments or UDP datagrams through any ports other than the ones prescribed by the system administrator.

port number   A number used to identify the requested service (such as SMTP or FTP) when connecting to a TCP/IP host. Some example port numbers include 80 (HTTP), 20 (FTP), 69 (TFTP), 25 (SMTP), and 110 (POP3).

Post Office Protocol version 3 (POP3)   One of the two client-level e-mail protocols that receive e-mail from SMTP servers. POP3 uses TCP port 110. *See also* Internet Message Access Protocol (IMAP).

potentially unwanted program (PUP)   Application installed on a computer that has negative or undesired effects, such as adware, browser "helper" extensions, and so on.

PowerShell   Command-line interface and programming language in Windows.

predictive analysis   Using software, often artificial intelligence, to look for trends to anticipate any upcoming problems.

Presentation layer   *See* Open Systems Interconnection (OSI) seven-layer model.

Pretty Good Privacy (PGP)   Cryptography application and protocol suite used in asymmetric cryptography. PGP is proprietary, but it also has an open-source equivalent,

Gnu Privacy Guard (GPG). Both use the web-of-trust model rather than a public key infrastructure.

preventive control   A security control that serves to prevent undesirable actions. Unlike a deterrent control, users do not require knowledge of a preventive control for it to be effective.

principle of least privilege   Security principle that states that users should receive only the privileges that they need to do their jobs and no more than that.

privacy impact assessment (PIA)   Part of a business impact analysis, a report that determines the impact on the privacy of the individuals whose data is being stored and ensures that the organization has sufficient security controls applied to be within compliance of applicable laws or standards.

private cloud   Software, platforms, and infrastructure, delivered via the Internet or an internal corporate intranet, which are solely for the use of one organization.

privilege creep   The process that occurs over time, as personnel are transferred or moved within an organization, that leads to individuals accumulating privileges they no longer require. Privilege creep is prevented by auditing an individual's necessary rights, permissions, and privileges periodically and when they are transferred or moved within the organization.

privilege escalation   The process of accessing a system at a lower authentication level and upgrading (escalating) authentication to a more privileged level to present attack opportunities.

privileges   Assigned rights to perform specialized actions on systems and within the network.

probability   The likelihood—over a defined period of time—of someone or something damaging assets.

procedures   Formally documented step-by-step processes that detail how to perform a particular task. Procedures are usually mandatory and support an organization's policies.

promiscuous mode   A mode of operation for a network card in which an attacker can detect and capture all traffic on a network, rather than only the traffic that is intended for its host. Also called *monitor mode* in Linux.

Protected Extensible Authentication Protocol (PEAP)   An authentication protocol that uses a password function based on MS-CHAPv2 with the addition of an encrypted TLS tunnel similar to EAP-TLS.

protected health information (PHI)   Specific information related to an individual's healthcare that is protected by law, both as individual data elements and in aggregate. PHI includes any information that could be connected back to an individual, including medical diagnosis, conditions, or treatment, as well as billing or insurance information. *See also* Health Insurance Portability and Accountability Act (HIPAA).

protocol   An agreement that governs the procedures used to exchange information between cooperating entities; usually includes how much information is to be sent, how often it is sent, how to recover from transmission errors, and who is to receive the information.

protocol analyzer   A software or hardware tool that has the capability to collect and analyze network traffic information. Also sometimes referred to as a *packet analyzer* or *packet sniffer*.

protocol suite   A set of protocols that are commonly used together and operate at different levels of the OSI seven-layer model.

provenance   Historical trail of data, from time of creation/creator, changes over time, handlers of the data, and current state.

provisioning   The process of moving an application from a development environment to a production environment. Also, creating and establishing a user account, along with its related rights, privileges, and permissions. May also refer to the initial configuration of a mobile or computing device.

proximity reader   A system that detects a token, smart card, or other security device when the device is within a specific physical range of distance from the reader. Proximity readers typically use radio-frequency (RF) signals to detect devices, which commonly have specialized active or passive RF signal chips embedded in them.

proxy server   A network security device that acts as an intermediary between internal client devices and an external untrusted network, such as the Internet. The proxy makes requests on behalf of the client and services those requests as they come back from the untrusted network. External resources are not given any information about the client.

public cloud   A cloud environment in which a third-party provider delivers software, platforms, or infrastructure via the Internet to customers for a fee.

Public Key Cryptographic Standards (PKCS)   A set of proprietary standards developed by RSA Security that dictates types and formats of different digital certificates and files.

public key cryptography   A method of encryption and decryption that uses two different keys: a public key for encryption and a private key for decryption.

public key infrastructure (PKI)   The formal system used for creating, using, and managing digital certificates throughout their life cycle.

PUP   *See* potentially unwanted program (PUP).

purple team   Group in a pentesting exercise that either acts as an intermediary between the red and blue teams or is made up of both red and blue elements to conduct both attacks and defense.

Python   Widely used programming language.

QA   *See* quality assurance (QA).

QoS   *See* quality of service (QoS).

qualitative assessment   A risk assessment method that uses informed but subjective information and produces descriptive values for likelihood and impact. Also called *qualitative risk assessment.*

quality assurance (QA)   Processes in application development used to ensure that the production code meets customer requirements while staying as close to error-free as possible.

quality of service (QoS)   Router feature that enables control over the bandwidth of different protocols coming through the router.

quantitative assessment   A risk assessment method that uses numerical or other non-subjective data to provide estimates for likelihood and impact values. Also called *quantitative risk assessment.*

quarantine network   An isolated network in which non-secure hosts that do not meet network standards are placed until they meet security standards and can be connected to the normal network.

RACE Integrity Primitives Evaluation Message Digest (RIPEMD)   Hashing algorithm developed as an open standard; it comes in 128-bit, 160-bit, 256-bit, and 320-bit versions.

radio-frequency identification (RFID)   Technology used to tag or identify an item by responding to radio signals.

radio-frequency interference (RFI)   The phenomenon in which a wireless signal is disrupted by a radio signal from another device.

RAID   *See* redundant array of inexpensive disks (RAID).

rainbow table   A binary dictionary file that also includes hashed entries; used in password cracking scenarios.

ransomware   A specific type of malware in which the computer user is forced to pay a sum of money to the malicious attacker in exchange for decrypting and restoring the user's important data.

Raspberry Pi   SoC computing system that runs a variety of Linux distros, including the dedicated Raspberry OS; designed by the Raspberry Pi Foundation to bring computing to the developing world and used as an inexpensive computing device for many embedded systems.

RC4   *See* Rivest Cipher version 4 (RC4).

real evidence   A type of best evidence usually characterized by physical objects.

real-time operating system (RTOS)   Programming that runs hardware designed to respond with no delay, such as anti-lock braking systems and other safety features.

recovery agent   A designated person or entity who has the authority to recover lost keys or data in the event the person holding the keys is not available.

recovery control   A type of control used to recover systems or data. Restoration of a backup could be considered a recovery control in the event of a data loss, just as the use of an alternate processing site could be used to recover operations in the event of a disaster. Recovery controls are typically temporary or one-time requirements until other controls that are normally used are back in operation.

recovery point objective (RPO)   The maximum amount of data that can be lost for the organization, after which the business cannot recover or would suffer significant loss.

recovery site   As part of a disaster recovery plan, a location for relocating an organization. *See* cold site, hot site, warm site.

recovery time objective (RTO)   The maximum amount of time that a resource may remain unavailable before an unacceptable impact on other system resources occurs.

red team   Attacking group in a pentesting exercise that emulates potential attacker techniques.

redundancy   To have more than one of some functioning feature of a system or even another complete system. Used to enhance resiliency.

redundant array of inexpensive disks (RAID)   A way to create a fault-tolerant storage system that uses multiple hard disks configured in an array. RAID has six levels. Level 0 uses byte-level striping and provides no fault tolerance. Level 1 uses mirroring or duplexing. Level 2 uses bit-level striping. Level 3 stores error-correcting information (such as parity) on a separate disk and data striping on the remaining drives. Level 4 is level 3 with block-level striping. Level 5 uses block-level and parity data striping. Sometimes referred to as *redundant array of independent disks.*

refactoring   Reprogramming a device driver's internals so that the device driver responds to all of the normal inputs and generates all the regular outputs but also generates malicious output.

registration authority (RA)   An additional element often used in larger organizations to help offset the workload of the certificate authority. The RA assists by accepting user requests and verifying their identities before passing along the request to the certificate authority.

regulations   Rules of law or policy that govern behavior in the workplace, such as what to do when a particular event occurs.

remote access   The capability to access a computer from outside the physical facility in which it resides. Remote access requires communications hardware, software, and network connections. Examples of remote access include access through a remote access server or through a VPN connection.

Remote Access Service (RAS)   Hardware and software that allows remote users from outside the network to connect into the internal network, as if they were physically located inside the network. Remote access service handles connection, identification, authentication, and authorization processes.

remote access Trojan (RAT)   A remote administration tool maliciously installed as a Trojan horse to give a remote user some level of control of an infected system.

Remote Authentication Dial-In User Service (RADIUS)   An AAA standard created to support ISPs with hundreds, if not thousands, of modems in hundreds of computers to connect to a single central database. RADIUS consists of three types of devices: the RADIUS server that has access to a database of user names and passwords, a number of network access servers that control the modems, and a group of systems that dial into the network.

Remote Desktop Protocol (RDP)   A protocol used to access the graphical desktop on a remote host, typically a Windows computer. RDP uses TCP port 3389.

remote lock   A security feature that enables an administrator to remotely lock a mobile device in the event of its loss or theft in order to prevent unauthorized access to the device.

remote wiping   A security feature that enables an administrator to remotely wipe a mobile device in the event of its loss or theft in order to prevent unauthorized access to the data on the device.

replay attack   An attempted attack in which user credentials are intercepted and retransmitted to the receiving end in order to authenticate to a network or resource.

repository   Storage area for data files (*file repository*) or code (*code repository*).

request for comments (RFC)   Formal document from the Internet Engineering Task Force (IETF) that defines standards that apply to the Internet.

residual risk   Amount of risk remaining after accounting for controls.

RFI   *See* radio-frequency interference (RFI).

RFID   *See* radio-frequency identification (RFID).

rights   Abilities or privileges to perform certain actions on a host, system, or network. Also sometimes referred to as *privileges*.

RIPEMD (RACE Integrity Primitives Evaluation Message Digest)   *See* RACE Integrity Primitives Evaluation Message Digest (RIPEMD).

risk   The possibility of a negative event occurring that will impact or harm an asset or an organization.

risk appetite   Relative term of how much risk is perceived by an organization.

risk assessment   A comprehensive assessment of the risk posture of a system or organization; typically involves formulation of threats, assets, impacts, and likelihood. A risk assessment often uses threat and vulnerability assessments, as well as penetration testing, to gather data on risk to the asset or organization.

risk control assessment   Use of an outside source to inspect and judge the quality of internal controls.

risk control self-assessment   Use of an internal source to inspect and judge the quality of internal controls.

risk factors   Elements that contribute to risk; risk factors can be either external to the organization or internal.

risk management   The process of how an organization evaluates, protects, and recovers from threats and attacks that take place on its networks.

risk management framework (RMF)   The major steps and flows of the complex process of applying security controls in an organized and controlled fashion. The NIST Risk Management Framework (RMF) described in NIST Special Publication (SP) 800-37, Revision 2, for example, has become the *de facto* RMF for the IT industry.

risk matrix   Table that plots the likelihood of occurrence of a risk against the severity of the impact.

risk posture   Overall scope of risk for an organization.

risk register   Scatter-plot graph that compares probability to impact; used for detecting otherwise easily missed risks.

risk response   The reaction an organization has to particular risk; the four general risk responses are risk mitigation, avoidance, transference, and acceptance.

Rivest Cipher 4 (RC4)   Symmetric streaming cipher popularly used in WEP, SSL, and earlier versions of TLS. It uses key sizes that range from 40 to 2048 bits in length.

Rivest-Shamir-Adleman (RSA) algorithm   Widely used asymmetric algorithm used for generating the public and private key pairs used in public key cryptography.

rogue access point (rogue AP)   An unauthorized wireless access point (WAP) installed in a computer network.

role-based access control (RBAC)   An access control model based upon the definition of specific roles that have specific rights and privileges assigned to them. Rights and permissions are not assigned on an individual basis; rather, individuals must be assigned to a role by an administrator.

root account   Credentials granted to a user that has complete power over the resource as well as the complete serving system. Windows calls this account *administrator*. In macOS and Linux/UNIX, this account is called *root*.

rootkit   Type of malware that is hidden in operating system files and functions, typically by replacing those files and functions with files that can perform malicious or unknown actions. It is normally able to evade most common antivirus solutions.

round   An iteration of the cryptographic process used by algorithms during the encryption and decryption process.

route   Command to display and edit a host's routing table.

router   A hardware device used to connect physically separate local area networks together. Routers direct traffic based upon logical Internet protocol addresses and also eliminate broadcast domains, since broadcasts cannot normally cross router connections to different networks.

RTOS   *See* real-time operating system (RTOS).

rule-based access control   An access control model in which access to different resources is strictly controlled on the basis of specific rules configured and applied to the resource. Rules may entail time of day, originating host, and type of action conditions. Rule-based access control models are typically seen on network security devices such as routers and firewalls.

rule-based system   A system that uses a preconfigured set of rules to allow or disallow access to other systems, networks, or resources.

salt   An arbitrary value, usually created by the application or operating system storing passwords, added to the end of a password before it is hashed.

sandboxing   The practice of keeping applications running in their own separate memory, storage, and program space, preventing their interaction and sharing of data or resources.

Sarbanes–Oxley Act (SOX)   US law enacted in 2002, part of which requires private businesses to retain critical records for specific time periods.

SCADA   *See* supervisory control and data acquisition (SCADA).

scalability   The capability to support future network growth beyond its current needs.

scanless   Python command-line utility and library for using Web sites that can perform port scans.

screened subnet   Network architecture situated between an untrusted network and a protected network that acts as a protective buffer zone between the two networks. Traditionally called a *demilitarized zone (DMZ)*.

script kiddies   Derogatory term for poorly skilled threat actors who take advantage of relatively easy-to-use scripts or programs developed by others to carry out attacks.

scytale   A baton or stick, used in Roman times, that used a strip of parchment wound around it several times, upon which writing was placed to ensure its confidentiality. The parchment would then be unreadable unless wound around an exactly sized similar baton.

SDV   *See* software defined visibility (SDV).

SEAndroid   *See* Security Enhanced Linux (SELinux).

secure boot   Use of TPM and UEFI to assure boot integrity.

Secure Copy Protocol (SCP)   A utility in the Secure Shell (SSH) suite of secure utilities that allows the user to copy files between two hosts.

Secure FTP (SFTP)   Tunneling a normal (non-secure) File Transfer Protocol session over SSH to provide security.

Secure Hash Algorithm (SHA)   A series of hashing algorithms developed by NIST and the NSA, which include SHA-1, SHA-2, and most recently SHA-3 (based upon the Keccak hash function).

Secure MIME (S/MIME)   Secure version of the Multipurpose Internet Mail Extensions (MIME) protocol built into every e-mail client that enables users to make e-mail attachments.

Secure Real-time Transport Protocol (SRTP)   A secure Real Time Protocol extension that enables protected voice and video communication.

Secure Shell (SSH)   A secure remote connection/terminal emulation program that is not only a protocol but also a suite of secure utilities. SSH uses TCP port 22 and is found natively on UNIX and Linux systems. It can also be ported to Windows systems.

Secure Sockets Layer (SSL)   A deprecated secure Application layer protocol that relies on digital certificates and public/private keys to set up authentication and encryption services between two hosts. Its successor, TLS, is used to provide security services for various unsecure protocols, such as HTTP, SMTP, and FTP. *See* Transport Layer Security (TLS).

security as a service (SECaaS)   Subset of software as a service (SaaS) that focuses on bundling security solutions.

Security Assertion Markup Language (SAML)   A format for a client and server to exchange authentication and authorization data securely. SAML defines three roles for making this happen: principle, identity provider (IdP), and service provider.

security control   A policy, action, or safeguard, usually defined by an authoritative security agency (e.g., NIST), designed to mitigate security risks in the environment as much as possible. Controls are usually characterized in *families* and are audited annually for compliance.

Security Enhanced Linux (SELinux)   Mandatory access control mechanism that provides security for Android devices; also called *SEAndroid*.

security guard   A person who is responsible for controlling access to physical resources such as buildings, secure rooms, and other physical assets.

security hacker   A person with the technical skills to gain access to computer systems. *See also* hacker.

security identifier (SID)   A numerical identifier in Windows systems used to identify a specific account or group. Similar to the concept of user IDs (UIDs) in UNIX- and Linux-based systems.

security information and event management (SIEM)   Refers to the technologies and products used to integrate security information management and security event management information into a centralized interface, providing real-time event correlation and analysis.

security log   A log that tracks anything that affects security, such as successful and failed logons and logoffs. It can be manually or automatically generated. Also referred to as an *audit log*.

security orchestration, automation, and response (SOAR)   Toolset designed to assist security professionals react to incidents with intelligence and automation.

security policy   Internal organizational governance that directs how security will be addressed regarding people, systems, and data.

security posture   Security status of every aspect of an organization. Also called *cybersecurity posture*.

Security Technical Implementation Guide (STIG)   Cybersecurity standard for a product, created by one or more organizations; helps organizations configure products securely.

security token   Physical device that enables authentication to a resource. In an online identity management system (IMS), a device such as a smartphone can receive authentication prompts via an app, like you find with Steam games. This authentication prompt is a security token that enables a user to access restricted resources. Also called a *secure token*.

SELinux   *See* Security Enhanced Linux (SELinux).

semi-authorized hacker   *See* gray hat hacker.

separation of duties   A personnel security concept that states a single individual should not perform all critical or privileged-level duties.

service level agreement (SLA) A contractual agreement, signed by an organization and a third-party provider, that details the level of security, data availability, and other protections afforded the organization's data held by the third party.

service set identifier (SSID) A basic network name for a wireless network, including both basic service set (BSS) networks, which use single access points, and extended service set (ESS) networks, which use multiple access points.

session A particular communications session between two hosts or programs communicating via a network.

session hijacking The interception of a valid computer session to get authentication information or other sensitive data.

Session layer *See* Open Systems Interconnection (OSI) seven-layer model.

shadow IT Information technology systems installed without the knowledge or consent of the main IT department.

shared account (or generic account) An account commonly used by more than one person, where all the users know its user name and password. Shared accounts should be avoided when possible, since they provide no accountability or non-repudiation services for actions taken on a system or network.

shim Library that responds to inputs that a device driver wasn't designed to handle. Used in shim attacks or shimming.

shoulder surfing Social engineering attack whereby the attacker surreptitiously views what a victim is typing by looking over the victim's shoulder or passing by the victim.

SID *See* security identifier (SID).

signature A specific pattern of bits or bytes that is unique to a particular virus. Virus scanning software maintains a library of signatures and compares the contents of scanned files against this library to detect infected files.

signature-based system A system that uses signatures to scan for attacks or viruses and then alerts the administrator.

Simple Mail Transfer Protocol (SMTP) An unsecure messaging protocol used to send e-mail messages to other hosts. It uses TCP port 25 by default.

Simple Network Management Protocol (SNMP) A protocol used to manage network devices. It uses ports 161 and 162.

single loss expectancy (SLE) The loss incurred when an asset has been affected by a negative event. It is calculated as follows: SLE = asset value (AV) × exposure factor (EF).

single point of failure A system component that has no backup, redundancy, or fault tolerance, such that if that component fails, the entire system fails.

single sign-on (SSO)   A security mechanism whereby a user needs to log in only once and their credentials are valid throughout the entire enterprise network, granting them access to various resources without the need to use a different set of credentials or continually re-identify themselves.

single-factor authentication   A form of authentication that uses only one of the following authentication factors: something you know, something you are, or something you have.

site survey   A process by which an administrator determines all of the potential issues and problems that may be associated with installing or upgrading a wireless network. Site survey considerations include distance limitations, electromagnetic interference, power output levels, and so on.

site-to-site   A type of VPN connection that uses two concentrators, placed in separate locations. All of the hosts in each location go through their own respective VPN concentrator to contact the distant-end VPN concentrator, thus allowing them access into the other network.

skimming   Attack designed to pick up PIN codes, ZIP codes, or CVV codes from users or credit cards; often used with card readers such as ATMs and gasoline pumps.

small office/home office (SOHO)   *See* SOHO (small office/home office).

smart card   Physical device used for authentication; size and shape of a typical credit card.

smishing   Phishing attack that uses SMS texts instead of e-mail.

SMTP (Simple Mail Transfer Protocol)   *See* Simple Mail Transfer Protocol (SMTP).

smurf attack   A type of hacking attack in which an attacker floods a network with ping packets sent to the broadcast address from a spoofed source address. All hosts that receive this ICMP message will respond to the spoofed address, flooding the victim with replies and possibly causing a denial-of-service condition on the host.

Sn1per   Pentesting reconnaissance framework and automated attack tool.

snapshot   A point-in-time backup of the system state of a virtual machine. A snapshot allows an administrator to restore the virtual machine's operating state in case of a system crash or failure. It should not be considered a complete backup of a virtual machine.

sniffer   A piece of software or hardware that intercepts network traffic. Also referred to as a *protocol analyzer*. Wireshark is a popular network sniffer.

SNMP (Simple Network Management Protocol)   *See* Simple Network Management Protocol (SNMP).

SOAR   *See* security orchestration, automation, and response (SOAR).

SoC   *See* system on a chip (SoC).

social engineering   The process of using or manipulating people inside an organization to gain access to facilities or network infrastructures.

social media analysis   Potential employee screening technique that checks online accounts—such as Facebook, Instagram, LinkedIn—for any past, unwelcome behavior; done as part of a *background check.*

software as a service (SaaS)   A third-party, cloud-based service that offers outsourced use of software by an organization; this allows an organization to use licensed software at a lower cost than buying, installing, and maintaining software. *See also* cloud computing service.

software defined visibility (SDV)   Application programming interface code added to network devices to ensure awareness of those devices to defensive tools, such as IDS/IPS/firewalls.

SOHO (small office/home office)   A classification of networking equipment, usually marketed to consumers or small businesses, that focuses on low price and ease of configuration. SOHO networks differ from enterprise networks, which focus on flexibility and maximum performance.

SOHO firewall   A simple firewall designed for a SOHO environment, often built into the firmware of a SOHO router.

SOX   *See* Sarbanes–Oxley Act of 2002 (SOX).

spam   Unsolicited, and potentially harmful, e-mail. May be used to launch phishing or other malicious attacks.

spam over instant messaging (SPIM)   A type of phishing attack that is similar to spam but takes place over instant messaging applications and systems.

spear phishing   A phishing attack that targets very specific users in an organization, such as network administrators or security personnel.

specialized system   Computing device dedicated to a specific task, such as medical, vehicle, and utility control, often with proprietary hardware and programming; a CompTIA catch-all category for an SoC-based system that's not an embedded system.

SPIM   *See* spam over instant messaging (SPIM).

spoofing   The act of impersonating a host, usually through impersonating its IP or MAC address.

spyware   Any program that sends information about your system or your actions over the Internet.

SQL (Structured Query Language)   A language created by IBM that relies on simple English statements to perform database queries. SQL enables databases from different manufacturers to be queried using a standard syntax.

SQL injection An attack using malformed SQL statements input into a Web form to cause a database to give up more information than the user is authorized to view or to cause it to execute commands, potentially resulting in unauthorized modification, creation, or deletion of data.

SSH *See* Secure Shell (SSH).

SSH File Transfer Protocol (SFTP) One method for sending FTP traffic over a Secure Shell (SSH) session using native SSH commands and methods. Note that this is not the same thing as *tunneling* regular FTP traffic over SSH (referred to as *FTP over SSH*, which is called *Secure FTP*).

SSID broadcast A wireless access point feature that announces the WAP's SSID to make it easy for wireless clients to locate and connect to it. By default, most WAPs regularly broadcast their SSID. For security purposes, some entities propose disabling this broadcast.

SSL (Secure Sockets Layer) *See* Secure Sockets Layer (SSL).

SSL VPN A type of VPN that uses SSL encryption. Clients connect to the VPN server using a standard Web browser, with the traffic secured using SSL. The two most common types of SSL VPNs are SSL portal VPNs and SSL tunnel VPNs.

standard A formally documented level of performance or process that supports security policies.

standard operating procedures (SOPs) Usually a written document depicting the procedures and actions taken for a variety of circumstances that is provided to new hires to read.

state actor In a security sense, a government-directed attack. Also known as *nation state*.

stateful firewall Software or network appliance that can inspect packets as a stream to detect anomalous patterns, such as a corruption or disruption, and can take appropriate measures.

stateless firewall Software or network appliance that examines every incoming packet individually, using addressing and port numbers to determine whether to block or allow.

static code analyzer A debugging tool that reads the source code but does not run the code.

static host A nonstandard device that uses Internet-based services and receives an IP address on a network. Examples include household appliances, automotive equipment, and game consoles. Commonly part of the concept of the Internet of Things.

steganography The science of hiding information in other data.

STIG *See* Security Technical Implementation Guide (STIG).

STIX   *See* Structured Threat Information eXpression (STIX).

storage area network (SAN)   A server that can take a pool of hard disks and present them over the network as any number of logical disks using block-level storage.

stream cipher (or algorithm)   An encryption method that encrypts a single bit at a time. Streaming ciphers are much faster than block ciphers. RC4 is an example of a streaming cipher.

Structured Threat Information eXpression (STIX)   Specification sponsored by the US Department of Homeland Security (DHS) for facilitating cybersecurity information sharing, enabling communication among organizations by providing a common language to represent information.

subnet   An independent network in a TCP/IP internetwork.

subnet mask   The value used in TCP/IP settings to divide the IP address of a host into its component parts: network ID and host ID.

subnetting   Taking a single class of IP addresses and dividing it into multiple smaller groups.

substitution cipher   Type of cipher that substitutes different letters of the alphabet for other letters.

succession planning   The process of identifying people who can take over certain critical positions (usually on a temporary basis) in case the people holding those positions are incapacitated or otherwise unavailable.

supervisory control and data acquisition (SCADA)   A system that has the basic components of a distributed control system (DCS), yet is designed for large-scale, distributed processes and functions with the idea that remote devices may or may not have ongoing communication with the central control.

supplicant   A client computer in a RADIUS network.

switch   A network device that offers multiple client connections to a network and has the added capability to limit collision domains. Some switches also offer the capability to create virtual LANs (VLANs), segmenting traffic by logical subnet and eliminating broadcast domains.

symmetric cryptography   Form of cryptography that uses only a single key for both encryption and decryption.

SYN flood   A network attack in which an attacker continually sends the first sequence (SYN) of the TCP three-way handshake but never completes the handshake process, causing the victim host to have to repeatedly acknowledge traffic and use up resources.

syslog   A logging facility often found in UNIX or Linux systems; it can collect logs from multiple systems at once for ease of administration.

system (or software) development life cycle (SDLC) A framework describing the entire useful life of a system or software, which usually includes phases relating to requirements definition, design, development, acquisition, implementation, sustainability, and disposal. CompTIA refers to SDLC as the *software development life cycle*, which narrows in on the development of an application.

system log A log file that records issues dealing with the overall system, such as system services, device drivers, or configuration changes.

system on a chip (SoC) Computer design where all processing components reside on a single circuit board (including CPU, RAM, BIOS, networking, Wi-Fi, and physical peripheral interfaces).

system resiliency Adding technologies and processes to computing equipment and networks that don't stop attacks, but enable the equipment and networks to recover easily. Methods to increase resiliency include non-persistence, redundancy, and automation.

tabletop exercise A type of group review to measure the effectiveness of a business continuity plan or other security procedure.

tail Linux/UNIX terminal command that displays the last ten lines of a text file.

tailgating An attempt by an unauthorized person to physically access the facility by closely following an authorized person into it.

TAXII *See* Trusted Automated eXchange of Intelligence Information (TAXII).

TCG *See* Trusted Computing Group (TCG).

TCP three-way handshake A three-segment conversation between TCP hosts to establish and start a data transfer session. The conversation begins with a SYN request by the initiator. The target responds with a SYN response and an ACK to the SYN request. The initiator confirms receipt of the SYN ACK with an ACK. Once this handshake is complete, data transfer can begin.

tcpdump Linux/UNIX protocol analyzer.

TCP/IP model An architecture model that is based on the TCP/IP protocol suite and defines and standardizes the flow of data between computers. The following lists the four layers:

- **Layer 1** The *Link layer (Network Interface layer)* is similar to OSI's Data Link and Physical layers (Layers 1 and 2). The Link layer consists of any part of the network that deals with frames.

- **Layer 2** The *Internet layer* is the same as OSI's Network layer. Any part of the network that deals with pure IP packets—getting a packet to its destination—is on the Internet layer.

- **Layer 3** The *Transport layer* combines the features of OSI's Transport layer. It is concerned with the assembly and disassembly of data, as well as connection-oriented and connectionless communication.

- **Layer 4** The *Application layer* combines the features of the top three layers of the OSI model. It consists of the processes that applications use to initiate, control, and disconnect from a remote system.

TCP/IP suite The collection of all the protocols and processes that make TCP over IP communication over a network possible.

tcpreplay Tool for editing and replaying pcap (Wireshark captures) files.

TCPView Windows-based GUI tool from Sysinternals that provides a graphical netstat.

technical controls Security control category characterized by all of the technical configuration options needed to protect a device or system. Also sometimes referred to as a *logical control*.

Telnet An older, non-secure program that enables users to remotely access systems.

temperature monitor A device used in monitoring and maintaining data center temperatures.

TEMPEST The NSA's security standard that is used to prevent radio-frequency emanation by using specialized enclosures and shielding.

Temporal Key Integrity Protocol (TKIP) The encryption mechanism used with Wi-Fi Protected Access (WPA). Each transmitted packet is sent with a different key, making it difficult to conduct an initialization vector attack on the protocol.

Terminal Access Controller Access Control System Plus (TACACS+) A proprietary protocol developed by Cisco to support AAA in a network with many routers and switches. It is similar to RADIUS in function, but uses TCP port 49 by default and separates authorization, authentication, and accounting into different parts.

tethering Sharing a cellular connection with another system via USB.

theHarvester Tool for gathering information (such as subdomain names and e-mail accounts) from publicly available sources.

thin client Computing system, often composed of keyboard, mouse, and monitor, that accesses computing resources (operating system, processing, applications, storage) remotely.

threat A negative event or occurrence that exploits a vulnerability in an asset.

threat actor Anyone or anything that has the motive and resources to attack another enterprise's IT infrastructure; also called a *threat agent*.

threat agent Any entity that initiates a threat; also called a *threat actor*.

threat assessment   A form of assessment that identifies all potential threats and threat actors that may affect the system or organization.

threat feeds   Real-time data streams generated by threat monitoring tools used for analysis by cybersecurity professionals.

threat hunting   Process of locating cyber attacks and mitigating them as soon as discovered.

threat intelligence   Collection of information about past, current, and potential threats to an organization.

threat intelligence sources   Resources combed by analysts, such as vulnerability databases, academic journals, social media, and more, to gain threat intelligence. Also called *research sources*.

threat map   Graphical representation of the geographical source and target of an attack.

threat vector   A particular method used by a threat actor to initiate a threat against a vulnerability.

Ticket-Granting Ticket (TGT)   A ticket that is issued to a client by an authentication server in a Kerberos realm and is later used by the client to gain a service ticket with which to access a resource.

time-based one-time password (TOTP)   A one-time-use-only password used to authenticate one communications session; not only can it be used only one time, it also has a very short lifespan and cannot be used outside of that time period.

time-of-check to time-of-use (TOCTOU)   Race condition where exploits can happen between the program checking the state of something and doing something about the results.

TOCTOU   *See* time-of-check to time-of-use (TOCTOU).

tokenization   Replacing a sensitive piece of information, such as a credit card number, with a random value for security purposes.

TPM   *See* Trusted Platform Module (TPM).

tracert (also traceroute)   A command-line utility used to follow the path a packet takes between two hosts.

tracert –6 (also traceroute6)   A command-line utility that checks a path from the station running the command to a destination host. Adding the –6 switch to the command line specifies that the target host uses an IPv6 address. tracerout6 is a Linux command that performs a traceroute to an IPv6 addressed host.

transitive trust   A trust between multiple systems or networks, such that if system A trusts system B, then system A will also automatically trust system C if system B also trusts system C.

Transmission Control Protocol (TCP)   A transport-layer protocol that establishes a defined connection with the sending and receiving hosts before a data segment transmission session begins. TCP also manages segment sequencing and retransmission of lost segments through the use of sequence numbers.

Transmission Control Protocol/Internet Protocol (TCP/IP)   A set of communication protocols developed by the US Department of Defense that enables dissimilar computers to share information over a network.

Transport layer   *See* Open Systems Interconnection (OSI) seven-layer model.

Transport Layer Security (TLS)   A more secure update to the SSL protocol that works with almost any TCP application. It uses TCP port 443, as does SSL. Provides security services for various unsecure protocols, such as HTTP and FTP.

transposition cipher   A type of cipher that transposes or changes the order of characters in a message using some predetermined method that both the sender and receiver are aware of.

trap   An alert sent to an administrative station due to an unusual event that occurs on a SNMP-managed device. A trap is a specific event configured with a certain threshold. If a configured threshold is reached for a particular event, the trap is triggered and the notification or alert is sent to the management console.

trend analysis   The process of collecting information from various sources over time and analyzing it for patterns or trends relating to resource access or network traffic.

Triple DES   An algorithm that is viewed as a replacement for DES and essentially puts plaintext blocks to the same type of encryption processes three distinct times; it uses three separate 56-bit keys.

Trojan horse   A form of malware that masquerades as a program with a legitimate purpose, so that a user will be tempted to run it, but performs malicious actions on the system when executed. The name is derived from the famed Greek Trojan horse.

trust relationship   An established security relationship between two entities or systems, such that they trust each other's user accounts database and allow unfettered authentication and authorization to each other's resources.

Trusted Automated eXchange of Intelligence Information (TAXII)   Specification sponsored by the US Department of Homeland Security (DHS) for facilitating cybersecurity information sharing through services and message exchanges.

Trusted Computing Group (TCG)   IT industry organization anchored by AMD, Hewlett-Packard, IBM, Intel, and Microsoft that works to make PC hardware and software interoperable.

trusted OS   A specialized version of an operating system, created and configured for high-security environments.

Trusted Platform Module (TPM) A hardware chip embedded in a device that provides for cryptographic key generation and storage functions. It is often used in computers for drive encryption and authentication processes.

trusted user A user that is trusted to the extent that they may be allowed higher-level privileges on a system or with a resource.

TTP *See* adversary tactics, techniques, and procedures (TTP).

tunnel An encrypted link between two systems, regardless of the network they reside on, that protects traffic between those systems from interception or modification.

two-factor authentication A method of security authentication that requires two separate means of authentication; for example, some sort of physical token that, when inserted, prompts for a password.

Twofish A symmetric block algorithm that was one of the five finalists in the competition to become AES. It uses 128-bit block sizes; 16 rounds of encryption; and 128-bit, 192-bit, and 256-bit key sizes.

typosquatting A method of attack in which a malicious actor purchases a similar sounding or slightly misspelled domain name that's a close match to a legitimate organization in an effort to trick a user into visiting that domain instead of the legitimate one.

unauthorized hacker *See* black hat hacker.

UAV *See* unmanned aerial vehicle (UAV).

UEM *See* Unified Endpoint Management (UEM).

unencrypted channel Unsecure communication between two hosts that pass data between them in unencrypted form, or clear text. HTTP, FTP, and the Telnet protocols are examples of connections that use unencrypted channels.

Unified Endpoint Management (UEM) Device management software that provides an enterprise with centralized control over all endpoints, such as mobile devices and wearables.

Unified Threat Management (UTM) The concept of implementing multipurpose security devices that perform a wide variety of functions, including firewall, proxy, VPN, and data loss prevention functions.

uninterruptible power supply (UPS) A device that supplies continuous clean power to a computer system and protects against power outages and sags.

UNIX A popular computer software operating system used on many Internet host systems.

unknown environment test *See* black box test (or blind box test).

unmanned aerial vehicle (UAV)   Flying device controlled by radio signals (often Wi-Fi or cellular), equipped with cameras and storage options for capturing images and sound in remote areas; commonly called a *drone*.

unsecure protocol   A protocol that transfers data between hosts in an unencrypted, clear text format. HTTP, FTP, and Telnet are examples of unsecure protocols.

URL hijacking   Type of attack similar to typosquatting (using misspelled domain names), where an attacker uses a fake URL to lure users to a non-legitimate Web site.

user account   A logically created system identifier that binds to a particular individual and is used to tie a user to a particular action or allowed actions.

User Datagram Protocol (UDP)   A Transport layer protocol that is used to carry datagrams between two hosts; it does not rely on established connections, nor does it manage data sequencing or retransmission of lost data.

user identifier (UID)   Identifies a particular user in UNIX and Linux operating systems. It is very similar to the concept of a security identifier (SID) used in Windows systems.

user-level security   A security system in which each user has an account and password for a resource, and access to resources is based on user identity on that particular system. Also called *peer* or *workgroup-level security*, it is a decentralized security model.

VBA   *See* Virtual Basic for Applications (VBA).

Virtual Basic for Applications (VBA)   A compiled general-purpose programming language.

virtual local area network (VLAN)   A subnet of a LAN that has been logically created on a switch device. VLANs are used to separate hosts in two logical networks, eliminate broadcast domains, and allow for better management and segregation of hosts by function, location, or security requirements.

virtual machine (VM)   A virtual computer accessed through a program called a *hypervisor* or *virtual machine manager*. A VM runs *inside* an actual operating system, essentially enabling you to run two or more operating systems at once.

virtual machine manager (VMM)   *See* hypervisor.

virtual private network (VPN)   A technology used to securely connect to an organization's internal network by tunneling unsecure protocols and data over a secure connection through an unsecure external network, such as the Internet, to a secure device known as a *VPN concentrator*.

virus   A piece of malicious software that must be propagated through a definite user action.

virus definition (or signature) files   Data file updates that enable virus protection software to recognize the viruses on a system by their characteristics and remove or quarantine them. Virus definitions should be updated often. Also called *signature files*, depending on the virus protection software in use.

vishing   An attack method that uses Voice over IP (VoIP) telephone systems to carry out phishing attacks.

Voice over IP (VoIP)   A set of technologies used to send telephony and voice services over standard Internet Protocol networks.

vulnerability   A potential weakness in an infrastructure, network, host, or even a person or organization that a threat might exploit.

vulnerability assessment   A type of security assessment in which vulnerabilities for a system are discovered and documented.

vulnerability database   Collection of all the known problem areas or weaknesses in deployed software hosted by a government or organization (e.g., NIST's *National Vulnerability Database*).

vulnerability scanner   A tool that scans a network for potential attack vectors.

walkthrough test   A type of group review to measure the effectiveness of a business continuity plan or other security measure; more thorough than a tabletop exercise.

warchalking   An older, obscure practice of secretly marking the location of unsecured wireless networks by drawing specialized symbols on sidewalks and walls with chalk to let others know about the wireless network.

war driving   The practice of driving through an area and scanning for unsecured wireless networks with the intention of connecting to them for free wireless access or hacking into them.

warm site   A facility with all of the physical resources, computers, and network infrastructure needed to recover from a primary site disaster. A warm site does not have current backup data, and it may take a day or more to recover and install backups before business operations can recommence.

waterfall   A linear software development life cycle model.

watering hole attack   Type of social engineering attack that targets a group within an organization based on patterns in Web usage.

Web services   Applications and processes that can be accessed over a network through a Web server, rather than being accessed locally on the client machine. Web services include things such as Web-based e-mail, network-shareable documents, spreadsheets and databases, and many other types of cloud-based applications.

web-of-trust   A model used between users of digital certificates and key pairs to trust each other's keys. This model is primarily used in small groups of users, and instead of using a centralized certificate issuing authority, it relies on the trust that individual users have in each other. PGP, when used in small groups, typically uses this model.

WEP   *See* Wired Equivalent Privacy (WEP).

whaling   A specific phishing attack targeted at large targets, such as senior executives. This attack normally is more complex and makes more use of specific information gathered through social engineering.

white box test   A penetration test in which the tester has full knowledge of the target systems and network through information provided by the network administrator. This test is usually conducted to verify known vulnerabilities, as well as to discover potentially unknown vulnerabilities and exploit them. Called a *known environment* test on some IT certification exams.

white hat hacker   A security professional who uses his or her abilities and knowledge to help secure networks; also known as an *ethical hacker* or *authorized hacker.*

white team   Group in a pentesting exercise that enforces the rules of engagement.

whitelisting   *See* allow/block list.

Wi-Fi   The name given to the consumer and commerce wireless technologies that use the Institute of Electrical and Electronics Engineers (IEEE) 802.11 wireless standards; "Wi-Fi" is a trademarked name belonging to the Wi-Fi Alliance.

Wi-Fi analyzer   Any device that finds and documents all wireless networks in the area. Also known as a *wireless analyzer.*

Wi-Fi Protected Access (WPA)   A wireless security protocol, developed by a consortium of vendors, that addresses the weaknesses of Wired Equivalent Privacy (WEP). WPA offers security enhancements such as dynamic encryption key generation (keys are issued on a per-user and per-session basis), an encryption key integrity-checking feature, user authentication through the industry-standard Extensible Authentication Protocol (EAP), and other advanced features that WEP lacks. WPA was intended as a temporary measure while awaiting the adoption of the official IEEE 802.11i standard, also known as *WPA2.*

Wi-Fi Protected Access 2 (WPA2)   The common name for the official IEEE 802.11i standard, which includes the use of the Advanced Encryption Standard as the de facto encryption algorithm. It is also backward-compatible with the WPA standard in most cases, since it can fall back to using the Temporal Key Integrity Protocol (TKIP), the standard encryption mechanism in WPA.

Wi-Fi Protected Access 3 (WPA3)   Successor to WPA2 wireless encryption standard. Institutes Simultaneous Authentication of Equals (SAE) to provide substantially better security than its predecessor. Requires a minimum encryption of AES-128 in CCM mode for WPA3-Personal and much higher for WPA3-Enterprise modes.

Wi-Fi Protected Setup (WPS)   Automated and semi-automated process to connect a wireless device to a WAP. The process can be as simple as pressing a button on the device or pressing the button and then entering a PIN code. WPS has several security issues and was later proven to be ineffective in establishing a secure wireless network.

wildcard certificate   Certificate issued by a CA that applies to a domain rather than a specific URL. Subject Alternate Name (SAN) extensions to X.509 reduce the risk involved with wildcard certificates by listing supported URLs.

Windows Firewall   The firewall that has been included in Windows operating systems since Windows XP through Windows 10. Originally named Internet Connection Firewall (ICF), Microsoft renamed it Windows Firewall in XP Service Pack 2.

Wired Equivalent Privacy (WEP)   The first attempt at wireless security protocols, introduced in the older IEEE 802.11b standard, which uses RC4 as its encryption algorithm. It is susceptible to many attacks, including initialization vector attacks and weak keys attacks.

wireless access point (WAP)   A network device that connects wireless network nodes to other wireless or wired networks. Many WAPs are combination devices that act as high-speed hubs, switches, bridges, and routers, all rolled into one.

wireless analyzer   *See* Wi-Fi analyzer.

Wireshark   A popular network protocol analyzer; it can be used on either wired or wireless networks.

witness   A person who sees an event. In computer forensics, the term "witness" takes on a different meaning. While people can testify that they visually saw someone enter data into the system or remove hardware, for example, most computer transactions that occur are "witnessed" by computers and equipment, not actual people. A person can witness a printout or what's shown on the screen of a computer, but data can be altered before it is printed out or shown on the screen, so the value of an actual physical witness to an event in a computer forensics case may be limited. *See also* expert witness.

workgroup   A method of organizing computers, users, and resources in a small environment; does not require an Active Directory domain. A workgroup configuration uses decentralized user-level security, where resources are located on individual hosts, and the user of each computer decides how other users access those resources.

worm   A very special form of malware that can replicate itself to other systems on a network by taking advantage of security weaknesses in networking protocols. Unlike a virus, a worm does not require user action or intervention to infect other files.

WPA   *See* Wi-Fi Protected Access (WPA).

WPA2   *See* Wi-Fi Protected Access 2 (WPA2).

WPA2-Enterprise   A version of WPA2 that is used in large enterprise environments and typically uses more advanced authentication technologies, such as IEEE 802.1X port authentication, and a RADIUS server for authentication.

WPA3   *See* Wi-Fi Protected Access 3 (WPA3).

X.509   A popular standard for the format, creation, use, and management of digital certificates.

XaaS   *See* anything as a service (XaaS).

XMAS attack   A network-based attack in which specific TCP flags are set to the "on" position; many hosts are not configured to properly deal with the specific combination, and it may cause a denial-of-service attack on the host.

XML injection   A specific type of injection attack that injects malformed XML into a Web application, causing data modification or destruction or the execution of arbitrary code on the system.

XOR function   Mathematical function that looks at each bit of plaintext and performs a mathematical eXclusive OR operation on it.

zero trust architecture (ZTA)   NIST guidelines that recommend organizations require proper authentication and authorization in all interactions with assets; published in NIST SP 800-207, *Zero Trust Architecture*.

zero-day attack   A new attack that uses a vulnerability that has yet to be identified and for which no known mitigation or patch exists.

Zigbee   Low-bandwidth, low-power communication protocols used in some IoT devices.

zombie   A single computer that is under the control of an operator and is used in a botnet attack. *See also* botnet.

ZTA   *See* zero trust architecture (ZTA).

INDEX

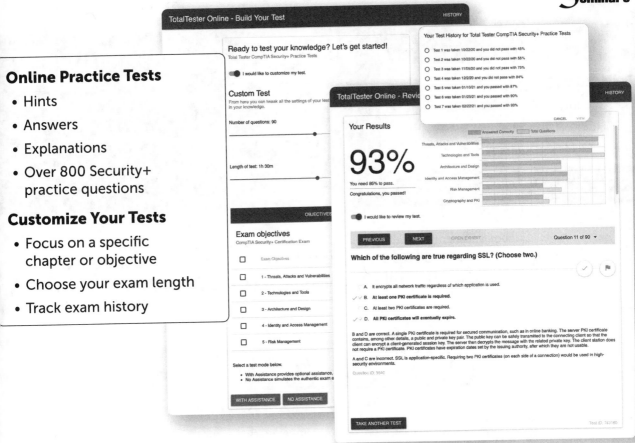
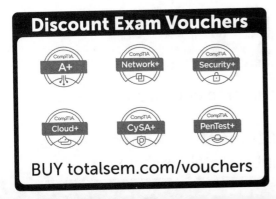

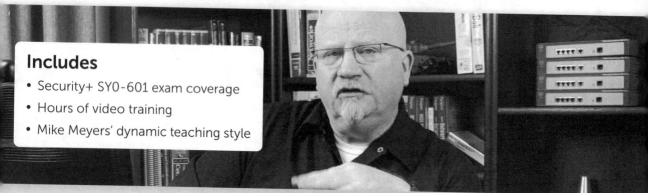